CLYMER

HONDA
VFR700F & VFR750F • 1986-1997

The world's finest publisher of mechanical how-to manuals

PRIMEDIA
Business Magazines & Media

P.O. Box 12901, Overland Park, Kansas 66282-2901

Copyright ©1998 PRIMEDIA Business Magazines & Media Inc.

FIRST EDITION
First Printing August, 1994

SECOND EDITION
First Printing December, 1998
Second Printing March, 2003

Printed in U.S.A.

CLYMER and colophon are registered trademarks of PRIMEDIA Business Magazines & Media Inc.

ISBN: 0-89287-711-1

Library of Congress: 97-75347

AUTHOR: Ed Scott.

TECHNICAL PHOTOGRAPHY: Randy Stephens and Ed Scott.

TECHNICAL ILLUSTRATIONS: Mitzi McCarthy.

WIRING DIAGRAMS: Robert Caldwell.

COVER: Mark Clifford Photography, Los Angeles, California. Honda VFR750F courtesy of Rice Honda of La Puente, La Puente, California.

TOOLS AND EQUIPMENT: K & L Supply Co. at www.klsupply.com.

All rights reserved. Reproduction or use, without express permission, of editorial or pictorial content, in any manner, is prohibited. No patent liability is assumed with respect to the use of the information contained herein. While every precaution has been taken in the preparation of this book, the publisher assumes no responsibility for errors or omissions. Neither is any liability assumed for damages resulting from use of the information contained herein. Publication of the servicing information in this manual does not imply approval of the manufacturers of the products covered.

All instructions and diagrams have been checked for accuracy and ease of application; however, success and safety in working with tools depend to a great extent upon individual accuracy, skill and caution. For this reason, the publishers are not able to guarantee the result of any procedure contained herein. Nor can they assume responsibility for any damage to property or injury to persons occasioned from the procedures. Persons engaging in the procedure do so entirely at their own risk.

CONTENTS

QUICK REFERENCE DATA IX

CHAPTER ONE
GENERAL INFORMATION 1

    Manual organization
    Notes, cautions and warnings
    Safety first
    Service hints
    Serial numbers
    Parts replacement
    Torque specifications
    Fasteners
    Lubricants
    RTV gasket sealant
    Threadlock
    Gasket remover
    Expendable supplies
    Basic hand tools
    Test equipment
    Precision measuring tools
    Cleaning solvent
    Other special tools
    Mechanic's tips
    Ball bearing replacement
    Oil seals
    Riding safety

CHAPTER TWO
TROUBLESHOOTING 35

    Operating requirements
    Troubleshooting instruments
    Starting the engine
    Emergency troubleshooting
    Engine starting troubleshooting
    Engine performance
    Engine noises
    Engine lubrication
    Clutch
    Gearshift linkage
    Transmission
    Electrical troubleshooting
    Test equipment
    Basic test procedures
    Electrical problems
    Charging system
    Ignition system troubleshooting
    Starter system troubleshooting
    Carburetor troubleshooting
    Excessive vibration
    Front suspension and steering
    Brake problems

CHAPTER THREE
PERIODIC LUBRICATION, MAINTENANCE AND TUNE-UP 63

    Routine checks
    Maintenance intervals
    Tires and wheels
    Battery
    Periodic lubrication
    Periodic maintenance
    Tune-up
    Ignition timing
    Carburetor adjustment

CHAPTER FOUR
ENGINE 122

Engine principles
Servicing engine in frame
Engine
Cylinder head cover
Camshafts (1986-1989 models)
Camshafts (1990-on models)
Cylinder heads
Rocker arms assemblies (1986-1989 models)
Valves and valve components

Oil pan, oil strainer and oil pump
Oil cooler
Alternator
Cylinder block and crankcase
Piston and connecting rods
Starter clutch assembly, starter reduction gear
  and primary drive gear
Break-in procedure

CHAPTER FIVE
CLUTCH SYSTEM 221

Clutch
Clutch hydraulic system
Master cylinder

Slave cylinder
Bleeding the clutch system

CHAPTER SIX
GEARSHIFT MECHANISM AND TRANSMISSION 242

Engine drive sprocket and cover
External shift mechanism
Transmission

Transmission and internal shift operation
Transmission
Internal shift mechanism

CHAPTER SEVEN
FUEL, EMISSION CONTROL AND EXHAUST SYSTEMS 274

Air filter housing
Carburetor operation
Carburetor service
Carburetor assembly
Carburetor overhaul
Carburetor adjustments
Throttle cable replacement
Choke cable replacement
Fuel tank
Fuel shutoff valve
Fuel filler cap

Fuel pump
Fuel filter
Gasoline/alcohol blend test
Crankcase breather system (U.S. only)
Evaporative emission control system
  (California models only)
Secondary air supply system
  (1986-on U.S., 1988-on Switzerland,
  1992-on Austria models)
Exhaust system

Chapter One
General Information

Chapter Two
Troubleshooting

Chapter Three
Periodic Lubrication, Maintenance and Tune-up

Chapter Four
Engine

Chapter Five
Clutch System

Chapter Six
Gearshift Mechanism and Transmission

Chapter Seven
Fuel, Emission Control and Exhaust Systems

Chapter Eight
Electrical System

Chapter Nine
Liquid Cooling System

Chapter Ten
Front Suspension and Steering

Chapter Eleven
Rear Suspension

Chapter Twelve
Brakes

Chapter Thirteen
Fairing Components

Index

Wiring Diagrams

CLYMER PUBLICATIONS
PRIMEDIA Business Magazines & Media
Chief Executive Officer Timothy M. Andrews
President Ron Wall

EDITORIAL

Editor
James Grooms

Associate Editor
Jason Beaver

Technical Writers
Ron Wright
Ed Scott
George Parise
Mark Rolling
Michael Morlan
Jay Bogart

Production Supervisor
Dylan Goodwin

Lead Production Editor
Shirley Renicker

Production Editors
Greg Araujo
Shara Pierceall

Associate Production Editors
Susan Hartington
Holly Messinger
Darin Watson

Technical Illustrators
Steve Amos
Mitzi McCarthy
Bob Meyer
Mike Rose

MARKETING/SALES AND ADMINISTRATION

Vice President,
PRIMEDIA Business Directories & Books
Rich Hathaway

Marketing Manager
Elda Starke

Advertising & Promotions Coordinator
Melissa Abbott

Associate Art Directors
Chris Paxton
Tony Barmann

Sales Manager/Marine
Dutch Sadler

Sales Manager/Motorcycles
Matt Tusken

Sales Coordinator
Marcia Jungles

Operations Manager
Patricia Kowalczewski

Sales Manager/Manuals
Ted Metzger

Customer Service Manager
Terri Cannon

Customer Service Supervisor
Ed McCarty

Customer Service Representatives
Susan Kohlmeyer
April LeBlond
Courtney Hollars
Jennifer Lassiter
Ernesto Suarez
Shawna Davis

Warehouse & Inventory Manager
Leah Hicks

The following books and guides are published by PRIMEDIA Business Directories & Books.

CLYMER®

More information available at *primediabooks.com*

CONTENTS

QUICK REFERENCE DATA IX

CHAPTER ONE
GENERAL INFORMATION 1

    Manual organization
    Notes, cautions and warnings
    Safety first
    Service hints
    Serial numbers
    Parts replacement
    Torque specifications
    Fasteners
    Lubricants
    RTV gasket sealant
    Threadlock
    Gasket remover
    Expendable supplies
    Basic hand tools
    Test equipment
    Precision measuring tools
    Cleaning solvent
    Other special tools
    Mechanic's tips
    Ball bearing replacement
    Oil seals
    Riding safety

CHAPTER TWO
TROUBLESHOOTING 35

    Operating requirements
    Troubleshooting instruments
    Starting the engine
    Emergency troubleshooting
    Engine starting troubleshooting
    Engine performance
    Engine noises
    Engine lubrication
    Clutch
    Gearshift linkage
    Transmission
    Electrical troubleshooting
    Test equipment
    Basic test procedures
    Electrical problems
    Charging system
    Ignition system troubleshooting
    Starter system troubleshooting
    Carburetor troubleshooting
    Excessive vibration
    Front suspension and steering
    Brake problems

CHAPTER THREE
PERIODIC LUBRICATION, MAINTENANCE AND TUNE-UP 63

    Routine checks
    Maintenance intervals
    Tires and wheels
    Battery
    Periodic lubrication
    Periodic maintenance
    Tune-up
    Ignition timing
    Carburetor adjustment

CHAPTER FOUR
ENGINE 122

Engine principles
Servicing engine in frame
Engine
Cylinder head cover
Camshafts (1986-1989 models)
Camshafts (1990-on models)
Cylinder heads
Rocker arms assemblies (1986-1989 models)
Valves and valve components

Oil pan, oil strainer and oil pump
Oil cooler
Alternator
Cylinder block and crankcase
Piston and connecting rods
Starter clutch assembly, starter reduction gear
  and primary drive gear
Break-in procedure

CHAPTER FIVE
CLUTCH SYSTEM 221

Clutch
Clutch hydraulic system
Master cylinder

Slave cylinder
Bleeding the clutch system

CHAPTER SIX
GEARSHIFT MECHANISM AND TRANSMISSION 242

Engine drive sprocket and cover
External shift mechanism
Transmission

Transmission and internal shift operation
Transmission
Internal shift mechanism

CHAPTER SEVEN
FUEL, EMISSION CONTROL AND EXHAUST SYSTEMS 274

Air filter housing
Carburetor operation
Carburetor service
Carburetor assembly
Carburetor overhaul
Carburetor adjustments
Throttle cable replacement
Choke cable replacement
Fuel tank
Fuel shutoff valve
Fuel filler cap

Fuel pump
Fuel filter
Gasoline/alcohol blend test
Crankcase breather system (U.S. only)
Evaporative emission control system
  (California models only)
Secondary air supply system
  (1986-on U.S., 1988-on Switzerland,
  1992-on Austria models)
Exhaust system

CHAPTER EIGHT
ELECTRICAL SYSTEM 313

Electrical connectors
Battery negative terminal
Charging system
Voltage regulator/rectifier
Alternator
Transistorized ignition system
Ignition spark unit (1986-1989 models)
Ignition control module (1990-on models)
Ignition coil
Crankshaft pulse generator

Camshaft pulse generator (1986 models only)
Starting system
Starter motor
Starter relay switch
Clutch diode
Lighting system
Switches
Electrical components
Fuses

CHAPTER NINE
LIQUID COOLING SYSTEM 373

Hoses and hose clamps
Cooling system check
Pressure check
Radiator
Cooling fan

Thermostat and housing
Water pump
Engine coolant crossover pipe
   (1986-1989 models)
Hoses

CHAPTER TEN
FRONT SUSPENSION AND STEERING 386

Front wheel
Front hub
Wheels
Tires
Tubeless tire changing
Tire repairs
Handlebar

Steering head and stem
Steering head bearing race
Front forks
Front forks (1986-1989)
Anti-dive front suspension (1986-1989 models)
Front forks (1990-on models)

CHAPTER ELEVEN
REAR SUSPENSION 436

Rear wheel
Rear hub (1986-1989 models)
Driven flange assembly (1986-1989 models)
Drive sprocket and drive chain
Shock absorber (1986-1989 models)
Shock absorber (1990-on models)
Shock absorber linkage (1986-1989 models)

Shock absorber linkage (1990-1993 models)
Shock absorber linkage (1994-on models)
Swing arm (1986-1989 models)
Swing arm (1990-on models)
Rear axle bearing holder and driven sprocket
   (1990-on models)
Driven sprocket (1990-on models)

CHAPTER TWELVE
BRAKES 472

Disc brakes
Front brake pad replacement
Front brake caliper
Front master cylinder
Rear disc brake
Rear brake pad replacement
Rear caliper
Rear master cylinder
Brake hose replacement
Brake disc—front and rear
Bleeding the system
Rear brake pedal

CHAPTER THIRTEEN
FAIRING COMPONENTS 517

Seat
Side covers (1986-1989 models)
Tailpiece
Front fairing

INDEX 538

WIRING DIAGRAMS 542

QUICK REFERENCE DATA

TIRE INFLATION PRESSURE (COLD)*

Load	Tire pressure Front psi	kPa	Rear psi	kPa
Solo riding	36	250	42	290
Dual riding	36	250	42	290

*Tire inflation pressure for factory equipped tires. Aftermarket tires may require different inflation pressure.

RECOMMENDED LUBRICANTS AND FLUIDS

Engine oil	
Temperature 15° F (–8° C) and up	SAE 20W/40 or SAE 20W/50, API grade SF or SG
Temperature 15° F (–8° C) and below	SAE 10W/30 or SAE 10W/40, API grade SF or SG
Brake fluid	DOT 4
Clutch hydraulic fluid	DOT 4
Battery refilling (non-sealed type)	Distilled water
Fork oil	
1986-1989	ATF (automatic transmission fluid)
1990-on	Pro Honda Suspension fluid SS-7
Cables and pivot points	Cable lube or SAE 10W/30 motor oil
Fuel	Regular unleaded
Drive chain	SAE 30-50 motor oil

ENGINE OIL CAPACITY

Model	Oil change Liters	U.S. qt.	Oil and filter change Liters	U.S. qt.	Overhaul Liters	U.S. qt.
1986-1989	3.0	3.2	–	–	4.0	4.2
1990-1993	2.9	3.1	3.1	3.3	4.0	4.2
1994-on	2.9	3.1	3.1	3.3	3.8	4.0

MAINTENANCE AND TUNE UP TIGHTENING TORQUES

Item	N•m	ft.-lb.
Oil drain plug	38	27
Side stand		
Pivot bolt	8	6
Pivot bolt locknut	40	29
Rear axle nut (1986-1989)	90-105	65-77
Rear wheel nuts (1990-on)	110	80
Rear axle bearing holder pinch bolt (1990-on)	55	40
Valve adjuster locknut (1986-1989)	21-25	15-18
Spark plugs	12	9

TUNE-UP SPECIFICATIONS

Valve clearance	
1986-1989	
Intake	0.10-0.13 mm (0.004-0.005 in.)
Exhaust	0.18-0.20 mm (0.007-0.008 in.)
1990-on	
Intake	0.13-0.19 mm (0.005-0.007 in.)
Exhaust	0.22-0.28 mm (0.009-0.011 in.)
Spark plug type	
Standard heat range	
1986-1989	NGK DPR9EA-9, ND X27EPR-U9
1990-1993	NGK CR8EH9, ND U24FER9
1994-on	NGK CR9EH9, ND U27FER9
Cold climate*	
1986-1989	NGK DPR8EA-9, ND X24EPR-U9
1990-1993	–
1994-on	NGK CR8EH9, ND U24FER9
Extended high-speed riding	
1986-1989	–
1990-1993	NGK CR9EH9, ND U27FER9
1994-on	–
Spark plug gap	0.8-0.9 mm (0.03-0.04 in.)
Idle speed	
1986-1989	
U.S.	1,200 ± 100 rpm
U.K.	1,000 ± 100 rpm
1990-1993	
49-state, Canada	1,000 ± 100 rpm
California, U.K.,	
Australia, Spain	1,200 ± 100 rpm
Switzerland	1,200 ± 50 rpm
1994-on	1,100 ± 100 rpm
Firing order	1, 3, 2, 4

* Cold climate = below 5° C (41° F)

FORK OIL CAPACITY AND DIMENSIONS

Front fork oil capacity (each fork leg)	
1986-1989	
Right-hand fork	358 ml (12.1 oz.)
Left-hand fork	370 ml (12.5 oz.)
1990-1991	
U.S.	383 ml (13.4 oz.)
U.K. and Canada	394 ml (13.8 oz.)
1992-1993	386 ml (13.5 oz.)
1994-on	412 ml (14.5 oz.)
Front fork oil level dimension	
1986-1989	153 mm (6.02 in.)
1990-1991	
U.S. and U.K.	175 mm (6.89 in.)
Canada	187 mm (7.36 in.)
1992-1993	
U.S., Canada and U.K.	178 mm (7.01 in.)
1994-on	177 mm (6.97 in.)
Fork oil type	
1986-1989	ATF (automatic transmission fluid)
1990-on	Pro Honda Suspension fluid SS-7

REPLACEMENT BULBS

1986-1987 U.S. and Canadian Models

Item	Voltage/wattage
Headlight (high/low beam)	12V 60/55W
Taillight/brakelight	12V 8/27W
Directional signal	
Front	12V 23/8W
Rear	12V 23W
License plate light	12V 8W
Instrument and indicator lights	12V 3.4W

1990-on U.S. and Canadian Models

Item	Voltage/wattage/candle power
Headlight (high/low beam)	12V 45/45W
Taillight/brakelight	12V 8/27W
1990-1993	12V 32/3cp
1994-on	12V 32/2cp
Directional signal	
Front	
1990-1993	12V 32/3cp
1994-on	12V 23/8W
Rear	
1990-1993	12V 32cp
1994-on	12V 23W
License plate light	
1990-1993	12V 4cp
1994-on	12V 8W
Instrument and indicator lights	
1990-1993	12V 3.4W
1994-on	12V 1.7W

1986-1989 Other than U.S. and Canadian Models

Item	Voltage/wattage
Headlight (high/low beam)	12V 60/55W
Position light	12V 4W
Taillight/brakelight	12V 5/21W
Directional signal	12V 21W
Instrument and indicator lights	12V 3.4W

1990-on Other than U.S. and Canadian Models

Item*	Voltage/wattage/candle power
Headlight (high/low beam)	
1990-1991	
E, IT, SA, SW	12V 60/55W
G, ED, F, FI, SD, SP, U	12V 60W, 12V 60/55W
1992-on	
E, IT, SP	12V 60/55W
AR, ED, F, G, SW	12V 60W, 12V 60/55W
U	12V 45/45W
Position light	12V 5W
Taillight/brakelight	12V 5/21W
Directional signal	12V 21W
Instrument, clock lights	12V 1.7W
Indicator lights	12V 3.4W

* AR = Austria, E = United Kingdom, ED = Europe, F = France, FI = Finland, G = Germany, IT = Italy, ND = No. Europe, SP = Spain, SW = Switzerland, U = Australia.

CLYMER®
HONDA
VFR700F & VFR750F • 1986-1997

INTRODUCTION

Honda introduced the VFR700-750 in 1986, and in typical Honda fashion created a versatile machine that set new standards. Availability in the U.S. included three models for 1986: VFR700F, VFR700F2 and VFR750F. In 1987 the VFR700F2 continued for the U.S. market, but the VFR's were not seen again on U.S. shores until the arrival of the VFR750F in 1990. However, the 750 cc version was available in the U.K. for 1988 and 1989. By combining cutting edge technological innovations from the VFR's racing cousins (RC30, RC45 and NR750) without sacrificing real world rideability, Honda created a new breed of machine.

The heart of the VFR is its V-4 powerplant. After some reliability problems on the VFR's predecessor the VF, Honda developed the complex liquid cooled DOHC engine into an engine capable of extreme performance without sacrificing everyday reliability. With loads of low-end torque and smooth high-speed operation due to the inherent qualities of the V-4 design, the VFR was an immediate hit on the street.

In 1990 the model received a major redesign that included a single sided rear swing and redesigned cylinder heads. The new swing arm was unheard of on anything less than exotic items seen on the racetrack. For the valve train, valve actuation via rocker arms was dropped in favor of shim and bucket operation. A new frame, seating position and bodywork furthered the development of what was becoming a quintessential sport touring machine. But with all of the improvements the machine began to sacrifice its 'sport' edge by putting on the pounds. To reverse this trend, in 1994, the frame, wheels, fork, swing arm, chain, foot pegs, handlebars, side and center stands, passenger grab rails, and exhaust system were redesigned to reduce weight. In all over 300 changes, including new bodywork based on the aggressive and futuristic look of the NR750, were incorporated into the 1994 model.

In 1998 the VFR750F gave way to the next generation—the VFR800FI. But for over a decade Honda's quality craftsmanship and high standards provided VFR750F owners a machine with cutting edge features and the ability for everyday use.

CHAPTER ONE

GENERAL INFORMATION

This Clymer shop manual covers the Honda VFR700F and VFR750F from 1986-1997. **Table 1** lists the chassis numbers (VIN) for models covered in this manual. The text provides complete information on maintenance, tune-up, repair and overhaul. Hundreds of photos and drawings guide the reader through every job.

A shop manual is a reference tool and as in all Clymer manuals, the chapters are thumb-tabbed. Important items are indexed at the end of the book. All procedures, tables and figures are designed for the reader who may be working on the motorcycle for the first time. Frequently used specifications and capacities from individual chapters are summarized in the *Quick Reference Data* section at the front of the manual.

Troubleshooting, tune-up, maintenance and repair are not difficult, if you know what tools and equipment to use and what to do. Step-by-step instructions guide you through jobs ranging from simple maintenance to complete engine and suspension overhaul.

This manual can be used by anyone from a first time do-it-yourselfer to a professional mechanic. Detailed drawings and clear photographs give you all the information you need to do the work right.

Some procedures will require the use of special tools. The resourceful mechanic can, in many cases, think of acceptable substitutes for special tools, there is always another way. This can be as simple as using a few pieces of threaded rod, washers and nuts to remove or install a bearing or fabricating a tool from scrap material. However, using a substitute for a special too is not recommended as it can be dangerous to and may damage the part. If you find that a tool can be designed and safely made, but will require some type of machine work, you may want to search out a local community college or high school that has a machine shop curriculum. Some shop teachers welcome outside work that can be used as practical shop applications for advanced students.

Tables 1-6 are at the end of the chapter.

MANUAL ORGANIZATION

This chapter provides general information useful to Honda vehicle owners and mechanics. In addition, information in this chapter discusses the tools and techniques for preventive maintenance, troubleshooting and repair.

Chapter Two provides methods and suggestions for quick and accurate diagnosis and repair of problems. Troubleshooting procedures discuss typical symptoms and logical methods to pinpoint the trouble.

Chapter Three explains all periodic lubrication and routine maintenance necessary to keep your Honda operating well. Chapter Three also includes recommended tune-up procedures, eliminating the need to consult other chapters constantly on the various assemblies.

Subsequent chapters describe specific systems, providing disassembly, repair, assembly and adjustment procedures in simple step-by-step form. If a repair is impractical for a home mechanic, it is so indicated. It is usually faster and less expensive to take such repairs to a dealer or competent repair shop. Specifications concerning a specific system are included at the end of the appropriate chapter.

NOTES, CAUTIONS AND WARNINGS

The terms NOTE, CAUTION and WARNING have specific meanings in this manual. A NOTE provides additional information to make a step or procedure easier or clearer. Disregarding a NOTE could cause inconvenience, but would not cause damage or personal injury.

A CAUTION emphasizes areas where equipment damage could occur. Disregarding a CAUTION could cause permanent mechanical damage; however, personal injury is unlikely.

A WARNING emphasizes areas where personal injury or even death could result from negligence. Mechanical damage may also occur. WARNINGS are to be taken seriously. In some cases, serious injury and death have resulted from disregarding similar warnings.

SAFETY FIRST

Professional mechanics can work for years and never sustain a serious injury. If you observe a few rules of common sense and safety, you can enjoy many safe hours servicing your own machine. If you ignore these rules you can hurt yourself or damage the equipment.

1. Never use gasoline as a cleaning solvent.

WARNING
Gasoline should only be stored in an approved safety gasoline storage container, properly labeled. Spilled gasoline should be wiped up immediately.

2. Never smoke or use a torch in the vicinity of flammable liquids, such as cleaning solvent, in open containers.

3. If welding or brazing is required on the machine, remove the fuel tanks to a safe distance, at least 50 feet away.

4. Use the proper sized wrenches to avoid damage to fasteners and injury to yourself.

5. When loosening a tight or stuck nut, be guided by what would happen if the wrench should slip. Be careful; protect yourself accordingly.

6. When replacing a fastener, make sure to use one with the same measurements and strength as the old one. Incorrect or mismatched fasteners can result in damage to your Honda and possible personal injury. Beware of fastener kits that are filled with cheap and poorly made nuts, bolts, washers and cotter pins. Refer to *Fasteners* in this chapter for additional information.

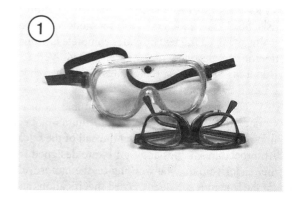

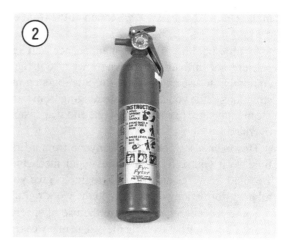

GENERAL INFORMATION

7. Keep all hand and power tools in good condition. Wipe grease and oil from tools after using them. They are difficult to hold and can cause injury. Replace or repair worn or damaged tools.

8. Keep your work area clean and uncluttered.

9. Wear safety goggles during all operations involving drilling, grinding, the use of a cold chisel or any time you feel unsure about the safety of your eyes. Safety goggles (**Figure 1**) should also be worn when solvent and compressed air are used to clean parts.

WARNING
The improper use of compressed air is very dangerous. Using compressed air to dust off your clothes, bike or workbench can cause flying particles to be blown into your eyes or skin. Never direct or blow compressed air into your skin or through any body opening (including cuts) as this can cause severe injury or death. Compressed air should be used carefully; never allow children to use or play with compressed air.

10. Keep an approved fire extinguisher nearby (**Figure 2**). Be sure it is rated for gasoline (Class B) and electrical (Class C) fires.

11. When drying bearings or other rotating parts with compressed air, never allow the air jet to rotate the bearing or part. The air jet is capable of rotating them at speeds far in excess of those for which they were designed. The bearing or rotating part is very likely to disintegrate and cause serious injury and damage. To prevent bearing damage when using compressed air, hold the inner bearing race (**Figure 3**) by hand.

12. Never work on the upper part of the bike while someone is working underneath it.

13. Never carry sharp tools in your pockets.

14. There is always a right way and wrong way to use tools. Learn to use them the right way.

SERVICE HINTS

Most of the service procedures covered are straightforward and can be performed by anyone reasonably handy with tools. It is suggested, however, that you consider your own capabilities carefully before attempting any operation involving major disassembly.

1. Front, as used in this manual, refers to the front of the motorcycle; the front of any component is the end closest to the front of the motorcycle. The left- and right-hand side refer to the position of the parts as viewed by a rider sitting on the seat and facing forward. For example, the throttle control is on the right-hand side. These rules are simple, but confusion can cause a major inconvenience during service.

2. Whenever servicing the engine or a suspension component, the bike should be secured in a safe manner. When the bike is parked on its sidestand or centerstand (optional on some models), check the stand to make sure the bike is secure before walking away from it. Block the front and rear wheels if they remain on the ground.

3. Repairs go much faster and easier if the bike is clean before you begin work. There are special cleaners for washing the engine and related parts. Spray or brush on the cleaning solution, following the manufacturer's directions. Rinse parts with a garden hose. Clean all oily or greasy parts with cleaning solvent as you remove them.

WARNING
Never use gasoline as a cleaning agent. It presents an extreme fire hazard. Be sure to work in a well-ventilated area when using cleaning solvent. Keep a fire extinguisher, rated for gasoline fires, handy in any case.

4. Much of the labor charged for by mechanics is to remove and disassemble other parts to reach the

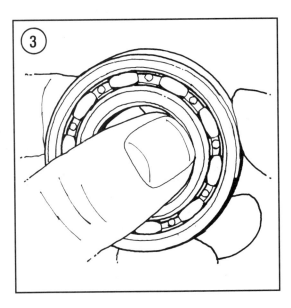

defective unit. It is usually possible to perform the preliminary operations yourself and then take the defective unit to the dealer for repair.

5. Once you have decided to tackle the job yourself, read the entire section completely while looking at the actual parts before starting the job. Make sure you have identified the proper procedure. Study the illustrations and text until you have a good idea of what is involved in completing the job satisfactorily. If special tools or replacement parts are required, make arrangements to get them before you start. It is frustrating and time-consuming to get partly into a job and then be unable to complete it.

NOTE
Some of the procedures or service specifications listed in this manual may not be applicable if your Honda has been modified or if it has been equipped with non-stock equipment. When modifying or installing non-stock equipment, file all printed instruction or technical information regarding the new equipment in a folder or notebook for future reference. If your Honda was purchased second hand, the previous owner may have installed non-stock parts. If necessary, consult with your dealer or the accessory manufacturer on components that may affect tuning or repair procedures.

6. Simple wiring checks can be easily made at home, but knowledge of electronics is almost a necessity for performing tests with complicated test gear.

CAUTION
Improper testing can sometimes damage an electrical component.

7. Disconnect the negative battery cable (**Figure 4**) as described under *Battery* in Chapter Three when working on or near the electrical, clutch or starter systems and before disconnecting any wires. On all models covered in this manual, the negative terminal will be marked with a minus (–) sign and the positive terminal with a plus (+) sign.

WARNING
Never disconnect the positive (+) battery cable unless the negative (–) cable has been disconnected. Disconnecting the positive cable while the negative cable is still connected may cause a spark. This could ignite the hydrogen gas given off by the battery, causing an explosion.

8. During disassembly, keep a few general cautions in mind. Force is rarely needed to get things apart. If parts are a tight fit, such as a bearing in a case, there is usually a tool designed to separate them. Never use a screwdriver to pry parts with machined surfaces such as crankcase halves. You will mar the surfaces and end up with leaks.

9. Make diagrams (or take a Polaroid picture) wherever similar-appearing parts are found. For instance, crankcase bolts are often not the same length. You may think you can remember where everything came from—but mistakes are costly. There is also the possibility that you may be sidetracked and not return to work for days or even weeks, in which time the carefully laid out parts may have become disturbed.

10. Tag all similar internal parts for location and mark all mating parts for position (A, **Figure 5**). Record number and thickness of any shims as they

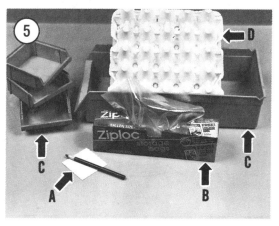

GENERAL INFORMATION

are removed; measure with a vernier caliper or micrometer. Small parts such as bolts can be identified by placing them in plastic sandwich bags (B, **Figure 5**). Seal and label them with masking tape.

11. Place parts from a specific area of the engine (e.g. cylinder heads, cylinders, clutch, transmission, etc.) into plastic boxes (C, **Figure 5**) to keep them separated.

12. When disassembling transmission shaft assemblies, use an egg flat (type that restaurants get their eggs in) (D, **Figure 5**) and set the parts from the shaft in one of the depressions in the same order in which they were removed.

13. Wiring should be tagged with masking tape and marked as each wire is removed. Again, do not rely on memory alone, especially if the wiring was changed by a previous owner.

14. Finished surfaces should be protected from physical damage or corrosion. Keep gasoline off painted surfaces.

15. Use penetrating oil on frozen or tight bolts, then strike the bolt head a few times with a hammer and punch (use a screwdriver on screws). Avoid the use of heat where possible, as it can warp, melt or affect the temper of parts. Heat also ruins finishes, especially paint and plastics.

16. Some parts will require the use of a puller or press during disassembly and reassembly. If a part is difficult to remove or install, find out why before proceeding.

17. Cover all openings after removing parts or components to prevent dirt, small tools, etc. from falling in.

18. Recommendations are occasionally made to refer service or maintenance to a Honda dealer or independent Honda repair shop. In these cases, the work will be done more quickly and economically than if you performed the job yourself.

19. In procedural steps, the term "replace" means to discard a defective part and replace it with a new or exchange unit. Overhaul means to remove, disassemble, inspect, measure, repair or replace defective parts, reassemble and install major systems or parts.

20. Some operations require the use of a hydraulic press. It would be wiser to have these operations performed by a shop equipped for such work, rather than to try to do the job yourself with makeshift equipment that may damage your machine.

21. When assembling parts, be sure all shims and washers are replaced exactly as they came out.

22. Whenever a rotating part butts against a stationary part, look for a shim or washer.

23. Always use new gaskets and O-rings during reassembly.

24. If it becomes necessary to purchase gasket material to make a gasket, measure the thickness of the old gasket (at an uncompressed point) and purchase gasket material with the same approximate thickness.

25. Heavy grease can be used to hold small parts in place if they tend to fall out during assembly. However, keep grease and oil away from electrical and brake components.

26. Never use wire to clean out jets and air passages. They are easily damaged. Use compressed air to blow out the carburetor only if the diaphragm has been removed first.

27. A baby bottle makes a good measuring device. Get one that is graduated in fluid ounces and cubic centimeters. After it has been used for this purpose, do not let a child drink out of it as there will always be an oil residue in it.

28. Take your time and do the job right. Do not forget that a newly rebuilt engine must be broken in just like a new one.

SERIAL NUMBERS

You must know the model serial number and VIN number for registration purposes and when ordering replacement parts. The various serial numbers are located as follows:

    a. The engine serial number is on the right-hand upper surface of the cylinder block next to the clutch cover (**Figure 6**).

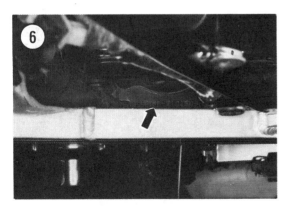

b. The frame serial number is stamped on the right-hand side of the steering head (**Figure 7**).

c. The vehicle identification number (VIN) is on the safety certification label on the right-hand side of the frame (**Figure 8**) on 1986-1989 models or on the left-hand side of the frame (**Figure 9**) on 1990-on models.

d. The carburetor identification number is located on the right-hand side of each carburetor body (**Figure 10**).

e. The color label is attached to the rear fender under the seat on early models and the frame tube cross member under the seat on later models. When ordering color-coded parts, always specify the color code indicated on the label.

PARTS REPLACEMENT

When you order parts from the dealer or other parts distributor, always order by frame and engine serial numbers. Refer to **Table 1**. Compare new parts to old before purchasing them. If they are not alike, have the parts manager explain the difference to you.

TORQUE SPECIFICATIONS

Torque specifications throughout this manual are given in Newton meters (N·m) and foot-pounds (ft.-lb.). Newton meters have been adopted in place of meter kilograms (mkg) in accordance with the International Modernized Metric System. Tool manufacturers offer torque wrenches calibrated in both Newton meters and foot-pounds.

Existing torque wrenches calibrated in meter kilograms can be used by performing a simple conversion. All you have to do is move the decimal point one place to the right; for example, 3.5 mkg = 35 N·m. This conversion is accurate enough for mechanical work even though the exact mathematical conversion is 3.5 mkg = 34.3 N·m.

Table 2 lists general torque specifications for nuts and bolts that are not listed in the respective chapters. To use the table, first determine the size of the bolt or nut. Use a vernier caliper and measure the inside dimension of the nut (**Figure 11**) and across the threads for a bolt (**Figure 12**).

GENERAL INFORMATION

FASTENERS

The materials and designs of the various fasteners used on your Honda are not arrived at by chance or accident. Fastener design determines the type of tool required to work the fastener. Fastener material is carefully selected to decrease the possibility of physical failure.

Nuts, bolts and screws are manufactured in a wide range of thread patterns. To join a nut and bolt, the diameter of the bolt and the diameter of the hole in the nut must be the same. It is just as important that the threads on both be properly matched.

The best way to tell if the threads on 2 fasteners are matched is to turn the nut on the bolt (or the bolt into the threaded hole in a piece of equipment) with fingers only. Be sure both pieces are clean. If much force is required, check the thread condition on each fastener. If the thread condition is good but the fasteners jam, the threads are not compatible. A thread pitch gauge (**Figure 13**) can also be used to determine pitch. Honda motorcycles are manufactured with metric standard fasteners. The threads are cut differently than those of American fasteners (**Figure 14**).

Most threads are cut so that the fastener must be turned clockwise to tighten it. These are called right-hand threads. Some fasteners have left-hand threads; they must be turned counterclockwise to be tightened. Left-hand threads are used in locations where normal rotation of the equipment would tend to loosen a right-hand threaded fastener.

ISO Metric Screw Threads

ISO (International Organization for Standardization) metric threads come in 3 standard thread

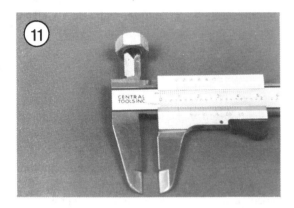

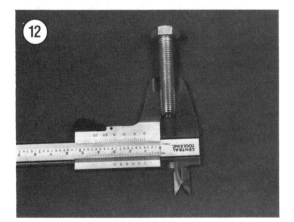

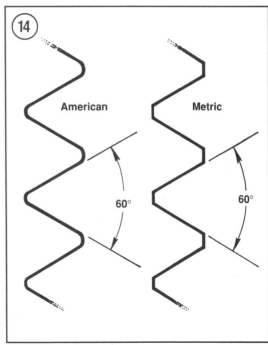

sizes: coarse, fine and constant pitch. The ISO coarse pitch is used for most all common fastener applications. The fine pitch thread is used on certain precision tools and instruments. The constant pitch thread is used mainly on machine parts and not for fasteners. The constant pitch thread is used on all metric thread spark plugs.

ISO metric threads are specified by the capital letter M followed by the diameter in millimeters and the pitch (or the distance between each thread) in millimeters separated by the sign ×. For example, a M8 × 1.25 bolt is one that has a diameter of 8 millimeters with a distance of 1.25 millimeters between each thread. Use a vernier caliper and measure the inside dimension of the nut (**Figure 11**) and across the threads for a bolt (**Figure 12**).

Machine Screws

There are many different types of machine screws. **Figure 15** shows a number of screw heads requiring different types of turning tools. Heads are also designed to protrude above the metal (round) or to be slightly recessed in the metal (flat). See **Figure 16**.

Bolts

Commonly called bolts, the technical name for these fasteners is cap screw. Metric bolts are described by the diameter and pitch (or the distance between each thread). For example, a M8 × 1.25 bolts is one that has a diameter of 8 millimeters and a distance of 1.25 millimeters between each thread. The measurement across 2 flats on the head of the bolt (**Figure 17**) indicates the proper wrench size to be used. Use a vernier caliper and measure across the threads (**Figure 12**) to determine the bolt diameter and to measure the bolt length (**Figure 18**).

Nuts

Nuts are manufactured in a variety of types and sizes. Most are hexagonal (6-sided) and fit on bolts, screws and studs with the same diameter and pitch.

Figure 19 shows several types of nuts. The common nut is generally used with a lockwasher. Self-locking nuts have a nylon insert which prevents the nut from loosening; no lockwasher is required. Wing nuts are designed for fast removal by hand. Wing

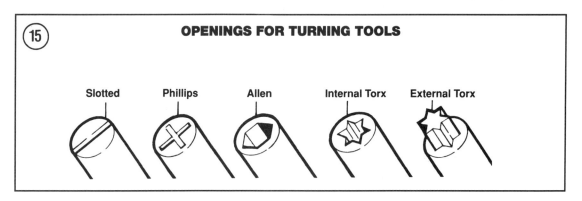

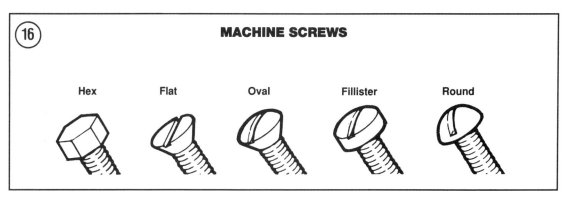

GENERAL INFORMATION

nuts are used for convenience in non-critical locations.

To indicate the size of a nut, manufacturers specify the diameter of the opening and the thread pitch. This is similar to bolt specifications, but without the length dimension. The measurement across 2 flats on the nut (**Figure 20**) indicates the proper wrench size to be used.

Self-locking Fasteners

Several types of bolts, screws and nuts incorporate a system that develops an interference between the bolt, screw, nut or tapped hole threads. Interference is achieved in various ways: by distorting threads, coating threads with dry adhesive or nylon, distorting the top of an all-metal nut, using a nylon insert in the center or at the top of a nut, etc.

Self-locking fasteners offer greater holding strength and better vibration resistance. Some self-locking fasteners can be reused if in good condition. Others, like the nylon insert nut, form an initial locking condition when the nut is first installed; the nylon forms closely to the bolt thread pattern, thus reducing any tendency for the nut to loosen. When the nut is removed, the locking efficiency is greatly reduced. For greatest safety, it is recommended that you install new self-locking fasteners whenever they are removed.

Washers

There are 2 basic types of washers: flat washers and lockwashers. Flat washers are simple discs with a hole to fit a screw or bolt. Lockwashers are designed to prevent a fastener from working loose due to vibration, expansion and contraction. Lockwashers should be installed between the bolt head or nut and a flat washer. **Figure 21** shows several types of washers. Washers are also used in the following functions:

a. As spacers.

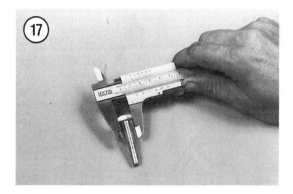

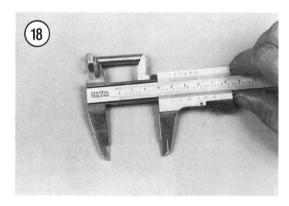

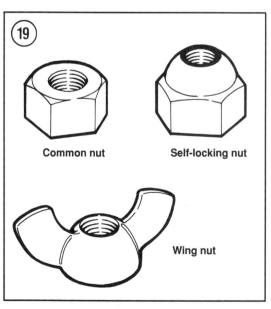

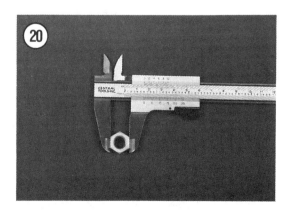

b. To prevent galling or damage of the equipment by the fastener.
c. To help distribute fastener load during torquing.
d. As fluid seals (copper or laminated washers).

Note that flat washers are often used between a lockwasher and a fastener to provide a smooth bearing surface. This allows the fastener to be turned easily with a tool.

NOTE
As much care should be given to the selection and purchase of washers as that given to bolts, nuts and other fasteners. Beware of washers that are made of thin and weak materials. These will deform and crush the first time they are used in a high torque application.

Cotter Pins

Cotter pins (**Figure 22**) are used to secure fasteners in a special location. The threaded stud, bolt or axle must have a hole in it. Its nut or nut lock piece has castellations around its upper edge into which the cotter pin fits to keep it from loosening. When properly installed, a cotter pin is a positive locking device.

The first step in properly installing a cotter pin is to purchase one that will fit snugly when inserted through the nut and the mating thread part. This should not be a problem when purchasing cotter pins through a Honda dealer; you can order them by their respective part numbers. However, when you purchase them at a hardware or automotive store, keep this in mind. The cotter pin should not be so tight that you have to drive it in and out, but you do not want it so loose that it can move or float after it is installed.

Before installing a cotter pin, tighten the nut to the recommended torque specification. If the castellations in the nut do not line up with the hole in the bolt or axle, tighten the nut until alignment is achieved. Do not loosen the nut to make alignment. Insert a new cotter pin through the nut and hole, then tap the head lightly to seat it. Bend one arm over the flat on the nut and the other against the top of the axle or bolt (**Figure 22**). Cut the arms to a suitable length to prevent them from snagging on clothing, or worse, your hands, arms or legs; the exposed arms will cut flesh easily. When the cotter pin is bent and its arms cut to length, it should be tight. If you can wiggle the cotter pin, it is improperly installed.

Cotter pins should not be reused as their ends may break and allow the cotter pin to fall out and perhaps the fastener to unscrew itself.

Circlips

Circlips can of be internal or external design. They are used to retain items on shafts (external type) or within tubes (internal type). In some applications,

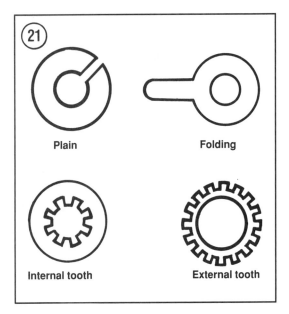

Plain   Folding

Internal tooth   External tooth

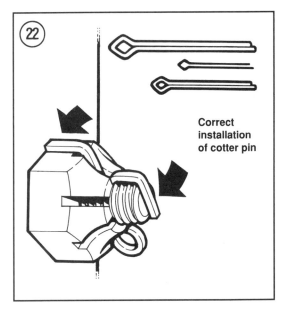

Correct installation of cotter pin

GENERAL INFORMATION

circlips of varying thicknesses are used to control the end play of parts assemblies. These are often called selective circlips. Circlips should be replaced during installation, as removal weakens and deforms them.

Two basic styles of circlips are available: machined and stamped circlips. Machined circlips (**Figure 23**) can be installed in either direction (shaft or housing) because both faces are machined, thus creating two sharp edges. Stamped circlips (**Figure 24**) are manufactured with one sharp edge and one rounded edge. When installing stamped circlips in a thrust situation, the sharp edge must face away from the part producing the thrust. When installing circlips, observe the following:

a. Circlips should be removed and installed with circlip pliers. See *Circlip Pliers* in this chapter.
b. Compress or expand circlips only enough to install them.
c. After the circlip is installed, make sure it is completely seated in its groove.

Transmission circlips become worn with use and increase side play. For this reason, always use new circlips whenever a transmission is to be reassembled.

LUBRICANTS

Periodic lubrication assures long life for any type of equipment. The type of lubricant used is just as important as the lubrication service itself, although in an emergency the wrong type of lubricant is better than none at all. The following paragraphs describe the types of lubricants most often used on motorcycle equipment. Be sure to follow the manufacturer's recommendations for lubricant types.

If any unique lubricant is recommended by Honda, it is specified in the service procedure.

Generally, all liquid lubricants are called "oil." They may be mineral-based (including petroleum bases), natural-based (vegetable and animal bases), synthetic-based or emulsions (mixtures). "Grease" is an oil to which a thickening base has been added so that the end product is semi-solid. Grease is often classified by the type of thickener added; lithium soap is commonly used.

Engine Oil

Four-cycle oil for motorcycle and automotive engines is graded by the American Petroleum Institute (API) and the Society of Automotive Engineers (SAE) in several categories. Oil containers display these ratings on the top or label (**Figure 25**).

API oil grade is indicated by letters; oils for gasoline engines are identified by an S.

Viscosity is an indication of the oil's thickness. The SAE uses numbers to indicate viscosity; thin oils have low numbers while thick oils have high numbers. A "W" after the number indicates that the

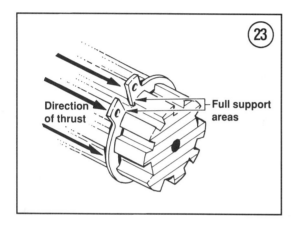

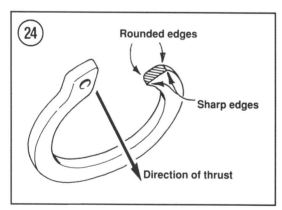

viscosity testing was done at low temperature to simulate cold-weather operation. Engine oils fall into the 5W-30 and 20W-50 range.

Multi-grade oils (for example 10W-40) are less viscous (thinner) at low temperatures and more viscous (thicker) at high temperatures. This allows the oil to perform efficiently across a wide range of engine operating conditions. The lower the number, the better the engine will start in cold climates. Higher numbers are usually recommended for engine running in hot weather conditions.

Grease

Greases are graded by the National Lubricating Grease Institute (NLGI). Greases are graded by number according to the consistency of the grease; these range from No. 000 to No. 6, with No. 6 being the most solid. A typical multipurpose grease is NLGI No. 2. For specific applications, equipment manufacturers may require grease with an additive such as molybdenum disulfide (MOS2).

RTV GASKET SEALANT

Room temperature vulcanizing (RTV) sealant is used on some pre-formed gaskets and to seal some components. RTV is a silicone gel supplied in tubes and can be purchased in a number of different colors.

Moisture in the air causes RTV to cure. Always place the cap on the tube as soon as possible when using RTV sealants. RTV has a shelf life of one year and will not cure properly when the shelf life has expired. Check the expiration date on RTV tubes before using and keep partially used tubes tightly sealed.

Applying RTV Sealant

Clean all gasket residue from mating surfaces. Surfaces should be clean and free of oil and dirt. Remove all RTV gasket material from blind attaching holes, as it can cause a "hydraulic" effect and affect bolt torque.

Apply RTV sealant in a continuous bead. Circle all mounting holes unless otherwise specified. Torque mating parts within 10 minutes after application.

THREADLOCK

A chemical locking compound should be used on all bolts and nuts, even if they are secured with lockwashers. A locking compound will lock fasteners against vibration loosening and seal against leaks. Loctite 242 (blue) and 271 (red) are recommended for many threadlock requirements described in this manual (**Figure 26**).

Loctite 242 (blue) is a medium strength threadlock and component disassembly can be performed with normal hand tools. Loctite 271 (red) is a high strength threadlock and heat or special tools, such as a press or puller, may be required for component disassembly.

Applying Threadlock

Surfaces should be clean and free of oil, grease, dirt and other residue; clean threads with an aerosol electrical contact cleaner before applying the Loctite. When applying Loctite, use a small amount. If too much is used, it can work its way down the threads and stick parts together not meant to be stuck.

GASKET REMOVER

Stubborn gaskets can present a problem during engine service as they can take a long time to remove. Consequently, there is the added problem of secondary damage occurring to the gasket mating surfaces from the incorrect use of gasket scraping tools. To quickly and safely remove stubborn gaskets, use a spray gasket remover. Spray gasket remover can be purchased through automotive parts

GENERAL INFORMATION

houses. Follow the manufacturer's directions for use.

EXPENDABLE SUPPLIES

Certain expendable supplies are required during maintenance and repair work. These include grease, oil, gasket cement, wiping rags and cleaning solvent. Ask your dealer for the silicone lubricants, contact cleaner and other products which make maintenance simpler and easier (**Figure 27**). Cleaning solvent or kerosene is available at some service stations or hardware stores.

BASIC HAND TOOLS

Many of the tuning and maintenance procedures in this manual can be carried out with simple hand tools and test equipment familiar to the average home mechanic. Keep your tools clean and in a tool box. Keep them organized with the sockets and related drives together, the open-end combination wrenches together, etc. After using a tool, wipe off dirt and grease with a clean cloth and return the tool to its correct place.

Top-quality tools are essential; they are also more economical in the long run. If you are now starting to build your tool collection, stay away from the "advertised specials" featured at some parts houses, discount stores and chain drug stores. These are usually a poor grade tool that can be sold cheaply and that is exactly what they are *cheap*. They are usually made of inferior material, and are thick, heavy and clumsy. Their rough finish makes them difficult to clean and they usually don't last very long. If it is ever your misfortune to use such tools, you will probably find out that the wrenches do not fit the heads of bolts and nuts correctly and damage the fastener.

Quality tools are made of alloy steel and are heat treated for greater strength. They are lighter and better balanced than cheap ones. Their surface is smooth, making them a pleasure to work with and easy to clean. The initial cost of good-quality tools may be more but they are cheaper in the long run. Don't try to buy everything in all sizes in the beginning; do it a little at a time until you have the necessary tools.

The following tools are required to perform virtually any repair job. Each tool is described and the recommended size given for starting a tool collection. Additional tools and some duplicates may be added as you become familiar with your Honda. Honda motorcycles are built with metric fasteners. If you are starting your collection now, buy metric sizes.

Screwdrivers

The screwdriver is a very basic tool, but if used improperly it will do more damage than good. The slot on a screw has a definite dimension and shape. Through improper use or selection, a screwdriver can damage the screw head, making removal of the screw difficult. A screwdriver must be selected to conform to the shape of the screw head used. Two basic types of screwdrivers are required: standard (flat- or slot-blade) screwdrivers (**Figure 28**) and Phillips screwdrivers (**Figure 29**).

Note the following when selecting and using screwdrivers:

a. The screwdriver must always fit the screw head. If the screwdriver blade is too small for the

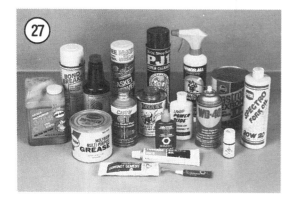

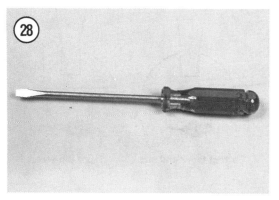

screw slot, damage may occur to the screw slot and screwdriver. If the blade is too large, it cannot engage the slot properly and will result in damage to the screw head.

b. Standard screwdrivers are identified by the length of their blade. A 6 in. screwdriver has a blade six inches long. The width of the screwdriver blade will vary, so make sure that the blade engages the screw slot the complete width of the screw.

c. Phillips screwdrivers are sized according to their point size. They are numbered one, two, three and four. The degree of taper determines the point size; the No. 1 Phillips screwdriver will be the most pointed. The points become more blunt as their number increases.

NOTE
You should also be aware of another screwdriver similar to the Phillips, and that is the Reed and Prince tip. Like the Phillips, the Reed and Prince screwdriver tip forms an "X" but with one major exception, the Reed and Prince tip has a much more pointed tip. The Reed and Prince screwdriver should never be used on Phillips screws and vise versa. Intermixing these screwdrivers will cause damage to the screw and screwdriver. If you have both types in your tool box and they are similar in appearance, you may want to identify them by painting the screwdriver shank underneath the handle.

d. When selecting screwdrivers, note that you can apply more power with less effort with a longer screwdriver than with a short one. Of course, there will be situations where only a short handle screwdriver can be used. Keep this in mind though, when having to remove tight screws.

e. Because the working end of a screwdriver receives quite a bit of abuse, you should purchase screwdrivers with hardened-tips. The extra money will be well spent.

Screwdrivers are available in sets which often include an assortment of common and Phillips blades. If you buy them individually, buy at least the following:

a. Common screwdriver—5/16 × 6 in. blade.
b. Common screwdriver—3/8 × 12 in. blade.

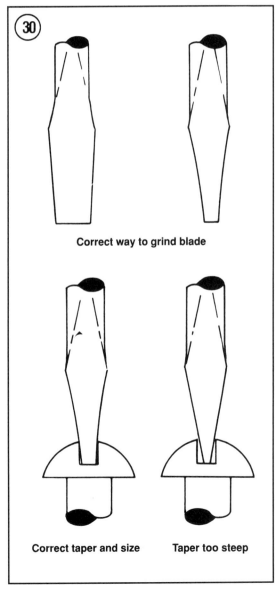

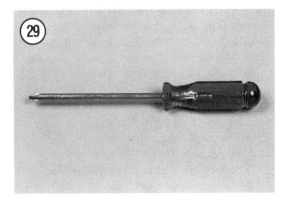

GENERAL INFORMATION

c. Phillips screwdriver—size 2 tip, 6 in. blade.

d. Phillips screwdriver—size 3 tip, 6 and 8 in. blade.

Use screwdrivers only for driving screws. Never use a screwdriver for prying or chiseling metal. Do not try to remove a Phillips, Torx or Allen head screw with a standard screwdriver (unless the screw has a combination head that will accept either type); you can damage the head so that the proper tool will be unable to remove it.

Keep screwdrivers in the proper condition and they will last longer and perform better. Always keep the tip of a standard screwdriver in good condition. **Figure 30** shows how to grind the tip to the proper shape if it becomes damaged. Note the symmetrical sides of the tip.

Pliers

Pliers come in a wide range of types and sizes. Pliers are useful for cutting, bending and crimping. They should never be used to cut hardened objects or to turn bolts or nuts. **Figure 31** shows several pliers useful in repairing your Honda.

Each type of pliers has a specialized function. Slip-joint pliers are general purpose pliers and are used mainly for holding things and for bending. Needlenose pliers are used to hold or bend small objects. Water pump pliers can be adjusted to hold various sizes of objects; the jaws remain parallel to grip around objects such as pipe or tubing. There are many more types of pliers.

CAUTION
Pliers should not be used for loosening or tightening nuts or bolts. The pliers' sharp teeth will grind off the nut or bolt corners and damage it.

CAUTION
If slip-joint or water pump pliers are going to be used to hold an object with a finished surface, wrap the object with tape or cardboard for protection.

Vise-grip Pliers

Vise-grip pliers (**Figure 32**) are used to hold objects very tightly while another task is performed on the object. While vise-grip pliers work well, caution should be followed with their use. Because vise-grip pliers exert more force than regular pliers, their sharp jaws can permanently scar the object. In addition, when vise-grip pliers are locked into position, they can crush or deform thin wall material.

Vise-grip pliers are available in many types for more specific tasks.

Circlip Pliers

Circlip pliers (**Figure 33**) are special in that they are only used to remove or install circlips. When purchasing circlip pliers, there are two kinds to distinguish from. External pliers (spreading) are used to remove circlips that fit on the outside of a shaft. Internal pliers (squeezing) are used to remove circlips which fit inside a housing.

WARNING
Because circlips can sometimes slip and "fly off" during removal and installation, always wear safety glasses when servicing them.

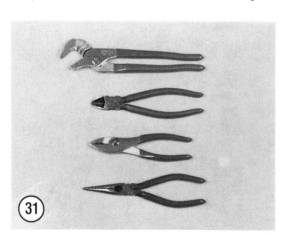

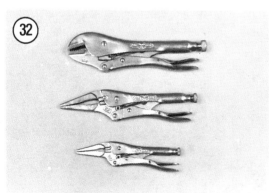

Box-end, Open-end and Combination Wrenches

Box-end and open-end wrenches (**Figure 34**) are available in sets or separately in a variety of sizes. The size number stamped near the end refers to the distance between 2 parallel flats on the hex head bolt or nut.

Box-end wrenches are usually superior to open-end wrenches. Open-end wrenches grip the nut on only 2 flats. Unless a wrench fits well, it may slip and round off the points on the nut. The box-end wrench grips on all 6 flats. Both 6-point and 12-point openings on box-end wrenches are available. The 6-point gives superior holding power; the 12-point allows a shorter swing.

Combination wrenches, which are open on one side and boxed on the other, are also available. Both ends are the same size.

No matter what style of wrench you choose, proper use is important to prevent personal injury. When using a wrench, get into the habit of pulling the wrench toward you. This technique will reduce the risk of injuring your hand if the wrench should slip. If you have to push the wrench away from you to loosen or tighten a fastener, open and push with the palm of your hand; your fingers and knuckles will be out of the way if the wrench slips. Before using a wrench, always think ahead as to what could happen if the wrench should slip or if the fastener strips or breaks.

Adjustable Wrenches

An adjustable wrench can be adjusted to fit nearly any nut or bolt head which has clear access around its entire perimeter. Adjustable wrenches are best used as a backup wrench to keep a large nut or bolt from turning while the other end is being loosened or tightened with a proper wrench. See **Figure 35**.

Adjustable wrenches have only two gripping surfaces which makes them more subject to slipping off the fastener and damaging the part and possibly your hand. See *Box-end, Open-end and Combination Wrenches* in this chapter.

These wrenches are directional; the solid jaw must be the one transmitting the force. If you use the adjustable jaw to transmit the force, it will loosen and possibly slip off.

Adjustable wrenches come in all sizes but something in the 6 to 8 in. range is recommended as an all-purpose wrench.

Socket Wrenches

This type is undoubtedly the fastest, safest and most convenient to use. Sockets which attach to a ratchet handle (**Figure 36**) are available with 6-point

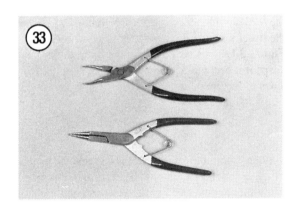

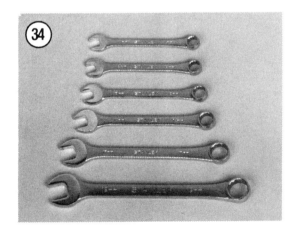

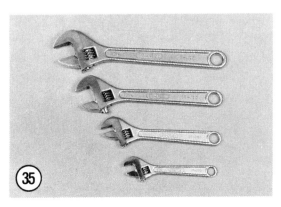

GENERAL INFORMATION

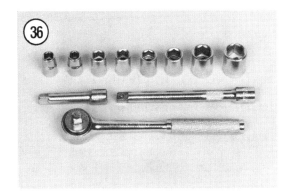

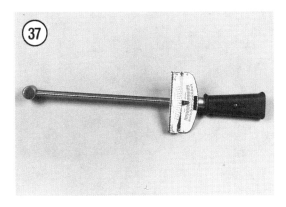

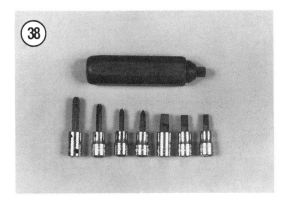

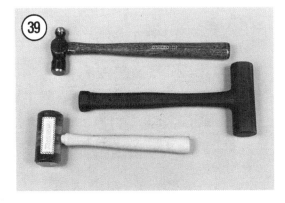

or 12-point openings and 1/4, 3/8, 1/2 and 3/4 in. drives. The drive size indicates the size of the square hole which mates with the ratchet handle.

Torque Wrench

A torque wrench (**Figure 37**) is used with a socket to measure how tightly a nut or bolt is installed. They come in a wide price range and with either 3/8 or 1/2 in. square drive. The drive size indicates the size of the square drive which mates with the socket.

Impact Driver

This tool makes removal of tight fasteners easy and eliminates damage to bolts and screw slots. Impact drivers and interchangeable bits (**Figure 38**) are available at most large hardware and motorcycle dealers. Don't purchase a cheap one as it won't work as well and will require more force than a moderately priced one. Sockets can also be used with a hand impact driver. However, make sure the socket is designed for use with an impact driver or air tool. Do not use regular hand type sockets, as they may shatter during use.

Hammers

The correct hammer (**Figure 39**) is necessary for repairs. A hammer with a face (or head) of rubber or plastic or the soft-faced type that is filled with buckshot is sometimes necessary in engine tear downs. Never use a metal-faced hammer on engine or suspension parts, as severe damage will result in most cases. Ball-peen or machinist's hammers will be required when striking another tool, such as a punch or impact driver. When striking a hammer against a punch, cold chisel or similar tool, the face of the hammer should be at least 1/2 in. larger than the head of the tool. When it is necessary to strike hard against a steel part without damaging it, a brass hammer should be used. A brass hammer can be used because brass will give when striking a harder object.

When using hammers, note the following:

a. Always wear safety glasses when using a hammer.

b. Inspect hammers for damaged or broken parts. Repair or replace the hammer as required. Do not use a hammer with a taped handle.
c. Always wipe oil or grease off of the hammer before using it.
d. The head of the hammer should always strike the object squarely. Do not use the side of the hammer or the handle to strike an object.
e. Always use the correct hammer for the job.

Allen Wrenches

Allen wrenches (**Figure 40**) are available in sets or separately in a variety of sizes. These sets come in metric and SAE size, so be sure to buy a metric set. Allen bolts are sometimes called socket bolts.

Honda uses Allen bolts throughout the bike. Sometimes the bolts are difficult to reach and it is suggested that a variety of Allen wrenches be purchased (e.g. socket driven, T-handle and extension type) as shown in **Figure 40**.

Tap and Die Set

A complete tap and die set (**Figure 41**) is a relatively expensive tool. But when you need a tap or die to clean up a damaged thread, there is really no substitute. Be sure to purchase one for metric threads when working on your Honda.

Tire Levers

When changing tires, use a good set of tire levers (**Figure 42**). Never use a screwdriver in place of a tire lever; refer to Chapter Twelve for tire changing procedures using these tools. Before using the tire levers, check the working ends of the tool and remove any burrs. Don't use a tire lever for prying anything but tires. **Figure 42** shows a regular pair of 10 in. long tire levers. However, for better leverage when changing tires on your Honda, you may want to invest in a set of 16 in. long tire irons. These can be ordered through your dealer.

Drivers and Pullers

These tools are used to remove and install oil seals, bushings, bearings and gears. These will be called out during service procedures in later chapters as required.

TEST EQUIPMENT

Multimeter or Volt-ohm Meter

This instrument (**Figure 43**) is invaluable for electrical system troubleshooting and service. A few of its functions may be duplicated by homemade test equipment, but for the serious mechanic it is a must.

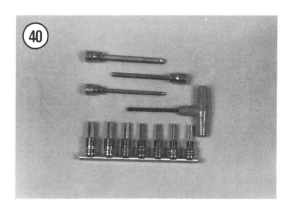

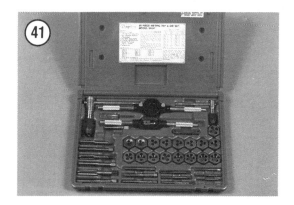

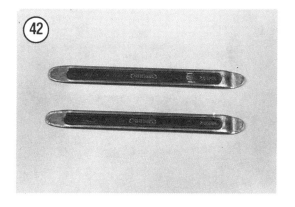

GENERAL INFORMATION

Its uses are described in the applicable section of the book.

Compression Gauge

An engine with low compression cannot be properly tuned and will not develop full power. A compression gauge measures engine compression. The one shown in **Figure 44** has a flexible stem with an extension that can allow you to hold it while turning the engine over. Open the throttle all the way when checking engine compression. See Chapter Three.

Cylinder Leak Down Tester

By positioning a cylinder on its compression stroke so that both valves are closed and then pressurizing the cylinder, you can isolate engine problem areas (e.g. leaking valve, damaged head gasket, broken, worn or stuck piston rings) by listening for escaping air through the carburetors, exhaust pipe, cylinder head mating surface, etc. To perform this procedure, a leak down tester (**Figure 45**) and an air compressor are required. This procedure is described in Chapter Three. Cylinder leak down testers can be purchased through Honda dealers, accessory tool manufacturers and automotive tool suppliers.

Portable Tachometer

A portable tachometer is necessary for tuning (**Figure 46**). Ignition timing and carburetor adjustments must be performed at specified engine speeds. The best instrument for this purpose is one with a low range of 0-1,000 or 0-2,000 rpm and a high range of 0-4,000 rpm. Extended range (0-6,000 or 0-8,000 rpm) instruments lack accuracy at lower speeds. The instrument should be capable of detecting 25 rpm on the low range.

Timing Light

Suitable timing lights range from inexpensive neon bulb types to powerful Xenon strobe lights (**Figure 47**). A light with an inductive pickup is recommended to prevent any possible damage to ignition wiring.

PRECISION MEASURING TOOLS

Measurement is an important part of servicing your Honda. When performing many of the service procedures in this manual, you will be required to make a number of measurements. These include basic checks such as engine compression and spark plug gap. As you become more involved with engine disassembly and service, measurements will be required to determine the condition of the piston and cylinder bore, crankshaft runout and so on. When making these measurements, the degree of accuracy will dictate which tool is required. Precision measuring tools are expensive. If this is your first experience at engine service, it may be more worthwhile to have the checks made at a dealer. However, as your skills and enthusiasm increase for doing your own service work, you may want to begin purchasing some of these specialized tools. The following is a description of the measuring tools required during engine overhaul.

Refer to **Table 3** for decimal and metric equivalents and to **Table 4** for a conversion table.

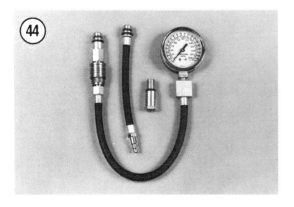

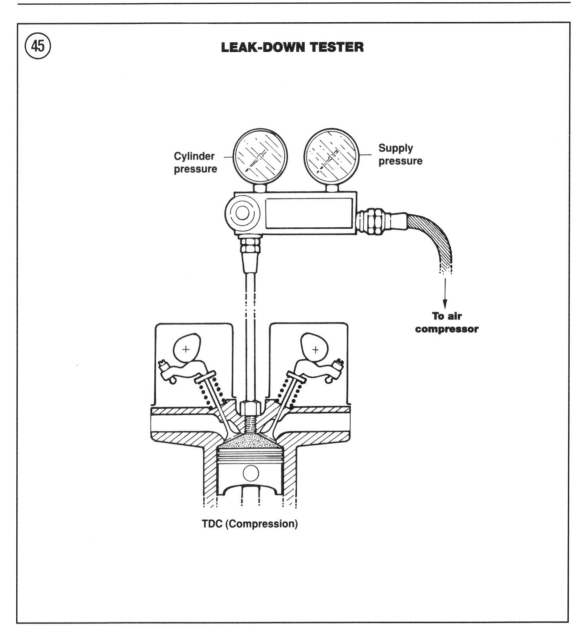
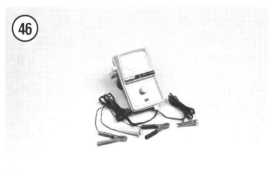

GENERAL INFORMATION

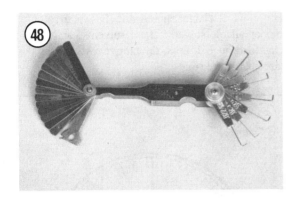

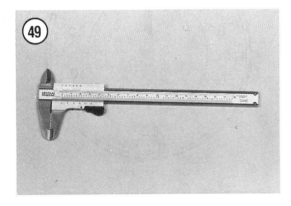

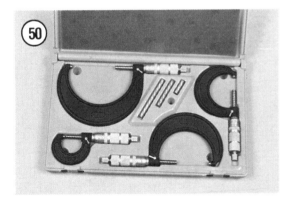

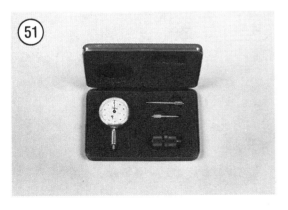

Feeler Gauge

The feeler gauge (**Figure 48**) is made of either a piece of a flat or round hardened steel of a specified thickness. Wire gauges are used to measure spark plug gap. Flat gauges are used for all other measurements.

Vernier Caliper

This tool (**Figure 49**) is invaluable when it is necessary to measure inside, outside and depth measurements with close precision. It can be used to measure the thickness of shims and thrust washers. It is perhaps the most often used measuring tool in the motorcycle service shop. Vernier calipers are available in a wide assortment of styles and price ranges.

Outside Micrometers

The outside micrometer (**Figure 50**) is used for very exact measurements of close-tolerance components. It can be used to measure the outside diameter of a piston as well as for shims and thrust washers. Outside micrometers will be required to transfer measurements from bore, snap and small hole gauges. Micrometers can be purchased individually or in a set.

Dial Indicator

Dial indicators (**Figure 51**) are precision tools used to check crankshaft and drive shaft runout limits. For motorcycle repair, select a dial indicator with a continuous dial (**Figure 52**).

Cylinder Bore Gauge

The cylinder bore gauge is a very specialized precision tool. The gauge set shown in **Figure 53** is comprised of a dial indicator, handle and a number of length adapters to adapt the gauge to different bore sizes. The bore gauge can be used to make cylinder bore measurements such as bore size, taper and out-of-round. An outside micrometer must be used together with the bore gauge to determine bore dimensions.

Small Hole Gauges

A set of small hole gauges (**Figure 54**) allows you to measure a hole, groove or slot ranging in size up to 14 mm (1/2 in). An outside micrometer must be used together with the small hole gauge to determine bore dimensions.

Telescoping Gauges

Telescoping gauges (**Figure 55**) can be used to measure hole diameters. Like the small hole gauge, the telescoping gauge does not have a scale gauge for direct readings. An outside micrometer is required to determine bore dimensions.

Screw Pitch Gauge

A screw pitch gauge (**Figure 56**) determines the thread pitch of bolts, screws, studs, etc. The gauge is made up of a number of thin plates. Each plate has a thread shape cut on one edge to match one thread pitch. When using a screw pitch gauge to determine a thread pitch size, try to fit different blade sizes onto the bolt thread until both threads match.

Surface Plate

A surface plate can be used to check the flatness of parts or to provide a perfectly flat surface for minor resurfacing of cylinder head or other critical gasket surfaces. While industrial quality surface plates are quite expensive, the home mechanic can improvise. A thick metal plate can be put to use as a surface plate. The metal surface plate shown in **Figure 57** has a piece of sandpaper or dry wall surface sanding sheets glued to its surface that is used for cleaning and smoothing cylinder head and crankcase mating surfaces.

NOTE
Check with a local machine shop on the availability and cost of having a metal plate resurfaced for use as a surface plate.

CLEANING SOLVENT

With the environmental concern that is prevalent today concerning the disposal of hazardous solvents, the home mechanic should select a water soluble, biodegradable solvent. These solvents can be purchased through dealers, automotive parts houses and large hardware stores.

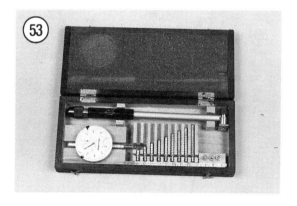

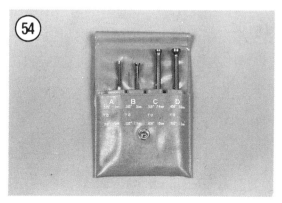

GENERAL INFORMATION

Selecting a solvent is only one of the problems facing the home mechanic when it comes to cleaning parts. You need some type of tank to clean parts as well as to store the solvent. There are a number of manufacturers offering different types and sizes of parts cleaning tanks. While a tank may seem a luxury to the home mechanic, you will find that it will quickly pay for itself through its efficiency and convenience. When selecting a parts washer, look for one that can recycle and store the solvent, as well as separate the sludge and contamination from the clean solvent. Most important, check the warranty, if any, as it pertains to the tank's pump. Like most tools, when purchasing a parts washer, you get what you pay for.

WARNING
Having a stack of clean shop rags on hand is important when performing engine work. However, to prevent the possibility of fire damage from spontaneous combustion from a pile of solvent-soaked rags, store them in a lid-sealed metal container until they can be washed or discarded.

NOTE
To avoid absorbing solvent and other chemicals into your skin while cleaning parts, wear a pair of petroleum-resistant rubber gloves. These can be purchased through industrial supply houses or well-equipped hardware stores.

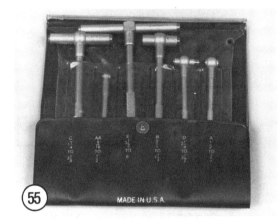

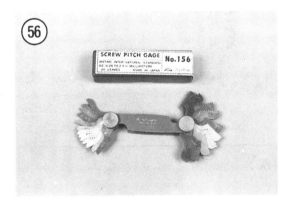

OTHER SPECIAL TOOLS

A few other special tools may be required for major service. These are described in the appropriate chapters and are available from Honda dealers or other manufacturers as indicated.

MECHANIC'S TIPS

Removing Frozen Nuts and Screws

When a fastener rusts and cannot be removed, several methods may be used to loosen it. First, apply penetrating oil such as Liquid Wrench or WD-40 (available at hardware or auto supply stores). Apply it liberally and let it penetrate for 10-15 minutes. Rap the fastener several times with a small hammer; do not hit it hard enough to cause damage. Reapply the penetrating oil if necessary.

For frozen screws, apply penetrating oil as described, then insert a screwdriver in the slot and rap the top of the screwdriver with a hammer. This loosens the rust so the screw can be removed in the normal way. If the screw head is too chewed up to use this method, grip the head with vise-grip pliers and twist the screw out.

Avoid applying heat unless specifically instructed, as it may melt, warp or remove the temper from parts.

Remedying Stripped Threads

Occasionally, threads are stripped through carelessness or impact damage. Often the threads can be cleaned up by running a tap (for internal threads on nuts) or die (for external threads on bolts) through the threads. See **Figure 58**. To clean or repair spark plug threads, a spark plug tap can be used.

If an internal thread is damaged, it may be necessary to install a Helicoil (**Figure 59**) or some other type of thread insert. These kits have all of the necessary parts to repair a damaged internal thread.

If it is necessary to drill and tap a hole, refer to **Table 5** for metric tap drill sizes.

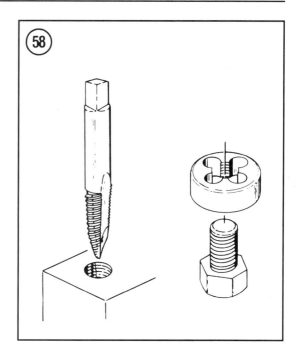

Removing Broken Screws or Bolts

When the head breaks off a screw or bolt, several methods are available for removing the remaining portion.

If a large portion of the remainder projects out, try gripping it with vise-grip pliers. If the projecting portion is too small, file it to fit a wrench or cut a slot in it to fit a screwdriver. See **Figure 60**.

If the head breaks off flush, use a screw extractor. To do this, center punch the exact center of the remaining portion of the screw or bolt. Drill a small hole in the screw and tap the extractor into the hole. Back the screw out with a wrench on the extractor. See **Figure 61**.

Removing Broken or Damaged Studs

If a stud is broken or the threads severely damaged, perform the following. A tube of Loctite 271 (red), 2 nuts, 2 wrenches and a new stud will be required during this procedure (**Figure 62**). Studs that are stripped or damaged will require the use of a stud remover.

1. Thread two nuts onto the damaged stud. Then tighten the 2 nuts against each other so that they are locked.

NOTE
If the threads on the damaged stud do not allow installation of the 2 nuts, you

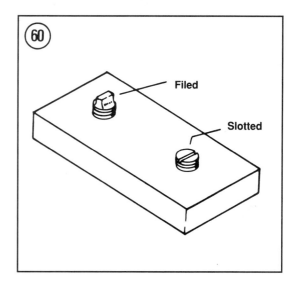

GENERAL INFORMATION

will have to remove the stud with a stud remover.

2. Turn the bottom nut counterclockwise and unscrew the stud.
3. Threaded holes with a bottom surface should be blown out with compressed air as dirt buildup in the bottom of the hole may prevent the stud from being torqued properly. If necessary, use a bottoming tap to true up the threads and to remove any deposits.
4. Install 2 nuts on the top half of the new stud as in Step 1. Make sure they are locked securely.
5. Coat the bottom half of a new stud with Loctite 271 (red).
6. Turn the top nut clockwise and thread the new stud securely.
7. Remove the nuts and repeat for each stud as required.
8. Follow Loctite's directions on cure time before assembling the component.

BALL BEARING REPLACEMENT

Ball bearings (**Figure 63**) are used throughout your Honda's engine and chassis to reduce power loss, heat and noise resulting from friction. Because ball bearings are precision made parts, they must be maintained by proper lubrication and maintenance. When a bearing is found to be damaged, it should be replaced immediately. However, when installing a new bearing, care should be taken to prevent damage to the new bearing. While bearing replacement is described in the individual chapters where applicable, the following can be used as a guideline.

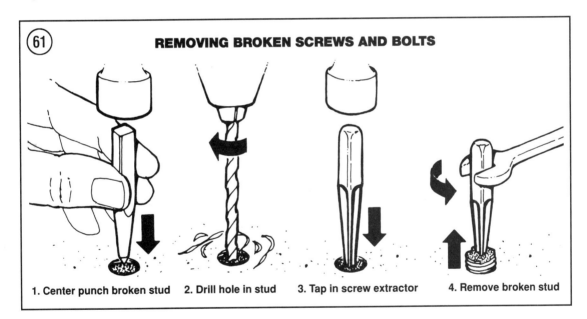

61 REMOVING BROKEN SCREWS AND BOLTS
1. Center punch broken stud
2. Drill hole in stud
3. Tap in screw extractor
4. Remove broken stud

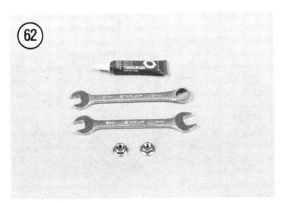

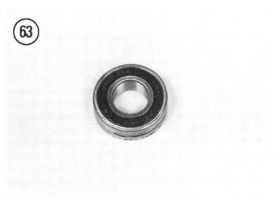

NOTE
Unless otherwise specified, install bearings with the manufacturer's mark or number on the bearing facing outward.

Bearing Removal

While bearings are normally removed only when damaged, there may be times when it is necessary to remove a bearing that is in good condition. Depending on the situation, you may be able to remove the bearing without damaging it. However, bearing removal in some situations, no matter how careful you are, will cause bearing damage. Care should always be given to bearings during their removal to prevent secondary damage to the shaft or housing. Note the following when removing bearings.

1. When using a puller to remove a bearing on a shaft, care must be taken so that shaft damage does not occur. Always place a piece of metal between the end of the shaft and the puller screw. In addition, place the puller arms next to the inner bearing race. See **Figure 64**.

2. When using a hammer to remove a bearing from a shaft, do not strike the hammer directly against the shaft. Instead, use a brass or aluminum spacer between the hammer and shaft (**Figure 65**). In addition, make sure to support both bearing races with wood blocks as shown in **Figure 65**.

3. The most ideal method of bearing removal is with a hydraulic press. However, certain procedures must be followed or damage may occur to the bearing, shaft or case half. Note the following when using a press:

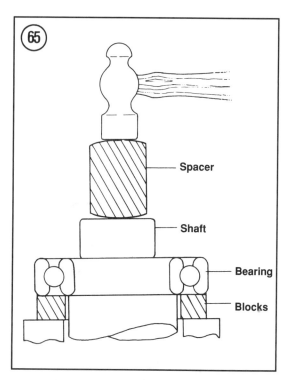

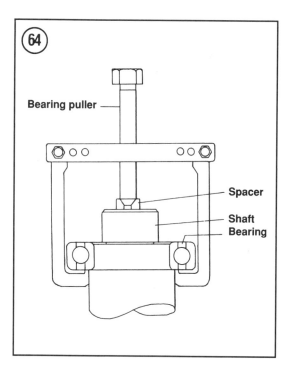

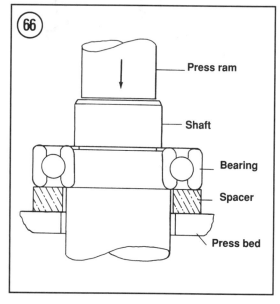

GENERAL INFORMATION

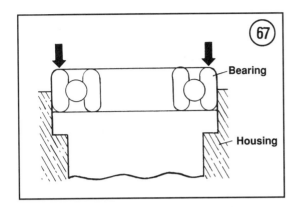

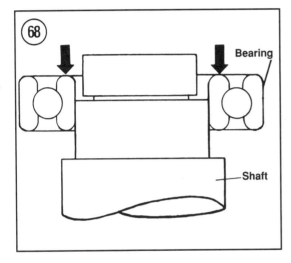

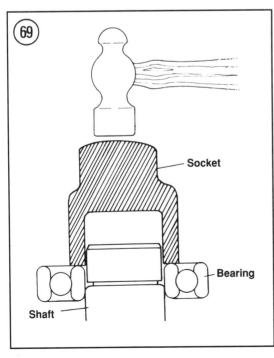

a. Always support the inner and outer bearing races with a suitable size wood or aluminum spacer ring (**Figure 66**). If only the outer race is supported, the balls and/or the inner race will be damaged.

b. Always make sure the press ram (**Figure 66**) aligns with the center of the shaft. If the ram is not centered, it may damage the bearing and/or shaft.

c. The moment the shaft is free of the bearing, it will drop to the floor. Secure or hold the shaft to prevent it from falling.

Bearing Installation

1. When installing a bearing in a housing, pressure must be applied to the outer bearing race (**Figure 67**). When installing a bearing on a shaft, pressure must be applied to the inner bearing race (**Figure 68**).

2. When installing a bearing as described in Step 1, some type of driver will be required. Never strike the bearing directly with a hammer or the bearing will be damaged. When installing a bearing, a piece of pipe or a socket with an outer diameter that matches the bearing race will be required. **Figure 69** shows the correct way to use a socket and hammer when installing a bearing over a shaft.

3. Step 1 describes how to install a bearing in a case half and over a shaft. However, when installing a bearing over a shaft and into a housing at the same time, a snug fit will be required for both outer and inner bearing races. In this situation, a spacer must be installed underneath the driver tool so that pressure is applied evenly across both races. See **Figure 70**. If the outer race is not supported as shown in **Figure 70**, the balls will push against the outer bearing track and damage it.

Shrink Fit

1. *Installing a bearing over a shaft:* When a tight fit is required, the bearing inside diameter will be smaller than the shaft. In this case, driving the bearing on the shaft using normal methods may cause bearing damage. Instead, the bearing should be heated before installation. Note the following:

a. Secure the shaft so that it can be ready for bearing installation.

b. Clean the bearing surface on the shaft of all residue. Remove burrs with a file or sandpaper.

c. Fill a suitable pot or beaker with clean mineral oil. Place a thermometer (rated higher than 248° F [120° C]) in the oil. Support the thermometer so that it does not rest on the bottom or side of the pot.

d. Remove the bearing from its wrapper and secure it with a piece of heavy wire bent to hold it in the pot. Hang the bearing in the pot so that it does not touch the bottom or sides of the pot.

e. Turn the heat on and monitor the thermometer. When the oil temperature rises to approximately 248° F (120° C), remove the bearing from the pot and quickly install it. If necessary, place a socket on the inner bearing race and tap the bearing into place. As the bearing chills, it will tighten on the shaft so you must work quickly when installing it. Make sure the bearing is installed all the way.

2. *Installing a bearing in a housing:* Bearings are generally installed in a housing with a slight interference fit. Driving the bearing into the housing using normal methods may damage the housing or cause bearing damage. Instead, the housing should be heated before the bearing is installed. Note the following:

CAUTION
Before heating the crankcases in this procedure to remove the bearings, wash the cases thoroughly with detergent and water. Rinse and rewash the cases as required to remove all traces of oil and other chemical deposits.

a. The housing must be heated to a temperature of about 212° F (100° C) in an oven or on a hot plate. An easy way to check to see that it is at the proper temperature is to drop tiny drops of water on the case as it heats up; if they sizzle and evaporate immediately, the temperature is correct. Heat only one housing at a time.

CAUTION
*Do not heat the housing with a torch (propane or acetylene) **never** bring a flame into contact with the bearing or housing. The direct heat will destroy the case hardening of the bearing and will likely warp the housing.*

b. Remove the housing from the oven or hot plate and hold onto the housing with a kitchen pot holder, heavy gloves or heavy shop cloths-it is hot.

NOTE
A suitable size socket and extension works well for removing and installing bearings.

c. Hold the housing with the bearing side down and tap the bearing out. Repeat for all bearings in the housing.

d. While heating up the housing halves, place the new bearings in a freezer if possible. Chilling them will slightly reduce their overall diameter while the hot housing assembly is slightly larger due to heat expansion. This will make installation much easier.

NOTE
Always install bearings with the manufacturer's mark or number facing outward.

e. While the housing is still hot, install the new bearing(s) into the housing. Install the bearings by hand, if possible. If necessary, lightly tap the bearing(s) into the housing with a socket placed on the outer bearing race. Do not install new

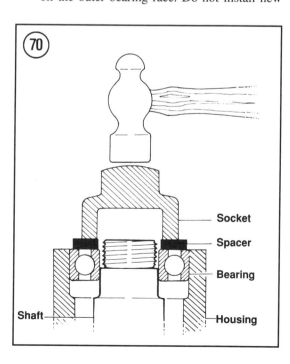

GENERAL INFORMATION

bearings by driving on the inner bearing race. Install the bearing(s) until it seats completely.

OIL SEALS

Oil seals (**Figure 71**) are used to contain oil, water, grease or combustion gasses in a housing or shaft. Improper removal of a seal can damage the housing or shaft. Improper installation of the seal can damage the seal. Note the following:

a. Prying is generally the easiest and most effective method of removing a seal from a housing. However, always place a rag underneath the pry tool to prevent damage to the housing.

b. Grease should be packed in the seal lips before the seal is installed.

c. Oil seals should always be installed so that the manufacturer's numbers or marks face out.

d. Oil seals should be installed with a socket placed on the outside of the seal as shown in **Figure 72**. Make sure the seal is driven squarely into the housing. Never install a seal by hitting against the top of the seal with a hammer.

RIDING SAFETY

General Tips

1. Read your owner's manual and know your machine.
2. Check the throttle and brake controls before starting the engine.
3. Know how to make an emergency stop.
4. Never add fuel while anyone is smoking in the area or when the engine is running.
5. Never wear loose scarves, belts or boot laces that could catch on moving parts.
6. Always wear eye and head protection and protective clothing to protect your entire body. Today's riding apparel is very stylish and you will be ready for action as well as being well protected.
7. Riding in the winter months requires a good set of clothes to keep your body dry and warm; otherwise your entire trip may be miserable. If you dress properly, moisture will evaporate from your body. If you become too hot and if your clothes trap the moisture, you will become cold. Even mild temperatures can be very uncomfortable and dangerous when combined with a strong wind or traveling at high speed. See **Table 6** for wind chill factors. Always dress according to what the wind chill factor is, not the ambient temperature.
8. Never allow anyone to operate the bike without proper instruction. This is for their bodily protection and to keep your machine from damage or destruction.
9. Use the "buddy system" for long trips, just in case you have a problem or run out of gas.
10. Never attempt to repair your machine with the engine running except when necessary for certain tune-up procedures.
11. Check all of the machine components and hardware as described in Chapter Three, especially the wheels and the steering.

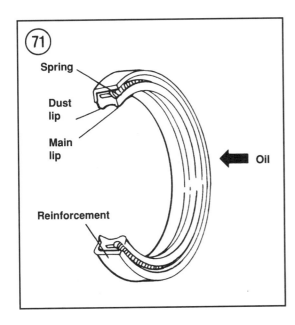

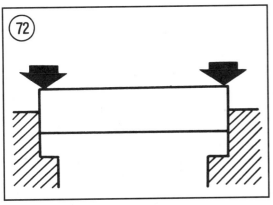

Operating Tips

1. Avoid dangerous terrain.

2. Keep the headlight, turn signal lights and taillight free of dirt.

3. Always steer with both hands.

4. Be aware of the terrain and avoid operating the bike at excessive speed.

5. Do not panic if the throttle sticks. Turn the engine stop switch to the OFF position.

6. Do not tailgate. Rear end collisions can cause injury and machine damage.

7. Do not mix alcoholic beverages or drugs with riding—ride straight.

8. Check your fuel supply regularly. Do not travel farther than your fuel supply will permit you to arrive at the next fuel stop.

Table 1 ENGINE AND FRAME SERIAL NUMBERS

Year/model	U.S. and Canadian models Engine number	Frame number
1986 VFR750F		
49-State	RC24E-2000485-on	RC240-GM000008-on
California	RC24E-2000519-on	RC241-GM000002-on
Canada	RC24E-2004245-2009403	RC24-GM000042-GM002395
1986 VFR700F		
49-State	RC26E-2000004-2004121	RC260-GM000003-GM001826
California	RC26E-2000008-2004359	RC261-GM000002-on GM001036
1986 VFR700F2		
49-State	RC26E-2000065-2001875	RC262-GM000001-GM000500
California	RC26E-2000237-2001470	RC263-GM000001-on GM000500
1987 VFR700F2		
49-State	RC26E-2100001-on	RC262-HM100001-on
California	RC26E-2100001-on	RC263-HM100001-on
1990 VFR750F*		
49-State	RC36E-2006112-2010294	RC360-LM000009-LM000788
California	RC36E-2006122-2010154	RC361-LM000011-LM000227
Canada	RC36E-2006107-2007619	RC362-LM000001-LM000227
1991 VFR750F		
49-State	RC36E-2100001-2104507	RC360-MM100001-MM101581
California	RC36E-2100001-2104645	RC361-MM100001-MM100403
Canada	RC36E-2103773-2106238	RC362-MM100001-MM100200
(continued)		

GENERAL INFORMATION

Table 1 ENGINE AND FRAME SERIAL NUMBERS (continued)

Year/model	U.S. and Canadian models* Engine number	Frame number
1992 VFR750F		
49-State	RC36E-2201394-2208553	RC360-NM200008-NM200817
California	RC36E-2201399-2202943	RC361-NM200006-on NM200186
Canada	RC36E-2200060-2207012	RC362-MM200001-MM200082
1993 VFR750F		
49-State	RC36E-2300001-on	RC360-PM300001-on
California	RC36E-2300001-on	RC361-PM300001-on
Canada	RC36E-2300060-on	RC362-PM300001-on
1994 VFR750F		
49-State	RC36E-2400068-on	RC360-RM400003-on
California	RC36E-2300001-on	RC361-RM400001-on
1995 VFR750F		
49-State	RC36E-2500001-2503493	RC360*SM500001-SM501271
California	RC36E-2501214-2503555	RC361*SM500001-SM500248
1996 VFR750F		
49-State	RC36E-2600001-on	RC360*TM600001-on
California	RC36E-2600001-on	RC361*TM600001-on
1997 VFR750F		
49-State	RC36E-2700001-on	RC360*VM700001-on
California	RC36E-2700001-on	RC361*VM700001-on

Year/model	U.K. models** Engine number	Frame number
1986 VFR750F	RC24E-2000000-on	RC24-20000000-on
1987 VFR750F	RC24E-2100000-on	RC24-21000000-on
1988 VFR750F	RC24E-2200000-on	RC24-22000000-on
1989 VFR750F	RC24E-2300000-on	RC24-23000000-on
1990 VFR750F	RC36E-2000000-on	RC36-20000000-on
1991 VFR750F	RC36E-2100000-on	RC36-21000000-on
1992 VFR750F		
Australia	RC36E-2200000-on	RC36U-NM2200001-on
Other than Australia	RC36E-2200000-on	RC36-22000000-on
1993 VFR750F	–	–
1994 VFR750F	–	–
1995 VFR750F	N/A	N/A
1996 VFR750F	N/A	N/A
1997 VFR750F	N/A	N/A

* There were no 1988 and 1989 VFR750F U.S. models. There were no 1987-1989 VFR750F Canadian models.
** AR= Austria, E= United Kingdom, ED= Europe, F= France, FI= Finland, G= Germany, IT= Italy, ND= No. Europe, SP= Spain, SW= Switzerland, U =Australia.

Table 2 STANDARD TIGHTENING TORQUES

Bolt and nut (mm)	N•m	ft.-lb.
5 mm bolt and nut	4.5-6.0	3-4
6 mm bolt and nut	8-12	6-9
8 mm bolt and nut	18-25	13-18
10 mm bolt and nut	30-40	22-29
12 mm bolt and nut	50-60	36-43
5 mm screw	4.5-5.0	3-4
6 mm screw	7-11	5-8
6 mm bolt with 8 mm head	7-11	5-8
6 mm flange bolt and nut	10-14	7-10
8 mm flange bolt and nut	24-30	17-22
10 mm flange bolt and nut	35-45	25-32

Table 3 DECIMAL AND METRIC EQUIVALENTS

Fractions	Decimal in.	Metric mm	Fractions	Decimal in.	Metric mm
1/64	0.015625	0.39688	33/64	0.515625	13.09687
1/32	0.03125	0.79375	17/32	0.53125	13.49375
3/64	0.046875	1.19062	35/64	0.546875	13.89062
1/16	0.0625	1.58750	9/16	0.5625	14.28750
5/64	0.078125	1.98437	37/64	0.578125	14.68437
3/32	0.09375	2.38125	19/32	0.59375	15.08125
7/64	0.109375	2.77812	39/64	0.609375	15.47812
1/8	0.125	3.1750	5/8	0.625	15.87500
9/64	0.140625	3.57187	41/64	0.640625	16.27187
5/32	0.15625	3.96875	21/32	0.65625	16.66875
11/64	0.171875	4.36562	43/64	0.671875	17.06562
3/16	0.1875	4.76250	11/16	0.6875	17.46250
13/64	0.203125	5.15937	45/64	0.703125	17.85937
7/32	0.21875	5.55625	23/32	0.71875	18.25625
15/64	0.234375	5.95312	47/64	0.734375	18.65312
1/4	0.250	6.35000	3/4	0.750	19.05000
17/64	0.265625	6.74687	49/64	0.765625	19.44687
9/32	0.28125	7.14375	25/32	0.78125	19.84375
19/64	0.296875	7.54062	51/64	0.796875	20.24062
5/16	0.3125	7.93750	13/16	0.8125	20.63750
21/64	0.328125	8.33437	53/64	0.828125	21.03437
11/32	0.34375	8.73125	27/32	0.84375	21.43125
23/64	0.359375	9.12812	55/64	0.859375	22.82812
3/8	0.375	9.52500	7/8	0.875	22.22500
25/64	0.390625	9.92187	57/64	0.890625	22.62187
13/32	0.40625	10.31875	29/32	0.90625	23.01875
27/64	0.421875	10.71562	59/64	0.921875	23.41562
7/16	0.4375	11.11250	15/16	0.9375	23.81250
29/64	0.453125	11.50937	61/64	0.953125	24.20937
15/32	0.46875	11.90625	31/32	0.96875	24.60625
31/64	0.484375	12.30312	63/64	0.984375	25.00312
1/2	0.500	12.70000	1	1.00	25.40000

Table 4 CONVERSION TABLE

Multiply	By	To get equivalent of
Length		
Inches	25.4	Millimeter
Inches	2.54	Centimeter
Miles	1.609	Kilometer
Feet	0.3048	Meter
Millimeter	0.03937	Inches
Centimeter	0.3937	Inches
Kilometer	0.6214	Mile
Meter	3.281	Mile
Fluid volume		
U.S. quarts	0.9463	Liters
U.S. gallons	3.785	Liters
U.S. ounces	29.573529	Milliliters
Imperial gallons	4.54609	Liters
Imperial quarts	1.1365	Liters
Liters	0.2641721	U.S. gallons
Liters	1.0566882	U.S. quarts
Liters	33.814023	U.S. ounces

(continued)

GENERAL INFORMATION

Table 4 CONVERSION TABLE

Fluid volume (continued)		
Liters	0.22	Imperial gallons
Liters	0.8799	Imperial quarts
Milliliters	0.033814	U.S. ounces
Milliliters	1.0	Cubic centimeters
Milliliters	0.001	Liters
Torque		
Foot-pounds	1.3558	Newton-meters
Foot-pounds	0.138255	Meters-kilograms
Inch-pounds	0.11299	Newton-meters
Newton-meters	0.7375622	Foot-pounds
Newton-meters	8.8507	Inch-pounds
Meters-kilograms	7.2330139	Foot-pounds
Volume		
Cubic inches	16.387064	Cubic centimeters
Cubic centimeters	0.0610237	Cubic inches
Temperature		
Fahrenheit	(F − 32°) × 0.556	Centigrade
Centigrade	(C × 1.8) + 32	Fahrenheit
Weight		
Ounces	28.3495	Grams
Pounds	0.4535924	Kilograms
Grams	0.035274	Ounces
Kilograms	2.2046224	Pounds
Pressure		
Pounds per square inch	0.070307	Kilograms per square centimeter
Kilograms per square centimeter	14.223343	Pounds per square inch
Kilopascals	0.1450	Pounds per square inch
Pounds per square inch	6.895	Kilopascals
Speed		
Miles per hour	1.609344	Kilometers per hour
Kilometers per hour	0.6213712	Miles per hour

Table 5 METRIC TAP DRILL SIZE

Metric size	Drill equivalent	Decimal fraction	Nearest fraction
3 × 0.50	No. 39	0.0995	3/32
3 × 0.60	3/32	0.0937	3/32
4 × 0.70	No. 30	0.1285	1/8
4 × 0.75	1/8	0.125	1/8
5 × 0.80	No. 19	0.166	11/64
5 × 0.90	No. 20	0.161	5/32
6 × 1.00	No. 9	0.196	13/64
7 × 1.00	16/64	0.234	15/64
8 × 1.00	J	0.277	9/32
8 × 1.25	17/64	0.265	17/64
9 × 1.00	5/16	0.3125	5/16
9 × 1.25	5/16	0.3125	5/16
10 × 1.25	11/32	0.3437	11/32
10 × 1.50	R	0.339	11/32
11 × 1.50	3/8	0.375	3/8
12 × 1.50	13/32	0.406	13/32
12 × 1.75	13/32	0.406	13/32

Table 6 WINDCHILL FACTOR

Estimated Wind Speed in MPH	Actual Thermometer Reading (° F)*											
	50	40	30	20	10	0	−10	−20	−30	−40	−50	−60
	Equivalent Temperature (° F)*											
Calm	50	40	30	20	10	0	−10	−20	−30	−40	−50	−60
5	48	37	27	16	6	−5	−15	−26	−36	−47	−57	−68
10	40	28	16	4	−9	−21	−33	−46	−58	−70	−83	−95
15	36	22	9	−5	−18	−36	−45	−58	−72	−85	−99	−112
20	32	18	4	−10	−25	−39	−53	−67	−82	−96	−110	−124
25	30	16	0	−15	−29	−44	−59	−74	−88	−104	−118	−133
30	28	13	−2	−18	−33	−48	−63	−79	−94	−109	−125	−140
35	27	11	−4	−20	−35	−49	−67	−82	−98	−113	−129	−145
40	26	10	−6	−21	−37	−53	−69	−85	−100	−116	−132	−148
**												
	Little Danger (for properly clothed person)				**Increasing Danger**				**Great Danger**			
								• Danger from freezing of exposed flesh •					

* To convert Fahrenheit (°F) to Celsius (°C), use the following formula: °C = 5/9 × (°F - 32).
** Wind speeds greater than 40 mph have little additional effect.

CHAPTER TWO

TROUBLESHOOTING

Every motorcycle engine requires an uninterrupted supply of fuel and air, proper ignition and adequate compression. If any of these are lacking, the engine will not run.

Diagnosing mechanical problems is relatively simple if you use orderly procedures and keep a few basic principles in mind.

The troubleshooting procedures in this chapter analyze typical symptoms and show logical methods of isolating causes. These are not the only methods. There may be several ways to solve a problem, but only a systematic approach can guarantee success.

Never assume anything. Do not overlook the obvious. If you are riding along and the bike suddenly quits, check the easiest, most accessible problem spots first.

If nothing obvious turns up in a quick check, look a little further. Learning to recognize and describe symptoms will make repairs easier for you or a mechanic at the shop. Describe problems accurately and fully. Saying that it won't run isn't the same thing as saying it quit at high speed and won't start, or that "it sat in my garage for 3 months and then wouldn't start."

Gather as many symptoms as possible to aid in diagnosis. Note whether the engine lost power gradually or all at once. Remember that the more complicated a machine is, the easier it is to troubleshoot because symptoms point to specific problems.

After the symptoms are defined, areas which could cause problems are tested and analyzed. Guessing at the cause of a problem may provide the solution, but it can easily lead to frustration, wasted time and a series of expensive, unnecessary parts replacements.

You do not need fancy equipment or complicated test gear to determine whether repairs can be attempted at home. A few simple checks could save a large repair bill and lost time while the bike sits in a dealer's service department. On the other hand, be realistic and don't attempt repairs beyond your abilities. Service departments tend to charge heavily for putting together a disassembled engine that may have been abused. Some won't even take on such a job, so use common sense and don't get in over your head.

OPERATING REQUIREMENTS

An engine needs 3 basics to run properly: correct fuel/air mixture, compression and a spark at the correct time (**Figure 1**). If one or more are missing, the engine will not run. Four-stroke engine operating principles are described under *Engine Principles* in Chapter Four.

If the machine has been sitting for any length of time and refuses to start, check and clean the spark plugs and then look to the gasoline delivery system. This includes the fuel tank, fuel shutoff valve and fuel line to the carburetor. Gasoline deposits may have formed and gummed up the carburetor jets and air passages. Gasoline tends to lose its potency after standing for long periods. Condensation may contaminate the fuel with water. Drain the old fuel (fuel tank, fuel lines and carburetors) and try starting with a fresh tankful.

TROUBLESHOOTING INSTRUMENTS

Refer to Chapter One for a list of the instruments needed.

STARTING THE ENGINE

When experiencing engine starting troubles, it is easy to work out of sequence and forget basic engine starting procedures. The following sections list factory recommended starting procedures for the VFR700F and VFR750F engine at the following ambient temperatures and engine conditions:
   a. Cold engine with normal air temperature.
   b. Cold engine with low air temperature.
   c. Warm engine and/or high air temperature.
   d. Flooded engine.

Starting Notes

1. A sidestand ignition cut-off system is used on 1990-on models. The position of the sidestand will affect engine starting. Note the following:
   a. The engine cannot start when the sidestand is down and the transmission is in gear.
   b. The engine can start when the sidestand is down and the transmission is in NEUTRAL. The engine will stop if the transmission is put in gear with the sidestand down.
   c. The engine can be started when the sidestand is up and the transmission is in NEUTRAL or in gear with the clutch lever pulled in.

2. Before starting the engine, shift the transmission into NEUTRAL and confirm that the engine stop switch is at RUN.

3. Turn the ignition switch to ON and confirm the following:
   a. The neutral indicator light is ON (when transmission is in NEUTRAL).
   b. The engine oil pressure warning light is ON.

4. The engine is now ready to start. Refer to the starting procedure in this section that best meets the air temperature and engine condition.

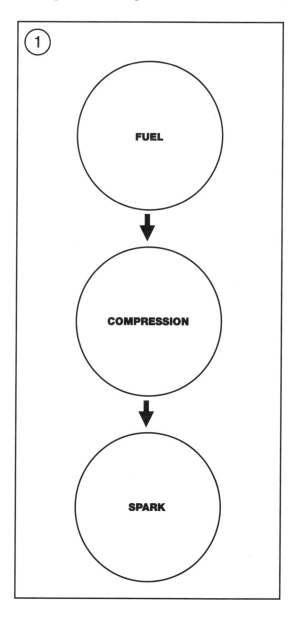

TROUBLESHOOTING

5. If the engine is idled at a fast speed for more than 5 minutes and/or the throttle is snapped on and off repeatedly at normal air temperatures, the exhaust pipes may discolor.

6. Excessive choke use can cause an excessively rich fuel mixture. This condition can wash oil off of the piston and cylinder walls, causing piston and cylinder scuffing.

CAUTION
Once the engine starts, the red oil pressure warning light should go off in a few seconds. If the light stays on longer than a few seconds, stop the engine immediately. Check the engine oil level as described in Chapter Three. If the oil level is okay, the oil pressure may be too low or the oil pressure switch may be shorted. Check the oiling system and correct the problem before starting the engine. If the oil pressure switch is okay, the system is warning you that some type of stoppage has occurred in the lubrication system and that oil is not being delivered to engine components. Severe engine damage will occur if the engine is run with low oil pressure. Refer to Engine Lubrication in this chapter.

NOTE
Do not operate the starter motor for more than 5 seconds at a time. Wait approximately 10 seconds between starting attempts.

Starting Procedure

Cold engine with normal air temperature

Normal air temperature is considered to be between 50-95° F (10-35° C).
1. Perform the procedures under *Starting Notes*.
2. Install the ignition key and turn the ignition switch to ON.
3. Pull the choke lever (**Figure 2**) to the fully ON position.
4. Depress the starter button (**Figure 3**) and start the engine. Do not open the throttle.

NOTE
When a cold engine is started with the throttle open and the choke ON, a lean mixture will result and cause hard starting.

5. With the engine running, operate the choke lever as required to keep the engine idle at 1,500-2,500 rpm.
6. After approximately 30 seconds, push the choke lever to the fully OFF position. If the idling is rough, open the throttle lightly until the engine warms up.

Cold engine with low air temperature

Low air temperature is considered to be 50° F (10° C) or lower.
1. Perform the procedures under *Starting Notes*.
2. Install the ignition key and turn the ignition switch to ON.
3. Pull the choke lever (**Figure 2**) to the fully ON position.
4. Depress the starter button (**Figure 3**) and start the engine. Do not open the throttle when pressing the starter button.
5. Once the engine is running, open the throttle slightly to help warm the engine. Continue warming the engine until the choke can be turned to the fully

OFF position and the engine responds to the throttle cleanly.

Warm engine and/or high air temperature

High air temperature is considered to be 95° F (35° C) or higher.
1. Perform the procedures under *Starting Notes*.
2. Install the ignition key and turn the ignition switch to ON.
3. Open the throttle slightly and depress the starter button (**Figure 3**). Do not use the choke.

Flooded engine

If the engine will not start after a few attempts it may be flooded. If you smell gasoline after attempting to start the engine, and the engine did not start, the engine is probably flooded. To start a flooded engine:
1. Turn the engine stop switch off.
2. Push the choke lever (**Figure 2**) to the OFF position.
3. Open the throttle completely and depress the starter button (**Figure 3**) for 5 seconds. Then release the start button and close the throttle.
4. Wait 10 seconds, then continue with Step 5.
5. Turn the engine stop switch on.
6. Turn the ignition switch on.
7. Open the throttle slightly and depress the starter button to start the engine. Do not use the choke.

EMERGENCY TROUBLESHOOTING

When the bike is difficult to start, or won't start at all, it doesn't help to wear down the battery by using the electric starter. Check for obvious problems even before getting out your tools. Go down the following list step by step. Do each one; you may be embarrassed to find the engine stop switch off, but that is better than wearing down the battery. If the bike still will not start, refer to the appropriate troubleshooting procedure in this chapter.
1. Is there fuel in the tank? Open the filler cap and rock the bike. Listen for fuel sloshing around.

> *WARNING*
> *Do not use an open flame to check in the tank. A serious explosion is certain to result.*

2. Is the fuel supply valve in the ON position? On 1986-1989 models, turn the valve to the ON position (**Figure 4**) and on 1990-on models turn the valve to the RES position (**Figure 5**). This will ensure you get the last remaining gas.
3. Is the engine stop switch (**Figure 6**) in the correct position? The engine should start and operate when the switch is in the RUN position. This switch is used primarily as an emergency or safety switch. Check that the switch is in the RUN position when starting the engine. Test the switch as described under Switches in Chapter Eight.
4. Are the spark plug caps on tight? Remove the fuel tank as described under *Fuel Tank Removal/Installation* in Chapter Seven. Push the spark plug caps (**Figure 7**) on all 4 cylinders and slightly rotate them to clean the electrical connection between the plug and the connector.
5. Is the choke lever (**Figure 2**) in the right position? The choke lever should be OFF for a warm engine and ON for a cold engine.

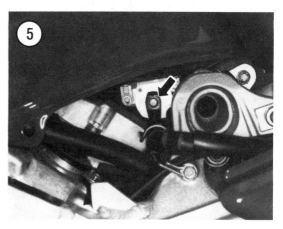

TROUBLESHOOTING

ENGINE STARTING TROUBLESHOOTING

An engine that refuses to start or is difficult to start is very frustrating. More often than not, the problem is very minor and can be found with a simple and logical troubleshooting approach.

First, review the steps under *Engine Starting Procedures* in this chapter. You may have been working out of sequence and flooded the engine. If the engine will not start by following the engine starting steps, continue with this section.

The following are beginning points from which to isolate engine starting problems.

NOTE
Do not operate the starter motor for more than 5 seconds at a time. Wait approximately 10 seconds between starting attempts.

Engine Fails to Start (Spark Test)

Perform the following spark test to determine if the ignition system is operating properly.

1. Remove all of the spark plugs as described in Chapter Three.

NOTE
If the spark plugs are wet after attempting to start the engine or if they appear fouled, refer to ***Fuel System*** *in this chapter.*

2. Connect each spark plug wire and connector to a spark plug and touch each spark plug base to a good ground like the engine cylinder head. Position the spark plugs so you can see the electrode.

WARNING
During the next step, do not hold the spark plugs or connectors with your fingers or a serious electrical shock may result. If necessary, use a pair of insulated pliers to hold the spark plugs or wires. The high voltage generated by the ignition system could produce serious or fatal shocks.

3. Crank the engine over with the starter. A fat blue spark should be evident across each spark plug electrode. If the spark is good, continue with Step 4. If the spark is weak or if there is no spark, perform Step 6.

NOTE
If the starter does not operate or if the starter motor rotates but the engine does not turn over, refer to ***Engine Will Not Crank*** *in this section.*

4. Check engine compression as described in Chapter Three. If the compression is good, perform Step 5. If the compression is low, check for one or more of the following:
   a. Valve clearance too tight.
   b. Leaking cylinder head gasket.
   c. Cracked or warped cylinder head.
   d. Worn piston rings, pistons and cylinders.
   e. Valve stuck open.
   f. Seized valve.
   g. Worn or damaged valve seat(s).
   h. Incorrect valve timing.

5. Disconnect the fuel tube at the carburetor and insert the open end into a clear, glass container. Turn the fuel valve (**Figure 4** or **Figure 5**) to ON, RES and OFF. A steady flow of fuel should be noticed with the fuel valve in the ON and RES positions. The

fuel flow should stop with the fuel valve in the OFF position. If the fuel flow is okay, perform Step 6. If there is no fuel flow or if the flow is slow and intermittent, check for one or more of the following conditions:
   a. Empty fuel tank.
   b. Plugged fuel tank cap vent hole.
   c. Clogged fuel filter or fuel line.
   d. Stuck or clogged carburetor fuel valve.
6. If the spark was weak or if there was no spark at one or more plugs, note the following:
   a. If there is no spark at all of the plugs, there may be a problem in the input side of the ignition system (spark unit [1986-1989 models] or ignition control module [1990-on models], pulse generator, sidestand switch or neutral switch). Test these parts as described in Chapter Eight.
   b. If there is no spark at one of the spark plugs, the spark plug is probably faulty or there is a problem with the spark plug wire or plug cap. Replace the spark plug and retest. If there is still no spark at that one plug, test the spark plug wire and plug cap as described in Chapter Eight. If those test good, the problem may be in the primary side of the ignition system (ignition coil or spark unit [1986-1989 models] or ignition control module [1990-on models]). Test these parts as described in Chapter Eight.

Engine is Difficult to Start

Check for one or more of the following possible malfunctions:
   a. Fouled spark plug(s).
   b. Improperly adjusted choke.
   c. Intake manifold air leak.
   d. Contaminated fuel system.
   e. Improperly adjusted carburetors.
   f. Ignition system malfunction.
   g. Weak ignition coil(s).
   h. Poor compression.
   i. Engine and transmission oil too heavy.

Engine Will Not Crank

Check for one or more of the following possible malfunctions:
   a. Blown fuse.
   b. Discharged battery.
   c. Defective starter motor, starter solenoid or start switch.
   d. Seized piston(s).
   e. Seized crankshaft bearings.
   f. Broken connecting rod.
   g. Locked-up transmission or clutch assembly.

ENGINE PERFORMANCE

In the following check list, it is assumed that the engine runs, but is not operating at peak performance. This will serve as a starting point from which to isolate a performance malfunction. Where ignition timing is mentioned as a problem, remember that there is no method of adjusting the ignition timing. If you check the ignition timing with a timing light as described in Chapter Three and it is incorrect, there is a faulty part within the ignition system. The individual parts must be checked and the faulty part(s) replaced.

Engine Will Not Start or Is Hard to Start

   a. Fuel tank empty.
   b. Obstructed fuel line, fuel shutoff valve or fuel filter.
   c. Sticking float valve in carburetor(s).
   d. Carburetors incorrectly adjusted.
   e. Improper starter valve (choke) operation.
   f. Improper throttle operation.
   g. Fouled or improperly gapped spark plug(s).
   h. Ignition timing incorrect.
   i. Broken or shorted ignition coil(s).
   j. Weak or faulty spark unit (1986-1989 models) or ignition control module (1990-on models), cam pulse generator (1986) or pulse generator(s).
   k. Improper valve timing.
   l. Faulty fuel pump.
   m. Clogged air filter element.
   n. Contaminated fuel.
   o. Engine flooded with fuel.
   p. Improper valve clearance.

Engine Starts but Then Stops

   a. Incorrect choke adjustment.
   b. Incorrect pilot air screw setting (closed).
   c. Incorrect ignition timing.

TROUBLESHOOTING

    d. Contaminated fuel.
    e. Faulty fuel pump.
    f. Intake manifold air leak.

Engine Will Not Idle

    a. Carburetors incorrectly adjusted (too lean or too rich).
    b. Fouled or improperly gapped spark plug(s).
    c. Leaking head gasket(s) or vacuum leak.
    d. Ignition timing incorrect.
    e. Improper valve timing.
    f. Obstructed fuel line or fuel shutoff valve.
    g. Low engine compression.
    h. Starter valve (choke) stuck in the open position.
    i. Incorrect pilot screw adjustment.
    j. Clogged slow jet(s) in the carburetor(s).
    k. Clogged air filter element.
    l. Improper valve clearance.
    m. Valve(s) and valve seat(s) require service.

Poor High Speed Performance

1. Check ignition timing as described in Chapter Three. If ignition timing is correct, perform Step 2. If the timing is incorrect, test the following ignition system components as described in Chapter Eight:
    a. Spark unit (1986-1989 models) or ignition control module (1990-on models).
    b. Cam pulse generator (1986).
    c. Pulse generator.
    d. Ignition coils.
2. Check the valve clearance as described in Chapter Three. Note the following:
    a. If the valve clearance is correct, perform Step 3.
    b. If the clearance is incorrect, readjust the valves and test ride the bike once again.
3. Disconnect the fuel tube at the carburetor and insert the open end into a clear, glass container. Turn the fuel valve to ON, RES and OFF. A steady flow of fuel should be noticed with the fuel valve in the ON and RES positions. The fuel flow should stop with the fuel valve in the OFF position. If the fuel flow is okay, perform Step 4. If there is no fuel flow or if the flow is slow and intermittent, check for one or more of the following conditions:
    a. Empty fuel tank.
    b. Plugged fuel tank cap vent hole.
    c. Clogged fuel filter or fuel line.

4. Remove the carburetors as described in Chapter Seven. Then remove the float bowls and check for stuck or clogged carburetor fuel inlet valve, contamination and plugged jets. If any contamination is found, disassemble and clean each carburetor. You should also pour out and discard the remaining fuel in the fuel tank and flush the fuel tank thoroughly. If no contamination was found and the jets were not plugged, perform Step 5.
5. Incorrect valve timing and worn or damaged valve springs can cause poor high speed performance. If the valve timing was set just prior to the bike experiencing this type of problem, the valve timing may be incorrect. If the valve timing was not set or changed, and you performed all of the other inspection procedures in this section without locating the problem area, the cylinder head cover should be removed and the valve train assembly inspected.

Low or Poor Engine Power

1. Support the bike with the rear wheel off the ground, then spin the rear wheel by hand. If the wheel spins freely, perform Step 2. If the wheel does not spin freely, check for the following conditions:
    a. Dragging rear brake.
    b. Drive chain damaged or adjusted too tightly.
    c. Excessive rear axle tightening torque (1986-1989).
    d. Worn or damaged rear wheel bearings.
2. Check the clutch adjustment and operation. If the clutch slips, refer to *Clutch* in this chapter.
3. If Steps 1 and 2 did not locate the problem, test ride the bike and accelerate lightly. If the engine speed increased according to throttle position, perform Step 4. If the engine speed did not increase, check for one or more of the following problems:
    a. Clogged or damaged air filter.
    b. Restricted fuel flow.
    c. Clogged fuel tank cap vent.
    d. Incorrect choke adjustment or operation.
    e. Clogged or damaged muffler.
4. Check for one or more of the following problems:
    a. Low engine compression.
    b. Fouled spark plug(s).
    c. Clogged carburetor jet(s).
    d. Incorrect ignition timing.
    e. Incorrect valve clearance.
    f. Incorrect oil level (too high or too low).
    g. Contaminated oil.
    h. Worn or damaged valve train assembly.

i. Engine overheating.

Engine Overheating

a. Incorrect coolant level.
b. Incorrect carburetor adjustment or jet selection.
c. Improper spark plug heat range.
d. Cooling system malfunction.
e. Clogged radiator and/or cooling fins.
f. Oil level low.
g. Oil not circulating properly.
h. Valves leaking.
i. Heavy engine carbon deposits.
j. Dragging brake(s).
k. Clutch slipping.

**Engine Overheating
(Cooling System Malfunction)**

Note the above, then proceed with the following items:
a. Clogged radiator.
b. Thermostat stuck closed.
c. Worn or damaged radiator cap.
d. Water pump worn or damaged.
e. Fan relay malfunction.
f. Thermostatic fan switch malfunction.
g. Damaged fan blade(s).
h. Clogged or blocked coolant passages in radiator, hoses or engine.

Excessive Exhaust Smoke and Engine Runs Roughly

a. Clogged air filter element.
b. Carburetor adjustment incorrect, mixture too rich.
c. Choke not operating correctly.
d. Water or other contaminants in fuel.
e. Clogged fuel line.
f. Spark plugs fouled.
g. Ignition coil defective.
h. Loose or defective ignition circuit wire.
i. Short circuit from damaged wire insulation.
j. Loose battery cable connection(s).
k. Valve timing incorrect.

Engine Lacks Acceleration

a. Carburetor mixture too lean.
b. Clogged fuel line.
c. Improper ignition timing.
d. Dragging brake(s).
e. Slipping clutch.

Engine Backfires

a. Improper ignition timing.
b. Carburetors improperly adjusted.
c. Lean fuel mixture.

Engine Misfires During Acceleration

a. Improper ignition timing.
b. Lean fuel mixture.

ENGINE NOISES

Often the first evidence of an internal engine problem is a strange noise. That knocking, clicking or tapping sound which you never heard before may be warning you of impending trouble.

While engine noises can indicate problems, they are difficult to interpret correctly; inexperienced mechanics can be seriously misled by them.

Professional mechanics often use a special stethoscope (which looks like a doctor's stethoscope) for isolating engine noises. You can do nearly as well with a "sounding stick" which can be an ordinary piece of doweling, or a section of small hose. By placing one end in contact with the area to which you want to listen and the other end to the front of your ear (not directly on your ear), you can hear sounds emanating from that area. The first time you do this, you may be confused at the strange sounds coming from even a normal engine. If you can, have an experienced friend or mechanic help you sort out the noises.

Consider the following when troubleshooting engine noises:

1. *Knocking or pinging during acceleration*– Caused by using a lower octane fuel than recommended. May also be caused by poor fuel. Pinging can also be caused by a spark plug of the wrong heat range or carbon build-up in the combustion chamber. Refer to *Correct Spark Plug Heat Range* and *Compression Test* in Chapter Three.

TROUBLESHOOTING

2. *Slapping or rattling noises at low speed or during acceleration*–May be caused by piston slap, i.e., excessive piston-cylinder wall clearance.

NOTE
Piston slap is easier to detect when the engine is cold and before the pistons have expanded. Once the engine has warmed up, piston expansion reduces piston-to-cylinder clearance.

3. *Knocking or rapping while decelerating*–Usually caused by excessive rod bearing clearance.
4. *Persistent knocking and vibration occurring every crankshaft rotation*–Usually caused by worn rod or main bearing(s). Can also be caused by broken piston rings or damaged piston pins.
5. *Rapid on-off squeal*–Compression leak around cylinder head gasket or spark plug(s).
6. *Valve train noise*–Check for the following:
   a. Valves adjusted incorrectly.
   b. Loose valve adjuster (1986-1989).
   c. Valve sticking in guide.
   d. Low oil pressure.
   e. Damaged rocker arm or holder (1986-1989).

ENGINE LUBRICATION

An improperly operating engine lubrication system will quickly lead to engine seizure. The engine oil level should be checked weekly and topped up, as described in Chapter Three. Oil pump service is described in Chapter Four.

Oil Consumption High or Engine Smokes Excessively

a. Worn valve guides.
b. Worn or damaged piston rings.

Excessive Engine Oil Leaks

a. Clogged air filter breather hose.
b. Loose engine parts.
c. Damaged gasket sealing surfaces.

Black Smoke

a. Clogged air filter.
b. Incorrect carburetor fuel level (too high).
c. Choke stuck.
d. Incorrect main jet (too large).

White Smoke

a. Worn valve guide.
b. Worn valve oil seal.
c. Worn piston ring oil ring.
d. Excessive cylinder and/or piston wear.
e. Coolant leaking into cylinders.

Oil Pressure Too High

a. Clogged oil filter.
b. Clogged oil gallery or metering orifices.
c. Pressure relief valve stuck closed.

Low Oil Pressure

a. Low oil level.
b. Damaged oil pump.
c. Clogged oil screen.
d. Clogged oil filter.
e. Internal oil leakage.
f. Pressure relief valve stuck open.

No Oil Pressure

a. Damaged oil pump.
b. Excessively low oil level.
c. No oil.
d. Internal oil leakage.
e. Damaged oil pump drive chain.
f. Damaged oil pump drive shaft.

Oil Pressure Warning Light Stays On

a. Low oil pressure.
b. No oil pressure.
c. Damaged oil pressure switch.
d. Short circuit in warning light circuit.

Oil Level Too Low

a. Oil level not maintained at correct level.
b. Worn piston rings.
c. Worn cylinder.
d. Worn valve guides.
e. Worn valve stem seals.

f. Piston rings incorrectly installed during engine overhaul.
g. External oil leakage.
h. Oil leaking into the cooling system.

Oil Contamination

a. Blown head gasket allowing coolant leakage.
b. Water contamination.
c. Oil and filter not changed at specified intervals or when abnormal operating conditions demand more frequent changes.

CLUTCH

The basic clutch troubles and causes are listed in this section.

Excessive Clutch Lever Operation

If the clutch lever is too hard to pull in, check the following:
a. Clogged hydraulic system.
b. Sticking slave cylinder piston.
c. Damaged clutch lifter bearing.
d. Push rod bent.

Rough Clutch Operation

This condition can be caused by excessively worn, grooved or damaged clutch housing slots.

Clutch Slippage

If the engine sounds like it is winding out without accelerating, the clutch is probably slipping. Some of the main causes of clutch slipping are:
a. Worn clutch plates.
b. Weak clutch springs.
c. No clutch lever free play.
d. Loose clutch lifter bolts.
e. Damaged clutch lifter.
f. Engine oil additive being used (clutch plates contaminated).

Clutch Drag

If the clutch will not disengage or if the bike creeps with the transmission in gear and the clutch disengaged, the clutch is dragging. Some of the main causes of clutch drag are:
a. Excessive clutch lever free play.
b. Warped clutch plates.
c. Damaged clutch lifter.
d. Loose clutch housing locknut.
e. Clutch lifter rod improperly installed.
f. Engine oil level too high.
g. Incorrect oil viscosity.
h. Engine oil additive being used.

GEARSHIFT LINKAGE

The gearshift linkage assembly connects the gearshift pedal (external shift mechanism) to the shift drum (internal shift mechanism).

The external shift mechanism can be examined after removing engine drive sprocket cover and the shift mechanism cover. The internal shift mechanism can only be examined once the engine has been removed from the frame and the crankcase disassembled. Common gearshift linkage troubles and checks to make are listed below.

Transmission Jumps out of Gear

a. Loose stopper arm bolt.
b. Damaged stopper arm.
c. Weak or damaged stopper arm spring.
d. Loose or damaged shifter cam.
e. Bent shift fork shaft(s).
f. Bent or damaged shift fork.
g. Worn gear dogs or slots.
h. Damaged shift drum grooves.

Difficult Shifting

a. Damaged clutch system.
b. Air in the clutch hydraulic system.
c. Incorrect oil viscosity.
d. Bent shift fork shaft(s).
e. Bent or damaged shift fork(s).
f. Worn gear dogs or slots.
g. Damaged shift drum grooves.

TRANSMISSION

Transmission symptoms are sometimes hard to distinguish from clutch symptoms. Common transmission troubles and checks to make are listed below. Refer to Chapter Six for transmission service procedures. Prior to working on the transmission, make sure the clutch and gearshift linkage assembly are not causing the trouble.

Difficult Shifting

a. Damaged clutch system.
b. Air in the clutch hydraulic system.
c. Incorrect oil viscosity.
d. Bent shift fork shaft(s).
e. Bent or damaged shift fork(s).
f. Worn gear dogs or slots.
g. Damaged shift drum grooves.

Jumps out of Gear

a. Loose or damaged shift drum stopper arm.
b. Bent or damaged shift fork(s).
c. Bent shift fork shaft(s).
d. Damaged shift drum grooves.
e. Worn gear dogs or slots.
f. Broken shift linkage return spring.

Incorrect Shift Lever Operation

a. Bent shift lever.
b. Stripped shift lever splines.
c. Damaged shift lever linkage.

Excessive Gear Noise

a. Worn bearings.
b. Worn or damaged gears.
c. Excessive gear backlash.

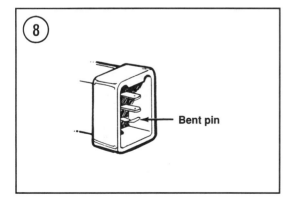

ELECTRICAL TROUBLESHOOTING

This section describes the basics of electrical troubleshooting, how to use test equipment and the basic test procedures with the various pieces of test equipment.

Electrical troubleshooting can be very time-consuming and frustrating without proper knowledge and a suitable plan. Refer to the wiring diagrams at the end of the book and at the individual system diagrams included with the *Charging System, Ignition System* and *Starting System* sections in this chapter. Wiring diagrams will help you determine how the circuit should work by tracing the current paths from the power source through the circuit components to ground. Also check any circuits that share the same fuse, ground or switch, etc. If the other circuits work properly, the shared wiring is okay and the cause must be in the wiring used only by the suspect circuit. If all related circuits are faulty at the same time, the probable cause is a poor ground connection or a blown fuse(s).

As with all troubleshooting procedures, analyze typical symptoms in a systematic procedure. Never assume anything and don't overlook the obvious like a blown fuse or an electrical connector that has separated. Test the simplest and most obvious cause first and try to make tests at easily accessible points on the bike.

Preliminary Checks and Precautions

Prior to starting any electrical troubleshooting procedure, perform the following:

a. Check the main fuse; make sure it is not blown. Replace if necessary.
b. Check the individual fuse(s) for each circuit; make sure it is not blown. Replace if necessary.
c. Inspect the battery. Make sure it is fully charged, the electrolyte level is correct (non-maintenance free batteries) and that the battery leads are clean and securely attached to the battery terminals. Refer to *Battery* in Chapter Eight.
d. Disconnect each electrical connector in the suspect circuit and check that there are no bent metal pins on the male side of the electrical connector (**Figure 8**). A bent pin will not connect to its mating receptacle in the female end of the connector, causing an open circuit.

e. Check each female end of the connector. Make sure that the metal connector on the end of each wire (**Figure 9**) is pushed all the way into the plastic connector. If not, carefully push them in with a narrow blade screwdriver.
f. Check all electrical wires where they enter the individual metal connector in both the male and female plastic connector.
g. Make sure all electrical connectors within the connector are clean and free of corrosion. Clean, if necessary, and pack the connectors with a dielectric grease.
h. After all is checked out, push the connectors together and make sure they are fully engaged and locked together (**Figure 10**).
i. Never pull on the electrical wires when disconnecting an electrical connector-pull only on the connector plastic housing.
j. Never use a self-powered test light on circuits that contain solid-state devices. The solid-state devices may be damaged.

TEST EQUIPMENT

Test Light or Voltmeter

A test light can be constructed of a 12-volt light bulb with a pair of test leads carefully soldered to the bulb. To check for battery voltage (12 volts) in a circuit, attach one lead to ground and the other lead to various points along the circuit. Where battery voltage is present the light bulb will light.

A voltmeter is used in the same manner as the test light to find out if battery voltage is present in any given circuit. The voltmeter, unlike the test light, will also indicate how much voltage is present at each test point. When using a voltmeter, attach the red lead (+) to the component or wire to be checked and the negative (–) lead to a good ground.

Self-powered Test Light and Ohmmeter

A self-powered test light can be constructed of a 12-volt light bulb, a pair of test leads and a 12-volt battery. When the test leads are touched together the light bulb will go on.

Use a self-powered test light as follows:
a. Touch the test leads together to make sure the light bulb goes on. If not, correct the problem prior to using it in a test procedure.
b. Disconnect the bike's battery or remove the fuse(s) that protects the circuit to be tested.
c. Select 2 points within the circuit where there should be continuity.
d. Attach one lead of the self-powered test light to each point.
e. If there is continuity, the self-powered test light bulb will come on.
f. If there is no continuity, the self-powered test light bulb will not come on indicating an open circuit.

An ohmmeter can be used in place of the self-powered test light. The ohmmeter, unlike the test light, will also indicate how much resistance is present between each test point. Low resistance means good continuity in a complete circuit. Before using an ohmmeter, it must first be calibrated. This is done by touching the leads together and turning the ohms calibration knob until the meter reads zero.

CAUTION
An ohmmeter must never be connected to any circuit which has power applied to it. Always disconnect the battery negative lead before using the ohmmeter.

Jumper Wire

When using a jumper wire, always install an inline fuse/fuse holder (available at most auto supply stores or electronic supply stores) to the jumper wire. Never use a jumper wire across any load (a component that is connected and turned on). This would result in a direct short and will blow the fuse(s) and/or damage components and wiring in that circuit.

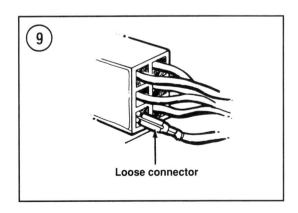

Loose connector

TROUBLESHOOTING

BASIC TEST PROCEDURES

Voltage Testing

Unless otherwise specified, all voltage tests are made with the electrical connector still connected. Insert the test leads into the backside of the connector and make sure the test lead touches the electrical wire or metal connector within the connector. If the test lead only touches the wire insulation you will get a false reading.

Always check both sides of the connector, as one side may be loose or corroded, thus preventing electrical flow through the connector. This type of test can be performed with a test light or a voltmeter A voltmeter will give the best results.

NOTE
If using a test light, it doesn't make any difference which test lead is attached to ground.

1. Attach the negative test lead (if using a voltmeter) to a good ground (bare metal). Make sure the part used for ground is not insulated with a rubber gasket or rubber grommet.
2. Attach the positive test lead (if using a voltmeter) to the point (electrical connector, etc.) you want to check.
3. Turn the ignition switch on. If using a test light, the test light will come on if voltage is present. If using a voltmeter, note the voltage reading. The reading should be within 1 volt of battery voltage (12 volts). If the voltage is 11 volts or less there is a problem in the circuit.

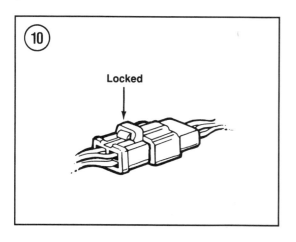

Voltage Drop Test

A voltage drop of 1 volt means there is a problem in the circuit. All components within the circuit are designed for low resistance in order to conduct electricity with a minimum loss of voltage.
1. Connect the voltmeter positive test lead to the end of the wire or switch closest to the battery.
2. Connect the voltmeter negative test lead to the other end of the wire or switch.
3. Turn the components on in the circuit.
4. A voltage reading of 1 volt or more indicates excessive resistance in the circuit. A reading equal to battery voltage indicates an open circuit.
5. Check the circuit for loose or dirty connections within an electrical connector(s).

Continuity Test

A continuity test is made to determine if the circuit is complete with no opens in either the electrical wires or components within that circuit.

Unless otherwise specified, all continuity tests are made with the electrical connector still connected. Insert the test leads into the backside of the connector and make sure the test lead touches the electrical wire or metal connector within the connector. If the test lead only touches the wire insulation, you will get a false reading.

Always check both sides of the connectors, as one side may be loose or corroded, thus preventing electrical flow through the connector. This type of test can be performed with a self-powered test light or an ohmmeter. An ohmmeter will give the best results.

If using an ohmmeter, calibrate the meter by touching the leads together and turning the ohms calibration knob until the meter reads zero. This is necessary in order to get accurate results.
1. Disconnect the battery negative lead as described under *Battery* in Chapter Three.
2. Attach one test lead (test light or ohmmeter) to one end of the part of the ciruclt to be tested.
3. Attach the other test lead to the other end of the part of the circuit to be tested.
4. The self-powered test light will come on if there is continuity. The ohmmeter will indicate either a low or no resistance (means good continuity in a complete circuit) or infinite resistance (means an open circuit).

Testing for a Short with a Self-powered Test Light or Ohmmeter

This test can be performed with either a self-powered test light or an ohmmeter.

1. Disconnect the battery negative lead as described under *Battery* in Chapter Three.
2. Remove the blown fuse from the fuse panel.
3. Connect one test lead of the test light or ohmmeter to the load side (battery side) of the fuse terminal in the fuse panel.
4. Connect the other test lead to a good ground (bare metal). If necessary, scrape away paint from the frame or engine (retouch later with paint). Make sure the part used for a ground is not insulated with a rubber gasket or rubber grommet.
5. With the self-powered test light or ohmmeter attached to the fuse terminal and ground, wiggle the wiring harness relating to the suspect circuit at 6 in. (15.2 cm) intervals. Start next to the fuse panel and work your way away from the fuse panel. Watch the self-powered test light or ohmmeter as you progress along the harness.
6. If the test light blinks or the needle on the ohmmeter moves, there is a short-to-ground at that point in the harness.

Testing For a Short with a Test Light or Voltmeter

This test can be performed with either a test light or voltmeter.

1. Remove the blown fuse from the fuse panel.
2. Connect the test light or voltmeter across the fuse terminals in the fuse panel. Turn the ignition switch on and check for battery voltage (12 volts).
3. With the test light or voltmeter attached to the fuse terminals, wiggle the wiring harness relating to the suspect circuit at 6 in. (15.2 cm) intervals. Start next to the fuse panel and work your way away from the fuse panel. Watch the test light or voltmeter as you progress along the harness.
4. If the test light blinks or the needle on the voltmeter moves, there is a short-to-ground at that point in the harness.

ELECTRICAL PROBLEMS

If light bulbs burn out frequently, the cause may be excessive vibration, loose connections that permit sudden current surges or the installation of the wrong type of bulb.

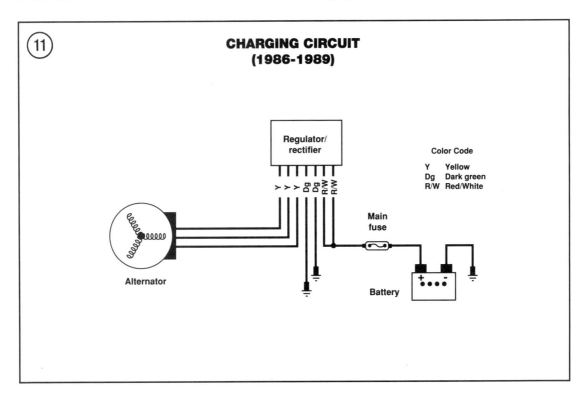

TROUBLESHOOTING

Most light and ignition problems are caused by loose or corroded ground connections. Check these prior to replacing a light bulb or electrical component.

CHARGING SYSTEM

The charging system consists of the battery, alternator and a voltage regulator/rectifier. Refer to **Figure 11** for 1986-1989 models or **Figure 12** for 1990-on models. A 30 amp main fuse protects the circuit.

Alternating current generated by the alternator is rectified to direct current. The voltage regulator maintains the voltage to the battery and additional electrical loads (lights, ignition, etc.) at a constant voltage regardless of variations in engine speed and load.

The basic charging system complaints are:
a. Battery discharging.
b. Battery overcharging.

Battery Discharging

1. Check all of the connections. Make sure they are tight and free of corrosion.
2. Perform the *Charging System Leakage Test* as described in Chapter Eight. Note the following:
   a. Current leakage under 1.2 mA, perform Step 3.
   b. Current leakage 1.2 mA or higher, perform Step 4.
3. Perform the *Regulator/Rectifier Unit Resistance Test* as described in Chapter Eight. Note the following:
   a. If the resistance readings are correct, perform the *Wiring Harness Test* as described in Chapter Eight. If the wiring harness tests are correct, the ignition switch is probably faulty; test the ignition switch as described in Chapter Eight.
   b. If the resistance readings are incorrect, replace the regulator/rectifier unit and retest.
4. Perform the *Charging Voltage Test* in Chapter Eight. Note the following:
   a. If the test readings are correct, perform Step 5.
   b. If the test readings are incorrect, perform Step 6.
5. Test the battery with the Honda battery tester (part No. 07GMJ-0010000). Note the following:

NOTE
If you do not have access to the battery tester, remove the battery from the bike and take it to a Honda dealer for testing.

   a. If the test readings are correct, the battery is faulty or the charging system is being overloaded, probably from accessory electrical items.

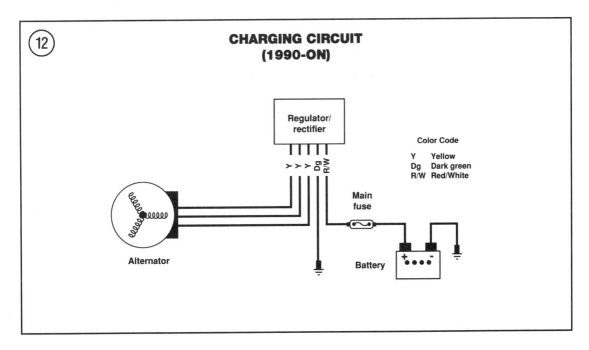

b. If the test readings are incorrect, check for an open circuit in the wiring harness and for dirty or loose-fitting terminals; clean and repair as required.

6. Perform the battery charging line and ground line tests as described under *Wiring Harness Test* in Chapter Eight. Note the following:

a. If the test readings are correct, perform Step 7.

b. If the test readings are incorrect, check for an open circuit in the wiring harness and for dirty or loose-fitting terminals; clean and repair as required.

7. Perform the charging coil line tests as described under *Wiring Harness Test* in Chapter Eight. Note the following:

a. If the test readings are incorrect, perform Step 8.

b. If the test readings are correct, perform Step 9.

8. Perform the *Charging Coil Resistance Test* as described in Chapter Eight. Note the following:

a. If the test readings are correct, check for a dirty or loose-fitting alternator electrical connector; clean and repair as required.

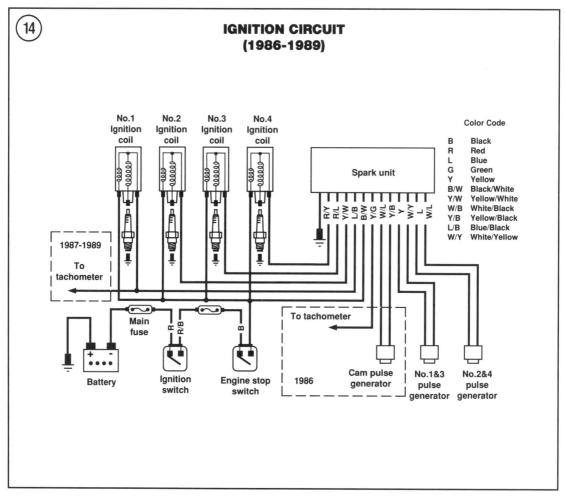

TROUBLESHOOTING

b. If the test readings are incorrect, replace the alternator assembly as described in Chapter Eight.

9. Perform the *Regulator/Rectifier Unit Resistance Test* as described in Chapter Eight. Note the following:

   a. If the resistance readings are correct, the battery is faulty. Replace the battery and retest.
   b. If the resistance readings are incorrect, replace the regulator/rectifier unit and retest.

Battery Overcharging

If the battery is overcharging, the regulator/rectifier unit (**Figure 13**) is faulty. Replace the regulator/rectifier unit as described in Chapter Eight.

IGNITION SYSTEM TROUBLESHOOTING

The ignition system consists of 4 ignition coils, 1 spark unit (1986-1989 models) or 1 ignition control module (1990-on models), 2 crankshaft driven pulse generators and 4 spark plugs. On 1986 models there was an additional camshaft pulse generator mounted on the front cylinder head.

Refer to **Figure 14** for 1986-1989 models or **Figure 15** for 1990-on models.

The basic ignition system complaints are:

a. No spark at all 4 spark plugs.
b. No spark at one spark plug.

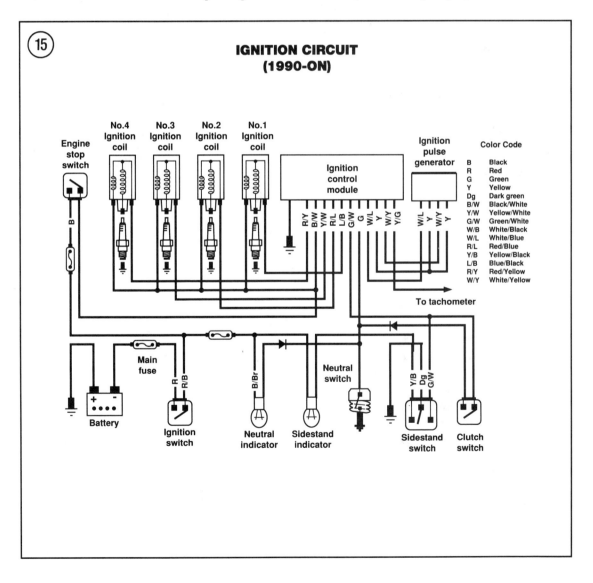

c. *1990-on:* Engine starts and runs but sidestand switch does not operate.

Prior to troubleshooting the ignition system, perform the following:

1. Check the battery to make sure it is fully charged and in good condition. A weak battery will result in a slower engine cranking speed.
2. Perform the spark test as described under *Engine Fails to Start (Spark Test)* in this chapter. Then refer to the appropriate ignition system complaint.
3. Because a loose or dirty electrical connector can prevent the ignition system from operating properly, check for dirty or loose-fitting connector terminals. The ignition system electrical diagrams and the wiring diagrams at the end of this book can be used to locate the appropriate electrical connectors. Also, refer to *Preliminary Checks and Precautions* under *Electrical Troubleshooting* in this chapter for additional information.

No Spark at All Four Spark Plugs

1986-1989 models

1. Check for dirty or loose-fitting connector terminals as previously described. Clean and repair as required.

> *NOTE*
> *If the ignition system does not operate properly after inspecting and cleaning the connector terminals, proceed with Step 2.*

2. Remove the seat as described in Chapter Thirteen.
3. Remove both side covers and tailpiece (A, **Figure 16**) as described in Chapter Thirteen.
4. Remove the rear turn signal mounting bracket as described in Chapter Thirteen.
5. Remove the screws securing the spark unit cover (B, **Figure 16**) and remove the cover.
6. Use Honda tester 07508-0013200 to test the spark unit. If the spark unit is good, *no fire* should be seen in the Off, P and Ext tester positions and *fire* should be seen in the On1 and On2 tester positions. Note the following:
    a. If the spark unit tests good, perform Step 7.
    b. If good results are not recorded, then replace the spark unit with a known good unit.

7. Disconnect the pulse generator 6-wire coupler (**Figure 17**).
8. Connect an ohmmeter between the yellow and white/yellow terminals and between the blue and white/blue terminals. Read the resistance on the ohmmeter. It should be 450-550 ohms. Note the following:
    a. If the resistance reading is incorrect, the pulse generator is faulty and should be replaced.
    b. If the resistance reading is correct, check for an open circuit between the spark unit and the pulse generator. If there is no open circuit, check the pulse generator connector for dirty or loose-fitting terminals. Perform Step 9.
9. On 1986 models only, perform the following:
    a. Disconnect the cam pulse generator 2-wire coupler (**Figure 18**).

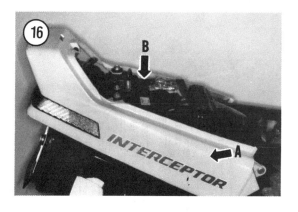

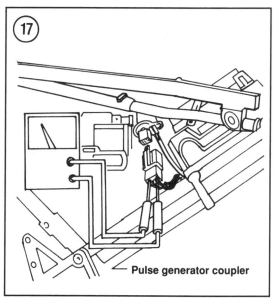

TROUBLESHOOTING

b. Connect an ohmmeter between the two wire terminals. Read the resistance on the ohmmeter. It should be 400-500 ohms. Note the following:

1. If the resistance reading is incorrect, the pulse generator is faulty and should be replaced.

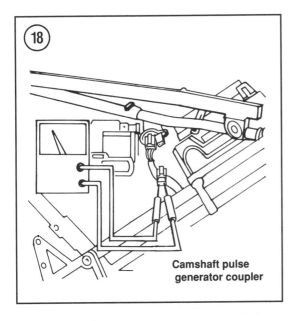

Camshaft pulse generator coupler

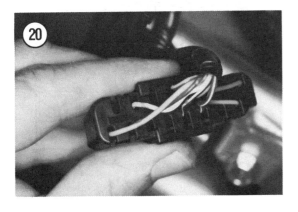

2. If the resistance is correct, check for an open circuit between the spark unit and the cam pulse generator. If there is no open circuit, check the cam pulse generator connector for dirty or loose-fitting terminals.

10. Reverse to install all previously removed parts.

1990-on models

1. Check for dirty or loose-fitting connector terminals as previously described. Clean and repair as required.

NOTE
If the ignition system does not operate properly after inspecting and cleaning the connector terminals, proceed with Step 2.

2. Remove both side covers and tailpiece as described in Chapter Thirteen.

3. Disconnect the ignition control module electrical connector (**Figure 19**).

4. Connect a voltmeter between the ignition control module connector black/white terminal (+) and the green terminal (−) (**Figure 20**).

5. Turn the ignition switch to ON and the engine stop switch to RUN. Read the voltage indicated on the voltmeter. It should be 12 volts. Note the following:

   a. If battery voltage is shown, perform Step 6.
   b. If there is no battery voltage, check for a faulty ignition or engine stop switch as described in Chapter Eight. If both switches test okay, check for an open circuit in the wiring harness or for dirty or loose-fitting connector terminals.
   c. Turn the ignition switch to OFF.

6. Connect an ohmmeter between the ignition control module connector yellow and white/yellow terminals and yellow and white/blue terminals (**Figure 20**). Read the resistance on the ohmmeter. It should be 450-550 ohms. Note the following:

   a. If the resistance reading is incorrect, perform Step 7.
   b. If the resistance reading is correct, perform Step 8.

7. Measure the pulse generator resistance as described under *Pulse Generator Resistance Test* in Chapter Eight. Note the following:

   a. If the resistance reading is incorrect, the pulse generator is faulty and should be replaced.

b. If the resistance reading is correct, check for an open circuit between the ignition control module and the pulse generator.

NOTE
*The pulse generator connector is located on the right-hand side (**Figure 21**). Remove the right-hand side middle fairing to expose the connector.*

NOTE
When switching between ohmmeter scales, always cross the test leads and zero the meter to assure a correct reading.

8. Connect an ohmmeter between the ignition control module connector light green and green terminals (**Figure 20**). The ohmmeter should show continuity with the transmission in NEUTRAL and should show no continuity (infinity) with the transmission in gear. Note the following:
   a. If the readings were incorrect, perform Step 9.
   b. If the readings were correct, perform Step 10.

9. Test the neutral switch as described in Chapter Eight. Note the following:
   a. If the neutral switch is faulty, replace it and retest.
   b. If the neutral switch is okay, check for an open circuit between the neutral switch and the ignition control module.

10. Connect an ohmmeter between the ignition control module connector green/white and green terminals (**Figure 20**). The ohmmeter should show continuity with the sidestand retracted and no continuity with the sidestand down. Note the following:
   a. If the readings were correct at both sidestand test positions, the ignition control module is faulty and should be replaced.
   b. If the readings were incorrect at both sidestand test positions, perform Step 11.

11. Test the sidestand switch as described in Chapter Eight. Note the following:
   a. If the sidestand switch is faulty, replace it and retest.
   b. If the sidestand switch is okay, check for an open circuit between the sidestand switch and the ignition control module.

12. Reverse to install all previously removed parts.

No Spark at One Spark Plug

If there is no spark at one spark plug, replace the plug and repeat the spark test. If the new plug will not fire, perform the following.

1A. *1986-1989:* If there is no spark at one of the front cylinders, then remove the lower fairing assembly as described in Chapter Thirteen. If there is no spark at one of the rear cylinders, then remove the seat.

1B. *1990-on:* Remove the left-middle fairing to test the left-hand cylinder coils and the right-middle fairing to test the right-hand cylinder coils.

2. Measure the coil's secondary resistance as described under *Ignition Coil Resistance Test* in Chapter Eight. Note the following:
   a. If the test results are incorrect, perform Step 3.
   b. If the test results are correct, repeat the spark test by switching the ignition coils. If you now have a spark, the original coil is faulty and should be replaced.

3. Remove the spark plug wire from the ignition coil and repeat the test made in Step 2. Note the following:
   a. If the test results are still incorrect, the ignition coil is faulty and should be replaced.
   b. If the test results are now correct, check for poor contact between the spark plug wire and coil. If this is okay, the spark plug wire is faulty and should be replaced.

4. Reverse to install all previously removed parts.

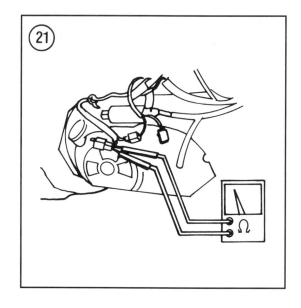

TROUBLESHOOTING

Engine Starts and Runs but Sidestand Switch Does Not Operate (1990-On)

When the engine is running and the transmission is in NEUTRAL, it should continue to run when the sidestand is moved down. When the engine is running and the transmission is in gear, the engine should stop when the sidestand is moved down.

1. Check that the sidestand switch indicator on the instrument panel works properly. Note the following:
    a. If the sidestand switch indicator does not work properly, perform Step 2.
    b. If the sidestand switch indicator works properly, check for an open circuit in the green/white sidestand switch wire.
2. Check the sidestand switch continuity as described in Chapter Eight. Note the following:
    a. If there is no continuity, the sidestand switch is faulty; replace the switch and retest.
    b. If there is continuity, check for a burned out sidestand switch bulb, for an open circuit in the green/white wire or for dirty or loose-fitting sidestand switch connector terminals.

STARTER SYSTEM TROUBLESHOOTING

The starting system consists of the starter motor, starter gears, solenoid, starter button, ignition switch, clutch switch, neutral switch, main and auxiliary fuses and battery.

Refer to the following illustrations:
a. **Figure 22**: 1986-1989 models.
b. **Figure 23**: 1990-1993 models.
c. **Figure 24**: 1994 models.

When the starter button is pressed, it allows current flow through the solenoid coil. The coil contacts close, allowing electricity to flow from the battery to the starter motor.

CAUTION
Do not operate the starter for more than 5 seconds at a time. Let it rest approximately 10 seconds, then use it again.

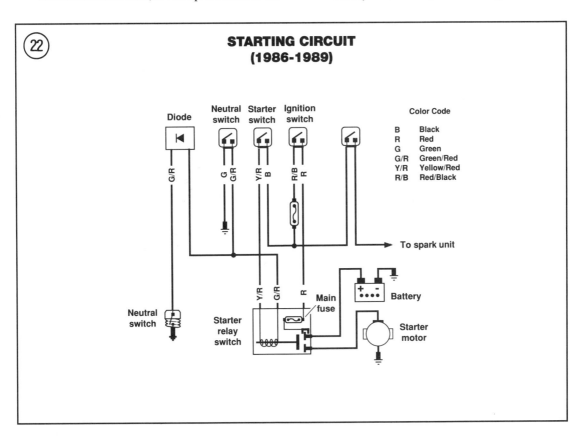

The starter should turn when the starter button is depressed when the transmission is in neutral and the clutch disengaged. If the starter does not operate properly, perform the following test procedures. Starter troubleshooting is grouped under the following:

a. Starter motor does not turn.
b. Starter motor turns slowly.
c. Starter motor turns but the engine does not.
d. Starter motor and engine turn but the engine does not start.

1. Check the battery to make sure it is fully charged and in good condition. Refer to Chapter Eight for battery service.
2. Check the starter cables for loose or damaged connections.
3. Check the battery cables for loose or damaged connections. Then check the battery state of charge as described under *Battery Testing* in Chapter Eight.
4. If the starter does not operate correctly after making these checks and adjustments, perform the test procedure that best describes the starting trouble.

Starter Motor Does Not Turn

1A. *1986-1989:* Remove the right side cover as outlined in Chapter Thirteen to expose the starter relay switch (**Figure 25**).

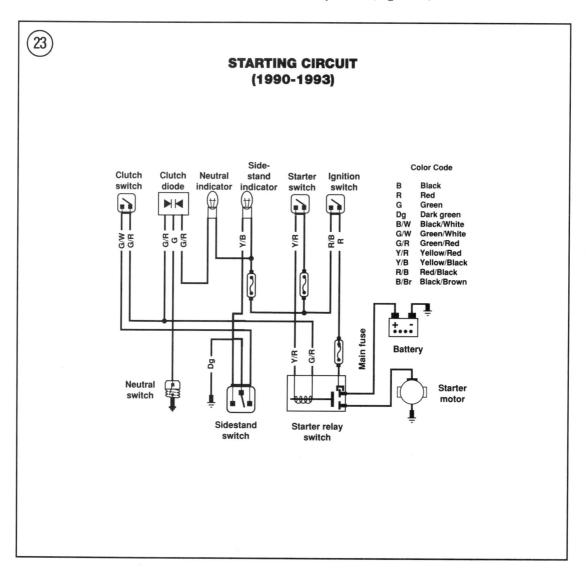

TROUBLESHOOTING

1B. *1990-on:* Remove the seat to expose the starter relay switch (**Figure 26**).

2. Check the starter relay connector for dirty or loose-fitting terminals. Clean and repair as required.

3. Check the starter relay switch. Turn the ignition switch on and depress the starter switch button. When the starter button is depressed, the starter relay switch should click once. Note the following:
   a. If there was a click, perform Step 4.
   b. If there was no click, perform Step 5.

CAUTION
Because of the large amount of current that will flow from the battery to the starter in Step 4, a large cable should be used to make the connection.

4. Remove the starter from the motorcycle as described in Chapter Eight. Using an auxiliary battery, apply battery voltage directly to the starter. The starter should turn when battery voltage is directly applied. Note the following:

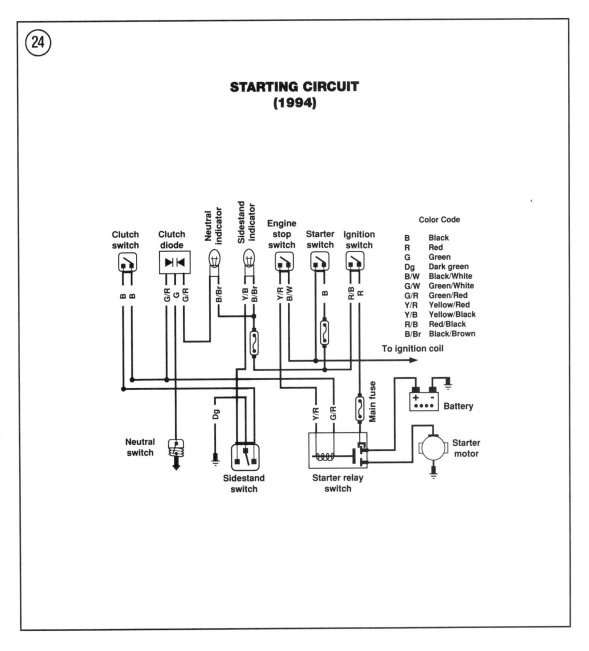

a. If the starter motor does not turn, disassemble and inspect the starter motor as described in Chapter Eight. Test the starter components and replace worn or damaged parts as required.

b. If the starter motor turns, check for loose or damaged starter cables. If the cables are okay, check the starter relay switch as described in Chapter Eight. Replace the starter relay switch if necessary.

5A. *1986-1989:* Remove the starter relay switch (**Figure 25**). Note the following:

a. Connect the positive lead of a fully charged 12-volt battery to the starter relay switch Yellow/Red wire terminal and the battery negative wire to the Green/Red wire terminal.

b. Connect an ohmmeter between the battery lead terminal and the starter motor lead terminal.

c. There should be continuity when the battery leads are connected to the starter relay switch and no continuity when they are disconnected.

5B. *1990-on:* Disconnect the starter relay switch connector and perform the following continuity tests:

a. Connect an ohmmeter between the starter relay switch connector (**Figure 26**) and the clutch switch diode connector green/red terminals. The ohmmeter should show continuity with the transmission in NEUTRAL and the clutch lever released.

b. Connect an ohmmeter between the starter relay switch connector green/red terminal (**Figure 26**) and the clutch switch ground green/red terminal. The ohmmeter should show continuity with the transmission in any gear and with the clutch lever pulled in and the sidestand up.

c. Connect an ohmmeter between the starter relay switch connector green/red terminal (**Figure 26**) and the sidestand switch green/red terminal. The ohmmeter should show continuity with the transmission in any gear and with the clutch lever pulled in and the sidestand up.

d. Reconnect the starter relay switch electrical connector (**Figure 26**).

6. If continuity was shown in each test, perform Step 7. If there is no continuity in one or more tests, check for dirty or loose-fitting terminals; clean and repair as required and retest. Then check for a short circuit in the wiring. If the connectors and wiring are okay, test the following components as described in Chapter Eight:

a. Clutch switch.
b. Clutch switch diode.
c. Neutral switch.
d. Sidestand switch (1990-on).

7. Pull the rubber cover away from the starter relay switch electrical connector to expose the wire terminals in the connector. Refer to **Figure 25** for 1986-1989 models or **Figure 26** for 1990-on models. Then connect a voltmeter between the starter relay switch connector yellow/red terminal (+) and ground (−). Turn the ignition switch to ON and the engine stop switch to RUN. Press the starter button and read the voltage indicated on the voltmeter. It should be 12 volts. Turn the ignition switch off and note the following:

a. If battery voltage is shown, perform Step 8.

b. If no battery voltage is shown, check for a blown main or sub-fuse; see *Fuses* in Chapter Eight. If the fuses are okay, check for an open circuit in the wiring harness or for dirty or loose-fitting terminals. If the wiring and connectors are okay, check for a faulty ignition and/or starter switch as described in Chapter Eight.

8. Test the starter relay switch as described in Chapter Eight. Note the following:

a. If the starter relay switch is normal, check for dirty or loose-fitting terminals in its connector block.

b. If the starter relay switch is faulty, replace it and retest.

Starter Motor Turns Slowly

If the starter motor turns slowly and all engine components and systems are normal, perform the following:

TROUBLESHOOTING

1. Test the battery as described in Chapter Eight.
2. Check for the following:
   a. Loose or corroded battery terminals.
   b. Loose or corroded battery ground cable.
   c. Loose starter motor cable.
3. Remove, disassemble and bench test the starter as described under *Starter* in Chapter Eight.
4. Check the starter for binding during operation. Disassemble the starter and check the armature shafts for bending or damaged. Also check the starter clutch as described in Chapter Four.

Starter Motor Turns but the Engine Does Not

If the starter motor turns but the engine does not, perform the following:
1. If the starter motor is running backwards and the starter was just reassembled or if the starter motor cables were disconnected and then reconnected to the starter:
   a. The starter motor was reassembled incorrectly.
   b. The starter motor cables were incorrectly installed.
2. Check for a damaged starter clutch (Chapter Four).
3. Check for a damaged or faulty starter pinion gear (Chapter Four).
4. Check for damaged starter reduction gears (Chapter Four).

Starter Relay Switch Clicks but Engine Does Not Turn Over

1. Excessive reduction gear friction.
2. Crankshaft cannot turn over because of mechanical failure.

Starter Motor Works with the Transmission in Neutral but Does Not Turn with the Transmission in Gear with the Clutch Lever Pulled in and the Sidestand Up (1990-on)

1. Turn the ignition switch on and move the sidestand up and down while watching the sidestand switch indicator light. Note the following:
   a. If the indicator light works properly, perform Step 2.
   b. If the indicator light does not work, check for a blown bulb, damaged sidestand switch (Chapter Eight) or an open circuit in the wiring harness.
2. Test the clutch switch as described in Chapter Eight. Note the following:
   a. Clutch switch okay, perform Step 3.
   b. Clutch switch faulty, replace switch and retest.
3. Test the sidestand switch as described in Chapter Eight. Note the following:
   a. Sidestand switch okay, perform Step 4.
   b. Sidestand switch faulty, replace switch and retest.
4. Check for an open circuit in the wiring harness. Check for loose or damaged electrical connector.

CARBURETOR TROUBLESHOOTING

The following lists isolate basic carburetor problems under specific complaints.

Engine Will Not Start

If the engine will not start and you have determined that the electrical and mechanical systems are working correctly, check the following:
1. If there is no fuel going to the carburetors, note the following:
   a. Clogged fuel tank breather cap hole.
   b. Clogged fuel tank-to-carburetor tube.
   c. Clogged fuel valve screen.
   d. Defective fuel pump.
   e. Incorrect float adjustment.
   f. Stuck or clogged fuel valve in carburetor.
2. If the engine is flooded (too much fuel), note the following:
   a. Flooded carburetors. Fuel valve in carburetor stuck open.
   b. Clogged air filter element.

3. A faulty emission control system (if equipped) can cause fuel problems. Note the following:
   a. Faulty purge control valve (PCV).
   b. Faulty air injection control valve (AICV).
   c. Loose, disconnected or plugged emission control system hoses.
4. If you have not located the problem in Steps 1-3, check for the following:
   a. Contaminated or deteriorated fuel.
   b. Intake manifold air leak.
   c. Clogged pilot or choke circuit.

Engine Starts but Idles and Runs Poorly or Stalls Frequently

An engine that idles roughly or stalls may have one or more of the following problems:
   a. Clogged air cleaner.
   b. Contaminated fuel.
   c. Incorrect pilot screw adjustment.
   d. Incorrect carburetor synchronization.
   e. Incorrect idle speed.
   f. Bystarter or slow circuit clogged.
   g. Loose, disconnected or damaged fuel and emission control vacuum hoses.
   h. Intake air leak.
   i. Lean fuel mixture.
   j. Rich fuel mixture.
   k. Faulty secondary air supply system on U.S. models.

Incorrect Fast Idle Speed

A fast idle speed can be due to one of the following problems:
   a. Faulty bystarter valve.
   b. Incorrect choke cable free play.
   c. Incorrect carburetor synchronization.

Poor Gas Mileage and Engine Performance

Poor gas mileage and engine performance can be caused by infrequent engine tune-ups. Check your records to see when your bike was last tuned up and compare against the recommended tune-up service intervals in Chapter Three. If the last tune-up was within the specified service intervals, check for one or more of the following problems:
   a. Clogged air filter.
   b. Clogged fuel system.
   c. Loose, disconnected or damaged fuel and emission control vacuum hoses.

Rich Fuel Mixture

A rich carburetor fuel mixture can be caused by one or more of the following conditions:
   a. Clogged or dirty air filter.
   b. Worn or damaged fuel valve and seat.
   c. Clogged air jets.
   d. Incorrect float level (too high).
   e. Bystarter valve damaged or stuck ON.
   f. Flooded carburetors.

Lean Fuel Mixture

A lean carburetor fuel mixture can be caused by one or more of the following conditions:
   a. Clogged carburetor air vent hole.
   b. Clogged fuel filter.
   c. Restricted fuel line.
   d. Intake air leak.
   e. Incorrect float level (too low).
   f. Worn or damaged fuel valve.
   g. Faulty throttle valve.
   h. Faulty vacuum piston.
   i. Faulty fuel pump.
   j. Faulty secondary air supply system (U.S. models).

Engine Backfires

   a. Lean fuel mixture.
   b. Incorrect carburetor adjustment.

Engine Misses During Acceleration

When there is a pause before the engine responds to the throttle, the engine is missing. An engine miss can occur when starting from a dead stop or at any speed. An engine miss may be due to one of the following:
   a. Lean fuel mixture.
   b. Faulty ignition coil secondary wires; check for cracking, hardening or bad connections.
   c. Faulty vacuum hoses; check for kinks, splits or bad connections.

TROUBLESHOOTING

    d. Vacuum leaks at the carburetor and/or intake manifold(s).
    e. Fouled spark plug(s).
    f. Low engine compression, especially at one cylinder only. Check engine compression as described in Chapter Three. Low compression can be caused by worn engine components.

EXCESSIVE VIBRATION

Usually, excessive vibration is caused by loose engine mounting hardware.

If mounting hardware is okay, vibration can be difficult to find without disassembling the engine.

FRONT SUSPENSION AND STEERING

Poor handling may be caused by improper tire pressure, a damaged or bent frame or front steering components, a worn front fork assembly, worn wheel bearings or dragging brakes.

Bike Steers to One Side

  a. Bent axle.
  b. Bent frame.
  c. Worn or damaged front wheel bearings.
  d. Worn or damaged swing arm pivot bearings.
  e. Damaged steering head bearings.
  f. Uneven front fork adjustment.
  g. Incorrectly installed wheels.

Suspension Noise

  a. Loose mounting fasteners.
  b. Damaged fork(s) or rear shock absorber.
  c. Incorrect front fork oil.

Wobble/Vibration

  a. Loose front or rear axle.
  b. Loose or damaged wheel bearing(s).
  c. Damaged wheel rim(s).
  d. Damaged tire(s).
  e. Loose swing arm pivot bolt.
  f. Unbalanced tire and wheel.

Hard Suspension (Front Forks)

  a. Insufficient tire pressure.
  b. Damaged steering head bearings.
  c. Incorrect steering head bearing adjustment.
  d. Bent fork tubes.
  e. Binding slider.
  f. Incorrect fork oil.
  g. Plugged fork oil hydraulic passage.

Hard Suspension (Rear Shock Absorbers)

  a. Excessive tire pressure.
  b. Bent damper rod.
  c. Incorrect shock adjustment.
  d. Damaged shock absorber bushing(s).
  e. Damaged shock absorber bearing.
  f. Damaged swing arm pivot bearing.

Soft Suspension (Front Forks)

  a. Insufficient tire pressure.
  b. Insufficient fork oil level or fluid capacity.
  c. Incorrect oil viscosity.
  d. Weak or damaged fork springs.

Soft Suspension (Rear Shock Absorbers)

  a. Insufficient tire pressure.
  b. Weak or damaged shock absorber spring.
  c. Damaged shock absorber.
  d. Incorrect shock absorber adjustment.
  e. Leaking damper unit.

BRAKE PROBLEMS

Sticking disc brakes may be caused by a stuck piston(s) in a caliper assembly or warped pad shim(s).

Brake Drag

  a. Clogged brake hydraulic system.
  b. Sticking caliper pistons.
  c. Sticking master cylinder piston.

d. Incorrectly installed brake caliper.
e. Warped brake disc.
f. Sticking caliper side slide pin.
g. Incorrect wheel alignment.

Brakes Grab

a. Contaminated brake pads.
b. Incorrect wheel alignment.
c. Warped brake disc.

Brake Squeal or Chatter

a. Contaminated brake pads.
b. Incorrectly installed brake caliper.
c. Warped brake disc.

d. Incorrect wheel alignment.
e. Anti-rattle spring missing in caliper.

Soft or Spongy Brake Lever or Pedal

a. Low brake fluid level.
b. Air in brake hydraulic system.
c. Leaking brake hydraulic system.

Hard Brake Lever or Pedal Operation

a. Clogged brake hydraulic system.
b. Sticking caliper pistons.
c. Sticking master cylinder piston.
d. Glazed or worn brake pads.

CHAPTER THREE

PERIODIC LUBRICATION, MAINTENANCE AND TUNE-UP

Your bike can be cared for by two methods: preventive and corrective maintenance. Because a motorcycle is subjected to tremendous heat, stress and vibration—even in normal use—preventive maintenance prevents costly and unexpected corrective maintenance. When neglected, any bike becomes unreliable and actually dangerous to ride. When properly maintained, your Honda is one of the most reliable bikes available and will give many miles and years of dependable, fast and safe riding. By maintaining a routine service schedule as described in this chapter, costly mechanical problems and unexpected breakdowns can be prevented.

The procedures presented in this chapter can be easily performed by anyone with average mechanical skills. **Table 1** is a suggested factory maintenance schedule. **Tables 1-9** are located at the end of this chapter.

NOTE
Where differences occur relating to the United Kingdom (U.K.) models they are identified. If there is no (U.K.) designation relating to a procedure, photo or illustration it is identical to the United States (U.S.) models.

ROUTINE CHECKS

The following pre-ride inspection checks should be performed at the start of each riding day.

Engine Oil Level

Refer to *Engine Oil Level Check* under *Periodic Lubrication* in this chapter.

Fuel

All VFR700F and VFR750F engines are designed to use gasoline that has a pump octane number (R+M)/2 of 86 or higher or a gasoline with a research octane number of 91 or higher. The pump octane number is normally displayed at service station gas pumps. Using a gasoline with a lower octane number can cause pinging or spark knock, both of which can lead to engine damage. Unleaded fuel is recommended because it reduces engine and spark plug deposits.

When choosing gasoline and filling the fuel tank, note the following:

a. When filling the tank, do not overfill it. There should be no fuel in the filler neck (tube located between the fuel cap and tank).
b. To help meet clean air standards in some areas of the United States and Canada, oxygenated fuels are being used. Oxygenated fuels are conventional gasolines that are blended with an alcohol or ether compound to increase the gasoline's octane. When using an oxygenated fuel, make sure that it meets the minimum octane rating as previously specified.
c. Because oxygenated fuels can damage plastic and paint, make sure not to spill fuel onto the fuel tank during fuel stops.
d. An ethanol (ethyl or grain alcohol) gasoline that contains more than 10 percent ethanol by volume may cause engine starting and performance related problems.
e. A methanol (methyl or wood alcohol) gasoline that contains more than 5 percent methanol by volume may cause engine starting and performance related problems. Gasoline that contains methanol must have corrosion inhibitors to protect the metal, plastic and rubber parts in the fuel system from damage.
f. Honda states that you can use a gasoline containing up to 15 percent MTBE (Methyl Tertiary Butyl Ether) by volume.
g. If your bike is experiencing fuel system damage or performance related problems from the use of oxygenated fuels, consult with a mechanic in an area where this type of fuel is widely sold and used.

Coolant Level

The coolant reserve tank is mounted behind the left-hand side cover on 1986-1989 models and the right-hand middle fairing on 1990-on models.

WARNING
Because the cooling fan can come on when the ignition switch is in the ON position, keep your hands, tools and clothing away from the fan when performing the following.

1. Start the engine and allow it to idle until it reaches normal operating temperature.
2. Turn the engine off.

3. Hold the bike upright and check the coolant level in the coolant reserve tank. The level should be between the "UPPER" and "LOWER" level marks. Refer to **Figure 1** for 1986-1989 models or **Figure 2** for 1990-on models.

4. If necessary, add coolant as follows:
   a. On 1986-1989 models, remove the left-hand side cover. On 1990-on models, remove the right-hand middle fairing.
   b. Remove the coolant reserve tank cap and add a 50:50 mixture of distilled water and antifreeze into the reserve tank (not the radiator) to bring the level to the "UPPER" mark.

NOTE
*If the coolant tank is empty, there may be a leak in the cooling system. Wait until the engine cools to room temperature and then remove the radiator cap and check the level in the radiator. If necessary, refer to **Cooling System Inspection** in this chapter.*

PERIODIC LUBRICATION, MAINTENANCE AND TUNE-UP

> **WARNING**
> *Do not remove the radiator cap when the engine is hot. The coolant is under pressure and scalding and severe burns could result.*

c. Reinstall the reserve tank cap.

d. Install the left-hand side cover on 1986-1989 models and the right-hand middle fairing on 1990-on models.

Tire Pressure

Tire pressure must be checked with the tires cold. Correct tire pressure depends on the load you are carrying. See **Table 2**. See *Tires and Wheels* in this chapter.

Brake Operation

Check that both brakes (front and rear) operate with full hydraulic advantage. Check the front and rear brake fluid level as described under *Disc Brake Fluid Level Inspection* in this chapter. Check that there is no brake fluid leakage from the reservoirs, master cylinders, calipers or brake lines.

Drive Chain

Lubricate the drive chain and check the chain slack as described under *Drive Chain Lubrication* and *Drive Chain Adjustment* in this chapter. Adjust the chain slack and align the chain if necessary.

Throttle

Sitting on the bike, with the brake ON, the transmission in NEUTRAL and with the engine idling, move the handlebars from side to side, making sure the idle does not increase or decrease by itself. Check that the throttle opens and closes smoothly in all steering positions.

Engine Stop Switch

The engine stop switch (**Figure 3**) is designed primarily as an emergency switch. It is part of the right-hand switch assembly next to the throttle housing and it has 2 operating positions: OFF and RUN. When the switch is in the OFF position, the engine will not start or run. In the RUN position, the engine should start and run with the ignition switch on while pressing the starter button. With the engine idling, move the switch to OFF. The engine should turn off.

Sidestand Ignition Cut-off System Inspection (1990-on Models)

1. Support the bike on its centerstand (optional) or in an upright position if not equipped with a centerstand.

2. Check the sidestand spring. Make sure the spring is in good condition and has not lost tension.

3. Swing the sidestand down and up a few times. The sidestand should swing smoothly and the spring should provide proper tension.

4. While sitting on the motorcycle, shift the transmission into NEUTRAL and move the sidestand up.

5. Start the engine and allow it to warm up. Then pull in the clutch lever and shift the transmission into gear.

6. Lower the sidestand with your foot. The engine should stop as the sidestand is lowered.

7. If the sidestand did not operate as described, inspect the sidestand switch as described in Chapter Eight.

Lights, Brakelight and Horn

With the engine running, check the following.

1. Pull the front brake lever and check that the brake light comes on.

2. Push the rear brake pedal and check that the brake light comes on soon after you have begun depressing the pedal.

3. Move the dimmer switch (A, **Figure 4**) up and down between the high and low positions, and check to see that both headlight elements are working.

4. Push the turn signal switch (B, **Figure 4**) to the left position and then to the right position and check that all 4 turn signal lights are working.

5. Push the horn button (C, **Figure 4**) and note that the horn blows loudly.

6. If the horn or any light failed to work properly, refer to Chapter Eight.

MAINTENANCE INTERVALS

The services and intervals shown in **Table 1** are recommended by the factory. Strict adherence to these recommendations will insure long life from your Honda. If the bike is run in an area of high humidity, the lubrication services must be done more frequently to prevent possible rust damage.

For convenience when maintaining your motorcycle, most of the services shown in **Table 1** are described in this chapter. Those procedures which require more than minor disassembly or adjustment are covered elsewhere in the appropriate chapter. The *Table of Contents* and *Index* can help you locate a particular service procedure.

TIRES AND WHEELS

Tires and wheels should be checked prior to each ride and daily when traveling.

Tire Pressure

Tire pressure should be checked and adjusted to maintain the tire profile, good traction and handling and to get the maximum life out of the tire. A simple, accurate gauge (**Figure 5**) can be purchased for a few dollars and should be carried in your motorcycle tool kit. Tire pressure should be checked when the tires are cold. The appropriate tire pressures are shown in **Table 2**.

NOTE
*After checking and adjusting the air pressure, make sure to reinstall the air valve cap (**Figure 6**). The cap prevents small pebbles and dirt from collecting in the valve stem; this could allow air leakage or result in incorrect tire pressure readings.*

NOTE
A loss of air pressure may be due to a loose or damaged valve core. Put a few drops of water on the top of the valve core. If the water bubbles, tighten the valve core and recheck. If air is still leaking from the valve after tightening it, replace the valve stem assembly.

Tire Inspection

The tires take a lot of punishment so inspect them periodically for excessive wear. Inspect the tires for the following:

a. Deep cuts and imbedded objects (i.e., stones, nails, etc.). If you find a nail or other object in a tire, mark its location with a light crayon prior to removing it. This will help to locate the hole for repair. Refer to Chapter Ten for tire changing and repair information.

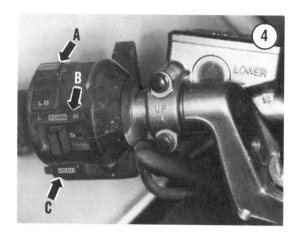

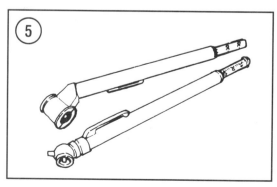

PERIODIC LUBRICATION, MAINTENANCE AND TUNE-UP

b. Flat spots.
c. Cracks.
d. Separating plies.
e. Sidewall damage.

NOTE
Tubeless tires have the ability to self-seal when punctured. If the foreign object was very small, air leakage may be very slow. Check the tires carefully and if necessary, wash the tires to obtain a better view of the tread.

Tire Wear Analysis

Abnormal tire wear should be analyzed to determine its causes. The most common causes are the following:

a. *Incorrect tire pressure:* Check tire pressure as described in this chapter.
b. Overloading.
c. Incorrect wheel alignment.

d. *Incorrect wheel balance:* The tire/wheel assembly should be balanced when installing a new tire and then re-balanced each time the tire is removed and reinstalled.
e. Worn or damaged wheel bearings.

Incorrect tire pressure is the biggest cause of abnormal tire wear (**Figure 7**). Under-inflated tires will result in higher tire temperatures, hard or imprecise steering and abnormal tire wear. Overinflated tires will result in a hard ride and abnormal tire wear. Examine the tire tread, comparing wear in the center of the contact patch with tire wear at the edge of the contact patch. Note the following:

a. If a tire shows excessive wear at the edge of the contact patch, but the wear at the center of the contact patch is okay, the tire has been under-inflated.
b. If a tire shows excessive wear in the center of the contact patch, but the wear at the edge of the contact patch is okay, the tire has been overinflated.

Tread Depth

Check local traffic regulations concerning minimum tread depth. Measure the tread depth at the center of tire and to the center of the tire tread (**Figure 8**) using a tread depth gauge (**Figure 9**) or a small ruler. Honda recommends that original equipment tires be replaced when the front tire tread depth is 1.5 mm (1/16 in.) or less, when the rear tread depth is 2.0 mm (3/32 in.) or less or when tread wear indicators appear at the designated area on the tire indicating the minimum tread depth.

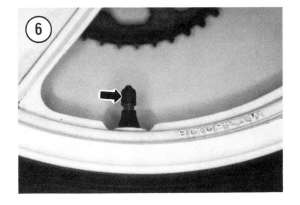

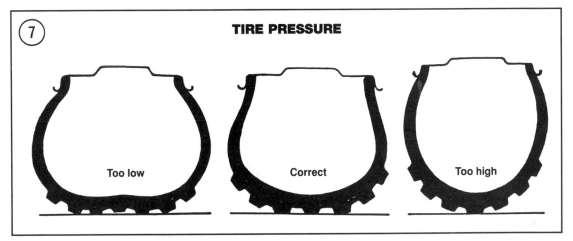

Rim Inspection

Frequently inspect the wheel rims. If a rim has been damaged, it might have been knocked out of alignment. Improper wheel alignment can cause severe vibration and result in an unsafe riding condition. If the rim is damaged, the wheel must be replaced as it cannot be repaired.

BATTERY

Removal and Installation

1986-1989 models

1. Remove the right-hand side cover as described in Chapter Thirteen.
2. Remove the battery bracket bolt (A, **Figure 10**), then swing the bracket (B, **Figure 10**) out of the way.
3. First disconnect the battery negative (–) (A, **Figure 11**) and then the positive (+) (B, **Figure 11**) cables from the battery.
4. Unhook the battery vent tube (C, **Figure 11**) from the battery. Leave it routed through the bike's frame.
5. Slide the battery out of the box in the frame.
6. Wipe off any of the highly corrosive residue that may have dripped from the battery during removal.
7. Clean the battery box in the frame of any corrosion and road dirt. Clean up any rust that may have occurred from corrosion and touch up with paint.
8. After the battery has been refilled, recharged or replaced, install it by reversing these removal steps.

NOTE
If the end of the vent tube that attaches to the battery has started to crack or

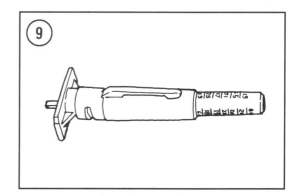

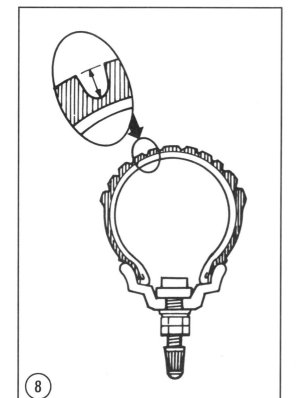

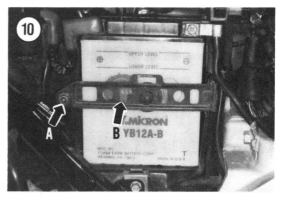

PERIODIC LUBRICATION, MAINTENANCE AND TUNE-UP

deteriorate, cut off that bad short section, then reattach the good section of hose to the battery fitting.

CAUTION
If you removed the vent tube from the frame, be sure to route it so that residue will not drain onto any part of the bike's frame. The tube must be free of bends or twists as any restriction may pressurize the battery and damage it.

1990-on models

1. Remove the seat as described in Chapter Thirteen.
2. Unhook the strap (A, **Figure 12**) securing the battery or battery cover.
3. On models so equipped, remove the cover (B, **Figure 12**).
4. First disconnect the battery negative (–) (A, **Figure 13**), then the positive (+) (B, **Figure 13**) cables from the battery.
5. Lift the battery out of the holder.
6. Clean the battery holder in the frame of any corrosion and road dirt. Clean up any rust that may have occurred from corrosion and touch up with paint.
7. After the battery has been recharged or replaced, install it by reversing these removal steps.

Electrolyte Level Check (Non-Maintenance Free Battery)

The battery is the heart of the electrical system. It should be checked and serviced frequently. Most electrical system troubles can be attributed to neglect of this vital component.

The electrolyte level should be maintained between the 2 marks on the battery case (**Figure 14**). If the electrolyte level is low, remove the battery from the bike so it can be thoroughly serviced and checked.

WARNING
Protect your eyes, skin and clothing. If electrolyte gets into your eyes, flush your eyes thoroughly with clean water and get prompt medical attention.

CAUTION
Be careful not to spill battery electrolyte on painted or polished surfaces. The liquid contains sulfuric acid that is highly corrosive and will damage the finish. If it is spilled, wash it off immediately with soapy water and thoroughly rinse with clean water.

1. Set the battery on a stack of newspapers or shop cloths (**Figure 15**) to protect the work surface of your workbench.
2. Remove the filler caps (**Figure 16**) from the battery cells and add distilled water to correct the

fluid level. Never add electrolyte (acid) to correct the level.

NOTE
If distilled water has been added, reinstall the battery caps and gently shake the battery for several minutes to mix the existing electrolyte with the new water.

CAUTION
If distilled water is going to be added to a battery in freezing or near freezing weather, add it to the battery, dress warmly and then ride the bike for a minimum of 30 minutes. This will help mix the just-added water into the electrolyte in the battery. Distilled water is lighter than electrolyte and will float on top of the electrolyte if it is not mixed in properly. If the water stays on the top, it may freeze and fracture the battery case.

3. After the fluid level has been corrected and the battery allowed to stand a few minutes, remove the battery caps and check the specific gravity of the electrolyte in each cell with a hydrometer (**Figure 17**). Refer to *Testing (Non-maintenance Free Battery)* in this chapter.

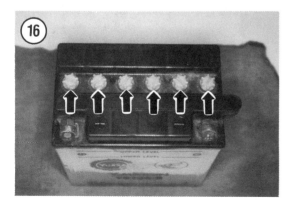

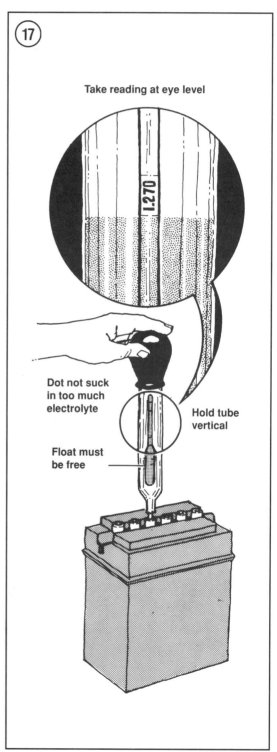

PERIODIC LUBRICATION, MAINTENANCE AND TUNE-UP

Testing (Non-Maintenance Free Battery)

Hydrometer testing is the best way to check battery condition. Use a hydrometer with numbered graduations from 1.100 to 1.300 rather than one with just color-coded bands. To use the hydrometer, squeeze the rubber ball, insert the tip into the cell and release the pressure on the ball. Draw enough electrolyte to float the weighted float inside the hydrometer. Note the number in line with the surface of the electrolyte (**Figure 18**); this is the specific gravity for this cell. Squeeze the rubber ball again and return the electrolyte to the cell from which it came.

The specific gravity of the electrolyte in each battery cell is an excellent indication of that cell's condition. A fully charged cell will read form 1.260-1.280, which a cell in good condition reads from 1.230-1.250 and anything below 1.140 is discharged.

If the cells test in the poor range, the battery requires recharging. The hydrometer is useful for checking the progress of the charging operation.

Inspection and Testing (Maintenance Free Battery)

The battery electrolyte level cannot be serviced. Never attempt to remove the sealing bar cap from the top of the battery (C, **Figure 13**). This bar cap was removed for initial filling of electrolyte prior to delivery of the bike or battery and is not to be removed thereafter. The battery does not require periodic electrolyte inspection or refilling.

> *WARNING*
> *Even though the battery is a sealed type, protect your eyes, skin and clothing; electrolyte is corrosive and can cause severe burns and permanent injury. The battery case may be cracked and leaking electrolyte. If electrolyte gets into your eyes, flush your eyes thoroughly with clean, running water and get immediate medical attention. Safety glasses should be worn when servicing the battery.*

1. Remove the battery from the motorcycle as described in this chapter. Do not clean the battery while it is mounted in the motorcycle.
2. Clean the battery case with a solution of warm water and household dish washing detergent. Rinse thoroughly with clean water.
3. Inspect the physical condition of the battery. Look for bulges or cracks in the case, leaking electrolyte or corrosion build-up.
4. Clean the battery terminals, bolts and cable ends with sandpaper and then rinse with water.
5. Check the cables for signs of chafing, deterioration or other damage.
6. Connect a voltmeter between the battery negative and positive leads (**Figure 19**). Note the following:

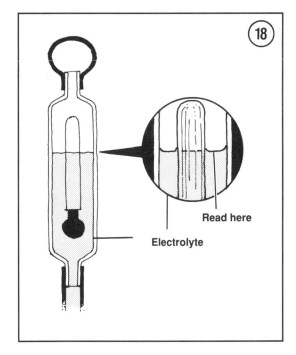

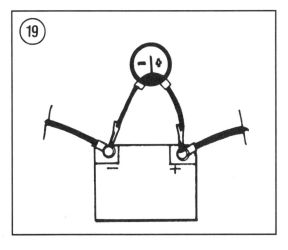

a. If the battery voltage is greater than 12.8 volts (at 20° C [68° F]), the battery is fully charged.

b. If the battery voltage is below 12.3 volts (at 20° C [68° F]), the battery is undercharged and requires charging.

7. If the battery is undercharged, recharge it as described in this chapter. Then test the charging system as described in Chapter Two.

**Charging
(Non-Maintenance Free Battery)**

*WARNING
During the charging process, highly explosive hydrogen gas is released from the battery. The battery should be charged only in a well-ventilated area away from any open flames (including pilot lights on home gas appliances). Do not allow any smoking in the area. Never check the charge by arcing (connecting pliers or other metal objects) across the terminals; the resulting spark can ignite the hydrogen gas.*

*CAUTION
Always remove the battery from the bike's frame before connecting the battery charger. Never recharge a battery in the bike's frame; the corrosive mist that is emitted during the charging process will corrode all surrounding surfaces.*

1. Set the battery on a stack of newspapers or shop cloths (**Figure 15**) to protect the work surface of your workbench. During the charging process, there may be an acid-based mist emitted from the battery cells from the charging bubble action. This mist is corrosive and will damage any surrounding surface. Properly discard the shop rags or newspapers after the charging process is completed.

2. Connect the positive (+) charger lead to the positive (+) battery terminal and the negative (–) charger lead to the negative (–) battery terminal.

3. Remove all vent caps (**Figure 16**) from the battery, set the charger to 12 volts and switch the charge ON. If the output of the charger is variable, it is best to select a low setting—1 1/2 to 2 amps. Normally, a battery should be charged at a slow charge rate of 1/10 its given capacity.

*CAUTION
The electrolyte level must be maintained at the upper level during the charging cycle; check and refill as necessary.*

4. The charging time depends on the discharged condition of the battery. The chart in **Figure 20** can be used to determine approximate charging times at different specific gravity readings. For example, if the specific gravity of your battery is 1.180, the approximate charging time would be 6 hours.

5. After the battery has been charged for about 6 hours, turn the charger OFF, disconnect the leads and check the specific gravity of each cell. It should be within the limits specified in **Table 3**. If it is, and remains stable for 1 hour, the battery is considered charged.

6. Clean the battery terminals and surrounding case. Coat the terminals with a thin layer of dielectric grease to retard the corrosion and decomposition of the battery terminals.

7. To ensure good electrical contact, cables must be clean and tight on the battery's terminals. Refer to *Battery Electrical Cable Connectors* in this chapter.

*CAUTION
Route the breather tube so that it does not drain onto any part of the frame. The tube must be free of bends or twists as any restriction may pressurize the battery and damage it.*

8. Reinstall the battery as described in this chapter.

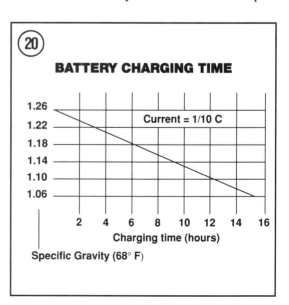

PERIODIC LUBRICATION, MAINTENANCE AND TUNE-UP

Charging
(Maintenance Free Battery)

On the maintenance free battery if recharging is required, a special type of battery charger must be used. Honda recommends the Cristie Battery Charger which has a built in battery tester along with a timer. It is recommended that the battery be recharged by a Honda dealer to avoid damage to a good battery that only requires recharging. The following procedure is included if you choose to recharge this type of battery.

If a battery not in use loses its charge within a week after charging, the battery is defective. A good battery should only self-discharge approximately 1 percent each day.

CAUTION
***Never** connect a battery charger to the battery with the battery cables still connected. **Always** disconnect the battery cables from the battery. During the charging procedure the charger may destroy the diodes within the voltage regulator/rectifier if the cables were left connected.*

WARNING
During the charging process, a small amount of highly explosive hydrogen gas is released from the battery. The battery should be charged only in a well-ventilated area away from any open flames (including pilot lights on home gas appliances). Do not allow any smoking in the area. Never check the charge of the battery by connecting screwdriver blades or other metal objects between the terminals; the resulting spark can ignite the hydrogen gas.

1. Remove the battery from the bike as described in this chapter.
2. Connect the positive (+) charger lead to the positive battery terminal and the negative (–) charger lead to the negative battery terminal.

CAUTION
*Do not exceed the recommended charging amperage rate or charging time on the battery charging time label (**Figure 21**) attached to the top of the battery.*

3. Set the charger at 12 volts. If the output of the charger is variable, it is best to select a low setting. Use the suggested charging amperage and length of charge time on the battery label (**Figure 21**). Normally, a battery should be charged at a slow charge rate of 1/10 its given capacity.
4. Turn the charger ON.
5. After the battery has been charged for the specified amount of time, turn the charger off, disconnect the leads.
6. Connect a voltmeter across the battery negative and positive terminals and measure the battery voltage. A fully charged battery should read 13.0-13.2 volts. If the voltage is 12.3 or less, the battery is undercharged.
7. If the battery remains stable for one hour, at the specified voltage, the battery is charged.
8. Clean the battery terminals and surrounding case. Coat the terminals with a thin layer of dielectric grease to retard the corrosion and decomposition of the battery terminals.
9. To ensure good electrical contact, cables must be clean and tight on the battery's terminals. Refer to *Battery Electrical Cable Connectors* in this chapter.
10. Reinstall the battery as described in this chapter.

New Battery Installation

When replacing the old battery with a new one, be sure it is charged completely before installing it. Failure to do so will reduce the life of the battery. Check with the dealer on the type of pre-service that the battery received. When replacing a maintenance free battery, be sure to install only another maintenance free battery.

NOTE
***Recycle your old battery.** When you replace the old battery, be sure to turn in*

*the old battery at that time. The lead plates and the plastic case can be recycled. Most motorcycle dealers will accept your old battery in trade when you purchase a new one, but if they will not, many automotive supply stores will. **Never** place an old battery in your household trash since it is illegal, in most states, to place any acid or lead (heavy metal) contents in landfills. There is also the danger of the battery being crushed in the trash truck and spraying acid on the truck or land fill operator.*

Battery Electrical Cable Connectors

To ensure good electrical contact between the battery and the electrical cables, the cables must be clean and free of corrosion.

1. If the electrical cable terminals are badly corroded, disconnect them from the bike's electrical system.
2. Thoroughly clean each connector with a wire brush and then with a baking soda solution. Rinse thoroughly with clean water and wipe dry with a clean cloth.
3. After cleaning, apply a thin layer of dielectric grease to the battery terminals before reattaching the cables.
4. If disconnected, connect the electrical cables to the bike's electrical system.
5. After connecting the electrical cables, apply a light coating of dielectric grease to the electrical terminals of the battery to retard corrosion and decomposition of the terminals.

PERIODIC LUBRICATION

Oil

Oil is graded according to its viscosity, which is an indication of how thick it is. The Society of Automotive Engineers (SAE) system distinguishes oil viscosity by numbers. Thick oils have higher viscosity numbers than thin oils.

Grease

A good-quality grease (preferably waterproof) should be used. Water does not wash grease off parts as easily as it washes oil off. In addition, grease maintains its lubricating qualities better than oil on long and strenuous rides.

In many cases in this book, a special grease called molybdenum disulfide grease is specified. It is used on some parts during engine reassembly and on some suspension components. Whenever this type of grease is specified it should be used, as it has special lubricating qualities. Be sure to use the proper grease, even though it may be more expensive than ordinary multipurpose grease.

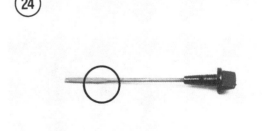

PERIODIC LUBRICATION, MAINTENANCE AND TUNE-UP

Engine Oil Level Check

The engine oil level is checked with the dipstick located on the right-hand crancase/clutch cover. Refer to **Figure 22** for 1986-1989 models or **Figure 23** for 1990-on models.

1. Place the bike on level ground. Have an assistant hold the bike upright.
2. Start the engine and let it idle for 2-3 minutes.
3. Stop the engine and allow the oil to settle for 2-3 minutes.
4. Unscrew the dipstick and wipe it clean. Reinsert the dipstick cap onto the threads in the hole; do not screw it it.
5. Remove the dipstick cap and check the oil level.
6. The level should be between the 2 level marks on the dipstick and now above the upper mark (Figure 24). If the level is below the lower mark, add the recommended oil (**Table 4**) through the fill cap opening to correct the level. Refer to **Figure 25** for 1986-1989 models or **Figure 26** for 1990-on models. Do not overfill.

Engine Oil and Filter Change

The factory-recommended oil and filter change interval is specified in **Table 1** or every three months. This assumes that the motorcycle is operated in moderate climates. The time interval is more important than the mileage interval because combustion acids, formed by gasoline and water vapor, will contaminate the oil even if the motorcycle is not run for several months. If a motorcycle is operated under dusty conditions, the oil will get dirty more quickly and should be changed more frequently than recommended.

Use only a detergent oil with an API classification of SF or SG. The classification is stamped on top of the can or printed on the container (**Figure 27**). Try always to use the same brand of oil. Use of oil additives is not recommended. Honda recommends the use of SAE 10W-40 oil viscosity under normal conditions. Refer to **Figure 28** for the correct weight

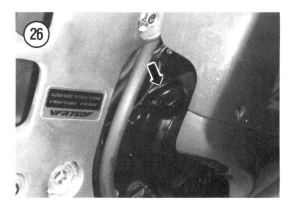

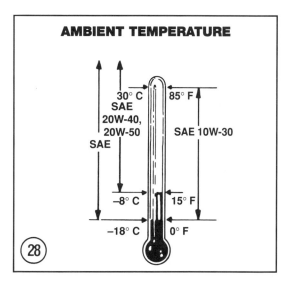

of oil to use under anticipated ambient temperatures (not engine oil temperature). Use of oil additives is not recommended as they may cause clutch slippage.

CAUTION
Honda does not recommend the use of vegetable, non-detergent or castor-based racing oils.

To change the engine oil and filter you will need the following:
a. Drain pan.
b. Funnel.
c. Wrench or sockeet to remove drain plug.
d. New drain plug washer (if necessary).
e. 4 quarts of oil (**Table 5**).
f. Oil filter element.
g. Socket-type oil filter wrench (**Figure 29**). See following NOTE.

NOTE
A socket-type oil filter wrench must be used when removing the oil filter because of the small working area between the oil filter, exhaust pipe and lower fairing.

NOTE
Never dispose of motor oil in the trash, on the ground, or down a storm drain. Many service stations accept used motor oil and waste haulers provide curbside used motor oil collection. Do not combine other fluids with motor oil to be recycled. To locate a recycler, contact the American Petroleum Institute (API) at www.recycleoil.org.

1. Start the engine and run it until it is at normal operating temperature, then turn it off.

NOTE
Warming the engine causes the oil to heat up, allowing it to flow freely and carry contamination and sludge with it.

2. Hold the bike upright to allow all of the oil to drain from the engine.

NOTE
It is not necessary to remove the lower fairing assembly when replacing the oil filter. It is shown removed in this procedure for clarity.

CAUTION
The engine, exhaust pipes and oil will be hot! Work quickly and carefully when removing the plug to avoid burning your hand.

3. Place a drip pan under the crankcase and remove the drain plug and washer. Refer to **Figure 30** for 1986-1989 models or **Figure 31** for 1990-on models.

4. Remove the oil fill cap and rest the cap on the fill hole; this will speed up the flow of oil. Refer to

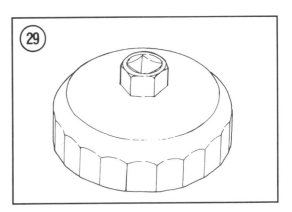

PERIODIC LUBRICATION, MAINTENANCE AND TUNE-UP

Figure 25 for 1986-1989 models or **Figure 26** for 1990-on models.

5. Let the oil drain for at least 15-20 minutes, then move the drain pan under the oil filter.

6. Put an oil filter wrench on the oil filter (**Figure 32**) turn the filter *counterclockwise* until oil begins to run out of the engine (**Figure 33**). Wait until the oil stops then loosen the filter all the way and remove it and the oil filter wrench.

7. Hold the oil filter over the drain pan and pour out any remaining oil. Place the old filter in a reclosable plastic bag and close it to prevent residual oil from draining out. Discard the used oil filter properly.

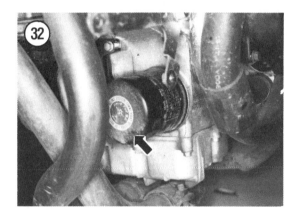

CAUTION
Prior to installing the new oil filter, clean off the crankcase mating surface with a lint-free cloth—do not allow any road dirt to enter the lubrication system.

8. Apply a light coat of new engine oil to the rubber seal on the new oil filter (**Figure 34**) and screw on the oil filter. Tighten the filter by hand until the filter's seal contacts the engine, then turn the filter an additional 3/4 turn.

NOTE
Over-tightening the filter may cause it to leak.

9. Replace the oil drain plug gasket if deformed.

10. Install the gasket onto the oil drain plug and thread the plug into the engine by hand. Then tighten the oil drain plug to the torque specification in **Table 6**. Refer to **Figure 30** for 1986-1989 models or **Figure 31** for 1990-on.

11. Remove the oil fill cap and fill the crankcase with the correct weight (**Table 4**) and quantity (**Table 5**) of oil.

12. Screw in the oil fill cap securely.

13. Start the engine and allow to idle; the oil pressure warning light should go out within 1-3 seconds. If it stays on, shut off the engine immediately and locate the problem. Do not run the engine with the oil pressure warning light on.

14. Let the engine idle and check for leaks.

15. Turn the engine off after 2-3 minutes and check the oil level as described in this chapter, adjust as necessary.

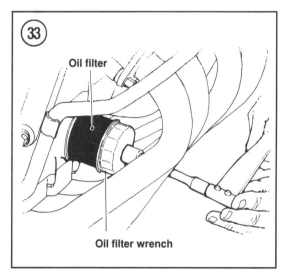

Oil filter
Oil filter wrench

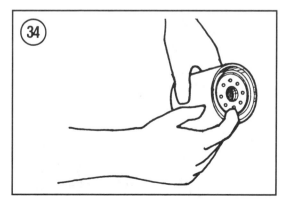

Front Fork Oil Change

The forks must be removed and partially disassembled for fork oil replacement and oil level adjustment. Refer to *Front Fork Disassembly and Reassembly* in Chapter Ten.

Control Cables

The throttle and choke control cables should be lubricated at the cable inspection intervals specified in **Table 1** or when they have become stiff or sluggish. At this time, they should also be inspected for fraying, and the cable sheath should be checked for chafing. The cables are relatively inexpensive and should be replaced when found to be faulty.

The cables should be lubricated with a cable lubricant and a cable lubricator (**Figure 35**).

CAUTION
*If the stock cables have been replaced with nylon-lined cables, do **not** oil them as described in the following procedure. Oil and most cable lubricants will cause the liner to expand, pinching the liner against the cable. Nylon lined cables are normally used dry. When servicing nylon-lined cables, follow the cable manufacturer's instructions.*

NOTE
The main cause of cable breakage or cable stiffness is improper lubrication. Maintaining the cables as described in this section will assure long service life.

1. Remove the fuel tank as described under *Fuel Tank Removal/Installation* in Chapter Seven. Fuel tank removal is necessary to gain access to the end of the choke and throttle cables where they are attached to the carburetor assembly.
2. Disconnect the choke cable from the choke lever as follows:
   a. Remove the screws securing the left-hand switch housing (**Figure 36**) and partially separate the housings.
   b. Disconnect the choke cable from the choke lever assembly.
3. Disconnect the throttle cables as follows:
   a. Loosen the throttle cable adjuster locknut (A, **Figure 37**) at the handlebar and loosen the throttle cable adjuster (B, **Figure 37**).
   b. Remove the screws securing the throttle cable/switch housing and partially separate the housings (**Figure 38**).
   c. Disconnect the throttle cables from the twist grip assembly.
4. Attach a cable lubricator (**Figure 35**) to the cable following the manufacturer's instructions.

5. Insert the nozzle of the lubricant can into the lubricator, press the button on the can and hold it down until the lubricant begins to flow out of the other end of the cable. If the lubricant flows out from the cable lubricator, the lubricator is not installed properly onto the end of the cable. You may have to install the lubricator a few times to get it to seal properly. Place a shop cloth at the end of the cable(s) to catch all excess lubricant that will flow out.

NOTE
If lubricant does not flow out the end of the cable, check the entire cable for fraying, bending or other damage.

NOTE
If you cannot get the cable lubricator to work at one end of the cable, install it onto the opposite cable end.

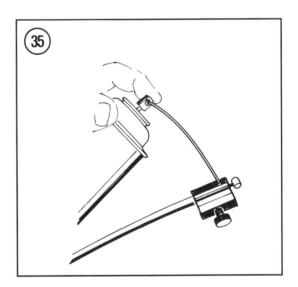

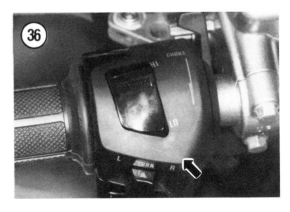

PERIODIC LUBRICATION, MAINTENANCE AND TUNE-UP

6. Remove the lubricator and wipe off all excess lubricant from the cable. Place a small amount of grease onto the cable barrel before reconnecting it. Reconnect and adjust the cable(s) as described in this chapter. Refer to:
   a. *Throttle Cable Adjustment.*
   b. *Choke Cable Adjustment.*

7. Install the fuel tank as described in Chapter Seven.

Brake and Clutch Lever Pivot Lubrication

Periodically, the brake and clutch lever pivot screws should be lubricated with a light-weight oil, such as machine oil or WD-40.

Rear Suspension Lubrication

The following rear suspension components should be cleaned and then lubricated with molybdenum disulfide grease. The rear suspension must be removed and partially disassembled (Chapter Eleven) to perform this service.

Honda does not list a specific mileage or time interval for lubricating the rear suspension.
   a. Swing arm pivot dust seal lips.
   b. Swing arm pivot needle bearings.
   c. Shock arm pivot dust seal lips.
   d. Shock arm pivot needle bearings.
   e. Shock link pivot dust seal lips.
   f. Shock link pivot needle bearings.
   g. Driven flange dust seal lips (1990-on).
   h. Bearing holder dust seal lips (1990-on).
   i. Bearing holder needle bearing (1990-on).

Brake System

The following brake components should be lubricated with silicone grease (specified for brake use) whenever the components are removed for service:
   a. Brake caliper boots (inside).
   b. Master cylinder rubber boots (inside).
   c. Rear brake caliper pin bolt sliding surface.
   d. Rear master cylinder pushrod.

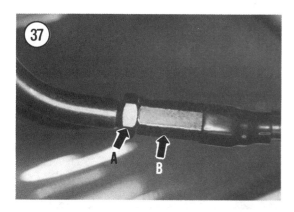

Speedometer Cable Lubrication (1986-1993 Models)

> *NOTE*
> *The 1994-on models are equipped with an electronic speedometer and are not equipped with a cable.*

The inner speedometer cable should be lubricated periodically or whenever needle operation is erratic. At the same time, check the outer cable for damage.

1. Remove the front fairing as described in Chapter Thirteen.

2. Unscrew the knurled speedometer cable ring (**Figure 39**) at the bottom of the speedometer housing.

3A. *1986-1989:* At the front wheel, remove the speedometer cable Phillips screw and pull the cable out of the speedometer gear housing.

3B. *1990-1993:* At the speedometer gear housing mounted on the drive sprocket cover, remove the Phillips head screw (A, **Figure 40**) and withdraw the cable (B, **Figure 40**) from the housing.

4. Attach a cable lubricator (**Figure 35**) to the cable following the manufacturer's instructions.

5. Insert the nozzle of the lubricant can into the lubricator, press the button on the can and hold it down until the lubricant begins to flow out of the other end of the cable. If the lubricant flows out from the cable lubricator, the lubricator is not installed properly onto the end of the cable. You may have to install the lubricator a few times to get it to seal properly. Place a shop cloth at the base of the speedometer cable or at the opening of the speedometer gear housing to catch all excess lubricant that will flow out.

NOTE
If lubricant does not flow out the end of the cable, check the entire cable for fraying, bending or other damage.

6. Remove the lubricator and wipe off all excess lubricant from the cable.

7A. *1986-1989:* Install the speedometer cable into the speedometer gear housing and secure with the Phillips head screw.

7B. *1990-1993:* Install the speedometer cable into the housing and install the Phillips head screw.

8. Reconnect the upper end of the speedometer cable to the speedometer housing (**Figure 39**) and tighten the ring securely.

9. Install the front fairing as described in Chapter Thirteen.

Steering Stem Lubrication

The retainer-type ball bearings used in the steering system should be removed, cleaned and lubricated with bearing grease as described in Chapter Ten.

Drive Chain Lubrication

Honda recommends SAE 80 or 90 gear oil for chain lubrication; it is less likely to be thrown off the chain than lighter oils. Many commercial drive chain lubricants are also available that do an excellent job.

NOTE
If the drive chain is very dirty, remove and clean it as described under Drive Chain Cleaning in Chapter Eleven before lubricating it as described in this procedure.

CAUTION
*The factory drive chain is equipped with O-rings between the side plates (**Figure 41**) that seal grease between the pins and bushings. To prevent O-ring damage, clean the chain with kerosene only. Do not use gasoline or other solvents that will cause the O-rings to swell or deteriorate. Refer to cleaning procedures in Chapter Eleven.*

1. Ride the bike a few miles to warm the drive chain. A warm chain increases lubricant penetration.
2. Support the bike so that the rear wheel clears the ground.
3. Oil the bottom chain run with SAE 80 or 90 gear oil or a commercial chain lubricant *recommended* for use on O-ring equipped drive chains. Concentrate on getting the oil down between the side plates of the chain links (**Figure 41**).

CAUTION
Not all commercial chain lubricants are recommended for use on O-ring equipped drive chains. Read the label

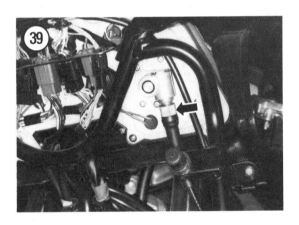

PERIODIC LUBRICATION, MAINTENANCE AND TUNE-UP

on the can carefully before use or purchase to be sure it is formulated for O-ring chains.

4. Rotate the chain and continue lubricating until the entire chain has been lubricated.

5. Wipe off any oil or chain lubricant that has run onto the swing arm or rear wheel.

Sidestand Pivot Bolt Lubrication

The sidestand pivot bolt should be periodically lubricated to ensure proper sidestand movement and support.

1. Support the bike so that it is off the sidestand.
2. On 1990-on models, remove the sidestand switch (Chapter Eight) and cover.
3. Raise the sidestand (A, **Figure 42**).

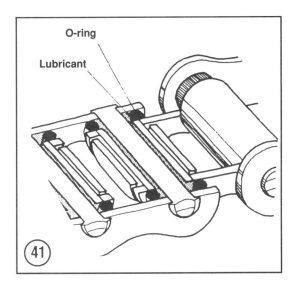

4. Using a spring hook tool or vise-grip pliers, remove the sidestand spring (B, **Figure 42**).

5. Remove sidestand locknut (C, **Figure 42**) and pivot bolt and slip the sidestand off of its bracket.

6. Clean all parts thoroughly in solvent and dry thoroughly.

7. Inspect the sidestand pivot bolt for metal fatigue or other damage. Also inspect the sidestand pivot bolt bracket for fatigue or damage that would allow the bike to fall when the sidestand is used.

CAUTION
Expensive fairing damage could result from sidestand failure should the bike fall over on its side.

8. Replace worn or damaged parts.

9. Apply a coat of molybdenum disulfide grease to the pivot bolt.

10. Install the sidestand by reversing these steps while noting the following:
   a. Tighten the sidestand pivot bolt to the torque specification in **Table 6**.
   b. Install and tighten the sidestand locknut to the torque specification in **Table 6**.
   c. Make sure the spring contacts the mounting bracket and sidestand completely.
   d. Operate the sidestand to make sure it pivots smoothly. If the spring feels weak or fatigued, replace it.
   e. On 1990-on models, install the sidestand switch (Chapter Eight) and test to make sure of proper operation as described in Chapter Two.
   f. On 1990-on models, install the sidestand cover.

Centerstand Pivot Shaft Lubrication (Models so Equipped)

Periodically, remove the centerstand pivot shaft and lubricate it with a coat of molybdenum disulfide grease. During installation, make sure the centerstand return spring is mounted properly and that the centerstand does not sag in its raised position. During installation, install a *new* cotter pin and bend the ends over completely to lock it.

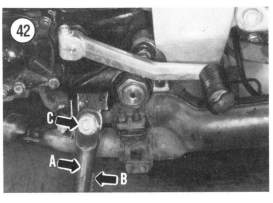

Brake Pedal Pivot Shaft Lubrication

The brake pedal should be removed, as described in Chapter Twelve, periodically and the pivot shaft lubricated with grease.

PERIODIC MAINTENANCE

Drive Chain Adjustment Inspection

To prevent drive chain tension related problems, adjust the chain at the intervals specified in **Table 1**. If the bike is operated at sustained high speeds or if it is repeatedly accelerated very hard, check the drive chain adjustment more often. Drive chain slack that exceeds 40 mm (1 5/8 in.) may damage the frame and/or swing arm.

1. Turn the engine off and shift the transmission into NEUTRAL.
2. Support the bike so that the rear wheel clears the ground.

NOTE
As drive chains stretch and wear in use, the chain will become tighter at one point. The chain must be checked and adjusted at this point.

3. Turn the rear wheel slowly, then stop it and check the chain tightness. Continue until you locate its tightest point. Mark this spot with chalk and turn the wheel so that the mark is located on the chain's lower run, midway between both drive sprockets. Check and adjust the drive chain as follows.

NOTE
*If the drive chain is kinked or feels tight, it may require cleaning and lubrication. Refer to **Drive Chain Lubrication** in this chapter. If the chain is still tight, it may be damaged due to swollen O-rings, damaged rollers, loose pins or binding links. Refer to **Drive Chain** in Chapter Eleven.*

4. Take the bike off its support and park it on its sidestand.

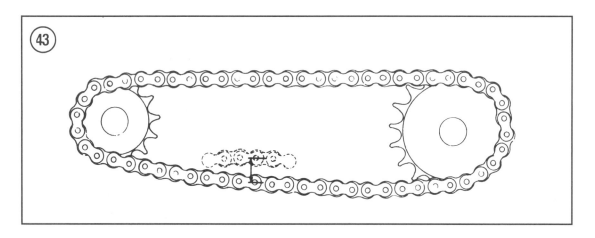

PERIODIC LUBRICATION, MAINTENANCE AND TUNE-UP

5. With thumb and forefinger, lift up and press down the chain at the center of the bottom chain run, measuring the distance the chain moves vertically (**Figure 43**).

6. The drive chain should have approximately 15-25 mm (5/8-1 in.) of vertical travel at midpoint (**Figure 43**). If necessary, adjust the chain in the following procedures.

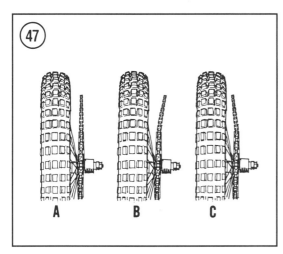

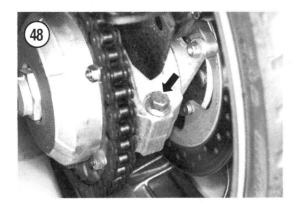

Drive Chain Adjustment

1986-1989 models

1. Loosen the axle nut on the right-hand side (**Figure 44**).
2. Loosen the axle adjuster locknut on both sides of the wheel.
3. Turn each adjuster nut (**Figure 45**) and equal number of turns to obtain the correct drive chain slack. Alignment is checked by observing the left- and right-hand adjuster marks; align the marks with the rear edge of the swing arm axle slots on both sides. Adjust the drive chain until the correct amount of free play is obtained (**Figure 43**).

> *NOTE*
> *A drive chain wear label is mounted on the left-hand side of the swing arm. If the arrow mark on the adjuster aligns with the red zone on the label (**Figure 46**), and the drive chain slack is correct, the drive chain is excessively worn and must be replaced as described under* ***Drive Chain*** *in Chapter Eleven.*

4. To verify the swing arm adjuster marks, remove the drive chain guard and check rear wheel alignment by sighting along the drive chain as it runs over the rear sprocket. It should not appear to bend sideways (**Figure 47**).
5. Tighten the rear axle nut to the torque specification in **Table 6**.
6. Tighten the adjusting nut (**Figure 45**) *lightly*. Then hold the adjusting nut with a suitable wrench and tighten the locknut. Repeat for the opposite side.
7. Recheck drive chain play.

1990-on models

1. Loosen the bearing holder pinch bolt (**Figure 48**).
2. Adjust the chain play using the pin spanner and handle tools located in the bike tool kit.
3. As viewed from the left-hand side of the swing arm, rotate the bearing holder as follows:
   a. **Figure 49**: *Clockwise* to tighten the drive chain and reduce drive chain play.
   b. **Figure 50**: *Counterclockwise* to loosen the drive chain and increase drive chain play.

CHAPTER THREE

NOTE
*A drive chain wear label is mounted on the drive chain guard. If the teeth of the drive sprocket align with the red zone on the label (**Figure 51**), and the drive chain slack is correct, the drive chain is excessively worn and must be replaced as described under **Drive Chain** in Chapter Eleven.*

4. Tighten the bearing holder pinch bolt (**Figure 48**) to the torque specification in **Table 6**.
5. Recheck drive chain play.

Swing Arm Slider Inspection

A slider is installed on the left-hand side of the swing arm to protect the swing arm from chain damage. The slider should be inspected frequently for advanced wear or damage that would allow the chain to cut into the swing arm. If necessary, replace the slider by removing the swing arm as described under *Swing Arm Removal/Installation* in Chapter Eleven and install a new slider (**Figure 52**).

Clutch Fluid Level Inspection

1. Support the bike so that it is upright and parked on level ground.
2. Turn the handlebars so that the master cylinder is level.
3. The fluid must be kept above the lower level line on the reservoir (**Figure 53**).

Adding Clutch Fluid

1. Clean the outside of the reservoir cover thoroughly with a dry rag and remove the two screws retaining the reservoir cover (**Figure 54**). Remove the cover, diaphragm plate and diaphragm.
2. The fluid level in the reservoir should be up to the upper level line. Add fresh DOT 4 brake fluid as required.

WARNING
Use hydraulic fluid from a sealed container and clearly marked DOT 4 only. Do not intermix different brands or types of hydraulic fluid as they may not be compatible. Do not intermix a silicone based (DOT 5) hydraulic fluid as it can cause clutch component damage, leading to clutch release system failure.

CAUTION
Be careful when handling hydraulic fluid. Do not spill it on painted or plated surfaces as it will destroy the surface. Wash the area immediately with soapy water and thoroughly rinse it off.

3. Reinstall the diaphragm, diaphragm plate and cover. Tighten the cover screws securely.

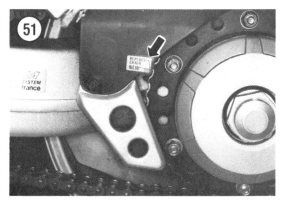

PERIODIC LUBRICATION, MAINTENANCE AND TUNE-UP

NOTE
*If the clutch fluid was so low as to allow air in the hydraulic system, the clutch will have to be bled. Refer to **Bleeding The System** in Chapter Five.*

Clutch Hydraulic Lines and Seals

Check the clutch lines between the master cylinder and the slave cylinder. If there is any leakage, tighten the connections and bleed the clutch as described in Chapter Five. If this does not stop the leak or if a line is obviously damaged, cracked or chafed, replace the line and seals and bleed the clutch.

Clutch Fluid Change

Every time you remove the reservoir cap a small amount of dirt and moisture enters the hydraulic fluid. The same thing happens if a leak occurs or when any part of the hydraulic system is loosened or disconnected. Dirt can clog the system and cause unnecessary wear. Water in the fluid vaporizes at high temperatures, impairing the hydraulic action and reducing clutch performance.

To change the clutch fluid, drain the clutch master cylinder as described under *Clutch Master Cylinder Removal/Installation* in Chapter Five. Add new hydraulic fluid to the master cylinder and bleed at the slave cylinder until the fluid leaving the slave cylinder is clean and free of contaminants and air bubbles. Refer to *Bleeding the System* in Chapter Five.

CAUTION
If the clutch operates correctly when the engine is cold or in cool weather, but operates erratically (or not at all) after the engine warms up or when riding in hot weather, there is air in the hydraulic line and the clutch system must be bled. Refer to Chapter Five.

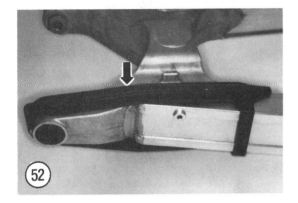

Disc Brake Inspection

The hydraulic brake fluid in the disc brake master cylinders should be checked every month. The disc brake pads should be checked at the intervals specified in **Table 1**. Brake pad replacement is described in Chapter Twelve.

Disc Brake Fluid Level Inspection

1. Support the bike so that it is upright and parked on level ground.
2. Turn the handlebars so that the front master cylinder is level.
3. The brake fluid must be kept above the lower level lines on both reservoirs. Refer to **Figure 55** for the front master cylinder and for the rear master cylinder reservoir refer to A, **Figure 56** for 1986-

1989 and 1994 models or **Figure 57** for 1990-1993 models.

Adding Brake Fluid

Front master cylinder

1. Clean the outside of the reservoir cover thoroughly with a dry rag and remove the two screws retaining the reservoir cover (**Figure 58**). Remove the cover, diaphragm plate and diaphragm.

2. The fluid level in the reservoir should be up to the upper level line. Add fresh DOT 4 brake fluid as required.

> *WARNING*
> *Use brake fluid from a sealed container and clearly marked DOT 4 only. Do not intermix different brands or types of hydraulic fluid as they may not be compatible. Do not intermix a silicone based (DOT 5) hydraulic fluid as it can cause brake component damage, leading to brake system failure.*

> *CAUTION*
> *Be careful not to spill brake fluid on painted or plated surfaces as it will destroy the surface. Wash immediately with soapy water and thoroughly rinse it off.*

3. Reinstall the diaphragm, diaphragm plate and cover (**Figure 58**). Tighten the cover screws securely.

> *NOTE*
> *If the brake fluid was so low as to allow air in the hydraulic system, the brakes will have to be bled. Refer to **Bleeding The System** in Chapter Twelve.*

Rear master cylinder

1A. *1986-1989:* Remove the right-hand side cover as described in Chapter Thirteen.

1B. *1990-on:* Remove the rear tailpiece/side cover assembly as described in Chapter Thirteen.

2. Clean the outside of the reservoir cover or cap thoroughly with a dry rag.

3A. *1986-1989 and 1994:* Unscrew the cap (**Figure 59**) and remove the cap, diaphragm plate and diaphragm.

3B. *1990-1993:* Remove the two screws retaining the reservoir cover (**Figure 60**) and remove the cover, diaphragm plate and diaphragm.

4. The fluid level in the reservoir should be up to the upper level line. Add fresh DOT 4 brake fluid as required.

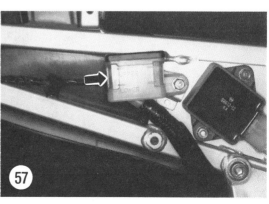

PERIODIC LUBRICATION, MAINTENANCE AND TUNE-UP

WARNING
Use brake fluid from a sealed container and clearly marked DOT 4 only. Do not intermix different brands or types of hydraulic fluid as they may not be compatible. Do not intermix a silicone based (DOT 5) hydraulic fluid as it can cause brake component damage, leading to brake system failure.

CAUTION
Be careful not to spill brake fluid on painted or plated surfaces as it will destroy the surface. Wash immediately with soapy water and thoroughly rinse it off.

5. Reinstall all parts. Make sure the cap is tightly secured and that the cover screws are tightened securely.

NOTE
*If the brake fluid was so low as to allow air in the hydraulic system, the brakes will have to be bled. Refer to **Bleeding The System** in Chapter Twelve.*

Disc Brake Lines and Seals

Check brake lines between the master cylinder and the brake caliper. If there is any leakage, tighten the connections and bleed the brakes as described in Chapter Twelve. If this does not stop the leak or if a line is obviously damaged, cracked or chafed, replace the line and seals and bleed the brake.

Disc Brake Pad Inspection

Refer to *Front Brake Pad Replacement* and *Rear Brake Pad Replacement* in Chapter Twelve. Check for pad wear at the service intervals specified in **Table 1**.

Disc Brake Fluid Change

Every time you remove the reservoir cap a small amount of dirt and moisture enters the brake fluid. The same thing happens if a leak occurs or when any part of the hydraulic system is loosened or disconnected. Dirt can clog the system and cause unnecessary wear. Water in the fluid vaporizes at high temperatures, impairing the hydraulic action and reducing brake performance.

To change brake fluid, drain the master cylinders as described under *Front Master Cylinder Removal/Installation* or *Rear Master Cylinder Removal/Installation* in Chapter Twelve. Add new fluid to the master cylinder and bleed at the caliper until the fluid leaving the caliper is clean and free of contaminants and air bubbles. Refer to *Bleeding the System* in Chapter Twelve.

WARNING
Use brake fluid from a sealed container and clearly marked DOT 4 only. Do not intermix different brands or types of hydraulic fluid as they may not be compatible. Do not intermix a silicone based (DOT 5) hydraulic fluid as it can cause brake component damage leading to brake system failure.

Front Brake Lever Adjustment

The position of the front brake lever, as measured from the tip of the lever to the handlebar grip, can be adjusted by rotating the brake lever adjuster wheel (A, **Figure 61**). After rotating the adjuster wheel, align the index mark on the adjuster wheel (A, **Figure 61**) with the arrow mark on the brake lever (B, **Figure 61**). Then apply and release the brake lever several times, checking that the adjuster wheel (A, **Figure 61**) rotates freely.

Front Brake Adjustment

Periodic adjustment of the front disc brake is not required because disc pad wear is automatically compensated. If there is excessive play in the front brake lever, check the front brake lever pivot hole and bolt for excessive wear. Replace worn parts. See *Front Master Cylinder* in Chapter Twelve. If the brake lever pivot bolt is okay, check for air in the brake line.

Rear Brake Pedal Height Adjustment

The rear brake pedal height, measured from the top of the footpeg (A, **Figure 62**) to the top of the brake pedal (B, **Figure 62**), should be set to your personal preference.
1. Park the bike on its centerstand or support it in a vertical position.
2. Check to be sure the brake pedal is in the at-rest position.
3. Loosen the rear master cylinder pushrod locknut (A, **Figure 63**) and turn the pushrod (B, **Figure 63**) in either direction to adjust rear brake pedal height. Tighten the locknut securely.
4. Recheck the brake pedal height and readjust if necessary.

5. Check the *Rear Brake Light Switch Adjustment* as described in this chapter.

Rear Brake Light Switch Adjustment

The rear brake light switch is mounted on the back of the right-hand footpeg bracket.
1. Turn the ignition switch ON.
2. Depress the brake pedal. The brake light should come on as the brake pedal is depressed. If necessary, adjust as follows.
3. Turn the rear brake light switch knurled adjuster ring (A, **Figure 64**) to move the switch body (B, **Figure 64**) up or down as required. Raising the switch will make the brake light come on earlier.

Clutch Lever Adjustment

Excessive clutch lever play prevents the clutch from disengaging and causes clutch drag. Too little or no clutch lever play does not allow the clutch to

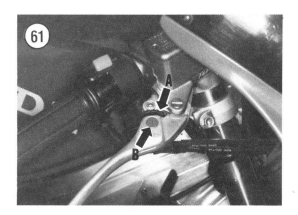

PERIODIC LUBRICATION, MAINTENANCE AND TUNE-UP

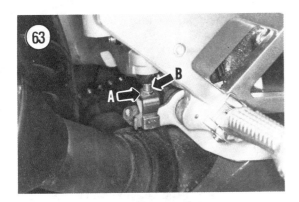

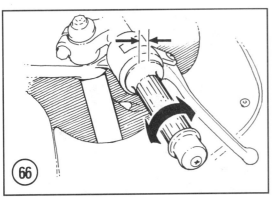

fully engage, resulting in clutch slippage. Both conditions cause unnecessary clutch wear.

The position of the clutch lever, as measured from the tip of the lever to the handlebar grip, can be adjusted by rotating the clutch lever adjuster wheel (A, **Figure 65**). After rotating the adjuster wheel, align the index mark on the adjuster wheel (A, **Figure 65**) with the arrow mark on the clutch lever (B, **Figure 65**). Then apply and release the clutch lever several times, checking that the adjuster wheel (A, **Figure 65**) rotates freely.

Throttle Cable Adjustment

Always check the throttle cable before you make any carburetor adjustments. Too much free play causes delayed throttle response; too little free play will cause unstable idling.

Check the throttle cable from grip to carburetors. Make sure they are not kinked or chafed. Replace the cables as a set.

Make sure that the throttle grip rotates smoothly from fully closed to fully open. Check at all steering positions.

Check that the throttle grip returns and closes properly in all steering positions. If not, lubricate the throttle cables as described in this chapter. At the same time, clean and lubricate the throttle grip housing with a light-weight oil. If the throttle will still not return properly, the cables are probably kinked or routed incorrectly.

Check free play at the throttle grip flange (**Figure 66**); Honda specifies 2-6 mm (3/32-1/4 in.) free play. If adjustment is required, proceed as follows.

> *WARNING*
> *If idle speed increases when the handlebar is turned to right or left, check throttle cable routing or for a damaged throttle cable(s). Correct this problem immediately. Do not ride the bike in this unsafe condition.*

1. To adjust free play at the throttle grip:
   a. Loosen the locknut (A, **Figure 67**) and turn the adjuster (B, **Figure 67**) in or out to achieve proper free play rotation.
   b. Tighten the locknut and recheck the adjustment.
2. To adjust free play at the carburetor assembly:

a. On 1986-1989 models, remove the left side cover. On 1990-on models, remove the left middle fairing. Refer to Chapter Thirteen.

b. Loosen the cable locknut (A, **Figure 68**) and turn the adjuster (B, **Figure 68**) in or out to achieve proper free play rotation.

c. Tighten the locknut and recheck the adjustment.

d. If necessary, fine tune adjustment at the throttle grip.

3. Operate the throttle grip a few times. The throttle grip should now be adjusted correctly. If not, the throttle cables may be stretched and should be replaced.

4. Reinstall all parts previously removed.

5. Sit on the seat and start the engine with the transmission in NEUTRAL. Turn the handlebars from right to left to check for abnormal idle speed variances due to improper cable routing.

WARNING
If idle speed increases when the handlebar is turned to right or left, check throttle cable routing. Do not ride the bike in this unsafe condition.

Choke Cable
Inspection and Adjustment

Inspect the choke cable at both ends for fraying or other damage.

The choke cable (A, **Figure 69**) is not provided with a cable adjuster. Instead, choke cable adjustment is initially made when the cable is installed and secured in its mounting bracket. To do this, align the end of the cable ferrule with the cable mounting bracket (B, **Figure 69**), then install the clamp (C, **Figure 69**) and secure it with its mounting screw.

The choke lever should move smoothly when pushed between the fully open (**Figure 70**) and fully closed (**Figure 71**) positions. When the choke lever is in its fully open position, there should be 1-2 mm (3/32-13/64 in.) of free play in the inner choke cable; to check, push the inner cable (D, **Figure 69**) with your finger. If the free play is incorrect, check that the cable is mounted in its mounting bracket correctly. If necessary, replace the choke cable.

Fuel and Vacuum Line Inspection

Inspect the condition of all fuel and vacuum lines for cracks or deterioration; replace if necessary. Make sure the hose clamps are in place and holding securely.

Emission Control Hoses
(1990-on U.S. and Switzerland Models)

A secondary air supply system (**Figure 72**) is used. An emission control information label is af-

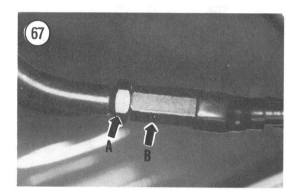

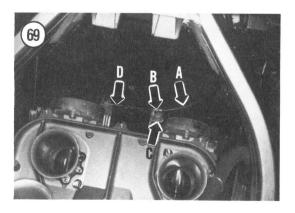

PERIODIC LUBRICATION, MAINTENANCE AND TUNE-UP

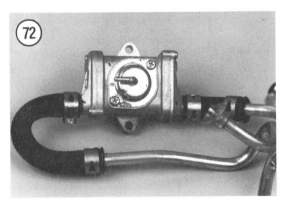

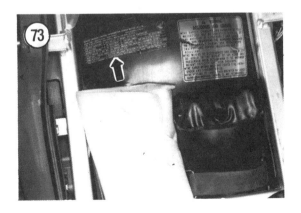

fixed to the rear inner fender (**Figure 73**). At the intervals specified in **Table 1**, check all emission control hoses for deterioration, damage or loose connections. Also check the charcoal canister housing for damage.

NOTE
When checking the secondary air supply system, look at the hoses carefully for heat damage. If any hose has been damaged from heat, check the reed valve as described in Chapter Seven.

Replace any parts or hoses as required.

Exhaust System

Check for leakage at all fittings. Tighten all bolts and nuts; replace any gaskets as necessary. Refer to *Exhaust System* in Chapter Seven.

Air Filter Element Replacement

The air filter element should be replaced at the service intervals specified in **Table 1**.

NOTE
*The service intervals specified in **Table 1** should be followed with general use. However, the air filter element should be replaced more often if the bike is ridden in dusty areas.*

The air filter removes dust and abrasive particles from the air before the air enters the carburetors and engine. A clogged air filter will decrease the efficiency and life of the engine. With a damaged air filter, very fine particles could enter the engine and cause rapid wear of the piston rings, cylinder and bearings while clogging small passages in the carburetors. Never run the bike without the air filter element installed.

Refer to **Figure 74** for this procedure.

1. Remove the fuel tank as described under *Fuel Tank Removal/Installation* in Chapter Seven.

2. Remove the air filter cover screws and lift the cover (**Figure 75**) off the air box.

3. Lift the air filter element (A, **Figure 76**) out of the air box.

NOTE
The intake sides of the carburetors (B, Figure 76) are now exposed. If the air filter element is going to be off the housing for some time, stuff clean rags into each carburetor opening to avoid dropping small screws or other parts into the carburetors.

4. At the specified service intervals (**Table 1**), replace the air filter element. If the bike's mileage is between replacement intervals, check the element for damage or dirt buildup; replace the element if necessary.
5. Check the inside of the air box for dust and other contamination.
6. Wipe out the interior of the air box with a damp cloth. Remove any foreign matter that may have passed through a broken element.
7. Install the air filter element so that it fits into the housing as shown in **Figure 77** with the "TOP" mark facing up.
8. Install the air filter cover (**Figure 75**) and its screws; tighten the screws securely. Check the housing cover to make sure it is seated completely around the lower housing.
9. Install the fuel tank as described in Chapter Seven.

Sub Air Filter Element
(1990-on Models)

1. Remove the fuel tank as described in Chapter Seven.
2. Remove the hose (A, **Figure 78**) from the sub air filter housing.
3. Remove the bolt and nut retaining the sub air filter assembly (B, **Figure 78**) and withdraw the assembly.
4. Remove the cover from the housing.
5. Remove the filter element from the housing and wash the filter in a non-flammable or high flash point solvent.

CAUTION
Because gasoline is a fire hazard, do not clean the air filter element with gasoline.

CAUTION
Do not wring or twist the filter when cleaning it. This harsh action could damage a filter pore. This would allow unfiltered air to enter the engine and cause severe and rapid wear.

6. After cleaning the filter, inspect it for any damage. Do not run an engine with a damaged filter as

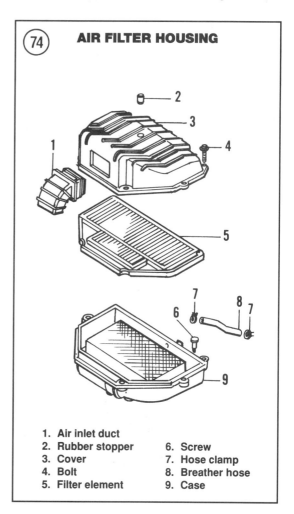

AIR FILTER HOUSING

1. Air inlet duct
2. Rubber stopper
3. Cover
4. Bolt
5. Filter element
6. Screw
7. Hose clamp
8. Breather hose
9. Case

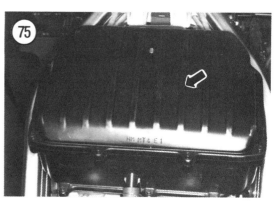

PERIODIC LUBRICATION, MAINTENANCE AND TUNE-UP

it may allow dirt to enter the engine and cause severe engine wear.

7. Set the filter aside and allow it to dry thoroughly.

CAUTION
A damp filter will not trap fine dust. Make sure the filter is completely dry before oiling it.

8. Properly oiling the filter element is a messy job. You may want to wear a pair of disposable rubber gloves when performing this procedure. Oil the filter as follows:

   a. Purchase a box of sandwich size reclosable bags. The bags can be used when cleaning the filter as well as for storing engine and carburetor parts during disassembly.

   b. Place the filter element into a sandwich bag.

   c. Pour Pro Honda Air Filter Oil, or a suitable equivalent foam air filter oil, onto the filter to soak it.

   d. Gently squeeze and release the filter to soak filter oil into the filter's pores. Repeat until all of the filter's pores are discolored with the oil.

   e. Remove the filter from the bag and check the pores for uneven oiling. This is indicated by light or dark areas. If necessary, soak the filter and squeeze it again.

   f. When the filter oiling is even, squeeze the filter a final time.

9. Remove the filter from the bag.

10. Install the filter element into the housing and install the cover.

11. Mount the sub air filter assembly (B, **Figure 78**) to the air box and attach the hose (A, **Figure 78**).

12. Install the fuel tank as described in Chapter Seven.

13. Pour the left over filter oil from the bag back into the bottle for reuse.

14. Dispose of the plastic bag and rubber gloves as described in local regulations.

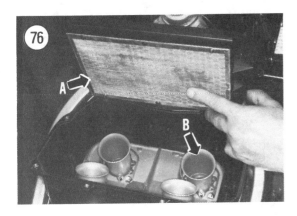

Steering Play

The steering head should be checked for looseness at the intervals specified in **Table 1**. Refer to *Steering Play* in Chapter Ten.

Cooling System Inspection

At the intervals indicated in **Table 1**, the following items should be checked. If you do not have the test equipment, the tests can be done by a Honda dealer, radiator shop or service station.

1A. *1986-1989:* Remove the front fairing right-hand side inner cover as described in Chapter Thirteen.

1B. *1990-on:* Remove the right-hand middle fairing as described in Chapter Thirteen.

WARNING
Do not remove the radiator cap when the engine is hot.

2. Remove the radiator cap (**Figure 79**).
3. Have the radiator cap pressure tested (**Figure 80**). The specified radiator cap relief pressure is 0.95-1.25 kg/cm^2 (14-18 psi). The cap must be able to sustain this pressure for 6 seconds. Replace the radiator cap if it does not hold pressure or if the relief pressure is too high or too low.
4. Leave the radiator cap off and have the cooling system pressure tested (**Figure 81**). The cooling system should be pressurized up to, but not exceeding 1.25 kg/cm^2 (18 psi). The system must be able to sustain this pressure for 6 seconds. Replace or repair any components that fail this test.

CAUTION
If test pressures exceed specifications, the radiator may be damaged.

5. Test the specific gravity of the coolant with an antifreeze tester (**Figure 82**) to ensure adequate temperature and corrosion protection. Never let the mixture become less than 40 percent antifreeze or corrosion protection will be impaired. See **Table 7** for antifreeze protection specifications.
6. Check all cooling system hoses for damage or deterioration. Replace any hose that is questionable. Make sure all hose clamps are tight.
7. Carefully clean any road dirt, bugs, mud, etc. from the radiator core. Use a whisk boom, compressed air or low-pressure water. If the radiator has been hit by a small rock or other item, *carefully* straighten out the fins with a screwdriver.

Coolant Change

The cooling system should be completely drained and refilled at the interval indicated in **Table 1**.

CAUTION
Use only a high-quality ethylene glycol antifreeze specifically labeled for use with aluminum engines. Do not use an alcohol-based antifreeze.

In areas where freezing temperatures occur, add a higher percentage of antifreeze to protect the system to temperatures far below those likely to occur. **Table 7** lists the recommended amount of antifreeze for protection. The following procedure must be performed when the engine is *cool*.

CAUTION
Be careful not to spill antifreeze on painted surfaces as it will destroy the surface. Wash immediately with soapy water and rinse thoroughly with clean water.

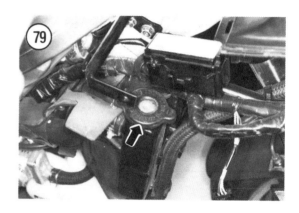

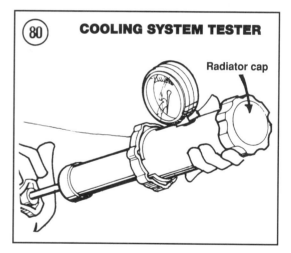

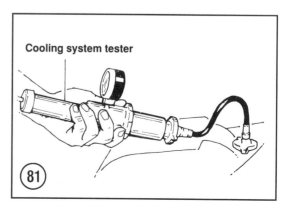

PERIODIC LUBRICATION, MAINTENANCE AND TUNE-UP

1. Support the bike so that it is level with both tires on the ground.

2A. *1986-1989:* Remove the left-hand fairing as described in Chapter Thirteen.

2B. *1990-on:* Remove the left-hand middle fairing and left-hand lower fairing as described in Chapter Thirteen.

3. Place a drain pan under the water pump on the left-hand side of the bike. Remove the water pump drain screw (**Figure 83**) and sealing washer.

WARNING
Do not remove the radiator cap when the engine is hot. Allow the cooling system to cool down prior to removing the radiator cap.

4. Remove the radiator cap (**Figure 79**) and allow the coolant to drain completely through the water pump drain hole.

5. Place a drain pan underneath the coolant reserve tank.

6. Disconnect the radiator siphon tube from the reserve tank and drain the coolant into the drain pan. Refer to **Figure 84** for 1986-1989 models or **Figure 85** for 1990-on models. Reconnect the siphon tube and secure it with its clamp.

7. Place a drain pan underneath the front cylinder head.

8. Remove the drain screws and washers (**Figure 86** and **Figure 87**) on the front cylinder head.

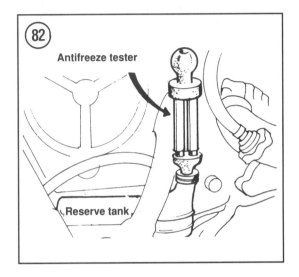

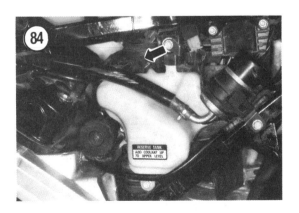

CHAPTER THREE

9. Reinstall the drain screw and sealing washer on the water pump cover (**Figure 83**). Replace the sealing washer, if necessary.

10. Reinstall the drain screws and sealing washers (**Figure 86** and **Figure 87**) on the front cylinder head. Replace the sealing washer, if necessary.

NOTE
When filling the radiator in Step 11, have an assistant lean the bike from side to side. This step will release air bubbles in the coolant mixture. Continue until the radiator is full.

11. Pour coolant through the radiator filler neck (**Figure 79**) very slowly. Use the recommended mixture of antifreeze and distilled water; see **Table 7** and **Table 8**. Fill to the radiator filler neck (just below the reservoir tank tube opening).

12. Fill the reserve tank to the UPPER level mark. Refer to **Figure 88** for 1986-1989 models or **Figure 89** for 1990-on models.

13. After filling the radiator, bleed the cooling system as follows:
   a. Start the engine and bring the idle up to 4,000-5,000 rpm.
   b. Snap the throttle a few times. When the radiator coolant level drops, add coolant to bring the level to the filler neck.
   c. When the radiator coolant level has stabilized, perform Step 14.

14. Install the radiator cap (**Figure 79**). Turn the radiator cap clockwise to the first stop. Then push the cap down and turn it clockwise until it stops and locks in place.

15. Start the engine and let it run at idle speed until the engine reaches normal operating temperature. Make sure there are no air bubbles in the coolant and that the coolant level in the reserve tank stabilizes at the correct level. Add coolant to the reserve tank as necessary. Refer to **Figure 88** for 1986-1989 models or **Figure 89** for 1990-on models.

16A. *1986-1989:* Install the left-hand fairing as described in Chapter Thirteen.

16B. *1990-on:* Install the left-hand middle fairing and left-hand lower fairing as described in Chapter Thirteen.

17. Test ride the bike and readjust the coolant level in the reserve tank as required.

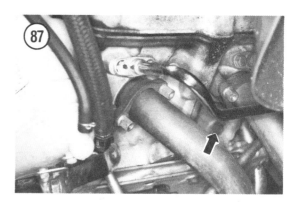

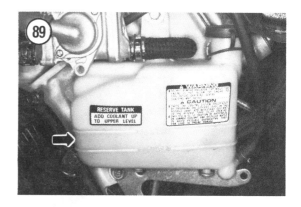

PERIODIC LUBRICATION, MAINTENANCE AND TUNE-UP

Front Headlight Aim

At the intervals in **Table 1**, check the front headlight aim as described in Chapter Eight. Adjust the headlight beam, if necessary.

Front Fork Air Pressure (1986-1989 Models)

The front fork air pressure must be checked when the forks are cold.

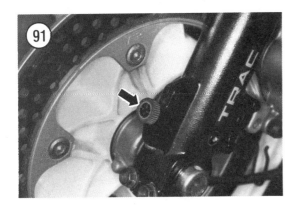

1. Raise the front wheel off the ground.
2. Remove the air valve cap (**Figure 90**) from both forks.
3. Use a low pressure gauge and measure the pressure of each fork. The recommended air pressure is 0-40 kPa (0-6 psi).
4. If air pressure is not within limits, use a hand air pump to add pressure or depress the needle in the air valve to release pressure. Make sure both forks are set at the same air pressure.
5. Reinstall the air valve caps and lower the front wheel to the ground.

Front Fork Anti-Dive System (1986-1989 Models)

The left fork is equipped with an anti-dive system. The four knob positions (**Figure 91**) are:
   a. Position 1—Light anti-dive damper force.
   b. Position 2—Medium anti-dive damper force.
   c. Position 3—Hard anti-dive damper force.
   d. Position 4—Maximum anti-dive damper force.

If the anti-dive system does not function properly, refer to Chapter Ten for service procedures.

Front Fork Spring Preload Adjustment (1992-on Models)

The spring preload can be adjusted by turning the adjuster screw (**Figure 92**) in the top of each fork cap. The adjuster is marked with 4 equally spaced grooves (**Figure 93**). These grooves can be used as alignment marks to ensure that both fork springs are adjusted equally. The standard setting is the third groove from the top of the adjuster.

> *WARNING*
> *Both fork springs must be adjusted to the **same setting**. If the springs are set on different settings, it will affect the motorcycle's handling which may lead to an accident. Make sure each adjuster ring is aligned correctly.*

1. Insert a flat-blade screwdriver into the slot in the adjuster (**Figure 92**) in the fork cap.
2. Turn the adjuster *clockwise* to increase preload or *counterclockwise* to decrease preload.
3. Repeat for the other fork assembly.

Front Suspension Check

1. Apply the front brake and pump the fork up and down as vigorously as possible. The forks should move smoothly. Check at the top of each slider and at the dust seal for oil leakage.
2. Make sure the upper (**Figure 94**) and lower (**Figure 95**) fork bridge pinch bolts are tight.
3. Check that the front axle pinch bolt(s) is tight. Refer to **Figure 96** for 1986-1989 models or **Figure 97** for 1990-on models.
4. Check that the front axle nut is tight. Refer to **Figure 98** for 1986-1989 models or **Figure 99** for 1990-on models.

> *WARNING*
> *If any of the previously mentioned bolts and nuts are loose, refer to Chapter Ten for correct procedures and torque specifications.*

Rear Shock Absorber Adjustment

1986-1989 spring preload

The spring preload adjust knob can be moved to any position between the LOW STS or HIGH positions. The LOW setting is the softest and the HIGH is the hardest, providing the maximum spring preload.

1. Remove the frame left-hand side cover.
2. Rotate the knob (**Figure 100**) to any of the settings from completely *counterclockwise* LOW or completely *clockwise* HIGH or any setting in between.
3. Always position the knob into one of the detents, NEVER in between detents.

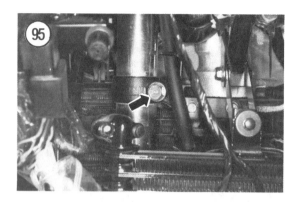

PERIODIC LUBRICATION, MAINTENANCE AND TUNE-UP

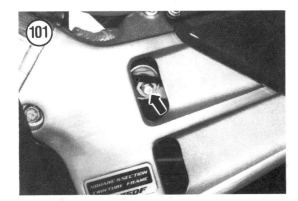

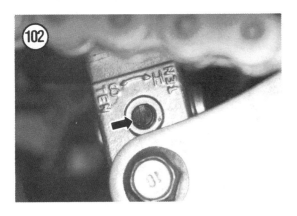

1990-on spring preload

1. Use the 8 × 12 mm open end wrench in the owner's tool kit and rotate the adjuster (**Figure 101**) in either direction to achieve the desired spring preload.
2. Turning the adjuster to any of the settings from completely *clockwise* HIGH or completely *counterclockwise* LOW or any setting in between.
3. Always position the knob into one of the detents, NEVER in between detents.

1990-on damping rebound

1. Use a flat-blade screwdriver and rotate the damping rebound adjuster (**Figure 102**) completely *clockwise*. This is the hardest setting. Rotate the adjuster completely *counterclockwise*. This is the softest setting.
2. The standard setting is when the adjuster is turned *counterclockwise* one full turn from the hardest setting. At this point the punch mark (A) will align with the reference mark (B) shown in **Figure 103**.

Rear Suspension Check

1. Support the bike so that the rear wheel is off the ground.

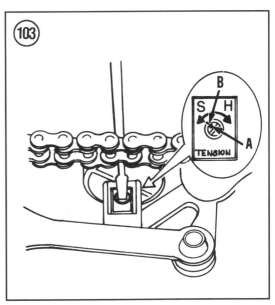

2. Check the rear shock absorber for any signs of leakage.

3. Push hard on the rear wheel sideways to check for side play in the rear swing arm bearings.

4. Check the tightness of the shock absorber upper (**Figure 104**) and lower (**Figure 105**) mounting nuts and bolts.

5. Check the tightness of the rear suspension bolts and nuts (**Figure 106**).

6A. *1986-1989:* Make sure the rear axle nut (**Figure 107**) is tight.

6B. *1990-on:* Make sure the bearing holder pinch bolt (**Figure 108**) is tight. Also check the rear wheel nuts (**Figure 109**) for tightness.

WARNING
If any of the previously mentioned nuts or bolts are loose, refer to Chapter Eleven for correct procedures and torque specifications.

Nuts, Bolts and Other Fasteners

Constant vibration can loosen may fasteners on a motorcycle. Check the tightness of all fasteners, especially those on:
  a. Engine mounting hardware.
  b. Engine crankcase covers.
  c. Handlebars and front forks.
  d. Gearshift lever.
  e. Sprocket bolts and nuts.
  f. Brake pedal and lever.
  g. Exhaust system.
  h. Lighting equipment.

TUNE-UP

A complete tune-up restores performance and power that is lost due to normal wear and deterioration of engine parts. Because engine wear occurs over a combined period of time and mileage, the engine tune-up should be performed at the intervals specified in **Table 1**. More frequent tune-ups may be required if the bike is ridden primarily in stop-and-go traffic.

On 1990-on U.S. and Switzerland models, the Vehicle Emission Control Information label is affixed to the rear inner fender (**Figure 110**). The VECI label lists tune-up information for your model.

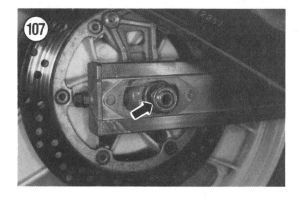

PERIODIC LUBRICATION, MAINTENANCE AND TUNE-UP

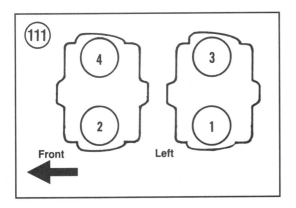

Table 9 lists tune-up specifications for all VFR700F and VFR750F models.

NOTE
*Always refer to the tune-up specifications on your bike's Vehicle Emission Control Information label located on the rear fender (**Figure 110**) if available. If specifications on the label differ from those in **Table 9**, use those on the label.*

Before starting a tune-up procedure, make sure to have all the necessary new parts on hand.

Because different systems in an engine interact, the procedures should be done in the following order:

a. Inspect fuel lines and fuel filter. Replace if necessary.
b. Inspect air filter element. Replace if necessary. Clean sub air filter element on 1990-on models.
c. Check and adjust valve clearances.
d. Check engine compression.
e. Check or replace the spark plugs.
f. Check the ignition timing.
g. Adjust carburetors (idle speed and synchronization).

To perform a tune-up on your Honda, you will need the following tools:

a. 18 mm spark plug wrench.
b. Socket wrench and assorted sockets.
c. Compression gauge.
d. Spark plug wire feeler gauge and gapper tool.
e. Flat feeler gauge set.
f. Ignition timing light.
g. Tune-up tachometer.
h. Manometer (carburetor synchronization tool).

Firing Order

The cylinder firing order for all Honda VFR700F and VFR750F engines is 1-3-4-2. The cylinders numbers (**Figure 111**) are as follows:

a. No. 1 cylinder-left rear.
b. No. 2 cylinder-left front.
c. No. 3 cylinder-right rear.
d. No. 4 cylinder-right front.

Valve Clearance Measurement (1986-1989 Models)

Valve clearance measurement and adjustment must be performed with the engine cold (below 35° C [95° F]). The correct valve clearance for all models is listed in **Table 9**. There are 2 exhaust valves and 2 intake valves per cylinder.

1. Remove the air filter housing as described in Chapter Seven.
2. Remove the cylinder head cover as described under *Cylinder Head Cover Removal/Installation* in Chapter Four.

NOTE
*If the rubber cylinder head cover gasket (**Figure 112**) is damaged, or if it came loose from the cover, pull the gasket off and clean the cover groove of all gasket and sealer residue. Then apply Three Bond 1521 or an equivalent rubber adhesive onto the cylinder head cover gasket surface groove and install the gasket into position. Doing this now will allow the gasket sealer to dry while you perform the following procedures.*

3. Remove the pulse generator rotor cover cap and O-ring (**Figure 113**).
4. Remove all of the spark plugs as described in this chapter. This will make it easier to rotate the engine.

NOTE
*In the following steps, rotate the engine with a socket on the starter clutch mounting bolt (**Figure 114**).*

5. Shift the transmission into NEUTRAL.
6. The correct valve clearance for both the intake and exhaust valves is listed in **Table 9**.

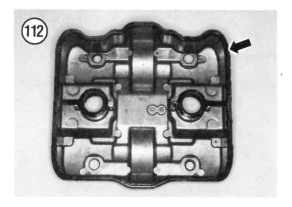

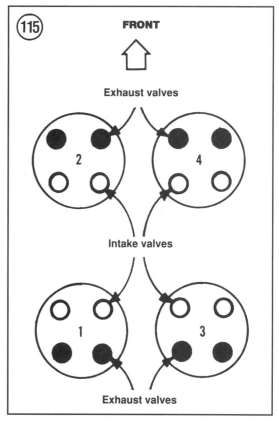

PERIODIC LUBRICATION, MAINTENANCE AND TUNE-UP

NOTE
*The No. 2 and 4 cylinders are at the front with the No. 2 cylinder on the left-hand side. Refer to **Figure 115**. The No. 1 and 3 cylinders are at the rear with the No. 1 on the left-hand side. The left-hand side refers to a rider sitting on the seat facing forward. The intake valves are located toward the center "V" of the engine (adjacent to the carburetors) and the exhaust valves are located at the front and rear of the engine (near the exhaust pipes).*

7. Rotate the crankshaft by turning the starter clutch mounting bolt (**Figure 114**). Rotate the crankshaft *clockwise* (as viewed from the left-hand side) until the "T 1" mark on the starter clutch (**Figure 116**) aligns with the clutch cover index mark (**Figure 117**). The No. 1 cylinder must be at top dead center (TDC) on the compression stroke. Check and record the clearances on both intake valves and both exhaust valves on the No. 1 cylinder.

NOTE
A cylinder at TDC of its compression stroke will have free play in all of its rocker arms, indicating that both pairs of intake and exhaust valves are closed.

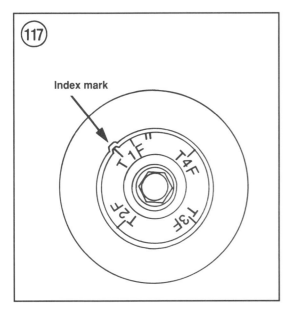

8. To measure the clearance, insert a flat feeler gauge (**Figure 118**) between *each* valve stem and the valve adjuster (**Figure 119**). The clearance is measured correctly when there is a slight drag on the feeler gauge when it is inserted and withdrawn. Write the clearance on piece of paper and identify it as to cylinder number and whether it is an intake or exhaust valve.

9. If the No. 1 cylinder clearance adjustment is necessary, adjust the valves as described in this chapter.

10. Rotate the crankshaft *clockwise* (as viewed from the left-hand side) 180° until the "T 3" mark on the starter clutch (**Figure 116**) aligns with the

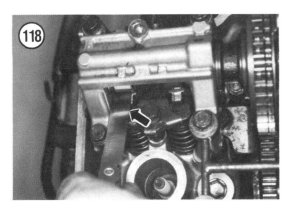

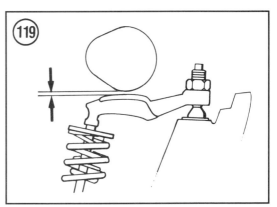

clutch cover index mark. The No. 3 cylinder must be at top dead center (TDC) on the compression stroke. Repeat Step 8 and check and record the clearances on both intake valves and both exhaust valves on the No. 3 cylinder.

11. If the No. 3 cylinder clearance adjustment is necessary, adjust the valves as described in this chapter.

12. Rotate the crankshaft *clockwise* (as viewed from the left-hand side) 270° until the "T 2" mark on the starter clutch (**Figure 116**) aligns with the clutch cover index mark (**Figure 120**). The No. 2 cylinder must be at top dead center (TDC) on the compression stroke. Repeat Step 8 and check and record the clearances on both intake valves and both exhaust valves on the No. 2 cylinder.

13. If the No. 2 cylinder clearance adjustment is necessary, adjust the valves as described in this chapter.

14. Rotate the crankshaft *clockwise* (as viewed from the left-hand side) 180° until the "T 4" mark on the starter clutch (**Figure 116**) aligns with clutch cover index mark. The No. 4 cylinder must be at top dead center (TDC) on the compression stroke. Repeat Step 8 and check and record the clearances on both intake valves and both exhaust valves on the No. 4 cylinder.

15. If the No. 4 cylinder clearance adjustment is necessary, adjust the valves as described in this chapter.

16. After all valve clearances are adjusted, install the following:
   a. Install the spark plugs as described in this chapter.
   b. Apply engine oil onto the pulse generator rotor cover cap O-ring and molybdenum disulfide grease onto the cap's threads. Install the cap and tighten securely.
   c. Make sure cylinder head cover rubber gasket (**Figure 112**) is in place and install the cover as described in Chapter Four.
   d. Install the air filter housing as described in Chapter Seven.

Valve Clearance Adjustment (1986-1989 Models)

The valves can be adjusted with the Honda special tools, Tappet Locknut Wrench (part No. 07GMA-ML70120) and Tappet Adjuster (part No. 07GMA-ML70110) or with a small box-end wrench and flat blade screwdriver.

Special tools

1. Position the cylinder that requires valve adjustment at TDC on the compression stroke as described under *Valve Clearance Measurement* in this chapter.
2. Install the special tools onto the valve adjuster.
3. Turn the locknut wrench portion of the tool (A, **Figure 121**) and back off the locknut.
4. Turn the adjuster portion of the tool (B, **Figure 121**) and screw the adjuster in or out so there is a slight resistance felt on the feeler gauge (**Figure 122**).

CAUTION
Be sure to tighten the locknut to the specified torque value. Failure to do so may result in the adjuster locknuts

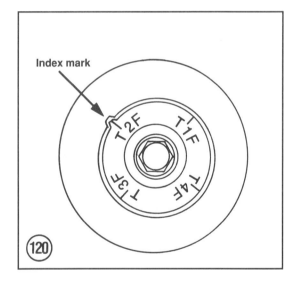

PERIODIC LUBRICATION, MAINTENANCE AND TUNE-UP

working loose and allowing incorrect valve clearances.

5. Hold the adjuster and tighten the locknut to the torque specification listed in **Table 6**. Then recheck the clearance to make sure the adjuster did not slip when the locknut was tightened.

6. Readjust if necessary, then remove the special tools.

Standard tools

1. Position the cylinder that requires valve adjustment at TDC on the compression stroke as described under *Valve Clearance Measurement* in this chapter.
2. Use a box-end wrench (A, **Figure 123**) and back off the locknut.
3. Use a flat bladed screwdriver (B, **Figure 123**) and screw the adjuster in or out so there is a slight resistance felt on the feeler gauge (**Figure 122**).

CAUTION
Be sure to tighten the locknut to the specified torque value. Failure to do so may result in the adjuster locknuts working loose and allowing incorrect valve clearances.

4. Hold the adjuster and tighten the locknut to the torque specification listed in **Table 6**. Then recheck the clearance to make sure the adjuster did not slip when the locknut was tightened.
5. Readjust if necessary, then remove the tools.

Valve Clearance Measurement (1990-on Models)

Valve clearance measurement and adjustment must be performed with the engine cold (below 35° C [95° F]). The correct valve clearance for all models is listed in **Table 9**. There are 2 exhaust valves and 2 intake valves per cylinder.

1. Remove the air filter housing as described in Chapter Seven.
2. Remove the cylinder head cover as described under *Cylinder Head Cover Removal/Installation* in Chapter Four.

NOTE
*If the rubber cylinder head cover gasket (**Figure 124**) is damaged, or if it came loose from the cover, pull the gasket off and clean the cover groove of all gasket and sealer residue. Then apply Three Bond 1521 or an equivalent rubber adhesive onto the cylinder head cover gasket surface groove and install the gasket into position with the IN mark and arrow facing toward the intake side of the cylinder head. Doing this now will allow the gasket sealer to dry while you perform the following procedures.*

3. Remove the pulse generator rotor cover cap and O-ring (**Figure 125**).

4. Remove all of the spark plugs as described in this chapter.

This will make it easier to rotate the engine.

NOTE
The following steps are shown with the engine removed from the frame and in some steps partially disassembled. Valve adjustment can be performed with the engine in the frame.

NOTE
*In the following steps, rotate the engine with a socket on the starter clutch mounting bolt (**Figure 126**).*

5. Shift the transmission into NEUTRAL.

6. The correct valve clearance for both the intake and exhaust valves is listed in **Table 9**.

NOTE
*The No. 2 and 4 cylinders are at the front with the No. 2 cylinder on the left-hand side. Refer to **Figure 115**. The No. 1 and 3 cylinders are at the rear with the No. 1 on the left-hand side. The left-hand side refers to a rider sitting on the seat facing forward. The intake valves are located toward the center "V" of the engine (adjacent to the carburetors) and the exhaust valves are located at the front and rear of the engine (near the exhaust pipes).*

7. Rotate the crankshaft by turning the starter clutch mounting bolt (**Figure 126**). Rotate the crankshaft *clockwise* (as viewed from the left-hand side) until the "T 1" mark on the starter clutch (**Figure 127**) aligns with the clutch cover index mark (**Figure 117**). The No. 1 cylinder must be at top dead center (TDC) on the compression stroke. Check and record the clearances on both intake valves and both exhaust valves on the No. 1 cylinder.

NOTE
*Write the clearance on a piece of paper and identify it as to the cylinder number and whether it is an intake or exhaust valve. **Figure 128** shows a typical chart and how you can keep track of the clearance measurements. The clearance dimensions will be used during the adjustment procedure, if adjustment is necessary.*

NOTE
A cylinder at TDC of its compression stroke will have free play in all of its rocker arms, indicating that both pairs of intake and exhaust valves are closed.

8. To measure the clearance, insert a flat feeler gauge between the camshaft lobe and the valve lifter (**Figure 129**). The clearance is measured correctly

PERIODIC LUBRICATION, MAINTENANCE AND TUNE-UP

when there is a slight drag on the feeler gauges when it is inserted and withdrawn. Write the clearance on a piece of paper and identify it as to cylinder number and whether it is an intake or exhaust valve.

9. If the No. 1 cylinder clearance adjustment is necessary, adjust the valves as described in this chapter.

10. Rotate the crankshaft *clockwise* (as viewed from the left-hand side) 180° until the "T 3" mark on the starter clutch (**Figure 127**) aligns with the clutch cover index mark. The No. 3 cylinder must be at top dead center (TDC) on the compression stroke. Repeat Step 8 and check and record the clearances on both intake valves and both exhaust valves on the No. 3 cylinder.

11. If the No. 3 cylinder clearance adjustment is necessary, adjust the valves as described in this chapter.

12. Rotate the crankshaft *clockwise* (as viewed from the left-hand side) 270° until the "T 2" mark on the starter clutch (**Figure 127**) aligns with the clutch cover index mark (**Figure 120**). The No. 2 cylinder must be at top dead center (TDC) on the compression stroke. Repeat Step 8 and check and record the clearances on both intake valves and both exhaust valves on the No. 2 cylinder.

13. If the No. 2 cylinder clearance adjustment is necessary, adjust the valves as described in this chapter.

14. Rotate the crankshaft *clockwise* (as viewed from the left-hand side) 180° until the "T 4" mark on the starter clutch (**Figure 127**) aligns with clutch cover index mark. The No. 4 cylinder must be at top dead center (TDC) on the compression stroke. Repeat Step 8 and check and record the clearances on both intake valves and both exhaust valves on the No. 4 cylinder.

15. If the No. 4 cylinder clearance adjustment is necessary, adjust the valves as described in this chapter.

16. After all valve clearances are adjusted, install the following:
   a. Install the spark plugs as described in this chapter.
   b. Apply engine oil onto the pulse generator rotor cover cap O-ring and molybdenum disulfide grease onto the cap's threads. Install the cap and tighten securely.
   c. Make sure cylinder head cover rubber gasket (**Figure 124**) is in place and install the cover as described in Chapter Four.
   d. Install the air filter housing as described in Chapter Seven.

Valve Clearance Adjustment (1990-on Models)

1. Remove the camshafts as described under *Camshaft Removal* in Chapter Four.
2. When removing the valve lifters and shims, note the following:
   a. The shims are mounted on top of the valve stem, underneath the valve lifters. Because a shim may stick to its valve lifter when the lifter is removed, remove the lifter carefully to prevent

CAMSHAFT SHIM CHART ↑ FRONT

EXHAUST				
	Cyl. No. 1	Cyl. No. 2	Cyl. No. 3	Cyl. No. 4
Clearance				
Shim No.				

INTAKE				
	Cyl. No. 1	Cyl. No. 2	Cyl. No. 3	Cyl. No. 4
Clearance				
Shim No.				

the shim from working loose and falling into the crankcase.

b. The valve lifters can be removed with a magnet or valve lapping tool.

c. The shims can be removed with a magnet or tweezers.

d. Clean the shims and valve lifters with solvent or contact cleaner. Dry with compressed air, if available.

e. The valve lifters and shims must be marked as to their original cylinder and valve mounting position to ensure correct valve clearance adjustment and reassembly. Use some type of divided tray or container, with each compartment labeled for cylinder and valve position, when performing the following.

3. Remove the valve lifter (A, **Figure 130**) and shim (B, **Figure 130**) for each valve to be adjusted. Label and store each lifter and shim assembly in a suitable container as previously mentioned in Step 2.

NOTE
*Always measure the thickness of the old shim with a micrometer to make sure of the exact thickness of the shim. If the shim is worn to less than the indicated thickness marked on it (**Figure 131**, typical), it will throw off calculations for a new shim. Measure the new shim to make sure it is marked correctly.*

4. Measure the thickness of the old shim with a micrometer (**Figure 132**) and record it on a piece of paper.

5. Using the recorded valve clearance, the specified valve clearance listed in **Table 9** and the old shim thickness, determine the new shim thickness with the following equation:

$$a = (b - c) + d$$

Where:

a is the new shim thickness.
b is the recorded valve clearance.
c is the specified valve clearance.
d is the old shim thickness.

NOTE
*The following numbers are for **example only**. Use the numbers written down during the **Valve Clearance Measurement** procedure.*

For example: If the recorded valve clearance is 0.05 mm, the old shim thickness is 1.870 mm and the specified valve clearance is 17 mm, then:

a = (0.05-0.17) + 1.870

a = 1.75 (new shim thickness).

NOTE
If the shim thickness exceeds 2.800 mm, the valve seat is heavily carboned and should be refaced.

6. Apply clean engine oil to both sides of the new shim.

7. Install the shim (B, **Figure 130**) and the valve lifter (A, **Figure 130**).

8. Repeat for each valve to be adjusted.

9. After all valve clearances are adjusted, install the following:

a. Install the camshafts as described under *Camshaft Installation* in Chapter Four.

b. Recheck the valve clearances as described in this chapter.

PERIODIC LUBRICATION, MAINTENANCE AND TUNE-UP

Compression Test

At every other tune-up, check cylinder compression. Record the results and compare them at the next tune-up. A running record will show trends in deterioration so that corrective action can be taken before complete failure.

The results, when properly interpreted, can indicate general cylinder, piston ring and valve condition.

1. Warm the engine to normal operating temperature. Shut the engine off. Make sure that the choke valve is completely open and that the engine stop switch is in the OFF position.

2. Place the bike on the centerstand or sidestand.

3. Disconnect the spark plug wires from all spark plugs.

4. Remove the spark plug from each cylinder as described in this chapter.

5. Connect the compression tester to one cylinder following manufacturer's instructions.

6. Open the throttle completely and using the starter, crank the engine over until there is no further rise in pressure. Maximum pressure is usually reached within 4-7 seconds of engine cranking.

NOTE
Do not turn the engine over more than absolutely necessary. When spark plug leads are disconnected, the electronic ignition will produce the highest voltage possible and the coils may overheat and be damaged.

7. Remove the tester and record the reading.

8. Repeat Steps 5-7 for the other cylinders.

When interpreting the results, actual readings are not as important as the difference between the readings. Readings should be about 1177-1569 kPa (171-227 psi). A maximum difference of 100 kPa (14 psi) between the cylinders is acceptable. Greater differences indicate worn or broken rings, leaking or sticking valves, a blown head gasket(s) or a combination of all.

If compression readings do not differ between the cylinders by more than 70 kPa (10 psi), the rings and valves are in good condition.

If a low reading (10% or more) is obtained on one of the cylinders, it indicates valve or ring trouble. To determine which, insert a small funnel into the spark plug hole and pour about a teaspoon of engine oil through it onto the top of the piston. Turn the engine over once to clear some of the excess oil, then take another compression test and record the reading. If the compression returns to normal, the valves are good but the rings are defective on that cylinder. If compression does not increase, the valves require servicing. A valve could be hanging open or a piece of carbon could be on a valve seat.

9. Install the spark plugs as described in this chapter and connect the spark plug wires.

Spark Plug Selection

Spark plugs are available in various heat ranges, hotter or colder than plugs originally installed at the factory.

Select plugs of a heat range designed for the loads and temperature conditions under which the bike will be run. The use of incorrect heat ranges can cause seized pistons, scored cylinder walls or damaged piston crowns.

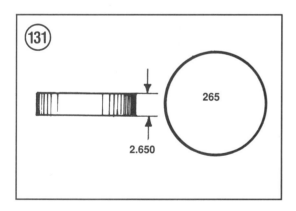

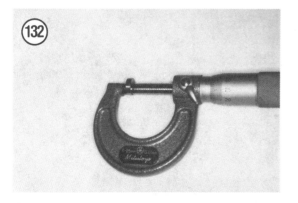

NOTE
Higher plug numbers designate colder plugs; lower plug numbers designate hotter plugs. For example, an NGK BP8ES plug is colder than an NGK BP7ES plug.

In general, use a hot plug for low speeds, low engine loads and low temperatures. Use a cold plug for high speeds, high engine loads and high temperatures. The plug should operate hot enough to burn off unwanted deposits, but not so hot that it is damaged or causes preignition. A spark plug of the correct heat range will show a light tan color on the portion of the insulator within the cylinder after the plug has been in service.

NOTE
In areas where seasonal temperature variations are great, the factory recommends a "2-plug system"—cold plugs for hard summer riding and hot plugs for slower winter operation.

The reach (length) of a plug is also important. A longer than normal plug could interfere with the valves and pistons, causing permanent and severe damage. Refer to **Figure 133**. The recommended spark plugs are listed in **Table 9**.

Spark Plug Removal/Cleaning

1A. On 1986-1989 models, remove both frame side covers as described in Chapter Thirteen.
1B. On 1990-on models, perform the following:
   a. Remove the lower portion of the front fairing on each side.
   b. Remove the lower center portion of the front fairing as described in Chapter Thirteen.
   c. On 1994 models, remove the tailpiece/side cover assembly as described in Chapter Thirteen.
   d. Remove the fuel tank rear mounting hardware and prop up the rear of the fuel tank to gain access to the rear set of spark plugs (No. 1 and No. 3).
2. Loosen the radiator upper mounting bolts (**Figure 134**).
3. Remove the radiator lower mounting bolts (**Figure 135**).
4. Carefully pivot the lower edge of the radiator assembly up and away from the front cylinder head cover. Secure it in this position with a piece of wire or Bungee cord.

NOTE
Figure 136 is shown with the fuel tank removed for clarity. It is not necessary

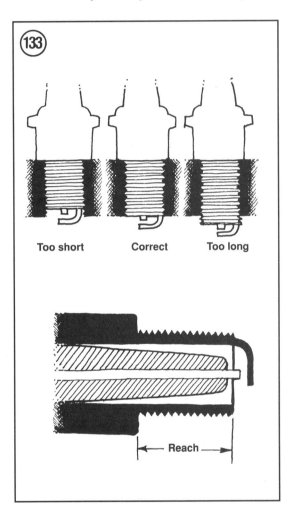

PERIODIC LUBRICATION, MAINTENANCE AND TUNE-UP

to remove the fuel tank to reach the No. 1 and No. 3 spark plugs.

5. Grasp the spark plug lead (**Figure 136**) as near to the plug as possible and pull it off the plug. If the boot is stuck to the plug, twist it slightly back and forth to break it loose.

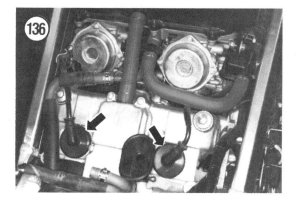

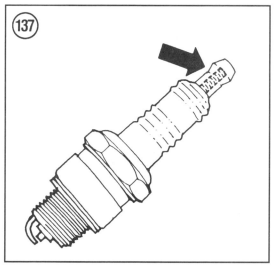

6. Blow away any dirt that has accumulated in the spark plug wells.

CAUTION
The dirt could fall into the cylinders when the plugs are removed, causing serious engine damage.

7. Remove all spark plugs with the spark plug wrench furnished in the owner's tool kit.

NOTE
If plugs are difficult to remove, apply penetrating oil around base of plugs and let it soak in about 10-20 minutes.

8. Inspect spark plug carefully. Look for a plug with broken center porcelain, excessively eroded electrodes and excessive carbon or oil fouling. Replace such plugs. If deposits are light, the plug may be cleaned in solvent with a wire brush or in a special spark plug sandblast cleaner. Regap the plug as explained in this chapter.

Spark Plug Gapping and Installation

New plugs should be carefully gapped to ensure a reliable, consistent spark. You must use a special spark plug gapping tool with a wire feeler gauge.

Be sure to replace all 4 spark plugs at the same time; all 4 plugs must be of the same heat range.

1. Remove the new plugs from the box. Do *not* screw in the small piece that is loose in each box (**Figure 137**); it is not used.

2. Insert a wire feeler gauge between the center and the side electrode of each plug (**Figure 138**). The correct gap is listed in **Table 9**. If the gap is correct, you will feel a slight drag as you pull the wire through. If there is no drag or the gauge won't pass

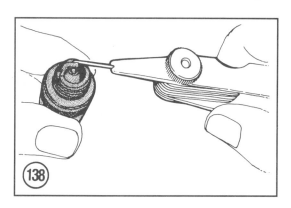

through, bend the side electrode *with the gapping tool* (**Figure 139**) to set the proper gap.

3. Put a *small* amount of anti-seize compound on the threads of each spark plug.

4. Install the spark plug into a spark plug wrench and extension.

5. Screw each spark plug in by hand until it seats. Very little effort is required. If force is necesary, you have a plug cross-threaded; unscrew it and try again.

6. Tighten the spark plugs an additional 1/2 turn after the gasket has made contact with the head or to the torque specification listed in **Table 6**. If you are reinstalling old, regapped plugs and are reusing the old gasket, only tighten an additional 1/4 turn.

NOTE
Do not overtighten. This will only squash the gasket and destroy its sealing ability.

7. Install each spark plug lead; make sure the head is on tight.

Reading Spark Plugs

Much information about engine and spark plug performance can be determined by careful examination of the spark plugs. This information is more valid after performing the following steps.

1. Ride the bike a short distance at full throttle in any gear.

2. Turn the engine kill switch to the OFF position before closing the throttle and simultaneously pull in the clutch or shift to NEUTRAL; coast and brake to a stop.

3. Remove the spark plugs and examine them. Compare then to **Figure 140**. If the insulator is white or burned, the plug is too hot and should be replaced with a colder one.

A too-cold plug will have sooty or oily deposits ranging in color rom dark brown to black. Replace with a hotter plug and check for too-rich carburetion or evidence of oil blowby at the piston rings.

If the plug has a light tan or gray colored deposit and no abnormal gap wear or electrode erosion is evident, the plug and the engine are running properly.

If the plug exhibits a black insulator tip, a damp and oily film over the firing end and a carbon layer over the entire nose, it is oil fouled. An oil fouled plug can be cleaned, but it is better to replace it.

If any one plug is found unsatisfactory, discard and replace all plugs.

IGNITION TIMING

The Honda VFR700F and VFR750F models are equipped with a transistorized ignition system. This system uses no breaker points and is non-adjustable. The timing should be checked to make sure all ignition components are operating correctly.

Incorrect ignition timing can cause a drastic loss of engine performance and efficiency. It may also cause overheating.

Ignition timing is to be checked on the No. 1 cylinder for 1986-1989 models or the No. 4 cylinder for 1990-on models. If the timing is correct on one of these cylinders, the other 3 cylinders will automatically be correct. Before starting on this procedure, check all electrical connections related to the ignition system. Make sure all connections are tight and free of corrosion and that all ground connections are tight.

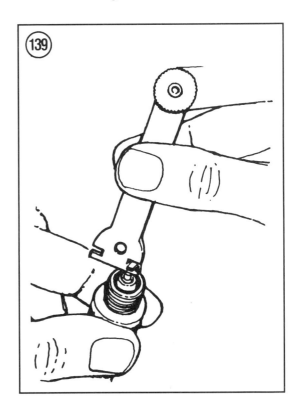

PERIODIC LUBRICATION, MAINTENANCE AND TUNE-UP

SPARK PLUG CONDITION

Normal
- Identified by light tan or gray deposits on the firing tip.
- Can be cleaned

Carbon-fouled
- Identified by black, dry fluffy carbon deposits on insulator tips, exposed shell surfaces and electrodes.
- Caused by too cold a plug, weak ignition, dirty air cleaner, too rich a fuel mixture, or excessive idling. Can be cleaned.

Oil-fouled
- Identified by wet black deposits on the insulator shell bore and electrodes.
- Caused by excessive oil entering combustion chamber through worn rings and pistons, excessive clearance between valve guides and stems, or worn or loose bearings. Can be cleaned. If engine is not repaired, use a hotter plug.

Gap-bridged
- Identified by deposit buildup closing gap between electrodes.
- Caused by oil or carbon fouling. If deposits are not excessive, the plug can be cleaned.

Overheated
- Identified by a white or light gray insulator with small black or gray brown spots and with bluish-burnt appearance of electrodes.
- Caused by engine overheating, wrong type of fuel, loose spark plugs, too hot a plug, or incorrect ignition timing. Replace the plug.

Sustained preignition
- Identified by melted electrodes and possibly blistered insulator. Metallic deposits on insulator indicates engine damage.
- Caused by wrong type of fuel, incorrect ignition timing or advance, too hot a plug, burned valves, or engine overheating. Replace the plug.

Refer to **Figure 141** for cylinder number locations.

1. Start the engine and let it reach normal operating temperature. Shut the engine OFF.
2. Remove the lower sections of the front fairing as described in Chapter Thirteen.
3. Place the bike on the centerstand or sidestand.
4. Remove the pulse generator rotor cover cap and O-ring (**Figure 142**).
5. Connect a portable tachometer following the manufacturer's instructions. The bike's tachometer is not accurate enough in the low rpm range for this adjustment.
6. Connect a timing light according the manufacturer's instructions to the number 1 (left rear) cylinder spark plug lead.
7. Start the engine and let it idle at the idle speed listed in **Table 9**; aim the timing light at the hole in the clutch cover and pull the trigger. If the timing mark "T1-F" aligns with the index mark on the clutch cover (**Figure 143**) the timing is correct.
8. Also check ignition advance as follows:
    a. Increase engine speed and pull the trigger.
    b. The "T1-F" marks should slowly rotate *counterclockwise* at approximately 2,000 rpm indicating that ignition timing is advancing.
9. If either idle or advance timing is incorrect, refer to Chapter Eight and check the spark units and the pulse generators.
10. Shut off the engine and disconnect the timing light and portable tachometer.
11. Apply engine oil onto the pulse generator rotor cover cap O-ring and molybdenum disulfide grease onto the cap's threads. Install the cap and tighten securely.

CARBURETOR ADJUSTMENT

Idle Speed

1. Attach a portable tachometer following the manufacturer's instructions.
2. Start the engine and let it warm up to normal operating temperature.

NOTE
The engine must be at normal operating temperature for the idle speed adjustment to be accurate.

3. Sit on the seat while the engine is idling. Move the handlebar from side to side without touching the throttle grip. If the engine speed increases when the wheel is turned, the throttle cable(s) may be damaged, incorrectly adjusted or they may be incorrectly routed through the frame. Correct this problem im-

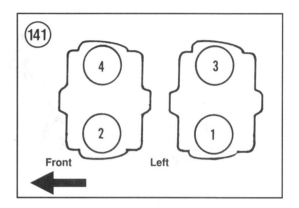

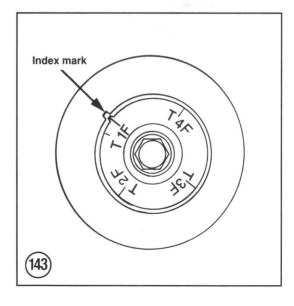

PERIODIC LUBRICATION, MAINTENANCE AND TUNE-UP

mediately. Do **not** ride the bike in this unsafe condition.

4. Set the idle speed by turning the throttle stop screw in to increase or out to decrease idle speed. The correct idle speed is listed in **Table 9**. Refer to the following for the location of the throttle stop screw:

  a. *1986-1989 models:* A, **Figure 144**.
  b. *1990-1993 models:* **Figure 145**.
  c. *1994-on models:* **Figure 146**.

5. Open and close the throttle a couple of times; check for variations in idle speed. Readjust if necessary.

WARNING
*With the engine idling, move the handlebar from side to side. If idle speed increases during this movement, the throttle cables may need adjusting or they may be incorrectly routed through the frame. Correct this problem immediately. Do **not** ride the bike in this unsafe condition.*

6. Shut the engine off and disconnect the portable tachometer.

Carburetor Synchronization

Carburetor synchronization is critical to engine performance because it synchronizes the vacuum in each carburetor's intake port, thereby ensuring that each carburetor delivers the same amount of air/fuel mixture to the cylinders. When the carburetors are properly synchronized the engine will warm up faster and there will be an improvement in throttle response, performance and mileage. When the carburetors are not synchronized, the engine will run rough, accelerate poorly and operate with reduced fuel economy.

Prior to synchronizing the carburetors, the air filter element must be clean and the valve clearances must be properly adjusted. The ignition timing must also be checked to make sure that all components within the ignition system are operating correctly.

This procedure requires the following tools:
  a. Carb-synch tool (vacuum gauge or mercury tube set). This tool measures how much partial vacuum is created in all 4 cylinders simultaneously. Carb-synch tools can be purchased through motorcycle dealers or mail-order parts houses.
  b. Auxiliary fuel tank. Because of the room required to install the vacuum gauges and make adjustments, the fuel tank must be removed when synchronizing the carburetors. To supply fuel to the carburetors during this procedure, an auxiliary fuel tank will be required. For this you can use a small displacement motorcycle fuel tank (purchased from a salvage yard) or a small tank from a discarded lawn mower. Auxiliary

fuel tanks for carburetor synchronization are also available on the aftermarket. Whatever type of fuel tank you use, however, make sure it does not leak and that it is mounted securely to the bike. Also make sure the tank's fuel valve and hose can supply an adequate amount of fuel to the engine.

WARNING
The following procedure should be performed in a well-ventilated area due to exhaust fumes, preferably outside your garage or workshop area.

1. Start the engine and warm it up fully.
2. Adjust the idle speed as described in this chapter, then turn the engine off.
3. Remove the fuel tank as described in Chapter Seven.
4. Install an auxiliary fuel tank onto the motorcycle and attach its fuel hose to the carburetors.

NOTE
Make sure the auxiliary fuel tank is mounted securely and positioned so that the connecting fuel hose is not kinked or obstructed.

WARNING
When supplying fuel by temporary means, make sure the fuel tank is secure and that all fuel lines are tight-no leaks.

NOTE
*The carburetor numbers match the cylinder numbers. Refer to **Figure 141** for cylinder number locations.*

5A. On 1986-1989 models, loosen and remove the vacuum plugs and washers. Refer to B, **Figure 144**.

NOTE
Some of the following steps are shown with the carburetors removed for clarity.

5B. On 1990-on models, perform the following:
 a. Disconnect the vacuum tube (**Figure 147**) from the carburetor vacuum joints on the front cylinder head (No. 1 and No. 3).

CAUTION
When removing the rubber caps in Step 5B, pinch the end of the cap to remove it. Pinching the rubber cap body and then trying to remove it can damage the cap.

 b. Pinch the end of the No. 2 and No. 4 carburetor rubber cap and remove them from the vacuum joints on the cylinder head.

6. If necessary, install carb-synch adapters into the vacuum port holes.

7. Mount the carb-synch tool onto the bike and connect a vacuum tube to each carburetor vacuum tube joint or carb-synch adaptor(s) following the manufacturer's instructions.

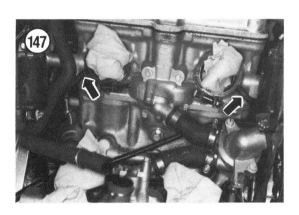

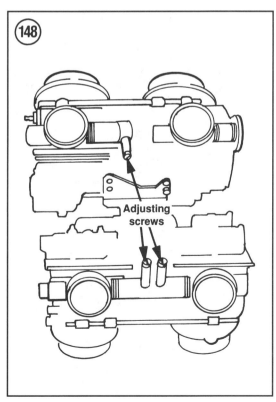

PERIODIC LUBRICATION, MAINTENANCE AND TUNE-UP

NOTE
On 1986-1993 models, the No. 2 carburetor is the base carburetor and has no synchronization screw. On 1994 models, the No. 1 carburetor is the base carburetor. The base carburetor has no synchronization screw and all other 3 carburetors must be synchronized to it.

8. Turn the auxiliary fuel tank petcock on and start the engine and let it idle at the speed listed in **Table 9**. Adjust the idle speed with the throttle stop screw, if necessary.

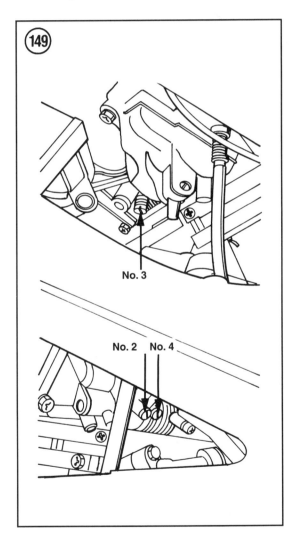

9. If the difference in gauge readings is 30 mm Hg (1.2 in. Hg) or less among all 4 cylinders, the carburetors are considered synchronized. If not, proceed as follows.

10A. On 1986-1993 models, turn the adjusting screws (**Figure 148**) and adjust the No. 1, No. 3 and No. 4 carburetors so that they each have the same gauge readings as the No. 2 carburetor. Snap the throttle a few times and recheck the synchronization readings. Readjust the idle speed and synchronization if required. Repeat a few times until all adjustments remain the same.

10B. On 1994-on models, turn the adjusting screws (**Figure 149**) and adjust the No. 2, No. 3 and No. 4 carburetors so that they each have the same gauge readings as the No. 1 carburetor. Snap the throttle a few times and recheck the synchronization readings. Readjust the idle speed and synchronization if required. Repeat a few times until all adjustments remain the same.

NOTE
To gain the utmost in performance and efficiency from the engine, adjust the carburetors so that the gauge readings are as close to each other as possible.

11. Reset the idle speed, stop the engine and install the vacuum plugs or reconnect the hose(s). Make sure the plugs and hose(s) are tight to prevent vacuum leaks.
12. Turn the petcock off and then shut the engine off.
13. Disconnect the vacuum gauge tubes and remove the adapters (if used).
14. Remove the carb-synch tool.
15. Remove the auxiliary fuel tank.
16A. On 1986-1989 models, install the vacuum plugs and washers.
16B. On 1990-on models, perform the following:
   a. Connect the vacuum tube (**Figure 147**) onto the carburetor vacuum joints on the front cylinder head (No. 1 and No. 3).
   b. Install the rubber cap onto the No. 2 and No. 4 carburetor vacuum joints on the cylinder head.
17. Install the fuel tank as described in Chapter Seven.

Tables 1-9 are on the following pages.

Table 1 MAINTENANCE SCHEDULE*

Prior to each ride	Inspect tires and rims and check inflation pressure
	Check steering for smooth operation with no excessive play or restrictions
	Check brake operation and for fluid leakage
	Check fuel supply. Make sure there is enough fuel for the intended ride
	Check for fuel leakage
	Check for coolant leakage
	Check all lights for proper operation
	Check engine oil level
	Check for smooth throttle operation
	Check gearshift pedal operation
	Check clutch operation and for fluid leakage
	Inspect drive chain
	Check drive chain tension; adjust if necessary
	Check drive chain slider for wear
Initial 600 miles (1,000 km)	Replace engine oil and filter
	Inspect entire brake system
	Check tightness of all fasteners
	Inspect steering head bearings
Every 600 miles (1,000 km)	Inspect, clean and lubricate drive chain
	Check drive chain slack; adjust if necessary
Every 4,000 miles (6,4000 km)	Replace all spark plugs (1986-1989 models)
	Clean and inspect spark plugs (1990-on models)
	Check idle speed; adjust if necessary
	Check brake fluid level in both brake master cylinders
	Check all brake system components
	Inspect the brake pads for wear
	Inspect the side stand operation
Every 8,000 miles (12,8000 km)	Inspect fuel lines for damage or leakage
	Check throttle operation
	Check choke operation
	Replace all spark plugs (1990-on models)
	Change engine oil and filter
	Check carburetor synchronization; adjust if necessary
	Inspect valve clearance (1986-1989 models); adjust if necessary
	Check coolant level in radiator and recovery tank; top off if necessary
	Inspect cooling system for leaks
	Inspect secondary air supply system (models so equipped)
	Inspect evaporation emission control system (models so equipped)
	Check brake fluid level in both brake master cylinders
	Check brake pad wear in all caliper assemblies
	Inspect entire brake system
	Inspect brake hoses (front and rear) for leakage
	Check brake light switch operation (front and rear)
	Check headlight aim
	Inspect entire clutch operating system
	Check fluid level in clutch master cylinder
	Inspect the side stand operation
	Check all suspension components for wear or damage
	Check tightness of all fasteners
	Inspect wheels and tires for wear or damage
	Inspect steering head bearings

(continued)

PERIODIC LUBRICATION, MAINTENANCE AND TUNE-UP

Table 1 MAINTENANCE SCHEDULE* (continued)

Every 12,000 miles (19,200 km)	Replace air filter element Drain and replace hydraulic brake fluid Drain and replace hydraulic clutch fluid
Every 16,000 miles (25,600 km)	Inspect valve clearance (1990-on models); adjust if necessary
Every 4 years	Replace all brake hoses Replace fuel lines Replace evaporative emission lines (models so equipped)

* This Honda factory maintenance schedule should be considered as a guide to general maintenance and lubrication intervals. Harder than normal use and exposure to mud, water, sand, high humidity, etc. (or if used for racing) will naturally dictate more frequent attention to most maintenance items.

Table 2 TIRE INFLATION PRESSURE (COLD)*

	Tire pressure			
	Front		Rear	
Load	psi	kPa	psi	kPa
Solo riding	36	250	42	290
Dual riding	36	250	42	290

*Tire inflation pressure for factory equipped tires. Aftermarket tires may require different inflation pressure.

Table 3 BATTERY STATE OF CHARGE

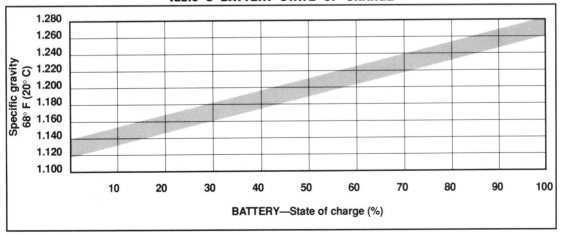

Table 4 RECOMMENDED LUBRICANTS AND FLUIDS

Engine oil	
Temperature 15° F (–8° C) and up	SAE 20W/40 or SAE 20W/50, API grade SF or SG
Temperature 15° F (–8° C) and below	SAE 10W/30 or SAE 10W/40, API grade SF or SG
Brake fluid	DOT 4
Clutch hydraulic fluid	DOT 4
Battery refilling (non-sealed type)	Distilled water
Fork oil	
1986-1989	ATF (automatic transmission fluid)
1990-on	Pro Honda Suspension fluid SS-7
Cables and pivot points	Cable lube or SAE 10W/30 motor oil
Fuel	Regular unleaded
Drive chain	SAE 30-50 motor oil

Table 5 ENGINE OIL CAPACITY

Model	Oil change		Oil and filter change		Overhaul	
	Liters	U.S. qt.	Liters	U.S. qt.	Liters	U.S. qt.
1986-1989	3.0	3.2	–	–	4.0	4.2
1990-1993	2.9	3.1	3.1	3.3	4.0	4.2
1994-on	2.9	3.1	3.1	3.3	3.8	4.0

Table 6 MAINTENANCE AND TUNE UP TIGHTENING TORQUES

Item	N•m	ft.-lb.
Oil drain plug	38	27
Side stand		
Pivot bolt	8	6
Pivot bolt locknut	40	29
Rear axle nut (1986-1989)	90-105	65-77
Rear wheel nuts (1990-on)	110	80
Rear axle bearing holder pinch bolt		
(1990-on)	55	40
Valve adjuster locknut (1986-1989)	21-25	15-18
Spark plugs	12	9

Table 7 ANTI-FREEZE PROTECTION

Ambient temperature	
–32° C (–25° F)	55% distilled water/45% coolant*
–37° C (–34° F)	50% distilled water/50% coolant*
–45° C (–48° F)	45% distilled water/55% coolant*

* Ethylene glycol type anti-freeze (coolant) for aluminum engines.

Table 8 COOLING SYSTEM CAPACITY

Item	Liters	U.S. qt.
Engine and radiator	2.3	2.4
Reserve tank	0.33	0.35
Total system	2.63	2.75

Table 9 TUNE-UP SPECIFICATIONS

Valve clearance	
1986-1989	
Intake	0.10-0.13 mm (0.004-0.005 in.)
Exhaust	0.18-0.20 mm (0.007-0.008 in.)
1990-on	
Intake	0.13-0.19 mm (0.005-0.007 in.)
Exhaust	0.22-0.28 mm (0.009-0.011 in.)
Spark plug type	
Standard heat range	
1986-1989	NGK DPR9EA-9, ND X27EPR-U9
1990-1993	NGK CR8EH9, ND U24FER9
1994-on	NGK CR9EH9, ND U27FER9
Cold climate*	
1986-1989	NGK DPR8EA-9, ND X24EPR-U9
1990-1993	–
1994-on	NGK CR8EH9, ND U24FER9
Extended high-speed riding	
1986-1989	–
1990-1993	NGK CR9EH9, ND U27FER9
1994-on	–
Spark plug gap	0.8-0.9 mm (0.03-0.04 in.)
Idle speed	
1986-1989	
U.S.	1,200 ± 100 rpm
U.K.	1,000 ± 100 rpm
1990-1993	
49-state, Canada	1,000 ± 100 rpm
California, U.K., Australia, Spain	1,200 ± 100 rpm
Switzerland	1,200 ± 50 rpm
1994-on	1,100 ± 100 rpm
Firing order	1, 3, 2, 4

* Cold climate–below 5° C (41° F)

CHAPTER FOUR

ENGINE

The VFR700F and VFR750F models are equipped with a liquid-cooled, 4-stroke, V-type 4 cylinder engine with double overhead camshafts. The crankshaft is supported by 4 main bearings and the camshafts are gear driven from the timing gear on the crankshaft. On 1986-1989 models, the camshafts operate rocker arms above each of the 4 valves per cylinder, with each valve having its own adjuster. On 1990-on models, the camshafts operate directly on top of the valve lifter and are adjusted by replacement shims located under the valve lifters.

The cylinders are an integral part of the upper crankcase, which is referred to in this manual as the cylinder block.

Engine lubrication is by wet sump, with the oil supply housed in the crankcase. The chain-driven oil pump supplies oil under pressure throughout the engine. One section of the oil pump delivers oil directly to the oil cooler while the other section feeds the oil to the engine assembly.

The starter motor is located under the front cylinder head and drives the starter clutch just forward of the clutch. All service procedures relating to the starter motor are covered in Chapter Eight.

This chapter provides procedures for the complete service and overhaul of the Honda V-4 engine. Although the clutch and the transmission are located within the engine, they are covered in separate chapters to simplify the presentation of this material. The clutch is covered in Chapter Five while the transmission is covered in Chapter Six.

Service procedures for all models are virtually the same. Where differences occur, they are identified.

Before starting any work, read the service hints in Chapter One. You will do a better job with this information fresh in your mind.

Table 1 provides complete engine specifications. **Tables 1-6** are located at the end of this chapter.

ENGINE PRINCIPLES

Figure 1 explains how the engine works. This will be helpful when troubleshooting or repairing the engine.

ENGINE

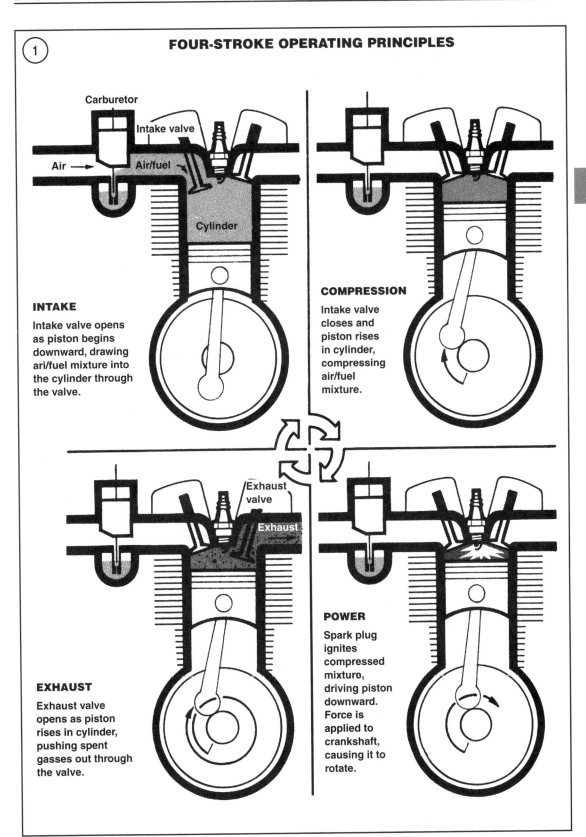

SERVICING ENGINE IN FRAME

The following components can be serviced while the engine is mounted in the frame (the bike's frame is a great holding fixture for breaking loose stubborn bolts and nuts):
 a. Camshaft assemblies.
 b. Front cylinder head.
 c. Rear cylinder head (1986-1989 only).
 d. Clutch assembly.
 e. External shift mechanism.
 f. Alternator.
 g. Pulse generator.
 h. Carburetor assembly.
 i. Starter motor.
 j. Oil pump.

NOTE
*The front cylinder head can be removed with the engine in the frame, but it's much easier to remove it after the engine is removed from the frame. On 1990-on models, the rear cylinder head **cannot** be removed with the engine in the frame (on 1986-1989 models it can) but the camshafts can be removed with the engine in the frame.*

ENGINE

Removal/Installation

One of the most important aspects of engine overhaul is removal and installation. Before removing the first bolt, collect a number of boxes, plastic bags and containers to have on hand so that you can identify and store the parts as they are removed. Have on hand a roll of masking tape and a permanent, waterproof marking pen to label each part or assembly as required. If the bike was purchased second hand, and it appears that some of the wiring may have been changed or replaced, label each electrical connection before disconnecting it.

A dirty engine is no fun to work on. After removing the front fairing assembly, clean the engine with a degreaser and water hose. Follow the instructions on the can and make sure to cover electrical components and the carburetor with plastic bags before using a chemical degreaser. To prevent a mess when using a degreaser, place old newspapers or cardboard underneath the bike. That way, the grease and grime will collect on the paper and not on the ground or on your driveway.

CAUTION
If the bike is equipped with the factory installed O-ring drive chain and you are going to use a degreaser, do not allow any of the degreaser to contact the chain. The chemicals in the degreaser will cause the O-rings to swell, permanently damaging the chain.

WARNING
The engine weighs approximately 80 kg (175 lb.). Due to this weight it is essential that a minimum of 2, preferably 3, people be used during engine removal and installation procedures.

CAUTION
The engine can be removed and installed with basic hand tools as described in Chapter One. However, a suitable size hydraulic floor jack and various blocks of wood are required to support and move the engine. Do not attempt engine removal without a hydraulic floor jack.

1. Place the bike on the centerstand (models so equipped) or sidestand.
2. Remove the seat, and on 1986-1989 models, the side covers as described in Chapter Thirteen.
3. Remove the front fairing assembly as described under *Front Fairing Removal/Installation* in Chapter Thirteen.
4. Disconnect the battery negative lead as described in Chapter Eight.
5. Remove the fuel tank as described under *Fuel Tank Removal/Installation* in Chapter Seven.
6. Drain the engine oil as described under *Engine Oil and Filter Change* in Chapter Three.
7. Drain the engine coolant as described under *Coolant Change* in Chapter Three.
8. Remove the radiator as described under *Radiator* in Chapter Nine.
9. Disconnect all coolant hoses from the engine components.
10. Disconnect the spark plug wires and tie them up out of the way.
11. Remove the exhaust system as described under *Exhaust System Removal/Installation* in Chapter Seven.

ENGINE

12. Remove the carburetor assembly as described under *Carburetor Removal/Installation* in Chapter Seven.
13. Remove the alternator as described in this chapter.
14. Remove the clutch as described under *Clutch Removal/Installation* in Chapter Five.
15. Remove the external shift mechanism as described under *External Shift Mechanism Removal/Installation* in Chapter Six.
16. Remove the clutch slave cylinder as described under *Clutch Slave Cylinder (Intact) Removal/Installation* in Chapter Five.
17. Remove the speedometer drive unit, drive sprocket and drive chain from the engine as described under *Drive Sprocket and Drive Chain Removal/Installation* in Chapter Six.
18. Remove the starter motor as described under *Starter Removal/Installation* in Chapter Eight.
19. On models so equipped, remove the evaporation canister as described in Chapter Seven.
20. On models so equipped, remove the secondary air supply valve as described in Chapter Seven.
21. Disconnect the engine ground strap, the thermo sensor wire, the oil pressure and the pulse generator electrical wire connectors.
22. Take a final look all over the engine to make sure everything has been disconnected.
23. Loosen, but do not remove, all engine mounting bolts and nuts.
24. Place a suitable size jack, with a piece of wood to protect the oil pan, under the engine. Apply a *small amount* of jack pressure up on the engine.

NOTE
There are many different bolt sizes and lengths, different combinations of brackets, spacers, fasteners, ground straps and different spacer lengths that are used to secure the engine to the frame. As each set of bolts, nuts, washers, spacers and brackets is removed, place each individual set in a separate plastic bag or box. This will save a lot of time when installing the engine.

CAUTION
Continually adjust jack height during engine removal and installation to prevent damage to the mounting bolt threads and hardware. Ideally, the jack should support the engine so its mounting bolts can be easily removed or installed.

WARNING
Due to the weight of the engine, the following steps must be taken slowly and carefully to avoid dropping the engine out of the frame, causing damage not only to the engine but to yourself and your helpers. Have a good supply of wood blocks on hand to support the engine as it is being removed from the frame.

25A. On 1986-1989 models, perform the following:

NOTE
*The spacers used between the engine mounting surfaces and the frame mounting points are made of stainless steel to slow heat transfer from the engine to the frame. Be sure to reinstall the same spacers and in their correct locations. Do **not** substitute a spacer made of a lesser material.*

   a. Remove the No. 1 and No. 3 ignition coils (A, **Figure 2**) from the frame and move them out of the way.
   b. Remove the front lower 10 mm mounting bolt (**Figure 3**) on each side.
   c. Remove the nut (**Figure 4**) from the rear lower through bolt. Withdraw the bolt (**Figure 5**) and don't lose the spacer on the left-hand side between the engine mounting surface and the frame.
   d. Remove the rear upper mounting bolt (**Figure 6**) on each side.

e. Remove the front upper mounting bolt and spacer (B, **Figure 2**) on each side.

f. Remove the center upper mounting bolt and spacer (**Figure 7**) on each side.

g. Proceed to Step 26.

25B. On 1990-on models, perform the following:

NOTE
*The spacers used between the engine mounting surfaces and the frame mounting points are made of stainless steel to slow heat transfer from the engine to the frame. Be sure to reinstall the same spacers and in their correct locations. Do **not** substitute a spacer made of a lesser material.*

a. On the left-hand side, remove the nut from the lower rear through bolt.

b. On the right-hand side, remove the lower rear through bolt. Remove the through bolt locknut and adjust bolt from the frame.

c. On the right-hand side, remove the upper rear bolt. Remove the bolt locknut and adjust bolt from the frame.

d. On each side, remove the upper front bolt (A, **Figure 8**) and upper rear bolt (B, **Figure 8**). Remove all components mounted under these bolts and move them out of the way. Don't lose the spacers (1 with each bolt) between the engine mounting surface and the frame.

e. On the left-hand side, remove the upper rear bolt (**Figure 9**). Don't lose the *thin* spacer between the engine mounting surface and the frame.

f. Proceed to Step 26.

CAUTION
The engine assembly is very heavy. This final step requires a minimum of 2, preferably 3, people to remove the engine from the frame safely.

26. Carefully and slowly lower the engine (on the wood blocks) down and out of the frame. Move it out far enough so that everyone can get a good hand hold on the engine.

27. Move the engine away from the frame and place the engine in an engine stand or take it to a work bench for further disassembly.

NOTE
Due to the weight of the complete engine assembly, it is suggested that all compo-

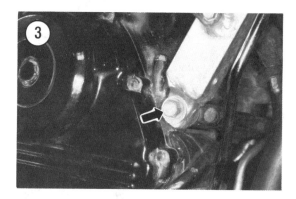

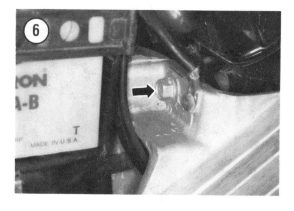

ENGINE

nents removed (except for the rear cylinder head assembly) be left off until the crankcase assembly is reinstalled into the frame. If you choose to install a completed engine assembly, it requires a minimum of 3 people.

28. Clean and inspect the exterior of the engine and all mounting hardware as described in this chapter.

29A. On 1986-1989 models, install by reversing these removal steps while noting the following:

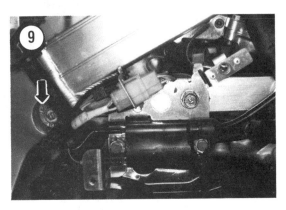

a. First install and tighten all bolt and nuts with the exception of the rear lower through bolt. Tighten the bolts and nuts to the torque specifications listed in **Table 2**.

b. Install the rear lower through bolt and tighten to the torque specifications listed in **Table 2**.

c. Install the nut onto the rear lower through bolt and tighten to the torque specifications listed in **Table 2**.

d. Fill the crankcase with the recommended type and quantity of engine oil and coolant. Refer to Chapter Three.

e. Start the engine and check for leaks.

29B. On 1990-on models, install by reversing these removal steps while noting the following:

a. Apply a light coat of multipurpose grease to the rear lower through bolt.

b. On the right-hand side, install the adjusting bolt (A, **Figure 10**) and tighten fully by hand.

c. Insert the rear through bolt (B, **Figure 10**) through the adjusting bolt and align the flats on the head of the bolt with the cut-out in the adjusting bolt.

d. Tighten the adjusting bolt (A, **Figure 11**) by tightening the through bolt (B, **Figure 11**) with an Allen wrench. Tighten to the torque specification listed in **Table 2**.

e. Install the locknut on the adjusting bolt. Using Honda special tool (part No. 07HMA-MR70200) (**Figure 12**), or equivalent, tighten to the torque specification listed in **Table 2**.

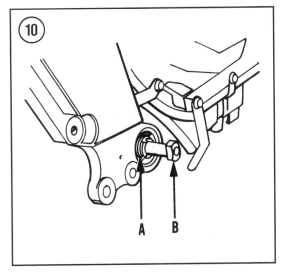

f. On the left-hand side, install the nut onto the through bolt and tighten to the torque specification listed in **Table 2**.

g. Install and tighten all other engine mounting bolts and tighten to the torque specification listed in **Table 2**.

h. On the right-hand side, install the rear upper adjusting bolt (**Figure 13**) and tighten to the torque specification listed in **Table 2**.

i. Onto the adjusting bolt (A, **Figure 14**), install the locknut (B, **Figure 14**). Using Honda special tool (part No. 07HMA-MR70200), or equivalent, tighten to the torque specification listed in **Table 2**.

j. Install the through bolt (**Figure 15**) and tighten to the torque specification listed in **Table 2**.

k. Fill the crankcase with the recommended type and quantity of engine oil and coolant. Refer to Chapter Three.

l. Start the engine and check for leaks.

Exterior Cleaning and Inspection

1. Clean all of the engine mount bolts, nuts, spacers and brackets in solvent and dry thoroughly.

2. Clean the engine mounting bolt hole threads with contact cleaner.

3. Replace worn, bent or damaged fasteners.

4. Clean the drive sprocket, mounting bolt and washer in solvent and dry thoroughly. Inspect the sprocket for wear as described in Chapter Eleven.

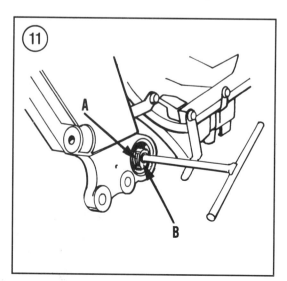

5. Check the coolant hoses for cracks, leakage or other damage. Replace if necessary.

6. Check the wire harness routing in the frame. Check the harness cover and wires for chafing or other damage that could cause an electrical problem later on. Replace harness cable guides and clips as required.

7. Clean all of the disconnected electrical connectors with contact cleaner.

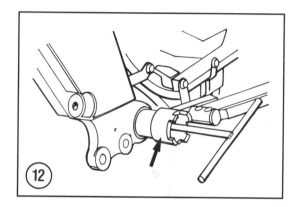

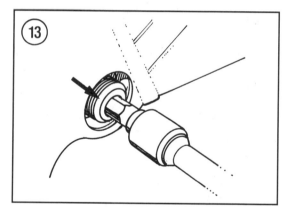

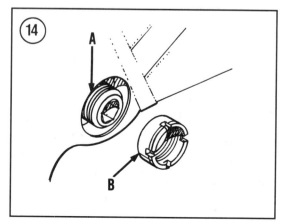

ENGINE

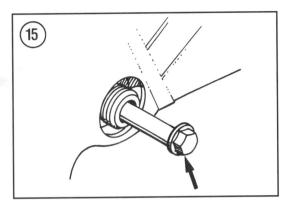

8. Check the ignition coil mounting bolts for tightness.

9. Check all of the frame mounting bolt holes for damage.

10. Inspect the air filter and replace it if necessary as described in Chapter Three.

CYLINDER HEAD COVER

Removal

1. Place the bike on the centerstand (models so equipped) or sidestand.

2. Remove the seat, and on 1986-1989 models, the side covers as described in Chapter Thirteen.

3. Remove the lower sections of the front fairing assembly as described under *Front Fairing Removal/Installation* in Chapter Thirteen.

4. Disconnect the battery negative lead as described in Chapter Eight.

5. Drain the engine oil as described under *Engine Oil and Filter Change* in Chapter Three.

6. Remove the fuel tank as described under *Fuel Tank Removal/Installation* in Chapter Seven.

7. Disconnect the breather tube (A, **Figure 16**) from the rear cylinder head cover.

8. Remove the air filter housing (B, **Figure 16**) as described in Chapter Seven.

9. To remove the front cylinder head cover, remove the radiator (A, **Figure 17**) as described in Chapter Seven.

10. Label and disconnect the spark plug caps at the spark plugs. Refer to B, **Figure 17** and C, **Figure 16**. Position the caps up and away from the cylinder head cover.

NOTE
Figure 18 is shown with the engine removed from the frame for clarity. It is not necessary to remove the engine to remove the cylinder head cover(s).

11. Using a crisscross pattern, loosen the bolts (A, **Figure 18**) securing the cylinder head cover to the cylinder head.

12. Remove the bolts and washers.

13. Remove the cylinder head cover (B, **Figure 18**) and gasket.

Installation

1. Inspect the rubber gasket around the perimeter (A, **Figure 19**) of the cylinder head cover and around the spark plug holes (B, **Figure 19**). If the gasket is starting to deteriorate or harden, it should be replaced.

NOTE
The new rubber cylinder head cover gasket must be installed onto the cylinder head cover using the following method to help prevent an oil leak.

2. Replace the cylinder head cover gasket as follows:
   a. Remove the old gasket (**Figure 20**) and clean off all gasket sealer residue from the cylinder head cover.
   b. Clean the gasket groove around the perimeter of the cover with an aerosol electrical contact cleaner and wipe dry.
   c. Apply ThreeBond 1521, or an equivalent rubber adhesive, to the gasket groove in the cover following the manufacturer's instructions.
   d. On 1990-on models, position the gasket with the IN mark facing toward the intake valve side of the cover.
   e. Install the gasket (**Figure 20**) into the cover groove.

NOTE
The rear cylinder head cover has the raised breather chamber.

3. Install the cylinder head cover (B, **Figure 18**) onto the cylinder head.

NOTE
*Make sure the cylinder head cover gasket is correctly positioned around each spark plug hole or oil will leak into the spark plug cavity. The oil will then drain out the hole on the front side of the cylinder head below the exhaust port. The oil leakage looks like a seeping cylinder head gasket. On 1990-on models, make sure the half-circles (C, **Figure 19**) of the gasket fit correctly into the receptacles (D, **Figure 19**) in the cylinder head.*

4. Install the cylinder head cover bolt washers (A, **Figure 21**) so that the "UP" mark on each washer faces up.
5. Install the cylinder head cover bolts and washer (B, **Figure 21**) hand-tight at this time.
6. Tighten the cylinder head cover bolts in a crisscross pattern to the torque specification listed in **Table 2**.

NOTE
*On 1986-1989 models, the cylinder number (**Figure 22**) is cast into the cover.*

7. Connect the spark plug caps to the correct spark plugs. Refer to (B, **Figure 17**) and (C, **Figure 16**).
8. If the front cylinder head cover was removed, install the radiator (A, **Figure 17**) as described in Chapter Seven.
9. Install the air filter housing (B, **Figure 16**) as described in Chapter Seven.
10. Connect the breather tube (A, **Figure 16**) onto the rear cylinder head cover. Make sure the hose clamp is secure.

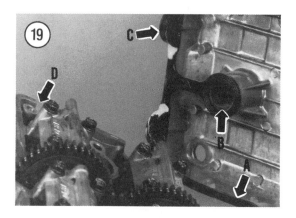

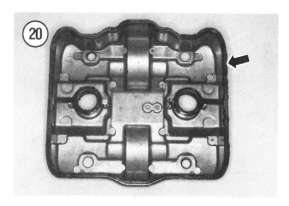

ENGINE

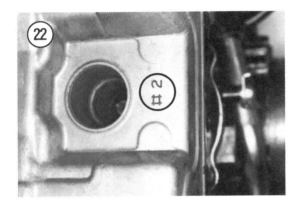

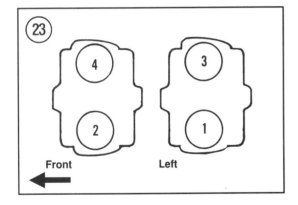

11. Install the fuel tank as described under *Fuel Tank Removal/Installation* in Chapter Seven.
12. Refill the engine with the specified type and quantity of oil as described in Chapter Three.
13. Connect the battery negative lead as described in Chapter Eight.
14. Install the lower sections of the front fairing assembly as described in Chapter Thirteen.
15. Install the seat, and on 1986-1989 models, the side covers as described in Chapter Thirteen.

CAMSHAFTS (1986-1989 MODELS)

This procedure shows the removal and installation of the camshafts in the front cylinder head. This procedure is identical for both the front and rear cylinder heads with the exception of the timing marks on the pulse generator cover. These differences are noted in the procedure.

The cylinders numbers (**Figure 23**) are as follows:
a. No. 1 cylinder-left rear.
b. No. 2 cylinder-left front.
c. No. 3 cylinder-right rear.
d. No. 4 cylinder-right front.

NOTE
The camshafts can be removed with the engine in the frame but it is much easier with the engine removed. This procedure is shown with the engine removed.

Removal

NOTE
Prior to removing the engine, shift the transmission into NEUTRAL.

1. Remove the engine as described in this chapter.
2. Remove all of the spark plugs as described in Chapter Three. This will make it easier to rotate the engine.
3. Remove both cylinder head covers (**Figure 24**) as described in this chapter.
4. Remove the pulse generator rotor cover cap and O-ring on the clutch cover.

NOTE
*In the following steps, rotate the engine with a socket on the starter clutch mounting bolt (**Figure 25**).*

5A. For the *front* cylinder head, perform the following:
   a. Rotate the crankshaft by turning the starter clutch mounting bolt (**Figure 25**).
   b. Rotate the crankshaft *clockwise* (as viewed from the left-hand side) until the "T 2" mark on the starter clutch (**Figure 26**) aligns with the clutch cover index mark (**Figure 27**).

   NOTE
   A cylinder at TDC of its compression stroke will have free play in all of its rocker arms, indicating that both pairs of intake and exhaust valves are closed.

   c. The No. 2 cylinder must be at top dead center (TDC) on the compression stroke. If the No. 2 cylinder is not at TDC on the compression stroke; rotate the crankshaft one full turn (360°) and make sure the "T 2" mark again aligns with the clutch cover index mark (**Figure 27**).

5B. For the *rear* cylinder head, perform the following:
   a. Rotate the crankshaft by turning the starter clutch mounting bolt (**Figure 25**).
   b. Rotate the crankshaft *clockwise* (as viewed from the left-hand side) until the "T 1" mark on the starter clutch (**Figure 26**) aligns with the clutch cover index mark (**Figure 28**).

   NOTE
   A cylinder at TDC of its compression stroke will have free play in all of its rocker arms, indicating that both pairs of intake and exhaust valves are closed.

   c. The No. 1 cylinder must be at top dead center (TDC) on the compression stroke. If the No. 1 cylinder is not at TDC on the compression

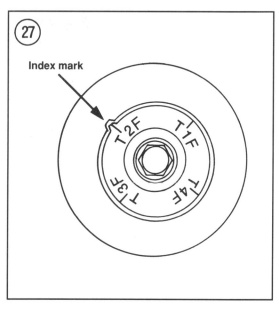

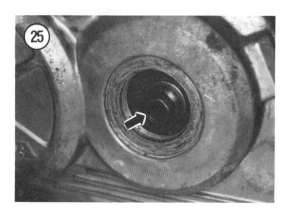

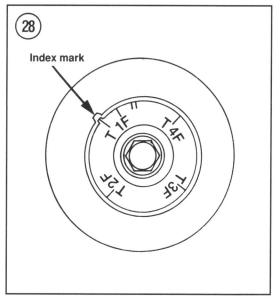

ENGINE

stroke; rotate the crankshaft one full turn (360°) and make sure the "T 1" mark again aligns with the clutch cover index mark (**Figure 28**).

6. Using an open end wrench and screwdriver (**Figure 29**), loosen all valve adjusters. This is to take the strain off the camshaft holders during removal.

7. Using a crisscross pattern, loosen the bolts in 2-3 stages securing the camshaft holders (**Figure 30**) and the oil pipe assembly. Remove all but the center 4 bolts.

8. Remove the center 4 bolts (**Figure 31**) securing the oil pipe assembly and remove the oil pipe assembly.

CAUTION
*The camshaft holders **must** be reinstalled in their correct locations during installation. They have taken a wear set with the camshafts and if reinstalled incorrectly, they can cause accelerated wear on both parts.*

9. The camshaft holders are marked at the factory indicating their location in the cylinder head. Refer to the following and to **Figure 32** for proper identification and locations of these holders:
   a. There are 3 raised letters (A, **Figure 33**) cast into each holder.
   b. One letter is an "F" and the other is an "R." At the factory one of these letters was chiseled off to indicate either the front or rear cylinder head location. The *missing* letter indicates the cylinder location.
   c. If the "F" has been removed (B, **Figure 33**), this holder belongs in the front cylinder head.
   d. If the "R" has been removed, this holder belongs in the rear cylinder head.

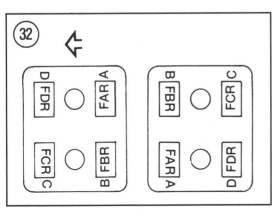

e. The center letter "A," "B," "C" or "D" indicated the holders' location within the cylinder head. Refer to **Figure 32** for these locations.

f. If these marks have been removed incorrectly or are no longer visible, use a permanent marking pen and mark each holder prior to removal using the layout in **Figure 32**.

10. Remove the bolts securing the camshaft holders.

11. Lift straight up and remove the intake camshaft and both camshaft holders as an assembly (A, **Figure 34**). Don't lose the locating dowels.

12. Lift straight up and remove the exhaust camshaft and both camshaft holders as an assembly (B, **Figure 34**). Don't lose the locating dowels.

13. If necessary, repeat Step 5-12 for the camshafts in the other cylinder head. Refer to Step 5 and realign the timing mark for the other cylinder head.

Disassembly/Inspection/Assembly

It is suggested that each set of camshafts and camshaft holders be disassembled, inspected and reassembled to prevent the intermixing of parts.

1. Remove the camshaft holders (**Figure 35**) from each camshaft as follows:
   a. Turn the assembly over.

   CAUTION
   *Do **not** pull the camshaft straight out of the holder without first aligning the camshaft lobe with the cutout in the holder. If alignment is not correct, the camshaft and/or the holder will be damaged.*

   b. Rotate the camshaft to align the camshaft lobe (A, **Figure 36**) with the cutout in the camshaft holder (B, **Figure 36**).
   c. Carefully withdraw the camshaft from the holder, being careful to not scratch or damage the lobes against the opening in the holder.
   d. Remove both holders from each camshaft assembly (**Figure 37**).

2. Check the camshaft bearing journals for wear and scoring (A, **Figure 38**).

3. Check the camshaft lobes for wear (B, **Figure 38**). The lobes should not be scored and the edges should be square. Slight damage may be removed with a silicon carbide oilstone. Use No. 100-200 grit initially, then polish with a No. 280-320 grit.

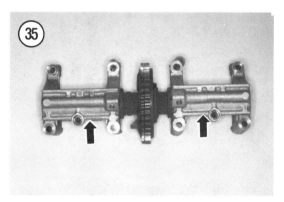

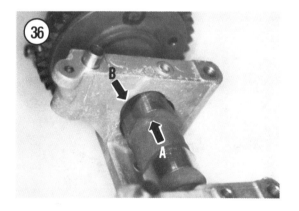

ENGINE

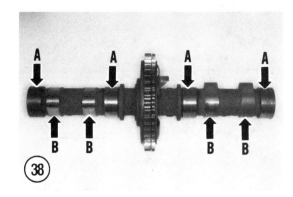
38

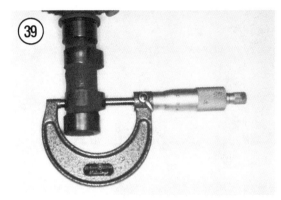
39

40

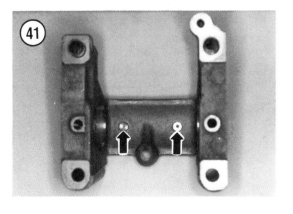
41

42

4. Even though the camshaft lobe surface appears to be satisfactory, with no visible signs of wear, the camshaft lobes must be measured with a micrometer as shown in **Figure 39**. Replace the camshaft(s) if worn beyond the service limits listed in **Table 1**.

5. Measure the runout of the camshaft with a dial indicator and V-blocks. Use 1/2 of the total runout and compare to the service limits listed in **Table 1**.

6. Inspect the camshaft driven gear teeth (**Figure 40**) for wear; replace if necessary.

7. Make sure the oil holes in the camshaft holders are open. Refer to **Figure 41** and **Figure 42**. If necessary, clean out with a piece of wire and blow out with compressed air. Thoroughly clean the camshaft holder in solvent after cleaning out the oil holes to remove any sludge.

CAUTION
Never replace only 1 camshaft holder even if only 1 of the pair is damaged. If you replace just one, you will have a mis-matched set which will result in premature camshaft bearing surface wear.

8. Check the camshaft bearing bores in the camshaft holders. They should not be scored or excessively worn. If replacement is necessary, the camshaft holders are sold and replaced as a matched pair for that camshaft. The pair are machined as a set during manufacturing and must be replaced as a set.

9. Inspect each bearing holder (**Figure 37**) for wear, cracks or other damage. If damaged, replace as a matched pair; refer to preceeding CAUTION.

10. Inspect the camshaft and camshaft holders as described in this chapter.

11. Clean the oil pipe assembly with solvent. Make sure all pipes are open and clean. Apply compressed air to all openings and make sure none are clogged.

12. Install the camshaft holders (**Figure 35**) onto each camshaft as follows:
   a. The camshafts are marked (**Figure 43**) with either an "IN" (intake) (**Figure 44**) or "EX" (exhaust) and "FR" (front cylinders) (**Figure 45**) or "RR" (rear cylinders).
   b. Refer to *Removal* Step 9 for the correct location of the camshaft holders within the cylinder heads so the holders can be properly matched with the correct camshaft.

   CAUTION
   *Do **not** install the camshaft straight onto the holder without first aligning the camshaft lobe with the cutout in the holder. If alignment is not correct the camshaft and/or the holder will be damaged.*

   c. Assemble the correct camshaft with the correct pair of camshaft holders (**Figure 37**).
   d. Apply a coat of molybdenum disulfide grease or clean engine oil to the bearing surfaces of the camshaft and the holders.
   e. Align the camshaft lobe (A, **Figure 36**) with the cutout in the camshaft holder (B, **Figure 36**).
   f. Carefully install the holder onto each end of the camshaft being careful to not scratch or damage the lobes against the opening in the holder during installation.
   g. Install the holders (**Figure 35**) onto each camshaft assembly until they bottom out on the shoulder (**Figure 46**).
   h. Assemble both sets of camshaft assemblies (**Figure 47**) for each cylinder head.

Camshaft Bearing Clearance Measurement

1. Measure the camshaft bearing journal O.D. with a micrometer. Measure the center journals and both end journals (**Figure 48**). Compare to the wear limits in **Table 1**. If the camshaft bearing journal is less than the service limit dimension specified, replace the camshaft.
2. Measure the camshaft holder bearing journal I.D. (**Figure 49**) with a bore gauge. Measure the center journal and the end journal of each holder. Compare to the wear limits in **Table 1**. If the camshaft holder bearing journal is greater than the service limit di-

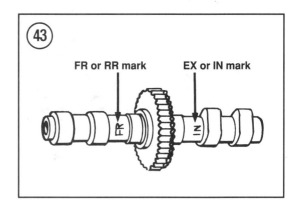

ENGINE

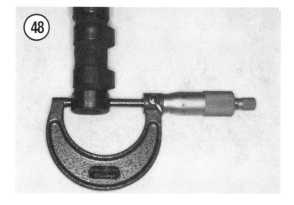

mension specified, replace the camshaft holders as a *matched pair*.

3. Subtract the camshaft bearing outer diameter from the holder's inner diameter. This will give you the oil clearance between the 2 parts. Compare to the wear limits in **Table 1**.

Camshaft Installation
(When Both Front and Rear Cylinders
Camshafts Were Removed)

NOTE
*Use this procedure only if **both front and rear** cylinders' camshafts were removed.*

1. Make sure all rocker arms are correctly indexed into their holder grooves (**Figure 50**). The rocker arms must be located correctly so the camshafts can be installed without any type of interference. If this alignment is incorrect, the rocker arm, holder and camshaft may be damaged during camshaft assembly installation.
2. Rotate the crankshaft by turning the starter clutch mounting bolt (**Figure 25**).
3. Rotate the crankshaft *clockwise* (as viewed from the left-hand side) until the "T 1" mark on the starter clutch (**Figure 26**) aligns with the clutch cover index mark (**Figure 28**).

NOTE
First install the camshaft assemblies into the rear cylinder head assembly, then the front cylinder head. Steps 4-11 are performed on the rear cylinder head assembly.

4. Install the camshaft holder locating dowels in the rear cylinder head or in the holders (**Figure 51**).
5. Align the index mark on the right-hand end of the camshaft with the index mark on the right-hand camshaft holder (**Figure 52**).
6. Install one of the camshaft assemblies into the rear cylinder head assembly. Engage the camshaft sub-gears with the idle gears by depressing the camshaft holders by hand while slightly rotating the crankshaft back and forth.
7. Repeat for the other camshaft assembly.

CAUTION
Very expensive damage could result from improper camshaft sub-gear and

idle gear alignment. Recheck your work several times to make sure alignment is correct.

8. After both rear camshaft assemblies are installed, recheck the timing marks as follows:
   a. The index mark on the right-hand end of both camshafts must still be aligned with the index mark on the right-hand camshaft holder (**Figure 52**).
   b. The "T 1" mark on the starter clutch (**Figure 26**) must still be aligned with the clutch cover index mark (**Figure 28**).
   c. All 3 of these marks *must be aligned correctly* at this time otherwise camshaft timing will be incorrect.
   d. If any of these 3 marks are incorrect, realign the components at this time—do *not* proceed if alignment marks are incorrect.

9. Install all of the bolts securing the camshaft holders with the exception of the 4 in the center that hold the oil pipe assembly in place. Tighten all of these bolts finger-tight.

10. Install the oil pipe assembly and the 4 bolts. Tighten these bolts finger-tight.

11. After all bolts are installed, using a crisscross pattern tighten the bolts in 2-3 stages to the torque specification listed in **Table 2**.

NOTE
*The following steps are performed on the **front** cylinder head assembly.*

12. To install the front cylinder head camshafts, rotate the crankshaft by turning the starter clutch mounting bolt (**Figure 25**).

13. Rotate the crankshaft *clockwise* (as viewed from the left-hand side) 450° until the "T 2" mark on the starter clutch (**Figure 26**) aligns with the clutch cover index mark (**Figure 27**).

14. Install the camshaft holder locating dowels in the front cylinder head or the holders (**Figure 51**).

15. Align the index mark on the right-hand end of the camshaft with the index mark on the right-hand camshaft holder (**Figure 52**).

16. Install one of the camshaft assemblies (**Figure 53**) into the front cylinder head assembly. Engage the camshaft sub-gears with the idle gears by depressing the camshaft holders by hand while slightly rotating the crankshaft back and forth.

17. Repeat for the other camshaft assembly (**Figure 54**).

CAUTION
Very expensive damage could result from improper camshaft sub-gear and idle gear alignment. Recheck your work several times to make sure alignment is correct.

18. After both front camshaft assemblies are installed, recheck the timing marks as follows:

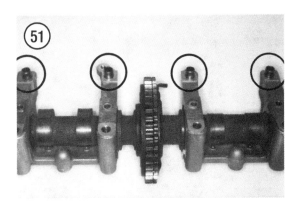

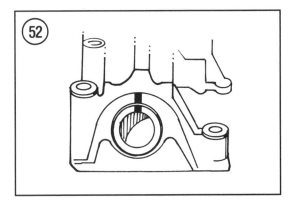

ENGINE

a. The index mark on the right-hand end of both camshafts must still be aligned with the index mark on the right-hand camshaft holder (**Figure 52**).

b. The "T 2" mark on the starter clutch (**Figure 26**) must still be aligned with the clutch cover index mark (**Figure 27**).

c. All 3 of these marks *must be aligned correctly* at this time otherwise camshaft timing will be incorrect.

d. If any of these 3 marks are incorrect, realign the components at this time—do *not* proceed if alignment marks are incorrect.

19. Install all of the bolts securing the camshaft holders with the exception of the 4 in the center that hold the oil pipe assembly in place. Tighten all of these bolts finger-tight.

20. Install the oil pipe assembly and the 4 bolts. Tighten these bolts finger-tight.

21. After all bolts are installed, using a crisscross pattern tighten the bolts in 2-3 stages to the torque specification listed in **Table 2**.

22. Adjust the valve clearance as described under *Valve Adjustment (1986-1989 Models)* in Chapter Three.

Camshaft Installation
(With The Rear Cylinder Camshafts Only Removed)

> *NOTE*
> *If the engine has been disturbed (crankshaft rotated) after the rear cylinders camshafts were removed, the engine must be **zeroed in** again to ensure proper camshaft timing with the front cylinder.*

1. Rotate the crankshaft by turning the starter clutch mounting bolt (**Figure 55**).

2. Rotate the crankshaft *clockwise* (as viewed from the left-hand side) until the "T 2" mark on the starter clutch (**Figure 56**) aligns with the clutch cover index mark (**Figure 57**).

3. Remove the front cylinder head cover as described in this chapter.

> *NOTE*
> *A cylinder at TDC of its compression stroke will have free play in all of its rocker arms, indicating that both pairs of intake and exhaust valves are closed.*

4. On the *front* cylinder head, make sure the No. 2 cylinder is at TDC on the compression stroke. Wiggle the rocker arms and if any are under tension, the cylinder is not at TDC. If the No. 2 cylinder is not at TDC on the compression stroke; rotate the crankshaft one full turn (360°) and make sure the "T 2" mark again aligns with the clutch cover index mark (**Figure 57**).

5. Rotate the crankshaft *clockwise* (as viewed from the left-hand side) 3/4 turn (270°) until the "T 1" mark on the starter clutch (**Figure 56**) aligns with the clutch cover index mark (**Figure 58**).

6. Make sure all rocker arms are correctly indexed into their holder grooves (**Figure 50**). The rocker arms must be located correctly so the camshafts can be installed without any type of interference. If this alignment is incorrect, the rocker arm, holder and camshaft may be damaged during camshaft assembly installation.

7. Install the camshaft holder locating dowels in the rear cylinder head or the holders (**Figure 51**).

8. Align the index mark on the right-hand end of the camshaft with the index mark on the right-hand camshaft holder (**Figure 52**).

9. Install one of the camshaft assemblies into the rear cylinder head assembly. Engage the camshaft sub-gears with the idle gears by depressing the camshaft holders by hand while slightly rotating the crankshaft back and forth.

10. Repeat for the other camshaft assembly.

CAUTION
Very expensive damage could result from improper camshaft sub-gear and idle gear alignment. Recheck your work several times to be sure alignment is correct.

11. After both rear camshaft assemblies are installed, the timing marks on the front and rear camshafts and holders should look like the marks shown in **Figure 59**. Recheck the timing marks as follows:
    a. The index mark on the right-hand end of both rear camshafts must still be aligned with the index mark on the right-hand camshaft holder (**Figure 52**).
    b. The "T 1" mark on the starter clutch (**Figure 56**) must still be aligned with the clutch cover index mark (**Figure 58**).
    c. All 3 of these marks *must be aligned correctly* at this time otherwise camshaft timing will be incorrect.
    d. If any of these 3 marks are incorrect, realign the components at this time—do *not* proceed if alignment marks are incorrect.

12. Install all of the bolts securing the camshaft holders with the exception of the 4 in the center that hold the oil pipe assembly in place. Tighten all of these bolts finger-tight.

13. Install the oil pipe assembly and the 4 bolts. Tightent these bolts finger-tight.

14. After all bolts are installed, using a crisscross pattern tighten the bolt in 2-3 stages to the torque specification listed in **Table 2**.

15. Adjust the valve clearance as described under *Valve Adjustment (1986-1989 Models)* in Chapter Three.

16. Install both rear and front cylinder head covers as described in this chapter.

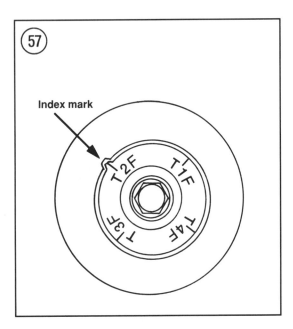

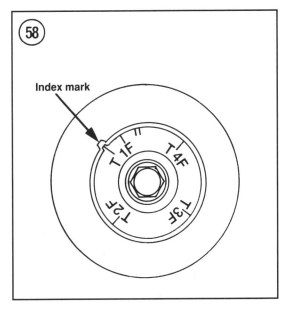

ENGINE

Camshaft Installation
(With The Front Cylinder Camshafts Only Removed)

NOTE
The camshafts for the rear cylinders must be installed prior to installing the camshafts for the front cylinders.

NOTE
If the engine has been disturbed (crankshaft rotated) after the front cylinders camshafts were removed, the engine must be zeroed in again to ensure proper camshaft timing with the rear cylinder.

1. Rotate the crankshaft by turning the starter clutch mounting bolt (**Figure 55**).
2. Rotate the crankshaft *clockwise* (as viewed from the left-hand side) until the "T 1" mark on the starter clutch (**Figure 56**) aligns with the clutch cover index mark (**Figure 58**).
3. Remove the rear cylinder head cover as described in this chapter.

NOTE
A cylinder at TDC of its compression stroke will have free play in all of its rocker arms, indicating that both pairs of intake and exhaust valves are closed.

4. On the *rear* cylinder head, make sure the No. 1 cylinder is at TDC on the compression stroke. Wiggle the rocker arms and if any are under tension the cylinder is not at TDC. If the No. 1 cylinder is not at TDC on the compression stroke; rotate the crankshaft one full turn (360°) and make sure the "T 1" mark again aligns with the clutch cover index mark (**Figure 58**).
5. Rotate the crankshaft *clockwise* (as viewed from the left-hand side) 1 1/4 turns (450°) until the "T 2" mark on the starter clutch (**Figure 56**) aligns with the clutch cover index mark (**Figure 57**).
6. Make sure all rocker arms are correctly indexed into their holder grooves (**Figure 50**). The rocker arms must be located correctly so the camshafts can be installed without any type of interference. If this alignment is incorrect, the rocker arm, holder and camshaft may be damaged during camshaft assembly installation.
7. Install the camshaft holder locating dowels in the front cylinder head or the holders (**Figure 51**).
8. Align the index mark on the right-hand end of the camshaft with the index mark on the right-hand camshaft holder (**Figure 52**).
9. Install one of the camshaft assemblies into the front cylinder head assembly. Engage the camshaft sub-gears with the idle gears by depressing the camshaft holders by hand while slightly rotating the crankshaft back and forth.
10. Repeat for the other camshaft assembly.

CAUTION
Very expensive damage could result from improper camshaft sub-gear and idle gear alignment. Recheck your work several times to be sure alignment is correct.

11. After both rear camshaft assemblies are installed, the timing marks on the front and rear camshafts and holders should look like the marks shown in **Figure 60**. Recheck the timing marks as follows:
   a. The index mark on the right-hand end of both front camshafts must still be aligned with the index mark on the right-hand camshaft holder (**Figure 52**).
   b. The "T 2" mark on the starter clutch (**Figure 56**) must still be aligned with the clutch cover index mark (**Figure 57**).
   c. All 3 of these marks *must be aligned correctly* at this time otherwise camshaft timing will be incorrect.

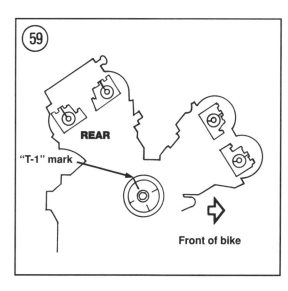

d. If any of these 3 marks are incorrect, realign the components at this time—do *not* proceed if alignment marks are incorrect.

12. Install all of the bolts securing the camshaft holders with the exception of the 4 in the center that hold the oil pipe assembly in place. Tighten all of these bolts finger-tight.
13. Install the oil pipe assembly and the 4 bolts. Tighten these bolts finger-tight.
14. After all bolts are installed, using a crisscross pattern tighten the bolt in 2-3 stages to the torque specification listed in **Table 2**.
15. Adjust the valve clearance as described under *Valve Adjustment (1986-1989 Models)* in Chapter Three.
16. Install both front and rear cylinder head covers as described in this chapter.

CAMSHAFTS
(1990-ON MODELS)

This procedure shows the removal and installation of the camshafts in the front cylinder head. This procedure is identical for both the front and rear cylinder heads with the exception of the timing marks on the pulse generator cover. These differences are noted in the procedure.

The cylinders' numbers (**Figure 61**) are as follows:

a. No. 1 cylinder-left rear.
b. No. 2 cylinder-left front.
c. No. 3 cylinder-right rear.
d. No. 4 cylinder-right front.

NOTE
The camshafts can be removed with the engine in the frame, but it is much easier with the engine removed. This procedure is shown with the engine removed.

Removal

NOTE
Prior to removing the engine, shift the transmission into NEUTRAL.

1. Remove the engine as described in this chapter.
2. Remove all of the spark plugs as described in Chapter Three. This will make it easier to rotate the engine.
3. Remove both cylinder head covers (**Figure 62**) as described in this chapter.
4. Remove the pulse generator rotor cover cap and O-ring on the clutch cover.

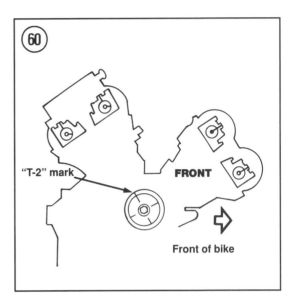

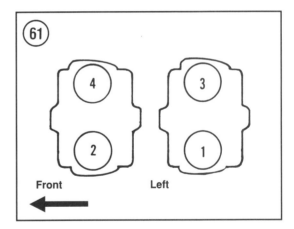

ENGINE

NOTE
*In the following steps, rotate the engine with a socket on the starter clutch mounting bolt (**Figure 63**).*

5A. For the *front* cylinder head, perform the following:

a. Rotate the crankshaft by turning the starter clutch mounting bolt (**Figure 63**).
b. Rotate the crankshaft *clockwise* (as viewed from the left-hand side) until the "T 2" mark on the starter clutch (**Figure 64**) aligns with the clutch cover index mark (**Figure 65**).

NOTE
A cylinder at TDC of its compression stroke will have both camshaft lobes facing away from the valve lifter surfaces, indicating both pairs of intake and exhaust valves are closed.

c. The No. 2 cylinder must be at top dead center (TDC) on the compression stroke. If the No. 2 cylinder is not at TDC on the compression stroke; rotate the crankshaft one full turn (360°) and make sure the "T 2" mark again aligns with the clutch cover index mark (**Figure 65**).

5B. For the *rear* cylinder head, perform the following:

a. Rotate the crankshaft by turning the starter clutch mounting bolt (**Figure 63**).
b. Rotate the crankshaft *clockwise* (as viewed from the left-hand side) until the "T 1" mark on the starter clutch (**Figure 64**) aligns with the clutch cover index mark (**Figure 66**).

NOTE
A cylinder at TDC of its compression stroke will have free play in all of its rocker arms, indicating that both pairs of intake and exhaust valves are closed.

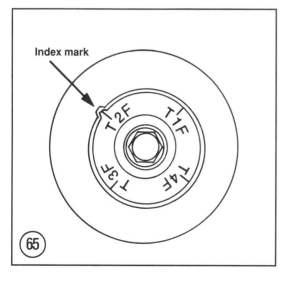

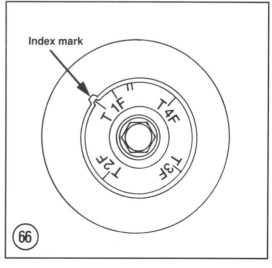

c. The No. 1 cylinder must be at top dead center (TDC) on the compression stroke. If the No. 1 cylinder is not at TDC on the compression stroke; rotate the crankshaft one full turn (360°) and make sure the "T 1" mark again aligns with the clutch cover index mark (**Figure 66**).

6. Using a crisscross pattern, loosen the bolts securing the camshaft holders in 2-3 stages.

CAUTION
*The camshaft holders **must** be reinstalled in their correct locations during installation. They have taken a wear set with the camshafts and if reinstalled in the wrong location can cause accelerated wear on both parts. Keep the camshaft holders and their mounting bolts together in sets, this will make installation easier.*

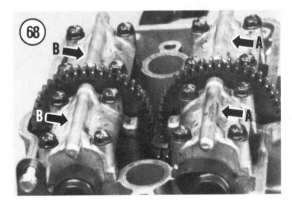

7. The camshaft holders are marked indicating their location in the cylinder head. Refer to the following for proper identification and locations of these holders:
   a. One of the letters "A," "B," "C" or "D" is cast into the top surface of each camshaft holder (A, **Figure 67**) and the same letters are cast into the top surface of the cylinder head (B, **Figure 67**). These letters must be matched up during installation.
   b. If these marks on the camshaft holders are no longer visible, use a permanent marking pen and mark each holder with the corrosponding letter ("A," "B," "C" or "D") on the cylinder head (B, **Figure 67**) prior to removal.

NOTE
The camshaft holder bolts installed in the locating dowels are of a different length.

8. Using a crisscross pattern, loosen the bolts securing the camshaft holders in 2-3 stages, then remove the bolts.

9. Lift straight up and remove the intake camshaft holders (A, **Figure 68**). Don't lose the locating dowels.
10. Lift straight up and remove the exhaust camshaft holders (B, **Figure 68**). Don't lose the locating dowels.
11. Lift straight up and remove both the intake and exhaust camshafts from the cylinder head.

ENGINE

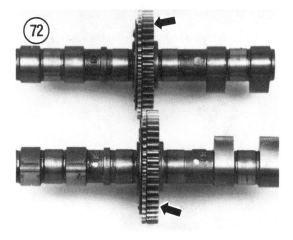

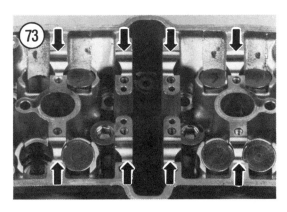

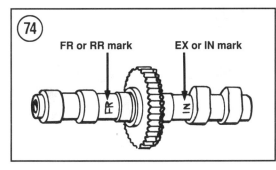

12. If necessary, repeat Steps 5-11 for the camshafts in the other cylinder head. Refer to Step 5 and realign the timing mark for the other cylinder head.

Inspection

1. Check the camshaft bearing journals for wear and scoring (**Figure 69**).
2. Check the camshaft lobes for wear (**Figure 70**). The lobes should not be scored and the edges should be square. Slight damage may be removed with a silicon carbide oilstone. Use No. 100-200 grit initially, then polish with a No. 280-320 grit.
3. Even though the camshaft lobe surface appears to be satisfactory, with no visible signs of wear, the camshaft lobes must be measured with a micrometer as shown in **Figure 71**. Replace the camshaft(s) if worn beyond the service limits listed in **Table 1**.
4. Measure the runout of the camshaft with a dial indicator and V-blocks. Use 1/2 of the total runout and compare to the service limits listed in **Table 1**.
5. Inspect the camshaft driven gear teeth (**Figure 72**) for wear; replace if necessary.
6. Make sure the oil holes in the camshaft holders are open. If necessary, clean out with a piece of wire and blow out with compressed air. Thoroughly clean the camshaft holder in solvent after cleaning out the oil holes to remove any sludge.
7. Check the camshaft bearing bores in the cylinder head (**Figure 73**) and camshaft holders. They should not be scored or excessively worn. If replacement is necessary, the cylinder head and the camshaft holders must be replaced as a set.
8. Inspect each bearing holder for wear, cracks or other damage. If replacement is necessary, the cylinder head and the camshaft holders must be replaced as a set.

Camshaft Bearing Clearance Measurement

This procedure requires the use of a Plastigage set. The camshafts must be installed into the cylinder heads. Prior to installation, wipe all oil residue from each camshaft bearing journal and bearing surface in the head and all camshaft holders.

1. Each camshaft is identified for correct placement in its respective location in the cylinder heads and is marked as shown in **Figure 74**. They are identified as follows:

a. "EX" "RR"—exhaust rear cylinders.
b. "IN" "RR"—intake, rear cylinders.
c. "EX" "FR"—exhaust front cylinders.
d. "IN" "FR"—intake, front cylinders.

2. The camshaft holders are marked indicating their locations in the cylinder head. Refer to the following for proper indentification and locations of these holders:
   a. One of the letters "A," "B," "C" or "D" is cast into the top surface of each camshaft holder (A, **Figure 67**).
   b. The same letters are cast into top surface of the cylinder head (B, **Figure 67**). These letters must be matched up during installation.
3. Install each camshaft into its correct location in the head. Position the camshaft lobes so they are not depressing any rocker arms.
4. Wipe all oil from camshaft bearing journals prior to using the Plastigage material.
5. Place a strip of Plastigage material on top of each camshaft bearing journal, parallel to the camshaft.
6. Place all camshaft holders, with locating dowels in place, in their correct positions onto the camshafts.
7. Install all camshaft holder bolts and the bolts. Install finger-tight at first, then tighten in a crisscross pattern to the torque specification listed in **Table 2**.

NOTE
Do not rotate either camshaft with the Plastigage material in place.

8. Gradually remove the bolts in a crisscross pattern. Pull the camshaft holders carefully stright up and remove them from the camshafts.
9. Measure the width of the flattened Plastigage according to manufacturer's instructions.
10. If the clearance exceeds the wear limit in **Table 1**, measure the camshaft bearing journals with a micrometer (**Figure 75**) and compare to the wear limits in **Table 1**. If the camshaft bearing journal is less than the dimension specified, replace the camshaft. If the camshaft is within specifications, the cylinder head and camshaft holders must be replaced as a set.

CAUTION
Remove all particles of Plastigage material from all camshaft bearing journals and camshaft holders. This material must not be left in the engine, as it can plug up a small oil control orifice and cause severe engine damage.

Camshaft Installation (When Both Front and Rear Cylinders Camshafts Were Removed)

NOTE
*Use this procedure only if **both front and rear** cylinders camshafts were removed.*

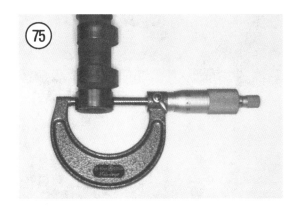

ENGINE

NOTE
*The camshafts have different timing marks—do not confuse them during installation. The timing marks on the front cylinder head camshafts are **arrows**. The timing marks on the rear cylinder head camshafts are lines and are referred to as **timing mark** in the text.*

1. Make sure valve lifters are correctly installed onto their specific valves (**Figure 76**).
2. Rotate the crankshaft by turning the starter clutch mounting bolt (**Figure 63**).
3. Rotate the crankshaft *clockwise* (as viewed from the left-hand side) until the "T 1" mark on the starter clutch (**Figure 64**) aligns with the clutch cover index mark (**Figure 66**).

NOTE
First install the camshaft and camshaft holders into the rear cylinder head assembly, then the front cylinder head. Steps 4-10 are performed on the rear cylinder head assembly.

4. Apply molybdenum disulfide grease or oil to the camshaft lobes and to the top surface of the valve lifters.
5. Install the camshafts into the rear cylinder head as follows:

   a. The camshaft driven gears are marked with a timing mark (A, **Figure 77**) and timing arrow (B, **Figure 77**) on the right-hand face.
   b. Position the camshafts with this side facing toward the right-hand side of the engine.
   c. Install one camshaft and then the other camshaft into the rear cylinder head with the marks *facing away from each other*.
   d. Align the *timing mark* (A, **Figure 77**) with the top surface on the rear cylinder head as shown in **Figure 78**. Engage the camshaft sub-gears with the idle gears by depressing the camshaft by hand while slightly rotating the crankshaft back and forth.

6. Install the camshaft holder locating dowels in the rear cylinder head or in the holders.
7. Install the camshaft holders into their correct positions in the rear cylinder head. The camshaft holders are marked, indicating their locations in the cylinder head. Refer to the following for proper identification and locations of these holders:

   a. One of the letters "A," "B," "C" or "D" is cast into the top surface of each camshaft holder (A, **Figure 67**).
   b. The same letters are cast into top surface of the cylinder head (B, **Figure 67**).

CAUTION
Very expensive damage could result from improper camshaft sub-gear and idle gear alignment. Recheck your work several times to make sure alignment is correct.

8. After both rear camshaft assembles are installed, recheck the timing marks as follows:

   a. The camshaft *timing mark* on each camshaft must still be *facing away from each other* and be aligned with the the top surface of the rear cylinder head as shown in **Figure 78**. Also refer to **Figure 79** and **Figure 80**.
   b. The "T 1" mark on the starter clutch (**Figure 64**) must still be aligned with the clutch cover index mark (**Figure 66**).
   c. All 3 of these marks *must be aligned correctly* at this time, otherwise camshaft timing will be incorrect.
   d. If any of these 3 marks are incorrect, realign the components at this time—do *not* proceed if alignment marks are incorrect.

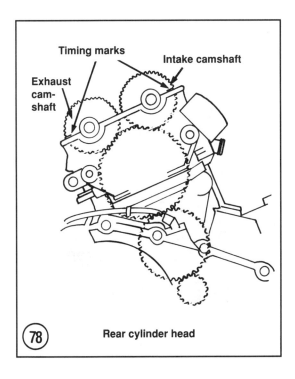

Rear cylinder head

9. Install all of the bolts securing the camshaft holders. Tighten these bolts finger-tight.

10. After all bolts are installed, using a crisscross pattern tighten the bolts in 2-3 stages to the torque specification listed in **Table 2**.

NOTE
*The following steps are performed on the **front** cylinder head assembly.*

11. Apply molybdenum disulfide grease or oil to the camshaft lobes and to the top surface of the valve lifters.

12. To install the front cylinder head camshafts, rotate the crankshaft by turning the starter clutch mounting bolt (**Figure 63**).

13. Rotate the crankshaft *clockwise* (as viewed from the left-hand side) 1 1/4 turns (450°) until the "T 2" mark on the starter clutch (**Figure 64**) aligns with the clutch cover index mark (**Figure 65**).

14. Install the camshafts into the front cylinder head as follows:
   a. The camshaft driven gears are marked with a timing arrow (B, **Figure 77**) on the right-hand face.
   b. Position the camshafts with this side facing toward the right-hand side of the engine.
   c. Install one camshaft and then the other camshaft into the front cylinder head with the arrrows *facing away from each other*.
   d. Aligning the *timing arrow* (B, **Figure 77**) with the top surface of the front cylinder head as shown in **Figure 81**. Engage the camshaft sub-gears with the idle gears by depressing the camshaft by hand while slightly rotating the crankshaft back and forth.

15. Install the camshaft holder locating dowels in the front cylinder head or in the holders.

16. Install the camshaft holders into their correct positions in the front cylinder head. The camshaft holders are marked indicating their locations in the cylinder head. Refer to the following for proper identification and locations of these holders:
   a. One of the letters "A," "B," "C" or "D" is cast into the top surface of each camshaft holder (A, **Figure 67**).
   b. The same letters are cast into top surface of the cylinder head (B, **Figure 67**).

CAUTION
Very expensive damage could result from improper camshaft sub-gear and idle gear alignment. Recheck your work several times to make sure alignment is correct.

17. After both rear camshaft assemblies are installed, recheck the timing marks as follows:
   a. The camshaft *timing arrow* on each camshaft must still be *facing away from each other* and are aligned with the the top surface of the front cylinder head as shown in **Figure 81** and **Figure 82**.
   b. The "T2" mark on the starter clutch (**Figure 65**) must still be aligned with the clutch cover index mark (**Figure 65**).
   c. All 3 of these marks *must be aligned correctly* at this time otherwise camshaft timing will be incorrect.
   d. If any of these 3 marks are incorrect, realign the components at this time—do *not* proceed if alignment marks are incorrect.

18. Install all of the bolts securing the camshaft holders. Tighten these bolts finger-tight.

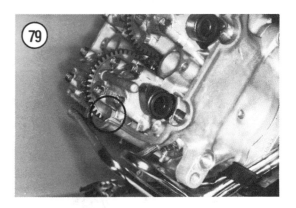

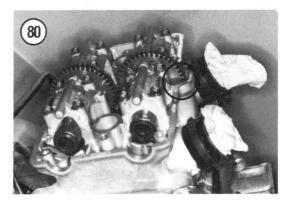

ENGINE

19. After all bolts are installed, using a crisscross pattern tighten the bolts in 2-3 stages to the torque specification listed in **Table 2**.

Camshaft Installation
(With The Rear Cylinder Camshafts Only Removed)

NOTE
*If the engine has been disturbed (crankshaft rotated) after the rear cylinders camshafts were removed, the engine must be **zeroed in** again to ensure proper camshaft timing with the front cylinder.*

1. Make sure valve lifters and shims are correctly installed onto their specific valves (**Figure 76**).
2. Remove the front cylinder head cover as described in this chapter.
3. Rotate the crankshaft by turning the starter clutch mounting bolt (**Figure 63**).
4. Rotate the crankshaft *clockwise* (as viewed from the left-hand side) until the "T 2" mark on the starter clutch (**Figure 64**) aligns with the clutch cover index mark (**Figure 65**).

NOTE
A cylinder at TDC of its compression stroke will have both camshaft lobes facing away from the valve lifter surfaces, indicating both pairs of intake and exhaust valves are closed.

5. The No. 2 cylinder must be at top dead center (TDC) on the compression stroke. If the No. 2 cylinder is not at TDC on the compression stroke; rotate the crankshaft one full turn (360°) and make sure the "T 2" mark again aligns with the clutch cover index mark (**Figure 65**).
6. Rotate the crankshaft *clockwise* (as viewed from the left-hand side) 3/4 turn (270°) until the "T 1" mark on the starter clutch (**Figure 64**) aligns with the clutch cover index mark (**Figure 66**).
7. Apply molybdenum disulfide grease or oil to the camshaft lobes and to the top surface of the valve lifters.
8. Install the camshafts into the rear cylinder head as follows:
    a. The camshaft driven gears are marked with a timing mark (A, **Figure 77**) and timing arrow (B, **Figure 77**) on the right-hand face.
    b. Position the camshafts with this side facing toward the right-hand side of the engine.
    c. Install one camshaft and then the other camshaft into the rear cylinder head with the marks *facing away from each other*.
    d. Aligning the *timing mark* (A, **Figure 77**) with the top surface on the rear cylinder head as shown in **Figure 78**. Engage the camshaft subgears with the idle gears by depressing the camshaft by hand while slightly rotating the crankshaft back and forth.
9. Install the camshaft holder locating dowels in the rear cylinder head or in the holders.

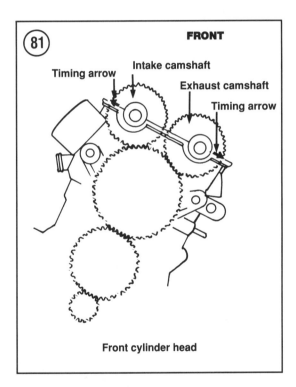

81

FRONT

Timing arrow
Intake camshaft
Exhaust camshaft
Timing arrow

Front cylinder head

82

10. Install the camshaft holders into their correct positions in the rear cylinder head. The camshaft holders are marked indicating their locations in the cylinder head. Refer to the following for proper identification and locations of these holders:
 a. One of the letters "A," "B," "C" or "D" is cast into the top surface of each camshaft holder (A, **Figure 67**).
 b. The same letters are cast into top surface of the cylinder head (B, **Figure 67**).

> *CAUTION*
> *Very expensive damage could result from improper camshaft sub-gear and idle gear alignment. Recheck your work several times to make sure alignment is correct.*

11. After both rear camshaft assemblies are installed, recheck the timing marks as follows:
 a. The camshaft *timing mark* on each camshaft must still be *facing away from each other* and be aligned with the the top surface of the rear cylinder head as shown in **Figure 78**. Also refer to **Figure 79** and **Figure 80**.
 b. The "T 1" mark on the starter clutch (**Figure 64**) must still be aligned with the clutch cover index mark (**Figure 66**).
 c. All 3 of these marks *must be aligned correctly* as shown in **Figure 83** at this time otherwise camshaft timing will be incorrect.
 d. If any of these 3 marks are incorrect, realign the components at this time—do *not* proceed if alignment marks are incorrect.

12. Install all of the bolts securing the camshaft holders. Tighten these bolts finger-tight.

13. After all bolts are installed, using a crisscross pattern tighten the bolts in 2-3 stages to the torque specification listed in **Table 2**.

Camshaft Installation
(With The Front Cylinder Camshafts Only Removed)

> *NOTE*
> *If the engine has been disturbed (crankshaft rotated) after the rear cylinders camshafts were removed, the engine must be **zeroed in** again to ensure proper camshaft timing with the front cylinder.*

1. Make sure valve lifters and shims are correctly installed onto their specific valves (**Figure 76**).

2. Remove the rear cylinder head cover as described in this chapter.

3. Rotate the crankshaft by turning the starter clutch mounting bolt (**Figure 63**).

4. Rotate the crankshaft *clockwise* (as viewed from the left-hand side) until the "T 1" mark on the starter clutch (**Figure 64**) aligns with the clutch cover index mark (**Figure 66**).

> *NOTE*
> *A cylinder at TDC of its compression stroke will have both camshaft lobes facing away from the valve lifter surfaces, indicating both pairs of intake and exhaust valves are closed.*

5. The No. 1 cylinder must be at top dead center (TDC) on the compression stroke. If the No. 1 cylinder is not at TDC on the compression stroke; rotate the crankshaft one full turn (360°) and make sure the "T 1" mark again aligns with the clutch cover index mark (**Figure 66**).

6. Rotate the crankshaft *clockwise* (as viewed from the left-hand side) 1 1/4 turn (450°) until the "T 2" mark on the starter clutch (**Figure 64**) aligns with the clutch cover index mark (**Figure 65**).

7. Apply molybdenum disulfide grease or oil to the camshaft lobes and to the top surface of the valve lifters.

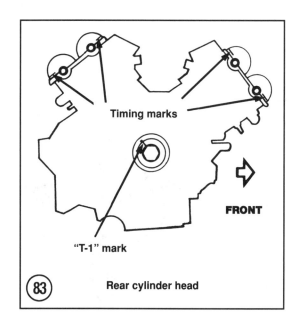

83 Rear cylinder head — Timing marks, "T-1" mark, FRONT

ENGINE

8. Install the camshafts into the rear cylinder head as follows:

  a. The camshaft driven gears are marked with a timing mark (A, **Figure 77**) and timing arrow (B, **Figure 77**) on the right-hand face.

  b. Position the camshafts with this side facing toward the right-hand side of the engine.

  c. Install one camshaft and then the other camshaft into the front cylinder head with the arrows *facing away from each other*.

  d. Aligning the *timing arrrow* (B, **Figure 77**) with the top surface on the front cylinder head as shown in **Figure 81**. Engage the camshaft sub-gears with the idle gears by depressing the camshaft by hand while slightly rotating the crankshaft back and forth.

9. Install the camshaft holder locating dowels in the front cylinder head or in the holders.

10. Install the camshaft holders into their correct positions in the front cylinder head. The camshaft holders are marked indicating their locations in the cylinder head. Refer to the following for proper identification and locations of these holders:

  a. One of the letters "A," "B," "C" or "D" is cast into the top surface of each camshaft holder (A, **Figure 67**).

  b. The same letters are cast into top surface of the cylinder head (B, **Figure 67**).

CAUTION
Very expensive damage could result from improper camshaft sub-gear and idle gear alignment. Recheck your work several times to make sure alignment is correct.

11. After both front camshaft assemblies are installed, recheck the timing marks as follows:

  a. The camshaft *timing arrows* on each camshaft must still be *facing away from each other* and are aligned with the the top surface of the front cylinder head as shown in **Figure 81** and **Figure 82**.

  b. The "T 2" mark on the starter clutch (**Figure 64**) must still be aligned with the clutch cover index mark (**Figure 65**).

  c. All 3 of these marks and arrows *must be aligned correctly* as shown in **Figure 84** at this time otherwise camshaft timing will be incorrect.

  d. If any of these 3 marks and arrows are incorrect, realign the components at this time—do *not* proceed if alignment marks are incorrect.

12. Install all of the bolts securing the camshaft holders. Tighten these bolts finger-tight.

13. After all bolts are installed, using a crisscross pattern tighten the bolts in 2-3 stages to the torque specification listed in **Table 2**.

CYLINDER HEADS

Either cylinder head can be removed first. On 1986-1989 models, the front and rear cylinder heads can be removed with the engine in the frame but it is much easier with the engine removed. On 1990-on models only the front cylinder can be removed with the engine in the frame; to remove the rear cylinder head, the engine *must* be removed from the frame.

This sequence is shown with the engine removed.

Removal
(1986-1989 Models)

1. Remove the engine as described in this chapter.

2. Remove the camshafts as described in this chapter.

3. Remove the 8 mm bolt and copper washer (**Figure 85**) securing the camshaft gear case to the V-portion of the cylinder block.

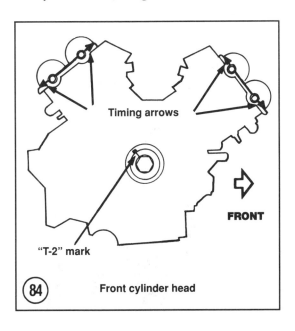

4. Remove the bolts securing the coolant pipe right- and left-hand caps (A, **Figure 86**) to the top of the cylinder block.

5. Remove the caps and connecting pipe (B, **Figure 86**) assembly from the cylinder block. Remove the O-ring seals from the cylinder block and discard them.

6. If necessary, on 1986 models' front cylinder head, remove the bolts (A, **Figure 87**) securing the camshaft pulse generator assembly (B, **Figure 87**) and remove the assembly.

7. Remove the bolts (A, **Figure 88**) securing the oil line to the cylinder head and the cylinder block. Remove the oil line (B, **Figure 88**) and O-ring seal (**Figure 89**).

8. Loosen the 9 mm bolts (A, **Figure 90**) securing the camshaft gear case.

9. To prevent warpage of the head, loosen the remaining cylinder head bolts 1/2 turn at a time in a crisscross pattern. Refer to A, **Figure 91** for 9 mm bolts or B, **Figure 91** for 6 mm bolts.

NOTE
*The camshaft gear case assembly is marked (**Figure 92**) with an "F" (front) or "R" (rear) indicating which cylinder head it goes with. If this mark is no longer visible, mark it with a scribe or permanent marking pen. This will assure that the camshaft gear case is reinstalled into the correct cylinder head.*

10. Remove the camshaft gear case bolts and pull the camshaft gear case assembly (B, **Figure 90**) straight up and out of the cylinder head.

11. Remove the remaining bolts.

12. Loosen the head by tapping around the perimeter with a rubber or plastic mallet. If necessary, *gently* pry the head loose with a broad-tipped screwdriver on the side of each head.

13. Pull the cylinder head straight up and off the cylinder block.

14. Remove the head gasket and dowel pins.

15. Place a clean shop rag into the cam gear case opening in the block to prevent entry of foreign matter.

16. Inspect the cylinder heads as described in this chapter.

17. Repeat this procedure for the other cylinder head.

ENGINE

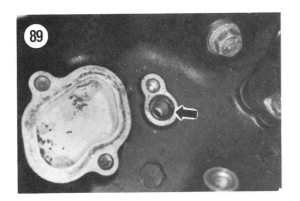

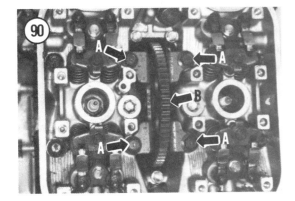

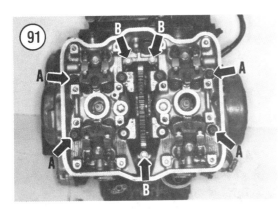

Installation
(1986-1989 Models)

1. Make sure all traces of old gasket material have been removed from the cylinder head and the cylinder block mating surfaces.

2. Install the 2 locating dowels in the lower corner of the cylinder block.

3. Position the cylinder head gasket with the "UP" mark facing up and install the new head gasket. Make sure all gasket holes align with the openings in the cylinder block.

4. Install the cylinder head straight down onto the cylinder block.

5. Install the 4 outer (9 mm × 90 mm) bolts to locate the cylinder head and tighten finger-tight.

NOTE
*Be sure to install the correct camshaft gear case assembly into the cylinder head. Refer to the mark (**Figure 92**), either an "F" (front) or "R" (rear) indicating which cylinder head it goes with.*

6. Position the camshaft gear case with the lower mounting tab (A, **Figure 93**) toward the intake side of the cylinder head.

CAUTION
*Make sure the camshaft gear case lower gear is properly meshed with the cranshaft timing gear prior to finger-tightening the mounting bolts. The gear case mounting surface **must** be sitting directly on top of the cylinder head mating surface with no air gap between the 2 surfaces. If there is an air gap, the 2 gears are not properly meshed and this*

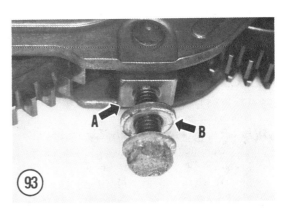

154

must be corrected prior to tightening the mounting bolts.

7. Install the camshaft gear case straight down into the cylinder head. If the gear case mounting surface is not flush with the top surface of the cylinder head; slightly rotate the cam upper gear back and forth so the lower gear will mesh properly with the crankshaft timing gear. Install the 4 (9 mm × 95 mm) bolts securing the gear case. Tighten finger-tight.

8. Install the remaining 9 mm (9 mm × 90 mm) bolts (A, **Figure 91**) and the 6 mm bolts (B, **Figure 91**) into the cylinder head.

9. Install the 8 mm bolt (**Figure 85**) and copper washer (B, **Figure 93**) securing the camshaft gear case to the cylinder block. Tighten finger-tight.

10. Tighten the cylinder head bolts in a crisscross pattern to the torque specification listed in **Table 2**. Tighten the bolts in the following sequence:
   a. 9 mm camshaft gear case bolts (A, **Figure 90**).
   b. 9 mm cylinder head bolts (A, **Figure 91**).
   c. 6 mm cylinder head bolts (B, **Figure 91**).
   d. 8 mm camshaft gear case bolt (**Figure 85**).

11. Make sure the oil control orifice (A, **Figure 94**) is in place in the cylinder head receptacle (B, **Figure 94**).

NOTE
Apply a light coat of sealant to the cylinder block oil line bolts prior to installation.

12. Install a new O-ring seal (**Figure 89**) and install the oil line (B, **Figure 88**) and the bolts (A, **Figure 88**) securing the oil line to the cylinder head and the cylinder block.

13. If removed, on 1986 models' front cylinder head, install the camshaft pulse generator assembly (B, **Figure 87**) and bolts (A, **Figure 87**) to the front cylinder head.

14. Tighten the oil bolts securely.

15. Install the coolant pipe as follows:
   a. Install a new upper seal on the metal pipe.
   b. Install a new O-ring seal (A, **Figure 95**) on the connecting pipe.
   c. Install new O-ring seals (B, **Figure 95**) under the right- and left-hand caps.
   d. Install the caps (A, **Figure 86**) and connecting pipe (B, **Figure 86**) assembly from the cylinder block.

CHAPTER FOUR

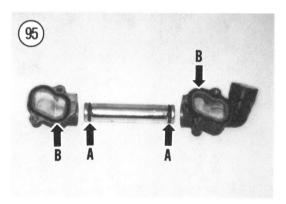

ENGINE

e. Apply a liquid sealant to the cap threads prior to installation and tighten them securely.
16. Install the camshafts as described in this chapter.
17. Repeat this procedure for the other cylinder head.
18. Install the engine as described in this chapter.

Removal
(1990-on Models)

1. Remove the engine as described in this chapter.
2. Remove the camshafts as described in this chapter.
3. Remove all valve lifters (A, **Figure 96**) and shims as described under *Valves* in this chapter.

NOTE
*Only one of the two 6 mm bolts is visible in **Figure 96**. Make sure to remove both bolts.*

4. Remove the 2 center 6 mm bolts (B, **Figure 96**).
5. To prevent warpage of the head, loosen the remaining 9 mm cylinder head bolts (C, **Figure 96**) 1/2 turn at a time in a crisscross pattern.

6. Remove the 9 mm bolts and washers.
7. Loosen the head by tapping around the perimeter with a rubber or plastic mallet. If necessary, *gently* pry the head loose with a broad-tipped screwdriver on the side of each head.
8. Pull the cylinder head straight up and off the cylinder block.
9. Remove the head gasket and dowel pins.

NOTE
*In **Figure 97** the bolts have already been removed. The arrows show the location of the bolts for each cylinder head.*

10. Remove the 8 mm camshaft gear case bolt (**Figure 97**) and sealing washer from the V-portion of the cylinder block.

NOTE
*The camshaft gear case assembly is marked (A, **Figure 98**) with an "F" (front) or "R" (rear) indicating which cylinder head it goes with. If this mark is no longer visible, mark it with a scribe or permanent marking pen. This will assure that the camshaft gear case is reinstalled into the correct cylinder head.*

11. Remove the camshaft gear case bolts and washers (**Figure 99**) and pull the camshaft gear case assembly straight up and out of the cylinder block. Don't lose the 2 locating dowels within 2 of the mounting bosses in the case assembly. These dowels must be reinstalled in the correct location during installation.
12. Place a clean shop rag into the cam gear case opening in the block to prevent entry of foreign matter.
13. Inspect the cylinder heads as described in this chapter.
14. Repeat this procedure for the other cylinder head.

Installation
(1990-on Models)

1. Make sure all traces of old gasket material have been removed from the cylinder head and the cylinder block mating surfaces.

CHAPTER FOUR

NOTE
*Be sure to install the correct camshaft gear case assembly into the cylinder block. Refer to the mark (A, **Figure 98**), either an "F" (front) or "R" (rear) indicating which cylinder head it goes with.*

CAUTION
*The camshaft gear case 2 locating dowels must be be properly installed in the cylinder block. They **must be** pushed down all the way until they bottom out. If they are not pushed down all the way the camshaft gear case will not be installed down far enough into the cylinder block. If the camshaft gear case is held up by the locating dowels, the gear case gears will not properly mesh with the crankshaft timing gears as shown in **Figure 100**. This would result in costly engine damage.*

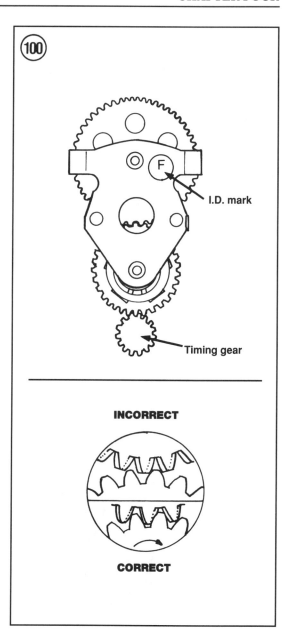

2. Install the 2 camshaft gear case locating dowels into their receptacles in the cylinder block. *Push the dowels in until they bottom out.*

3. Position the camshaft gear case with the lower bolt mounting tab (B, **Figure 98**) toward the V-portion of the cylinder block.

CAUTION
*Make sure the camshaft gear case lower gear is properly meshed with the crankshaft timing gear prior to finger-tightening the mounting bolts. The gear case mounting surface **must** be sitting directly on top of the cylinder block mating surface (A, **Figure 101**) with no air gap between the 2 surfaces. If there is an air gap, the 2 gears are not properly meshed, or the locating dowels were not properly installed in Step 2. This must be corrected prior to tightening the mounting bolts.*

4. Install the camshaft gear case straight down into the cylinder block. If the gear case mounting surface is not flush with the top surface of the cylinder head; slightly rotate the cam upper gear back and forth so the lower gear will mesh properly with the crankshaft timing gear. Install the four 6 mm bolts (**Figure 99**) and washers (B, **Figure 101**) securing the gear case. Tighten finger-tight.

ENGINE

5. Install the 8 mm camshaft gear case bolt (**Figure 97**) and new sealing washer into the V-portion of the cylinder block.

6. Tighten the 6 mm bolts in a crisscross pattern in 2-3 stages to the torque specification listed in **Table 2**.

7. Tighten the 8 mm bolt in 2-3 stages to the torque specification listed in **Table 2**.

8. Position the cylinder head gasket with the "UP" mark (A, **Figure 102**) facing up and install the new head gasket (B, **Figure 102**). Make sure all gasket holes align with the openings in the cylinder block.

9. Install the locating dowels (C, **Figure 102**) in the lower corners of the crankcase block.

10. Install the cylinder head straight down onto the cylinder block.

11. Apply clean engine oil cylinder head bolt threads and to the underside seating surface of the bolt heads.

12. Install the eight 9 mm bolts (C, **Figure 96**) and the two 6 mm bolts (B, **Figure 96**).

13. Tighten the cylinder head bolts in a crisscross pattern to the torque specification listed in **Table 2**. Tighten the bolts in the torque sequence shown in **Figure 103**.

14. Install the camshafts as described in this chapter.

15. Repeat this procedure for the other cylinder head.

16. Install the engine as described in this chapter.

Cylinder Head Inspection
(All Years)

NOTE
After removing the cylinder head, check the top and bottom mating surfaces for any indications of leakage. Also check the head gasket for signs of leakage. A blown gasket could indicate possible cylinder head warpage or other damage.

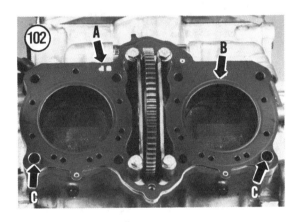

1. Before cleaning the head and removing the valves, perform the following leakage test:
   a. Set the cylinder head so that the exhaust ports face up, then pour solvent or kerosene into each port opening.
   b. Turn the head over slightly and check each exhaust valve area on the combustion chamber side. If the valves and seats are in good condition, there should be no fluid leakage. If an area is wet, the valve seat is not sealing correctly. This can be caused by a damaged valve seat and/or valve face or a bent or damaged valve. The valve(s) should be removed and the valve(s) and seat(s) inspected for wear or damage as described under *Valve and Valve Components* in this chapter.
   c. Repeat for the intake valve side of the cylinder head.

2. Remove all traces of old gasket material from the cylinder head (**Figure 104**) and the cylinder block (A, **Figure 105**) mating surface.

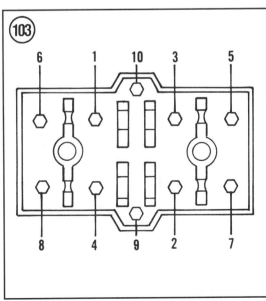

CAUTION
If the combustion chambers are cleaned while the valves are removed, the valve seat in the cylinder head will probably be damaged. A damaged or even slightly scratched valve seat will cause poor valve seating.

3. *Without removing the valves*, remove all carbon deposits from both combustion chambers with a wire brush. A blunt screwdriver or chisel may be used if care is taken not to damage the head, valves and spark plug threads.

4. Examine the spark plug threads in the cylinder head for damage. If damage is minor or if the threads are dirty or clogged with carbon, use a spark plug thread tap to clean the threads following the manufacturer's instructions. If thread damage is severe, the thread can be restored by installing a steel thread insert. Thread insert kits can be purchased at automotive supply stores or you can have the inserts installed by a Honda dealer or machine shop.

NOTE
When using a thread tap to clean spark plug threads, coat the tap with an aluminum tap cutting fluid or kerosene.

NOTE
Spark plug threads in an aluminum cylinder head are commonly damaged due to galling, cross-threading and overtightening. It is easy to cross-thread spark plugs on this engine because the plug holes are set deeply and hard to get to. To prevent galling, always apply an anti-seize compound on the plug threads before installation and do not overtighten.

5. After all carbon is removed from the combustion chambers (**Figure 106**) and valve intake and exhaust ports, clean the entire head in solvent.

NOTE
If the cylinder head was bead-blasted, make sure to clean the head thoroughly with solvent and then with hot water and soap afterwards. Residual grit seats in small crevices and other areas and can be hard to remove. Chase each exposed thread with a tap to remove grit between the threads or you may damage a thread later. Residual grit left in the engine will cause premature piston, ring and bearing wear.

6. Check for cracks in the combustion chamber and exhaust ports. A cracked head must be replaced.

7. Examine the piston crowns. The crowns should show no signs of wear or damage. If the crown appears pecked or spongy-looking (B, **Figure 105**), also check the spark plug, valves and combustion chamber for aluminum deposits. If these deposits are found, the cylinder(s) is suffering from excessive heat caused by a lean fuel mixture or preignition.

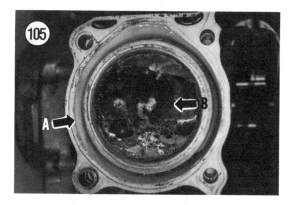

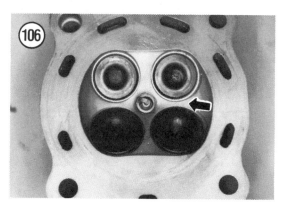

ENGINE

CAUTION
Do not clean the piston crowns with the cylinder assembled on the crankcase. Carbon scraped from the tops of the pistons will fall between the cylinder wall and piston and onto the piston rings. Because carbon grit is very abrasive, premature cylinder, piston and ring wear will occur. If the piston crowns have heavy deposits of carbon, remove the pistons as described in this chapter and clean them while removed from the engine. Excessive carbon build-up on the piston crowns reduces piston cooling, raises engine compression and causes overheating.

8. After the cylinder head has been thoroughly cleaned, place a straightedge across the gasket surface at several points. Measure warp by inserting a feeler gauge between the straightedge and cylinder head at each location. Maximum allowable warpage is listed in **Table 1**. Warpage or nicks in the cylinder head surface could cause an air leak and result in overheating. If warpage exceeds this limit, the cylinder head must be resurfaced by a Honda dealer or qualified machine shop or replaced.

9. Check the exhaust pipe studs (**Figure 107**) for looseness or thread damage. Slight thread damage can be repaired with a thread file or die. If thread damage is severe, replace the damaged stud(s) as described in Chapter One.

10. Inspect the intake pipes (**Figure 108**) for cracks, deterioration or damage. If they are damaged in any way they should be replaced to avoid an unwanted vacuum leak.

11. Check the valves and valve guides as described under *Valves and Valve Components* in this chapter.

12. On 1986-1989 models, clean the external oil line assembly (**Figure 109**) with solvent. Make sure the pipe is open and clean. Apply compressed air to all openings and make sure none are clogged.

Camshaft Gear Case Inspection

The camshaft gear case assembly cannot be disassembled. If any portion is faulty, the entire assembly must be replaced.

1. Inspect both gears for wear, damage, chipped or missing teeth. Refer to **Figure 110** for 1986-1989 models or **Figure 111** for 1990-on models. If either

gear is damaged, inspect the mating gear on the camshafts or crankshaft timing gear for possible damage.

2. Inspect the thin lower split gear (**Figure 112**) for wear or damage. Also check the springs (**Figure 113**) for wear, damage or sagging.

3. Make sure the assembly rivets (A, **Figure 114**) are tight. The holding plates on each side of the gears must be held together tightly to avoid any play in the gears.

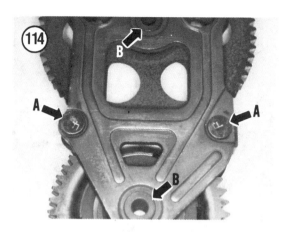

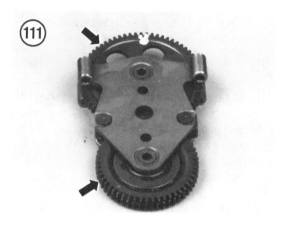

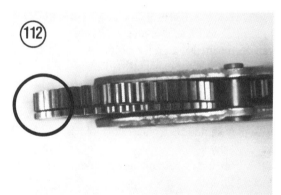

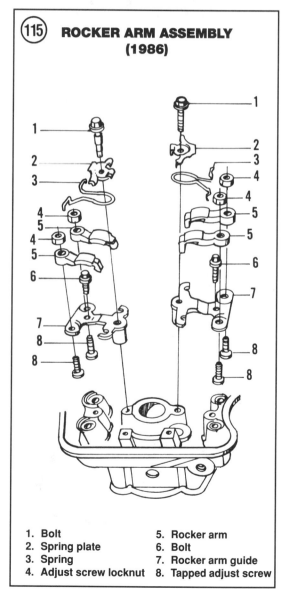

ROCKER ARM ASSEMBLY (1986)

1. Bolt
2. Spring plate
3. Spring
4. Adjust screw locknut
5. Rocker arm
6. Bolt
7. Rocker arm guide
8. Tapped adjust screw

ENGINE

4. Inspect the gear bearings (B, **Figure 114**). Rotate the gears and listen for any bearing noise or play.

ROCKER ARMS ASSEMBLIES (1986-1989 MODELS)

Removal/Installation

Refer to the following illustrations for this procedure:
a. **Figure 115**: 1986 models.
b. **Figure 116**: 1987-1989 models.

NOTE
If working on a well-run in engine (high mileage), keep the rocker arm assembly parts together as a set. Mark these sets relating to the cylinder number and intake or exhaust. These parts have developed a wear pattern that relates to the camshaft and the valve stem and each set should be reinstalled in its original location to prevent rapid wear from mis-matched sets of parts.

1. Remove the cylinder head as described in this chapter.
2A. On 1986 models, perform the following:
   a. Remove the bolts (**Figure 117**) securing the rocker arm assembly to the cylinder head.
   b. Remove the rocker arm assembly.
2B. On 1987-1989 models, perform the following:
   a. Remove the nuts securing the rocker arm assembly to the cylinder head.
   b. Remove the spring and guide, then remove the collars from the mounting studs in the cylinder head.
   c. Remove the nut securing each rocker arm to the threaded stud in the cylinder head and remove each rocker arm.
3. Install by reversing these removal steps while noting the following:
   a. On 1986 models, refer to **Figure 118** for correct alignment of all parts after installation.
   b. On 1987-1989 models, be sure to install the collar onto the threaded stud prior to installing the guide and spring.
   c. On 1987-1989 models, refer to **Figure 119** for correct alignment of all parts after installation.

Disassembly/Inspection/Assembly (1986 Models)

1. Inspect the rocker arm where it rides on the camshaft lobe (**Figure 120**) and where it rides on the valve stem (**Figure 121**). If worn or damaged, replace the rocker arm(s).

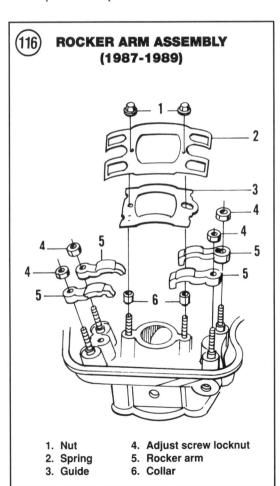

ROCKER ARM ASSEMBLY (1987-1989)

1. Nut
2. Spring
3. Guide
4. Adjust screw locknut
5. Rocker arm
6. Collar

2. To remove the rocker arm (A, **Figure 122**), unscrew the adjust screw (B, **Figure 122**) and remove the rocker arm from the rocker arm guide (C, **Figure 122**) and tappet adjust screw.

3. Inspect the spring plate and mounting bolt (**Figure 123**) for wear or damage. Replace any worn or damaged parts.

4. Inspect tappet adjust screw pivot (**Figure 124**) for wear or damage. These pivots cannot be replaced and if damage is severe the cylinder head must be replaced.

5. Assemble by reversing these disassembly steps.

Inspection
(1987-1989 Models)

1. Inspect the rocker arm where it rides on the camshaft lobe and where it rides on the valve stem. If worn or damaged, replace the rocker arm(s).

2. Inspect the spring and guide for wear or damage. Replace any worn or damaged parts.

3. Inspect tappet adjust screw pivot for wear or damage.

Rocker Arm Pivot Bolt
Removal/Installation
(1987-1989 Models)

1. Remove the locknut and rocker arm from the adjust screw.

2. Install a 8 × 16 mm dowel pin onto the pivot bolt then reinstall the locknut against the dowel pin.

3. Hold the locknut (A, **Figure 125**) with a wrench and slowly tighten the adjust screw. Continue to tighten the adjust screw until it works free from the pivot seat (B, **Figure 125**) in the cylinder head.

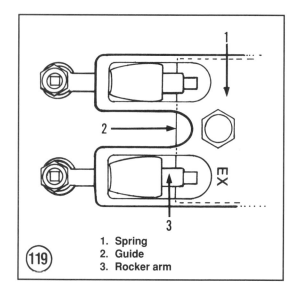
1. Spring
2. Guide
3. Rocker arm

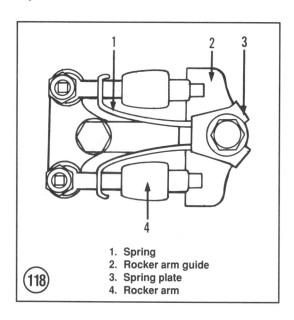
1. Spring
2. Rocker arm guide
3. Spring plate
4. Rocker arm

ENGINE

4. Remove the adjust screw, locknut and dowel pin.

NOTE
If the threads on the adjust screw are damaged, proceed to Step 5.

5. Tighten the locknut on the adjust screw with the rocker arm in place.

6. Install a small solid spacer under the rocker arm, then push down on the end of the rocker arm (A, **Figure 126**). Pushing down on the end of the rocker arm should release the adjust screw from the pivot seat (B, **Figure 126**) in the cylinder head.

7. Repeat for any additional adjust screws as necessary.

8. To install the adjust screw, perform the following:
   a. Install the adjust screw and locknut onto the rocker arm.
   b. Install the rocker arm (A, **Figure 127**), locknut and adjust screw (B, **Figure 127**) into the pivot seat (C, **Figure 127**) on the cylinder head.
   c. Install a suitable size socket (D, **Figure 127**) onto the locknut and rest it on the top surface of the rocker arm.
   d. Keep the rocker arm and adjust screw in a true vertical line to the pivot socket. Carefully tap on the end of the socket and drive the adjust nut in to the pivot socket in the cylinder head.

VALVES AND VALVE COMPONENTS

General practice among those who do their own service is to remove the cylinder head(s) and take it to a dealer or machine shop for inspection and serv-

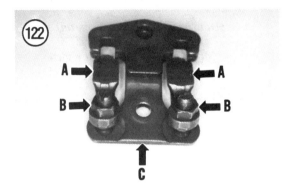

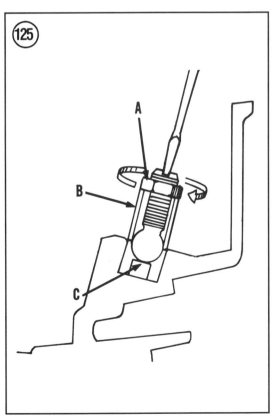

ice. This is because correct valve service requires a number of special tools. The following procedures describe how to check for valve component wear and to determine what type of service is required. In most cases, valve troubles are caused by poor valve seating, worn valve guides and burned valves. A valve spring compressor is required to remove and install the valves.

This procedure is included for those who choose to do their own valve service.

Valve Removal

Refer to the following illustrations for this procedure:

a. **Figure 128**: 1986-1989 models.

b. **Figure 129**: 1990-on models.

On 1990-on models, each set of valve springs and related parts is located within a recess in the cylinder head. This recess is the area that the valve lifter rides within. It is a machined surface and it must be protected against damage during valve component removal and installation.

On 1990-on models, several Honda special tools are required to avoid damage to the cylinder head. They are as follows:

a. Tappet hole protector (part No. 07HMG-MR70001).

b. Valve spring compressor (part No. 07757-0010000).

c. Valve spring compressor attachment (part No. 07959-KM30101).

NOTE
This procedure is shown on a 1986-1989 model cylinder head. Valve removal and installation is the same on all models with some minor variations. Where differences occur, they are identified.

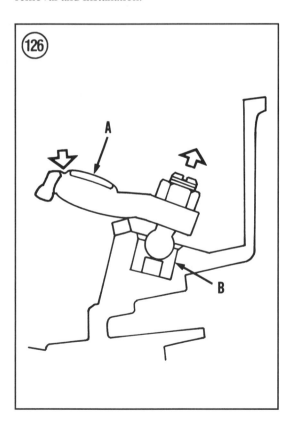

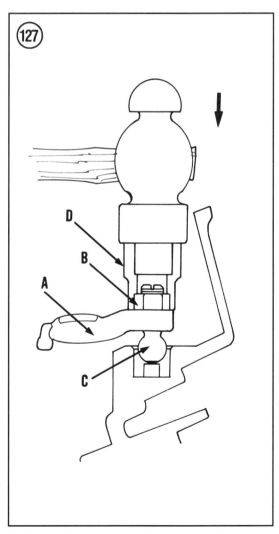

ENGINE

1. Remove the cylinder head(s) as described in this chapter.

2A. On 1986-1989 models, remove the rocker arm assemblies as described in this chapter.

2B. On 1990-on models, remove each valve lifter (A, **Figure 130**) and shim (B, **Figure 130**) from the cylinder head, making sure to store each set in a divided container and labeled as to its original position in the cylinder head(s), so the sets are not mixed up during reassembly.

CAUTION
To avoid loss of spring tension, do not compress the springs any more than necessary to remove the keepers.

3. On 1990-on models, perform the following:

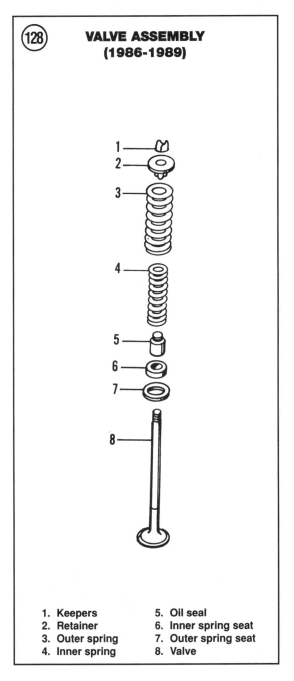

VALVE ASSEMBLY (1986-1989)

1. Keepers
2. Retainer
3. Outer spring
4. Inner spring
5. Oil seal
6. Inner spring seat
7. Outer spring seat
8. Valve

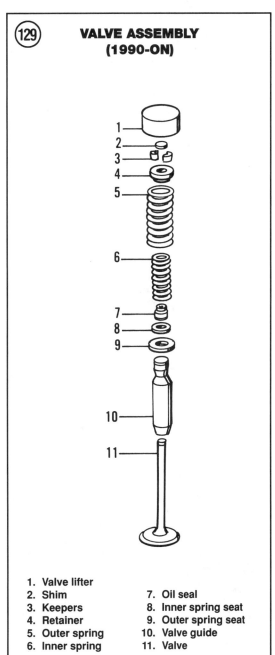

VALVE ASSEMBLY (1990-ON)

1. Valve lifter
2. Shim
3. Keepers
4. Retainer
5. Outer spring
6. Inner spring
7. Oil seal
8. Inner spring seat
9. Outer spring seat
10. Valve guide
11. Valve

a. Install the tappet hole protector into the valve lifter sliding surface of the valve being removed.

NOTE
The tappet hole protector protects the valve lifter sliding surface in the cylinder head from damage.

b. If you are using the Honda valve spring compressor, install the attachment onto the end of the compressor.

4. Install a valve spring compressor squarely over the valve retainer with other end of tool placed against the valve head (**Figure 131**).

5. Tighten the valve spring compressor until the valve keepers separate. Lift valve keepers out through the valve spring compressor with needlenose pliers or tweezers (**Figure 132**).

6. Gradually loosen the valve spring compressor and remove it from the head. Remove the retainer (**Figure 133**).

7. Remove the outer spring (**Figure 134**) and inner spring (**Figure 135**).

8. Remove the outer spring seat (**Figure 136**)

ENGINE

136

137

9. Remove the inner spring seat (**Figure 137**).

CAUTION
Remove any burrs from the valve stem grooves before removing the valve; otherwise, the valve guides will be damaged. ***Figure 138*** *shows the area to be deburred.*

10. Turn the cylinder head over and remove the valve (**Figure 139**).

11. Pull the oil seal (**Figure 140**) off of the valve guide.

12. Mark all parts as they are removed so that they will be installed in their same locations. Refer to **Figure 141** for a typical set of valve parts (1990-on model shown).

13. Repeat for all intake and exhaust valves.

NOTE
Do not remove the valve guides unless they require replacement.

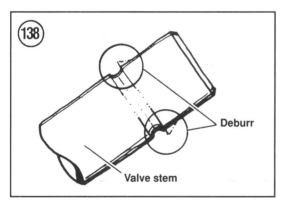

138

140

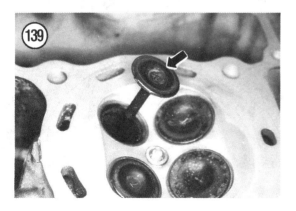

139

141

Inspection

Table 1 lists valve specifications and service limits.

1. Using a motor-driven wire brush, remove carbon deposits from the valve heads. Work carefully so that you do not gouge or damage the valve seating surface. Then clean the valves in solvent and dry thoroughly.

2. Inspect the contact surface (**Figure 142**) of each valve for burning, pitting or other signs of wear. Unevenness of the valve face is an indication that the valve is not serviceable. If the wear on a valve is too extensive to be corrected by hand-lapping the valve into its seat, the valve should be replaced. The valve face surface cannot be ground and must be replaced if defective. Valves should be hand-lapped only.

3. Inspect the valve stems for wear and roughness. Check the valve cotter grooves for damage.

4. Measure each valve stem for wear with a micrometer (**Figure 143**). If worn beyond specifications in **Table 1**, the valve must be replaced.

5. Honda recommends reaming the valve guides to remove any carbon build-up before checking and measuring the guides in the following steps. Ream the guides as described under *Valve Guide Replacement* in this chapter. If you do not have the correct size reamer, remove carbon and varnish from the valve guides with a stiff spiral wire brush. Then clean the valve guides with solvent to wash out all metal particles. Dry with compressed air.

6. Insert each valve into its respective valve guide and move it up and down by hand. The valve should move smoothly with no sign of binding or roughness.

NOTE
If you do not have the required measuring devices, proceed to Step 9.

7. Measure and record each valve guide inside diameter with a small hole gauge or inside micrometer (**Figure 144**). Compare measurements with the service limit in **Table 1**.

8. Subtract the measurement made in Step 4 from the measurement made in Step 7. The difference is the valve stem-to-guide clearance. See specification in **Table 1** for correct clearance. Replace any guide or valve that is not within tolerance. Valve guide replacement is described later in this chapter.

9. If a small hole gauge or inside micrometer is not available, insert each valve in its guide. Hold the valve just slightly off its seat and rock it sideways or use a dial indicator with its plunger against the upper valve stem (**Figure 145**). If the valve rocks more than slightly, the guide is probably worn and should be replaced. As a final check, take the cylinder head to a dealer or machine shop and have the valve guides accurately measured.

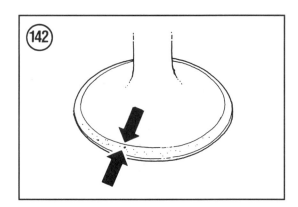

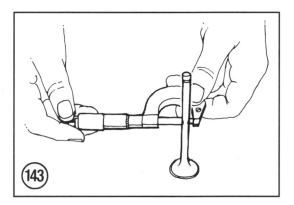

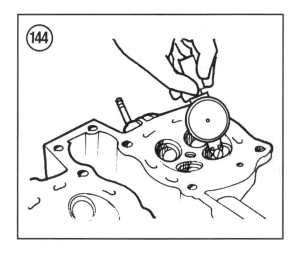

ENGINE

10. Measure each valve spring length with a vernier caliper (**Figure 146**). All should be within the length specified in **Table 1** with no bends or distortion. Replace defective springs in pairs, both the inner and the outer.

11. Check the valve spring retainer and valve keepers. If they are in good condition, they may be reused; replace in pairs as necessary.

12. On 1990-on models, perform the following:
   a. Measure the valve lifter outside diameter.
   b. Measure the lifter bore inside diameter in the cylinder head.
   c. If worn to the service limit in **Table 1**, the valve lifters and/or cylinder head must be replaced.

13. Inspect the valve seats as described under *Valve Seat Inspection* in this chapter.

Valve Guide Replacement

Worn valve guides can create excessive valve stem-to-guide clearance or valve wobble. In such cases, the guides must be replaced. This job should be done by a dealer, as special tools and considerable expertise are required. If the valve guide is replaced, also replace its valve.

The valve guides must be removed and installed with special tools that are available from a Honda dealer. See a Honda dealer for part numbers.

1. Place the new valve guides in a freezer for approximately 1 hour prior to heating up the cylinder head. Chilling them will slightly reduce their outside diameter, while the hot cylinder head is slightly larger due to heat expansion. This will make valve guide installation much easier.

> *NOTE*
> *Because flangeless valve guides are used, the measurements required in Step 2 are critical for proper valve guide and valve operation.*

2. Measure the height of the exposed valve guide projection from the cylinder head surface with a vernier caliper (**Figure 147**). Record each valve guide projection height. The correct valve guide projection specifications for intake and exhaust valves are listed in **Table 1**.

3. Remove the screws securing the intake pipes (**Figure 148**) onto the cylinder head. Remove the intake pipe prior to placing the cylinder head in the oven.

> *NOTE*
> *There **may** be a residual oil or solvent odor left in the oven after heating the cylinder head. If you use a household oven; first check with the person who*

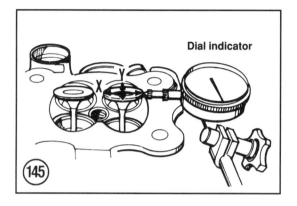

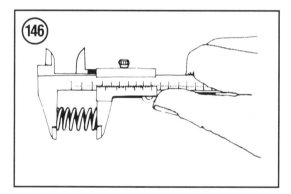

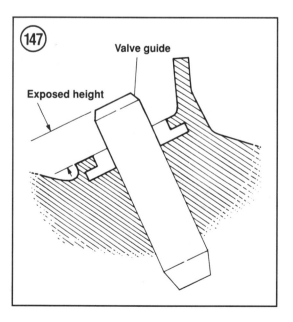

uses the oven for food preparation to avoid getting into trouble.

NOTE
To monitor the cylinder head temperature when heating it in Step 4, use heat indicator sticks, available at welding supply stores. Follow the manufacturer's directions when using the sticks.

4. The valve guides are installed with a slight interference fit. Place the cylinder head in a heated shop oven or on a hot plate. Heat the cylinder head to a temperature between 130-140° C (275-290° F). Do not heat the cylinder head beyond 150° C (300° F).

CAUTION
Do not heat the cylinder head with a torch (propane or acetylene); never bring a flame into contact with the cylinder head or valve guide. The direct heat will destroy the case hardening of the valve guide and will likely cause warpage of the cylinder head.

WARNING
Heavy, insulated gloves must be worn when performing this procedure the cylinder head will be very hot.

5. Remove the cylinder head from the oven or hot plate and place it onto wood blocks with the combustion chamber facing up. Make sure the cylinder head is properly supported on the wood blocks.

6. From the combustion chamber side of the cylinder head, drive out the old valve guide with a hammer and the correct size Honda valve guide driver (**Figure 149**). Discard valve guides after removing them. Never reinstall a valve guide that has been removed, as it is no longer true nor within tolerance.

7. Reheat the cylinder as described in Step 4, then remove and install it onto the wood blocks so that the valve spring side faces up (combustion side down).

NOTE
The same Honda valve guide driver tool is used for both removal and installation of the valve guide.

8. From the top side (valve spring side) of the cylinder head, drive in the new valve guide (**Figure 150**) until the projection height of the valve guide is within the specifications listed in **Table 1** and shown in **Figure 147**.

9. Repeat for each valve guide.

10. After the cylinder head has cooled to room temperature, ream the new valve guides as follows:
  a. Use the Honda 4.5 mm Valve Guide Reamer when reaming the valve guides. See your Honda dealer for the correct part number.
  b. Mount the reamer in a tap wrench.
  c. Apply cutting oil to both the new valve guide and the valve guide reamer.

CAUTION
***Always** rotate the valve guide reamer **clockwise** when removing and installing it in the valve guides. If the reamer is rotated counterclockwise, you will dull its cutting surfaces and damage the guide.*

  d. Rotate the reamer clockwise as shown in **Figure 151**. Continue to rotate the reamer and work it down through the entire length of the new valve

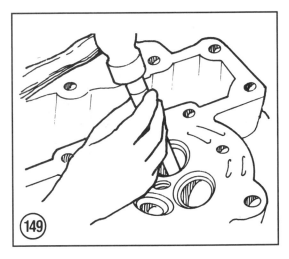

ENGINE

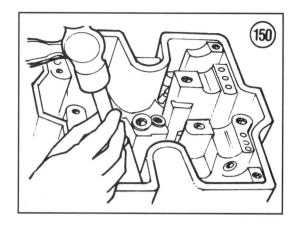

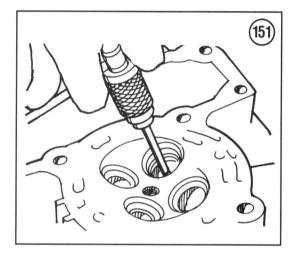

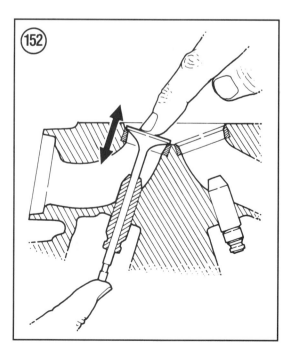

guide. Apply additional cutting oil during this procedure.

e. Rotate the reamer *clockwise* until the reamer has traveled all the way through the new valve guide.

f. Rotate the reamer *clockwise* and withdraw the reamer from the valve guide.

11. If necessary, repeat for any other valve guide.
12. Thoroughly clean the cylinder head and valve guides with solvent to wash out all metal particles. Dry with compressed air.
13. Measure the valve guide inside diameter with a small hole gauge or bore gauge (**Figure 144**). The valve guide should be within the service specifications listed in **Table 1**.
14. Reface the valve seats as described in this chapter.

Valve Seat Inspection

1. Clean the valves of all carbon, then rinse in solvent as described under Valve Inspection in this chapter.
2. The most accurate method of checking the valve seat width and position is to use Prussian blue or machinist's dye, available from auto parts stores. To check the valve seat with Prussian blue or machinist's dye, perform the following:

NOTE
Install the valves in their original locations when performing the following.

a. Thoroughly clean the valve face and valve seat with contact cleaner.
b. Spread a thin layer of Prussian blue or machinist's dye evenly on the valve face.
c. Insert the valve into its guide.
d. Support the valve with your fingers (**Figure 152**) and tap the valve up and down in the cylinder head. Do not rotate the valve or a false reading will result.
e. Remove the valve and examine the impression left by the Prussian blue or machinist's dye. If the impression left in the dye (on the valve or in the cylinder head) is not even and continuous and the valve seat width is not even and continuous within the specified tolerance in **Table 1**, the cylinder head valve seat must be reconditioned.

3. Closely examine the valve seat in the cylinder head (**Figure 153**). It should be smooth and even with a polished seating surface.

4. If the valve seat is okay, install the valve as described in this chapter.

5. If the valve seat is not correct, recondition the valve seat as described in this chapter.

Valve Seat Reconditioning

Special valve seat cutter tools and considerable expertise are required to recondition the valve seats in the cylinder head properly. You can save considerable money by removing the cylinder head(s) and taking just the cylinder head(s) to a dealer or machine shop and have the valve seats ground.

The following procedure is provided if you choose to perform this task yourself.

While the valve seat for both the intake valves and exhaust valves are machined to the same angles, different cutter sizes are required. The following Honda valve seat cutters (**Figure 154**) are required:

   a. 24.5 mm valve seat cutter (EX 45°).
   b. 29 mm valve seat cutter (IN 45°).
   c. 25 mm valve flat cutter (EX 32°).
   d. 30 mm valve flat cutter (IN 32°).
   e. 30 mm valve interior cutter (EX 60°).
   f. 26 mm valve interior cutter (IN 60°).
   g. 4.5 mm cutter holder.

NOTE
Follow the manufacturer's instructions when using valve facing equipment.

1. Carefully rotate and insert the solid pilot into the valve guide. Make sure the pilot is correctly seated.
2. Install the 45° cutter and T-handle onto the solid pilot.
3. Using the 45° cutter, descale and clean the valve seat with one or two turns (**Figure 155**).

CAUTION
*Measure the valve seat contact in the cylinder head (**Figure 156**) after each cut to make sure the contact area is correct and to avoid removing too much material. Overgrinding will sink the valves too far into the cylinder head, requiring replacement of the cylinder head.*

4. If the seat is still pitted or burned, turn the 45° cutter additional turns until the surface is clean. Refer to the previous CAUTION to avoid removing too much material from the cylinder head.

5. Measure the valve seat with a vernier caliper (**Figure 156**). Record the measurement to use as a reference point when performing the following.

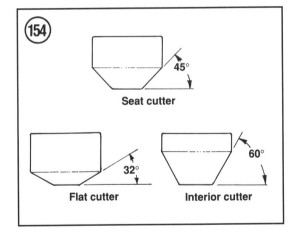

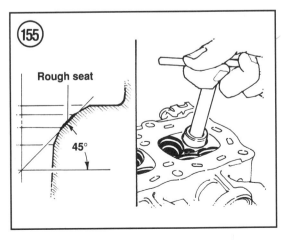

CAUTION
The 32° cutter removes material quickly. Work carefully and check your progress often.

6. Install the 32° cutter onto the solid pilot and lightly cut the seat to remove 1/4 of the existing valve seat (**Figure 157**).

7. Install the 60° cutter onto the solid pilot and lightly cut the seat to remove the lower 1/4 of the existing valve seat (**Figure 158**).

8. Measure the valve seat with a vernier caliper (**Figure 156**). Then fit the 45° cutter onto the solid pilot and cut the valve seat to the specified seat width listed in **Table 1**. See **Figure 159**.

9. When the valve seat width is correct, check valve seating as follows.

10. Remove the solid pilot from the cylinder head.

11. Inspect the valve seat-to-valve face impression as follows:

   a. Clean the valve seat with contact cleaner.
   b. Spread a thin layer of Prussian Blue or machinist's dye evenly on the valve face.
   c. Insert the valve into its guide.
   d. Support the valve with your fingers (**Figure 152**) and tap the valve up and down in the cylinder head. Do not rotate the valve or a false reading will result.
   e. Remove the valve and examine the impression left by the Prussian blue or machinist's dye.
   f. Measure the valve seat width as shown in **Figure 156**. Refer to **Table 1** for the correct seat width.
   g. The valve contact area should be approximately in the center of the valve seat area.

12. If the contact area is too high on the valve, or if it is too wide, use the 32° cutter and remove a portion of the top area of the valve seat material to lower or narrow the contact area (**Figure 157**).

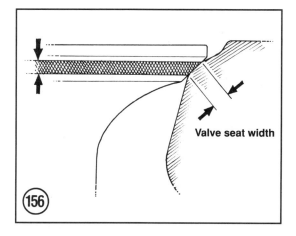

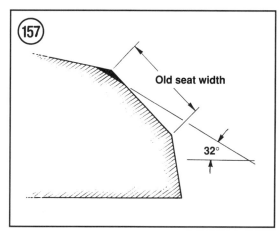

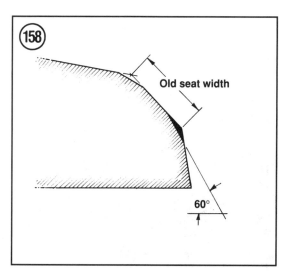

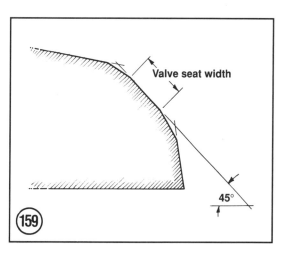

13. If the contact area is too low on the valve, or if it is too wide, use the 60° cutter and remove a portion of the lower area to raise and narrow the contact area (**Figure 158**).
14. After the desired valve seat position and angle is obtained, use the 45° cutter and very lightly clean off any burrs that may have been caused by the previous cuts.
15. When the contact area is correct, lap the valve as described in this chapter.
16. Repeat Steps 1-15 for all remaining valve seats.
17. Thoroughly clean the cylinder head and all valve components in solvent, then clean with detergent and hot water and finish with a final rinsing in cold water. Dry with compressed air. Then apply a light coat of engine oil to all non-aluminum metal surfaces to prevent any rust formation.

Valve Lapping

Valve lapping is a simple operation which can restore the valve seat without machining if the amount of wear or distortion is not too great.

This procedure should only be performed after determining that the valve seat width and outside diameter are within specifications.

1. Smear a light coating of fine grade valve lapping compound on the valve face seating surface.
2. Insert the valve into the head.
3. Wet the suction cup of the lapping stick and stick it onto the head of the valve (**Figure 160**). Lap the valve to the seat by spinning the lapping stick in both directions. Every 5 to 10 seconds, rotate the valve 180° in the valve seat to prevent uneven seat wear. Continue this action until the mating surfaces on the valve and seat are smooth and equal in size.
4. Closely examine valve seat in cylinder head (**Figure 153**). It should be smooth and even with a smooth, polished seating "ring."
5. Thoroughly clean the valves and cylinder head in solvent to remove all grinding compound. Compound left on the valves or cylinder head will cause excessive wear to engine components.
6. After the valve assemblies have been installed into the head, check the valve seal as follows:
   a. Support the head so that the combustion side faces down and pour a small amount of solvent into each intake port.
   b. There should be no leakage past the seat. If leakage occurs, combustion chamber will appear wet. If fluid leaks past any of the seats, disassemble that valve assembly and repeat the lapping procedure until there is no leakage.
   c. Repeat for the exhaust valves.

Valve Installation

Following your reference marks made during removal, install the valves in their original locations.

Refer to the following illustrations for this procedure:
   a. **Figure 128**: 1986-1989 models.
   b. **Figure 129**: 1990-on models.

NOTE
Oil seals should be replaced whenever a valve is removed.

1. Carefully slide a new oil seal (**Figure 140**) over the valve guide.
2. Turn the cylinder head over.

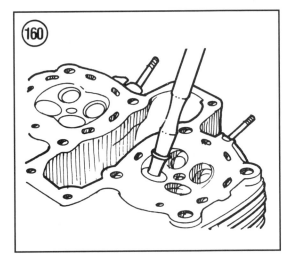

ENGINE

3. Coat a valve stem with molybdenum disulfide grease. To avoid damage to the valve stem seal, turn the valve slowly while inserting the valve into the cylinder head (**Figure 139**).

4. Install the inner spring seat (**Figure 137**).

5. Install the outer spring seat (**Figure 136**).

6. Position the inner spring with the close wound coils going in first (**Figure 161**) and install the inner spring.

7. Position the outer spring with the close wound coils going in first (**Figure 162**) and install the outer spring.

8. Install the retainer (**Figure 133**).

9. On 1990-on models, install the tappet hole protector into the valve lifter sliding surface; see the NOTE preceding Step 3 under *Valve Removal*.

CAUTION
To avoid loss of spring tension, do not compress the springs any more than necessary to install the keepers.

10. Compress the valve spring with a compressor tool and install the valve keepers (**Figure 132**).

Make sure both keepers fit snugly into the rounded groove in the valve stem.

11. Gradually loosen the valve spring compressor and remove it from the head.

12. Gently tap the end of the valve stem with a plastic hammer. This will ensure that the keepers (**Figure 163**) are properly seated.

13. Repeat for all valve assemblies.

14. Install the cylinder head as described under *Cylinder Head Installation* in this chapter.

OIL PAN, OIL STRAINER AND OIL PUMP

The oil strainer and oil pump are mounted within the lower crankcase and both can be removed with the engine in the frame. This procedure is shown with the engine removed from the frame for clarity.

Refer to **Figure 164** for this procedure.

Removal

1. Place the bike on the centerstand (models so equipped) or sidestand.

2. Remove the clutch as described under *Clutch Removal/Installation* in Chapter Five.

3. Remove the exhaust system as described under *Exhaust System Removal/Installation* in Chapter Seven.

4. Remove the bolt and washer (**Figure 165**) securing the oil pump drive sprocket. Remove the drive sprocket from the shaft. The sprocket can remain on the drive chain.

5. Remove the bolts securing the oil pan (**Figure 166**) and remove the oil pan and gasket. Discard the gasket as a new one must be installed.

6. Pull straight out and remove the oil strainer (**Figure 167**) from the oil pump.

7. Remove the bolts (and 1 nut on 1994 models) securing the oil crossover pipes and remove all 4 oil pipes (**Figure 168**). Don't lose the O-ring seals on each end where the pipes fit into the oil pump and the crankcase.

8. Remove the bolts (**Figure 169**) securing the oil pump assembly and remove the assembly. Don't lose the 2 locating dowels in the crankcase. Sometimes the dowels may stay with the oil pump.

9. Inspect the oil pan (**Figure 170**) for fractures or cracks. If the pan is damaged, replace it.

10. Inspect the oil pump as described in this chapter.

CHAPTER FOUR

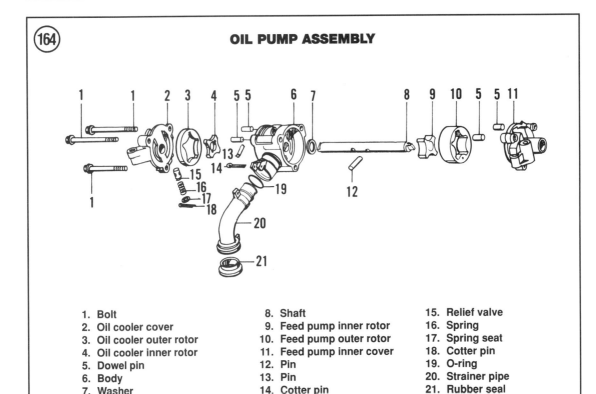

OIL PUMP ASSEMBLY

1. Bolt
2. Oil cooler cover
3. Oil cooler outer rotor
4. Oil cooler inner rotor
5. Dowel pin
6. Body
7. Washer
8. Shaft
9. Feed pump inner rotor
10. Feed pump outer rotor
11. Feed pump inner cover
12. Pin
13. Pin
14. Cotter pin
15. Relief valve
16. Spring
17. Spring seat
18. Cotter pin
19. O-ring
20. Strainer pipe
21. Rubber seal

ENGINE

169

170

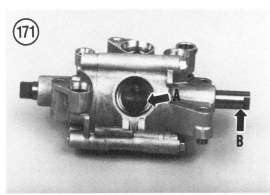

171

Installation

1. If the oil pump was disassembled, prime the oil pump. Add clean engine oil into the inlet opening (A, **Figure 171**) in the oil pump. Rotate the shaft (B, **Figure 171**) and continue to add oil and rotate the shaft until the oil comes out of the outlet openings (**Figure 172**).

2. Install the 2 locating dowels (**Figure 173**) in the oil pump.

3. Install the oil pump and tighten the bolts securely (**Figure 169**).

4. Check the condition of the O-ring seals on each end of the crossover pipes. Replace both on each pipe if either is starting to harden or deteriorate.

5. Install the crossover pipes (**Figure 168**) and push them down until they are completely seated in the crankcase and the oil pump. Install the bolts (or nut) securing the pipes and tighten securely.

6. Make sure the rubber seal is in place in the oil strainer pipe.

7. Install the strainer and align the notch on the strainer with the raised tab on the oil pump strainer pipe. Push the strainer on until it bottoms out.

8. Install a new pan gasket, then install the the oil pan and bolts. Tighten the bolts securely.

9. The "IN" mark (**Figure 174**) on the oil pump driven sprocket must face in toward the crankcase. Align the slot in the driven sprocket with the tab on the oil pump shaft (**Figure 175**). Install the washer and bolt (**Figure 176**) and tighten the bolt securely.

10. Install the clutch assembly as described in Chapter Five.

11. Install the exhaust system as described in Chapter Seven.

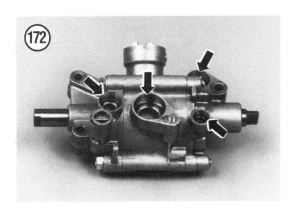

172

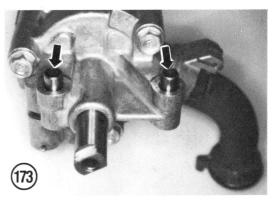

173

CHAPTER FOUR

12. Refill the engine with the recommended type and quantity of engine oil as described in Chapter Three.
13. Start the engine and check for leaks.

Disassembly

The oil pump has two sets of rotors. The secondary thin set of rotors pumps the oil directly to the oil cooler while the primary thicker set of rotors pumps oil to the engine assembly.

NOTE
Replacement parts are not available for the oil pump. If any of the external or internal components are worn or damaged, the entire oil pump assembly must be replaced.

1. Remove the cotter pin (**Figure 177**) securing the relief valve. Discard the cotter pin—never reuse a cotter pin, as it may break and fall out.
2. Remove the spring seat (**Figure 178**), spring and relief valve.

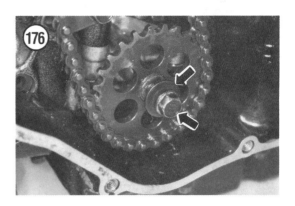

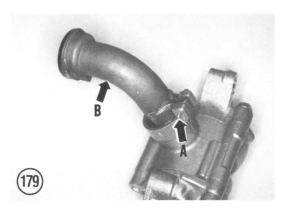

ENGINE

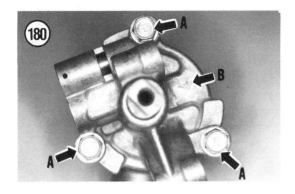

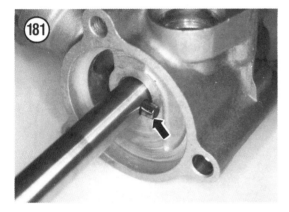

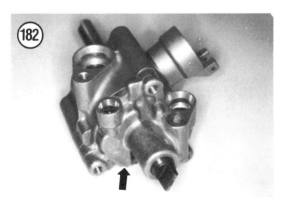

3. Remove the cotter pin (A, **Figure 179**) and remove the oil strainer pipe (B, **Figure 179**) from the oil pump. Discard the cotter pin—never reuse a cotter pin, as it may break and fall out.

4. Remove the bolts (A, **Figure 180**) securing the oil cooler side pump cover to the pump body. Remove the pump cover (B, **Figure 180**).

5. Remove the oil cooler side inner and outer rotors.

6. Remove the pin (**Figure 181**) from the shaft.

7. Turn the oil pump assembly around and remove the feed pump side cover (**Figure 182**) from the body and shaft.

8. Remove the feed pump side inner and outer rotors.

9. Remove the pin and washer (**Figure 183**) from the shaft.

10. Withdraw the shaft (A, **Figure 184**) from the body. Note the shaft-to-body orientation. This will help during installation.

11. Clean all parts in solvent and thoroughly dry. Coat all parts with fresh oil prior to installation.

Inspection

1. Inspect both sets of inner and outer rotors (**Figure 185**) for scratches and abrasion.

2. Inspect both outer covers and body (**Figure 186**) for cracks.

3. Inspect the inner surface of both outer covers (**Figure 187**) for severe scratches caused by the rotors.

4. Inspect the interior passageways of the oil pump body (**Figure 188**). Make sure that all oil sludge and foreign matter is removed.

5. Inspect the oil pump drive shaft (**Figure 189**) for wear or damage.

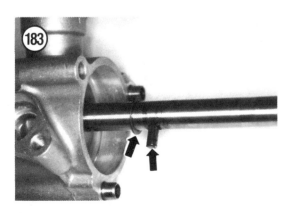

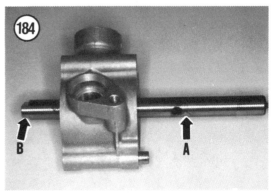

6. Inspect the oil strainer screen for breaks or damage. Replace if deteriorated or damaged.

7. Install the drive shaft into the body.

8. Install the feed side inner and outer rotors into the pump body.

9. Check the clearance between the inner tip and outer rotor (**Figure 190**) with a flat feeler gauge. If the clearance is greater than the service limit in **Table 1**, the oil pump must be replaced.

10. Check the clearance between the outer rotor and the body (**Figure 191**) with a flat feeler gauge. If the clearance is greater than the service limit in **Table 1** the oil pump must be replaced.

11. Check the rotor side clearance with a straightedge and flat feeler gauge. If the clearance is greater than the service limit in **Table 1** the oil pump must be replaced.

12. Remove the feed side inner and outer rotors from the pump body and turn the body over.

13. Install the oil cooler side inner and outer rotors into the pump body.

14. Check the clearance between the inner tip and outer rotor (**Figure 192**) with a flat feeler gauge. If the clearance is greater than the service limit in **Table 1**, the oil pump must be replaced.

15. Check the clearance between the outer rotor and the body (**Figure 193**) with a flat feeler gauge. If the clearance is greater than the service limit in **Table 1**, the oil pump must be replaced.

16. Check the rotor side clearance with a straightedge and flat feeler gauge. If the clearance is greater than the service limit in **Table 1**, the oil pump must be replaced.

17. Remove the oil cooler side inner and outer rotors and the shaft from the pump body.

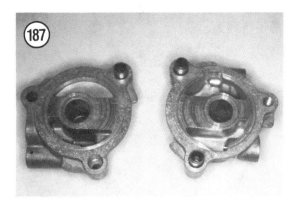

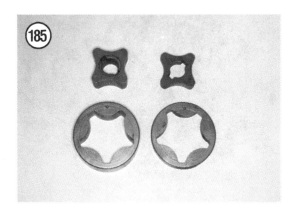

ENGINE

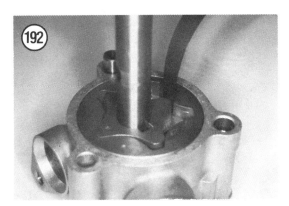

Assembly

1. Apply clean engine oil to all rotating parts prior to assembly.

2. Position the shaft (A, **Figure 184**) with the oil pump drive sprocket end (B, **Figure 184**) going in first and install the shaft into the body.

3. Install the washer and pin (**Figure 183**) onto the shaft.

4. Position the feed pump inner rotor (A, **Figure 194**) with the recess for the pin side going on first.

5. Install the feed pump inner rotor and index it into the pin and washer (B, **Figure 194**).

6. Install the feed pump outer rotor (**Figure 195**) onto the inner rotor.

7. Push the inner and outer rotors and shaft into the body until they stop (A, **Figure 196**).

8. If removed, install the locating dowels (B, **Figure 196**) into the body and install the feed pump side cover (**Figure 182**). Push the cover on until it bottoms out on the body.

9. Turn the oil pump assembly around.

10. Install the pin (**Figure 181**) into the shaft.

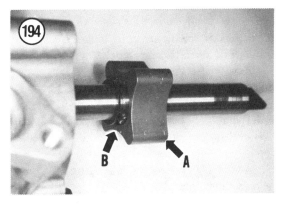

11. Install the oil cooler side inner rotor and index it properly with the pin on the shaft (**Figure 197**).

12. Install the oil cooler side outer rotor (A, **Figure 198**) and index it properly with the inner rotor.

13. If removed, install the locating dowels (B, **Figure 198**) into the body and install the oil cooler pump side cover (B, **Figure 180**). Push the cover on until it bottoms out on the body.

14. Install the bolts (A, **Figure 180**) securing the oil cooler side pump cover to the pump body and tighten securely.

15. After the oil pump is assembled, turn the shaft and make sure the oil pump turns freely with no binding.

16. Install relief valve, spring and the spring seat (**Figure 199**).

17. Install a new cotter pin (**Figure 177**) securing the relief valve. Bend the ends over completely.

18. Prime the oil pump. Add clean engine oil into the inlet opening in the oil pump. Rotate the shaft and continue to add oil and rotate the shaft until the oil comes out of the outlet openings (**Figure 200**).

19. Install a new O-ring seal (A, **Figure 201**) on the oil strainer pipe where it fits into the oil pump body.

20. Carefully scrub the strainer screen with a soft toothbrush; do not damage the screen.

21. Inspect the strainer screen for broken areas. This would allow small foreign particles to enter the oil pump and cause damage. If broken in any area, replace the strainer.

22. Install the oil strainer pipe (B, **Figure 179**) into the oil pump body. Install a new cotter pin (A, **Figure 179**) and bend the ends over completely. Never reuse a cotter pin as it may break and fall out.

23. Install a new rubber seal (B, **Figure 201**) onto the oil strainer pipe.

24. Install the oil pump assembly.

NOTE
*If the condition of the oil pump is doubtful, run the **Oil Pump Pressure Test** described in this chapter.*

Oil Pump Pressure Test

If the oil pump output is doubtful, the following test can be performed.

1. Warm the engine up to normal operating temperature (80° C [176° F]). Shut off the engine.

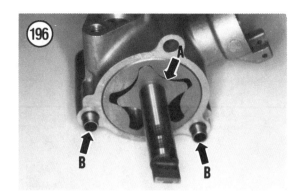
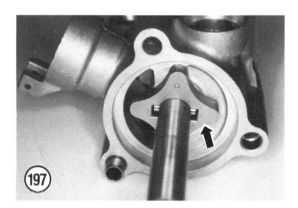
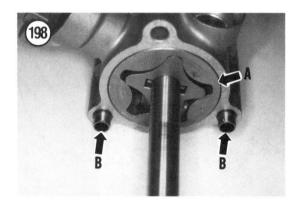
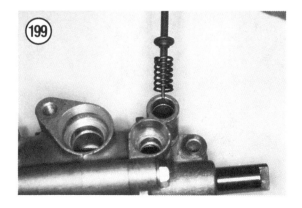

ENGINE

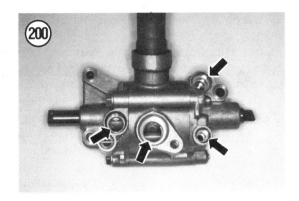

200

201

202

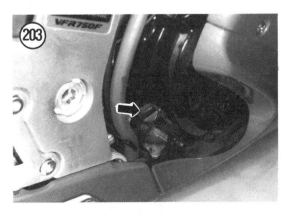

203

2. Place the bike on the centerstand (models so equipped) or side stand.

3. Check the engine oil level as follows:
   a. Allow the oil to settle.
   b. Unscrew the dipstick/filler cap and wipe it clean. Refer to **Figure 202** for 1986-1989 models or **Figure 203** for 1990-on models.
   c. Reinsert the dipstick/filler cap onto the threads in the hole; do not screw it in.
   d. Remove the dipstick/filler cap and check the oil level.
   e. The level should be between the 2 lines. If the level is below the lower line, add the recommended type engine oil to correct the level.

NOTE
Do not run this test with the oil level low or the test readings will be false.

4. Remove the right-hand lower fairing assembly as described under *Front Fairing Removal/Installation* in Chapter Thirteen.

5. Slide back the rubber boot (A, **Figure 204**) and remove the electrical wire from the oil pressure sending switch.

6. Remove the oil pressure sending switch (B, **Figure 204**).

7. Screw a portable oil pressure gauge into the switch hole in the crankcase.

NOTE
These can be purchased in an automotive or motorcycle supply store or from a Honda dealer. The Honda parts are No. 07506-3000000 (Oil Pressure Gauge) and No. 07510-4220100 (Oil Pressure Gauge Attachment).

204

8. Start the engine and run it at 5,000 rpm. The standard pressure is 490-588 kPa (71-85 psi) at 5,000 rpm and at 80° C (176° F). If the pressure is less than specified, the oil pump must be replaced.

9. Remove the portable oil pressure gauge.

10. Apply ThreeBond sealant, or equivalent, to the switch threads prior to installation. Tighten the switch to the torque specifications listed in **Table 2**.

11. Install the electrical wire to the top of the switch and tighten the screw securely. Make sure this connection is free of any oil residue or corrosion. It must make good electrical contact.

12. Slide the rubber boot back into position.

OIL COOLER

The factory equipped oil cooler is mounted to the front fairing mounting bracket below the headlight area.

Removal/Installation

Refer to **Figure 205** for this procedure.

1. Remove the lower fairing sections as described under *Front Fairing Removal/Installation* in Chapter Thirteen.

2. Drain the engine oil and remove the oil filter as described under *Engine Oil and Filter Change* in Chapter Three.

3. Place the drain pan underneath the oil cooler lines at the front of the crankcase.

4. Thoroughly clean off all road dirt and oil residue from the crankcase where the oil cooler lines are attached. This will prevent any foreign matter from entering the crankcase after the oil cooler lines are removed.

5. Remove the bolts securing both oil cooler lines (**Figure 206**) to the crankcase. Pull the oil lines away from the crankcase and allow the residual oil to drain out. Don't lose the O-ring seal behind each oil line fitting.

6. Place some shop cloths on top of the front fender to catch any oil that may spill out during oil cooler removal.

7. Remove the bolts (A, **Figure 207**) securing the oil cooler line to each side of the oil cooler.

8. Disconnect the oil line (B, **Figure 207**) from the oil cooler. Pull the oil line away from the oil cooler. Some additional residual oil will drain out the lower end of the line. Don't lose the O-ring seal behind each oil line fitting.

9. Release the hose clamp and disconnect the drain hose (C, **Figure 207**) from the oil cooler.

10. Repeat Step 7-9 for the other oil line and drain hose.

11. Move all electrical cables (A, **Figure 208**) out of the way in front of the oil cooler.

NOTE
The oil cooler will still be full of oil. In the next step, either plug the fittings at each end of the cooler with corks, duct tape or your fingers and try to hold the cooler horizontal while removing it

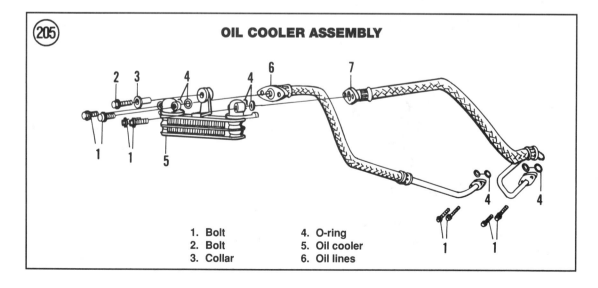

205 OIL COOLER ASSEMBLY

1. Bolt
2. Bolt
3. Collar
4. O-ring
5. Oil cooler
6. Oil lines

ENGINE

from the frame to avoid spilling oil on the front fender, wheel and brake caliper.

12. Remove the 2 bolts on 1986-1989 models or single bolt (B, **Figure 208**) on 1990-on models securing the oil cooler to the front fairing mounting bracket.

13. Carefully remove the oil cooler from the frame area being careful to not spill any oil out of the cooler. Wipe up any spilled oil immediately.

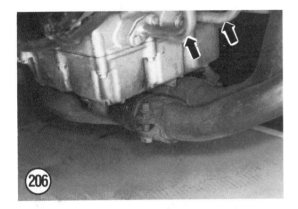

14. If necessary, remove any tie wraps or clamps and remove the oil lines from the frame. Be careful not to bend the metal sections of the lines during removal.

15. Install by reversing these steps while noting the following:
   a. Clean off all road dirt and oil residue from the oil cooler assembly prior to installation.
   b. Install *new* O-ring seals at all fittings during installation.
   c. Apply new engine oil to the O-rings before installing them.
   d. Install a new oil filter and refill the engine with the recommended type and quantity oil as described in Chapter Three.
   e. After starting the engine, check the oil cooler, drain plugs and coolant hose for leaks.

ALTERNATOR

An alternator is a form of electrical generator in which a magnetized field called a rotor revolves within a set of stationary coils called a stator. As the rotor revolves, alternating current is induced in the stator. The current is then rectified to direct current and used to operate the electrical accessories on the motorcycle and to charge the battery. The rotor is permanently magnetized.

The alternator rotor and stator testing procedures are covered in Chapter Eight.

Refer to the following illustrations for this procedure:
   a. **Figure 209**: 1986-1989 models.
   b. **Figure 210**: 1990-on models.

Rotor
Removal/Installation

NOTE
This procedure is shown on a 1986-1989 model. Where differences occur between these models and the 1990-on models, they are identified.

1. Place the bike on the centerstand (models so equipped) or sidestand.

2. Remove the lower fairing sections as described under *Front Fairing Removal/Installation* in Chapter Thirteen.

3. Disconnect the battery negative lead as described in Chapter Eight.

4. On 1990-on models, disconnect the alternator stator 3-pin white electrical connector containing 3 yellow wires from the main harness on the right-hand side of the bike.

5. Remove the bolts securing the alternator cover (**Figure 211**) and remove the cover and the gasket.

6. Remove the bolt (A, **Figure 212**) and washer (B, **Figure 212**) securing the alternator rotor.

7. Shift the transmission into gear and have an assistant apply the rear brake. This will keep the rotor from turning while removing the bolt.

CAUTION
Don't try to remove the rotor without a puller; any attempt to do so will ultimately lead to some form of damage to the engine and/or rotor. Many aftermarket pullers are available from motorcycle dealers or mail order houses. The cost of one of these pullers is low and it makes an excellent addition to any mechanic's tool box. If you can't buy or borrow one, have the dealer remove the rotor.

8. Screw in the rotor puller until it stops. Use the Honda rotor puller (part No. 07933-3290001 or 07733-0020001), K & N rotor puller (part No. 81-0170) (**Figure 213**) or equivalent.

9. Turn the rotor puller with a wrench until the rotor is free.

NOTE
If the rotor is difficult to remove, strike the end of the puller (not the rotor as it will be damaged) with a hammer a few times. This will usually break it loose.

CAUTION
If normal rotor removal attempts fail, do not force the puller, as the threads may be stripped out of the rotor, causing expensive damage. Take the bike to a dealer and have the rotor removed.

10. Remove the rotor from the crankshaft. Unscrew and remove the rotor puller from the rotor.

11. Inspect the inside of the rotor (**Figure 214**) for small bolts, washers or other metal "trash" that may have been picked up by the magnets. These small metal bits can cause severe damage to the alternator stator assembly.

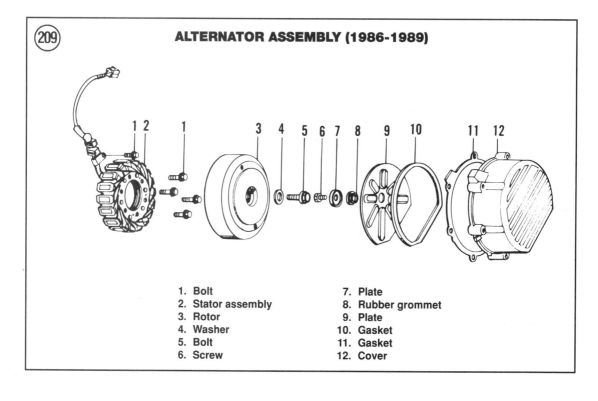

ALTERNATOR ASSEMBLY (1986-1989)

1. Bolt
2. Stator assembly
3. Rotor
4. Washer
5. Bolt
6. Screw
7. Plate
8. Rubber grommet
9. Plate
10. Gasket
11. Gasket
12. Cover

ENGINE

12. Inspect the keyway (**Figure 215**) for wear or damage. If damage is severe, replace the rotor.

13. Install by reversing these removal steps while noting the following:

   a. Use an aerosol electrical contact cleaner and clean all oil residue from the crankshaft taper where the rotor slides onto and the matching tapered surface in the rotor. This is to assure a good tight fit of the rotor onto the crankshaft.

   b. Be sure to install the washer (B, **Figure 212**) under the bolt.

   c. Tighten the rotor bolt (A, **Figure 212**) to torque specification listed in **Table 2**.

   d. Make sure the electrical connector is tight and free of corrosion.

Stator
Removal/Installation

NOTE
This procedure is shown on a 1986-1989 model. Where differences occur

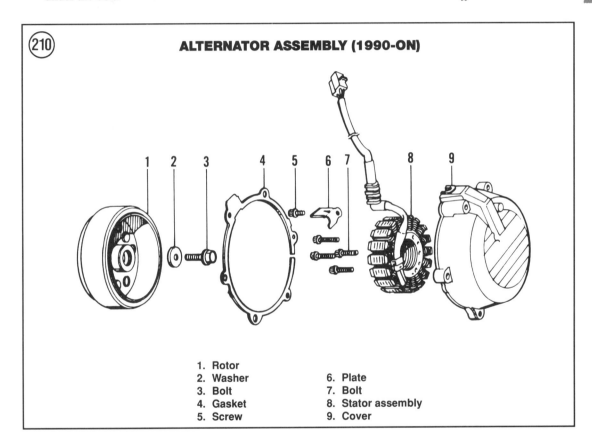

ALTERNATOR ASSEMBLY (1990-ON)

1. Rotor
2. Washer
3. Bolt
4. Gasket
5. Screw
6. Plate
7. Bolt
8. Stator assembly
9. Cover

between these models and the 1990-on models, they are identified.

1. Remove the alternator rotor as described in this chapter.
2. On 1986-1989 models, disconnect the alternator stator 3-pin white electrical connector containing 3 yellow wires from the main harness.
3. Remove the electrical harness from the clips on the frame and engine.
4A. On 1986-1989 models, perform the following:
   a. Remove the bolt and wire clamp (A, **Figure 216**) securing the wire to the cylinder block.
   b. Remove the bolts (B, **Figure 216**) securing the alternator stator to the cylinder block and crankcase.
   c. Carefully pull the rubber grommet (C, **Figure 216**) and electrical wire harness from the cylinder block and remove the wires from the frame. Note the path of the wire harness, as it must be routed the same during installation.
4B. On 1990-on models, perform the following:
   a. Remove the bolt and wire clamp (A, **Figure 217**) securing the wire to the alternator cover.
   b. Remove the bolts (B, **Figure 217**) securing the alternator stator to the alternator cover.
   c. Carefully pull the rubber grommet and electrical wire (C, **Figure 217**) harness from the alternator cover.
5. Install by reversing these removal steps while noting the following:
   a. Be sure to install the wire clamp securing the wiring. If the clamp is left off the rotor may rub against the wires, wear off the insulation and cause a short in the circuit.
   b. Make sure the rubber grommet is correctly positioned in the cylinder block groove (1986-1989 models) or alternator cover groove (1990-on models).
   c. Make sure that the electrical wire harness is routed through the frame exactly as before.
   d. Make sure the electrical connector is free of corrosion and is tight.

CYLINDER BLOCK AND CRANKCASE

The cylinder block and crankcase are made of die-cast aluminum and matched as a set. The mating of the 2 parts is a precision fit with no gasket at the

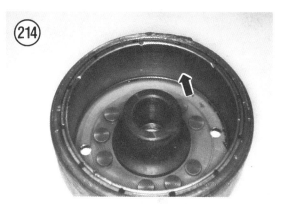

ENGINE

joint, only a thin layer of gasket sealer. The cylinder block and crankcase should be handled carefully during cleaning and inspection to avoid damaging the bearing and mating surfaces.

The cylinders are an integral part of the upper crankcase, which is referred to as the cylinder block. The lower portion is referred to as the crankcase.

Service to the lower end requires that the engine be removed from the bike's frame.

Disassembly

1. Remove the engine from the frame as described in this chapter.
2. Remove the following exterior assemblies from the cylinder block/crankcase assembly:
    a. Cylinder heads: this chapter.
    b. Alternator: this chapter.
    c. Starter clutch: this chapter.
    d. Oil pan, oil pump: this chapter.
    e. External shift mechanism: Chapter Six.
    f. Clutch: Chapter Five.
    g. Water pump: Chapter Nine.
    h. Starter motor: Chapter Eight.
    i. Neutral switch: Chapter Eight.
    j. Oil pressure switch: Chapter Eight.

CAUTION
The bolts had a thread locking agent applied to the threads during assembly and may be difficult to loosen. Use an inpact driver and applicable socket to break the bolts loose.

3. Remove the bolts securing the transmission main shaft bearing retainer (**Figure 218**) and remove the retainer.
4. Loosen the cylinder block bolts in 2-3 stages in a crisscross pattern to avoid warpage. Remove all bolts. Refer to **Figure 219** and **Figure 220**.
5. Turn the engine upside down on the workbench.

CAUTION
When removing the crankcase bolts, leave the eight 9 mm crankshaft bearing bolts for last.

6. Loosen the crankcase bolts in 2-3 stages in a crisscross pattern to avoid warpage. Loosen the bolts in the following order:
    a. A, **Figure 221**: 6 mm bolts.
    b. B, **Figure 221**: 8 mm bolts.

190   CHAPTER FOUR

c. **Figure 222**: 9 mm bolts.

7. Tap around the perimeter of the crankcase and cylinder block with a plastic mallet—do not use a metal hammer, as it will cause damage.

8. Pull the crankcase off of the cylinder block. Don't lose the locating dowels.

CAUTION
If it is necessary to pry the crankcase apart, do it very carefully so that you do not mar the gasket surfaces. If you do, the cases will leak and must be replaced as a set. They cannot be repaired.

9. Remove the transmission assemblies as described under *Transmission Removal* in Chapter Six.

10. Remove the gearshift drum and forks as described under *Internal Gearshift Mechanism Removal/Installation* in Chapter Six.

11. Remove the pistons and connecting rods as described in this chapter.

12. Remove the crankshaft as described in this chapter.

NOTE
In the following step, the numbers assigned to the bearing inserts relate to the cylinder numbers (1, 2, 3 and 4) as shown in Figure 223.

13. Remove the crankshaft main bearing inserts from the cylinder block (upper) and crankcase (lower). Mark the back sides of the inserts with a "1," "2," "3" and "4" and "U" (upper) or "L" (lower). Start from the left-hand side, so they can be reinstalled into the same position (**Figure 224**).

NOTE
The left-hand side refers to the engine as it sits in the bike's frame—not necessarily as it sits on your workbench. If the cylinder block or crankcase is turned over, be sure to compensate for that.

Inspection

The following procedure requires the use of highly specialized and expensive measuring instruments. If such instruments are not readily available, have the measurements performed by a dealer or qualified machine shop.

NOTE
The cylinders bores must be cleaned thoroughly before attempting any measurements, if not thoroughly cleaned, incorrect readings may be obtained.

1. Remove all old gasket residue material from both the cylinder block and crankcase mating surfaces.

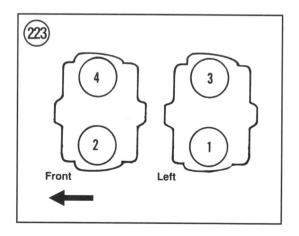

ENGINE

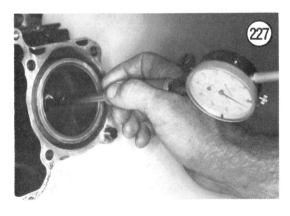

2. Soak with solvent any old cylinder head gasket material that may be stuck to the top surface of the cylinder block (**Figure 225**). Use a broad-tipped *dull* chisel and gently scrape off all gasket residue. Do not gouge the sealing surfaces, as oil and air leaks will result.

3. Thoroughly clean the inside and outside of the cylinder block and the crankcase with cleaning solvent. Dry with compressed air. Make sure there is no solvent residue left in either part, as it will contaminate the new engine oil.

4. Check all bolts and threaded holes for stripping, cross-threading or deposit buildup. Threaded holes should be blown out with compressed air, as dirt buildup in the bottom of a hole may prevent the bolt from being torqued properly. Replace damaged bolts and washers.

5. Inspect machined surfaces for burrs, cracks or other damage (**Figure 226**). Repair minor damage with a fine-cut file or oilstone.

6. Make sure that all oil passages throughout the cylinder block and crankcase are clean.

7. Apply a light coat of engine oil to the cylinder walls to prevent any rust formation.

8. After the cylinder block has been thoroughly cleaned, place a straightedge across the cylinder block/cylinder head gasket surfaces at several points. Measure the warpage by inserting a flat feeler gauge between the straightedge and the cylinder block at each location. There should be no warpage; if a small amount is present, it can be resurfaced by a dealer or qualified machine shop. If the cylinder head is warped in any direction by 0.10 mm (0.004 in.) or more, it must be replaced.

9. Measure the cylinder bores with a cylinder gauge (**Figure 227**) or inside micrometer at points near the top, in the middle and toward the bottom as shown in **Figure 228**. Measure in 2 axes—in line with the piston pin and at 90° to the pin. If the taper or out-of-round is greater than 0.05 mm (0.002 in.), the cylinders must be rebored to the next oversize and new pistons and rings installed. Rebore all cylinders even though only one cylinder requires boring. All 4 cylinders must be the same size after boring is completed.

NOTE
The new pistons should be obtained first before the cylinder block is rebored so that the pistons can be measured; slight manufacturing tolerances must be taken

into account to determine the actual size and the working clearance. Each cylinder must be bored to match one specific piston only. The standard and service limit dimensions for piston-to-cylinder clearance are listed in **Table 1**.

NOTE
*The maximum wear limit for cylinder bores is listed in **Table 1**. If any cylinder is worn to this limit, the cylinder block and the lower crankcase must be replaced as a set. Never rebore a cylinder if the finished rebored diameter will be to this dimension or larger.*

10. If the cylinders are not worn past the service limit, check the bore surface (A, **Figure 229**) carefully for scratches or gouges. If damaged in any way, the bore will require boring and reconditioning.

11. If the cylinders require reboring, remove all dowel pins (B, **Figure 229**) from the cylinder block prior to taking it to a dealer or machine shop for service.

12. After the cylinders have been serviced, perform the following:

CAUTION
A combination of soap and hot water is the only solution that will completely clean cylinder walls. Solvent and kerosene cannot wash fine grit out of cylinder crevices. Any grit left in the cylinders will act as a grinding compound and cause premature wear to the new rings.

a. Wash each cylinder bore in hot soapy water. This is the only way to clean the cylinders of the fine grit material left from the bore and honing procedure.
b. Also wash out any fine grit material from the cooling cores surrounding each cylinder.
c. After washing the cylinder walls, run a clean white cloth through each cylinder wall. It should *not* show any traces of grit or debris. If the rag is the slightest bit dirty, the wall is not thoroughly cleaned and must be rewashed.
d. After the cylinder is cleaned, lubricate the cylinder walls with clean engine oil to prevent the cylinder liners from rusting.

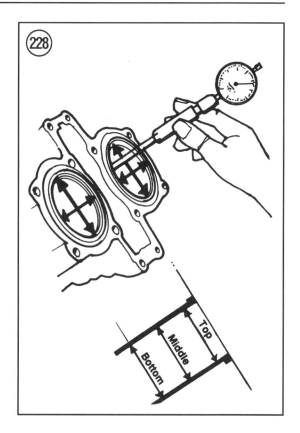

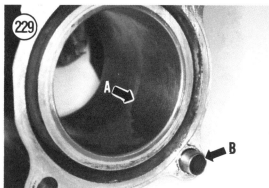

ENGINE

13. Make sure the oil control orifices in the crankcase are clear and open. Refer to **Figure 230** and **Figure 231**. Clean out with compressed air.

14. Inspect the threads for the oil filter. Clean off with a wire brush if necessary. If the threads are damaged, clean them up with an appropriate size metric thread die.

Do not coat this area with sealant

Assembly

Prior to installation of all parts, coat rotating surfaces, not gasket sealing surfaces, with assembly oil or engine oil. Assemble with the cylinder block upside-down.

NOTE
In the following step, the numbers assigned to the bearing inserts relate to the cylinder numbers (1, 2, 3 and 4).

1. Install the main bearing inserts in both the cylinder block and the crankcase. If reusing old bearings, make sure that they are installed in the same location (**Figure 224**). Refer to marks made in *Disassembly*, Step 13.
2. Install the gearshift drum and forks as described in Chapter Six.
3. Install the transmission shafts as described in Chapter Six. Move the gears on both shafts into the NEUTRAL psotion.
4. Install the piston/connecting rods as described in this chapter.
5. Apply assembly oil to the main bearing inserts. Install the crankshaft assembly as described in this chapter.
6. Install the locating dowels (A, **Figure 224**) at the side and at the rear (A, **Figure 232**).
7. Position the oil control orifice with the larger opening facing down toward the cylinder block and install the oil control orifice and O-ring (B, **Figure 232**). into the cylinder block.
8. Make sure both the crankcase and the cylinder block sealing surfaces are clean and dry. Clean both surfaces with aerosol electrical contact cleaner and wipe dry with a lint-free cloth.

NOTE
Use ThreeBond No. 1207, or equivalent gasket sealer. When selecting an equivalent, avoid thick and hard-setting materials.

9. Apply a light coat of gasket sealer to the sealing surfaces of the cylinder block (C, **Figure 232**) and the crankcase (B, **Figure 224**). Cover only flat surfaces, not curved bearing surfaces. Make the coating as thin as possible or the cases can shift and hammer out the bearings. Do not apply sealant close to the edge of the bearing inserts (**Figure 233**) as it would restrict oil flow.

NOTE
Make sure the crankshaft main bearing inserts are correctly positioned and still locked in place.

10. In the crankcase, rotate the shift drum into NEUTRAL. The shift forks will automatically locate in the NEUTRAL position.

11. Position the crankcase onto the cylinder block. Set the rear portion down first and lower the rear while making sure the shift forks engage properly into the transmission assemblies as follows:
   a. Right- and left-hand shift forks into the countershaft gears.
   b. Center shift fork into the mainshaft gear.

12. Lower the crankcase completely, making sure the locating dowels are seated correctly.

CAUTION
*Do not install any crankcase bolts until the sealing surface around the entire crankcase perimeter has seated completely as shown in **Figure 234**.*

13. Prior to installing any bolts, slowly spin the transmission countershaft, turn the shift drum by hand and shift the transmission through all 5 gears. This is done to check to make sure the shift forks are properly engaged.

14. Apply clean engine oil to the threads and to the under side seating area of all crankcase bolts. Refer to **Figure 235** and install the crankcase bolts only finger-tight at this time.

15. Tighten all bolts in 2-3 stages in a crisscross pattern. Tighten to the torque specifications listed in **Table 2**.

16. Turn the crankcase assembly over.

CAUTION
Be sure to install the sealing washers under the two 10 mm bolts on the left-hand side. Failure to do so will result in an oil leak.

17. Apply clean engine oil to the threads and to the under side seating area of all cylinder block bolts. Refer to **Figure 236** and install the cylinder block only finger-tight at this time.

18. Tighten all bolts in 2-3 stages in a crisscross pattern. Tighten to the torque specifications listed in **Table 2**.

19. Install the transmission main shaft bearing retainer (**Figure 218**). Apply red Loctite (No. 271) to the bolt threads prior to installation and tighten the screws securely.

20. Install the following exterior assemblies onto the crankcase:
   a. Oil pressure switch: Chapter Eight.
   b. Neutral switch: Chapter Eight.
   c. Starter motor: Chapter Eight.
   d. Water pump: Chapter Nine.
   e. Clutch: Chapter Five.
   f. External shift mechanism: Chapter Six.

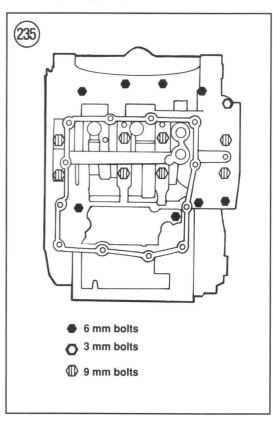

● 6 mm bolts
◯ 3 mm bolts
⬢ 9 mm bolts

ENGINE

g. Oil pan, oil pump: this chapter.
h. Starter clutch: this chapter.
i. Alternator: this chapter.
j. Cylinder heads: this chapter.

21. Install the engine as described in this chapter.
22. Fill the crankcase with the recommended type and quantity of engine oil. Refer to Chapter Three.

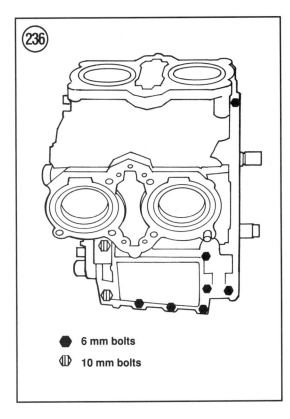

- ⬢ 6 mm bolts
- ⬗ 10 mm bolts

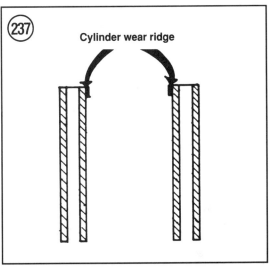

Cylinder wear ridge

23. Fill the cooling system with the recommended coolant. Refer to Chapter Three.

PISTON AND CONNECTING RODS

The engine must be removed from the frame and the crankcase disassembled in order to remove the pistons and connecting rods. The pistons and connecting rods are removed through the top of the cylinder bore.

Piston and Connecting Rod Removal

1. Remove the engine as described in this chapter.
2. Separate the cylinder block and the crankcase as described in this chapter.
3. Measure the connecting rod big end side clearance. Insert a flat feeler gauge between a connecting rod big end and either crankshaft machined web. Record the clearance for each connecting rod and compare to the specifications listed in **Table 1**. If the clearance is greater than specified, replace the connecting rods and/or crankshaft.
4. Mark the piston crown with the corresponding cylinder number so the piston will be reinstalled in the correct cylinder. Refer to **Figure 223** for cylinder numbers.

CAUTION
*If disassembling a well run-in engine, inspect the top of the cylinder bores for a ridge where the piston ring reaches the top of its travel (**Figure 237**). Perform Step 5 only if there is a ridge present.*

5. If there is a ridge at the top of any cylinder bore, the ridge must be removed with an automotive type ridge reamer. Do one cylinder at a time as follows:
   a. Rotate the crankshaft until the piston in the cylinder to be worked on is at the bottom of its travel.
   b. Place an oil-soaked shop cloth down into that cylinder over the piston to collect the cuttings. Remove the ridge and/or deposits from the top of the cylinder bore with a ridge reamer.
   c. Turn the crankshaft until that piston is at top dead center and remove the rag and the cuttings. Make sure to remove *all cuttings* as they may scratch the cylinder wall during piston removal.

Make sure that *none* of the cuttings fall into the water jacket surrounding the cylinder bore.

d. Repeat for all cylinders.

6. Split the crankcases as described under *Crankcase Disassembly* in this chapter.

7. Remove the transmission main shaft assembly.

NOTE
Prior to disassembly, mark the rods and caps. Number them "1," "2," "3" and "4" (Figure 238) starting from the left-hand side. The left-hand side refers to the engine sitting in the bike frame—not as it sits on your workbench. A center punch and hammer will also work. Use single, double, triple or four dots to mark the rods and caps. The No. 4 rod and piston assembly are already removed.

8. Remove the nuts (**Figure 239**) securing the connecting rod caps and remove the caps.

9. Carefully remove the connecting rods and piston assemblies out through the top of the cylinder bore.

10. Mark the back of each bearing insert with the cylinder number and "U" (upper) or "L" (lower).

Piston and Connecting Rod Installation

1. Apply molybdenum disulfide grease to the bearing inserts, crankpins and connecting rod bolt threads.

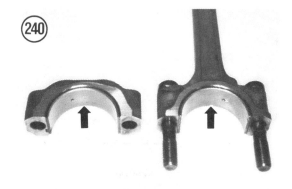

CAUTION
Do not interchange the bearing inserts from the front and rear connecting rods. The location of the oil hole in the insert is in a different location, and if interchanged, it will block the oil hole in the connecting rod. This misalignment will restrict oil flow, causing expensive engine damage.

NOTE
If the old bearing inserts are reused, be sure they are installed into their original positions; refer to Removal, Step 9.

2. Install the bearing inserts into each connecting rod and cap (**Figure 240**). Align the oil holes in the upper bearing inserts (**Figure 241**). Make sure they are locked into place correctly (**Figure 242**).

ENGINE

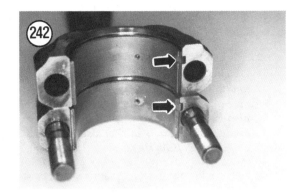

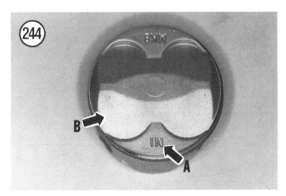

3. Install a piece of rubber or vinyl tubing onto the connecting rod bolts (**Figure 243**) so the crankshaft bearing surface will not be damaged by the connecting bolts during installation.

4. Apply a light coat of engine oil to the cylinder walls and to the piston rings prior to installation.

5. Install a piston ring compressor onto the piston.

6. Position the piston with the "IN" mark (A, **Figure 244**) toward the V-portion (intake side) of the cylinder block.

7. Carefully install the piston and connecting rod assembly into the correct cylinder (**Figure 245**).

8. Remove the ring compressor and carefully push the piston and connecting rod assembly all the way down. Guide the connecting rod onto the crankshaft so the bearing surface will not be damaged by the connecting rod during installation.

CAUTION
Be sure to install the correct rod cap onto its respective connecting rod. Refer to marks made during disassembly (Figure 246).

9. Install the connecting rods caps and nuts (**Figure 239**). Tighten the cap nuts evenly in 2-3 steps to the torque specifications listed in **Table 2**.

10. After all rod caps have been installed, carefully rotate the crankshaft several times and check that the bearings are not too tight. Make sure there is no binding.

Piston Disassembly

WARNING
The edges of all piston rings are very sharp. Be careful when handling them to avoid cut fingers.

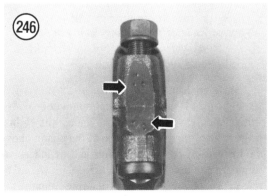

1. Remove the piston rings as described in this chapter.

2. Before removing the piston, place the connecting rod in a vise with soft jaws. Rock the piston as shown in **Figure 247**. Any rocking motion (do not confuse with the normal sliding motion) indicates wear on the piston pin or piston pin bore (more likely a combination of both). Mark the piston, pin and rod so they will be reassembled in the same set.

NOTE
Discard the piston circlips. New circlips must be installed during reassembly.

3. Remove the clip (**Figure 248**) from each side of the piston pin bore. Hold your thumb over one edge of the clip when removing it to prevent it from springing out.

4. Use a proper size wooden dowel or socket extension and push out the piston pin.

CAUTION
Be careful when removing the pin to avoid damaging the connecting rod. If it is necessary to tap the pin gently to remove it, be sure that the piston is properly supported.

5. If the piston pin is difficult to remove, heat the piston and pin with a small butane torch. The pin will probably push right out. If not, heat the piston to about 60° C (140° F), i.e., until it is too warm to touch, but not excessively hot. If the pin is still difficult to push out, use a special tool as shown in **Figure 249**.

6. Lift the piston off the connecting rod.

Piston Inspection

NOTE
Make sure to renumber the piston crowns after performing Step 1. Used pistons must be reinstalled in their original cylinders.

1. Carefully clean the carbon from the piston crown (B, **Figure 244**) with a chemical remover or with a soft scraper. Do not remove or damage the carbon ridge around the circumference of the piston above the top ring. If the pistons, rings and cylinders are found to be dimensionally correct, they can be reused. The removal of the carbon ring from the top edge of the pistons will promote excessive oil consumption.

CAUTION
Do not wire brush piston skirts or ring lands. The wire brush removes aluminum and increases piston clearance. It also rounds the corners of the ring lands, which results in decreased support for the piston rings.

2. After cleaning the piston, examine the crown. There should be no wear or damage. If the crown appears pecked or spongy-looking, also check the

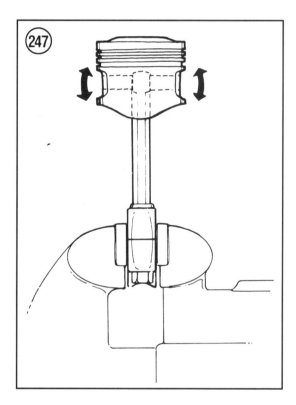

ENGINE

spark plug, valves and combustion chamber for aluminum deposits. If these deposits are found, the cylinder(s) is suffering from excessive heat caused by a lean fuel mixture or preignition.

3. Examine each ring groove for burrs, dented edges and wide wear. Pay particular attention to the top compression ring groove, as it usually wears more than the other grooves. Because the oil rings are constantly bathed in oil, these rings and grooves wear little compared to compression rings and their grooves. If there is evidence of oil ring groove wear or if the oil ring assembly is tight and difficult to remove, the piston skirt may have collapsed due to excessive heat and is permanently deformed. Replace the pistons.

4. Check the oil control holes (**Figure 250**) in the piston for carbon or oil sludge buildup. Clean the holes with a small diameter drill bit by hand.

5. Check the piston skirts (**Figure 251**) for cracks or other damage. If a piston(s) shows signs of partial seizure (bits of aluminum build-up on the piston skirts), the pistons should be replaced and the cylinders bored (if necessary) to reduce the possibility of engine noise and further piston seizure.

NOTE
If the piston skirts are worn or scuffed unevenly from side to side, the connecting rod may be bent or twisted.

6. Measure the piston pin bore (**Figure 252**) with a telescoping gauge and measure the outside diameter of the piston pin with a micrometer (**Figure 253**). Compare against dimensions given in **Table 1**. Replace the piston and piston pin as a set if either is worn.

7. Inspect the piston pin for chrome flaking or cracks. Replace if necessary.

8. Oil the piston pin and install it in the connecting rod. Slowly rotate the piston pin and check for radial play (**Figure 254**). If any play exists, the piston pin should be replaced, providing the connecting rod bore is in good condition.

9. Inspect the piston pin clip groove (**Figure 255**) on each side of the piston. If the groove is damaged, replace the piston.

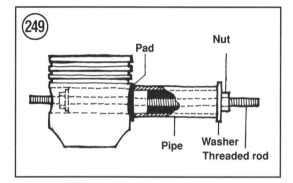

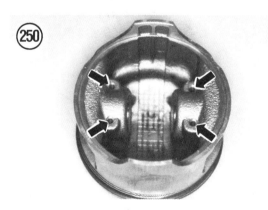

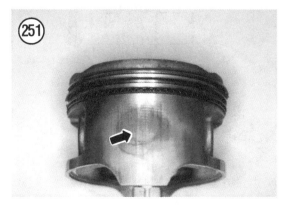

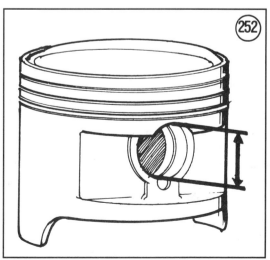

10. Install a new piston pin circlip in each piston circlip groove and check the groove for wear or circlip looseness by pulling the circlip from side to side. If the circlip has any side play, the groove is worn and the piston must be replaced. Discard these clips after removing them.

11. Measure piston-to-cylinder clearance as described under *Piston Clearance* in this chapter.

12. If damage or wear indicate piston replacement, select new pistons as described under *Piston Clearance* in this chapter.

Piston Clearance Measurement

1. Make sure the piston and cylinder walls are clean and dry.
2. Measure the inside diameter of the cylinder bore at a point 13 mm (1/2 in.) from the upper edge with a bore gauge.
3. Measure the outside diameter of the piston across the skirt (**Figure 256**) at right angles to the piston pin. Measure at a distance 10 mm (0.4 in.) up from the bottom of the piston skirt.
4. Piston clearance is the difference between the maximum piston diameter and the minimum cylinder diameter. Subtract the dimension of the piston from the cylinder dimension. If the clearance exceeds the dimension listed in **Table 1** the cylinder should be rebored to the next oversize and a new piston installed.

NOTE
If the cylinder diameters are still within specification, new pistons can be installed without reboring. New pistons will take up some of the excessive piston-to-cylinder clearance. Check carefully before deciding to rebore or to just use new pistons.

5. To establish a final overbore dimension with a new piston, add the new piston skirt measurement to the specified piston-to-cylinder clearance. This will determine the dimension for the cylinder overbore size. Remember, do not exceed the cylinder maximum inside diameter listed in **Table 1**.
6. Oversized pistons are available in 0.25 and 0.50 mm increments.

Piston Assembly

Refer to **Figure 257** for this procedure.

1. Apply molybdenum disulfide grease to the inside surface of the connecting rod small end. Apply fresh engine oil to the piston pin and piston pin bore.
2. Insert the piston pin into the piston until its end extends slightly beyond the inside of the boss (**Figure 258**).
3. The front cylinder connecting rods are marked "ML7-F" (**Figure 259**) or "MK8-F."
4. Place the front cylinder piston over the connecting rod, with the "IN" mark (A, **Figure 260**) facing in the same direction as the oil hole (B, **Figure 260**) on the rod. Be sure to install the correct piston (No. 1, 2, 3 or 4) onto the same rod from which it was removed.
5. The rear cylinder connecting rods are marked "ML7-R" OR "MK8-R."
6. Place the rear cylinder piston over the connecting rod, with the "IN" mark (A, **Figure 261**) facing in the opposite direction as the oil hole (B, **Figure 261**)

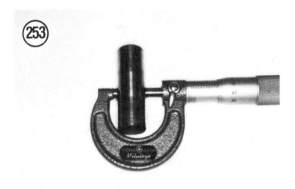

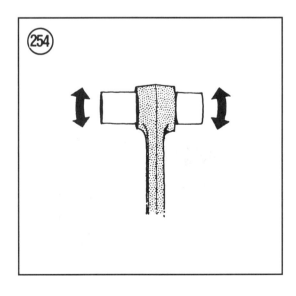

ENGINE

on the rod. Be sure to install the correct piston (No. 1, 2, 3 or 4) onto the same rod from which it was removed.

7. Line up the piston pin with the holes in the piston and connecting rod and push the pin into the piston (**Figure 262**) until its ends are even with the clip grooves.

NOTE
If the piston pin does not slide in easily, heat the piston with a hair dryer until it

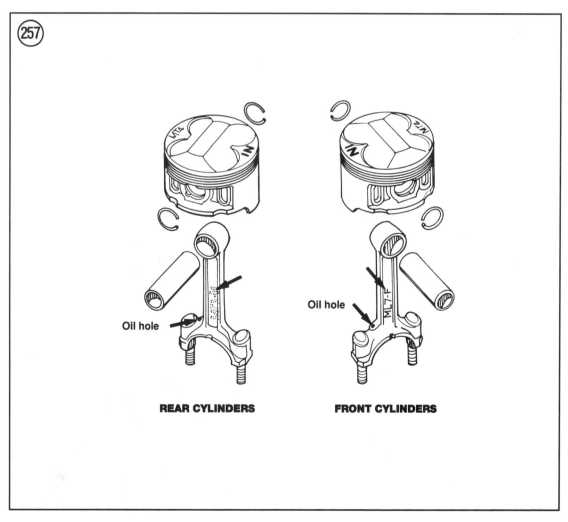

is too warm to touch but not excessively hot (60° C/140° F). Continue to drive the piston pin while holding the piston so the rod does not have to take any shock. Drive the piston pin in until it is centered in the rod. If the pin is still difficult to install, use the special tool used during the removal sequence.

NOTE
*In the next step, install the new clips with the gap away from the cutout in the piston (**Figure 263**).*

8. Install new piston pin clips in the ends of the pin boss. Make sure they are seated in the grooves.

9. Check installation by rocking the piston back and forth around the piston pin axis and from side to side along the axis. It should rotate freely back and forth but not from side to side.

10. Repeat Steps 1-9 for all remaining pistons.

11. Install the piston rings as described in this chapter.

Piston Rings
Removal/Installation

WARNING
The edges of all piston rings are very sharp. Be careful when handling them to avoid cut fingers.

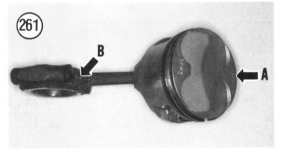

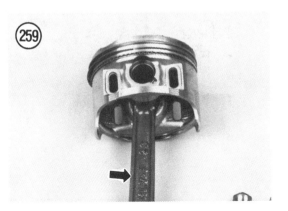

ENGINE

1. Measure the side clearance of each ring in its groove with a flat feeler gauge (**Figure 264**) and compare with dimensions listed in **Table 1**. If the clearance is greater than specified, the rings must be replaced. If the clearance is still excessive with the new rings, the piston must be replaced.

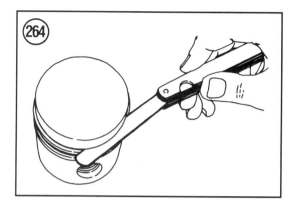

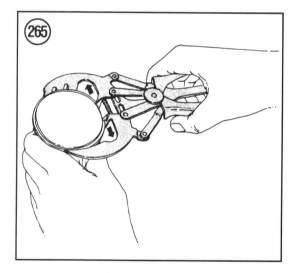

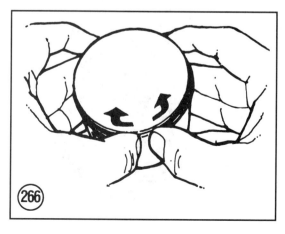

CAUTION
If you are going to reuse the piston rings, you must work carefully to prevent breakage. Used rings must be installed in their original positions; mark the rings to prevent incorrect reassembly.

NOTE
*There are two ways to remove the rings: with a ring expander tool (**Figure 265**) or with your hands (**Figure 266**). The ring expander tool is useful because it removes the rings without damaging them or scratching the piston. If you don't have a ring expander tool, remove the rings by carefully spreading their end gaps with your thumbs and sliding them off the top of the piston one at a time.*

2. Remove the top ring with a ring expander tool or by spreading the ring ends with your thumbs and lifting the ring up and over the piston. Repeat for the remaining rings one at a time.

3. Carefully remove all carbon from the ring grooves. Inspect grooves carefully for burrs, nicks or broken and cracked lands. Recondition or replace the piston if necessary.

4. Roll each ring around its piston groove as shown in **Figure 267** to check for binding. Minor binding may be cleaned up with a fine-cut file.

5. Measure the rings for wear as shown in **Figure 268**. Place each ring, one at a time, into the cylinder and push it in about 20 mm (3/4 in.) with the crown of the piston to ensure that the ring is square in the cylinder bore. Measure the gap with a flat feeler gauge and compare with dimensions listed in **Table 1**. If the gap is greater than specified, the ring(s) should be replaced. When installing new rings, measure their end gap in the same manner. If the gap is less than specified, carefully file the ends with a fine-cut file until the gap is correct.

6. Install the piston rings in the order shown in **Figure 269**.

NOTE
Install all rings with their markings facing up.

7. Install the piston rings—first the bottom, then the middle, then the top ring—by carefully spreading the ends with your thumbs and slipping the ring over

the top of the piston. Remember that the piston rings must be installed with the marks on them facing up toward the top of the piston.

8. Make sure the rings are seated completely in their grooves all the way around the piston and that the end gaps are distributed around the piston as shown in **Figure 269**. The important thing is that the ring gaps are not aligned with each other when installed.

9. If new rings are installed, measure the side clearance of each ring in its groove with a flat feeler gauge (**Figure 264**) and compare to dimensions listed in **Table 1**.

Connecting Rod Inspection

NOTE
If not already marked, prior to disassembly, mark the rods and caps. Number them "1," "2," "3" or "4" (Figure 246) starting from the left-hand side. The left-hand side refers to the engine sitting in the bike's frame—not as it sits on your workbench.

1. Remove the connecting rods and pistons as described in this chapter.

2. Clean the connecting rods and inserts in solvent and dry with compressed air.

3. Measure the inside diameter of the small end of the connecting rod (**Figure 270**) with an inside bore gauge. Check against the dimension listed in **Table 1**; replace the rod if necessary.

4. Check each rod for obvious damage such as cracks and burns.

5. Check the piston pin bore for wear or scoring.

6. Take the connecting rods to a machine shop and check for twisting and bending.

7. Examine the bearing inserts (**Figure 271**) for wear, bluish tint (burned), flaking, abrasion and scoring. They are reusable if in good condition. Make a note of the bearing color (if any) marked on the side of the insert if the bearing is to be discarded.

8. Remove the connecting rod bearing bolts and check them for cracks or twisting; if necessary, replace bolts and nuts and always in pairs.

9. Check bearing clearance as described in this chapter.

Connecting Rod Bearing Clearance Measurement

1. Clean the rod bearing surfaces of the crankshaft and the rod bearing inserts and measure the rod bearing clearance by performing the following steps.

2. Install the piston/connecting rod assemblies into the correct cylinders as described in this chapter.

3. Place a strip of Plastigage material over each rod bearing journal parallel to the crankshaft (**Figure**

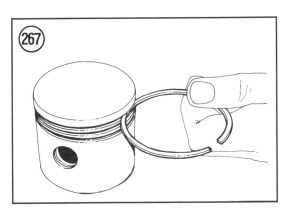

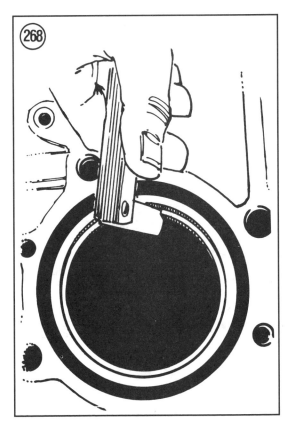

ENGINE

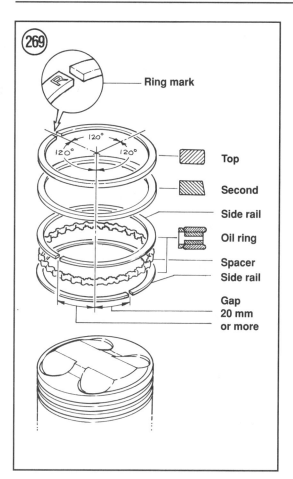

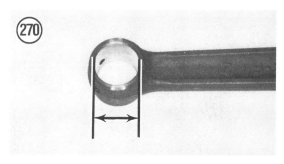

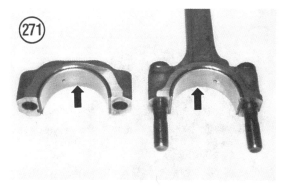

272). Do not place the Plastigage material over an oil hole in the crankshaft.

NOTE
Do not rotate the crankshaft while the Plastigage strips are in place.

4. Install the rod cap onto one rod and tighten the nuts to the torque specification listed in **Table 2**.

5. Remove the rod cap and measure the width of the flattened Plastigage material (**Figure 273**) following the manufacturer's instructions. Measure both ends of the Plastigage strip. A difference of 0.025 mm (0.001 in.) or more indicates a tapered journal. Confirm with a micrometer. New bearing clearance and the service limit are listed in **Table 1**. Remove all of the Plastigage material from the crankshaft journals and the connecting rods.

6. If the rod bearing clearance is greater than specified, select new bearings as described in this chapter.

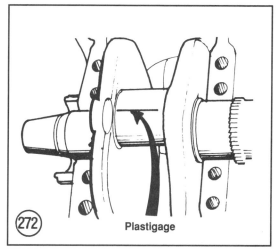

Connecting Rod Bearing Selection

1. Each crankpin counterweight is marked with a letter ("A," "B" or "C") as shown at A, **Figure 274**. Each letter code indicates the diameter of the adjacent crankpin journal (**Figure 275**).

NOTE
*Each crankpin counterweight is also marked with a number ("1," "2" or "3") as shown at C, **Figure 274**. The number code (C, **Figure 274**) is for the original main bearing journal diameter.*

NOTE
The letter on the left-hand end relates to the bearing insert in the left-hand side (No. 1 cylinder) and so on, working across from left to right. Remember, the left-hand side relates to the engine as it sits in the bike's frame, not as it sits on your workbench.

2. The connecting rod bearing I.D. code number ("1," "2" or "3") is marked on the side of each connecting rod and cap.
3. Select new connecting rod bearings by cross-referencing the crankpin code letter with the connecting rod number in **Table 3**. Where the 2 columns intersect, the new bearing insert color is indicated. **Table 4** lists the bearing insert color and thickness.

NOTE
Connecting rod bearings are color-coded on the side of the bearing insert.

4. After new bearings have been installed, recheck clearance by repeating this procedure. If a clearance is incorrect, remeasure the crankpin journal diameter with a micrometer (B, **Figure 274**). Replace crankshaft whenever a crankpin journal dimension (**Table 1**) is beyond the specified range of the stamped letter code.
5. Clean and oil the main bearing journals and insert faces.
6. After new bearings have been installed, recheck clearance by repeating this procedure.
7. Repeat Steps 1-6 for the other 3 cylinders.

Connecting Rod Selection

An alphabetical weight code ("A," "B" or "C") is marked on the side of each connecting rod and cap. When replacing a connecting rod, replace it with the same weight code as the original rod. If the same weight code replacement rod is unavailable, Honda states that you can replace it within one code letter of the original rod.

CAUTION
Mismatching connecting rod weight codes will cause abnormal engine vibration, leading to costly damage.

CRANKSHAFT

Removal/Installation

1. Separate the cylinder block and the crankcase as described in this chapter.

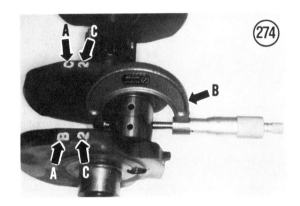

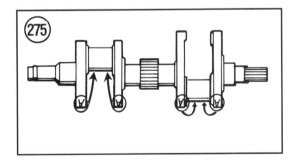

ENGINE

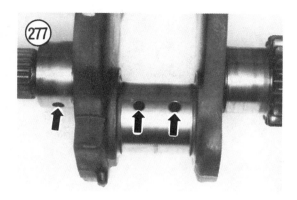

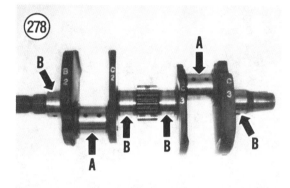

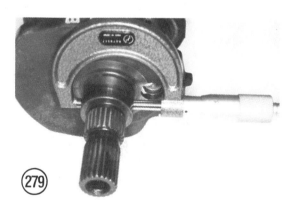

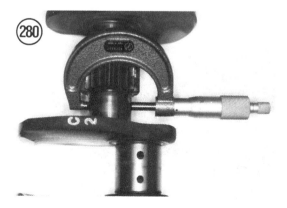

2. Remove the transmission assemblies as described under *Transmission Removal* in Chapter Six.

3. Remove the piston and connecting rod assemblies (A, **Figure 276**) from the crankshaft as described in this chapter.

4. Lift the crankshaft (B, **Figure 276**) up and out of the cylinder block.

5. Install by reversing these removal steps.

Inspection

1. Clean crankshaft thoroughly with solvent. Clean oil holes (**Figure 277**) with rifle cleaning brushes. Flush thoroughly with new solvent and dry with compressed air. Lightly oil all bearing journal surfaces immediately to prevent rust.

2. Carefully inspect each journal for scratches, ridges, scoring, nicks, etc. Very small nicks and scratches may be removed with fine emery cloth. Refer to A, **Figure 278** for connecting rod journals and B, **Figure 278** for main bearing journals. More serious damage must be removed by grinding—a job for a machine shop or dealer.

3. If the surface on all journals is satisfactory, measure the journals with a micrometer and check for out-of-roundness and taper. Refer to **Figure 279** and **Figure 280**.

4. Check the crankshaft for bending. Mount the crankshaft between accurate centers (lathe or crankshaft truing stand) and rotate it one full turn with a dial gauge contacting the center journal. Actual bend is half the reading shown on the gauge. If the runout exceeds the service limit in **Table 1**, replace the crankshaft.

CAUTION
*If the crankshaft timing gear is damaged, check both gears on both camshaft gear cases (**Figure 281**). They may be damaged also and may need to be replaced.*

5. Inspect the crankshaft timing gear for damaged, chipped or missing teeth (**Figure 282**). If damaged, the crankshaft must be replaced.

6. Inspect the splines (**Figure 283**) for the clutch on the right-hand end of the crankshaft. If damaged, the crankshaft must be replaced.

7. Inspect the Woodruff key and keyway (**Figure 284**) on the left-hand end of the crankshaft. If the

key is damaged, replace the key. If the keyway is damaged, the crankshaft must be replaced.

Crankshaft Main Bearing Clearance Measurement

1. Check the inside and outside surfaces of the bearing inserts for wear, bluish tint (burned), flaking abrasion and scoring. If the bearings are good, they may be reused. If any insert is questionable, replace the entire set.
2. Clean the bearing surfaces of the crankshaft and the main bearing inserts. Measure the main bearing clearance by performing the following steps.
3. Set the cylinder block upside down on the workbench on wood blocks.

NOTE
Used bearing inserts must be installed in their original locations.

4. Install the existing main bearing inserts into the cylinder block.
5. Install the crankshaft into the cylinder block.
6. Place a strip of Plastigage material over each main bearing journal parallel to the crankshaft (**Figure 285**). Do not place the Plastigage strip over an oil hole in the crankshaft.

NOTE
Do not rotate the crankshaft while the Plastigage strips are in place.

7. Install the existing bearing inserts into the crankcase.
8. Position the crankcase onto the cylinder block. Set the front portion down first and lower the rear. Join both parts and tap them together lightly with a plastic mallet—do not use a metal hammer, as it will damage the crankcase.

CAUTION
The crankcase and cylinder block should fit together without force. If they do not fit together completely, do not attempt to pull them together with the crankcase bolts. Separate them and investigate the cause of the interference. Do not risk damage by trying to force them together.

9. Apply oil to the threads of the 9 mm crankcase bolts and install them into the crankcase (**Figure**

ENGINE

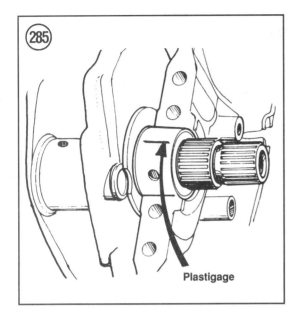

Plastigage

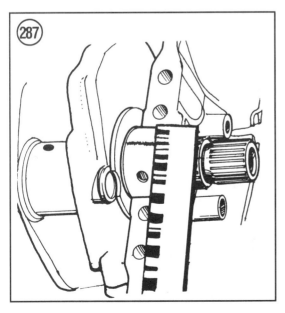

286). Tighten them in 2-3 steps in a crisscross pattern to the torque specification listed in **Table 2**.

10. Remove the 9 mm crankcase bolts in the reverse order of installation.

11. Carefully remove the crankcase from the cylinder block.

12. Measure the width of the flattened Plastigage material following manufacturer's instructions. Measure both ends of the Plastigage strip (**Figure 287**). A difference of 0.025 mm (0.001 in.) or more indicates a tapered journal. Confirm with a micrometer. New bearing clearance and service limit dimensions are listed in **Table 1**. Remove the Plastigage strips from all bearing journals.

13. If the bearing clearance is greater than specified, select new bearings as described in this chapter.

Crankshaft Main Bearing Selection

NOTE
The letter on the left-hand end of the set of letters relates to the bearing insert in the left-hand side and so on, working across from left to right. Remember, the left-hand side relates to the engine as it sits in the bike's frame, not as it sits on your workbench.

1. The cylinder block is marked with a series of 3 letters (A, B or C) that represent each main bearing crankpin journal (Nos. 1-4) reading from left to right. The letters are stamped on the upper rear section of the cylinder block on 1986-1989 models or on the right-hand side of the cylinder block by the No. 4 main bearing insert (**Figure 288**) on 1990-on models.

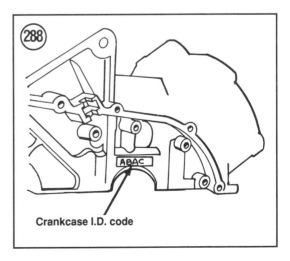

Crankcase I.D. code

2. Each crankshaft counterbalancer is stamped with a code number ("1," "2" or "3") that represents a crankshaft main journal outside diameter. Refer to C, **Figure 274** and **Figure 289**.

3. Select new main bearings by cross-referencing the crankpin code number with the main journal code letter in **Table 5**. Where the 2 columns intersect, the new bearing insert color is indicated. **Table 6** lists the bearing insert color and thickness.

4. After new bearings have been installed, recheck clearance by repeating this procedure. If a clearance is incorrect, remeasure the crankshaft journal with a

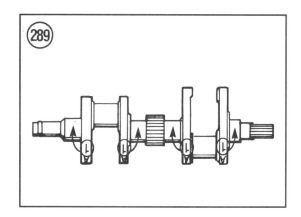

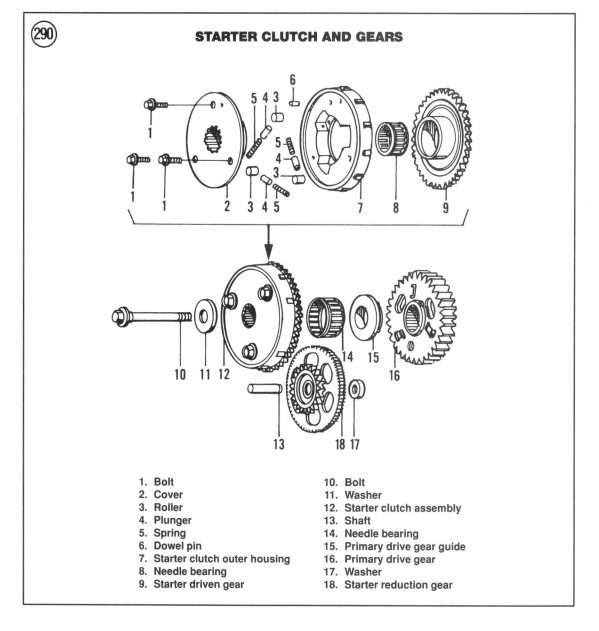

STARTER CLUTCH AND GEARS

1. Bolt
2. Cover
3. Roller
4. Plunger
5. Spring
6. Dowel pin
7. Starter clutch outer housing
8. Needle bearing
9. Starter driven gear
10. Bolt
11. Washer
12. Starter clutch assembly
13. Shaft
14. Needle bearing
15. Primary drive gear guide
16. Primary drive gear
17. Washer
18. Starter reduction gear

ENGINE

micrometer. Refer to **Figure 279** and **Figure 280**. Replace the crankshaft if a crankpin journal dimension is beyond the specified range of the stamped number code listed in **Table 5**. If the crankshaft is within specifications, the cylinder block and crankcase are worn and require replacement.

5. Clean and oil the main bearing journals and bearing inserts.

6. After new bearings have been installed, recheck clearance by repeating this procedure.

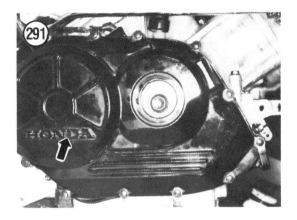

STARTER CLUTCH ASSEMBLY, STARTER REDUCTION GEAR AND PRIMARY DRIVE GEAR

The starter clutch assembly, starter gear and primary drive gear can be removed with the engine in the frame. The starter motor can be left in place, if desired. Starter removal is covered in Chapter Eight.

Refer to **Figure 290** for this procedure.

Removal/Installation

NOTE
This procedure is shown with the engine removed from the frame for clarity.

1. Remove the lower sections of the front fairing as described under *Front Fairing Removal/Installation* in Chapter Thirteen.

2. Place the bike on the centerstand (models so equipped) or sidestand.

3. Drain the engine oil as described under *Engine Oil and Filter Change* in Chapter Three.

4. Remove the bolts securing the right-hand crankcase cover (**Figure 291**) and remove the cover and gasket. Don't lose the 2 locating dowels.

5. Withdraw the shaft (A, **Figure 292**) and remove the starter reduction gear (B, **Figure 292**). Don't lose the washer behind the reduction gear.

NOTE
*If the starter clutch assembly is going to be disassembled, loosen the cover bolts (A, **Figure 293**) at this time. A thread locking agent was applied to the bolts during assembly and it will be difficult to loosen them once the assembly is removed from the engine.*

6. To keep the primary drive gear from turning while loosening the bolt, install a copper washer (or copper penny) between the clutch outer housing and the primary drive gear (**Figure 294**).

7. Remove the bolt and washer (B, **Figure 293**) securing the starter clutch assembly;

8. Remove the starter clutch assembly (C, **Figure 293**).

9. Remove the primary drive gear guide (**Figure 295**).

10. Remove the primary drive gear (**Figure 296**).

Starter Clutch
Disassembly/Inspection/Assembly

Refer to **Figure 290** for this procedure.

1. Place the starter clutch assembly with the gear side facing up. Rotate the starter driven gear (A, **Figure 297**) *clockwise* and pull up at the same time. Remove the starter driven gear from the starter clutch assembly (B, **Figure 297**).

2. Remove the needle bearing (**Figure 298**) from the starter clutch.

3. Inspect the teeth on the primary drive gear (**Figure 299**), the starter driven gear (A, **Figure 300**) and the reduction gear (**Figure 301**). Check for chipped or missing teeth. Look for uneven or excessive wear on the gear faces. Replace the gear(s) if necessary.

4. Inspect the inner surface (B, **Figure 300**) of the starter clutch gear where the needle bearing rides for wear or damage. Replace if necessary.

5. Inspect the outer surface (C, **Figure 300**) of the starter clutch gear flange where the needle bearing rides for wear or damage. Replace if necessary.

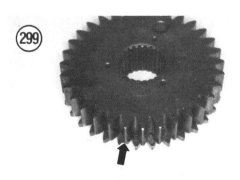

ENGINE

6. Check the needle bearing (**Figure 302**) for wear or damage. The needles must rotate freely. Replace if necessary.
7. Inspect the inner splines (**Figure 303**) of the primary drive gear for wear or damage. Replace the gear if necessry.
8. Inspect the damper springs (**Figure 304**) of the primary drive gear for wear or damage. Replace the gear if necessry.
9. Check the rollers (**Figure 305**) in the starter clutch assembly for uneven or excessive wear; replace as a set if any are bad.
10. To replace the rollers, perform the following:
    a. Remove the bolts (A, **Figure 306**) securing the starter clutch cover and remove the cover (B, **Figure 306**).
    b. Remove the rollers, plunger and spring from each receptacle as necessary.
    c. Inspect all parts and replace as necessary.
    d. Install the spring, plunger and roller into each receptacle.
    e. Align the dowel pin on the backside of the clutch cover with the depression in the starter clutch and install the cover.

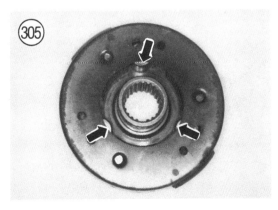

f. Apply blue Loctite (No. 242) to the bolt threads prior to installation. Install the bolts and tighten to the torque specifications listed in **Table 2**.

11. Install the shaft into the starter reduction gear (**Figure 307**) and rotate the gear on the shaft. Check for loose or rough rotation. Replace the defective part(s).

12. Install the needle bearing into the starter clutch assembly (**Figure 298**). Apply clean engine oil to the needle bearing.

13. Place the starter clutch with the needle bearing side facing up. Place the starter driven gear onto the starter clutch and rotate the starter driven gear *clockwise* and push down at the same time. Push the starter driven gear down until it bottoms out in the starter clutch assembly (**Figure 308**).

Installation

1. Partially install the primary drive gear onto the crankshaft. In order for both gears to mesh properly, use a screwdriver and align the split gear teeth on the primary drive gear with the clutch outer housing gear. Push the gear all the way on until it stops (**Figure 296**).

2. Position the guide with the recessed side (**Figure 309**) going on first and install the guide (**Figure 295**).

3. Align the wide groove in the starter clutch assembly splines (A, **Figure 310**) with the wide groove (B, **Figure 310**) on the shaft. Install the starter clutch assembly (C, **Figure 293**) and push it on all the way on until it stops.

4. Install the bolt (B, **Figure 293**) securing the starter clutch assembly. Install a copper washer (or copper penny) between the clutch outer housing and

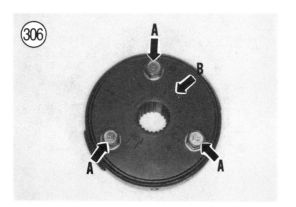

ENGINE

the primary drive gear. This will keep the primary drive gear from turning while tightening the bolt.

5. Tighten the bolt (B, **Figure 293**) to the torque specification listed in **Table 2**. Remove the copper washer or penny from the gears.

6. Install the shaft into the starter reduction gear and install the washer (**Figure 311**) onto the shaft.

7. Place the starter reduction gear, shaft and washer in place and mesh it properly with the starter gear and the starter clutch. Push the shaft in until it bottoms out.

8. Install 2 locating dowels (A, **Figure 312**) and new gasket (B, **Figure 312**).

9. Install the right-hand crankcase cover (**Figure 291**) and tighten the bolts securely.

10. Refill the engine with the recommended type and quantity of engine oil as described in Chapter Three.

11. Install the lower sections of the front fairing as described in Chapter Thirteen.

BREAK-IN PROCEDURE

If the rings were replaced, new pistons installed, the cylinders rebored or honed or major lower end work performed, the engine should be broken in just as though it were new. The performance and service life of the engine depends greatly on a careful and sensible break-in.

For the first 800 km (500 miles), no more than one-third throttle should be used and speed should be varied as much as possible within the one-third throttle limit. Prolonged steady running at one speed, no matter how moderate, is to be avoided as well as hard acceleration.

Following the *800 km (500 mile) Service* described in this chapter more throttle should not be used until the motorcycle has covered at least 1,600 km (1,000 miles) and then it should be limited to short bursts of speed until 2,410 km (1,500 miles) have been logged.

During this period, oil consumption will be higher than normal. It is therefore important to check and correct oil level frequently. At no time during the break-in or later should the oil level be allowed to drop below the bottom line on the dipstick; if the oil level is low, the oil will become overheated, resulting in insufficient lubrication and increased wear.

800 km (500 mile) Service

It is essential that the oil and filter be changed after the first 800 km (500 miles). In addition, it is a good idea to change the oil and filter at the completion of the break-in (about 2,410 km/1,500 miles) to ensure that all of the particles produced during break-in are removed from the lubrication system. The small added expense may be considered a smart investment that will pay off in increased engine life.

Tables 1-6 are on the following pages.

Table 1 ENGINE SPECIFICATIONS

	Specification	Wear limit
General		
Type and number of cylinders		
V-4 cylinder, DOHC, liquid cooled		
Bore × stroke		
700 cc	70.0 × 45.4 mm (2.76 × 1.79 in.)	
750 cc	70.0 × 48.6 mm (2.76 × 1.91 in.)	
Displacement		
700 cc	699 cc (42.7 cu. in.)	
750 cc	742 cc (45.7 cu. in.)	
Compression pressure	1,177-1,569 kPa (171-227 psi).	
Camshaft (1986-1989)		
Cam lobe height		
Intake	31.406-31.566 mm (1.2365-1.2428 in.)	31.370 mm (1.235 in.)
Exhaust	31.460-31.620 mm (1.2386-1.2449 in.)	31.43 mm (1.237 in.)
Journal O.D. (intake and exhaust)		
Center	27.929-27.950 mm (1.0996-1.1004 in.)	27.92 mm (1.099 in.)
Both ends	27.949-27.970 mm (1.1004-1.1012 in.)	27.94 mm (1.100 in.)
Camshaft holder I.D.	28.000-28.021 mm (1.1024-1.1032 in.)	28.03 mm (1.104 in.)
Journal oil clearance (intake and exhaust)		
Center	0.050-0.092 mm (0.0019-0.0036 in.)	0.110 mm (0.0036 in.)
Both ends	0.030-0.072 mm (0.0012-0.0028 in.)	0.090 mm (0.0035 in.)
Runout	–	0.03 mm (0.001 in.)
Camshaft (1990-on)		
Cam lobe height		
49-state, U.K., Canada		
Intake	36.280-36.440 mm (1.4283-1.4346 in.)	36.250 mm (1.427 in.)
Exhaust (1990-1993)	36.370-36.530 mm (1.4319-1.4382 in.)	36.340 mm (1.431 in.)
California		
Intake (1990-on)	33.980-34.140 mm (1.3378-1.3441 in.)	33.950 mm (1.3366 in.)
Exhaust (1990-1993)	35.270-35.430 mm (1.3886-1.3949 in.)	35.240 mm (1.3874 in.)
1994-on (49-state, U.K., Canada)		
Exhaust	36.070-36.230 mm (1.4201-1.4264 in.)	36.040 mm (1.419 in.)
1994-on (California)		
Exhaust	35.470-35.630 mm (1.3965-1.4028 in.)	35.440 mm (1.395 in.)
Journal O.D.		
Intake and exhaust	24.949-24.970 mm (0.9822-0.9831 in.)	24.94 mm (0.982 in.)
Camshaft holder/cylinder head I.D.	25.000-25.021 mm (0.9843-0.9851 in.)	–
Journal oil clearance		
Intake and exhaust	0.020-0.062 mm (0.0008-0.0024 in.)	0.100 mm (0.004 in.)
Runout	–	0.05 mm (0.002 in.)

(continued)

Table 1 ENGINE SPECIFICATIONS (continued)

	Specification	Wear limit
Cylinder head distortion	–	0.10 mm (0.004 in.)
Valves and valve springs (1986-1989)		
Valve stem O.D.		
Intake	5.475-5.490 mm (0.2156-0.2161 in.)	5.47 mm (0.215 in.)
Exhaust	5.445-5.470 mm (0.2148-0.2154 in.)	5.45 mm (0.214 in.)
Valve guide I.D.	5.500-5.515 mm (0.2165-0.2171 in.)	5.55 mm (0.219 in.)
Valve guide projection above cylinder head surface	14.0 mm (0.55 in.)	
Valve stem-to-guide clearance		
Intake	0.010-0.040 mm (0.0004-0.0016 in.)	0.08 mm (0.003 in.)
Exhaust	0.030-0.060 mm (0.0012-0.0024 in.)	0.10 mm (0.004 in.)
Valve head thickness	–	0.05 mm (0.002 in.)
Valve stem end length	–	2.5 mm (0.10 in.)
Valve seat width	1.0-1.3 mm (0.04-0.05 in.)	1.5 mm (0.06 in.)
Valve spring free length		
Inner	32.8 mm (1.29 in.)	31.3 mm (1.23 in.)
Outer	37.0 mm (1.46 in.)	35.4 mm (1.39 in.)
Valves and valve springs (1990-on)		
Valve stem O.D.		
Intake	4.475-4.490 mm (0.1762-0.1767 in.)	4.47 mm (0.176 in.)
Exhaust	4.465-4.480 mm (0.1758-0.1764 in.)	4.45 mm (0.175 in.)
Valve guide I.D.	4.500-4.512 mm (0.1772-0.1776 in.)	4.56 mm (0.179 in.)
Valve guide projection above cylinder head surface	15.4 mm (0.606 in.)	–
Valve stem-to-guide clearance		
Intake	0.010-0.037 mm (0.0004-0.0015 in.)	0.07 mm (0.0028 in.)
Exhaust	0.020-0.047 mm (0.0008-0.0019 in.)	0.10 mm (0.0039 in.)
Valve seat width	1.0 mm (0.04 in.)	1.5 mm (0.06 in.)
Valve spring free length		
Inner	34.2 mm (1.35 in.)	32.5 mm (1.28 in.)
Outer	38.1 mm (1.50 in.)	36.2 mm (1.43 in.)
Cylinders		
Bore	70.000-70.015 mm (2.755-2.756 in.)	70.100 mm (2.759 in.)
Cylinder/piston clearance	0.010-0.045 mm (0.0004-0.0018 in.)	0.100 mm (0.004 in.)
Out-of-round	–	0.10 mm (0.004 in.)
Pistons		
Outer diameter	69.970-6.990 mm (2.755-2.756 in.)	69.85 mm (2.750 in.)
Piston pin bore	17.002-17.008 mm (0.6694-0.6696 in.)	17.02 mm (0.670 in.)
Piston pin outer diameter	16.994-17.000 mm (0.6691-0.6693 in.)	16.98 mm (0.669 in.)
Piston-to-piston pin clearance	0.002-0.014 mm (0.0001-0.0005 in.)	0.04 mm (0.002 in.)

(continued)

Table 1 ENGINE SPECIFICATIONS (continued)

	Specification	Wear limit
Piston rings		
Number per piston		
Compression	2	–
Oil control	1	–
Ring end gap (1986-1989)		
Top and second	0.2-0.4 mm (0.008-0.016 in.)	0.55 mm (0.022 in.)
Oil (side rail)	0.20-0.80 mm (0.008-0.031 in.)	1.00 mm (0.039 in.)
Ring end gap (1990-on)		
Top	0.20-0.35 mm (0.008-0.014 in.)	0.5 mm (0.02 in.)
Second	0.35-0.50 mm (0.014-0.020 in.)	0.7 mm (0.03 in.)
Oil (side rail)	0.20-0.80 mm (0.008-0.031 in.)	1.00 mm (0.039 in.)
Connecting rods		
Piston pin hole I.D.	17.016-17.034 mm (0.6699-0.6706 in.)	17.040 mm (0.671 in.)
Big end side clearance	0.10-0.30 mm (0.004-0.012 in.)	0.40 mm (0.016 in.)
Big end oil clearance	0.030-0.052 mm (0.0012-0.0020 in.)	0.080 mm (0.003 in.)
Crankshaft		
Crankpin O.D.	33.991-34.003 mm (1.3382-1.3387 in.)	–
Crankpin journal oil clearance	0.023-0.045 mm (0.0009-0.0017 in.)	0.060 mm (0.002 in.)
Runout	–	0.03 mm (0.001 in.)

Table 2 ENGINE TIGHTENING TORQUES

Item	N•m	ft.lb.
Engine mounting bolts and nuts (1986-1989)		
Front lower 10 mm bolt	35-45	25-33
Front upper center bolt	25-30	18-22
Rear lower through bolt	10-12	7.2-9
Rear lower through bolt nut	50-60	36-43
Rear upper mounting bolt	35-45	25-33
Engine mounting bolts and nuts (1990-on)		
Front and rear upper bolts	40	28
Rear lower through bolt		
Adjusting bolt	9	7
Adjusting bolt locknut	55	40
Nut	55	40
Upper left-hand bolt	40	28
Upper right-hand bolt		
Adjust bolt	9	7
Adjust bolt locknut	55	40
Bolt	40	28
Cylinder head cover bolts	8-12	5.8-9
Camshaft holder and oil pipe bolts	10-14	7.2-10
Cylinder head bolts (1986-1989)		
6 mm bolts	10-14	7.2-10
8 mm bolts	24-30	17-22
9 mm bolts	35-39	25-28
(continued)		

ENGINE

Table 2 ENGINE TIGHTENING TORQUES (continued)

Item	N•m	ft.lb.
Cylinder head bolts (1990-on)		
6 mm bolts	12	9
8 mm bolts	45	33
Camshaft gear case bolts		
6 mm bolts	10	7
8 mm bolts	23	17
Oil pressure switch	10-14	7.2-10
Alternator rotor bolt	80-100	58-72
Oil pump mounting bolts	10-14	7.2-10
Crankcase bolts-lower		
6 mm	10-14	7.2-10
8 mm	21-25	15-18
9 mm	30-34	22-25
Cylinder block bolts-upper		
6 mm	10-14	7.2-10
10 mm	38-42	27-30
Connecting rod cap nuts	32-36	23-26
Starter clutch		
Cover bolts	38-42	27-30
Mounting bolt	80-100	58-72

Table 3 CONNECTING ROD BEARING SELECTION

	Crankpin journal OD size code		
	Letter A 35.995-36.000 mm (1.4171-1.4173 in.)	**Letter B** 35.989-35.994 mm (1.4169-1.4171 in.)	**Letter C** 35.982-35.988 mm (1.4166-1.4169 in.)
Connecting rod ID code			
Number 1 39.000-39.005 mm (1.5354-1.5356 in.)	Yellow	Green	Brown
Number 2 39.006-39.011 mm (1.5357-1.5359 in.)	Green	Brown	Black
Number 3 39.012-39.018 mm (1.5359-1.5361 in.)	Brown	Black	Blue

Table 4 CONNECTING ROD BEARING INSERT COLOR*

Color	Thickness range
Blue	Thick
Black	
Brown	Medium
Green	
Yellow	Thin

* Honda does not provide dimensions for these inserts.

Table 5 MAIN JOURNAL BEARING SELECTION

1986-1993 Models

Crankcase ID code	Main journal OD size code		
	Number 1 33.998-34.003 mm (1.3385-1.3387 in.)	**Number 2** 33.997-33.992 mm (1.3383-1.3385 in.)	**Number 3** 33.985-33.991 mm (1.3380-1.3382 in.)
Letter A 37.000-37.005 mm (1.4567-1.4569 in.)	Yellow	Green	Brown
Letter B 37.006-37.011 mm (1.4569-1.4572 in.)	Green	Brown	Black
Letter C 37.012-37.018 mm (1.4572-1.4574 in.)	Brown	Black	Blue

1994 Models

Crankcase ID code	Main journal OD size code		
	Number 1 34.007-34.013 mm (1.3389-1.3391 in.)	**Number 2** 34.001-34.006 mm (1.3386-1.3388 in.)	**Number 3** 33.995-34.000 mm (1.3368-1.3385 in.)
Letter A 37.000-37.005 mm (1.4567-1.4569 in.)	Yellow	Green	Brown
Letter B 37.006-37.011 mm (1.4569-1.4572 in.)	Green	Brown	Black
Letter C 37.012-37.018 mm (1.4572-1.4574 in.)	Brown	Black	Blue

Table 6 MAIN JOURNAL BEARING INSERT COLOR*

Color	Thickness range
Blue	Thick
Black	
Brown	Medium
Green	
Yellow	Thin

* Honda does not provide dimensions for these inserts.

CHAPTER FIVE

CLUTCH SYSTEM

This chapter contains repair and service information for the clutch system.

Table 1 and **Table 2** are located at the end of this chapter.

NOTE
Where differences occur relating to the United Kingdom (U.K.) models they are identified. If there is no (U.K.) designation relating to a procedure, photo or illustration it is identical to the United States (U.S.) models.

CLUTCH

The clutch is a wet, multiplate type which operates immersed in the engine oil. It is mounted on the right-hand end of the transmission main shaft. The outside clutch center is splined to the main shaft. The outer clutch housing can rotate freely on the main shaft and is geared to the primary driven gear splined to the end of the crankshaft.

The clutch release mechanism is hydraulic and requires no routine adjustment. The mechanism consists of a clutch master cylinder on the left-hand handlebar, a slave cylinder on the left-hand side of the engine just behind the alternator and a pushrod that rides within the channel in the transmission mainshaft.

The clutch is activated by hydraulic fluid pressure and is controlled by the clutch master cylinder. The hydraulic pressure generated by the master cylinder activates the clutch slave cylinder that in turn pushes the clutch pushrod. The clutch pushrod pushes on the lifter guide thus moving the pressure plate which disengages the clutch mechanism.

Refer to **Table 1** for all clutch torque specifications and to **Table 2** for clutch specifications.

Removal/Disassembly

Refer to **Figure 1** for this procedure.

NOTE
This procedure is shown with the engine removed from the frame for clarity. The clutch assembly can be removed with the engine in the frame.

1. Remove the lower sections of the front fairing as described under *Front Fairing Removal/Installation* in Chapter Thirteen.

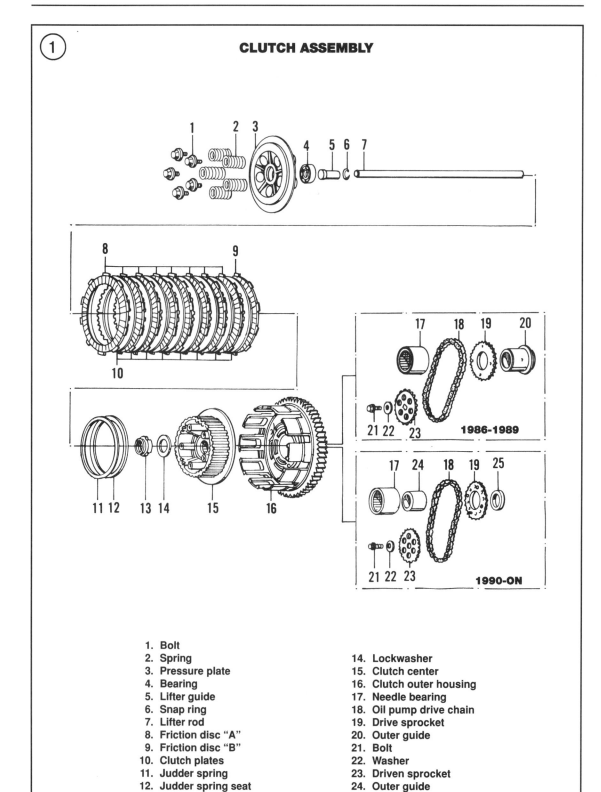

CLUTCH SYSTEM

2. Place the bike on the centerstand (models so equipped) or sidestand.

3. Drain the engine oil as described under *Engine Oil and Filter Change* in Chapter Three.

NOTE
Do not operate the clutch lever after the clutch assembly or slave cylinder is removed from the engine. If the lever is applied it will force the slave cylinder piston out of the body and make slave cylinder installation difficult.

4. Place a block of wood between the clutch lever and the hand grip to hold the lever in the released position. Secure the wood with a rubber band, a tie wrap or tape. This will prevent the clutch lever from being applied accidentally after the clutch slave cylinder is removed from the crankcase.

5. Remove the bolts securing the right-hand crankcase cover (**Figure 2**) and remove the cover and gasket. Don't lose the 2 locating dowels.

6. Remove the starter clutch assembly (**Figure 3**) as described in Chapter Four.

7. Remove the bolts (**Figure 4**) securing the clutch pressure plate springs and remove the springs (**Figure 5**).

8. Remove the clutch pressure plate (**Figure 6**).

9. Remove the lifter guide and ball bearing (**Figure 7**).

10. Withdraw the lifter rod (**Figure 8**) from the mainshaft.

11. Remove the clutch friction discs and clutch plates.

12. Unstake the locknut (**Figure 9**) from the groove in the mainshaft.

CAUTION
Do not clamp the "Grabbit" on too tight as it may damage the grooves in the clutch hub.

13. To keep the clutch hub from turning in the next step, attach a special tool such as the "Grabbit" (A, **Figure 10**) to the clutch hub (B, **Figure 10**).

14. Use Honda special tool (part No. 07724-0050001) or equivalent (**Figure 11**) and loosen the locknut (**Figure 12**).

15. Remove the locknut and the lockwasher (**Figure 13**).

16. Remove the clutch center (**Figure 14**).

17. Remove the clutch outer housing (**Figure 15**) and needle bearing (**Figure 16**).

NOTE
*On 1986-1989 models, there is a shoulder on the backside of the outer guide (**Figure 17**) located behind the oil pump gear that prevents the removal of the outer guide without first removing the oil pump drive gear, chain and driven gear.*

CLUTCH SYSTEM

18A. On 1986-1989 models, perform the following:

a. Remove the bolt (**Figure 18**) and washer securing the oil pump driven gear.

b. Remove the oil pump drive gear (A, **Figure 19**), driven gear (B, **Figure 19**) and chain (C, **Figure 19**) as an assembly.

c. Remove the outer guide (**Figure 20**).

18B. On 1990-on models, remove the outer guide from within the oil pump drive sprocket.

19. Remove the friction discs, clutch plates, judder spring and judder spring seat from the clutch center.

Inspection

Refer to **Table 1** for clutch specifications.

1. Clean all clutch parts (**Figure 21**) in petroleum-based solvent such as kerosene and thoroughly dry with compressed air.

NOTE
If any of the friction discs or clutch plates require replacement you should consider replacing all of them as a set to retain maximum clutch performance.

2. The friction material is made of cork that is bonded onto the aluminum disc for warp resistance and durability. Measure the thickness of each friction disc at several places around the disc as shown in **Figure 22**. Compare to the specifications listed in **Table 1**. Replace all friction discs if any one is found to be worn to the service limit or less. Do not replace only 1 or 2 discs.

3. Check the clutch plates for warpage on a surface plate such as a piece of plate glass (**Figure 23**). Compare to the specifications listed in **Table 1**. If any plate is warped to the service limit or more, replace the entire set of clutch plates. Do not replace only 1 or 2 plates.

4. Check both ends of the clutch lifter rod for wear or damage. Also roll the lifter rod on a surface plate such as a piece of plate glass (**Figure 24**) and check for bending. A bent lifter rod may bind inside the transmission mainshaft when under load. Replace as necessary.

5. Inspect the teeth of the outer housing (**Figure 25**) for damage. Remove any small nicks on the gear

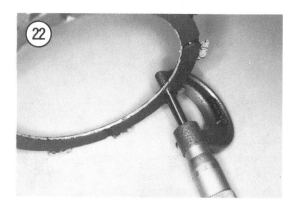

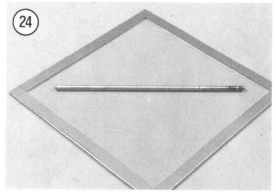

CLUTCH SYSTEM

25

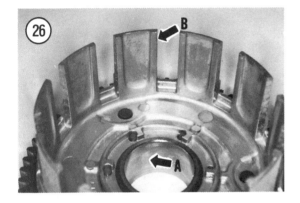

26

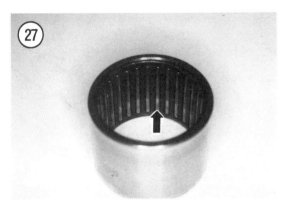

27

teeth with an oilstone. If damage is severe, the housing must be replaced. Also check the teeth and inner splines on the driven gear; it may also need replacing.

6. Inspect the needle bearing surface (A, **Figure 26**) within the clutch outer housing. Make sure it rotates smoothly with no signs of wear; replace if necessary.

7. Inspect the clutch outer housing needle bearing (**Figure 27**). Make sure it rotates freely with no signs of wear, replace if necessary.

8. Inspect the slots in the clutch outer housing (B, **Figure 26**) for cracks, galling or nicks where they come in contact with the friction disc tabs. If any severe damage is evident, the housing must be replaced.

9. Inspect the damper springs (**Figure 28**) in the backside of the clutch outer housing. Check for weak or sagging springs, replace the clutch outer housing if necessary.

10. Inspect the inner splines (**Figure 29**) in the clutch center for damage. Remove any small nicks with an oilstone. If damage is severe, the clutch center must be replaced.

11. Inspect the outer grooves (**Figure 30**) in the clutch center. If it shows signs of wear or galling the clutch center should be replaced.

12. Inspect the spring posts (**Figure 31**) in the clutch center. If any show signs of wear, galling or fractures the clutch center should be replaced.

13. Check the bearing and lifter guide (**Figure 32**). Make sure the bearing rotates smoothly with no signs of wear or damage. Replace if necessary.

14. Inspect the outer grooves (**Figure 33**) in the clutch pressure plate. If it shows signs of wear or galling the clutch pressure plate should be replaced.

28

29

15. Inspect the spring receptacles (**Figure 34**) in the clutch pressure plate. If either show signs of wear or galling the clutch pressure plate should be replaced.

16. Check the inner and outer surfaces of the outer guide (**Figure 35**) for signs of wear or damage. Replace if necessary.

17. Measure the inside diameter of the outer guide (**Figure 36**). Replace the outer guide if worn to the specification listed in **Table 1** or greater.

18. Install the outer guide into the needle bearing (**Figure 37**) and rotate the outer guide and check for wear. Replace either/or both parts if necessary.

Assembly/Installation

Refer to **Figure 1** for this procedure.

1. Assemble the parts onto the clutch center as follows:

> *NOTE*
> *If new friction discs and clutch plates are being installed, apply new engine oil to all surfaces to avoid having the clutch lock up when used for the first time.*

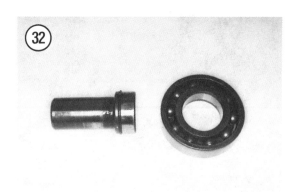

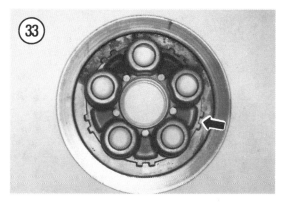

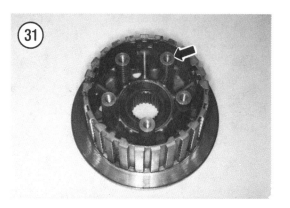

CLUTCH SYSTEM

a. Place the clutch center on the workbench with the splines facing up.

b. Install the judder spring seat onto the clutch center followed by the judder spring with the dished side facing in as shown in **Figure 38**.

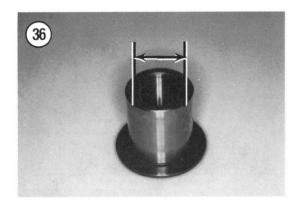

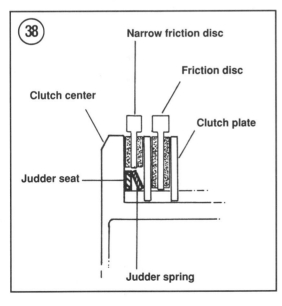

c. Install the only *narrow* friction disc "B" onto the clutch center with the judder spring seat and spring inboard of it. Make sure it seats correctly next to the spring. Refer to **Figure 38**.

d. Onto the narrow friction disc "B," install a clutch plate and then a friction disc "A" to hold the judder spring seat and spring in place.

2A. On 1986-1989 models, perform the following:

a. Position the outer guide with the shoulder side going on first and install the outer guide onto the mainshaft (**Figure 20**).

b. Engage the oil pump chain onto the drive and driven gears. Position the driven gear with the "IN" mark (A, **Figure 39**) facing in toward the crankcase.

c. Install this assembly onto the outer guide and onto the oil pump drive shaft (B, **Figure 39**). Correctly index the driven gear with the oil pump drive shaft (**Figure 40**) and push the assembly on until it bottoms out.

d. Install the bolt and washer (**Figure 41**) securing the oil pump driven gear and tighten to the torque specification listed in **Table 2**.

2B. On 1990-on models, install the outer guide (A, **Figure 42**) onto the mainshaft and into the oil pump drive sprocket (B, **Figure 42**).

3. Apply a good coat of clean engine oil to the needle bearing and install the needle bearing (**Figure 16**) onto the transmission shaft.

NOTE
***Figure 43** is shown with the outer housing and the oil pump drive gear removed for clarity.*

4. Rotate the oil pump drive sprocket (A, **Figure 43**) so the pins are lined up at the 12, 3, 6 and 9 o'clock positions.

CAUTION
The oil pump drive gear and the clutch outer housing must index properly or the housing will not go on all the way. The clutch will not operate properly nor will the oil pump rotate, resulting in severe engine damage.

5. Align the index holes in the backside of the outer housing (B, **Figure 43**) with the drive sprocket pins and install the clutch outer housing (**Figure 15**). Slowly rotate the oil pump driven gear back and forth until the pins and holes align properly. Push the housing on all the way and make sure that the pins and the holes are indexed properly.

6. Install the clutch center (**Figure 14**).

7. Install the lockwasher (**Figure 13**).

CAUTION
If the locknut has been removed several times it should be replaced with a new one. The shoulder that is staked down into the transmission shaft groove may be damaged or partially missing after

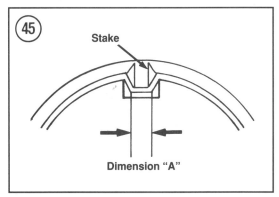

CLUTCH SYSTEM

being used several times. This shoulder must be solid when staked down into shaft in order to properly secure the clutch assembly.

8. Install a *new* locknut (**Figure 44**).
9. Use the same tool set-up used in *Removal* Step 13 and Step 14. Tighten the locknut to the torque specification listed in **Table 2**.
10. Remove the special tool from the clutch hub.
11. Using a center punch and hammer, stake the locknut into the groove in the mainshaft until Dimension "A" is 2.2-2.5 mm (0.08-0.09 in.) as shown in **Figure 45**.
12. Install the remaining clutch plates and friction discs "A," (**Figure 46**) alternating them until all are installed. The last item installed is a friction disc "A" (**Figure 47**).
13. Install the lifter rod (**Figure 8**) into the mainshaft.
14. Install the lifter guide and ball bearing (**Figure 7**).
15. Install the clutch pressure plate (**Figure 6**).
16. Install the clutch springs (**Figure 5**) and clutch bolts (**Figure 4**). Tighten the bolts securely.
17. Install the starter clutch assembly (**Figure 48**) as described in Chapter Four.
18. Make sure the locating dowels (A, **Figure 49**) are in place.
19. Install a new clutch cover gasket (B, **Figure 49**).
20. Install the right-hand crankcase cover (**Figure 50**) and bolts. Tighten the bolts securely in a crisscross pattern.
21. Remove the block of wood from between the clutch lever and the hand grip.
22. Refill the engine oil as described under *Engine Oil and Filter Change* in Chapter Three.

23. Install the lower sections of the front fairing as described in Chapter Thirteen.

24. Test ride the bike to make sure the clutch operates correctly.

CLUTCH HYDRAULIC SYSTEM

The clutch is actuated by hydraulic fluid pressure and is controlled by the hand lever on the clutch master cylinder. As clutch components wear, the fluid level drops in the reservoir and automatically adjusts for wear. There is no routine adjustment necessary or possible.

When working on the hydraulic clutch system, it is necessary that the work area and all tools be absolutely clean. Any tiny particles of foreign matter and grit in the clutch slave cylinder or the clutch master cylinder can damage the components. Also, sharp tools must not be used inside the slave cylinder or on the piston. If there is any doubt about your ability to correctly and safely carry out major service on the clutch hydraulic components, take the job to a dealer.

CAUTION
*Throughout the text, reference is made to hydraulic fluid. Hydraulic fluid is the same as DOT 4 brake fluid. Use only DOT 4 brake fluid; **do not use other types of fluids** as they are not compatible. Do not intermix silicone based (DOT 5) brake fluid as it can cause clutch component damage leading to clutch system failure.*

MASTER CYLINDER

Removal/Installation

CAUTION
Cover the surrounding area with a heavy cloth or plastic tarp to protect it from accidental hydraulic fluid spills. Wash fluid off any painted or plated surfaces immediately, as it will destroy the finish. Use soapy water and rinse completely.

1. Disconnect the electrical wires from the clutch switch.
2. Clean all dirt from the top of the cover.
3. Remove the screws securing the cover (A, **Figure 51**) and remove the cover, diaphragm plate and diaphragm.
4. If you have a shop syringe, draw all of the hydraulic fluid out of the master cylinder reservoir and discard it. *Never reuse clutch fluid.*
5. If the master cylinder is not going to be serviced, reinstall the diaphragm, diaphragm cover and cover to prevent the entry of foreign matter.
6. Pull back the rubber boot (**Figure 52**).
7. Place a shop cloth under the union bolt to catch any spilled hydraulic fluid that will leak out. Remove the union bolt (B, **Figure 51**) securing the clutch hose to the clutch master cylinder. Remove the clutch hose and place the loose end in a reclosable plastic bag to prevent entry of foreign matter. Tie the end up to the handlebar.
8. Remove the clamping bolts and clamp (C, **Figure 51**) securing the clutch master cylinder to the handlebar and remove the clutch master cylinder.
9. Install by reversing these removal steps, while noting the following:
   a. Position the clamp with the UP mark facing up and install the clamp.

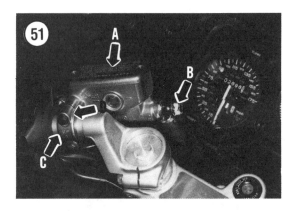

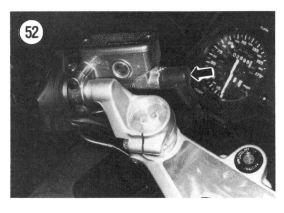

CLUTCH SYSTEM

b. Align the punch mark with the punch mark (D, **Figure 51**) on the handlebar.

c. Tighten the upper bolt first, then the lower. Tighten the bolts securely.

d. Install the clutch hose onto the clutch master cylinder. Be sure to place a sealing washer on each side of the fitting and install the union bolt. Tighten the union bolt to the torque specifications listed in **Table 2**.

e. Attach the electrical wires to the clutch switch.

f. Bleed the clutch as described in this chapter.

Disassembly

Refer to **Figure 53** for this procedure.

1. Remove the clutch master cylinder as described in this chapter.

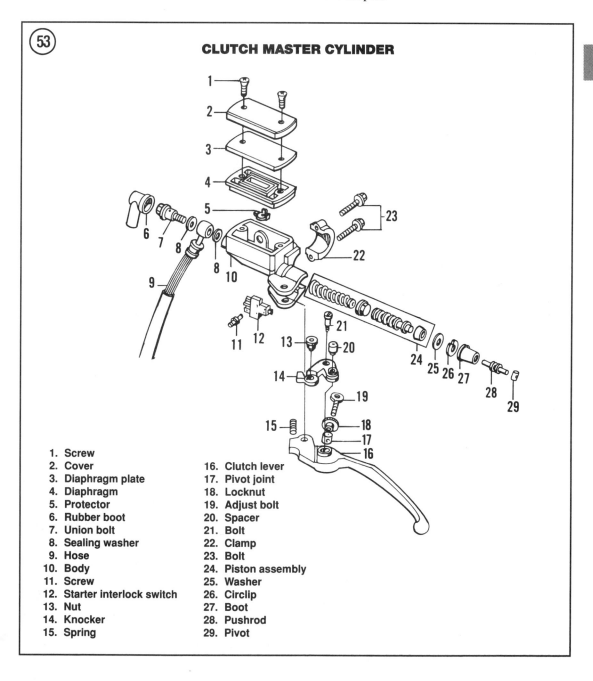

CLUTCH MASTER CYLINDER

1. Screw
2. Cover
3. Diaphragm plate
4. Diaphragm
5. Protector
6. Rubber boot
7. Union bolt
8. Sealing washer
9. Hose
10. Body
11. Screw
12. Starter interlock switch
13. Nut
14. Knocker
15. Spring
16. Clutch lever
17. Pivot joint
18. Locknut
19. Adjust bolt
20. Spacer
21. Bolt
22. Clamp
23. Bolt
24. Piston assembly
25. Washer
26. Circlip
27. Boot
28. Pushrod
29. Pivot

2. Remove the screw securing the clutch switch (A, **Figure 54**) and remove the switch.

3. Remove the bolt and nut (B, **Figure 54**) securing the clutch lever and remove the lever. Don't lose the small spring in the lever.

4. Remove the screws securing the cover (**Figure 55**) and remove the cover, diaphragm plate (**Figure 56**) and diaphragm; pour out any residual clutch fluid and discard it. *Never reuse clutch fluid.*

5. Remove the pushrod and end piece from the rubber boot.

6. Remove the rubber boot from the area where the hand lever actuates the internal piston.

7. Using circlip pliers, remove the internal circlip (**Figure 57**) from the body.

8. Remove the secondary cup and the piston assembly (A, **Figure 58**).

9. Remove the primary cup and spring (B, **Figure 58**).

10. Remove the protector (**Figure 59**) from the bottom of the reservoir.

Inspection

1. Clean all parts in denatured alcohol or fresh clutch fluid. Inspect the cylinder bore and piston contact surfaces for signs of wear and damage. If either part is less than perfect, replace it.

2. Check the end of the piston (A, **Figure 60**) for wear caused by the hand lever. Replace if worn.

3. Replace the piston if the secondary cup (B, **Figure 60**) requires replacement.

4. Inspect the primary cup and spring (C, **Figure 60**) for wear or deterioration. Replace if necessary.

5. Make sure the passages (**Figure 61**) on the bottom of the clutch fluid reservoir are clear. Clean out if necessary.

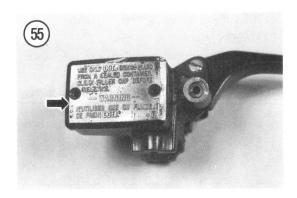

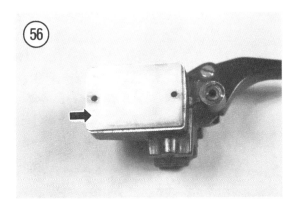

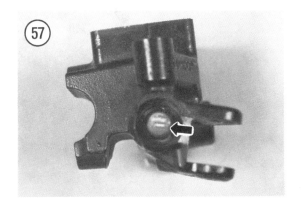

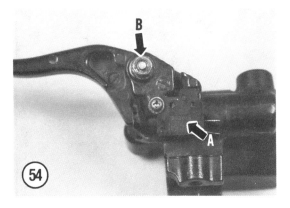

CLUTCH SYSTEM

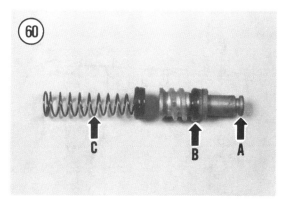

6. Check the reservoir cap and diaphragm (**Figure 62**) for damage and deterioration and replace as necessary.

7. Inspect the threads in the bore for the clutch hose union bolt. If the threads are slightly damaged; clean them up with a tap.

8. Check the hand lever pivot lugs (**Figure 63**) on the master cylinder body for elongation or cracks. Replace the body if necessary.

9. Measure the cylinder bore (**Figure 64**). Replace the master cylinder if the bore exceeds the specifications given in **Table 1**.

10. Measure the outside diameter of the piston as shown in **Figure 65** with a micrometer. Replace the piston assembly if it is less than the specifications given in **Table 1**.

11. Inspect the pivot hole (**Figure 66**) in the hand lever. If worn or elongated it must be replaced.

12. Inspect the adjustment bolt, locknut and knocker on the lever. Replace any worn parts.

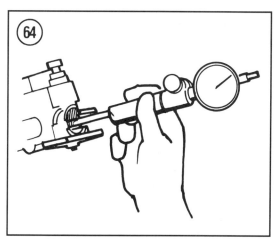

Assembly

1. Soak the new cups in fresh clutch fluid for at least 15 minutes to make them pliable. Coat the inside of the cylinder with fresh clutch fluid prior to the assembly of parts.

CAUTION
When installing the piston assembly, do not allow the cups to turn inside out as they will be damaged and allow clutch fluid leakage within the cylinder bore.

2. Install the spring, primary cup and piston assembly into the reservoir cylinder together. Install the spring (B, **Figure 58**) with the tapered end facing toward the primary cup.

NOTE
Be sure to install the primary cup with the open end in first, toward the spring.

3. Install the circlip (**Figure 57**) and slide in the rubber boot.
4. Install the protector (**Figure 59**) onto the bottom of the reservoir.
5. Install the diaphragm (**Figure 56**), diaphragm plate and cover (**Figure 55**). Do not tighten the cover screws at this time as fluid will have to be added later.
6. Make sure the small spring is in place within the lever end and install the clutch lever onto the master cylinder body. Tighten the bolt and nut securely.
7. Install the clutch switch. Tighten the screw securely but not too tight as the switch may be damaged.
8. Install the pushrod and end piece into the end of the rubber boot.
9. Install the master cylinder as described in this chapter.

Clutch Hose Assembly Replacement

There is no factory-recommended replacement interval but it is a good idea to replace the clutch hose assembly every four years or when it shows signs of cracking or damage. On 1986-1989 models, the hydraulic hose assembly consists of 2 flexible hoses, 1 section of metal tubing and fittings for union bolts at each end. On 1990 and later models, the hydraulic hose is one continuous flexible hose with fittings for union bolts at each end. On all models the hose assembly must be replaced as one unit.

CAUTION
Cover the front wheel, fender, front fairing and frame with a heavy cloth or plastic tarp to protect them from accidental spilling of hydraulic fluid. Wash the fluid off of any painted or plated surface immediately, as it will destroy the finish. Use soapy water and rinse completely.

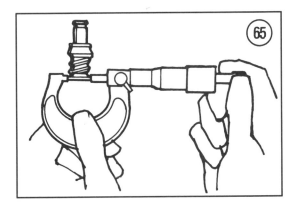

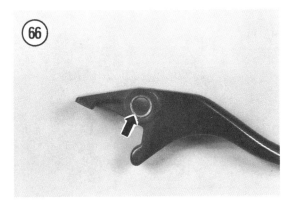

CLUTCH SYSTEM

1. Remove the left-hand lower section of the front fairing as described under *Front Fairing Removal/Installation* in Chapter Thirteen.
2. Remove the seat as described in Chapter Thirteen.
3. Remove the fuel tank as described under *Fuel Tank Removal/Installation* in Chapter Seven.
4. Drain the fluid from the entire system as follows:
   a. Attach a hose to the bleed valve on the clutch slave cylinder (A, **Figure 67**).
   b. Place the loose end into a container and open the bleed valve. Operate the clutch lever until all fluid is pumped out of the system.
   c. Close the bleed valve and remove the hose.

WARNING
Dispose of this fluid—never reuse hydraulic fluid. Contaminated fluid can cause clutch failure.

5. Place a container under the lower flexible portion of the hose at the clutch slave cylinder to catch any remaining fluid. Remove the union bolt and sealing washers (B, **Figure 67**) securing the hose to the clutch slave cylinder.
6. Disconnect the flexible hose and let any remaining fluid drain out into the container.
7. Pull back the rubber boot (**Figure 52**).
8. Place a shop cloth under the union bolt to catch any spilled hydraulic fluid that will leak out. Remove the union bolt (A, **Figure 68**) securing the clutch hose to the clutch master cylinder and disconnect the clutch hose (B, **Figure 68**).
9. Remove all bands and brackets securing the hose assembly to the frame and remove the hose assembly from the frame.

CAUTION
After removing the hose assembly, wash any hydraulic fluid off of any painted or plated surface immediately, as it will destroy the finish.

10. Install the hose assembly, new sealing washers and union bolts in the reverse order of removal. Be sure to install new sealing washers in the correct position on each side of each union bolt.
11. Tighten all union bolts to torque specifications listed in **Table 2**.
12. Refill the clutch master cylinder with fresh hydraulic brake fluid clearly marked DOT 4 only. Bleed the clutch system as described in this chapter.
13. Install the fuel tank, seat and the left-hand lower section of the front fairing.

SLAVE CYLINDER

Removal and installation are covered in 2 different ways. The first procedure is for removing the slave cylinder from the crankcase intact when no service procedures are going to be performed. The second procedure is for when the slave cylinder is going to be disassembled, inspected and serviced. Follow the correct procedure for your specific needs.

Refer to **Figure 69** for both procedures.

Removal/Installation (Intact)

This procedure is for removal and installation of the slave cylinder with the clutch hose still at-

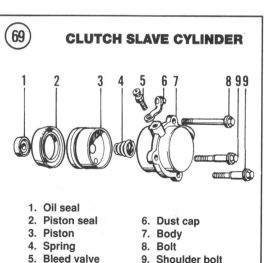

CLUTCH SLAVE CYLINDER
1. Oil seal
2. Piston seal
3. Piston
4. Spring
5. Bleed valve
6. Dust cap
7. Body
8. Bolt
9. Shoulder bolt

tached—not for the disassembly, inspection and service procedures.

1. Place a piece of wood between the clutch lever and the hand grip to hold the lever in the released position. Secure the piece of wood with a rubber band, tie wrap or tape. This will prevent the clutch lever from being applied accidentally after the clutch slave cylinder is removed from the crankcase.

NOTE
Do not operate the clutch lever after the slave cylinder is removed from the crankcase. If the clutch lever is applied it will force the piston out of the slave cylinder body and make installation difficult.

2. Remove the bolts (**Figure 70**) securing the clutch slave cylinder to the crankcase and withdraw the unit from the crankcase.
3. Tie the clutch slave cylinder up and out of the way.
4. Apply a light coat of high-temperature silicone grease (or hydraulic fluid) to the piston seal and the oil seal on the backside of the slave cylinder prior to installing the assembly.

NOTE
Inspect the piston seal and the oil seal. Replace if their condition is doubtful. If either seal is removed from the piston it must be replaced with a new seal.

5. Make sure the piston seal is still correctly seated in the groove in the piston. If not seated correctly, fluid will leak past the seal and render the clutch useless.

NOTE
Sometimes the piston will move out slightly from the slave cylinder body when the body is withdrawn from the crankcase during removal.

6. Withdraw the clutch lifter rod from the transmission mainshaft and use it to push the piston as far back in as possible into the slave cylinder body. Reinstall the clutch lifter rod into the transmission main shaft.
7. Install the slave cylinder onto the crankcase.
8. Make sure the lifter rod is inserted correctly into the receptacle in the slave cylinder piston.

NOTE
*After being positioned correctly into the crankcase, the slave cylinder assembly **may** stick out by about 3/8 in. from the mating surface of the crankcase. This is not a problem, as it is due to the pressure within the hydraulic system.*

9. Install the bolts securing the slave cylinder and gradually tighten the bolts in a crisscross pattern. Continue to tighten the bolts in this manner until the slave cylinder has bottomed out on the mating surface of the crankcase. Tighten the bolts securely.

Removal/Disassembly

This procedure is for a complete service procedure of removal, disassembly, inspection, assembly and installation of the slave cylinder.

1. Drain the hydraulic fluid from the entire system as follows:

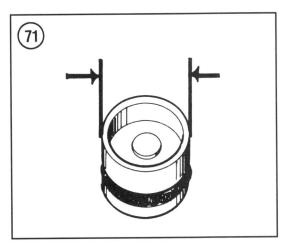

CLUTCH SYSTEM

a. Attach a hose to the bleed valve (A, **Figure 67**) on the clutch slave cylinder.
b. Place the loose end into a container and open the bleed valve.
c. Operate the clutch lever until all fluid is pumped out of the system.
d. Close the bleed valve and remove the hose.

WARNING
Dispose of this fluid—never reuse hydraulic fluid. Contaminated fluid can cause clutch failure.

2. Place a container under the lower flexible portion of the clutch hose at the clutch slave cylinder to catch any remaining fluid. Remove the union bolt and sealing washers (B, **Figure 67**) securing the hose to the clutch slave cylinder. Remove the hose and let any remaining fluid drain out into the container.
3. Remove the bolts (**Figure 70**) securing the clutch slave cylinder to the crankcase and withdraw the unit from the crankcase.

Inspection

1. To remove the piston, hold the slave cylinder body in your hand with the piston facing away from you. Place a clean shop cloth behind the piston. Carefully apply a *small* amount of compressed air in short spurts into the threaded hole where the union bolt was attached. The air pressure will force the piston out of the body.

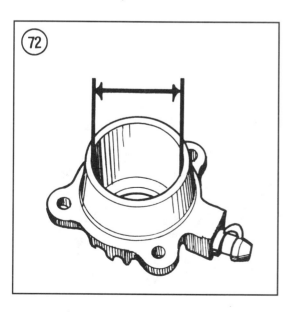

CAUTION
Be sure to catch the piston when it is pushed out of the body. Failure to do so will result in damage to the piston.

2. Remove the spring from the piston.
3. Check the spring for damage or sagging. Honda does not provide service limit dimensions for this spring. Replace the spring if its condition is doubtful.
4. Remove the oil seal and the piston seal from the piston; discard both seals.
5. Use a vernier caliper and measure the outside diameter of the piston as shown in **Figure 71**. Replace the piston if it is worn to the service limit listed in **Table 1**.
6. Use a vernier caliper and measure the inside diameter of the slave cylinder body as shown in **Figure 72**. Replace the body if it is worn to the service limit listed in **Table 1** or greater.

Assembly/Installation

1. Apply a light coat of high-temperature silicone grease (or hydraulic fluid) to the new piston seal and the oil seal prior to installation.
2. Install both seals onto the piston. Make sure the piston seal is correctly seated in the groove in the piston. If not seated correctly, fluid will leak past the seal and render the clutch useless.

NOTE
A new piston seal and oil seal must be installed every time the slave cylinder is removed.

3. Withdraw the clutch lifter rod from the transmission mainshaft and use it to push the piston all the way into the slave cylinder body. Reinstall the clutch lifter rod.
4. Install the slave cylinder onto the crankcase.
5. Make sure the lifter rod is inserted correctly into the receptacle in the slave cylinder piston.
6. Install the bolts and tighten in a crisscross pattern in 2-3 stages. Tighten the bolts securely.
7. Install the union bolt and sealing washers to the slave cylinder. Tighten the union bolts to the torque specification listed in **Table 2**.
8. Clean the top of the clutch master cylinder of all dirt and foreign matter. Remove the screws securing the top cover (**Figure 73**) and remove the cover,

diaphragm plate and the diaphragm. Fill the reservoir almost to the top lip; insert the diaphragm and install the cover loosely.

9. Bleed the clutch as described in this chapter.

BLEEDING THE CLUTCH SYSTEM

This procedure is not necessary unless the clutch feel spongy, there has been a leak in the system, a component has been replaced or the hydraulic fluid has been replaced.

CAUTION
Throughout the text reference is made to hydraulic fluid. Hydraulic fluid is the same as DOT 4 brake fluid. Use only DOT 4 fluid; **do not use other fluids** *as they are not compatible. Do not intermix silicone based (DOT 5) brake fluid as it can cause clutch component damage leading to clutch system failure.*

1. Remove the dust cap from the bleed valve on the clutch slave cylinder (A, **Figure 67**). Connect a length of clear tubing to the bleed valve on the clutch slave cylinder.
2. Place the other end of the tube into a clean container. Fill the container with enough fresh hydraulic fluid to keep the end submerged. The tube should be long enough so that a loop can be made higher than the bleed valve to prevent air from being drawn into the clutch slave cylinder during bleeding.

CAUTION
Cover the clutch slave cylinder and lower frame with a heavy cloth or plastic tarp to protect them from accidental fluid spilling. Wash any fluid off of any painted or plated surface immediately, as it will destroy the finish. Use soapy water and rinse completely.

3. Clean the top of the clutch master cylinder of all dirt and foreign matter. Remove the screws securing the top cover (**Figure 73**) and remove the cover, diaphragm plate and the diaphragm. Fill the reservoir almost to the top lip; insert the diaphragm and install the cap loosely.

CAUTION
Failure to install the diaphragm on the master cylinder will allow fluid to spurt out when the clutch lever is applied.

CAUTION
Use hydraulic fluid clearly marked DOT 4 only. Others may vaporize and cause clutch failure. Always use the same brand name; do not intermix as many brands are not compatible.

4. Slowly apply the clutch lever several times. Hold the lever in the applied position.
5. Open the bleed valve about one-half turn. Allow the lever to travel to its limit. When this limit is reached, tighten the bleed valve.
6. Occasionally tap the slave cylinder to loosen any trapped air bubbles that won't come up the normal way. As the fluid enters the system, the level will drop in the reservoir. Maintain the level at the top of the reservoir to prevent air from being drawn into the system.
7. Repeat Step 6 until the fluid emerging from the hose is completely free of bubbles.

NOTE
Do not allow the reservoir to empty during the bleeding operation or air will enter the system. If this occurs, the entire procedure must be repeated.

8. Hold the lever in, tighten the bleed valve, remove the bleed tube and install the bleed valve dust cap.
9. If necessary, add fluid to correct the level in the reservoir. It should be to the upper level line.
10. Install the reservoir diaphragm, diaphragm plate, cover and screws. Tighten the screws securely.

NOTE
The clutch lever will not have the same "feel" as the brake lever when the brake system has been bled properly. The clutch lever will still feel a little "soft"

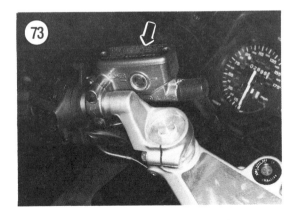

CLUTCH SYSTEM

compared to the brake lever after the bleeding procedure has been completed.

11. Test the feel of the clutch lever. It should be firm and should offer the same resistance each time it's operated. If it feels spongy, it is likely that there still is air in the system and it must be bled again. When all air has been bled from the system and the fluid level is correct in the reservoir, double-check for leaks and tighten all the fittings and connections.

12. Test ride the bike to make sure the clutch release system is operating correctly.

Table 1 CLUTCH SPECIFICATIONS

Item	Standard	Wear limit
Friction disc thickness (A and B)	2.92-3.08 mm (0.115-0.121 in.)	2.5 mm (0.10 in.)
Clutch plate warpage	–	0.30 mm (0.012 in.)
Clutch spring free length	44.4 mm (1.75 in.)	41.2 mm (1.62 in.)
Clutch slave cylinder		
Piston OD	35.650-35.675 mm (1.4035-1.4045 in.)	35.63 mm (1.403 in.)
Cylinder bore ID	35.700-35.762 mm (1.4055-1.4079 in.)	35.17 mm (1.409 in.)
Clutch master cylinder		
Piston OD	13.957-13.984 mm (0.5495-0.5506 in.)	13.94 mm (0.549 in.)
Cylinder bore ID	14.000-14.043 mm (0.5512-0.5524 in.)	14.06 mm (0.553 in.)
Starter clutch driven gear OD	47.175-47.200 mm (1.8573-1.8583 in.)	47.16 mm (1.857 in.)

Table 2 CLUTCH TIGHTENING TORQUES

Item	N•m	Ft.-lb.
Clutch locknut	80-100	58-72
Clutch union bolt	25-35	18-25
Oil pump driven gear bolt	15-20	11-14

CHAPTER SIX

GEARSHIFT MECHANISM AND TRANSMISSION

This chapter contains repair and service information for the external and internal shift mechanism and the 5-speed transmission.

To gain access to the internal shift mechanism and the transmission shafts, it is necessary to remove the engine from the frame and separate the crankcase from the cylinder block. Once the crankcase is separated, removal of both transmission shafts is a simple task of pulling the assemblies up and out of the cylinder block.

Tables 1-3 are located at the end of this chapter.

ENGINE DRIVE SPROCKET AND COVER

The engine drive sprocket is on the left-hand end of the transmission countershaft, behind the sprocket cover. The drive chain is endless as it has no master link. To remove the drive chain, remove the engine sprocket from the countershaft and remove the swing arm; see *Rear Swing Arm Removal/Installation* in Chapter Eleven.

Removal/Installation

1. Remove the lower section and the middle sections of the front fairing as described under *Front Fairing Removal/Installation* in Chapter Thirteen.
2. Place wood block(s) under each side of the frame to support the bike securely with the rear wheel off the ground.
3. On 1990-on models, remove the bolts securing the speedometer drive unit (A, **Figure 1**), or speed

GEARSHIFT MECHANISM AND TRANSMISSION

sensor unit (**Figure 2**) to the drive sprocket cover. Move the unit out of the way, it is not necessary to detach the cable or electrical wires from the unit.

4. Remove the clutch slave cylinder (B, **Figure 1**) as described under *Clutch Slave Cylinder Removal/Installation (Intact)* in Chapter Five. Move the slave cylinder out of the way.

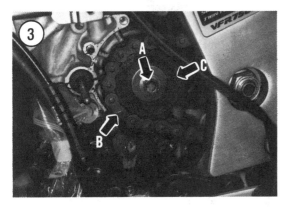

5. Remove the bolts securing the drive sprocket cover (C, **Figure 1**) and remove the cover.
6. Have an assistant apply the rear brake.
7. Loosen then remove the drive sprocket bolt and washer (A, **Figure 3**).
8. To provide slack in the drive chain, refer to *Drive Chain Adjustment* in Chapter Three. Loosen the rear wheel and push the rear wheel forward to achieve slack in the drive chain.
9. Remove the drive chain (B, **Figure 3**) and the drive sprocket (C, **Figure 3**) off the transmission shaft as an assembly.
10. Install by reversing these removal steps while noting the following:
    a. Position the drive chain on the sprocket, then slide the sprocket along with the drive chain onto the countershaft.
    b. Install the sprocket washer and bolt.
    c. Tighten the sprocket bolt to the torque specification listed in **Table 1**.
    d. On 1990-on models, when installing the speedometer (or speed sensor) unit, align the hex joint on the unit with the sprocket bolt hex head (A, **Figure 3**).
    e. Adjust the drive chain. See *Drive Chain Adjustment* in Chapter Three.

Inspection

Inspect the driven sprocket teeth (**Figure 4**). If the teeth are visibly worn or undercut, replace both the drive and driven sprockets along with the drive

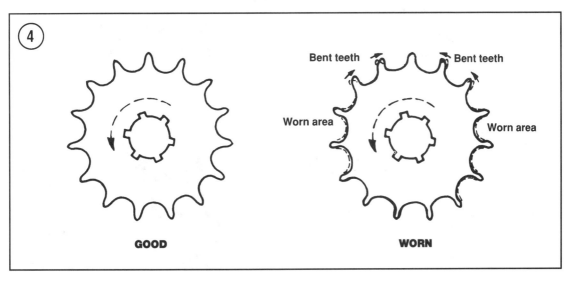

CHAPTER SIX

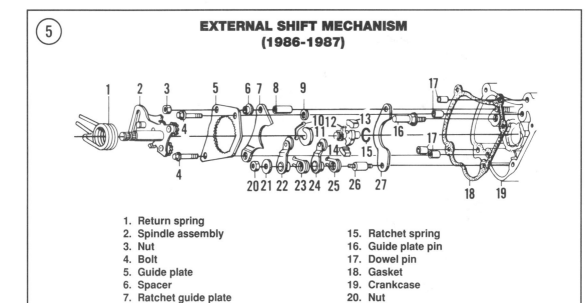

EXTERNAL SHIFT MECHANISM (1986-1987)

1. Return spring
2. Spindle assembly
3. Nut
4. Bolt
5. Guide plate
6. Spacer
7. Ratchet guide plate
8. Collar
9. Washer
10. Ratchet spring
11. Stopper washer
12. Drum shifter
13. Pawl
14. Pawl
15. Ratchet spring
16. Guide plate pin
17. Dowel pin
18. Gasket
19. Crankcase
20. Nut
21. Washer
22. Gearshift drum stopper
23. Spring
24. Neutral stopper
25. Spring
26. Stud bolt
27. Shift drum set plate

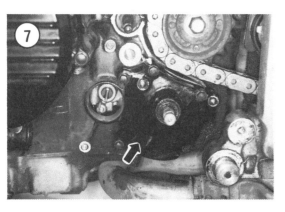

GEARSHIFT MECHANISM AND TRANSMISSION

chain. Never replace only one sprocket or the drive chain as a separate item; worn parts will cause rapid wear of the new component.

EXTERNAL SHIFT MECHANISM

The external shift mechanism is located on the left side of the engine and can be removed with the engine in the frame.

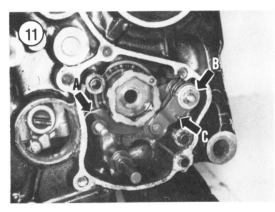

1986-1987 Models

Refer to **Figure 5** for this procedure.

Removal

> *NOTE*
> *Some steps in this procedure are shown with the engine removed from the frame for clarity. The gearshift linkage assembly can be removed with the engine in the frame.*

1. Remove the lower sections of the front fairing as described under *Front Fairing Removal/Installation* in Chapter Thirteen.
2. Place the bike on the centerstand (models so equipped) or sidestand.
3. Drain the engine oil as described under *Engine Oil and Filter Change* in Chapter Three.
4. Remove the engine drive sprocket cover as described in this chapter.
5. Remove the bolt (A, **Figure 6**) securing the gearshift arm to the gearshift spindle assembly. Move the gearshift arm (B, **Figure 6**) out of the way.
6. Remove the water pump (C, **Figure 6**) as described under *Water Pump Removal/Installation* in Chapter Nine.
7. Remove the bolts securing the gearshift linkage cover (**Figure 7**) and remove the cover and gasket. Don't lose the locating dowels.
8. Remove the 2 bolts (A, **Figure 8**) and one nut (B, **Figure 8**) securing the guide plate.
9. Remove the gearshift return spring (**Figure 9**).
10. Remove the spindle assembly, guide plate and ratchet guide plate as an assembly.
11. Remove the gearshift drum shifter assembly (A, **Figure 10**).
12. Remove the collar (A, **Figure 11**) from the crankcase stud.
13. Remove the nut and washer (B, **Figure 11**) and remove the gearshift drum stopper and neutral stopper arms and springs (C, **Figure 11**).

> *NOTE*
> *If the shift drum is going to be removed; perform Step 14, otherwise leave those parts in place.*

14. If the shift drum is going to be removed, remove the stud bolt (A, **Figure 12**) and shift drum set plate (B, **Figure 12**) as follows:

a. Screw 2 nuts (**Figure 13**) onto the stud bolt until they bottom out on the shoulder.
b. Using 2 wrenches (**Figure 14**) tighten the 2 nuts *against each other*. They must be tight as the outer nut will be used to unscrew the stud bolt.
c. Using the outer nut, unscrew the stud bolt (A, **Figure 12**) from the crankcase. Leave the 2 nuts attached to the stud bolt as they will be used during installation.
d. Remove the shift drum set plate (B, **Figure 12**).

Inspection

1. Inspect the gearshift spindle assembly return spring (**Figure 15**). If broken or weak it must be replaced.
2. Inspect the gearshift drum stopper arm and spring (A, **Figure 16**). If broken or weak, remove and replace the spring. Make sure the roller spins freely.
3. Inspect the neutral stopper arm and spring (B, **Figure 16**). If broken or weak, remove and replace the spring. Make sure the roller spins freely.
4. Inspect the gearshift spindle assembly shaft (**Figure 17**) for bending, wear or other damage; replace if necessary.
5. Inspect the gearshift spindle gears (**Figure 18**) for bending, wear or other damage; replace as an assembly if necessary.
6. Make sure the gearshift spindle assembly rotates freely within the guide plate (**Figure 19**). Replace the defective portion if necessary.
7. Inspect the gearshift spindle guide plate (**Figure 20**) for bending, wear or other damage; replace if necessary.
8. Inspect the gearshift drum shifter and pawls (**Figure 21**).

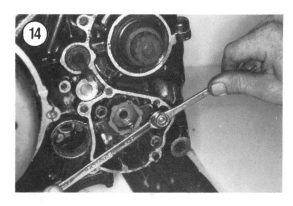

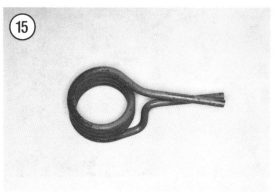

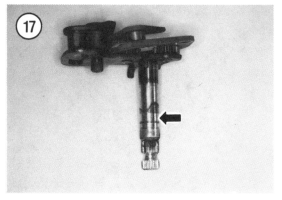

GEARSHIFT MECHANISM AND TRANSMISSION

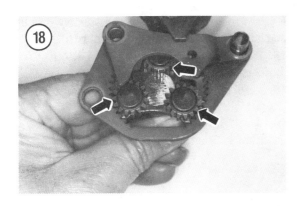

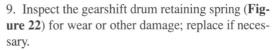

9. Inspect the gearshift drum retaining spring (**Figure 22**) for wear or other damage; replace if necessary.

10. Inspect the needle bearing dust seal (**Figure 23**) in the cover for wear or deterioration, replace if necessary.

11. Inspect the gearshift shaft needle bearing (**Figure 24**) in the cover. Rotate it with your fingers, it should rotate freely. If damaged, replace the cover as the bearing cannot be replaced.

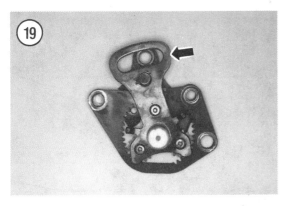

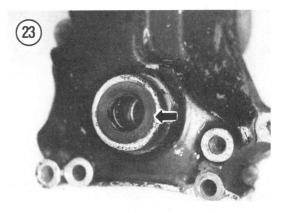

Installation

1. If removed, install the shift drum set plate (B, **Figure 12**), and the stud bolt (A, **Figure 12**). Tighten the stud bolt securely. Using 2 wrenches (**Figure 14**) loosen the outer nut (**Figure 13**) from the inner nut, then remove both nuts from the stud bolt.

2. Correctly position the springs onto the gearshift drum stopper and neutral stopper arms.

3. Install the neutral stopper arm and spring assembly.

4. Install the gearshift drum stopper and spring assembly (C, **Figure 11**), then install the washer and nut (B, **Figure 11**). Tighten the nut securely.

5. Install the collar (A, **Figure 11**) onto the crankcase stud.

6. Install the drum shifter (A, **Figure 10**) into shift drum receptacle. Rotate the drum shifter and align the punch mark on the ratchet pawl with the groove to the right of the punch mark on the shift drum (B, **Figure 10**).

7. Insert a 3.0 mm (0.12 in.) pin or drill bit (A, **Figure 25**) into the groove and lock the shift drum in place.

8. If removed, install the locating dowels (B, **Figure 25**) into the crankcase.

9. Install the collar (C, **Figure 25**) onto the crankcase stud.

10. Assemble the spindle assembly, guide plate and ratchet guide plate and install as an assembly (A, **Figure 26**).

11. Remove the 3.0 mm (0.12 in.) pin or drill bit (B, **Figure 26**).

12. Install the gearshift return spring (A, **Figure 27**). Make sure it is properly indexed onto the pin (B, **Figure 27**) on the spindle assembly.

13. Install the 2 bolts (A, **Figure 8**) securing the guide plate. Apply red Loctite (No. 271) to the threads on the stud prior to installing the nut. Install the nut (B, **Figure 8**) and tighten the bolts and nut securely.

14. Make sure the dowels are still in place and install a new gasket.

15. Install the gearshift linkage cover (**Figure 7**) and bolts and tighten the bolts securely.

16. Install the water pump (C, **Figure 6**) as described in Chapter Nine.

17. Align the punch marks on the gearshift arm and the gearshift spindle and install the gearshift arm (B, **Figure 6**) onto the gearshift spindle assembly. Install and tighten the clamping bolt (A, **Figure 6**).

18. Install the drive sprocket cover as described in this chapter.

19. Refill the engine oil and coolant as described in Chapter Three.

20. Install the lower sections of the front fairing as described in Chapter Thirteen.

1990 and Later Models

Refer to **Figure 28** for this procedure.

GEARSHIFT MECHANISM AND TRANSMISSION

Removal

1. Remove the lower sections of the front fairing as described under *Front Fairing Removal/Installation* in Chapter Thirteen.

2. Place the bike on the centerstand (models so equipped) or place wood blocks under the engine to support the bike securely.

3. Drain the engine oil as described under *Engine Oil and Filter Change* in Chapter Three.

4. Remove the drive sprocket cover as described in this chapter.

5. Remove the water pump as described under *Water Pump Cover Removal/Installation* in Chapter Nine.

6. Disconnect the electrical connector to the sidestand switch.

7. Remove the sidestand assembly as described in Chapter Thirteen.

8. Remove the bolt (A, **Figure 29**) securing the gearshift arm to the gearshift spindle assembly. Move the gearshift arm (B, **Figure 29**) out of the way.

NOTE
This procedure is shown with the engine removed from the frame for clarity. The gearshift linkage assembly can be removed with the engine in the frame.

9. Remove the bolts (**Figure 30**) securing the gearshift linkage cover and remove the cover and gasket. Don't lose the locating dowels.

10. Remove the spindle assembly (A, **Figure 31**).

11. Remove the collar (A, **Figure 32**) from the drum shifter.

NOTE
When the drum shifter is removed from the receptacle in the gearshift drum the pawls, plungers and collars may fall out. Be prepared to catch them to avoid losing any small parts.

12. Remove the bolts securing the guide plate (B, **Figure 32**) and remove the guide plate and drum shifter (C, **Figure 32**) as an assembly.

13. Remove the gearshift drum stopper arm spring, collar and stopper arm.

14. Remove both long dowel pins.

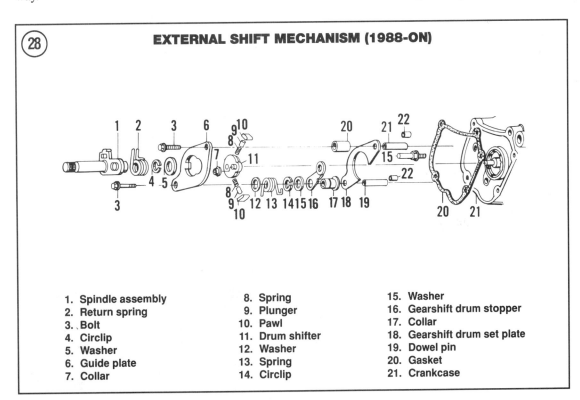

EXTERNAL SHIFT MECHANISM (1988-ON)

1. Spindle assembly
2. Return spring
3. Bolt
4. Circlip
5. Washer
6. Guide plate
7. Collar
8. Spring
9. Plunger
10. Pawl
11. Drum shifter
12. Washer
13. Spring
14. Circlip
15. Washer
16. Gearshift drum stopper
17. Collar
18. Gearshift drum set plate
19. Dowel pin
20. Gasket
21. Crankcase

NOTE
If the shift drum is going to be removed; perform Step 15, otherwise leave those parts in place.

15. If the shift drum is going to be removed, unscrew the drum pin from the shift drum and remove the shift drum center. Remove the locating dowel from the end of the shift drum.

Inspection

1. Inspect the return spring on the gearshift spindle assembly. If broken or weak it must be replaced.
2. Inspect the gearshift spindle assembly shaft for bending, wear or other damage; replace if necessary.
3. Inspect the gearshift drum shifter and the pawls, plungers and springs for wear.
4. Inspect the dust seal for wear or deterioration, replace if necessary.
5. Inspect the needle bearing in the cover. Rotate it with your fingers, it should rotate freely. If damaged, replace the cover as the bearing cannot be replaced.

Installation

1. If the shift drum center was removed, perform the following:
   a. Install the locating dowel into the end of the shift drum.
   b. Align the groove in the backside of the shift drum center with the locating pin and install the shift drum center.
   c. Push it on until it bottoms out.
   d. Apply red Loctite (No. 271) to the threads of the drum pin prior to installation and install the drum pin. Tighten the pin securely.
2. Install both long dowel pins and push them in until they bottom out.
3. Install the gearshift drum stopper arm spring, collar and stopper arm.
4. Install both sets of pawls, plungers and collars into the drum shifter. Install the drum shifter into the guide plate.
5. Apply red Loctite (No. 271) to the threads of the guide plate bolts prior to installation and install the guide plate and drum shifter assembly into the end of the shift drum center. Tighten the bolts securely.
6. Install the collar (A, **Figure 32**) onto the drum shifter.

7. Install the spindle assembly (A, **Figure 31**) and make sure the spindle is meshed properly with the collar (B, **Figure 32**).
8. Make sure the locating dowels are in place and install a new gasket.
9. Install the gearshift linkage cover and bolts (**Figure 30**) and tighten the bolts securely.
10. Align the punch marks on the gearshift arm and the gearshift spindle and install the gearshift arm onto the gearshift spindle assembly. Install and tighten the clamping bolt securely.
11. Install the side stand assembly as described in Chapter Thirteen.
12. Connect the electrical connector to the sidestand switch.
13. Install the water pump as described in Chapter Nine.
14. Install the drive sprocket cover as described in this chapter.
15. Refill the engine oil and coolant as described in Chapter Three.
16. Install the lower sections of the front fairing as described in Chapter Thirteen.

GEARSHIFT MECHANISM AND TRANSMISSION

TRANSMISSION

The transmission is located within the engine cylinder block. To gain access to the transmission and internal shift mechanism it is necessary to remove the engine from the frame and separate the crankcase from the cylinder block. Once the crankcase is separated, removal of both transmission shafts is a simple task of pulling the assemblies up and out of the cylinder block.

Pay particular attention to the location of spacers, washers and bearings during disassembly. If disassembling a used, well run-in engine for the first time by yourself, pay particular attention to any additional shims that may have been added by a previous owner. The shims may have been added to take up the tolerance of worn components. If all of the existing components are going to be reinstalled, these shims must be reinstalled in the same position as the shims have developed a wear pattern. If new parts are going to be installed these shims may be eliminated. This is something you will have to determine upon reassembly.

Specifications for the transmission components are listed in **Table 2**.

TRANSMISSION AND INTERNAL SHIFT OPERATION

Transmission

The transmission has 6 pairs of constantly meshed gears on the mainshaft and countershaft. Each pair of meshed gears gives one gear ratio. In each pair, one of the gears is locked to its shaft and always turns with it. The other gear is not locked to its shaft and can spin freely on it. Next to each free spinning gear is a third gear which is splined to the same shaft, always turning with it. This third gear can slide from side to side along the shaft splines. The side of the sliding gear and the free spinning gear have mating "dogs" and "slots." When the sliding gear moves up against the free spinning gear, the 2 gears are locked together via the "dogs" and "slots," locking the free spinning gear to its shaft. Since both meshed mainshaft and countershaft gears are now locked together on their shafts, power is transmitted to the drive sprocket at that gear ratio.

Shift Drum and Shift Forks

Each sliding transmission gear has a deep groove machined around its outside. The curved shift fork fingers ride in this groove, controlling the side-to-side sliding of the gear on its shaft. This movement determines the selection of the different gear ratios. Each shift fork slides back and forth on the shift fork shaft. The shift fork has a peg that rides in the machined groove in the shift drum. When the external shift mechanism rotates the shift drum, the zig-zag grooves in the shift drum move the shift forks thus sliding the gears back and forth. This action shifts the transmission from one gear to another.

TRANSMISSION

Removal/Installation

1. Disassemble the crankcase as described under *Cylinder Block and Crankcase Disassembly* in Chapter Four.
2. Remove the countershaft assembly (A, **Figure 33**) and main shaft assembly (B, **Figure 33**) from the upper crankcase.
3. Inspect the transmission shaft assemblies as described under *Preliminary Inspection* in this chapter.

NOTE
Prior to installation, coat all bearing surfaces with assembly oil.

4. If removed, install the countershaft bearing set ring (A, **Figure 34**) and bearing locating dowel (B, **Figure 34**) into the cylinder block.

5. Make sure the oil control orifice is in place in each side of the crankcase prior to installing the shaft assemblies. Refer to **Figure 35** and **Figure 36**.

6. Install the mainshaft assembly (**Figure 37**) into the cylinder block.

7. On 1986-1989 models, make sure the oil control orifice plate (**Figure 38**) is still in place.

8. Install the countershaft assembly (A, **Figure 39**) into the cylinder block. Make sure the large bearing is properly indexed into the set ring (**Figure 40**) and the small bearing (B, **Figure 39**) is properly indexed into the locating dowel.

9. After both transmission shaft assemblies are installed, perform the following:
   a. Hold onto the mainshaft (B, **Figure 33**) and rotate the countershaft (A, **Figure 33**). The countershaft should rotate freely. If it does not, shift the gear that is engaged so that both shafts are in NEUTRAL.
   b. Rotate both shaft assemblies by hand. Make sure there is no binding. This is the time to find that something may be installed incorrectly—not after the crankcase is completely assembled.

10. Reassemble the crankcase as described in Chapter Four.

Preliminary Inspection

After the transmission shaft assemblies have been removed from the crankcase, clean and inspect the

GEARSHIFT MECHANISM AND TRANSMISSION

assemblies prior to disassembling them. Hold the assembled shafts together so you won't lose any small parts from either end and place each assembled shaft into a large can or plastic bucket and thoroughly clean with a petroleum based solvent such as kerosene and a stiff brush. Dry with compressed air or let it sit on rags to drip dry. Repeat for the other shaft assembly.

1. After they have been cleaned, visually inspect the components of the assemblies for excessive wear. Any burrs, pitting or roughness on the teeth of a gear will cause wear on the mating gear. Minor roughness can be cleaned up with an oilstone but there's little point in attempting to remove deep scars.

NOTE
Defective gears should be replaced. It's a good idea to replace the mating gear on the other shaft even though it may not show as much wear or damage.

2. Carefully check the engagement dogs. If any are chipped, worn, rounded or missing, the affected gear must be replaced.

3. Rotate the transmission bearings on both shafts by hand. Refer to **Figure 41** and **Figure 42**. Check for looseness, noise and radial play. Any bearing that is suspect should be replaced as described in this chapter.

NOTE
If the transmission shafts were not blown dry with compressed air, make sure the oil applied in Step 4 totally saturates all 4 bearings. This will help displace any residual solvent residue.

4. If the transmission shafts are satisfactory and are not going to be disassembled, apply assembly oil or

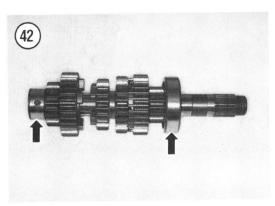

engine oil to all components and reinstall them in the crankcase as described in this chapter.

NOTE
If disassembling a used, well run-in (high mileage) transmission for the first time by yourself, pay particular attention to any additional shims that may have been added by a previous owner. These may have been added to take up the tolerance of worn components and must be reinstalled in the same position since the shims have developed a wear pattern. If new parts are going to be installed these shims may be eliminated. This is something you will have to determine upon reassembly.

Transmission Service Notes

1. A divided container, such as a restaurant type egg carton can be used to help maintain correct alignment and positioning of the parts. As you remove a part from the shaft set it in one of the depressions in the same position from which it was removed. Refer to **Figure 43** for the mainshaft and **Figure 44** for the

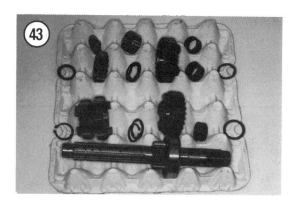

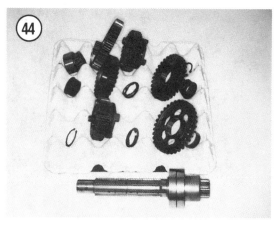

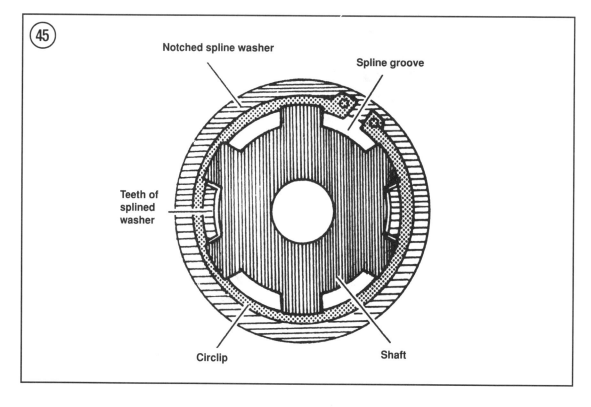

GEARSHIFT MECHANISM AND TRANSMISSION

countershaft. This is an easy way to remember the correct relationship of all parts.

2. The circlips are a tight fit on the transmission shafts. It is recommended to replace all circlips during reassembly.

3. When installing circlips, align the circlip opening with a spline groove as shown in **Figure 45** *not* on a spline.

4. Circlips and flat washers will have one sharp edge and one rounded edge (**Figure 46**). Install the circlips as described under shaft assembly.

5. Circlips will turn and fold over, making removal and installation difficult. To ease replacement, open the circlips with a pair of circlip pliers while at the same time holding the back of the circlip with a pair of pliers and remove them. Repeat for installation.

Mainshaft Disassembly/Inspection

Refer to the following illustrations for this procedure:

a. **Figure 47**: 1986-1989 models.

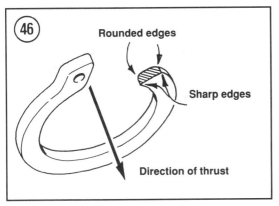

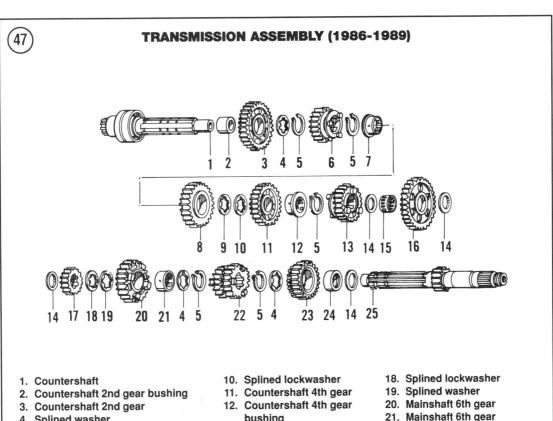

TRANSMISSION ASSEMBLY (1986-1989)

1. Countershaft
2. Countershaft 2nd gear bushing
3. Countershaft 2nd gear
4. Splined washer
5. Circlip
6. Countershaft 6th gear
7. Countershaft 3rd gear bushing
8. Countershaft 3rd gear
9. Splined washer
10. Splined lockwasher
11. Countershaft 4th gear
12. Countershaft 4th gear bushing
13. Countershaft 5th gear
14. Washer
15. Needle bearing
16. Countershaft 1st gear
17. Mainshaft 2nd gear
18. Splined lockwasher
19. Splined washer
20. Mainshaft 6th gear
21. Mainshaft 6th gear
22. Mainshaft 3rd/4th combination gear
23. Mainshaft 5th gear
24. Mainshaft 5th gear bushing
25. Mainshaft/1st gear

b. **Figure 48**: 1990-on models.

NOTE
This procedure is shown on a 1986-1989 model mainshaft assembly. Slight differences occur between this shaft assembly and the mainshaft used on the 1990-on models. The splined lockwashers and splined washers used to lock gears in place on the shaft have a slightly different shape, but they are removed and installed in the same manner on all models. Where differences occur between the two different mainshaft assemblies, they are identified.

1. Clean the shaft as described under *Preliminary Inspection* in this chapter.

NOTE
A helpful "tool" that should be used for transmission disassembly is a large egg flat (the type restaurants get their eggs in). See ***Figure 43****. As you remove a part from the shaft, set it in one of the depressions in the same position from which it was removed. This is an easy way to*

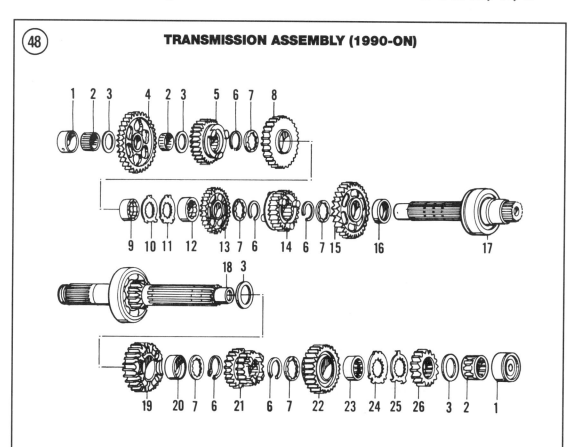

TRANSMISSION ASSEMBLY (1990-ON)

1. Needle bearing outer race
2. Needle bearing
3. Washer
4. Countershaft 1st gear
5. Countershaft 5th gear
6. Circlip
7. Splined washer
8. Countershaft 4th gear
9. Countershaft 4th gear bushing
10. Splined lockwasher
11. Splined washer
12. Countershaft 3rd gear bushing
13. Countershaft 3rd gear
14. Countershaft 6th gear
15. Countershaft 2nd gear
16. Countershaft 2nd gear bushing
17. Countershaft
18. Mainshaft/1st gear
19. Mainshaft 5th gear
20. Mainshaft 5th gear bushing
21. Mainshaft 3rd/4th combination gear
22. Mainshaft 6th gear
23. Mainshaft 6th gear bushing
24. Splined washer
25. Splined lockwasher
26. Mainshaft 2nd gear

GEARSHIFT MECHANISM AND TRANSMISSION

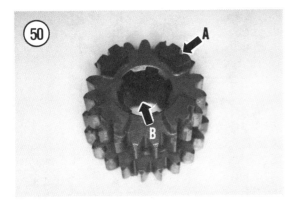

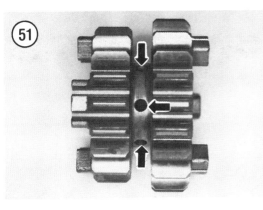

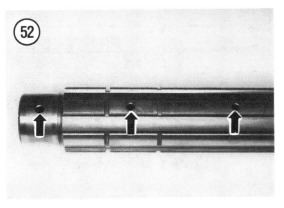

remember the correct relationship of all parts.

2. ON 1986-1989 models, remove the oil control orifice plate.

3. Slide off the bearing outer race, needle bearing and thrust washer.

4. Slide off the 2nd gear.

5. Slide off the splined lockwasher.

6. Rotate the splined washer in either direction to disengage the tangs from the grooves on the transmission shaft. Slide off the splined washer.

7. Slide off the 6th gear and the 6th gear bushing.

8. Slide off the splinded washer.

9. Remove the circlip and slide off the 3rd/4th combination gear.

10. Remove the circlip and splined washer.

11. Slide off the 5th gear and the 5th gear bushing.

12. Slide off the thrust washer.

13. If necessary, remove the ball bearing from the shaft.

NOTE
The 1st gear is part of the mainshaft. If the gear is defective, the shaft must be replaced.

14. Make sure that all gears slide smoothly on the main shaft splines.

15. Check each gear for excessive wear, burrs, pitting or chipped or missing teeth (**Figure 49**). Make sure the lugs (A, **Figure 50**) are in good condition.

16. Make sure the gear oil control holes (**Figure 51**) and bushing oil control holes are clear. Clean out with a piece of wire then rinse with solvent and blow out with compressed air.

17. On gears so equipped, inspect the inner splines (B, **Figure 50**) for burrs or nicks that would allow the gear to hang up on the shaft. Clean up if necessary.

18. Make sure the shaft oil control holes (**Figure 52**) are clear. Clean out with a piece of wire then rinse with solvent and blow out with compressed air.

19. Check the needle bearing (**Figure 53**). Make sure it rotates smoothly with no signs of wear or damage. Replace if necessary.

20. Check the shaft ball bearing (**Figure 54**). Make sure it rotates smoothly with no signs of wear or damage. Replace if necessary.

21. Measure the inside diameter (A, **Figure 55**) of the 5th and the 6th gears. Compare with the dimensions listed in **Table 1**.

22. Measure the inside diameter (B, **Figure 55**) and the outside diameter (C, **Figure 55**) of the 5th and the 6th gear bushings. Compare with the dimensions listed in **Table 1**.

23. Measure the outside diameter of the shaft (**Figure 56**) at the location of the 5th (A, **Figure 57**) and 6th gear bushings (B, **Figure 57**). Compare with the dimension listed in **Table 1**.

Mainshaft Assembly

NOTE
*It is a good idea to replace the circlips every time the transmission is disassembled to ensure proper gear alignment. Do **not** expand the circlip more than necessary to slide it over the shaft.*

1. Slide on the thrust washer (A, **Figure 58**).
2. Slide on the 5th gear bushing (B, **Figure 58**).
3. Position the 5th gear with the dog receptacle side going on last and slide on the 5th gear (**Figure 59**).

4. Slide on the splined washer (A, **Figure 60**) and circlip (B, **Figure 60**) with the sharp edge facing out. Make sure the circlip (**Figure 61**) is correctly seated in the mainshaft groove.

5. Position the 3rd/4th combination gear with the larger diameter 4th gear (**Figure 62**) going on first. Slide on the 3rd/4th combination gear (**Figure 63**).

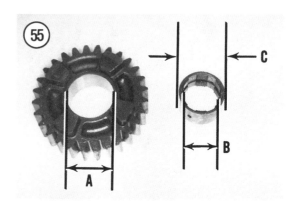

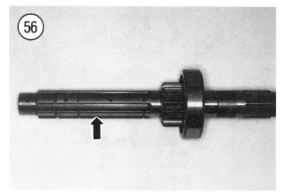

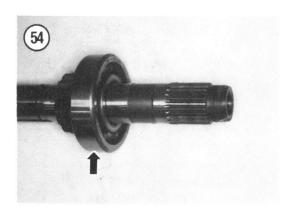

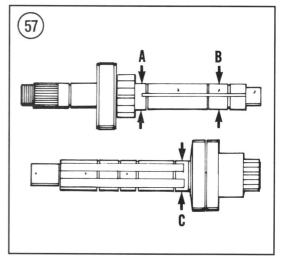

GEARSHIFT MECHANISM AND TRANSMISSION

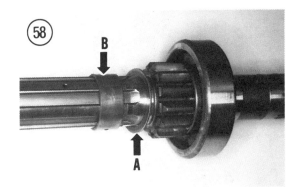

6. Install the circlip (**Figure 64**) with the sharp edge facing in. Make sure the circlip is correctly seated in the mainshaft groove.

7. Slide on the splined washer (**Figure 65**).

8. Align the oil hole in the 6th gear bushing with the oil hole in the mainshaft (A, **Figure 66**). This alignment is necessary for proper oil flow. Slide on the 6th gear bushing (B, **Figure 66**).

9. Position the 6th gear with the shift dog side going on first and slide on the 6th gear (**Figure 67**).

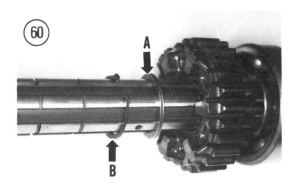

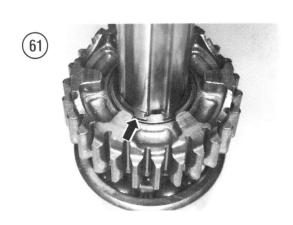

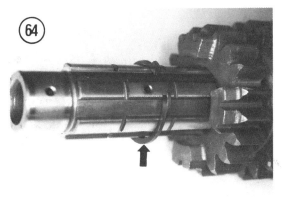

10. Slide on the splined washer (**Figure 68**). Rotate the splined washer in either direction to engage the tangs from the grooves on the transmission shaft (**Figure 69**).

11. Slide on the splined lockwasher (**Figure 70**) so the tangs go into the open areas of the splined washer and lock the washer in place (**Figure 71**).

12. Slide on the 2nd gear (**Figure 72**) and install the thrust washer (**Figure 73**).

13. Install the needle bearing (**Figure 74**) and outer race (**Figure 75**).

GEARSHIFT MECHANISM AND TRANSMISSION

14. On 1986-1989 models, install the oil control orifice plate (**Figure 76**).

15. After assembly is complete, refer to **Figure 77** for correct placement of all gears. Make sure all circlips are seated correctly in the main shaft grooves.

16. Make sure each gear engages properly with the adjoining gears where applicable.

Countershaft
Disassembly/Inspection

Refer to the following illustrations for this procedure:
   a. **Figure 47**: 1986-1989 models.
   b. **Figure 48**: 1990-on models.

NOTE
This procedure is shown on a 1986-1989 model countershaft assembly. Slight differences occur between this shaft assembly and the countershaft used on the 1990-on models. The splined lockwashers and splined washers used to lock gears in place on the

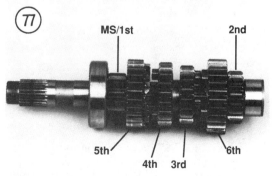

shaft have a slightly different shape, but they are removed and installed in the same manner on all models. Where differences occur between the two different countershaft assemblies, they are identified.

1. Clean the shaft as described under *Preliminary Inspection* in this chapter.

NOTE
A helpful "tool" that should be used for transmission disassembly is a large egg flat (the type restaurants get their eggs in). See **Figure 44**. *As you remove a part from the shaft, set it in one of the depressions in the same position from which it was removed. This is an easy way to remember the correct relationship of all parts.*

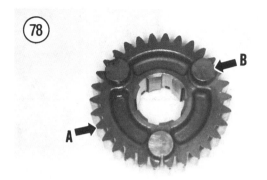

2. Slide off the bearing outer race, needle bearing and thrust washer.
3. Slide off the 1st gear and the 1st gear needle bearing.
4. Slide off the thrust washer and 5th gear.
5. Remove the circlip.
6A. On 1986-1989 models, slide off the 4th gear and the 4th gear bushing.
6B. On 1990-on models, slide off the splined washer, 4th gear and the 4th gear bushing.
7. Slide off the splinded lockwasher.
8. Rotate the splined washer in either direction to disengage the tangs from the grooves on the transmission shaft. Slide off the splined washer.
9. Slide off the 3rd gear and the 3rd gear bushing.
10. On 1990-on models, slide off the splined washer.
11. Remove the circlip and slide off the 6th gear.
12. Remove the circlip and splined washer.
13. Slide off the 2nd gear and the 2nd gear bushing.
14. Make sure that all gears slide smoothly on the countershaft splines.
15. Check each gear for excessive wear, burrs, pitting or chipped or missing teeth (A, **Figure 78**). Make sure the lugs (B, **Figure 78**) are in good condition.
16. Check the needle bearing (**Figure 79**). Make sure it rotates smoothly with no signs of wear or damage. Replace if necessary.

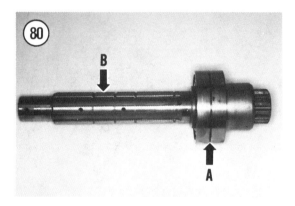

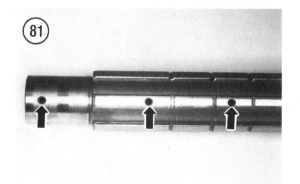

GEARSHIFT MECHANISM AND TRANSMISSION

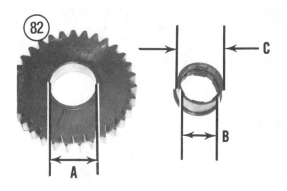

17. Check the shaft ball bearing (A, **Figure 80**). Make sure it rotates smoothly with no signs of wear or damage. Replace if necessary.
18. Make sure the shaft oil control holes (**Figure 81**) are clear. Clean out with a piece of wire then rinse with solvent and blow out with compressed air.
19. Measure the inside diameter (A, **Figure 82**) of the 2nd, 3rd and the 4th gears. Compare with the dimensions listed in **Table 1**.
20. Measure the inside diameter (B, **Figure 82**) and the outside diameter (C, **Figure 82**) of the 2nd, 3rd and the 4th gear bushings. Compare with the dimensions listed in **Table 1**.
21. Measure the outside diameter of the shaft (B, **Figure 80**) at the location of the 2nd, 3rd and the 4th gear bushings (C, **Figure 57**). Compare with the dimension listed in **Table 1**.

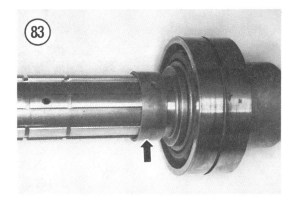

Countershaft Assembly

1. Apply a light coat of clean engine oil to all sliding surfaces prior to installing any parts.
2. Slide on the 2nd gear bushing (**Figure 83**).
3. Position the 2nd gear with the raised shoulder (**Figure 84**) going on first and slide on the 2nd gear (**Figure 85**).
4. Slide on the splined washer (A, **Figure 86**).
5. Install the circlip (B, **Figure 86**) with the sharp edge facing out. Make sure the circlip is correctly seated in the countershaft groove (**Figure 87**).
6. Position the 6th gear with the shift dog side going on last and slide the 6th gear on (**Figure 88**).
7. Install the circlip (**Figure 89**) with the sharp edge going on first. Make sure the circlip is correctly seated in the countershaft groove (**Figure 90**).
8. On 1990-on models, slide on the splined washer.

9A. On 1986-1989 models, perform the following:
   a. Align the oil hole in the 3rd gear bushing (A, **Figure 91**) with the oil hole in the countershaft (B, **Figure 91**). This alignment is necessary for proper oil flow.
   b. Position the 3rd gear bushing with the flange side (C, **Figure 91**) going on first. Slide on the 3rd gear bushing (**Figure 92**).
   c. Position the 3rd gear with the smooth side going on last and slide on the 3rd gear (**Figure 93**).
9B. On 1990-on models, perform the following:

GEARSHIFT MECHANISM AND TRANSMISSION

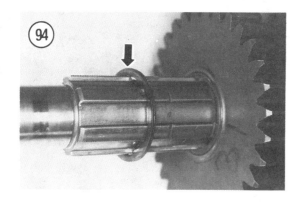

a. Slide on the 3rd gear bushing.
b. Position the 3rd gear with the smooth side going on last and slide on the 3rd gear.

10. Slide on the splined washer (**Figure 94**). Rotate the splined washer in either direction to engage the tangs from the grooves on the transmission shaft (**Figure 95**).

11. Slide on the splined lockwasher (**Figure 96**) so the tangs go into the open areas of the splined washer and lock the washer in place (**Figure 97**).

12. Slide on the 4th gear (A, **Figure 98**).

NOTE
*On all models, align the oil hole in the 4th gear bushing (B, **Figure 98**) with the oil hole in the countershaft (C, **Figure 98**). This alignment is necessary for proper oil flow.*

13A. On 1986-1989 models, position the 4th gear bushing with the flange side (**Figure 99**) going on last. Slide on the 4th gear bushing and push it all the way into the 4th gear (**Figure 100**).

13B. On 1990-on models, slide on the 4th gear bushing and push it all the way into the 4th gear.

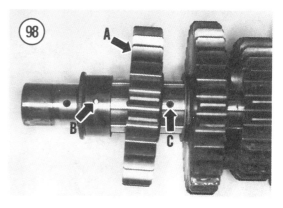

14. On 1990-on models, slide on the splined washer.

15. Install the circlip (**Figure 101**) with the sharp edge going on last. Make sure the circlip is correctly seated in the countershaft groove (**Figure 102**).

16. Position the 5th gear with the shift dog side going on last and slide the 5th gear on (**Figure 103**).

17. Slide on the thrust washer (**Figure 104**).

18. Slide on the 1st gear (**Figure 105**), then slide the 1st gear needle bearing into it (**Figure 106**).

19. Install the thrust washer (**Figure 107**).

GEARSHIFT MECHANISM AND TRANSMISSION

20. Slide on the needle bearing (**Figure 108**) and outer race (**Figure 109**).

21. If removed, install the oil seal (**Figure 110**).

22. Refer to **Figure 111** for correct placement of all gears. Make sure all circlips are correctly seated in the countershaft grooves.

23. After both transmission shafts have been assembled, mesh the 2 assemblies together in the correct position (**Figure 112**). Check that gear engages properly to the adjoining gear where applicable. This is your last check prior to installing the shaft assemblies into the crankcase; make sure they are correctly assembled.

INTERNAL SHIFT MECHANISM

Refer to **Figure 113** for this procedure.

Removal

1. Remove the external shift mechanism as described in this chapter.

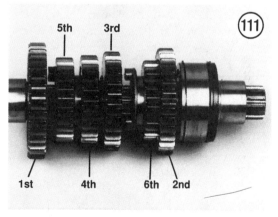

2. Disassemble the crankcase as described under *Cylinder Block and Crankcase Disassembly* in Chapter Four.

3. Remove both transmission shaft assemblies as described in this chapter.

4. If not removed during external gearshift removal, remove the stud bolt (A, **Figure 114**) and shift drum set plate (B, **Figure 114**) as follows:

   a. Screw 2 nuts (**Figure 115**) onto the stud bolt until they bottom out on the shoulder.

   b. Using 2 wrenches (**Figure 116**) tighten the 2 nuts *against each other*. They must be tight as the outer nut will be used to unscrew the stud bolt.

   c. Using the outer nut, unscrew the stud bolt (A, **Figure 114**) from the crankcase. Leave the 2 nuts attached to the stud bolt as they will be used during installation.

   d. Remove the shift drum set plate (B, **Figure 114**).

5. Mark the shift forks with a "R" (right-hand), "C" (center) and "L" (left-hand) side so they will be reinstalled in the same location (**Figure 117**).

6. On the right-hand side of the crankcase, withdraw the shift fork shaft and remove the shift forks.

7. Withdraw the shift drum out through the left-hand side of the crankcase.

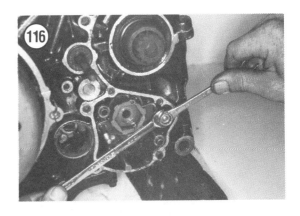

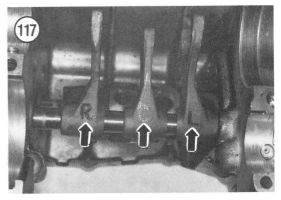

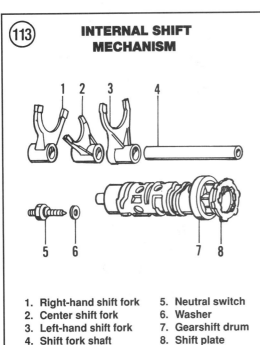

INTERNAL SHIFT MECHANISM

1. Right-hand shift fork
2. Center shift fork
3. Left-hand shift fork
4. Shift fork shaft
5. Neutral switch
6. Washer
7. Gearshift drum
8. Shift plate

GEARSHIFT MECHANISM AND TRANSMISSION

Inspection

Refer to **Table 3** for internal shift mechanism specifications.

1. Inspect each shift fork for signs of wear or cracking. Make sure the forks slide smoothly on their shaft. Replace any worn forks.

NOTE
*Check for any arc-shaped wear or burn marks (A, **Figure 118**) on the shift fork fingers. If this is apparent, the shift fork has come in contact with the gear, indicating that the fingers are worn beyond use and the fork must be replaced.*

2. Roll the shift fork shaft on a flat surface such as a piece of plate glass and check for bends. If the fork shaft is bent, it must be replaced.

3. Make sure the shift fork shaft oil control holes (A, **Figure 119**) are clear. Clean out with a piece of wire then rinse with solvent and blow out with compressed air.

4. Measure the outer diameter of the shift fork shaft with a micrometer (**Figure 120**). Replace the shaft if worn beyond the limit in **Table 3**.

5. Check the cam pin followers (B, **Figure 118**) in each shift fork for wear or burrs. If worn or damaged the shift fork must be replaced.

6. Measure the inside diameter of the shift forks with an inside micrometer (**Figure 121**). Replace any worn beyond the limit in **Table 3**.

7. Measure the width of the gearshift fingers with a micrometer (**Figure 122**). Replace any worn beyond the limit in **Table 3**.

8. Check the shift drum cam plate ramps for wear (A, **Figure 123**); replace if necessary.

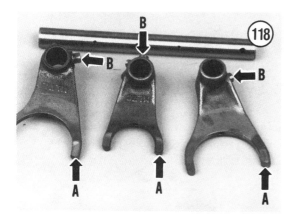
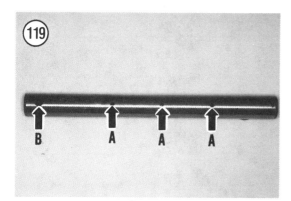

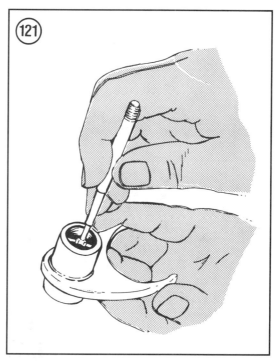

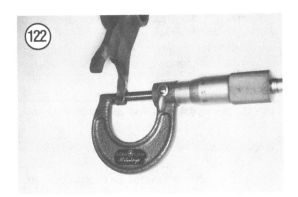

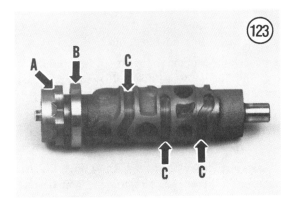

GEARSHIFT MECHANISM AND TRANSMISSION

9. Check the shift drum bearing (B, **Figure 123**). Make sure it operates smoothly with no signs of wear or damage. Replace if necessary.

10. Check the grooves in the shift drum (C, **Figure 123**) for wear or roughness. If any of the groove profiles have excessive wear or damage, replace the shift drum.

11. Inspect all bearing surfaces in the crankcase where the shift fork shaft and shift drum ride. Check for scoring or scratches. If severely damaged, the crankcase must be replaced.

Installation

1. Coat all bearing and sliding surfaces with assembly oil.
2. Install the shift drum into the left-hand side of the crankcase (**Figure 124**). Push it in until it seats completely (**Figure 125**).
3. Position the shift fork shaft with the large oil hole (B, **Figure 119**) and machined end going in last (toward the right-hand side) and start it into the crankcase (A, **Figure 126**).
4. Correctly position the right-hand shift fork (B, **Figure 126**) and push the shift fork shaft through it.
5. Correctly position the center shift fork (**Figure 127**) and push the shift fork shaft through it.
6. Correctly position the left-hand shift fork (**Figure 128**) and push the shift fork shaft through it.
7. Push the shift fork in until it bottoms out in the crankcase.
8. Rotate the shift fork shaft until the machined end with the cut-out is aligned with the cut-out in the crankcase (**Figure 129**). This alignment is necessary so the transmission bearing holder (**Figure 130**) can be installed correctly during crankcase assembly. This bearing holder secures the shift fork shaft within the crankcase.
9. Move the shift forks into position in the shift drum (**Figure 131**). Make sure the cam pin followers are indexed correctly in the shift drum grooves.
10. Install the transmission mainshaft as described in this chapter.
11. Assemble the crankcase as described under *Cylinder Block and Crankcase Assembly* in Chapter Four.
12. Install the external shift mechanism as described in this chapter.

Tables 1-3 are on the following pages.

Table 1 TRANSMISSION TIGHTENING TORQUES

Item	N•m	ft.-lb.
Drive sprocket bolt	50-54	36-39

Table 2 TRANSMISSION SPECIFICATIONS

Item	Specifications	Wear limit
Gear ID main shaft		
5th and 6th	28.000-28.021 mm (1.1024-1.1032 in.)	28.04 mm (1.104 in.)
Gear ID countershaft		
2nd, 3rd, 4th	31.000-31.025 mm (1.2205-1.2215 in.)	31.04 mm (1.222 in.)
Gear bushing OD		
Main shaft		
4th & 5th	27.959-27.980 mm (1.1007-1.1016 in.)	27.94 mm (1.100 in.)
Countershaft		
2nd	30.970-30.995 mm (1.2193-1.2203 in.)	30.95 mm (1.219 in.)
3rd & 4th	30.950-30.975 mm (1.2185-1.2195 in.)	30.93 mm (1.218 in.)
Gear bushing ID		
Main shaft		
5th & 6th	24.985-25.006 mm (0.9834-0.9845 in.)	25.03 mm (0.985 in.)
Countershaft		
2nd	28.000-28.021 mm (1.1024-1.1032 in.)	28.04 mm (1.104 in.)
3rd & 4th	27.995-28.016 mm (1.1022-1.1030 in.)	28.04 mm (1.104 in.)
Main shaft OD		
At 5th and 6th gear bushing location (A and B)	24.959-24.980 mm (0.9826-0.9835 in.)	24.95 mm (0.982 in.)
Countershaft OD		
At 2nd, 3rd 4th gear bushing location (C)	27.967-27.980 mm (1.1010-1.1016 in.)	27.96 mm (1.101 in.)
Bushing to shaft clearance		
Main shaft		
5th and 6th	0.005-0.047 mm (0.0002-0.0019 in.)	0.06 mm (0.002 in.)
Countershaft		
2nd	0.020-0.054 mm (0.0008-0.0021 in.)	0.06 mm (0.002 in.)
3rd and 4th	0.015-0.049 mm (0.0006-0.0019 in.)	0.06 mm (0.002 in.)
Gear to bushing clearance		
Main shaft		
5th and 6th	0.002-0.062 mm (0.00008-0.0024 in.)	0.10 mm (0.0039 in.)
Countershaft		
2nd	0.005-0.046 mm (0.0002-0.0018 in.)	0.09 mm (0.0035 in.)
3rd and 4th	0.025-0.066 mm (0.0010-0.0026 in.)	0.11 mm (0.0043 in.)

Table 3 INTERNAL SHIFT MECHANISM SPECIFICATIONS

Item	Specifications	Wear limit
Shift fork hole ID	14.016-14.034 mm (0.5518-0.5525 in.)	14.05 mm (0.553 in.)
Shift fork fingers	6.43-6.50 mm (0.253-0.256 in.)	6.1 mm (0.24 in.)
Shift fork shaft OD	13.973-13.984 mm (0.5501-0.5505 in.)	13.90 mm (0.547 in.)

CHAPTER SEVEN

FUEL, EMISSION CONTROL AND EXHAUST SYSTEMS

The fuel system consists of the fuel tank, shutoff valve, fuel pump, fuel filter, 4 down-draft Keihin constant velocity carburetors and the air filter.

The exhaust system consists of 4 exhaust pipes, a common collector and depending on model, either a single muffler or dual mufflers.

Models sold in California are equipped with an evaporative emission control system. All models sold in California and models since 1988 sold in Switzerland and 1992-on in Austria are equipped with secondary air supply systems.

This chapter includes service procedures for all parts of the fuel and exhaust systems. Carburetor specifications are listed in **Table 1** at the end of this chapter.

Air filter service is covered in Chapter Three.

NOTE
Where differences occur relating to the United Kingdom (U.K.) models, they are identified. If there is no (U.K.) designation relating to a procedure, photo or illustration, it is identical to the United States (U.S.) models.

AIR FILTER HOUSING

Removal/Installation

Refer to **Figure 1** for this procedure.
1. Remove the fuel tank as described in this chapter.
2. Disconnect the crankcase breather hose (A, **Figure 2**) from the air filter housing at the rear.

NOTE
*The air filter housing case mounting screws are located inside the case on 1986-1989 models or on the outside of the case as shown in **Figure 2** on 1990-on models.*

3. Remove the screws securing the air filter housing to the carburetor assembly air chamber. There are 3 screws (B, **Figure 2**) across the back, 3 at the front and 1 on each side.
4. Carefully pull the air filter housing up and out of the frame.
5. After removing the air filter case, stuff clean shop cloths into the 4 openings (A, **Figure 3**) in the carburetor intake tubes to prevent the entry of foreign matter into the carburetors.

FUEL, EMISSION CONTROL AND EXHAUST SYSTEMS

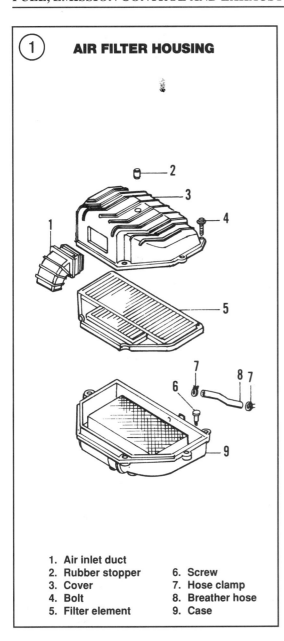

AIR FILTER HOUSING

1. Air inlet duct
2. Rubber stopper
3. Cover
4. Bolt
5. Filter element
6. Screw
7. Hose clamp
8. Breather hose
9. Case

6. On 1990-on models, if necessary, remove the bolt (A, **Figure 4**) and nut securing the sub-air filter assembly (B, **Figure 4**) and remove it. Don't lose the spacer between air filter mounting boss and the sub-air filter assembly.

7. Install by reversing these removal steps while noting the following:

   a. Inspect the sealing surface of the bottom of the air filter case and the mating surface on the carburetor assembly air filter base (B, **Figure 3**) for damage or dirt. Clean off if necessary to ensure a good air-tight fit between the 2 parts.

   b. On models so equipped, inspect the inner screen in the air filter case for damage, replace the case if necessary.

   c. Be sure to remove the shop cloths from the carburetor air intakes.

   d. Make sure the air filter case is correctly seated on the carburetor assembly air filter base before installing the screws. The alignment around the perimeter of these 2 parts must be correct or unfiltered air will enter the air chamber. If alignment is incorrect, this could lead to carburetor and engine damage.

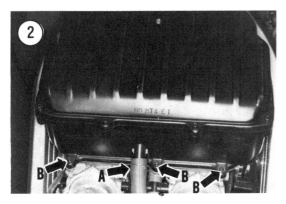

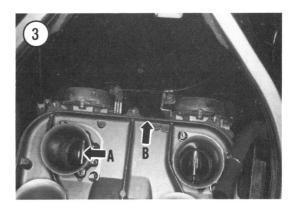

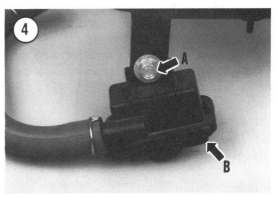

CARBURETOR OPERATION

An understanding of the function of each of the carburetor components and their relation to one another is a valuable aid for pinpointing a source of carburetor trouble.

The carburetor's purpose is to supply and atomize fuel and mix it in correct proportions with air that is drawn in through the air intake. At the primary throttle opening (idle), a small amount of fuel is siphoned through the pilot jet by the incoming air. As the throttle is opened further, the air stream begins to siphon fuel through the main jet and needle jet. The tapered needle increases the effective flow capacity of the needle jet as it is lifted, in that it occupies less area of the jet.

At full throttle the carburetor venturi is fully open and the needle is lifted far enough to permit the main jet to flow at full capacity.

The choke is a "bystarter" system in which the choke lever opens a valve rather than closing a butterfly in the venturi area as on many carburetors. In the open position, the slow jet discharges a stream of fuel into the carburetor venturi, enriching the mixture when the engine is cold.

CARBURETOR SERVICE

Carburetor service (removal and cleaning) should be performed when poor engine performance or hesitation is observed. If, after servicing the carburetors and making the adjustments described in this chapter, the motorcycle does not perform correctly (and assuming that other factors affecting performance are correct, such as ignition timing and condition, valve adjustment, etc.), the motorcycle should be checked by a dealer or a qualified performance tuning specialist.

Troubleshooting

Refer to Chapter Two.

e. Install the screws and tighten securely.

CARBURETOR ASSEMBLY

Removal/Installation

1. Support the bike securely.
2. Remove the seat as described in Chapter Thirteen.
3. Disconnect the battery negative lead as described in Chapter Eight.
4. Remove the fuel tank as described in this chapter.
5. Remove the front fairing lower side panels as described under *Front Fairing Removal/Installation* in Chapter Thirteen.

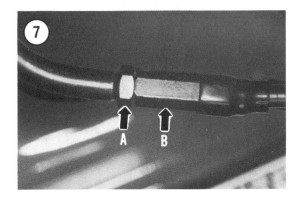

FUEL, EMISSION CONTROL AND EXHAUST SYSTEMS

6. Remove the air filter housing (A, **Figure 5**) as described in this chapter.

7. Disconnect the crankcase breather tube (B, **Figure 5**) from the cylinder head.

8. Loosen the clamping screw (A, **Figure 6**) and remove the choke cable from the clamp on the carburetor assembly.

9. Disconnect the choke cable (B, **Figure 6**) from the choke lever on the carburetor assembly.

10. At the hand throttle, loosen the throttle cable locknut (A, **Figure 7**) and turn the adjusting barrel (B, **Figure 7**) all the way in. This provides the necessary slack for ease of cable removal at the carburetor assembly.

11. Loosen the pull cable locknuts (A, **Figure 8**) and remove the pull cable from the clamp and from the rear receptacle (B, **Figure 8**) in the throttle wheel.

12. Loosen the push cable locknuts (C, **Figure 8**) and remove the push cable from the clamp and from the front receptacle (D, **Figure 8**) in the throttle wheel.

13. Move the throttle cables out of the way and secure them to the frame rail.

14. Disconnect the throttle stop adjust screw from the bracket on the frame. Refer to **Figure 9** for 1990-1993 models or **Figure 10** for 1994-on models.

15. Loosen the clamping screws (**Figure 11**) on all 4 carburetor bands.

16. Disconnect the fuel line (C, **Figure 5**) to the carburetor assembly. Plug the end of the fuel inlet line and the fuel fitting on the carburetor assembly to prevent the entry of dirt and foreign matter.

17. Pull the carburetors straight up and off the rubber intake tubes and remove the assembly from the engine and frame.

18. If necessary, remove the heat insulator plate in front of the top of the front cylinder assembly.

19. Install by reversing these removal steps while noting the following:

   a. Prior to installing the carburetor assembly, coat the inside surface of all 4 rubber intake tubes with Armor All or rubber lube. This will make it easier to install the carburetor throats into the intake tubes.

   b. Be sure the throttle cables and choke cable are correctly positioned in the frame—not twisted or kinked and without any sharp bends. Tighten the clamping screw and the locknuts securely.

CAUTION
The throttle cables are the push/pull type and must be installed as described in the following steps. **Do not interchange the 2 cables.**

c. Attach the "pull" throttle cable into the top portion of the bracket (A, **Figure 8**) and into the rear slot in the throttle wheel (B, **Figure 8**).
d. Attach the "push" throttle cable into the bottom portion of the bracket (C, **Figure 8**) and into the front slot in the throttle wheel (D, **Figure 8**).
e. Adjust the throttle cable as described under *Throttle Adjustment and Operation* in Chapter Three.
f. Adjust the choke as described in this chapter.
g. Test ride the bike slowly at first and make sure the throttle is operating correctly.

CARBURETOR OVERHAUL

Disassembly

Refer to the following illustrations for this procedure:
a. **Figure 12**: 1986-1989 models.
b. **Figure 13**: 1990-1993 models.
c. **Figure 14**: 1994-on models.

It is recommended that only one carburetor be disassembled and cleaned at a time. This will prevent an accidental interchange of parts.

All components that require cleaning can be removed from the carburetor body without separating the carburetors. If other parts require replacement, take the carburetor and air chamber assembly to a dealer.

NOTE
This procedure is shown on a 1991 model. Where differences occur among the different model years, they are noted in the procedure.

1. Remove the screws securing the carburetor top cover (**Figure 15**) to the body and remove the cover.
2. Remove the spring and vacuum piston/diaphragm assembly.
3A. On 1986-1993 models, perform the following:
   a. Put an 8 mm socket down into the vacuum piston/diaphragm assembly cavity.
   b. Place the socket on the needle holder and turn the holder 90° *counterclockwise* to unlock it from the tangs within the vacuum piston.
   c. Remove the needle holder, jet needle spring and the jet needle (**Figure 16**) from the vacuum piston.

CAUTION
Do not try to remove the jet needle holder by pushing it out from the bottom with the needle jet. If this is done, the internal components will be damaged.

3B. On 1994-on models, perform the following:
   a. Insert a 4 mm screw (A, **Figure 17**) (use one of the top cover screws) into the top of the needle jet holder (B, **Figure 17**).
   b. Pull the screw and needle jet holder out of the vacuum piston with a pair of pliers. Remove the screw.
   c. Remove all internal components (**Figure 18**).
4. Turn the carburetor assembly over.
5. Remove the screws securing the float bowl (**Figure 19**) to the main body and remove the float bowl.
6. Remove the gasket from the float bowl (**Figure 20**).
7. Carefully push out the float pin (A, **Figure 21**).
8. Lift the float (B, **Figure 21**) and needle valve (C, **Figure 21**) out of the main body.
9. Remove the float valve seat and filter (A, **Figure 22**).
10. Remove the main jet (B, **Figure 22**).
11. Remove the jet needle holder (C, **Figure 22**).
12. Remove the slow jet (D, **Figure 22**).
13. Do *not* try to remove the starter jet (E, **Figure 22**). It is pressed in place and will be damaged if removed.

NOTE
Pilot jet removal is only necessary if it has been misadjusted. Do not remove the pilot jets unless you suspect they are not functioning properly.

14. If pilot screw removal is necessary, perform the following:
   a. Use a pair of pliers and break off the limiter cap (**Figure 23**).

NOTE
Prior to removing the pilot screw, record the number of turns necessary until the screw lightly seats. Record the number

FUEL, EMISSION CONTROL AND EXHAUST SYSTEMS

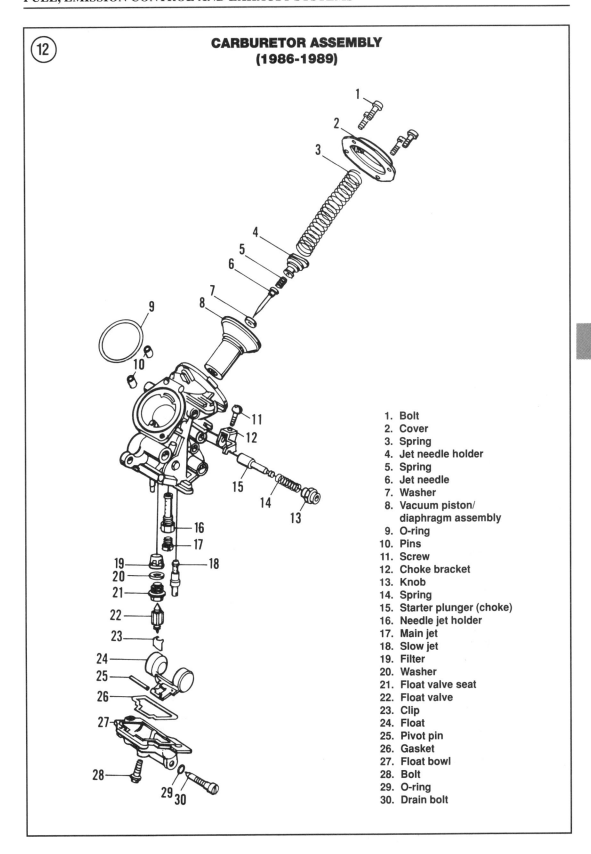

CARBURETOR ASSEMBLY (1986-1989)

1. Bolt
2. Cover
3. Spring
4. Jet needle holder
5. Spring
6. Jet needle
7. Washer
8. Vacuum piston/ diaphragm assembly
9. O-ring
10. Pins
11. Screw
12. Choke bracket
13. Knob
14. Spring
15. Starter plunger (choke)
16. Needle jet holder
17. Main jet
18. Slow jet
19. Filter
20. Washer
21. Float valve seat
22. Float valve
23. Clip
24. Float
25. Pivot pin
26. Gasket
27. Float bowl
28. Bolt
29. O-ring
30. Drain bolt

CARBURETOR ASSEMBLY
(1990-1993)

1. Bolt
2. Cover
3. Clip
4. Retainer
5. Spring
6. Jet needle holder
7. Spring
8. Spring holder
9. Jet needle
10. Washer
11. O-ring
12. Washer
13. Spring
14. Pilot screw
15. Cap
16. Knob
17. Spring
18. Starter plunger (choke)
19. Gasket
20. Pivot pin
21. Float
22. Gasket
23. Drain screw
24. O-ring
25. Float bowl
26. Bolt
27. Screw
28. Air cut off valve cover
29. O-ring
30. Spring
31. Diaphragm
32. Spring
33. Screw
34. Filter
35. Washer
36. Float valve seat
37. Float valve
38. Main jet
39. Jet needle holder
40. Slow jet
41. Body
42. Vacuum piston/ diaphragm assembly

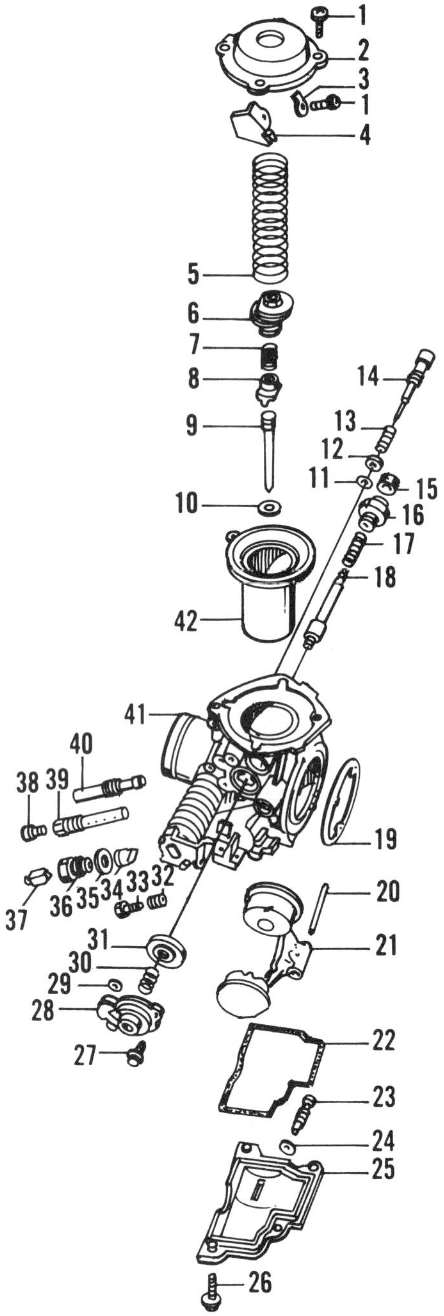

FUEL, EMISSION CONTROL AND EXHAUST SYSTEMS

CARBURETOR ASSEMBLY (1994-ON)

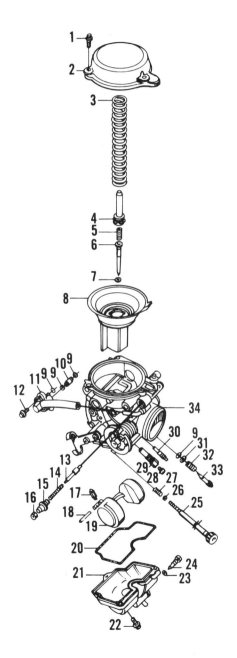

1. Bolt
2. Cover
3. Spring
4. Jet needle holder
5. Spring
6. Jet needle
7. Washer
8. Vacuum piston/diaphragm assembly
9. O-ring
10. Slow air jet
11. Air cut valve
12. Screw
13. Starter plunger (choke)
14. Spring
15. Knob
16. Cap
17. Float valve
18. Pivot pin
19. Float
20. Gasket
21. Float bowl
22. Screw
23. O-ring
24. Drain screw
25. Throttle stop screw
26. Washer
27. Spring
28. Main jet
29. Jet needle holder
30. Slow jet
31. Washer
32. Spring
33. Pilot screw
34. Body

ber of turns for each individual carburetor as the screws must be reinstalled into the exact same setting.

b. Unscrew the pilot jet, spring, washer and O-ring from the carburetor body.

NOTE
Further disassembly is neither necessary nor recommended. If throttle or choke shafts or butterflies are damaged, take the carburetor and air chamber assembly to a dealer for replacement.

Cleaning and Inspection

1. Remove the drain screw from the float bowl.

2. Thoroughly clean and dry all parts. Honda does not recommend the use of a caustic carburetor cleaning solvent. Instead, clean carburetor parts in a petroleum based solvent. Then rinse in clean water.

3. Allow the carburetor and parts to dry thoroughly before assembly and blow dry with compressed air. Blow out the jets and needle jet holder with compressed air.

4. Inspect all O-ring seals. O-ring seals tend to become hardened after prolonged use and heat and therefore lose their ability to seal properly.

CAUTION
*If compressed air is not available, allow the parts to air dry or use a clean lint-free cloth. Do **not** use a paper towel to dry carburetor parts, as small paper particles may plug openings in the carburetor body or jets.*

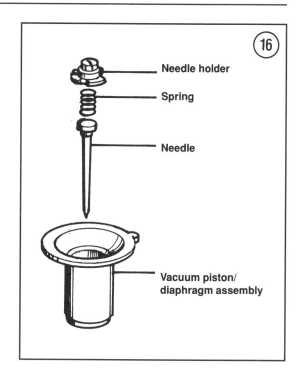

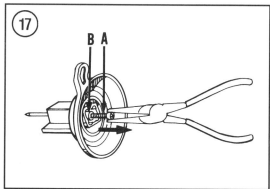

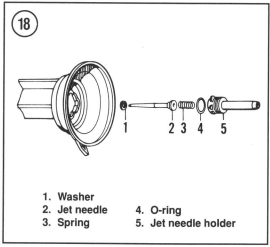

1. Washer
2. Jet needle
3. Spring
4. O-ring
5. Jet needle holder

FUEL, EMISSION CONTROL AND EXHAUST SYSTEMS

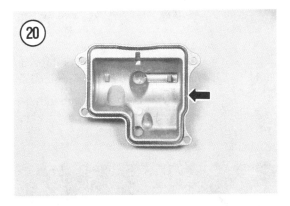

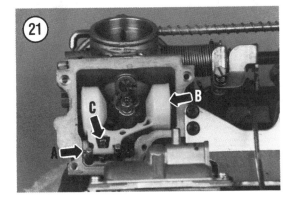

CAUTION
*Do **not** use a piece of wire to clean the jets as minor gouges can alter flow rate and upset the fuel/air mixture.*

5. Make sure all air openings in the carburetor body are clear. Blow out with compressed air if necessary.
6. Inspect the end of the float valve needle (**Figure 24**) and seat for wear or damage; replace either or both parts if necessary.
7. Inspect the pilot jet for wear or damage that may have occurred during removal.
8. Make sure the holes in the needle jet holder are clear. Clean out if they are plugged in any way. Replace the needle jet holder if you cannot unplug the holes.
9. Make sure the holes in the main jet and slow jet are clear. Clean out if they are plugged in any way. Replace the main jet or slow jet if you cannot unplug the holes.
10. Make sure the diaphragm is not cracked or starting to deteriorate. Replace if necessary.

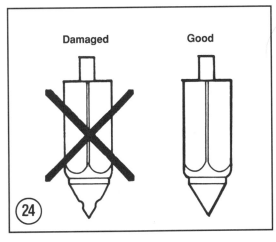

11. Inspect the jet needle for wear or damage; replace if necessary.

12. Inspect the float (**Figure 25**) for deterioration or damage. If the float is suspected of leakage, place it in a container of non-caustic solution and push it down. If the float sinks or if bubbles appear (indicating a leak); replace the float.

Assembly

1. If removed, screw the pilot screw into the exact same position (same number of turns) as recorded during disassembly.

NOTE
*If new pilot screws were installed, turn them out the number of turns indicated in **Table 1**, from the **lightly seated** position.*

2. Install the slow jet (D, **Figure 22**).
3. Install the jet needle holder (C, **Figure 22**).
4. Install the main jet (B, **Figure 22**).
5. Install the float valve seat and filter (A, **Figure 22**).
6. Install the needle valve onto the float.
7. Install the float (B, **Figure 21**) and needle valve (C, **Figure 21**) and install the float pin (A, **Figure 21**).
8. Inspect the float height and adjust if necessary. Refer to *Float Adjustment* in this chapter.
9. Install a new gasket into the float bowl (**Figure 20**).
10. Install the float bowl (**Figure 19**) and tighten the screws securely.
11A. On 1986-1993 models, to assemble the vacuum piston/diaphragm, perform the following:
   a. Install the jet needle, jet needle spring and needle holder (**Figure 16**).
   b. Place the 8 mm socket on the needle holder and turn the holder 90° *clockwise* to lock it into the tangs within the vacuum piston.
11B. On 1994-on models, to assemble the vacuum piston/diaphragm, perform the following:
   a. Apply a light coat of oil to the O-ring and install all internal components (**Figure 18**) into the vacuum piston.
   b. Insert the needle jet holder into the vacuum piston and push it down until it is completely seated.

12. Install the vacuum cylinder into the carburetor body. Align the tab on the diaphragm with the hole in the carburetor body.

13. Install the vacuum piston/diaphragm spring into the vacuum cylinder receptacle.

CAUTION
To keep the rubber diaphragm of the vacuum cylinder from tearing and also to make sure the diaphragm bead is properly seated, Honda suggests that the vacuum cylinder be held in the raised position until the top cover is installed.

14. Insert your finger into the carburetor throat and hold the vacuum cylinder in the raised position.

15. Align the hole in the diaphragm with the raised boss on the top cover. Install the top cover (**Figure 15**) and tighten the screws securely.

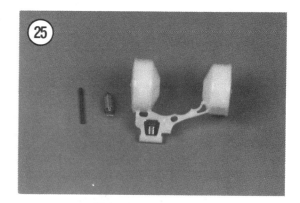

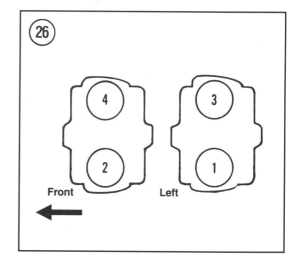

FUEL, EMISSION CONTROL AND EXHAUST SYSTEMS

CARBURETOR ADJUSTMENTS

Pilot Screw Adjustment (U.S., Canada and Switzerland Models)

The pilot screws are pre-set at the factory and do not require adjustment unless the carburetor is overhauled or the pilot screws replaced. A tachometer able to detect 50 rpm changes will be required for this procedure.

The carburetors are numbered the same as the cylinders; refer to **Figure 26**.

The following pilot screw wrench (or equivalent) will be required:
  a. 1989 Switzerland: Honda part No. 07KMA-MS60100.
  b. 1990-on U.S., U.K. and Switzerland: Honda part No. 07KMA-MS60100 and part No. 07PMA-MZ20110.
  c. Canada: Honda part No. 07908-4220201.

CAUTION
Tightening the pilot screw tightly against its seat will damage the pilot screw.

1. Install a new air filter element, as described in Chapter Three, before starting this procedure or the results will be inaccurate.
2. Synchronize the carburetors as described in Chapter Three.
3. For the preliminary adjustment, carefully turn the pilot screw on each carburetor in until it *lightly seats* and then back it out the number of turns listed in **Table 1**.
4. Start the engine and let it reach normal operating temperature. Stop-and-go riding for approximately 10-15 minutes is sufficient.
5. Connect a tachometer to the engine following the manufacturer's instructions.
6. Adjust the idle speed by turning the throttle stop screw to the idle speed listed in **Table 1**. Refer to the following for the location of the throttle stop screw:
  a. 1986-1989 models: **Figure 27**.
  b. 1990-1993 models: **Figure 28**.
  c. 1994-on models: **Figure 29**.
7. Turn each pilot screw *out* 1/2 turn from the initial setting of Step 3.
8. If the engine speed increases by 50 rpm or more, turn each pilot screw out by an additional 1/2 turn at a time until engine speed drops by 50 rpm or less.
9. Turn the idle adjust screw in or out again to achieve the desired idle speed listed in **Table 1**.
10A. On 1986-1989 and 1994-on models, perform the following:
  a. Turn the pilot screw on the No. 1 carburetor *in* until engine speed drops by 50 rpm.
  b. Turn the pilot screw on the No. 1 carburetor *out* 1 turn from the position obtained in Step 10A/a.
  c. Turn the idle adjust screw in or out again to achieve the desired idle speed listed in **Table 1**.
  d. Repeat this step for the No. 2, 3 and 4 carburetor pilot screws.

10B. On 1990-1993 models, perform the following:
  a. Turn the pilot screw on the No. 2 carburetor *in* until engine speed drops by 50 rpm.
  b. Turn the pilot screw on the No. 2 carburetor *out* 1 turn from the position obtained in Step 10B/a.
  c. Turn the idle adjust screw in or out again to achieve the desired idle speed listed in **Table 1**.
  d. Repeat this steps for the No. 1, 3 and 4 carburetor pilot screws.

11. Turn the engine off and disconnect the portable tachometer.

12. After this adjustment is completed, test ride the bike. Throttle response from idle should be rapid and without any hesitation. Readjust if necessary.

Float Adjustment

The carburetor assembly has to be removed and partially disassembled for this adjustment.

1. Remove the carburetors as described in this chapter.

2. Remove the screws securing the float bowls (**Figure 19**) to the main bodies and remove the float bowls.

3. Hold the carburetor assembly with the carburetor inclined 15-45° from vertical so that the float arm is just touching the float needle. Use a float level gauge (Honda part No. 07401-0010000 or equivalent) and measure the distance from the carburetor body to the float arm (**Figure 30**). The correct height is listed in **Table 1**.

4. Adjust by carefully bending the tang on the float arm.

5. If the float level is too high, the result will be a rich fuel/air mixture. If it is too low, the mixture will be too lean.

NOTE
The floats on all 4 carburetors must be adjusted at the same height to maintain the same fuel/air mixture to all 4 cylinders.

6. Reassemble and install the carburetors as described in this chapter.

Needle Jet Adjustment

The needle jet is *non-adjustable* on all models.

High Altitude Adjustment

If the bike is going to be ridden for any sustained period of time at high elevations (2,000 m [6,500 ft.]) the carburetors must be readjusted to improve performance and decrease exhaust emissions.

NOTE
*If this adjustment has been performed by a Honda dealer, there will be a Vehicle Emission Control Information Update Label attached to the top surface of the rear fender adjacent to the standard emission control label (**Figure 31**).*

1. Start the engine and let it reach normal operating temperature. Stop-and-go riding for approximately 10 minutes is sufficient. Turn off the engine.

2. Connect a portable tachometer following the manufacturer's instructions. The bike's tach is not accurate enough at low rpm.

NOTE
***Figure 23** is shown with the carburetor assembly partially removed from the engine for clarity. Do not remove the carburetor assembly for this procedure.*

3. Turn each pilot screw (**Figure 23**) *clockwise* 1/2 turn.

4. Restart the engine and adjust the idle speed by turning the throttle stop screw to the idle speed listed in **Table 1**. Refer to the following for the location of the throttle stop screw:
  a. 1986-1989 models: A, **Figure 27**.
  b. 1990-1993 models: **Figure 28**.
  c. 1994-on models: **Figure 29**.

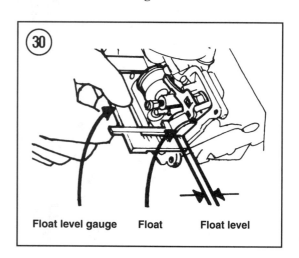

FUEL, EMISSION CONTROL AND EXHAUST SYSTEMS

5. Turn the engine off and disconnect the portable tachometer.

6. Install new pilot screw plugs as described in this chapter.

7. When the bike is returned to lower elevations (near sea level), the pilot screws must be returned to their original positions and the idle speed readjusted to the idle speed listed in **Table 1**.

Rejetting The Carburetors

Do not try to solve a poor running engine problem by rejetting the carburetors if all of the following conditions hold true:
  a. The engine has held a good tune in the past with the standard jetting.
  b. The engine has not been modified.
  c. The motorcycle is being operated in the same geographical region under the same general climatic conditions as in the past.
  d. The motorcycle was and is being ridden at average highway speeds.

If those conditions all hold true, the chances are that the problem is due to a malfunction in the carburetor or in another component that needs to be adjusted or repaired. Changing carburetor jet size probably won't solve the problem. Rejetting the carburetors may be necessary if any of the following conditions hold true:
  a. A non-standard type of air filter element is being used.
  b. A non-standard exhaust system is installed on the motorcycle.
  c. Any of the top end components in the engine (pistons, cams, valves, compression ratio, etc.) have been modified.

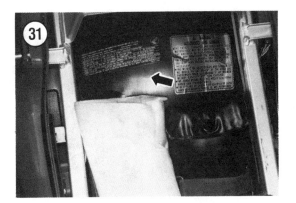

  d. The motorcycle is in use at considerably higher or lower altitudes or in a considerably hotter or colder climate than in the past.
  e. The motorcycle is being operated at considerably higher speeds than before and changing to colder spark plugs does not solve the problem.
  f. Someone has previously changed the carburetor jetting.
  g. The motorcycle has never held a satisfactory engine tune.

If it is necessary to rejet the carburetors, check with a dealer or motorcycle performance tuner for recommendations as to the size of jets to install for your specific situation.

If you do change the jets, do so only one size at a time. After rejetting, test ride the bike and perform a spark plug test; refer to *Reading Spark Plugs* in Chapter Three.

THROTTLE CABLE REPLACEMENT

1. Remove the seat as described in Chapter Thirteen.
2. Remove the fuel tank as described in this chapter.
3. Remove the front fairing as described under *Front Fairing Removal/Installation* in Chapter Thirteen.
4. Remove the air filter housing as described in this chapter.
5. At the hand throttle, loosen the throttle cable locknut (A, **Figure 7**) and turn the adjusting barrel (B, **Figure 7**) all the way in. This provides the necessary slack for ease of cable removal at the carburetor assembly.
6. Loosen the pull cable locknuts (A, **Figure 8**) and remove the pull cable from the clamp and from the rear receptacle (B, **Figure 8**) in the throttle wheel.
7. Loosen the push cable locknuts (C, **Figure 8**) and remove the push cable from the clamp and from the front receptacle (D, **Figure 8**) in the throttle wheel.
8. Move the throttle cables away from the throttle wheel.
9. Remove the screws securing the right-hand switch/throttle housing halves together (A, **Figure 32**).

NOTE
Use masking tape and label the old cables before removal. That way, you can use the old cables as a guide when in-

stalling the new cables as the 2 cables are different.

10. Remove the housing from the handlebar and disengage the throttle cables (B, **Figure 32**) from the throttle grip.

NOTE
The piece of string attached in the next step will be used to pull the new throttle cables back through the frame so they will be routed in exactly the same position as the old ones were.

11. Tie a piece of heavy string or cord to the carburetor end of the throttle cables. Wrap this end with masking or duct tape. Do not use an excessive amount of tape as it must be pulled through the frame loop during removal. Tie the other end of the string to the frame or air box.

12. At the throttle grip end of the cables, carefully pull the cables (and attached string) out through the frame, past the electrical harness and from behind the headlight housing. Make sure the attached string follows the same path as the cables through the frame.

13. Remove the tape and untie the string from the old cables.

14. Lubricate the new cables as described in Chapter Three.

15. Tie the string to the new throttle cables and wrap it with tape.

16. Carefully pull the string back through the frame routing the new cables through the same path as the old cables.

17. Remove the tape and untie the string from the cables and the frame.

18. Be sure the throttle cables are correctly positioned in the frame—not twisted or kinked and without any sharp bends.

CAUTION
*The throttle cables are the push/pull type and must be installed as described in the following steps. **Do not interchange the 2 cables**.*

19. Attach the "pull" throttle cable into the top portion of the bracket (A, **Figure 8**) and into the rear slot in the throttle wheel (B, **Figure 8**).

20. Attach the "push" throttle cable into the bottom portion of the bracket (C, **Figure 8**) and into the front slot in the throttle wheel (D, **Figure 8**).

21. Install the throttle/switch housing and tighten the screws securely.

22. Operate the throttle grip and make sure the carburetor throttle linkage is operating correctly, with no binding. If operation is incorrect or there is binding carefully check that the cables are attached correctly and there are no tight bends in the cables.

23. Install all parts that were removed as described in this chapter and other related chapters.

24. Adjust the throttle cable as described under *Throttle Adjustment and Operation* in Chapter Three.

25. Test ride the bike slowly at first and make sure the throttle is operating correctly.

CHOKE CABLE REPLACEMENT

1. Remove the seat as described in Chapter Thirteen.
2. Remove the fuel tank as described in this chapter.
3. Remove the front fairing as described in Chapter Thirteen.

FUEL, EMISSION CONTROL AND EXHAUST SYSTEMS

4. Remove the front fairing as described under *Front Fairing Removal/Installation* in Chapter Thirteen.

5. Remove the air filter housing as described in this chapter.

6. Loosen the clamping screw (A, **Figure 33**) and remove the choke cable from the clamp on the carburetor assembly.

7. Disconnect the choke cable (B, **Figure 33**) from the choke lever on the carburetor assembly.

8. Remove the screws securing the left-hand switch assembly (A, **Figure 34**) and remove the switch assembly from the handlebar.

9. Remove the choke cable (B, **Figure 34**) from the clutch lever assembly on the handlebar.

NOTE
The piece of string attached in the next step will be used to pull the new choke cable back through the frame so it will be routed in the same position as the old cable.

10. Tie a piece of heavy string or cord to the carburetor end of the choke cable. Wrap this end with masking or duct tape. Do not use an excessive amount of tape as it must be pulled through the frame loop during removal. Tie the other end of the string to the frame or air box.

11. At the choke lever end of the cable, carefully pull the cable (and attached string) out through the frame. Make sure the attached string follows the same path that the cable does through the frame.

12. Remove the tape and untie the string from the old cable.

13. Lubricate the new cable as described in Chapter Three.

14. Tie the string to the new choke cable and wrap it with tape.

15. Carefully pull the string back through the frame routing the new cable through the same path as the old cable.

16. Remove the tape and untie the string from the cable and the frame.

17. Install the choke cable onto the choke lever assembly.

18. Attach the choke cable to the carburetor choke linkage and tighten the clamping screw.

19. Install the left-hand switch assembly halves onto the handlebar and install the screws securing the halves together.

20. Operate the choke lever and make sure the carburetor choke linkage is operating correctly, with no binding. If operation is incorrect or there is binding carefully check that the cable is attached correctly and there are no tight bends in the cable.

21. Install all parts that were removed as described in this chapter and other related chapters.

FUEL TANK

Removal/Installation
(All U.S. Models and 1986-1989 U.K. Models)

WARNING
Do not store gasoline in an open container, since it is an extreme fire hazard. Store the gasoline in a sealed metal container, away from heat, sparks or flames.

Refer to the following illustrations for this procedure:

a. **Figure 35**: 1986-1987 U.S., 1986-1989 U.K. models.
b. **Figure 36**: 1990-on U.S. models.

1. Park and support the bike securely.

2. On 1986-1989 models, turn the fuel shutoff valve to the OFF position (**Figure 37**).

3. Remove the seat as described in Chpater Thirteen.

4. On 1986-1989 models, remove both side covers.

5. Disconnect the battery negative lead as described in Chapter Three.

6A. On 1986-1989 models, remove the front (**Figure 38**) and rear mounting bolts (**Figure 39**).

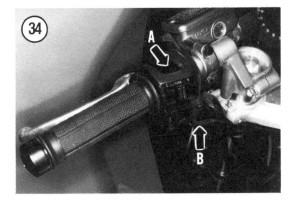

6B. On 1990-on models, remove the rear mounting bolt (**Figure 40**) and nut (**Figure 41**). Don't lose the metal spacer in the fuel tank mount.

7. Lift the rear of the fuel tank up and disconnect the fuel level sensor 2-pin or 3-pin electrical connector containing 2 or 3 wires as follows:
   a. 1986-1989 models: one green and one gray/black.
   b. 1990-on models: one brown/black, one gray/black, one green/black.

8. On 1994-on models, release the fuel level sensor from the clamp on the right-hand side of the frame.

9. On 1990-on models, turn the fuel shutoff valve to the OFF position (**Figure 42**).

10. Disconnect the fuel line (**Figure 43**) to the carburetor assembly. Plug the end with a golf tee to prevent the entry of dirt and foreign matter.

NOTE
In Step 11, disconnect the 2 tubes from the fuel tank—don't remove the fuel tank

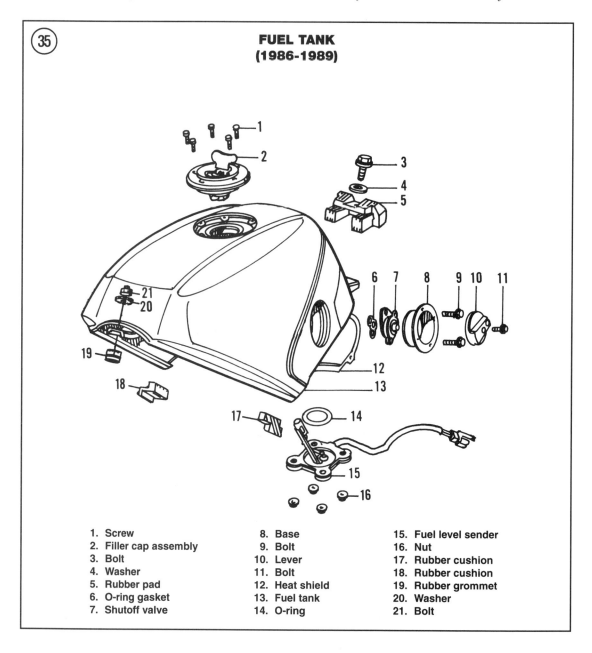

FUEL TANK (1986-1989)

1. Screw
2. Filler cap assembly
3. Bolt
4. Washer
5. Rubber pad
6. O-ring gasket
7. Shutoff valve
8. Base
9. Bolt
10. Lever
11. Bolt
12. Heat shield
13. Fuel tank
14. O-ring
15. Fuel level sender
16. Nut
17. Rubber cushion
18. Rubber cushion
19. Rubber grommet
20. Washer
21. Bolt

FUEL, EMISSION CONTROL AND EXHAUST SYSTEMS

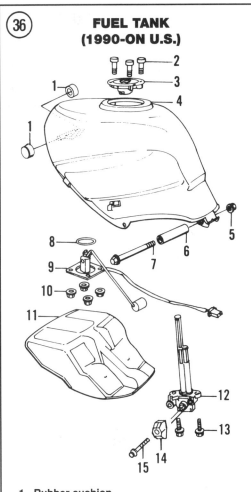

FUEL TANK (1990-ON U.S.)

1. Rubber cushion
2. Screw
3. Filler cap assembly
4. Fuel tank
5. Nut
6. Collar
7. Bolt
8. O-ring
9. Fuel level sender
10. Nut
11. Heat shield
12. Shutoff valve/filter
13. Bolt
14. Lever
15. Bolt

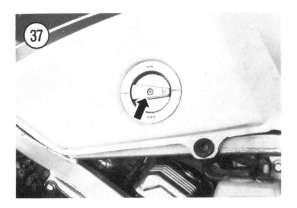

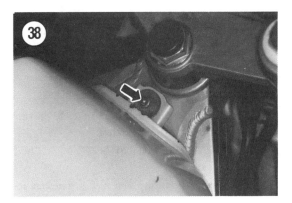

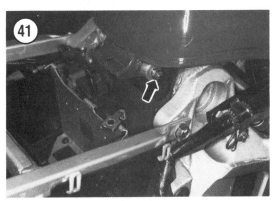

with these 2 tubes attached. Leave the 2 tubes routed correctly through the frame.

11. On 1994 models, disconnect the large overflow tube and the smaller breather tube from the base of the fuel tank. Plug the ends with a golf tee to prevent the entry of dirt and foreign matter.

12. Lift the fuel tank, slide it to the rear and remove it from the frame.

13. If necessary, drain the fuel into a fuel can approved for gasoline storage.

> **WARNING**
> *Do not store gasoline in an open container, since it is an extreme fire hazard. Store the gasoline in a sealed metal container, away from heat, sparks or flames.*

14. Inspect the fuel tank mount rubber dampers and replace if damaged or starting to deteriorate.

15. Install by reversing these removal steps while noting the following:
   a. On 1994 models, connect the large overflow tube and the smaller breather tube onto the base of the fuel tank.
   b. On 1994 models, if the overflow and breather tubes were removed from the frame, route them away from rear suspension components and the exhaust system. Make sure they are not pinched anywhere along the entire length of the tube.

Removal/Installation (1990-on U.K. Models)

> **WARNING**
> *Do not store gasoline in an open container, since it is an extreme fire hazard. Store the gasoline in a sealed metal container, away from heat, sparks or flames.*

Refer to **Figure 44** for this procedure.

1. Park and support the bike securely.
2. Remove the seat as described in Chapter Thirteen.
3. Disconnect the battery negative lead as described in Chapter Three.
4. Turn the fuel shutoff valve to the OFF position.

5. Remove the rear mounting bolt (**Figure 40**) and nut (**Figure 41**). Don't lose the metal spacer in the fuel tank mount.

6. Lift the rear of the fuel tank up and prop it in this position.

7. Remove the 2 outer screws (**Figure 45**) securing the fuel shutoff valve control cable bracket to the fuel tank.

8. Remove the inner screw (**Figure 45**) securing the collar and cable drum to the fuel shutoff valve.

9. Remove the collar and cable drum from the fuel shutoff valve.

10. Move the cable drum and cables out of the way.

11. Disconnect the fuel level sensor 2-pin electrical connector containing 2 wires (one gray/black and one green/black).

12. On 1994 models, release the fuel level sensor from the clamp on the right-hand side of the frame.

13. Disconnect the fuel line (**Figure 43**) to the carburetor assembly. Plug the end with a golf tee to prevent the entry of dirt and foreign matter.

14. On models so equipped, disconnect the drain and breather tubes from the base of the fuel tank.

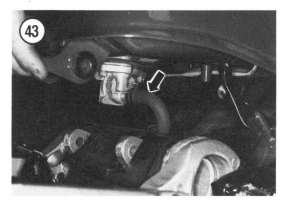

FUEL, EMISSION CONTROL AND EXHAUST SYSTEMS

FUEL TANK (1990-ON U.K.)

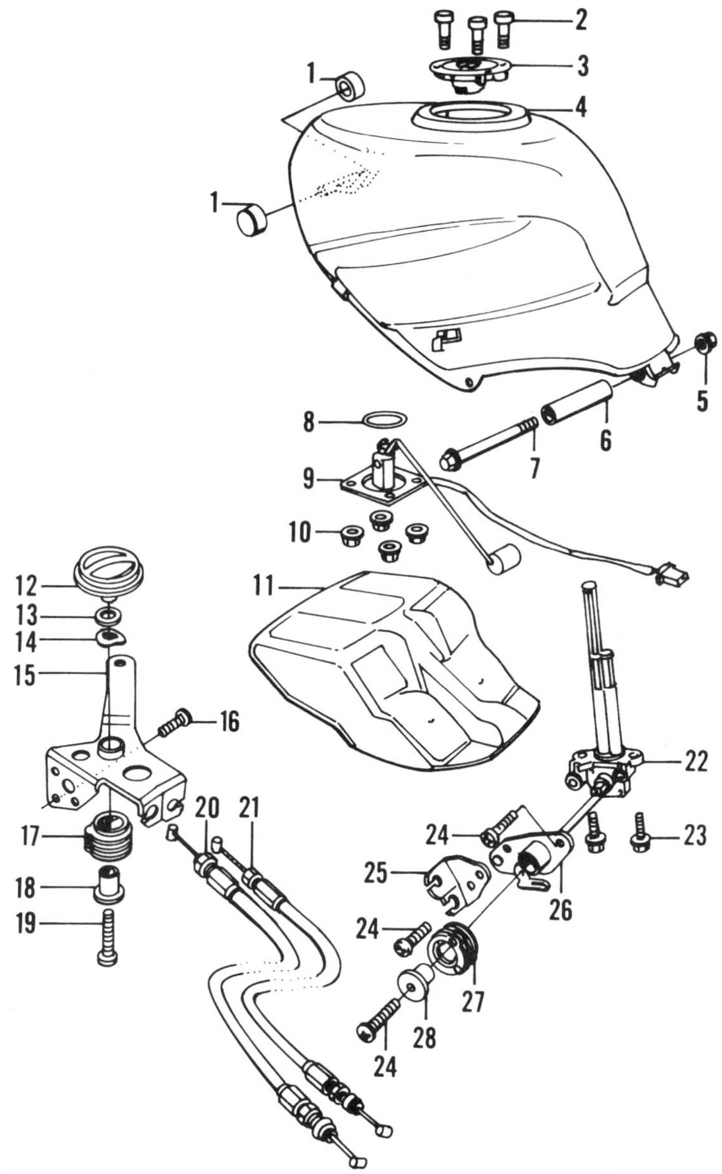

1. Rubber cushion
2. Screw
3. Filler cap assembly
4. Fuel tank
5. Nut
6. Collar
7. Bolt
8. O-ring
9. Fuel level sender
10. Nut
11. Heat shield
12. Control knob
13. Washer
14. Wave washer
15. Knob and cable bracket
16. Bolt
17. Cable drum-front
18. Collar
19. Bolt
20. Cable "A"
21. Cable "B"
22. Shutoff valve/filter
23. Screw
24. Screw
25. Cable bracket
26. Valve bracket
27. Cable drum-rear
28. Collar

15. Lift the fuel tank, slide it to the rear and remove it from the frame.

16. If necessary, drain the fuel into a fuel can approved for gasoline storage.

WARNING
Do not store gasoline in an open container, since it is an extreme fire hazard. Store the gasoline in a sealed metal container, away from heat, sparks or flames.

17. Inspect the fuel tank mount rubber dampers and replace if damaged or starting to deteriorate.

18. Install by reversing these removal steps while noting the following:

   a. If the control cables were removed from the drum, install the lower cable "A" onto the inner groove in the drum and the upper cable "B" onto the outer groove in the drum as shown in **Figure 46**.

   b. Apply a light coat of multipurpose grease to the collar sliding surfaces. Install the collar and align the cutout with the projection on the drum (**Figure 47**).

   c. Install the collar and screw and tighten the screw securely.

   d. After installation is complete, operate the fuel valve on the front fairing and check for smooth operation.

FUEL SHUTOFF VALVE

On 1990-on models, the fuel shutoff valve is equipped with a filter. There is also a separate inline fuel filter.

Removal/Installation

Refer to the following illustrations for this procedure:

a. **Figure 35**: 1986-1987 U.S., 1986-1989 U.K. models.

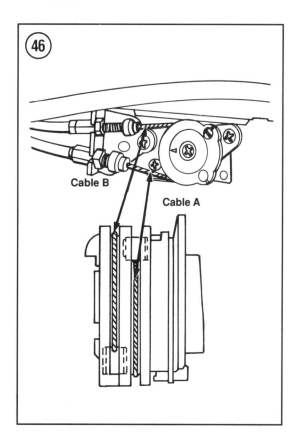

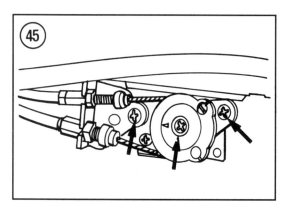

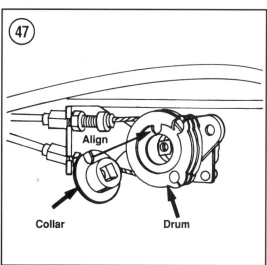

FUEL, EMISSION CONTROL AND EXHAUST SYSTEMS

b. **Figure 36**: 1990-on U.S. models.
c. **Figure 44**: 1990-on U.K. models.

The fuel tank should be almost empty to perform this procedure. Drain the fuel from the tank prior to removing the tank from the frame.

1. Remove the fuel tank as described in this chapter.
2. Place a blanket or some clean shop cloths on the workbench to protect the painted finish of the fuel tank.
3. On 1986-1989 models, lay the fuel tank on its right-hand side.

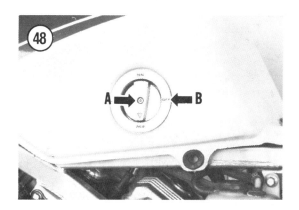

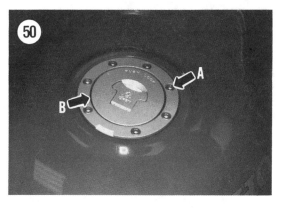

4A. On 1986-1989 models, perform the following:
   a. Remove the screw securing the lever (A, **Figure 48**).
   b. Remove the screws securing the base (B, **Figure 48**) and shutoff valve to the fuel tank.
   c. Remove the base and the shutoff valve from the fuel tank.
   d. Remove the rubber gasket assembly from the fuel tank.

4B. On 1990-on models, perform the following:
   a. Remove the bolts (A, **Figure 49**) securing the shutoff valve/filter and remove the shutoff valve/filter assembly (B, **Figure 49**).
   b. Remove the rubber gasket assembly from the fuel tank.

5. Inspect the rubber gasket assembly for deterioration or hardness. Replace if necessary.
6. Install by reversing these removal steps.
7. After installation is complete, thoroughly check for fuel leaks.

FUEL FILLER CAP

Removal/Installation

Refer to the following illustrations for this procedure:
   a. **Figure 35**: 1986-1987 U.S., 1986-1989 U.K. models.
   b. **Figure 36**: 1990-on U.S. models.
   c. **Figure 44**: 1990-on U.K. models.

The fuel tank should be almost empty to perform this procedure. Drain the fuel from the tank prior to removing the tank from the frame.

1. Remove and drain the fuel tank as described in this chapter.

WARNING
Do not store gasoline in an open container, since it is an extreme fire hazard. Store the gasoline in a sealed metal container, away from heat, sparks or flames.

2. Remove the filler cap mounting bolts (A, **Figure 50**) and remove the filler cap assembly (B, **Figure 50**).
3. Cover the fuel tank opening to prevent contamination.
4. Replace the filler cap if the rubber seal is worn or damaged.

5. Install by reversing these removal steps. Tighten the bolts securely.

FUEL PUMP

The fuel pump performance testing is covered under *Electrical Components* in Chapter Eight.

Removal/Installation

1A. On 1986-1989 models, remove the side covers as described in Chapter Thirteen.
1B. On 1990-on models, remove the tailpiece as described in Chapter Thirteen.
2. Remove the fuel tank as described in this chapter.
3. Disconnect the battery negative cable as described in Chapter Eight.
4. Disconnect the electrical connector (A, **Figure 51**) for the fuel pump.

NOTE
Mark the hoses and the fuel pump fittings so the hoses will be reconnected to the correct fittings during installation.

5. Disconnect both flexible fuel lines (B, **Figure 51**) from the fuel pump. Plug the ends of both fuel lines with golf tees to prevent fuel leakage.
6. Remove the bolt (C, **Figure 51**) securing the fuel pump mounting bracket to the frame.
7. Remove the mounting bracket and remove the fuel pump (D, **Figure 51**) from the rubber mount on the bracket.
8. Install by reversing these removal steps while noting the following:
   a. Be sure to install the fuel pump in the rubber mount.
   b. Connect the hoses to the correct fittings on the fuel pump.
   c. Make sure the hose clamps are on tight.
   d. Make sure the electrical connector is tight and free of corrosion.
   e. After installation is complete, thoroughly check for fuel leaks.

FUEL FILTER

1A. On 1986-1989 models, remove the side covers as described in Chapter Thirteen.
1B. On 1990-on models, remove the tailpiece as described in Chapter Thirteen.
2. Remove the fuel tank as described in this chapter.
3. Disconnect the fuel outlet flexible fuel line (A, **Figure 52**) from the fuel filter (B, **Figure 52**). Plug the end of the fuel line with a golf tee to prevent fuel leakage.
4. Disconnect the fuel inlet flexible fuel line (C, **Figure 52**) from the fuel filter and remover the filter. Plug the end of the fuel line with a golf tee to prevent fuel leakage.
5. Install by reversing these removal steps while noting the following:
   a. Position the filter with the arrow pointing toward the outlet side (toward the fuel pump).
   b. Make sure the hose clamps are on tight.
   c. After installation is complete, thoroughly check for fuel leaks.

GASOLINE/ALCOHOL BLEND TEST

Gasoline blended with alcohol is available in many areas. Most states and most fuel suppliers require labeling of gasoline pumps that dispense

FUEL, EMISSION CONTROL AND EXHAUST SYSTEMS

gasoline containing a certain percentage of alcohol (methyl or wood). If in doubt, ask the service station operator if their fuel contains any alcohol. A gasoline/alcohol blend, even if it contains co-solvents and corrosion inhibitors for methanol, may be damaging to the fuel system. It may also cause poor performance, hot engine restart or hot-engine running problems.

If you are not sure if the fuel you purchased contains alcohol, run this simple and effective test. A blended fuel doesn't look any different from straight gasoline so it must be tested.

WARNING
Gasoline is very volatile and presents an extreme fire hazard. Be sure to work in a well-ventilated area away from any open flames (including pilot lights on household appliances). Do not allow anyone to smoke in the area and have a fire extinguisher rated for gasoline fires handy.

During this test keep the following facts in mind:
a. Alcohol and gasoline mix together.
b. Alcohol mixes *easier* with water.
c. Gasoline and water do *not* mix.

NOTE
If cosolvents have been used in the gasoline, this test may not work with water. Repeat this test using automotive antifreeze instead of water.

NOTE
A very handy item is now available at some motorcycle dealers and motorcycle supply houses that is designed specifically for this test. It is a glass vial with a screw on cap (Figure 53). There are instructions printed on the side of the glass as to how to perform the test. If you purchase one of these items, follow the manufacturer's instructions.

Use a 8 oz. transparent baby bottle with a sealable cap.

1. Set the baby bottle on a level surface and add water up to the 1.5 oz mark. Mark this line on the bottle with a fine-line permanent marking pen. This will be the reference line used later in this test.

2. Add the suspect fuel into the baby bottle up to the 8 oz. mark.

3. Install the sealable cap and shake the bottle vigorously for about 10 seconds.

4. Set the baby bottle upright on the level surface used in Step 1 and wait for a few minutes for the mixture to settle down.

5. If there is *no* alcohol in the fuel, the gasoline/water separation line will be exactly on the 1.5 oz reference line made in Step 1.

6. If there *is* alcohol in the fuel, the gasoline/water separation line will be *above* the 1.5 oz. reference line made in Step 1. The alcohol has separated from the gasoline and mixed in with the water (remember it is easier for the alcohol to mix with water than gasoline).

WARNING
*After the test, discard the baby bottle or place it out of reach of small children. There will always be a gasoline and alcohol residue in it and should **not** be used to drink out of.*

CRANKCASE BREATHER SYSTEM (U.S. ONLY)

To comply with air pollution standards, the Honda VFR700F and VFR750F are equipped with a crankcase breather system. The system shown in **Figure 54** draws blowby gases from the crankcase and recirculates them into the fuel/air mixture and thus into the engine to be burned.

Make sure all hose clamps are tight on the hose between the air filter housing and the breather housing on the rear cylinder had cover. Check the hose (**Figure 55**) for deterioration and replace as necessary.

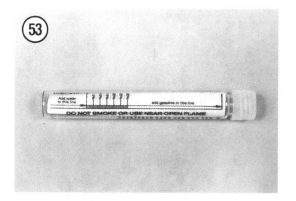

EVAPORATIVE EMISSION CONTROL SYSTEM (CALIFORNIA MODELS ONLY)

To comply with the California Air Resources Board, an evaporative emission control system (**Figure 56**) is installed on all models sold in California. A Vacuum Hose Routing Diagram Label is mounted on the top surface of the rear fender under the seat.

Fuel vapor from the fuel tank is routed into a charcoal canister. This vapor is stored when the engine is not running. When the engine is running these vapors are drawn through a purge control valve and into the carburetor to be burned. Make sure all hose clamps are tight. Check all hoses for deterioration and replace as necessary.

Prior to removing the hoses from any of the parts of these systems, mark the hose and the fitting with a piece of masking tape and identify where the hose goes. There are so many vacuum hoses on these models it can be very confusing where each one is supposed to be attached.

Component Removal/Installation

1. Remove the lower side panels of the front fairing and, on models so equipped, the lower cowl as described under *Front Fairing Removal/Installation* in Chapter Thirteen.

NOTE
Prior to removing the hoses from the PCV valve, mark the hose and the fitting with a piece of masking tape and identify where the hose goes.

2. Disconnect the hoses from the PCV valve going to the charcoal canister.
3. Pull the vacuum hoses from the clips on the frame.
4. Pull the PCV valve from the mounting tab on the frame.
5. Disconnect the hoses from the AVCV valve.
6. Pull the vacuum hoses from the clips on the frame.
7. Pull the AVCV valve from the mounting tab on the frame.
8. Remove the bolts securing the charcoal canister to the frame mounting bracket and remove the canister assembly.
9. Install by reversing these removal steps. Be sure to install the hoses onto their correct fittings on the components.

Purge Control Valve (PCV) Testing

Test the purge control valve (PCV) if the engine becomes difficult to restart once it has warmed up.

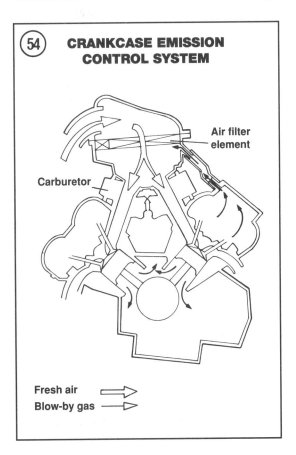

FUEL, EMISSION CONTROL AND EXHAUST SYSTEMS

1. Connect a vacuum pump to the PCV hose fitting that goes to the 3-way joint. Refer to the emission control decal on your bike for the correct hose fitting.

2. Apply 250 mm (9.8 in.) Hg of vacuum and watch the pump gauge. The vacuum should *not* bleed down. If the valve loses vacuum, the PCV is faulty and must be replaced.

3. Disconnect the vacuum pump.

4. Connect a vacuum pump to the PCV hose fitting that goes to the No. 1 carburetor body. Refer to the emission control decal on your bike for the correct hose fitting. See **Figure 57**, typical.

5. Apply 250 mm (9.8 in.) Hg of vacuum and watch the pump gauge. The vacuum should *not* bleed down. If the valve loses vacuum, the PCV is faulty and must be replaced.

6. Disconnect the vacuum pump.

7. Connect a vacuum pump to the PCV hose fitting that goes to the 3-way joint.

8. Connect a pressure pump to the PCV hose fitting that goes to the charcoal canister.

CAUTION
Do not use compressed air, as the PCV will be damaged internally. Use only a hand-operated pump.

9. Apply 250 mm (9.8 in.) Hg of vacuum to the PCV engine hose fitting. While the vacuum is applied,

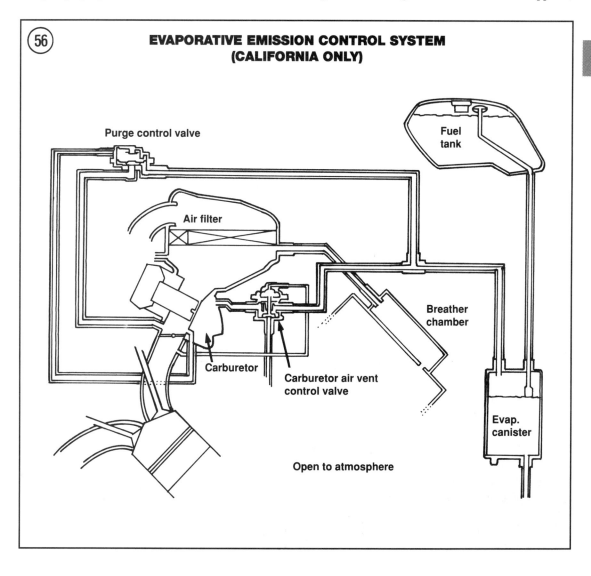

EVAPORATIVE EMISSION CONTROL SYSTEM (CALIFORNIA ONLY)

apply air pressure with the pressure pump. Air should blow out of the PCV carburetor hose fitting.

10. If air does not blow out as described in Step 9, the PCV is defective and must be replaced.

11. If the PCV checks out okay, reinstall it. If the PCV fails any one of these tests, install a new PCV.

Air Vent Control Valve (AVCV) Testing/Replacement

Test the AVCV valve if the engine becomes difficult to restart once it has warmed up.

1. Connect a vacuum pump to the AVCV No. 10 hose fitting that goes to the carburetors. Refer to the emission control decal on your bike for the correct hose fittings.

2. Apply 250 mm (9.8 in.) Hg of vacuum and watch the pump gauge. The vacuum should *not* bleed down. If the valve loses vacuum, the AVCV is faulty and must be replaced.

3. Disconnect the vacuum pump.

4. Install the vacuum pump to the AVCV air vent port and apply vacuum to the port. The vacuum should *not* bleed down. If the valve loses vacuum, the AVCV is faulty and must be replaced.

5. Disconnect the vacuum pump.

6. Connect the vacuum pump to the AVCV No. 10 fitting.

7. Connect a pressure pump to the AVCV air vent port.

CAUTION
Do not use compressed air, as the AVCV valve will be damaged internally. Use only a hand-held pump.

8. Apply vacuum to the AVCV fuel tank hose fitting. While the vacuum is applied, apply air pressure with the pressure pump. Air should blow out of the AVCV hose fitting that goes to the carburetor. If the air does *not* blow out, the AVCV is defective and must be replaced.

9. Plug the AVCV hose fitting that goes to the carburetor.

10. Repeat Step 8. While the vacuum is applied, apply air pressure with the pressure pump. The air supplied from the pump should *not* bleed out of the AVCv. If the air bleeds out, the AVCV is defective and must be replaced.

11. If the AVCV checks out okay, reinstall it. If the AVCV fails any one of these tests, install a new AVCV valve.

SECONDARY AIR SUPPLY SYSTEM (1986-ON U.S., 1988-ON SWITZERLAND, 1992-ON AUSTRIA MODELS)

The secondary air supply system improves emission performance by routing unburned filtered air into the exhaust port as shown in **Figure 58**.

NOTE
Honda does not provide any service procedures for the 1990-on models. On 1990-on models, the system is referred to as the Pulse Secondary Air Injection (PAIR) System.

Secondary Air Supply System Inspection (1986-1989 Models Only)

1. Start the engine and let it reach normal operating temperature.

2. Shut the engine off and support the bike securely.

3. Remove the lower side panels of the front fairing as described under *Front Fairing Removal/Installation* in Chapter Thirteen.

4. Make sure all vacuum tubes and pipes are not cracked or pinched. Replace any damaged tubes or pipes.

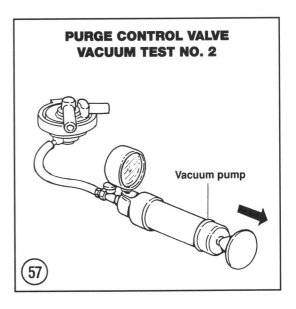

57. PURGE CONTROL VALVE VACUUM TEST NO. 2

FUEL, EMISSION CONTROL AND EXHAUST SYSTEMS

5. Make sure there are no exhaust leaks at the cylinder heads. Replace the gasket(s) and tighten the bolt(s) securely.

6. Remove the air filter housing as described in this chapter.

7. Check the secondary air port at the front of the carburetor air chamber assembly. The port should be clean and free of all carbon deposits.

8. If the secondary air port is carbon fouled, check the reed valves in the reed valve chamber as described in this chapter.

9. Disconnect the vacuum tube from the No. 4 carburetor 3-way joint intake pipe. Plug the fitting to prevent air from entering and causing a vacuum leak. Refer to the emission control decal on your bike for the correct hose fittings.

10. Connect a vacuum pump (Honda part No. ST-AH-260-MC7 or equivalent) to the vacuum tube disconnected in Step 7.

11. Start the engine and open the throttle slightly to make sure that air is sucked through the intake port in the air chamber. Place your thumb over the hose opening momentarily to feel if air is being sucked in or not.

12. If air is not being sucked in, check the air supply tube and vacuum tube for being clogged.

13. With the engine running, gradually apply 300-370 mm (11.8-14.6 in.) Hg of vacuum and watch the pump gauge to the vacuum tube.

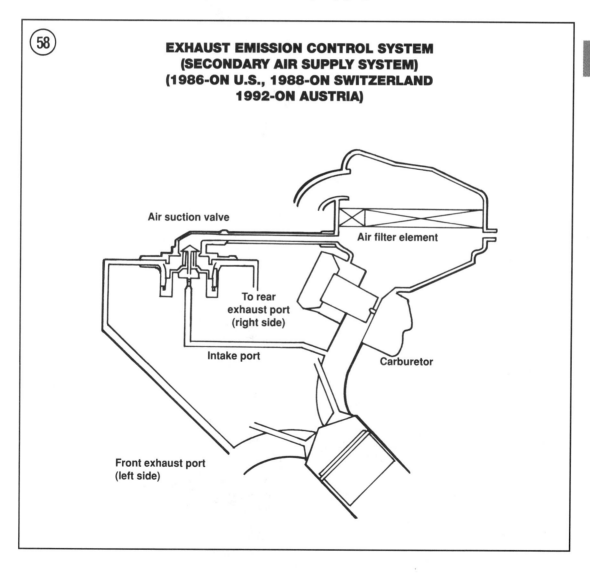

14. Check that the air intake port stops drawing air and that the vacuum does not bleed down. Place your thumb over the intake port opening momentarily to feel if air is being sucked in or not.
15. If air is still not being drawn in or the specified vacuum is not maintained, install a new air suction valve.
16. If after burn occurs on deceleration, even when the secondary air system is operating normally, check the muffler joint(s) for an exhaust gas leak.

Reed Valve Inspection

NOTE
The reed valves cannot be serviced. If defective, they must be replaced as an assembly. There is a reed valve at each end of the air suction valve assembly.

1. Remove the air suction valve assembly as described in this chapter.
2. Remove the screws securing the end cap on the air suction valve.
3. Remove the end cap and the reed valve assembly.
4. Check the reeds for damage or fatigue and replace if necessary.
5. Check the rubber seat for cracking or deterioration, or for clearance between the reed and the rubber seat. Replace the reed valve if necessary.
6. Repeat for the reed valve on the other side.

Air Injection Control Valve (AICV) Removal/Installation

1. Remove the lower side panels of the front fairing as described under *Front Fairing Removal/Installation* in Chapter Thirteen.

NOTE
The AICV assembly can be removed by itself or the entire assembly, AICV and air inlet pipes can be removed as an assembly.

2. Label, then disconnect the vacuum hose and intake pipes (A, **Figure 59**) at the AICV assembly. Refer to the emission control decal on your bike for correct hose fittings.

NOTE
*In **Figure 59** only 1 bolt is visible, be sure to remove both mounting bolts.*

3. Remove the bolts and lockwashers (B, **Figure 59**) securing the AICV to the cylinder block or frame.
4. Remove the air inlet pipe joint bolts (**Figure 60**). Then remove the air inlet pipes and O-ring gaskets.
5. Remove the AICV valve assembly.
6. Inspect the air inlet pipes and the valve assembly (**Figure 61**) for wear or damage. Make sure the end cap mounting screws are tight. Replace damaged air inlet pipe joint O-ring gaskets.
7. Install by reversing these removal steps.

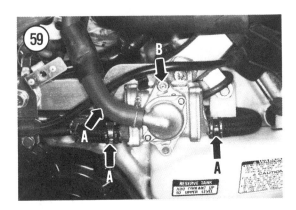

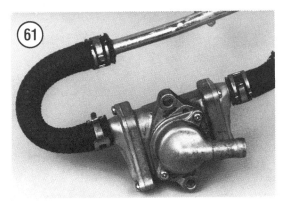

FUEL, EMISSION CONTROL AND EXHAUST SYSTEMS

EXHAUST SYSTEM

The exhaust system is a vital performance component and frequently, it is a vulnerable piece of equipment. Check the exhaust system for deep dents and fractures and repair or replace them immediately. Refer to **Figure 62** and **Figure 63**. Check the muffler frame mounting flanges for fractures and loose bolts. Check the cylinder head mounting flanges for tightness. A loose exhaust pipe connection can rob the engine of power.

The factory exhaust system consists of 4 exhaust pipes, a common collector and depending on model, either a single muffler or dual mufflers.

Removal/Installation
(1986-1989 Models)

Refer to the following illustrations for this procedure:

a. **Figure 64**: 1986-1987 models.

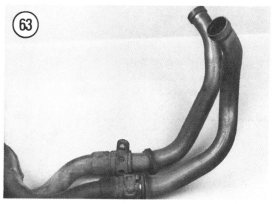

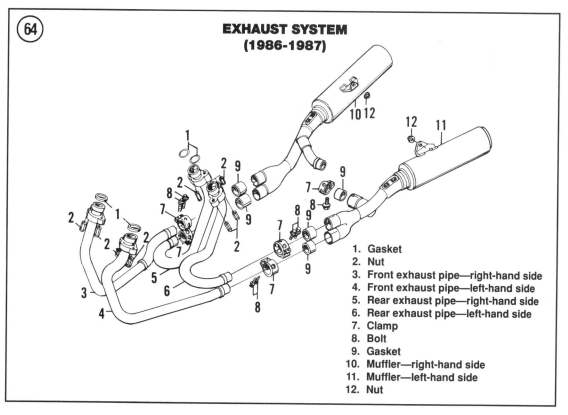

1. Gasket
2. Nut
3. Front exhaust pipe—right-hand side
4. Front exhaust pipe—left-hand side
5. Rear exhaust pipe—right-hand side
6. Rear exhaust pipe—left-hand side
7. Clamp
8. Bolt
9. Gasket
10. Muffler—right-hand side
11. Muffler—left-hand side
12. Nut

b. **Figure 65**: 1988-1989 models.

NOTE
This procedure is shown on a 1986 model.

1. Support the bike securely.
2. Remove the lower side panels of the front fairing as described under *Front Fairing Removal/Installation* in Chapter Thirteen.

WARNING
*Do not remove or service the exhaust system when it is **HOT**.*

NOTE
If it is difficult to separate two components, spray some WD-40 or equivalent into the joint and to the clamping bolts threads. This will help to loosen the joint.

3A. On 1986-1987 models, to remove the muffler, perform the following:
   a. Loosen the clamping bolts securing the exhaust pipes to the muffler (**Figure 66**).
   b. Loosen the clamping bolt on the muffler crossover pipe.
   c. Remove the bolt (**Figure 67**) and nut securing the muffler to the rear footpeg bracket.
   d. Pull the muffler toward the rear and pull it free from the exhaust pipes. Remove the muffler.
   e. Repeat for the other side.

3B. On 1986-1989 models, to remove the muffler, perform the following:
   a. Loosen the clamping bolt securing the muffler to the common collector.

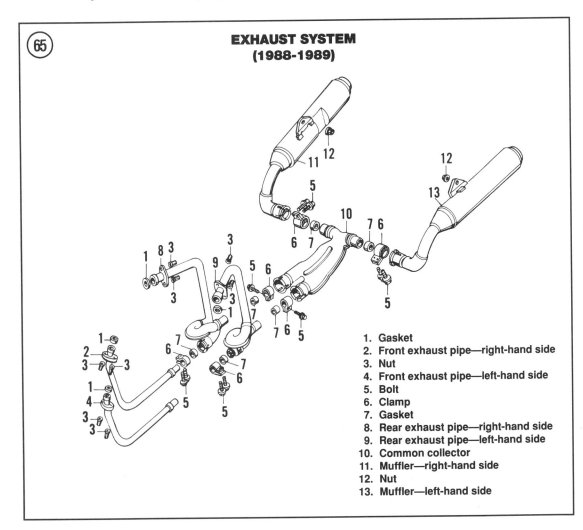

EXHAUST SYSTEM (1988-1989)

1. Gasket
2. Front exhaust pipe—right-hand side
3. Nut
4. Front exhaust pipe—left-hand side
5. Bolt
6. Clamp
7. Gasket
8. Rear exhaust pipe—right-hand side
9. Rear exhaust pipe—left-hand side
10. Common collector
11. Muffler—right-hand side
12. Nut
13. Muffler—left-hand side

FUEL, EMISSION CONTROL AND EXHAUST SYSTEMS

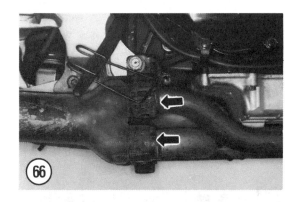

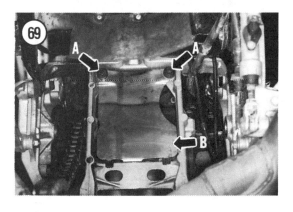

b. Remove the bolt and nut securing the muffler to the rear footpeg bracket.

c. Pull the muffler toward the side and pull it free from the common collector. Remove the muffler.

d. Repeat for the other side.

4. On 1988-1989 models, loosen the clamping bolts securing the common collector to the rear set of exhaust pipes and remove the common collector.

5. To remove the front exhaust pipes, perform the following:

   a. On 1986-1987 models, loosen the clamping bolts securing the front exhaust pipes to the muffler (**Figure 66**).

   b. On 1988-1989 models, loosen the clamping bolts securing the front exhaust pipes to the rear set of exhaust pipes.

   c. Remove the nuts (A, **Figure 68**) securing the front exhaust pipe/flange to the front cylinder head.

   d. Pull the exhaust pipe (B, **Figure 68**) down to clear the threaded studs on the front cylinder head, then pull toward the front and free it from the muffler or rear set of exhaust pipes.

   e. Repeat for the other front exhaust pipe.

6. To remove the rear exhaust pipes, perform the following:

   a. Remove the front set of exhaust pipes and the mufflers as described in Steps 3-5.

   b. Remove the rear wheel as described in Chapter Eleven.

   c. Remove the shock absorber as described in Chapter Eleven.

   d. Remove the bolts (A, **Figure 69**) securing the access panel and remove the panel (B, **Figure 69**).

   e. Remove the nuts (A, **Figure 70**) securing the rear exhaust pipe/flange to the rear cylinder head.

   f. Pull the exhaust pipe (B, **Figure 70**) down to clear the threaded studs on the rear cylinder head, then pull down and remove the exhaust pipe.

   g. Repeat for the other rear exhaust pipe.

7. Inspect the gaskets at all joints; replace as necessary.

8. Be sure to install a new gasket in each exhaust port in both cylinder heads.

9. Apply a light coat of multipurpose grease to the inside surface of the gaskets. This will make inser-

tion of the exhaust pipes into the respective fittings easier.

10. Move the assembly into position and install all bolts and nuts only finger-tight until the exhaust flange nuts are installed and securely tightened. This will minimize an exhaust leak at the cylinder heads.

11. Tighten all bolts and nuts securely.

12. After installation is complete, make sure there are no exhaust leaks.

13. Install the lower side panels of the front fairing as described in Chapter Thirteen.

Removal/Installation (1990-1993 Models)

Refer to **Figure 71** for this procedure.

1. Support the bike securely.

2. Remove the lower side panels of the front fairing as described under *Front Fairing Removal/Installation* in Chapter Thirteen.

3. Remove the bolts (A, **Figure 72**) securing the front right-hand footpeg bracket and move the bracket (B, **Figure 72**) out of the way.

4. Remove the rear wheel as described in Chapter Eleven.

WARNING
*Do not remove or service the exhaust system when it is **HOT**.*

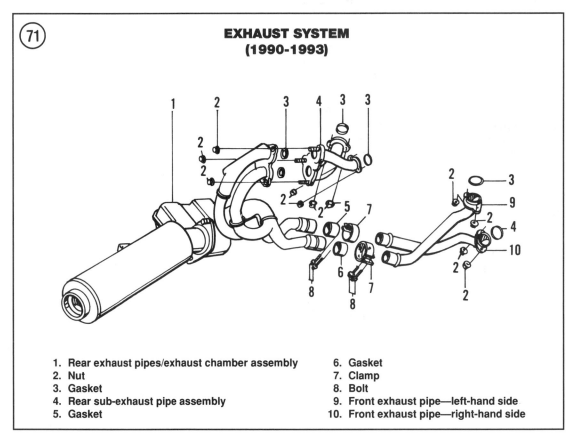

EXHAUST SYSTEM (1990-1993)

1. Rear exhaust pipes/exhaust chamber assembly
2. Nut
3. Gasket
4. Rear sub-exhaust pipe assembly
5. Gasket
6. Gasket
7. Clamp
8. Bolt
9. Front exhaust pipe—left-hand side
10. Front exhaust pipe—right-hand side

FUEL, EMISSION CONTROL AND EXHAUST SYSTEMS

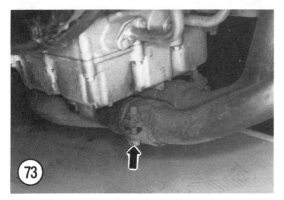

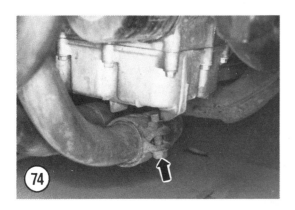

NOTE
If it is difficult to separate two components, spray some WD-40 or equivalent into the joint and to the clamping bolt's threads. This will help to loosen the joint.

5. To remove the front exhaust pipes, perform the following:

   a. Loosen the clamping bolts securing the front exhaust pipes to the rear exhaust pipes/exhaust chamber assembly. Refer to **Figure 73** and **Figure 74**.

   b. Remove the nuts securing both forward exhaust pipe flanges to the front cylinder head. Refer to **Figure 75** and **Figure 76**. Slide the flanges down.

   c. Pull the exhaust pipes down to clear the threaded studs on the front cylinder head, then pull toward the front and free them from the rear exhaust pipes/exhaust chamber assembly

   d. Remove both front exhaust pipes.

NOTE
The muffler and rear exhaust pipes/exhaust chamber assembly must be removed out through the bottom of the frame in Step 6. This assembly is fairly tall and requires vertical room for clearance. If you are unable to raise the bike sufficiently to clear this assembly along with the muffler, remove the muffler. This will decrease the mass of the assembly and may ease the removal process.

6. To remove the muffler and rear exhaust pipes/exhaust chamber assembly, perform the following:

a. Remove the nuts securing the rear exhaust pipes/exhaust chamber assembly to the rear sub-exhaust pipe assembly on the rear cylinder head.
b. Remove the bolt and nut securing the muffler to the rear right-hand footpeg assembly.
c. If necessary, remove the bolts, washers and flex joint (**Figure 77**) securing the muffler and remove the muffler.
d. Pull the rear exhaust pipes/exhaust chamber assembly to the rear to clear the threaded studs on the rear sub-exhaust pipe, then move down to clear the frame.
e. Remove the muffler and rear exhaust pipes/exhaust chamber assembly.

7. Remove the nuts securing the rear sub-exhaust pipe assembly to the rear cylinder head. Pull the rear sub-exhaust pipe assembly to the rear to clear the threaded studs on the rear cylinder head and remove it.

8. Inspect the gaskets at all joints; replace as necessary.

9. Be sure to install a new gasket in each exhaust port in both cylinder heads.

10. Apply a light coat of multipurpose grease to the inside surface of the gaskets. This will make insertion of the exhaust pipes into the respective fittings easier.

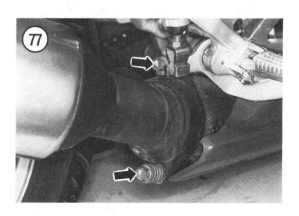

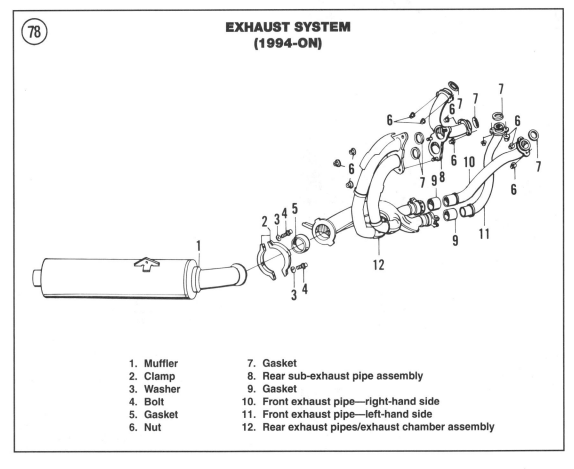

EXHAUST SYSTEM (1994-ON)

1. Muffler
2. Clamp
3. Washer
4. Bolt
5. Gasket
6. Nut
7. Gasket
8. Rear sub-exhaust pipe assembly
9. Gasket
10. Front exhaust pipe—right-hand side
11. Front exhaust pipe—left-hand side
12. Rear exhaust pipes/exhaust chamber assembly

FUEL, EMISSION CONTROL AND EXHAUST SYSTEMS

11. Move all assemblies into position and install all bolts and nuts only finger-tight until the exhaust flange nuts are installed and securely tightened. This will minimize an exhaust leak at the cylinder heads.
12. Tighten all bolts and nuts securely.
13. After installation is complete, make sure there are no exhaust leaks.
14. Tighten the front right-hand footpeg assembly mounting bolts securely.
15. Install the lower side panels of the front fairing as described in Chapter Thirteen.

Removal/Installation
(1994-on Models)

Refer to **Figure 78** for this procedure.
1. Support the bike securely.
2. Remove the lower side panels of the front fairing as described under *Front Fairing Removal/Installation* in Chapter Thirteen.
3. Remove the rear wheel as described in Chapter Eleven.
4. Remove the centerstand as follows:
   a. Use vise-grip pliers and disconnect the return spring from the centerstand spring bracket.
   b. Remove the spring bracket from the centerstand pivot shaft.
   c. Remove the Allen bolt securing the centerstand pivot shaft to the frame.
   d. Withdraw the pivot shaft from the left-hand side.
   e. Remove the centerstand from the frame. Don't lose the washer from the outer surface of the right-hand pivot point. It must be reinstalled in the same location during installation.
5. Remove the bolts (A, **Figure 72**) securing the front right-hand footpeg bracket and move the bracket (B, **Figure 72**) out of the way.

> **WARNING**
> *Do not remove or service the exhaust system when it is **HOT**.*

> **NOTE**
> *If it is difficult to separate two components, spray some WD-40 or equivalent into the joint and to the clamping bolt's threads. This will help to loosen the joint.*

6. Remove the bolts and washers securing the muffler clamp. Remove the muffler clamp.
7. Remove the bolt and nut securing the muffler to the rear right-hand footpeg assembly and remove the muffler.
8. To remove the front exhaust pipes, perform the following:
   a. Loosen the clamping bolts securing the front exhaust pipes to the rear exhaust pipes/exhaust chamber assembly. Refer to **Figure 73** and **Figure 74**.
   b. Remove the nuts securing both forward exhaust pipe flanges to the front cylinder head. Refer to **Figure 75** and **Figure 76**. Slide the flanges down.
   c. Pull the exhaust pipes down to clear the threaded studs on the front cylinder head, then pull toward the front and free them from the rear exhaust pipes/exhaust chamber assembly
   d. Remove both front exhaust pipes.
9. To remove the rear exhaust pipes/exhaust chamber assembly, perform the following:
   a. Remove the nuts securing the rear exhaust pipes/exhaust chamber assembly to the rear sub-exhaust pipe assembly on the rear cylinder head.
   b. Pull the rear exhaust pipes/exhaust chamber assembly to the rear to clear the threaded studs on the rear sub-exhaust pipe, then move down to clear the frame.
   c. Remove the rear exhaust pipes/exhaust chamber assembly.
10. Remove the nuts securing the rear sub-exhaust pipe assembly to the rear cylinder head. Pull the rear sub-exhaust pipe assembly to the rear to clear the threaded studs on the rear cylinder head and remove it.
11. Inspect the gaskets at all joints; replace as necessary.
12. Be sure to install a new gasket in each exhaust port in both cylinder heads.
13. Apply a light coat of multipurpose grease to the inside surface of the gaskets. This will make insertion of the exhaust pipes into the respective fittings easier.
14. Move all assemblies into position and install all bolts and nuts only finger-tight until the exhaust flange nuts are installed and securely tightened. This will minimize an exhaust leak at the cylinder heads.

15. Align the notches in the muffler clamps with the raised tabs on the outlet fitting of the rear exhaust pipes/exhaust chamber assembly (**Figure 79**). Install the clamps and bolts and tighten the bolts securely.

16. Tighten all bolts and nuts securely.

17. Move the muffler back into position and maintain a distance (Dimension A) of 25-35 mm (1-1 3/8 in.) between the muffler and the rear tire (**Figure 80**). Tighten the muffler bolt securely.

18. Install the centerstand assembly.

19. After installation is complete, make sure there are no exhaust leaks.

20. Install the lower side panels of the front fairing as described in Chapter Thirteen.

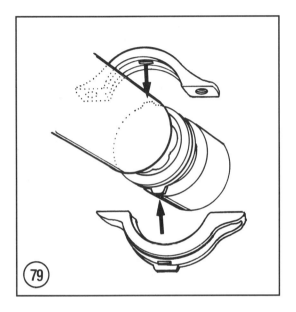

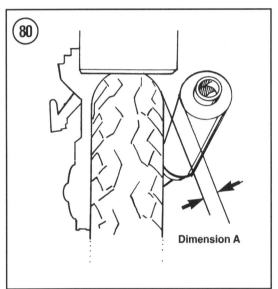

Table 1 CARBURETOR SPECIFICATIONS

1986-1987 U.S. and Canada	
Carburetor type	Keihin VD
Model No.	
VFR700F, VFR700II	
49-state	VDBAB
California	VDBCA
VFR750F	
49-state	VDBAA
California	VDBBA
Canada	VDBOD
Venturi diameter	34.5 mm (1.37 in.)
Needle clip position	fixed
Main jet No.	
Front	118
Rear	118
Pilot screw	pre-set
Initial opening	
49-state	2 1/2 turns out
California	2 turns out
Float level	
1986	9.0 mm (0.35 in.)
1987	7.0 mm (0.28 in.)
(continued)	

FUEL, EMISSION CONTROL AND EXHAUST SYSTEMS

Table 1 CARBURETOR SPECIFICATIONS (continued)

1990-on U.S. and Canada	
Carburetor type	Keihin VD or VP
Model No.	
1990-1991	
49-state	VDJBA
California	VDJCA
Canada	VDJ1A
1992-1993	
49-state	VDJJA
California	VDJKA
Canada	VDJ5A
1994	
49-state	VP34A
California	VP33A
Canada	VP35A
Venturi diameter	34.5 mm (1.37 in.)
Needle clip position	fixed
Main jet No.	
1990-1993	130
1994	
49-state and Canada	125
California	
Front	128
Rear	125
Slow jet	
49-state and Canada	40
California	
1990-1993	38
1994	40
Pilot screw	pre-set
Initial opening	
49-state	
1990-1991	1 1/2 turns out
1992-1993	1 7/8 turns out
1994	1 5/8 turns out
California	
1990-1991	2 1/2 turns out
1992-1993	2 turns out
1994	2 3/8 turns out
Canada	
1990-1991	2 1/4 turns out
1992-1993	1 7/8 turns out
1994	1 3/8 turns out
Float level	
1990-1993	9.0 mm (0.35 in.)
1994	13.7 mm (0.54 in.)
1986-1989 Other than U.S. and Canada	
Carburetor type	Keihin VD
Model No.*	
1986-1987	
AR, E, ED, F, G, IT, SP, U	VDB0B
1988-1989	
AR	VDJ0B
E, ED, F, G, IT, SP, U	VDJ0A
SW	VDJAA
Venturi diameter	34.5 mm (1.37 in.)
(continued)	

Table 1 CARBURETOR SPECIFICATIONS (continued)

1986-1989 Other than U.S. and Canada (continued)	
Needle clip position	fixed
Main jet No.	118
Pilot screw	pre-set
Initial opening	
1986-1987	2 1/2 turns out
1988-1989	2 3/8 turns out
Float level	
1986-1987	7.0 mm (0.28 in.)
1988-1989	9.0 mm (0.35 in.)

1990-on Other than U.S. and Canada	
Carburetor type	Keihin VD
Model No.*	
1990-1991	
ED, F, IT, ND	VDJ1A
E, SP, U	VDJ4A
G, AR, FI	VDJEA
SW	VDJDA
1992-on	
AR	VDJHA
E, SP, U	VDJ6A
G	VDJFA
ED, F, IT	VDJ5A
SW	VDJGA
Venturi diameter	34.5 mm (1.37 in.)
Needle clip position	fixed
Main jet No.	130
Slow jet	
1990	40
1991-on	
SW	38
Other than SW	40
Pilot screw	pre-set
Initial opening	
1990	
E, ED, F, IT, N, SW	2 1/8 turns out
G, AR, FI	1 3/4 turns out
SP, U	1 7/8 turns out
1991	
E, SP, U	1 7/8 turns out
AR, G, FI	1 3/4 turns out
ED, F, IT, ND	2 1/4 turns out
SW	2 5/8 turns out
1992-on	
E, SP, U	2 1/4 turns out
G	1 1/2 turns out
ED, F, IT, SW, AR	1 7/8 turns out
Float level	9.0 mm (0.35 in.)

* AR=Austria, E=United Kingdom, ED=Europe, F=France, FI=Finland, G=Germany, IT=Italy, ND=No. Europe, SP=Spain, SW=Switzerland, U=Australia.

CHAPTER EIGHT

ELECTRICAL SYSTEM

This chapter contains operating principles and service and test procedures for all electrical and ignition components. Information regarding the battery and spark plugs is covered in Chapter Three.

The electrical system includes the following systems:
   a. Charging system.
   b. Ignition system.
   c. Starting system.
   d. Lighting system.
   e. Directional signal system.
   f. Switches.
   g. Various electrical components.

Tables 1-4 are located at the end of this chapter.

NOTE
Where differences occur relating to the United Kingdom (U.K.) models, they are identified. If there is no (U.K.) designation relating to a procedure, photo or illustration, it is identical to the United States (U.S.) models.

NOTE
*Most motorcycle dealers and parts suppliers will not accept the return of any electrical part. When testing electrical components, three general requirements to make are: (1) that you follow the test procedures as described in this chapter; (2) that your test equipment is working properly; and (3) that you are familiar with the test equipment and its operation. If a test result shows that a component is defective, have a Honda dealer **retest** the component to verify your test results.*

ELECTRICAL CONNECTORS

The Honda VFR700F and VFR750F are equipped with many electrical components, connectors and wires. Corrosion-causing moisture can enter these electrical connectors and cause poor electrical connections, leading to component failure. Troubleshooting an electrical circuit with one or more corroded electrical connectors can be time-consuming and frustrating.

When reconnecting electrical connectors, pack them in a dielectric grease compound. Dielectric grease is especially formulated for sealing and waterproofing electrical connectors and will not interfere with the current flow through the electrical connectors. Use only this compound or an equivalent designed for this specific purpose. Do *not* use a substitute that may interfere with the current flow within the electrical connector. Do *not* use silicone sealant.

After cleaning both the male and female connectors, make sure they are thoroughly dry. Using this dielectric compound, pack the interior of one of the connectors prior to connecting the 2 connector halves. On multi-pin connectors, pack the male side and on single-wire connectors, pack the female side. Use a good-size glob so that it will squish out when the two halves are pushed together. For best results, the compound should fill the entire inner area of the connector. On multi-pin connectors, also pack the backside of both the male and female side with the compound to prevent moisture from entering the backside of the connector. After the connector is fully packed, wipe the exterior of all excessive compound.

Get into the practice of cleaning and sealing all electrical connectors every time they are unplugged. This may prevent a breakdown on the road and also save you time when troubleshooting a circuit.

Always make sure all ground connections are free of corrosion and are tight. **Figure 1** shows a typical ground connection used at various locations on the bike.

BATTERY NEGATIVE TERMINAL

Some of the component replacement procedures and some of the test procedures in this chapter require disconnecting the battery negative (–) lead as a safety precaution.

1986-1989 Models

1. Remove the frame right-hand side cover as described in Chapter Thirteen.
2. Disconnect the battery negative lead (**Figure 2**).
3. Move the negative lead (**Figure 3**) out of the way so it will not accidentally make contact with the battery negative terminal.
4. Connect the battery negative terminal and tighten the screw securely.
5. Install the frame right-hand side cover.

1990-on Models

1. Remove the seat as described in Chapter Thirteen.
2. Remove the rubber strap (A, **Figure 4**) and, on models so equipped, remove the cover (B, **Figure 4**).
3. Disconnect the battery negative lead (**Figure 5**).
4. Move the lead out of the way so it will not accidentally make contact with the battery negative terminal.

ELECTRICAL SYSTEM

5. Connect the battery negative terminal and tighten the screw securely.
6. Install the cover (models so equipped) and rubber strap.
7. Install the seat and make sure it is locked in place correctly.

CHARGING SYSTEM

The charging system consists of the battery, alternator and a voltage regulator/rectifier. Refer to **Figure 6** for 1986-1989 models or **Figure 7** or 1990-on models.

Alternating current generated by the alternator is rectified to direct current. The voltage regulator maintains the voltage to the battery and additional electrical loads (lights, ignition, etc.) at a constant voltage regardless of variations in engine speed and load.

A malfunction in the charging system generally causes the battery to remain undercharged. To prevent damage to the alternator and the regulator/rectifier when testing and repairing the charging system, note the following precautions:

1. Always disconnect the negative battery cable, as described in this chapter, before removing a component in the charging system.

2. When it is necessary to charge the battery, remove the battery from the motorcycle as described in this chapter.

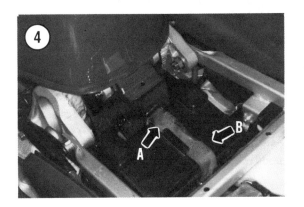

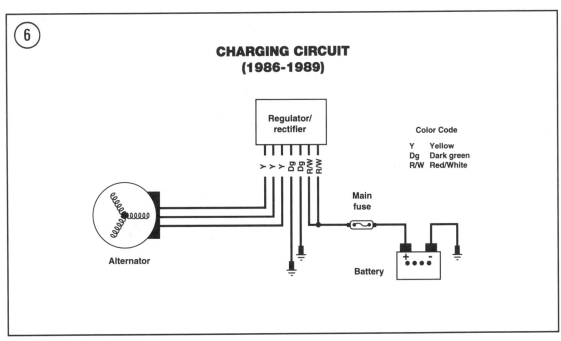

3. Inspect the physical condition of the battery. Look for bulges or cracks in the case, leaking electrolyte or corrosion build-up.

4. Check the wiring in the charging system for signs of chafing, deterioration or other damage.

5. Check the wiring for corroded or loose connections. Clean, tighten or reconnect as required.

**Leakage Test
(1986-1989 Models)**

Perform this test prior to performing the output test.

1. Remove the right-hand side cover.
2. Turn the ignition to the OFF position.
3. Disconnect the battery negative (–) lead as described in this chapter.
4. Connect a voltmeter between the battery ground cable and the negative terminal on the battery.
5. The voltmeter should read 0 volts.
6. If there is a voltage reading, this indicates a voltage drain in the system that will drain the battery.
7. Check all components of the charging system for any bare wires that may be shorting out which could cause the drain.

**Leakage Test
(1990-on Models)**

Perform this test before performing the output test.

1. Turn the ignition switch off.
2. Disconnect the battery negative (–) lead as described in this chapter.

CAUTION
Before connecting the ammeter into the circuit in Step 3, set the meter to its highest amperage scale. This will prevent a large current flow from damaging the meter or blowing the meter's fuse, if so equipped.

3. Connect an ammeter between the battery ground cable and the negative terminal on the battery (**Figure 8**).
4. Switch the ammeter between its highest to lowest amperage scale while reading the meter scale. The specified current leakage rate is 1.2 mA maximum.
5. A higher current leakage value indicates a continuous battery discharge. This could be caused by dirt and/or electrolyte that has collected on top of the battery or a crack in the battery case. These conditions provide a path which battery current can fol-

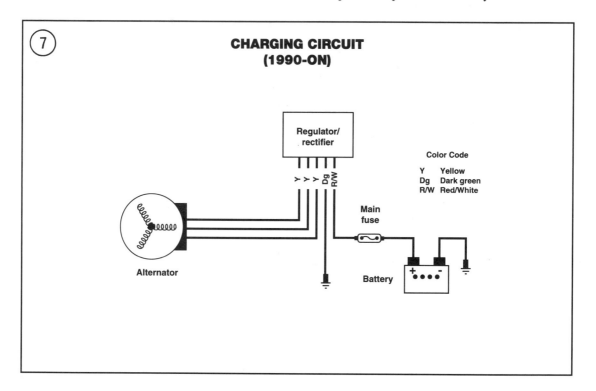

ELECTRICAL SYSTEM

low. Remove and clean the battery as described in this chapter. Then reinstall the battery and retest.

6. If the current leakage rate is still excessive, the probable causes are:
   a. Damaged battery.
   b. Short circuit in the system.
   c. Loose, dirty or faulty electrical connectors in the charging circuit.

7. Disconnect the ammeter from the battery and negative lead.

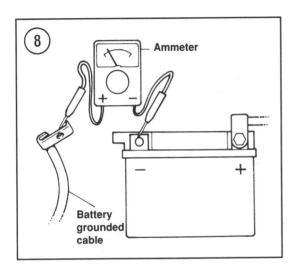

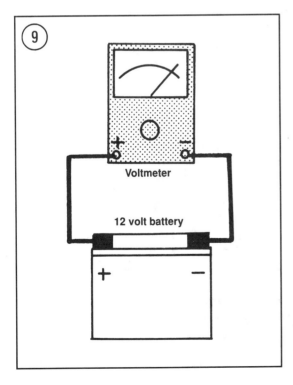

8. Connect the battery negative (–) lead.

Output Test
(1986-1989 Models)

Whenever charging system trouble is suspected, make sure the battery is fully charged and in good condition before going any further. Clean and test the battery as described under *Battery* in Chapter Three.

1. Prior to starting this test, start the bike and let it reach normal operating temperature. Usually 10-15 minutes of stop-and-go riding is sufficient, then turn off the engine.
2. Remove the right- and left-hand side covers and the seat as described in Chapter Thirteen.

NOTE
Do not disconnect either the positive or negative battery cables; they are to remain in the circuit as is.

3. Connect a 0-20 DC voltmeter to the battery terminals as shown in **Figure 9**.
4. Start the engine and gradually increase engine speed listed in **Table 1**. Check the voltage at the indicated engine speed listed under regulator regulated voltage in **Table 1**.
5. If the charging voltage is not within specifications, perform the following checks.
6. Check the wiring harness from the alternator to the battery for an open or short:
   a. At the voltage regulator white 4-pin electrical connector between the green wire and ground.
   b. At the voltage regulator white 4-pin electrical connector between both red/white connectors.
   c. Between the battery and the starter magnetic switch.
7. Check the electrical connectors and the main fuse for loose or poor connector contact.
8. Inspect the alternator stator coils as described in this chapter.
9. Repeat Steps 1-4 and if the regulated voltage is still not within specification, replace the voltage regulator/rectifier as described in this chapter.
10. Disconnect the voltmeter.
11. Install the right- and left-hand side covers and the seat.

Charging Voltage Test
(1990-on Models)

This procedure tests charging system operation. It does not measure maximum charging system output. **Table 1** lists charging system specifications.

For the following test results to be accurate, the battery voltage must be greater than 12.8 volts; measure battery voltage as described under *Battery* in Chapter Three. If the voltage is 12.8 volts or less, recharge the battery as described in Chapter Three.

1. Prior to starting this test, start the bike and let it reach normal operating temperature. Usually 10-15 minutes of stop-and-go riding is sufficient, then turn off the engine.
2. Remove both side covers and seat as described in Chapter Thirteen.
3. Remove the rubber strap (A, **Figure 4**) and on models so equipped, remove the cover (B, **Figure 4**).
4. Disconnect the starter relay switch connector at the starter relay switch (**Figure 10**) and remove the 30A fuse. Then reconnect the connector.
5. Connect a DC ammeter to the circuit as shown in **Figure 10**.

NOTE
Do not disconnect either the positive or negative battery cables; they are to remain in the circuit.

CAUTION
To protect the ammeter, do not connect an ammeter between the positive (+) and negative (−) battery terminals. The ammeter will burn out when the electric starter is operated.

6. Connect a 0-20 DC voltmeter to the battery terminals as shown in **Figure 8**.
7. Start the engine and allow it to idle.
8. Gradually increase engine speed from idle to the engine rpm listed in **Table 1**. Check the voltage and amperage at the indicated engine speed listed under regulator regulated voltage/amperage in **Table 1**.
9. If the ammeter shows a discharge when the engine speed is increased, the probable causes are:
   a. Faulty alternator.
   b. Overcharged battery.
   c. Short circuit in the system.
   d. Loose or dirty terminals between the alternator and the voltage regulator/rectifier.
10. If the ammeter shows charging when the engine speed is reduced, the probable causes are:
    a. Faulty voltage regulator/rectifier.
    b. Discharged battery.
11. If the output voltage is above 14-15 volts when the engine speed is increased, check the voltage regulator/rectifier as described in this chapter.
12. Turn the engine OFF.
13. Disconnect the voltmeter and ammeter.
14. Disconnect the starter relay switch connector at the starter relay switch and install the 30A fuse. Then reconnect the connector.
15. On models so equipped, install the battery cover. On all models, install the rubber strap securing the battery.
16. Install both side covers and seat as described in Chapter Thirteen.

Wiring Harness Test
(1990-on Models)

1. Remove the right-hand rear side cover as described in Chapter Thirteen.
2. Disconnect the regulator/rectifier 5-pin electrical connector (**Figure 11**).

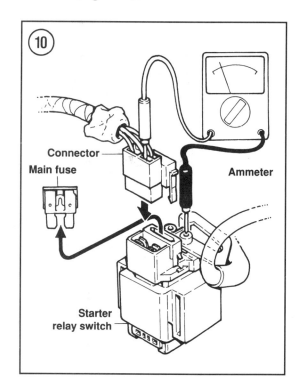

ELECTRICAL SYSTEM

NOTE
When performing the following tests, connect the test probes between the regulator/rectifier connector terminal pins on the wiring harness side of the connector, not on the regulator/rectifier side.

3. Check the battery charge lead as follows:
   a. Connect a voltmeter between the red/white (+) and a good engine ground.
   b. With the ignition switch off, read the voltage indicated on the voltmeter. It should be 12.9 volts or higher (battery voltage).
   c. If the battery voltage is less than specified, check the red/white wire, between the regulator/rectifier and starter relay, for damage.
   d. Disconnect the voltmeter leads.
4. Check the ground line as follows:
   a. Switch an ohmmeter to R × 1 and zero the test leads.
   b. Connect an ohmmeter between the green wire and a good engine ground.
   c. The ohmmeter should show continuity.
   d. If there is no continuity (high resistance), check the ground line for damage.
5. Check the charge coil line as follows:
   a. Switch an ohmmeter to R × 1 and zero the test leads.
   b. Touch one ohmmeter lead to one yellow wire and the other lead to another yellow wire and then to the other. Read the resistance on the ohmmeter after making each test connection.
   c. The ohmmeter should read 1.0-2.0 ohms (@ 20° C [68° F]). A higher reading indicates an open circuit.
   d. If the resistance reading is excessive, check for dirty or loose-fitting terminals or damaged wires.
6. Reconnect the regulator/rectifier electrical connector (**Figure 11**).
7. Install the right-hand side cover.

VOLTAGE REGULATOR/RECTIFIER

Testing
(1986-1989 Models)

1. Remove the left-hand side cover.
2. Disconnect the voltage regulator/rectifier (**Figure 12**) electrical connectors. One is a 3-pin electrical connector containing 3 yellow wires. The other is a 4-pin electrical connector containing 4 wires (2 green and 2 red/white).
3. Use an ohmmeter set at R × 1 and check continuity between the electrical connector terminals of the regulator/rectifier.

NOTE
The following steps are set up for a positive(+) ground ohmmeter. If a negative (–) ground ohmmeter is used, the test results will be the opposite.

4. Connect the positive (+) ohmmeter lead to the yellow terminal and the negative (–) ohmmeter lead to the green terminal. There should be continuity (low resistance).
5. Reverse the ohmmeter leads and repeat Step 4. This time there should be no continuity (infinite resistance).
6. Connect the positive (+) ohmmeter lead to the red/white terminal and the negative (–) ohmmeter lead to the yellow terminal. There should be continuity (low resistance).

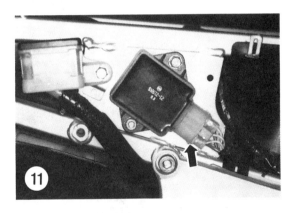

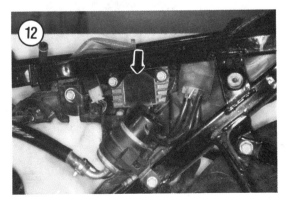

7. Reverse the ohmmeter leads and repeat Step 6. This time there should be no continuity (infinite resistance).

8. If the voltage regulator/rectifier fails any of these tests, the unit is faulty and must be replaced as described in this chapter.

9. If the voltage regulator/rectifier passes this test, reconnect the voltage regulator/rectifier electrical connectors and install the left-hand side cover.

Regulator/Rectifier Unit Resistance Test (1990-on Models)

Honda specifies the use of 2 multi-meters for accurate testing of the regulator/rectifier unit. These are the KOWA digital multimeter (part No. KS-AMH-32-003) and the SANWA analog multimeter (part No. 07308-0020001). Because of the different resistance value characteristics of the semiconductors used in these meters, the use of a different meter may give you an incorrect reading. These meters can be purchased through a Honda dealer or you can remove the regulator/rectifier unit and have the dealer test it for you.

1. Remove the seat and the rear tail piece/side cover as described in Chapter Thirteen.

2. Disconnect the regulator/rectifier unit electrical connector (**Figure 11**).

3A. Set the SANWA tester to the × k ohms scale.

3B. Set the KOWA tester to the × 100 ohms scale.

4. Refer to **Figure 13** for test connections and values. If any of the meter readings differ from the stated values, first check the condition of the battery

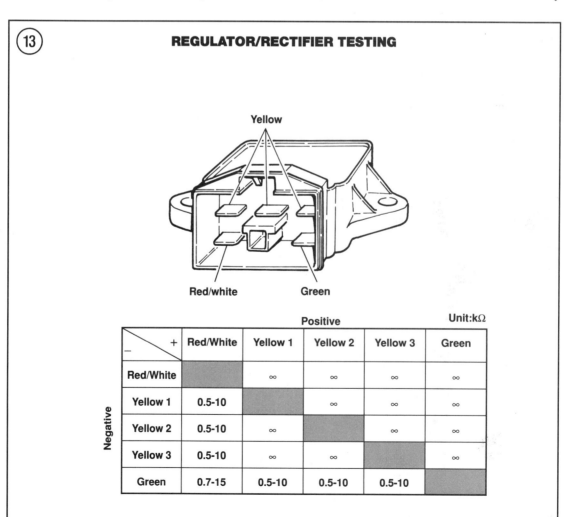

REGULATOR/RECTIFIER TESTING

− \ +	Red/White	Yellow 1	Yellow 2	Yellow 3	Green
Red/White		∞	∞	∞	∞
Yellow 1	0.5-10		∞	∞	∞
Yellow 2	0.5-10	∞		∞	∞
Yellow 3	0.5-10	∞	∞		∞
Green	0.7-15	0.5-10	0.5-10	0.5-10	

Unit: kΩ

ELECTRICAL SYSTEM

in the multimeter; an old battery can cause inaccurate readings. If the readings are still incorrect with a new battery, replace the regulator/rectifier unit as described in this chapter.

Voltage Regulator/Rectifier Removal/Installation

1986-1989 models

1. Remove the seat and left-hand side cover as described in Chapter Thirteen.
2. Disconnect the battery negative (–) lead as described in this chapter.
3. Disconnect the voltage regulator/rectifier electrical connectors. One is a 3-pin electrical connector containing 3 yellow wires. The other is a 4-pin electrical connector containing 4 wires (2 green and 2 red/white).
4. Remove the bolts securing the voltage regulator/rectifier (**Figure 12**) to the frame and remove it.
5. Install the voltage regulator/rectifier to the frame and tighten the bolts securely.
6. Install by reversing these removal steps while noting the following:
   a. Make sure all electrical connections are tight and free of corrosion.
   b. Connect the battery negative (–) lead.

1990-on models

1. Remove the seat and the rear tail piece/side cover as described in Chapter Thirteen.
2. Disconnect the battery negative (–) lead as described in this chapter.
3. Disconnect the regulator/rectifier unit electrical connector (A, **Figure 14**).

4. Remove the bolts (B, **Figure 14**) securing the voltage regulator/rectifier to the frame panel and remove it.
5. Install the voltage regulator/rectifier to the frame panel and tighten the bolts securely.
6. Install by reversing these removal steps while noting the following:
   a. Make sure all electrical connections are tight and free of corrosion.
   b. Connect the battery negative (–) lead.

ALTERNATOR

The alternator is a form of electrical generator in which a magnetized field called a rotor revolves around a set of stationary coils called a stator assembly. As the rotor revolves, alternating current is induced in the stator coils. The current is then rectified to direct current and is used to operate the electrical systems on the motorcycle and to keep the battery charged. The rotor is permanently magnetized.

Alternator rotor and stator assembly removal and installation are covered in Chapter Four.

Rotor Testing

The rotor is permanently magnetized and cannot be tested except by replacing it with a known good one. The rotor can lose magnetism from old age or a sharp hit. If defective, the rotor must be replaced; it cannot be remagnetized.

Stator Testing

1A. On 1986-1989 models, remove the left-hand side cover as described in Chapter Thirteen.
1B. On 1990-on models, remove the tailpiece assembly as described in Chapter Thirteen.
2. Disconnect the alternator stator 3-pin electrical connector containing 3 yellow wires.
3. Use an ohmmeter set at R × 1 and check continuity between each yellow terminal on the alternator stator side of the connector.
4. Replace the stator assembly if any yellow terminal shows no continuity (infinite resistance) to any other yellow terminal. This would indicate an open in the stator coil winding.

5. Use an ohmmeter set at R × 1 and check continuity from each yellow terminal on the alternator stator side of the connector and to ground.

6. Replace the stator assembly if any yellow terminal shows continuity (indicated resistance) to ground. This would indicate a short within the stator coil winding.

NOTE
Prior to replacing the stator assembly, check the electrical wires to and within the electrical connector for any opens or poor connections.

7. If the stator assembly fails either of these tests, it must be replaced as described under *Alternator Stator Removal/Installation* in Chapter Four.

TRANSISTORIZED IGNITION SYSTEM

All models covered in this manual are equipped with a transistorized electronic ignition system. The system uses no breaker points and is non-adjustable, but the timing should be checked to make sure all ignition components within the system are operating correctly.

The ignition system is computer controlled and is operated by the microprocessor within the ignitor unit.

The signal generators are mounted on the right-hand end of the crankshaft. On 1986 models, there was an additional camshaft pulse generator mounted on the front cylinder head. As the signal generator rotor is turned by the crankshaft, its signal is sent to the ignitor unit. This signal turns the ignitor unit

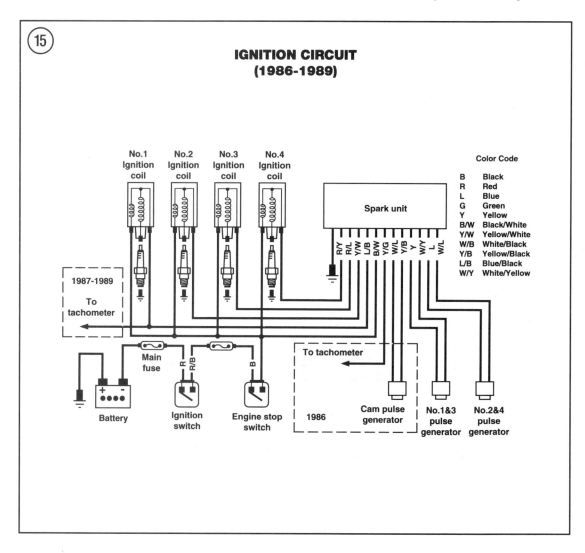

ELECTRICAL SYSTEM

transistor alternately ON and OFF. As the transistor is turned ON and OFF, the current passing through the primary windings of the ignition coil is also turned ON and OFF. Thus it induces the secondary current on the ignition coil's secondary windings and produces the current necessary to fire the spark plugs.

The ignition system consists of 4 ignition coils, 1 spark unit (1986-1989 models) or 1 ignition control module (1990-on models), 2 cranksaft driven pulse generators (plus a camshaft pulse generator on the 1986 models) and 4 spark plugs.

Refer to the following illustrations for the two different transistorized ignition systems:

a. **Figure 15**: 1986-1989 models.
b. **Figure 16**: 1990-on models.

Transistorized Ignition System Precautions

Certain measures must be taken to protect the ignition system. Damage to the micro-processor in the system may occur if the following precautions are not observed.

1. Never connect the battery backwards. If the connected battery polarity is wrong, damage will occur to the spark unit (1986-1989 models) or the ignition control module (1990-on models), the voltage regulator/rectifier and/or the alternator stator assembly.

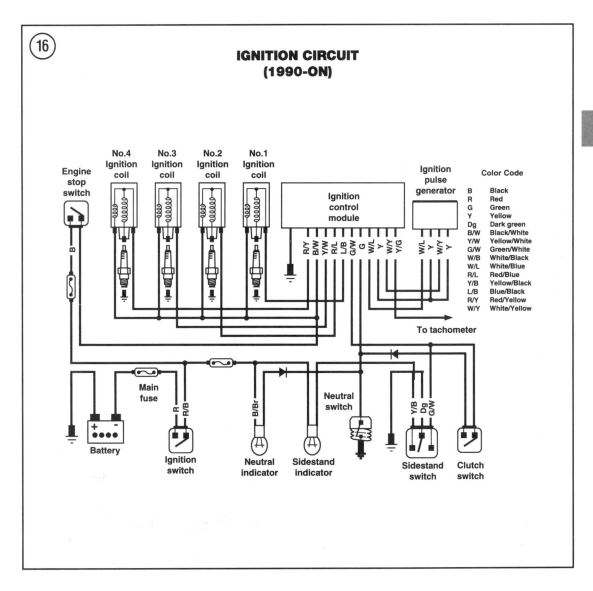

2. Do not disconnect the battery when the engine is running. A voltage surge will occur which will damage the voltage regulator/rectifier and possibly burn out the lights.
3. Keep all connections between the various units clean and tight. Be sure that the wiring connections are pushed together firmly to help keep out moisture.
4. Do not substitute another type of ignition coil.
5. Each component is mounted within a rubber vibration isolator. Always be sure that the isolator is in place when installing any units in the system.
6. Prior to inspecting or troubleshooting the ignition system, check the battery charge as described in this chapter. For the following test results to be accurate, the battery must be fully charged (12.9 volts or higher). A lower voltage reading will result with different and inaccurate test readings.
7. Do not turn the engine over unless all of the spark plugs are installed in the cylinder heads or are grounded against the engine.

IGNITION SPARK UNIT (1986-1989 MODELS)

Testing (All Models Including 1990-on)

Honda does not provide test procedures or specifications for the spark unit (1986-1989 models) or ignition control module (1990-on models). If the ignition coils and pulse generator test correctly as described in this chapter, and all related wiring and switches are in good condition, your last resort would be to replace the spark unit or ignition control module with a known good unit. However, this step could be expensive if performed by yourself and it is not the cause of the problem. Remember, if you purchase a new spark unit and it does not solve the ignition system problem, you may not be able to return the spark unit or ignition control module for a refund. Most motorcycle dealers will not accept returns on any electrical component since they could be damaged internally even though they look okay externally.

Replacement

1. Remove the seat as described in Chapter Thirteen.
2. Remove both side covers and tailpiece (A, **Figure 17**) as described in Chapter Thirteen.
3. Disconnect the battery negative lead as described in this chapter.
4. Remove the rear turn signal mounting bracket as described in Chapter Thirteen.
5. Remove the screws securing the spark unit cover (B, **Figure 17**) and remove the cover.
6. Remove the spark unit retainer and carefully partially remove the spark unit from the rubber mount.
7. Disconnect the electrical connectors going to the spark unit.
8. Install by reversing these removal steps. Make sure all electrical connections are tight and free of corrosion.

IGNITION CONTROL MODULE (1990-ON MODELS)

Testing

Refer to the preceding test procedure relating to all models covered in this manual.

Replacement

1. Remove the seat as described in Chapter Thirteen.
2. Remove both side covers and tailpiece as described in Chapter Thirteen.
3. Disconnect the battery negative lead as described in this chapter.
4. Disconnect the electrical connector (A, **Figure 18**) going to the ignition control module.
5. Carefully pull the ignition control module (B, **Figure 18**) out of the rubber mount (C, **Figure 18**) on the rear section of frame.

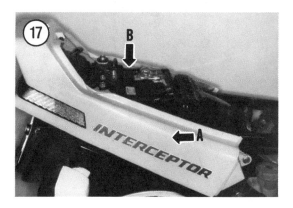

ELECTRICAL SYSTEM

6. Install by reversing these removal steps. Make sure all electrical connections are tight and free of corrosion.

IGNITION COIL

The ignition coil is a form of transformer which develops the high voltage required to jump the spark plug's gap. The only maintenance required is that of keeping the electrical connections clean and tight and occasionally checking to see that the coils are mounted securely.

There are 4 ignition coils; one for each spark plug.

Dynamic Test

Disconnect the high voltage lead from one of the spark plugs (refer to Chapter Three). Remove the spark plug from the cylinder head. Connect a new or known good spark plug to the high voltage lead and place the spark plug base on a good ground like the engine cylinder head. Position the spark plug so you can see the electrodes.

> *WARNING*
> *If it is necessary to hold the high voltage lead, do so with an insulated pair of pliers. The high voltage generated could produce serious or fatal shocks.*

Push the starter button to turn the engine over a couple of times. If a fat blue spark occurs, the coil is in good condition; if not it must be replaced. Make sure that you are using a known good spark plug for this test. If the spark plug used is defective, the test results will be incorrect.

Reinstall the spark plug in the cylinder head and reconnect the spark plug lead.

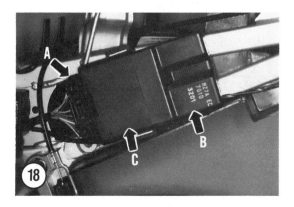

Ignition Coil Resistance Test

1. Remove the seat as described in Chapter Thirteen.
2. Remove the lower side fairing panels as described in Chapter Thirteen.
3. On 1994 models, remove the tailpiece assembly as described in Chapter Thirteen.
4. Disconnect all ignition coil wires (including the spark plug leads from the spark plugs) before testing.
5. Use an ohmmeter set at R × 1 and measure the primary coil resistance between the 2 terminal pins on the ignition coil. Read the resistance on the ohmmeter and compare to the specified resistance in **Table 2**.
6. Use an ohmmeter set on R × 1,000 and measure the secondary coil resistance between the spark plug lead and the terminal pin (with the spark plug cap attached). Read the resistance on the ohmmeter and compare to the specified resistance in **Table 2**.
7. If the secondary resistance is incorrect, remove the spark plug cap and remeasure the secondary resistance between the primary and secondary coil terminals on the coil. Read the resistance on the ohmmeter and compare to the specified resistance in **Table 2**. If the specified resistance is correct, replace the spark plug caps and repeat Step 5.
8. If any one coil reading was incorrect, the coil is faulty and must be replaced.
9. Repeat this procedure for the other 3 ignition coils.
10. Reconnect all ignition coil wires to the ignition coil.
11. On 1994-on models, install the tailpiece assembly as described in Chapter Thirteen.
12. Install the lower side fairing panels as described in Chapter Thirteen.

Removal/Installation

1. Remove the seat as described in Chapter Thirteen.
2. Remove the lower side fairing panels as described in Chapter Thirteen.
3. On 1994-on models, remove the tailpiece assembly as described in Chapter Thirteen.
4. Disconnect the battery negative lead as described in this chapter.
5. Disconnect the spark plug leads.

6. Disconnect the primary wire connectors from each coil to be removed.

NOTE
On 1994-on models, the ignition coils are attached to the frame in pairs; on all other models, the coils are attached independent of each other. The 1994-on model installation is not shown in Step 7.

7. Remove the bolts securing the ignition coils. Refer to **Figure 19** for a typical 1986-1989 model installation and to **Figure 20** for a typical 1990-1993 model installation. Remove the ignition coil(s).
8. Install by reversing these removal steps while noting the following:
    a. Make sure all electrical connections are tight and free of corrosion.
    b. Route the spark plug wires to the correct cylinder.

CRANKSHAFT PULSE GENERATOR

Resistance Test

In order to achieve accurate test results the pulse generator should be warm—at 20° C (68° F). If necessary use a hair dryer and warm the pulse generator coils.

1. Remove the seat as described in Chapter Thirteen.
2. Remove the lower side fairing panels as described in Chapter Thirteen.
3A. On 1986-1989 models, perform the following:
    a. Disconnect the 6-pin ignition pulse generator electrical connector containing 6 wires (one yellow, one white/yellow, one blue, one white/blue, and two black).
    b. Connect the ohmmeter leads between the white/yellow and the yellow leads and then between the white/blue and the blue leads (**Figure 21**).
    c. Read the resistance on the ohmmeter and compare to the specified resistance in **Table 2**.
3B. On 1990-on models, perform the following:
    a. Disconnect the 4-pin ignition pulse generator electrical connector containing 4 wires (one yellow, one white/yellow, one blue and one white/blue).
    b. Connect the ohmmeter leads between the white/yellow and the yellow leads and then between the yellow and the white/blue leads (**Figure 22**).
    c. Read the resistance on the ohmmeter and compare to the specified resistance in **Table 2**.

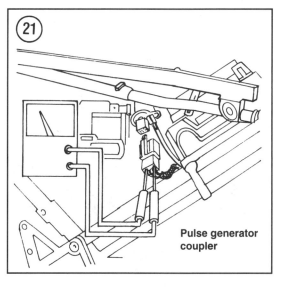

Pulse generator coupler

ELECTRICAL SYSTEM

c. Read the resistance on the ohmmeter and compare to the specified resistance in **Table 2**.

4. If the pulse generator coils do not meet these specifications, the ignition pulse generator assembly must be replaced as described in this chapter. It cannot be serviced.

Removal/Installation

NOTE
This procedure is shown with the engine removed from the frame for clarity. The ignition pulse generator assembly can be removed with the engine in the frame.

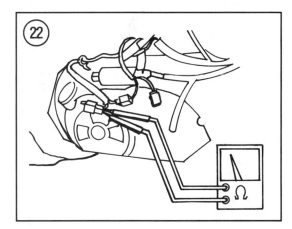

1. Remove the lower sections of the front fairing as described under *Front Fairing Removal/Installation* in Chapter Thirteen.
2. Disconnect the battery negative lead as described in this chapter.
3. Place the bike on the centerstand (models so equipped) or sidestand.
4. Drain the engine oil as described under *Engine Oil and Filter Change* in Chapter Three.

NOTE
Do not operate the clutch lever after the clutch assembly or slave cylinder is removed from the engine. If the lever is applied, it will force the slave cylinder piston out of the body and make slave cylinder installation difficult.

5. Place a block of wood between the clutch lever and the hand grip to hold the lever in the released position. Secure the wood with a rubber band, a tie wrap or tape. This will prevent the clutch lever from being applied accidentally after the clutch slave cylinder is removed from the crankcase.
6. Remove the bolts securing the right-hand crankcase cover (**Figure 23**) and remove the cover and gasket. Don't lose the 2 locating dowels.
7A. On 1986-1989 models, disconnect the 6-pin ignition pulse generator electrical connector containing 6 wires (one yellow, one white/yellow, one blue, one white/blue, and two black). Refer to **Figure 21** for location.
7B. On 1990-on models, disconnect the 4-pin ignition pulse generator electrical connector containing 4 wires (one yellow, one white/yellow, one blue and one white/blue). Refer to **Figure 22** for location.
8. Pull back the rubber boot (A, **Figure 24**) on the oil pressure warning switch and disconnect the electrical wire from the top of the switch. This electrical wire is part of the pulse generator wiring harness.
9A. On 1986-1989 models, remove the bolts securing each pulse generator (**Figure 25**) to the cylinder block.
9B. On 1990-on models, remove the bolts securing the pulse generator assembly (B, **Figure 24**) to the cylinder block.
10. Carefully remove the rubber grommet (C, **Figure 24**) and electrical wires from the cylinder block and remove the assembly from the frame.
11. Install by reversing these removal steps while noting the following:

CAUTION
In Step 11a, if the wiring harness mounting bracket is positioned under the pulse generator the pulse generator will be mounted at an angle, not in line with the raised bars on the starter clutch housing. If this occurs, the ignition system will not operate correctly.

a. On 1986-1989 models, first place the rear pulse generator (A, **Figure 26**) onto the cylinder block mounting studs (B, **Figure 26**), then place the wiring harness mounting bracket (C, **Figure 26**) on top of the pulse generator mounting tab and install the bolts. Tighten the bolts securely.

b. On 1990-on models, be sure to place the electrical harness for the front pulse generator behind the pulse generator mounting bracket (D, **Figure 24**). Tighten the bolts securely.

c. Make sure the rubber grommet (C, **Figure 24**) is installed correctly in the groove in the cylinder block.

d. Install a new gasket (A, **Figure 27**) and make sure the locating dowels (B, **Figure 27**) are in place in the crankcase. Install the right-hand crankcase/clutch cover and tighten the bolts securely in a crisscross pattern.

e. Refill the crankcase with the recommended type and quantity of oil as described in Chapter Three.

f. Make sure all electrical connections are free of corrosion and are tight.

CAMSHAFT PULSE GENERATOR (1986 MODELS ONLY)

Resistance Test

In order to achieve accurate test results the pulse generator should be warm—at 20° C (68° F). If necessary use a hair dryer and warm the pulse generator coils.

1. Remove the right-hand side cover.

2. Disconnect the 2-pin camshaft pulse generator electrical connector containing 2 wires (one white/black and one yellow/black).

3. Connect the ohmmeter leads between the 2 leads (**Figure 28**).

4. Read the resistance on the ohmmeter and compare to the specified resistance in **Table 2**.

5. If the pulse generator coil does not meet this specification, the camshaft pulse generator assembly must be replaced as described in this chapter. It cannot be serviced.

Removal/Installation

1. Remove the right-hand side cover.

2. Disconnect the battery negative lead as described in this chapter.

ELECTRICAL SYSTEM

3. Disconnect the 2-pin camshaft pulse generator electrical connector containing 2 wires (one white/black and one yellow/black). Refer to **Figure 28** for location.

4. Remove the carburetor assembly as described under *Carburetor Removal/Installation* in Chapter Seven.

NOTE
Figure 29 is shown with the engine removed from the frame and partially disassembled for clarity. The camshaft pulse generator can be removed with the engine in the frame.

5. Remove the bolts (A, **Figure 29**) securing the camshaft pulse generator (B, **Figure 29**) and remove it from the cylinder head. Discard the O-ring seal.

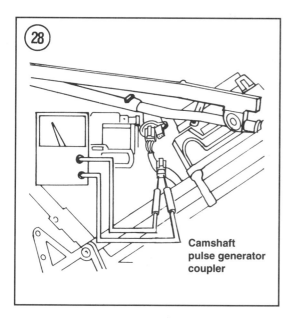

Camshaft pulse generator coupler

6. Install by reversing these removal steps while noting the following:
   a. Install a new O-ring seal and apply a light coat of clean engine oil to it prior to installation.
   b. Tighten the bolts securely.
   c. Make sure all electrical connections are free of corrosion and are tight.

STARTING SYSTEM

The starting system consists of the starter motor, starter gears, starter relay switch and the starter button. When the starter button is pressed, it allows current flow through the starter relay switch coil. The coil contacts close, allowing electricity to flow from the battery to the starter motor.

Refer to the following starter system illustrations:
   a. **Figure 30**: 1986-1989 models.
   b. **Figure 31**: 1990-1993 models.
   c. **Figure 32**: 1994-on models.

CAUTION
Do not operate the starter for more than 5 seconds at a time. Let it rest approximately 10 seconds, then use it again.

Troubleshooting

Basic starter troubleshooting procedures are described in Chapter Two.

STARTER MOTOR

Removal/Installation

1. Remove the lower sections of the front fairing as described under *Front Fairing Removal/Installation* in Chapter Thirteen.

2. Disconnect the battery negative lead as described in this chapter.

3. Remove the oil filter (**Figure 33**) as described under *Engine Oil and Filter Change* in Chapter Three.

4. Remove the bolts securing the external oil pipe (**Figure 34**) to the crankcase and move the lower end of the pipe out of the way. It is not necessary to remove the oil pipe.

5. Disconnect the electric cable from the starter.

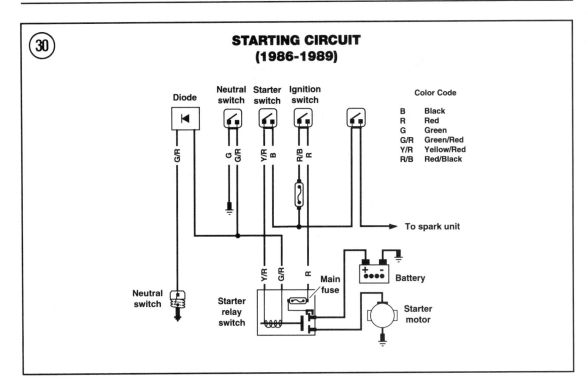

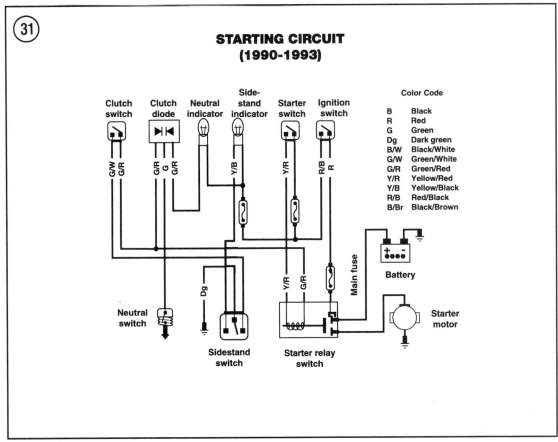

ELECTRICAL SYSTEM

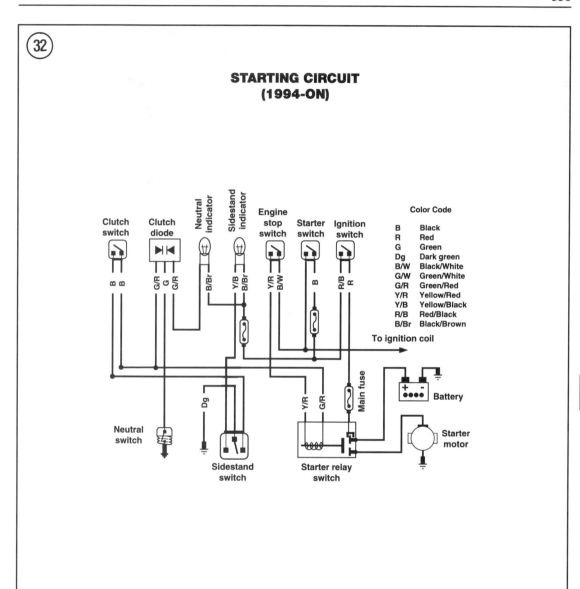

332 CHAPTER EIGHT

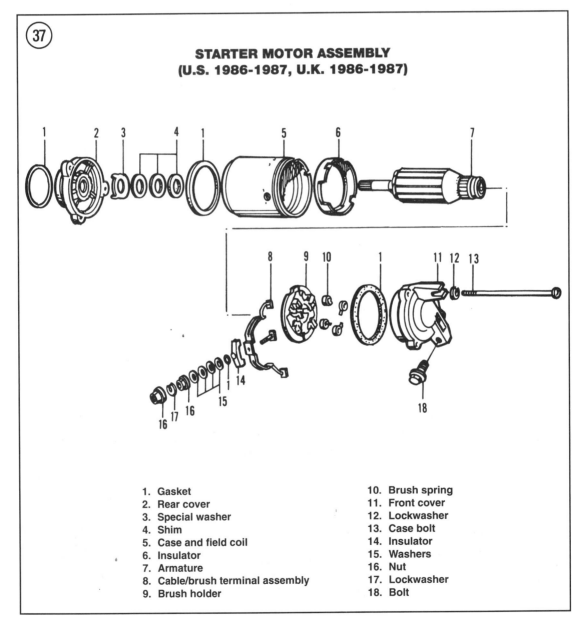

STARTER MOTOR ASSEMBLY (U.S. 1986-1987, U.K. 1986-1987)

1. Gasket
2. Rear cover
3. Special washer
4. Shim
5. Case and field coil
6. Insulator
7. Armature
8. Cable/brush terminal assembly
9. Brush holder
10. Brush spring
11. Front cover
12. Lockwasher
13. Case bolt
14. Insulator
15. Washers
16. Nut
17. Lockwasher
18. Bolt

ELECTRICAL SYSTEM

NOTE
Figure 35 is shown with the engine removed from the frame and partially disassembled for clarity. The starter motor can be removed with the engine in the frame.

6. Remove the bolts (A, **Figure 35**) securing the starter motor to the crankcase.
7. Pull the starter motor (B, **Figure 35**) to the left and remove the starter motor from the crankcase.
8. Install by reversing these removal steps while noting the following:
   a. Make sure the O-ring seal is in place on the external oil pipe. Move it into place on the crankcase, install the bolts and tighten securely.
   b. Make sure the electrical wire connection is tight and free of corrosion.
   c. Refill the crankcase with the recommended type and quantity of oil as described in Chapter Three.
   d. Start the engine and check for oil leaks.

Preliminary Inspection

The overhaul of a starter motor is best left to an expert. This procedure shows how to detect a defective starter.
Inspect the O-ring seal (A, **Figure 36**). O-ring seals tend to harden after prolonged use and heat and therefore lose their ability to seal properly. Replace as necessary.
Inspect the gear (B, **Figure 36**) for chipped or missing teeth. If damaged, the starter assembly must be replaced.

Disassembly

Refer to the following illustrations for this procedure:
   a. **Figure 37**: U.S. 1986-1987, U.K. 1986-1987.
   b. **Figure 38**: U.S. 1990-on, U.K. 1988-on.

1. Remove the case screws and washers (**Figure 39**), then separate the front and rear covers from the case.

NOTE
Write down the number of shims used on the shaft next to the commutator and next to the rear cover. Be sure to install the same number when reassembling the starter.

2. Remove the special washer and shims (**Figure 40**) from the rear cover end of the shaft.
3. Withdraw the armature coil assembly (**Figure 41**) from the rear end of the case.
4. Remove the brush holder assembly (**Figure 42**) from the front end of the case.

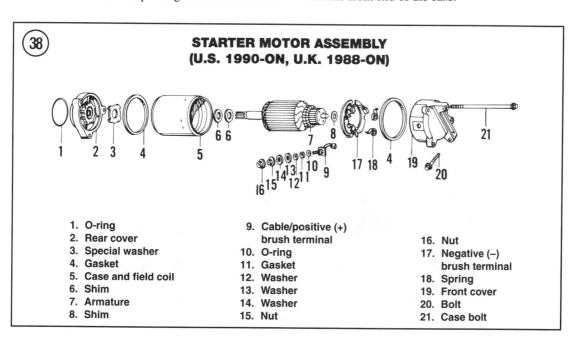

STARTER MOTOR ASSEMBLY (U.S. 1990-ON, U.K. 1988-ON)

1. O-ring
2. Rear cover
3. Special washer
4. Gasket
5. Case and field coil
6. Shim
7. Armature
8. Shim
9. Cable/positive (+) brush terminal
10. O-ring
11. Gasket
12. Washer
13. Washer
14. Washer
15. Nut
16. Nut
17. Negative (−) brush terminal
18. Spring
19. Front cover
20. Bolt
21. Case bolt

NOTE
Before removing the nuts and washers, write down their description and order. They must be reinstalled in the same order to insulate this set of brushes from the case.

5. Remove the nuts, washers and O-ring (**Figure 43**) securing the cable/brush terminal set. Remove the cable/brush terminal set (**Figure 44**).

CAUTION
Do not immerse the wire windings in the case or the armature coil in solvent as the insulation may be damaged. Wipe the windings with a cloth lightly moistened with solvent and thoroughly dry.

6. Clean all grease, dirt and carbon from all components.

Inspection

1. Measure the length of each brush (**Figure 45**) with a vernier caliper. If the length is 6.5 mm (0.26 in.) or less for any one of the brushes, the brush

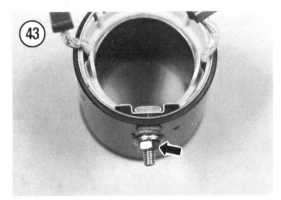

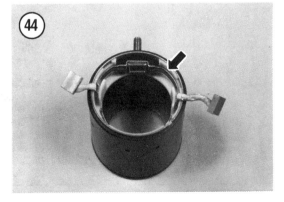

ELECTRICAL SYSTEM

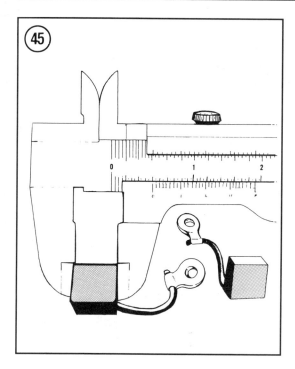

holder assembly and cable/brush terminal set must be replaced. The brushes cannot be replaced individually.

2. Inspect the commutator (**Figure 46**). The mica in a good commutator is below the surface of the copper bars as shown in **Figure 47**. On a worn commutator the mica and copper bars may be worn to the same level (**Figure 48**). If necessary, have the commutator serviced by a dealer or electrical repair shop.

3. Inspect the commutator copper bars for discoloration. If a pair of bars is discolored, grounded armature coils are indicated.

4. Use an ohmmeter and perform the following:

   a. Check for continuity between the commutator bars (**Figure 49**); there should be continuity (indicated resistance) between pairs of bars.

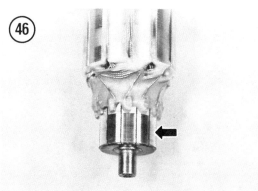

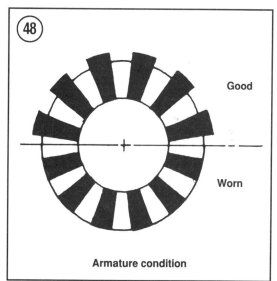

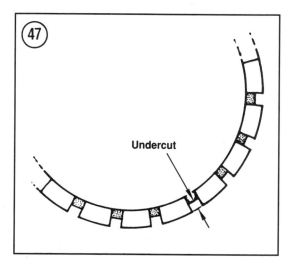

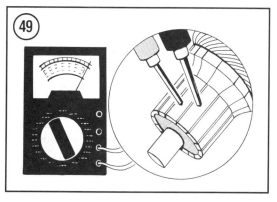

b. Check for continuity between the commutator bars and the shaft (**Figure 50**); there should be *no* continuity (infinite resistance).

c. If the unit fails either of these tests, the starter assembly must be replaced. The armature cannot be replaced individually.

5. Use an ohmmeter and perform the following:

a. Check for continuity between the starter cable terminal and the starter case (**Figure 51**); there should be continuity (indicated resistance).

b. Check for continuity between the starter cable terminal and the brush wire terminal; there should be *no* continuity (infinite resistance).

c. If the unit fails either of these tests, the starter assembly must be replaced. The case/field coil assembly cannot be replaced individually.

6. Inspect the oil seal and bushing (**Figure 52**) in the rear cover for wear or damage. If either is damaged, replace the starter assembly as these parts are not available separately.

7. Inspect the bushing (**Figure 53**) in the front cover for wear or damage. If it is damaged, replace the starter assembly as this part is not available separately.

8. Inspect the case/field coil assembly (**Figure 54**) for wear or damage. If it is damaged, replace the starter assembly as this part is not available separately.

9. Inspect the brush holder (**Figure 55**) for wear or damage. Replace if necessary.

10. Inspect the cable/brush terminal set (**Figure 56**) for wear or damage. Replace if necessary.

Assembly

1. Install the cable/brush terminal assembly (**Figure 44**).

NOTE
In the next step, reinstall all parts in the same order as noted during removal. This is essential in order to insulate this set of brushes from the case.

2. Install the O-ring, washers and nuts (**Figure 43**) securing the brush terminal set to the case.

3. Install the brush holder assembly onto the end of the case. Align the holder locating tab with the case notch (**Figure 57**).

4. Install the brushes into their receptacles (A, **Figure 58**).

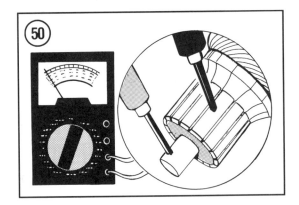

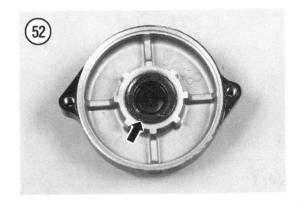

ELECTRICAL SYSTEM

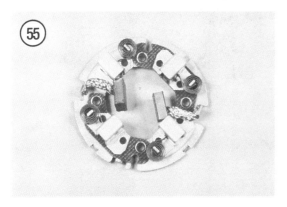

5. Install the brush springs (B, **Figure 58**) but do not place them against the brushes at this time.

6. Insert the armature coil assembly (**Figure 41**) in from the rear end of the case. Do not damage the brushes during this step.

7. Bring the end of the spring up and onto the backside of the brush (A, **Figure 58**) for correct spring-to-brush installation. Repeat for all remaining brushes.

8. Align the raised tab on the brush holder with the locating notch (**Figure 59**) in the front cover and install the front cover.

9. Install the shims and special washer (**Figure 40**) onto the rear cover end of the shaft.

10. Align the raised marks on the rear cover with the case.

11. Install the rear cover (A, **Figure 60**), then the case screws and washers (B, **Figure 60**). Make sure the marks are still aligned (**Figure 61**). Tighten the screws securely.

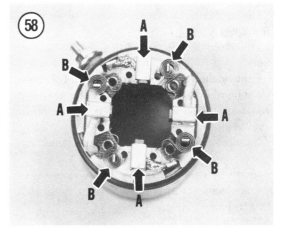

STARTER RELAY SWITCH

Testing

1. Remove the starter relay switch as described in this chapter.
2. Connect an ohmmeter to the starter relay switch terminals as shown in **Figure 62**.
3. Connect a 12 volt battery to the switch terminals as shown in **Figure 62**.
4. There should be continuity (indicated resistance).
5. If there is no continuity (infinite resistance), the starter relay switch is faulty and must be replaced.

Removal/Installation

1A. On 1986-1989 models, remove the seat and right-hand frame side cover as described in Chapter Thirteen.
1B. On 1990-on models, remove the seat as described in Chapter Thirteen.
2. Disconnect the negative battery lead (A, **Figure 63**) as described in this chapter.
3. Slide off the rubber protective boot.
4. Disconnect the main fuse electrical connector (A, **Figure 64**).
5. Disconnect the electrical wires from the top terminals.
6. Remove the starter relay switch from the rubber mounting receptacle on the frame. Refer to B, **Figure 64** for 1986-1989 models or B, **Figure 63** for 1990-on models.
7. Install a new main fuse in the new starter relay switch.
8. Install by reversing these removal steps. Make sure the electrical wire connections are tight and free of corrosion.

CLUTCH DIODE

Testing/Replacement

1. Remove the seat as described in Chapter Thirteen.

NOTE
The clutch diode, on 1994-on models, is located on the main wiring harness, under the front fairing on the right-hand side next to the right-hand directional signal electrical connector.

2. Disconnect the clutch diode from the wire harness. Refer to **Figure 65** for 1986-1988 models or **Figure 66** for 1990-1993 models.

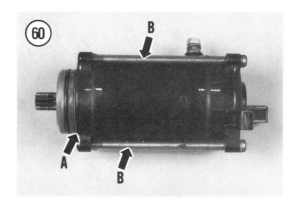

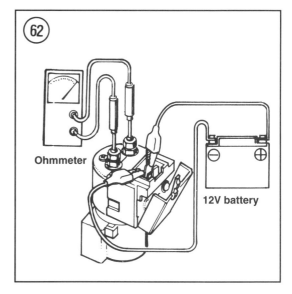

ELECTRICAL SYSTEM

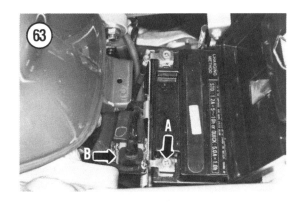

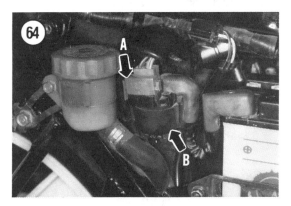

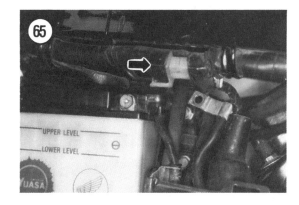

3. Set the ohmmeter to the R × 1 scale and zero the test leads.

4. Use an ohmmeter and check for continuity between the 2 terminals on the clutch diode (**Figure 67**). There should be continuity (low resistance) in the normal direction and no continuity (infinite resistance) in the reverse direction. Replace the diode if it fails this test.

LIGHTING SYSTEM

The lighting system consists of a headlight, taillight/brake light combination, license plate light, turn signals, indicator lights and illumination lights for the speedometer, tachometer and indicator lights on the instrument cluster. **Table 3** lists replacement bulbs for these components.

Always use the correct wattage bulb as indicated in this section. The use of a larger wattage bulb will give a dim light and a smaller wattage bulb will burn out prematurely.

Headlight Bulb Replacement

The headlight is equipped with a quartz halogen bulb and can be replaced without having to remove any of the fairing assembly components. Special handling of the quartz halogen bulb is required as specified in this procedure.

Refer to the following illustrations for this procedure:

a. **Figure 68**: 1986-1989 models.
b. **Figure 69**: 1990-on models.

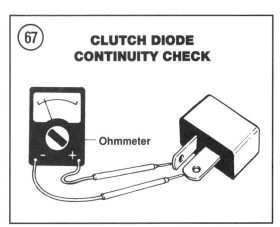

NOTE
This procedure is shown on a 1990-on model that is equipped with 2 bulbs. The procedure is the same as on prior years equipped with only 1 bulb.

1. Unplug the headlight bulb electrical connector (A, **Figure 70**) from the backside of the bulb(s).
2. Remove the rubber cover (B, **Figure 70**) from the back of the headlight bulb.

NOTE
The following steps are shown with the front fairing removed for clarity.

3. Disconnect the bulb retainer (**Figure 71**) and remove the headlight bulb (**Figure 72**).

CAUTION
Carefully read all instructions shipped with the replacement quartz halogen bulb. Do not touch the bulb glass with your fingers because of oil on your skin. Any traces of oil on the glass will drastically reduce the life of the bulb. Clean any traces of oil from the bulb with a cloth moistened in alcohol or lacquer thinner.

4. Replace with a new bulb assembly—do not touch the bulb with your fingers.
5. Assemble and install by reversing these removal steps while noting the following:
   a. Install the rubber cover with the TOP mark facing up.
   b. Adjust the headlight as described in this chapter.

Front Position Light Bulb Replacement (U.K. Models)

Refer to the following illustrations for this procedure:
   a. **Figure 68**: 1986-1989 models.

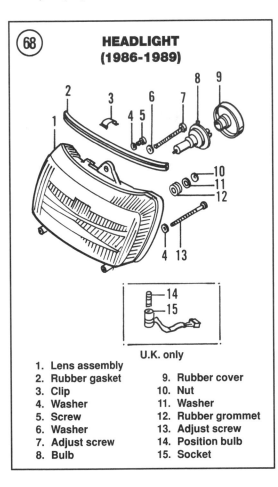
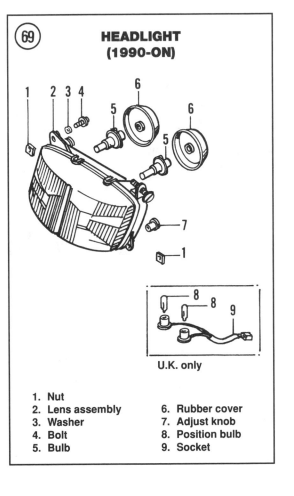

ELECTRICAL SYSTEM

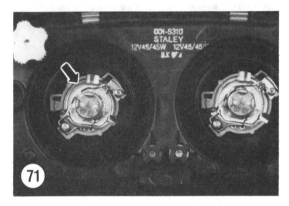

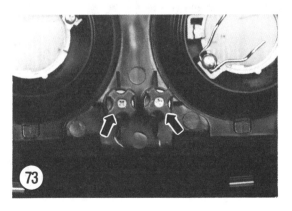

b. **Figure 69**: 1990-on models.

1. Reach in under the headlight assembly and carefully pull the bulb/socket assembly(ies) straight down and out.
2. Pull the bulb(s) straight out of the socket(s).
3. Replace the bulb and install the socket assembly. Make sure the socket assembly(ies) is pushed all the way in until it bottoms out. This is necessary to keep moisture out of the headlight housing.

Headlight Adjustment

Adjust the headlight horizontally and vertically according to Department of Motor Vehicle regulations in your area.

The headlight adjustment knobs are mounted on the backside of the headlight housing.

1986 models

1. To adjust the headlight horizontally, turn the lower left-hand knob; turn the knob either clockwise or counterclockwise until the aim is correct.
2. To adjust the headlight vertically, turn the upper right-hand knob; turn the knob either clockwise or counterclockwise until the aim is correct.

1987-1989 models

1. To adjust the headlight horizontally, turn the upper right-hand knob; turn the knob either clockwise or counterclockwise until the aim is correct.
2. To adjust the headlight vertically, turn the lower left-hand knob; turn the knob either clockwise or counterclockwise until the aim is correct.

1990-on models

NOTE
Figure 73 is shown with the headlight assembly removed for clarity. Do not remove the assembly for this procedure.

1. To adjust the headlight(s) horizontally, turn the lower center knob(s) (**Figure 73**); turn the knob(s) either clockwise or counterclockwise until the aim is correct.
2. To adjust the headlight(s) vertically, turn the upper knob(s). Refer to **Figure 74** or **Figure 75**. Turn

the knob(s) either clockwise or counterclockwise until the aim is correct.

Headlight Lens and Housing Assembly Removal/Installation

Refer to the following illustrations for this procedure:
  a. **Figure 68**: 1986-1989 models.
  b. **Figure 69**: 1990-on models.

1. Unplug the headlight bulb electrical connector (A, **Figure 76**) from the backside of the bulb(s).

2. Remove the front fairing (B, **Figure 76**) as described under *Front Fairing Removal/Installation* in this chapter.

3. Disconnect the battery negative lead as described in this chapter.

4. Remove the screws (C, **Figure 76**) securing the headlight housing to the front fairing and remove the lens and housing assembly (D, **Figure 76**) from the front fairing.

5. Install by reversing these removal steps while noting the following:
  a. Tighten all screws securely. Do not overtighten the screws as the plastic may fracture.
  b. Adjust the headlight as described in this chapter.

Taillight/Brake Light Replacement

Refer to the following illustrations for this procedure:
  a. **Figure 77**: 1986-1989 models.
  b. **Figure 78**: 1990-on models.

1. Remove the seat as described in Chapter Thirteen.

2. Rotate the bulb socket assembly (**Figure 79**) and withdraw the socket assembly from the backside of the taillight housing.

3. Inspect the socket assembly gasket and replace if it is damaged or deteriorated.

4. Replace the bulb(s) and install the socket assembly. Turn the socket assembly and make sure it is secure in the lens assembly. If not tightened correctly, water will enter the lens area.

5. Install the seat as described in Chapter Thirteen.

License Plate Light Replacement

Refer to the following illustrations for this procedure:
  a. **Figure 80**: 1986-1989 models.
  b. **Figure 81**: 1990-on models.

1. From behind the license plate holder (**Figure 82**), remove the nuts securing the license plate light base and light assembly.

2. Pull the license plate light cover, lens and gasket as an assembly from the socket base.

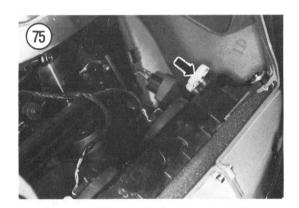

ELECTRICAL SYSTEM

3. Wash the inside and outside of the lens with a mild detergent and thoroughly wipe dry.

4. Inspect the lens gasket and replace if it is damaged or deteriorated.

5. Replace the bulb.

6. Install the gasket, lens and cover.

7. Tighten the nuts securely.

Front and Rear Directional Signal Bulb Replacement (1986-1989 Models)

1. Remove the screw on the underside of the directional signal housing, securing the lens assembly.

2. Carefully pull the lens assembly away from the housing.

3. Rotate the bulb socket assembly and withdraw the socket assembly from the lens assembly.

4. Inspect the socket assembly gasket and replace if it is damaged or deteriorated.

5. Wash the inside and outside of the lens with a mild detergent and wipe dry.

6. Replace the bulb and install the socket assembly. Turn the socket assembly and make sure it is secure in the lens assembly. If not tightened correctly, water will enter the lens area.

7. Install the lens assembly turn signal housing and install the screw on the base of the socket assembly.

Rear Directional Signal Bulb Replacement (1986-1993 Models)

1. Remove the screw (A, **Figure 83**) on the underside of the directional signal housing, securing the lens assembly.

2. Carefully pull the lens and socket assembly (B, **Figure 83**) away from the housing.

3. Rotate the bulb/socket assembly (C, **Figure 83**) and withdraw the socket assembly from the lens assembly.

4. Inspect the socket assembly gasket and replace if it is damaged or deteriorated.

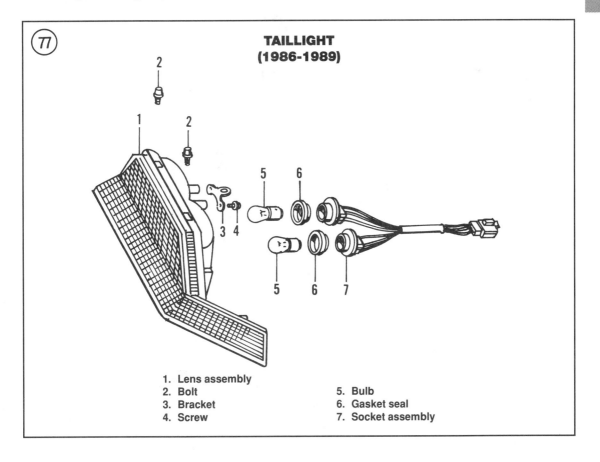

TAILLIGHT (1986-1989)

1. Lens assembly
2. Bolt
3. Bracket
4. Screw
5. Bulb
6. Gasket seal
7. Socket assembly

5. Wash the inside and outside of the lens with a mild detergent and wipe dry.

6. Replace the bulb (**Figure 84**) and install the socket assembly. Turn the socket assembly and make sure it is secure in the lens assembly. If not tightened correctly, water will enter the lens area.

7. Install the lens assembly turn signal housing and install the screw on the base of the socket assembly.

Front Directional Signal Bulb Replacement (1990-on Models)

NOTE
***Figure 85** is shown with the front fairing panel removed for clarity. It is not necessary to remove the panel to remove the bulb/socket assembly.*

1A. On 1990-1993 models, reach up under the front fairing and rotate the bulb/socket assembly (**Figure 85**) and withdraw the socket assembly from the lens assembly (**Figure 86**).

1B. On 1994-on models, perform the following:

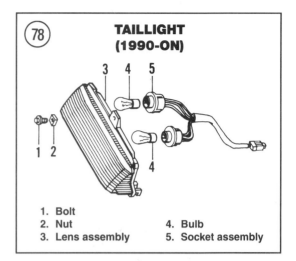

TAILLIGHT (1990-ON)

1. Bolt
2. Nut
3. Lens assembly
4. Bulb
5. Socket assembly

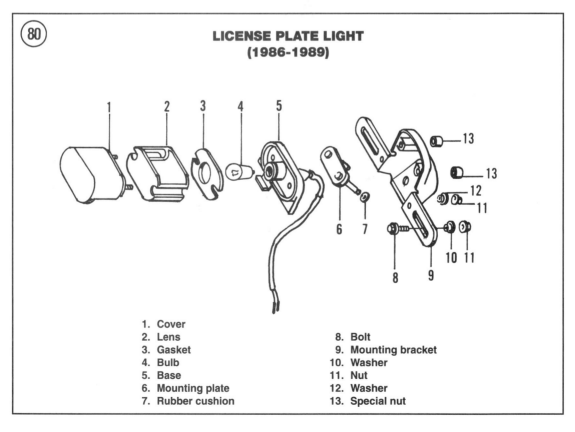

LICENSE PLATE LIGHT (1986-1989)

1. Cover
2. Lens
3. Gasket
4. Bulb
5. Base
6. Mounting plate
7. Rubber cushion
8. Bolt
9. Mounting bracket
10. Washer
11. Nut
12. Washer
13. Special nut

ELECTRICAL SYSTEM

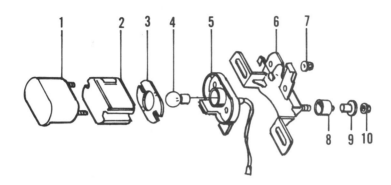

LICENSE PLATE LIGHT (1990-ON)

1. Cover
2. Lens
3. Gasket
4. Bulb
5. Base
6. Mounting plate
7. Special nut
8. Rubber cushion
9. Collar
10. Nut

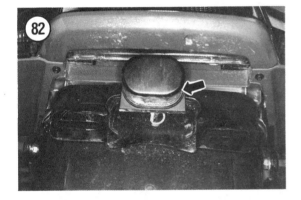

a. Remove the screw (A, **Figure 87**) on each side securing the front fairing lower cover (B, **Figure 87**) (below the headlight) and remove the lower cover.

b. Reach up under the front fairing and rotate the bulb/socket assembly (**Figure 85**) and withdraw the socket assembly from the lens assembly (**Figure 86**).

2. Rotate the bulb and remove it from the socket assembly.

3. Inspect the socket assembly gasket and replace if it is damaged or deteriorated.

4. Replace the bulb and install the socket assembly. Turn the socket assembly and make sure it is secure in the lens assembly. If not tightened correctly, water will enter the lens area.

5. On 1994-on models, install the lower cover and screws. Tighten the screws securely. Do not overtighten as the plastic cover may fracture.

**Rear Directional Signal
Bulb Replacement
(1994 Models)**

1. Reach up under the tail piece and rotate the bulb/socket assembly and withdraw the socket assembly from the lens assembly (**Figure 88**).

2. Rotate the bulb and remove it from the socket assembly.

3. Inspect the socket assembly gasket and replace if it is damaged or deteriorated.

4. Replace the bulb and install the socket assembly. Turn the socket assembly and make sure it is secure in the lens assembly. If not tightened correctly, water will enter the lens area.

**Directional Signal Assembly
Front and Rear (1986-1989 Models)
Rear (1990-1993 Models)
Removal/Installation**

1. Disconnect the electrical connector.

2. Disconnect the battery negative lead as described in this chapter.

3. Unscrew the nut (A, **Figure 89**) securing the assembly to the mounting bracket.

4. Remove the directional signal light assembly (B, **Figure 89**) from the mounting bracket.

5. Install by reversing these removal steps. Make sure the electrical connector is free of corrosion and is on tight.

**Front Directional Signal Assembly
Removal/Installation
(1990-on Models)**

1. Remove the front section of the front fairing as described under *Front Fairing Removal/Installation* in Chapter Thirteen.

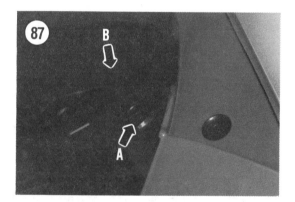

ELECTRICAL SYSTEM

2. Disconnect the battery negative lead as described in this chapter.

3. Remove the screw (A, **Figure 90**) securing the directional signal light assembly (B, **Figure 90**).

4. Carefully remove the assembly from the front fairing panel.

5. Install by reversing these removal steps. Make sure the electrical connector is free of corrosion and is on tight.

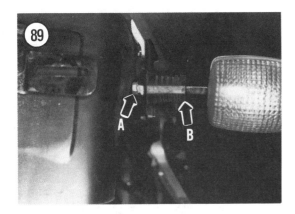

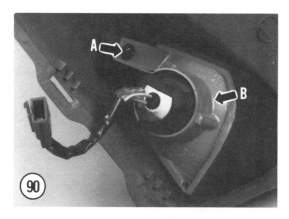

Rear Directional Signal Assembly Removal/Installation (1994-on Models)

1. Remove the tailpiece as described in Chapter Thirteen.

2. Disconnect the battery negative lead as described in this chapter.

3. Remove the screw securing the directional signal light assembly (**Figure 88**).

4. Carefully remove the assembly from the tailpiece.

5. Install by reversing these removal steps. Make sure the electrical connector is free of corrosion and is on tight.

Instrument Cluster Indicator Light and Meter Illumination Light Replacement

NOTE
Some of the light sockets are accessible without removing the instrument cluster. Others are located behind the instrument cluster mounting bracket which requires removal of the instrument cluster to gain access to the bulbs.

1. Remove the windshield from the front fairing as described in Chapter Thirteen.

2. If necessary, depending on the location of the light socket, remove the instrument cluster as described in this chapter.

3A. On 1986-1993 models, pull the defective bulb(s) and socket assembly (**Figure 91**) straight up and out of the instrument cluster base and replace with new ones.

3B. On 1994-on models, rotate the socket assembly (A, **Figure 92**) counterclockwise and pull socket and bulb assembly out of the instrument cluster. Remove the defective bulb(s) (B, **Figure 92**) from the socket and replace with new one(s).

4. Assemble and install by reversing these steps.

SWITCHES

Switches can be tested for continuity with an ohmmeter (see Chapter One) or a test light at the switch connector plug by operating the switch in each of its operating positions and comparing results with the switch operation. For example, **Figure 93** shows a continuity diagram for a typical ignition switch. It shows which terminals should show continuity when the ignition switch is in a given position.

When the ignition switch is in the PARK position, there should be continuity between terminals red and yellow/black. This is indicated by the line on the continuity diagram. An ohmmeter connected between these 2 terminals should indicate little or no resistance and a test lamp should light. When the ignition switch is OFF, there should be no continuity between the same terminals.

Testing

If the switch or button doesn't perform properly, replace it. Refer to the following figures when testing the switches:

a. Ignition switch (1986-1989): **Figure 93**.
b. Ignition switch (1990-on): **Figure 94**.
c. Engine start switch (1986-1989): **Figure 95**.
d. Engine start switch (1990-on): **Figure 96**.
e. Engine stop switch (1986-1989): **Figure 97**.
f. Engine stop switch (1990-on): **Figure 98**.
g. Headlight dimmer switch: **Figure 99**.
h. Directional signal switch: **Figure 100**.
i. Passing switch (U.K.): **Figure 101**.

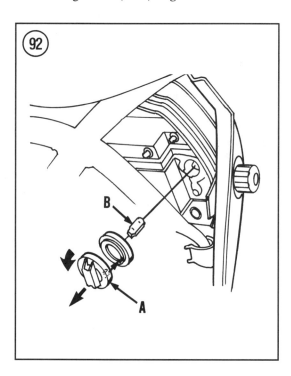

⑬ IGNITION SWITCH (1986-1989)

	BAT1	IG	FAN	TL1	TL2	PA
ON	●——	●——	●——	●——	●——	
OFF						
P	●——					●——
Color	R	R/BL	Bu/O	Br/W	Br	Y/Bl

⑭ IGNITION SWITCH (1990-ON)

	FAN	IG	BAT1
ON	●——	●——	●——
OFF			
LOCK			
Color	Bu/O	R/Bl	R

⑮ ENGINE START SWITCH (1986-1989)

	ST	BAT4	HL	BAT5
PUSH	●——	●——		
FREE			●——	●——
Color	Y/R	Bl	Bu/W	Bl/R

⑯ ENGINE START SWITCH (1990-ON)

	ST	BAT2	BAT4	HL
FREE			●——	●——
PUSH	●——	●——		
Color	Bl/W	Y/R	Bl/R	Bu/W

ELECTRICAL SYSTEM

97 **ENGINE STOP SWITCH (1986-1989)**

	BAT4	IG
OFF		
RUN	•—————•	
Color	Bl	Bl/W

98 **ENGINE STOP SWITCH (1990-ON)**

	IG	BAT2
OFF		
RUN	•—————•	
Color	Bl/W	Bl

99 **HEADLIGHT DIMMER SWITCH**

	HL	Lo	Hi
Lo	•———•		
(N)	•———•———•		
H	•———————•		
Color	Bu/W	W	Bu

100 **DIRECTIONAL SIGNAL SWITCH**

	W	R	L	P	PR	PL
R	•———•			•———•———•		
N				•———•———•		
L	•———————•			•———•		
Color	Gr	Lb	O	Br/W	Lb/W	O/W

j. Horn switch (1986-1989): **Figure 102**.
k. Horn switch (1990-on): **Figure 103**.
When testing switches, note the following:
a. First check the fuses as described under *Fuses* in this chapter.
b. Check the battery as described under *Battery* in Chapter Three; charge the battery to the correct state of charge, if required.
c. Disconnect the negative cable from the battery as described in this chapter, if the switch connectors are not disconnected in the circuit.

101 **PASSING SWITCH (U.K.)**

	BAT3	Hi
FREE		
PUSH	•—————•	
Color	W/G	Bu

102 **HORN SWITCH (1986-1989)**

	Ho	BAT2
FREE		
PUSH	•—————•	
Color	Lg	W/G

103 **HORN SWITCH (1990-ON)**

	Ho	BAT3
FREE		
PUSH	•—————•	
Color	Lg	W/G

CAUTION
Do not attempt to start the engine with the battery negative cable disconnected or you will damage the wiring harness.

d. When separating 2 connectors, depress the retaining clip and pull on the connector housings and *not* the wires (**Figure 104**).

NOTE
Connectors can be serviced by disconnecting them and cleaning with electrical contact cleaner. Multiple pin connectors should be packed with a dielectric compound (available at most automotive and motorcycle supply stores).

e. After locating a defective circuit, check the connectors to make sure they are clean and properly connected. Make sure there are no bent metal pins on the male side of the connector. Check all wires going into a connector housing to make sure each wire is properly positioned and that the wire end is not loose (**Figure 105**).
f. To connect connectors properly, push them together until they click and are locked into place (**Figure 106**).
g. When replacing handlebar switch assemblies, make sure the cables are routed correctly so that they are not crimped when the handlebar is turned from side to side.

**Ignition Switch
Removal/Installation**

1. Remove the front fairing as described under *Front Fairing Removal/Installation* in Chapter Thirteen.
2. Disconnect the battery negative lead as described in this chapter.
3A. On 1986-1989 models, in front of the instrument cluster, locate the ignition switch 6-pin electrical connector containing 6 wires (1 red, 1 red/black, 1 blue/orange, 1 brown/white, 1 brown and 1 yellow/black). Disconnect this electrical connector.
3B. On 1990-on models, in front of the instrument cluster, locate the ignition switch 6-pin electrical connector containing 5 wires (1 blue/orange, 1 red/black, 1 red and a brown jumper wire between 2 terminals) on the switch side and 3 wires on the harness side (1 blue/orange, 1 red/black and 1 red). Disconnect this electrical connector.
4. The ignition switch is mounted to the upper fork bridge by a bolt (**Figure 107**) on each side of the switch.
5. Remove the upper fork bridge (A, **Figure 108**) as described under *Steering Stem Removal/Installation* in Chapter Ten.

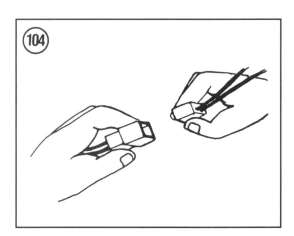

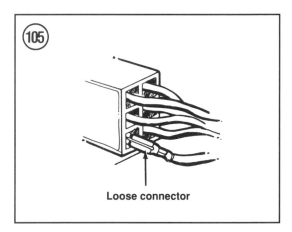

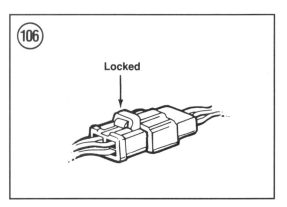

ELECTRICAL SYSTEM

6. Remove the bolts (**Figure 107**) securing the ignition switch assembly (B, **Figure 108**) to the lower surface of the upper fork bridge.

7. Install the new ignition switch onto the upper fork bridge and install the bolts. Tighten the bolts securely.

8. Install the upper fork bridge as described in Chapter Ten.

9. Pack the multiple pin connector with a dielectric compound.

10. Reconnect the 6-pin electrical connector. Make sure the electrical connector is free of corrosion and is tight.

11. Install the front fairing as described in Chapter Twelve.

Right-hand Combination Switch (Engine Start and Stop Switch) Removal/Installation

The right-hand combination switch assembly contains the engine start and the engine stop switch. If any portion of the switch is faulty the entire switch assembly must be replaced.

1. Remove the seat as described in Chapter Thirteen.

2. Disconnect the battery negative lead as described in this chapter.

3. Remove the fuel tank as described under *Fuel Tank Removal/Installation* in Chapter Seven.

4. Disconnect the front brake light switch electrical connector from the front master cylinder. The wires are part of the right-hand switch assembly.

5. Unhook the tie wraps and locate the engine start and stop switch 9-pin red electrical connector. Disconnect this electrical connector.

6. Remove the electrical wire harness from any clips on the frame and carefully pull the harness out from the frame.

7. Remove the screws securing the right-hand combination switch together and remove the switch assembly (**Figure 109**).

8. Install a new switch and tighten the screws securely. Do not overtighten the screws or the plastic switch housing may crack.

9. Reconnect the 9-pin red electrical connector and the connector to the front brake light switch.

10. Make sure the electrical connectors are free of corrosion and are tight. Install the tie wrap to hold the electrical wires to the frame.

11. Install the fuel tank as described in Chapter Seven.

12. Install the seat as described in Chapter Twelve.

Left-hand Combination Switch (Headlight Dimmer Switch, Turn Signal Switch, Horn Switch and, on U.K. Models, the Passing Switch) Removal/Installation

The left-hand combination switch assembly contains both the headlight dimmer switch, turn signal switch, horn switch and, on U.K. models, the passing switch. If any portion of the switch is faulty, the entire switch assembly must be replaced.

1. Remove the seat as described in Chapter Thirteen.
2. Disconnect the battery negative lead as described in this chapter.
3. Remove the fuel tank as described under *Fuel Tank Removal/Installation* in Chapter Seven.
4. Disconnect the starter interlock switch electrical connector from the clutch master cylinder. The wires are part of the left-hand switch assembly.
5. Follow the electrical wiring harness from the left-hand switch assembly on the handlebar to the wiring harness connection(s) in the frame area. There are several different combinations of multi-pin electrical connectors for this switch assembly for the various models covered in this manual. The main electrical connector is a 9-pin black connector and some models have 1 or more additional connectors for this switch. Disconnect all electrical connectors.
6. Remove the screws securing the left-hand combination switch together and remove the switch assembly (**Figure 110**).
7. Remove the electrical wire harness from any clips on the frame and carefully pull the harness out from the frame.
8. Install a new switch and tighten the screws securely. Do not overtighten the screws or the plastic switch housing may crack.
9. Reconnect all multi-pin electrical connector(s) and the wires to the starter interlock switch.
10. Make sure the electrical connector is free of corrosion and is tight. Install the tie wrap to hold the electrical wires to the front of the frame. The wires must be retained in this manner to allow room for the fuel tank.
11. Install the fuel tank as described in Chapter Seven.
12. Install the seat as described in Chapter Thirteen.

Starter Interlock Switch Removal/Installation

The starter interlock switch is mounted to the underside of the clutch master cylinder and is activated by the clutch lever.

1. Disconnect the battery negative lead as described in this chapter.
2. At the clutch lever assembly, disconnect the electrical wires from the connectors on the switch.
3. Remove the screw securing the clutch switch and remove the switch.
4. Install a new switch and tighten the screws securely.
5. Reconnect the electrical connectors.
6. Make sure the electrical connectors are free of corrosion and are tight.

Front Brake Light Switch Removal/Installation

The front brake light switch is mounted to the underside of the front brake master cylinder and is activated by the front brake lever.

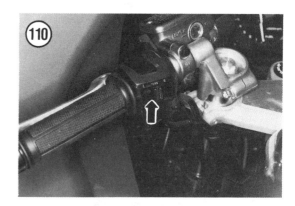

ELECTRICAL SYSTEM

1. Disconnect the battery negative lead as described in this chapter.
2. At the front brake lever assembly, disconnect the electrical wires from the connectors on the switch.
3. Remove the screws securing the front brake light switch to the front brake lever housing and remove the switch assembly.
4. Install a new switch and tighten the screws securely.
5. Reconnect the electrical connectors.
6. Make sure the electrical connectors are free of corrosion and are tight.

Rear Brake Light Switch Adjustment

The rear brake light switch is mounted on the back of the right-hand footpeg bracket.
1. Turn the ignition switch ON.
2. Depress the brake pedal. The brake light should come on as the brake pedal is depressed. If necessary, adjust as follows.
3. Turn the rear brake light switch knurled adjuster ring (A, **Figure 111**) to move the switch body (B, **Figure 111**) up or down as required. Raising the switch will make the brake light come on earlier.

NOTE
Some riders prefer the brake light to come on a little early. This way, they can tap the pedal without braking to warn drivers who are following too closely.

Rear Brake Light Switch Removal/Installation

The rear brake light switch is mounted on the back of the right-hand footpeg bracket.
1. Disconnect the battery negative lead as described in this chapter.
2. Remove the right-hand side cover as described in Chapter Thirteen.
3. Unhook the return spring (A, **Figure 112**) from the lower end of the switch.
4. Pull the switch assembly up and out of the mounting bracket (B, **Figure 112**).
5. Disconnect brake switch 2-pin white electrical connector from the wiring harness.
6. Install by reversing these removal steps while noting the following:
   a. Make sure the electrical connector is free of corrosion and is tight.
   b. Adjust the rear brake light switch as described in this chapter.

Neutral Switch Testing

1. Remove the lower portions of the front fairing as described under *Front Fairing Removal/Installation* in Chapter Thirteen.
2. Pull back the rubber boot and disconnect the electrical connector from the neutral switch (**Figure 113**).
3. Shift the transmission into NEUTRAL.
4. Set the ohmmeter to the R × 1 scale and zero the test leads.
5. Use an ohmmeter and check for continuity between the electrical terminal of the switch and to a good ground. There should be continuity (low resistance).
6. Shift the transmission into any gear.
7. Repeat Step 5. This time there should be no continuity (infinite resistance).

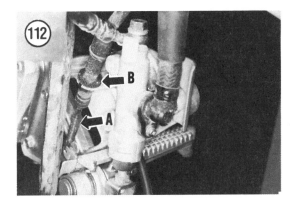

8. If the switch fails either of these tests, replace the switch as described in this chapter.
9. Reconnect the electrical connector to the switch and pull the rubber boot back over the top of the switch.
10. Install the lower portions of the front fairing as described in Chapter Thirteen.

Neutral Switch
Removal/Installation

1. Remove the lower portions of the front fairing as described under *Front Fairing Removal/Installation* in Chapter Thirteen.
2. Pull back the rubber boot and disconnect the electrical connector from the neutral switch (**Figure 113**).
3. Drain the engine oil as described under *Engine Oil and Filter Change* in Chapter Three.

NOTE
Figure 114 is shown with the engine removed from the frame and disassembled for clarity. It is not necessary to remove the engine from the frame for this procedure.

4. Unscrew the neutral switch (**Figure 114**) from the right-hand rear corner of the crankcase.
5. Apply gasket sealant to the switch threads prior to installation and install the switch. Tighten the switch securely.
6. Refill the engine with the recommended type and quantity of oil as described in Chapter Three.
7. Reconnect the electrical connector to the switch and pull the rubber boot back over the top of the switch.
8. Make sure the electrical connector is free of corrosion and is tight.
9. Install the lower portions of the front fairing as described in Chapter Thirteen.

Sidestand Check Switch
(1990-On Models)
Testing

1. Remove the tail piece as described in Chapter Thirteen.
2. On the left-hand side of the bike, above the fuel pump, disconnect the 3-pin green electrical connector (**Figure 115**) containing 3 wires (1 green/white, 1 yellow/black and 1 green).
3. Set the ohmmeter to the R × 1 scale and zero the test leads.
4. Use an ohmmeter and check for continuity between the electrical terminals of the switch as follows:
   a. *Sidestand down (**Figure 116**):* there should be continuity (low resistance) between the yellow/black and green terminals.
   b. *Sidestand up:* there should be continuity (low resistance) between the green/white and green terminals.
5. If the switch fails either of these tests, replace the switch as described in this chapter.
6. Reconnect the electrical connector to the switch.
7. Install the tail piece as described in Chapter Thirteen.

Sidestand Check Switch
(1990-On Models)
Removal/Installation

1. Remove the tail piece as described in Chapter Thirteen.

ELECTRICAL SYSTEM

2. On the left-hand side of the bike, above the fuel pump, disconnect the 3-pin green electrical connector (**Figure 115**) containing 3 wires (1 green/white, 1 yellow/black and 1 green).

3. Unhook the tie-wrap securing the electrical wires to the frame.

4. Place the bike on the sidestand.

5. Remove the stand check switch mounting bolt and remove the switch.

6. Align the switch's rotating pin with the indexing hole in the backside of the sidestand and install the switch. Install the mounting bolt and tighten securely.

7. Route the electrical wire harness through the frame and install the tie wraps securing the harness to the frame.

8. Reconnect the 3-pin green electrical connector (**Figure 115**).

9. Make sure the electrical connector is free of corrosion and is tight. Install the tie wrap to hold the electrical wires to the frame.

10. Install the tail piece as described in Chapter Thirteen.

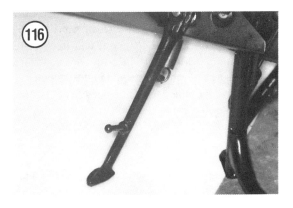

Oil Pressure Switch
Testing

1. Remove the lower sections of the front fairing as described under *Front Fairing Removal/Installation* in Chapter Thirteen.

2. Pull back the rubber boot (A, **Figure 117**) and disconnect the electrical connector from the oil pressure switch.

3. Turn the ignition switch to the ON position.

4. Ground the oil pressure switch electrical connector to the switch body. The oil pressure warning light should come on.

5. If the light does not come on, remove the light bulb from the instrument cluster and make sure it is not burned out. Replace the bulb if necessary. If the bulb is okay, proceed to Step 6.

6. With the oil pressure switch electrical connector grounded to the switch body, connect a 0-20 DC voltmeter to the connector and a good bare metal ground. There should be battery voltage.

7A. If battery voltage is present, but the oil pressure warning light does not come on, the oil pressure switch is defective and must be replaced as described in this chapter.

7B. If battery voltage is *not* present, and the oil pressure warning light does not come on, check for a loose electrical connection or break in the switch wire or a blown fuse in that circuit.

8. Reconnect the electrical connector to the switch and pull the rubber boot back over the top of the switch.

9. Make sure all of electrical connector is free of corrosion and is tight.

10. Install the lower portions of the front fairing as described in Chapter Thirteen.

Oil Pressure Switch
Removal/Installation

1. Remove the lower sections of the front fairing as described under *Front Fairing Removal/Installation* in Chapter Thirteen.

2. Pull back the rubber boot (A, **Figure 117**) and disconnect the electrical connector from the oil pressure switch.

3. Unscrew the oil pressure switch (B, **Figure 117**) from the cylinder block.

4. Apply a light coat of gasket sealer to the switch threads prior to installation. Install the switch and tighten securely.

5. Connect the oil pressure sending switch wire and tighten the screw securely.

6. Reconnect the electrical connector to the switch and pull the rubber boot back over the top of the switch.

7. Make sure all of electrical connector is free of corrosion and is tight.

8. Install the lower portions of the front fairing as described in Chapter Thirteen.

Fan Motor Switch Testing/Replacement

The fan motor switch controls the radiator fan according to engine coolant temperature. This switch is attached to the lower left-hand side of the radiator.

NOTE
If the cooling fan is not operating correctly, make sure that the cooling fan fuse has not blown prior to starting this test. Also clean off any rust or corrosion from the electrical terminals on the thermostatic switch.

1. Remove the lower sections of the front fairing as described under *Front Fairing Removal/Installation* in Chapter Thirteen.

2. Pull back the rubber boot (A, **Figure 118**) and disconnect the electrical connector from the fan motor switch.

3. Place a jumper wire between the fan motor switch electrical connector and a good ground.

4. Turn the ignition switch ON; the cooling fan should start running.

5A. If the fan does not run, either the fan or the wiring to the fan is faulty. Remove the jumper wire and perform the following:
  a. Turn the ignition switch OFF.
  b. Disconnect the 2-pin black electrical connector from the cooling fan motor.
  c. Connect a 0-20 DC voltmeter between the black/blue and green terminal on the wiring harness side of the connector.
  d. Turn the ignition switch ON. There should be battery voltage.
  e. If there is no battery voltage, check for a loose electrical connection or break in the fan motor wire or a blown fuse in that circuit.

5B. If the fan now runs, the fan motor switch may be defective; test the fan motors witch as follows:

WARNING
Wear safety glasses or goggles and gloves during this test. Protect yourself accordingly, as the coolant is heated to a high temperature.

  a. Turn the ignition switch OFF.
  b. Drain the cooling system as described under *Coolant Change* in Chapter Three.
  c. Pull back the rubber boot (A, **Figure 118**) and disconnect the electrical connector from the fan motor switch.
  d. Unscrew the fan motor switch (B, **Figure 118**) from the base of the radiator.
  e. Use an ohmmeter with alligator clips on the test lead ends. Attach the alligator clips to the electrical connectors on the switch. At room temperature there should be no continuity (infinite resistance).
  f. Suspend the switch or place the switch on a small piece of wood in a small pan of 50/50 mixture of distilled water and anti-freeze. The fan motor switch must be positioned so that all of its threads are submerged in the coolant.
  g. Place a thermometer in the pan of coolant (use a cooking or candy thermometer that is rated for temperatures higher than the test temperature). Do not let the switch or the thermometer touch the pan, as it will give a false readings.
  h. Heat the coolant slowly until the temperature reaches the following degrees: 1986-1989 mod-

ELECTRICAL SYSTEM

els, 98-102° C (208-216° F) or on 1990-on models, 93-97° C (199-207° F).

i. Maintain this temperature for at least 3 minutes before taking a reading. A sudden change in temperature will cause a different ohmmeter reading. After this 3 minute interval is completed, check the ohmmeter; there should be continuity (low resistance)

j. If the switch fails this test, the switch must be replaced.

k. Apply a silicone based sealant to the threads of the switch and install the switch in the radiator. Tighten the switch securely.

l. Refill the cooling system with the recommended type and quantity of coolant. Refer to Chapter Three.

6. Attach the electrical wires to the fan motor switch. Make sure the connections are tight and free from oil and corrosion. Pull the rubber boot back into position on the switch.

7. Install the lower sections of the front fairing as described in Chapter Thirteen.

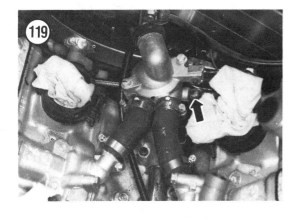

Thermo Sensor
Preliminary Testing

The coolant thermo sensor controls the temperature gauge on the instrument cluster. This sensor is attached to the thermostat housing.

1. Remove the right-hand lower section of the front fairing as described under *Front Fairing Removal/Installation* in Chapter Thirteen.

NOTE
Figure 119 *is shown with the carburetor assembly removed for clarity. It is not necessary to remove the carburetor assembly to gain access to the electrical connector.*

2. Disconnect the electrical connector from the thermo sensor. Refer to **Figure 120** for 1986-1989 models or **Figure 119** for 1990-on models.

3. Set the ohmmeter to the R × 1 scale and zero the test leads.

4. Use an ohmmeter and check for continuity between the thermostat housing and ground. There should be continuity (low resistance), indicating that the thermostat housing is grounded to the frame.

5. If there is no continuity (infinite resistance), check the housing mounting bolts for tightness. Also check for corrosion between the housing and its mounting surface. If corroded, clean off and repeat Step 4.

6. If there is still not continuity, remove the thermo sensor and test it in the following procedure.

Thermo Sensor
Removal/Final Testing/Installation

WARNING
Wear safety glasses or goggles and gloves during this test. Protect yourself accordingly, as the coolant is heated to a very high temperature and can result in severe burns if not handled properly.

1. Drain the cooling system as described under *Coolant Change* in Chapter Three.

2. Remove the temperature sensor from the thermostat housing.

3. Use an ohmmeter with alligator clips on the test lead ends. Attach one of the alligator clips to the electrical connector on the sensor. Attach the other alligator clip to the housing.

4. Suspend the sensor or place the sensor on a small piece of wood in a small pan of 50/50 mixture of distilled water and anti-freeze. The sensor must be positioned so that all of its threads are submerged in the coolant.

5. Place a thermometer in the pan of coolant (use a cooking or candy thermometer that is rated for temperatures higher than the test temperature). Do not let the sensor or the thermometer touch the pan, as it will give a false readings.

6. Heat the coolant slowly and check the resistance readings as listed in **Table 4**.

7. If the sensor readings do not correspond to those listed in **Table 4** during any of the temperature ranges, the sensor must be replaced.

8. Apply a silicone based sealant to the threads of the sensor and install the sensor in the thermostat housing. Tighten the sensor securely.

9. Connect the electrical connector to the temperature sensor. Make sure the connection is tight and free from corrosion.

10. Refill the cooling system as described under *Coolant Change* in Chapter Three.

11. Install the right-hand lower section of the front fairing as described in Chapter Thirteen.

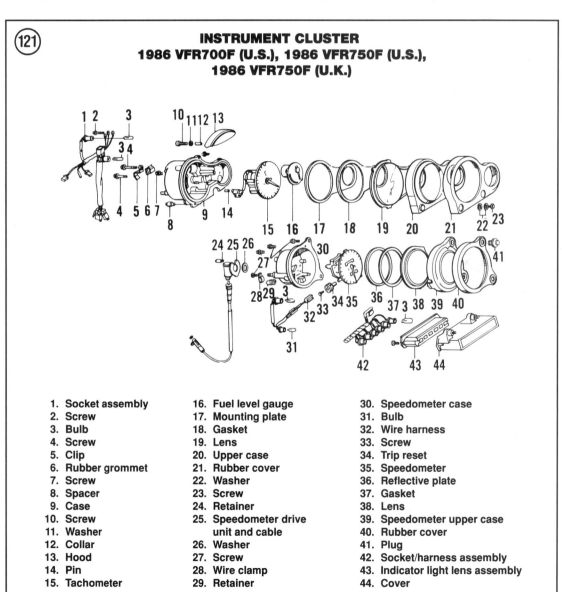

INSTRUMENT CLUSTER
1986 VFR700F (U.S.), 1986 VFR750F (U.S.),
1986 VFR750F (U.K.)

1. Socket assembly
2. Screw
3. Bulb
4. Screw
5. Clip
6. Rubber grommet
7. Screw
8. Spacer
9. Case
10. Screw
11. Washer
12. Collar
13. Hood
14. Pin
15. Tachometer
16. Fuel level gauge
17. Mounting plate
18. Gasket
19. Lens
20. Upper case
21. Rubber cover
22. Washer
23. Screw
24. Retainer
25. Speedometer drive unit and cable
26. Washer
27. Screw
28. Wire clamp
29. Retainer
30. Speedometer case
31. Bulb
32. Wire harness
33. Screw
34. Trip reset
35. Speedometer
36. Reflective plate
37. Gasket
38. Lens
39. Speedometer upper case
40. Rubber cover
41. Plug
42. Socket/harness assembly
43. Indicator light lens assembly
44. Cover

ELECTRICAL SYSTEM

ELECTRICAL COMPONENTS

This section contains information on electrical components other than switches.

Some of the test procedures covered in this section instruct taking a meter reading within the electrical connector attached to a specific part. Under these conditions, make sure that the meter test lead has penetrated into the connector and is touching the bare metal wire *not* the insulation on the wire. If the test lead does not touch the bare metal wire, the readings will be false and may lead to the unnecessary purchase of an expensive electrical part that cannot be returned for a refund. Most dealers and parts houses will not accept any returns on electrical parts.

If you are having trouble with some of these components, perform some quick preliminary checks and they may save you a lot of time.

a. Disconnect each electrical connector and check that there are no bent metal pins on the male side of the electrical connector. A bent pin will not connect to its mating receptacle in the female end of the connector, causing an open circuit.

b. Check each female end of the connector. Make sure that the metal connector on the end of each wire is pushed in all the way into the plastic connector. If not, carefully push them in with a narrow bladed screwdriver.

c. Check all electrical wires where they enter the individual metal connector in both the male and female plastic connector.

d. After all is checked out, push the connectors together and make sure they are fully engaged and locked together.

Instrument Cluster Removal/Installation

Refer to the following illustrations for this procedure:

a. **Figure 121**: 1986 VFR700F (U.S.), 1986 VFR750F (U.S.), 1986 VFR750F (U.K.) models.
b. **Figure 122**: 1986-1987 VFR700F2 (U.S.), 1986-1989 VFR750F2 (U.K.) models.
c. **Figure 123**: 1990-1993 models.
d. **Figure 124**: 1994-on models.

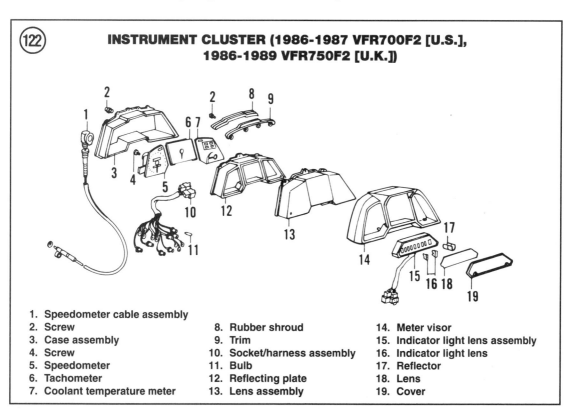

INSTRUMENT CLUSTER (1986-1987 VFR700F2 [U.S.], 1986-1989 VFR750F2 [U.K.])

1. Speedometer cable assembly
2. Screw
3. Case assembly
4. Screw
5. Speedometer
6. Tachometer
7. Coolant temperature meter
8. Rubber shroud
9. Trim
10. Socket/harness assembly
11. Bulb
12. Reflecting plate
13. Lens assembly
14. Meter visor
15. Indicator light lens assembly
16. Indicator light lens
17. Reflector
18. Lens
19. Cover

1. Disconnect the battery negative lead as described in this chapter.
2. Remove the front fairing (A, **Figure 125**) as described under *Front Fairing Removal/Installation* in Chapter Thirteen.
3. On 1990-1993 models, remove the headlight assembly as described in this chapter.
4A. On 1986-1993 models, disconnect all multi-pin electrical connectors attached to the instrument cluster.
4B. On 1994-on models, disconnect the 2 plug-in electrical connectors (1 blue and 1 green) from the backside of the instrument cluster.

NOTE
1994 models are equipped with an electronic speedometer, therefore no cable is used.

5. On 1986-1993 models, disconnect the speedometer cable (A, **Figure 126**) from the meter.
6. On 1990-1993 models, perform the following:

a. Unhook the meter front cover (B, **Figure 126**) from the meter cover and remove the front cover.
b. Remove the screws securing the meter cover (B, **Figure 125**) and remove the meter cover.

NOTE
C, Figure 125 is shown on a 1990-1993 model. The number of mounting nuts vary among the different models. Be sure to remove all nuts prior to removing the meter assembly.

7. Remove the nuts (C, **Figure 126**) securing the instrument cluster to the front fairing mounting bracket. Remove the instrument cluster (C, **Figure 125**).
8. Install by reversing these removal steps. Make sure the electrical connectors are free of corrosion and are tight.

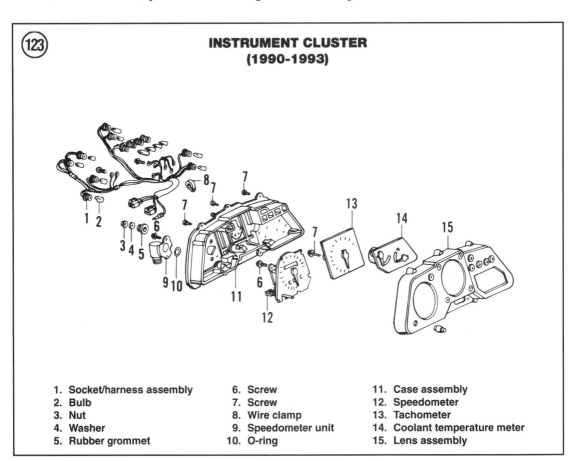

INSTRUMENT CLUSTER (1990-1993)

1. Socket/harness assembly
2. Bulb
3. Nut
4. Washer
5. Rubber grommet
6. Screw
7. Screw
8. Wire clamp
9. Speedometer unit
10. O-ring
11. Case assembly
12. Speedometer
13. Tachometer
14. Coolant temperature meter
15. Lens assembly

ELECTRICAL SYSTEM

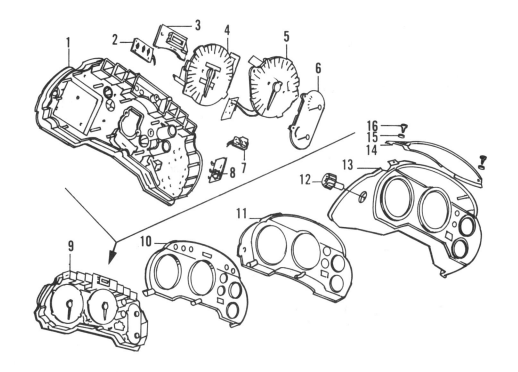

INSTRUMENT CLUSTER (1994-ON)

1. Case assembly
2. Indicator light panel
3. Lens
4. Speedometer
5. Tachometer
6. Coolant temperature meter
7. Connector
8. Display panel
9. Meter assembly
10. Reflective panel
11. Lens
12. Trip reset knob
13. Cover
14. Meter visor
15. Washer
16. Screw

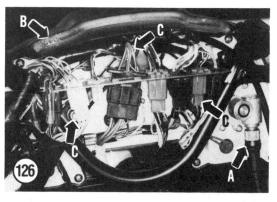

Coolant Temperature Gauge Testing

1. Remove the right-hand lower section of the front fairing as described under *Front Fairing Removal/Installation* in Chapter Thirteen.

NOTE
Figure 119 is shown with the carburetor assembly removed for clarity. It is not necessary to remove the carburetor assembly to gain access to the electrical connector.

2. Disconnect the electrical connector from the thermo sensor. Refer to **Figure 120** for 1986-1989 models or **Figure 119** for 1990-on models.
3. Turn the ignition switch ON.

CAUTION
In Step 4, do not short out the electrical connector for longer than a few seconds or the temperature gauge portion of the instrument cluster will be damaged.

4. *Momentarily*, touch the end of the thermo sensor electrical connector to a good ground like a fairing mounting bracket while observing the temperature gauge on the instrument cluster. The temperature gauge needle should move all the way up to the "H" mark on the gauge (A, **Figure 127**). Immediately "un-ground" the electrical connector to avoid damage to the temperature gauge.
5. Make sure the ignition switch is still in the ON position.
6. If the needle does *not* move, connect one of the test leads of a 0-20 DC voltmeter to the thermo sensor electrical connector, then *momentarily* ground the other test probe to the ground surface.
7. The meter needle should move to the "H" position and there should be battery voltage. Immediately "un-ground" the electrical connector to avoid damage to the temperature gauge.
8. If the meter needle does *not* move, but there is battery voltage present, the thermo sensor is faulty and must be replaced as described in this chapter.
9. If battery voltage is not present, check all electrical connectors within the circuit and also check for a blown fuse.
10. Repeat Step 6. If the needle still does not move, there is an open circuit in the wire, or the temperature gauge is faulty. First, make a continuity check on the wire and repair if possible. If this is not the problem, then the fuel and temperature assembly portion of the instrument cluster is faulty and must be replaced.

Tachometer Testing

1986-1989 models

1. Remove the front fairing as described under *Front Fairing Removal/Installation* in Chapter Thirteen.
2. Disconnect the 6-pin white electrical connector.
3. Turn the ignition switch ON.
4. Connect a 0-20 DC voltmeter to the black/brown and the green wire terminal on the wiring harness side of the electrical connector.
5. There should be battery voltage present.
6. If battery voltage is present, turn the ignition switch OFF.
7. Set the ohmmeter to the R × 1 scale and zero the test leads.
8. Use an ohmmeter and check for continuity of the yellow/green wire between the tachometer electrical connector and the electrical connector at the spark

ELECTRICAL SYSTEM

unit. If there is no continuity (infinite resistance), there is an open in the circuit.

9. Repair the open circuit.

10. If there is continuity in the yellow/green wire, then the tachometer unit of the instrument cluster is faulty and must be replaced.

11. Connect the 6-pin white electrical connector.

12. Install the front fairing as described in Chapter Thirteen.

1990-on models

1. Remove the front fairing as described under *Front Fairing Removal/Installation* in Chapter Thirteen.

2A. On 1990-1993 models, disconnect the 6-pin black electrical connector (A, **Figure 128**) and the single yellow/green electrical connector (B, **Figure 128**).

2B. On 1994-on models, disconnect the 10-pin green plug-in electrical connector from the backside of the instrument cluster.

3. Turn the ignition switch ON.

4. Connect a 0-20 DC voltmeter positive (+) probe to the yellow terminal in the connector (A, **Figure 129**) and the negative (–) probe to the single green/yellow connector (B, **Figure 129**) on the wiring harness side of the electrical connectors.

5. There should be battery voltage present.

6A. If battery voltage is present, turn the ignition switch OFF.

6B. If there is no battery voltage, check the wiring harness for an open circuit or a blown sub-fuse.

7. Remove the tailpiece as described in Chapter Thirteen.

8. Disconnect the electrical connector (**Figure 130**) from the ignition control module.

9. Set the ohmmeter to the R × 1 scale and zero the test leads.

10A. On 1990-1993 models, use an ohmmeter and check for continuity between the single yellow/green connector (A, **Figure 131**) and the green/yellow electrical connector at the ignition control module (B, **Figure 131**).

10B. On 1994-on models, use an ohmmeter and check for continuity between the yellow/green wire in the plug-in connector and the green/yellow electrical connector at the ignition control module (B, **Figure 131**).

11. If there is no continuity (infinite resistance), there is an open in the circuit. Repair the open circuit.

12. If there is continuity in the yellow/green wire, then the tachometer unit (**Figure 132**) of the instrument cluster is faulty and must be replaced.

13. Connect all electrical connectors.

14. Install the tailpiece and the front fairing as described in Chapter Thirteen.

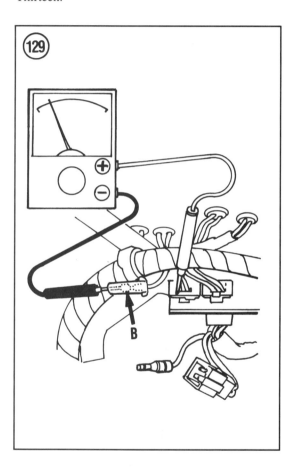

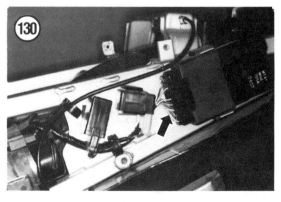

Headlight Relay Testing (1990-on Models)

If there is a problem with the headlight operation, either the headlight will not come on and/or go off, first make sure the headlight switch is operating correctly as described under *Switches* in this chapter, then check the headlight relay for proper operation.

Headlight does not shut off

1. Inspect the headlight switch as described in this chapter.
2. Inspect the headlight relay as described in the following procedure. If the relay is okay, inspect the headlight circuit or an open or short.

Headlight does not come on

1. Inspect the headlight switch as described in this chapter.
2. Check the headlight bulb. If burned out, replace the bulb.
3. Check the fuse. If blown, replace the fuse.

Headlight relay test

1. Remove the front fairing as described under *Front Fairing Removal/Installation* in Chapter Thirteen.
2. Disconnect the 4-pin black electrical connector from the headlight relay (A, **Figure 133**). Check for loose or corroded terminals and correct if necessary.
3. Set the ohmmeter to the R × 1 scale and zero the test leads.
4. Use an ohmmeter and check for continuity between the green wire terminal of the electrical connector and a good ground.
5A. If there is no continuity (infinity resistance) there is a short in that circuit. Repair or replace that circuit.
5B. If there is continuity (low resistance) perform Step 6.
6. Connect a 0-20 V DC voltmeter between the black/red and green terminals in the 4-pin electrical connector.
7A. If there is no battery voltage, check for an open circuit between the headlight relay and the fuse block.
7B. If there is battery voltage, perform Step 8 and test the headlight relay. If the headlight relay tests okay, check for an open circuit between the headlight relay and the headlight and/or the headlight relay and the left-hand combination switch assembly on the handlebar.
8. With the headlight relay disconnected and the cover removed, perform the following to the relay:
   a. Connect battery voltage to the blue and green terminals.
   b. Connect an ohmmeter between the black/red and black/blue terminals.
   c. There should be continuity (low resistance).
   d. If there is no continuity (infinity resistance), the headlight relay is faulty and must be replaced.

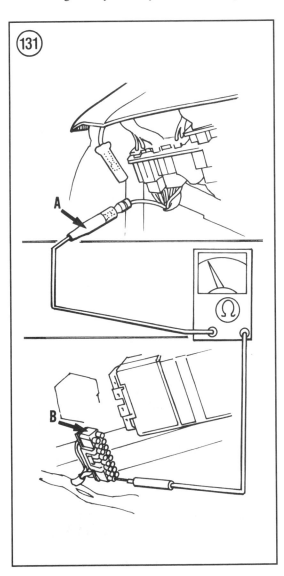

ELECTRICAL SYSTEM

9. Reconnect the 4-pin black electrical connector to the headlight relay (A, **Figure 133**).

10. Install the front fairing as described in Chapter Thirteen.

High beam relay test

1. Remove the front fairing as described under *Front Fairing Removal/Installation* in Chapter Thirteen.

2. Turn the ignition switch ON.

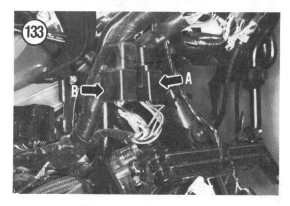

3. Move the headlight switch (**Figure 134**) from LO to HI while listening to the high beam relay. You should hear a "click" from the LO to the HO position.

4. If the relay does not click, disconnect the 4-pin black electrical connector from the high beam relay (B, **Figure 133**). Check for loose or corroded terminals and correct if necessary. Also check for a blown fuse and replace if necessary.

5. Connect a 0-20 V DC voltmeter between the blue and green terminals in the 4-pin electrical connector.

6A. If there is no battery voltage, check for an open circuit in the blue wire.

6B. If there is battery voltage, replace the high beam relay.

7. Reconnect the 4-pin black electrical connector to the high beam relay (B, **Figure 133**).

8. Install the front fairing as described in Chapter Thirteen.

Fuel Pump Flow Test

The electromagnetic fuel pump pumps fuel from the fuel tank to the carburetor assembly.

When the ignition switch is turned ON the electromagnet is energized, pulling the armature and the diaphragm up. This causes a vacuum and pulls fuel through the inlet check valve. As the armature reaches the limit of its upward travel, the contact points are opened in the switch and the circuit is broken. The electromagnet is pushed down by the return spring which in turn pushes the fuel through the outlet check valve and to the carburetor assembly. This continuing up and down movement moves or pumps the fuel from the fuel tank into the carburetors.

Fuel pump removal and installation are covered in Chapter Seven.

1A. On 1986-1989 models, remove the left-hand side cover.

1B. On 1990-on models, remove the tailpiece as described in Chapter Thirteen.

2. Turn the ignition switch OFF.

3. Remove the fuel pump relay from its rubber mount. Refer to **Figure 135** for 1986-1989 models or **Figure 136** for 1990-on models.

4. Connect a jumper wire between the black wire and the black/blue wire in the fuel pump relay electrical connector on the wire harness side (**Figure 137**).

5. Disconnect the fuel line going to the carburetors.
6. Place the loose end of the fuel line into a graduated beaker (**Figure 138**).
7. Turn the ignition switch to the ON position and allow the fuel to run out of the fuel line (into the graduated beaker) for 5 seconds.
8. Turn the ignition OFF.
9. Multiply the amount of fuel in the beaker by 12 ($12 \times 5 = 60$ seconds). This will give the fuel pump flow capacity for one minute.
10. The fuel pump minimum flow capacity for one minute is as follows:
    a. 1986-1989 models: 800 ml (27.1 U.S. oz., 28.2 Imp. oz.) per minute.
    b. 1990-on models: 900 cc (30.4 U.S. oz., 31.7 Imp. oz.) per minute.
11. If the fuel pump does not flow to the specified capacity, check the fuel pump relay circuit in the following procedure.
12. Reconnect the fuel line to the carburetors.
13. Disconnect the jumper wire from the fuel pump relay.
14. Install by reversing these removal steps. Make sure the electrical connector is free of corrosion and is tight.

Fuel Pump Relay
Testing/Replacement

1A. On 1986-1989 models, remove the left-hand side cover.
1B. On 1990-on models, remove the tailpiece as described in Chapter Thirteen.
2. Turn the ignition switch OFF.
3. Remove the fuel pump relay from its rubber mount. Refer to **Figure 135** for 1986-1989 models or **Figure 136** for 1990-on models.
4. Disconnect the electrical connector from the fuel pump relay. Inspect the contacts for corrosion or damage, repair if necessary. Reconnect the electrical connector.
5. Turn the ignition switch ON.
6. Connect a 0-20 DC voltmeter positive (+) probe to the black terminal on the wiring harness side of the electrical connector and the negative (−) probe to a good ground. There should be battery voltage. Disconnect the voltmeter.
7. Set the ohmmeter to the $R \times 1$ scale and zero the test leads.

8. Use an ohmmeter and check for continuity between the following terminals:
    a. Between the red/yellow electrical terminal in the wiring harness side of the fuel pump relay connector and the red/yellow electrical terminal of the ignition control module. There should be continuity (low resistance).

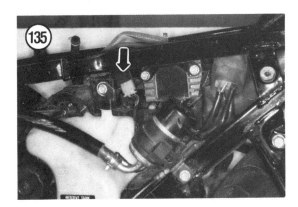

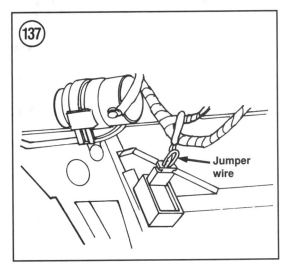

ELECTRICAL SYSTEM

b. Between the black/blue electrical terminal in the wiring harness side of the fuel pump relay connector and the black/blue electrical terminal of the fuel pump. There should be continuity (low resistance).

c. Disconnect the ohmmeter.

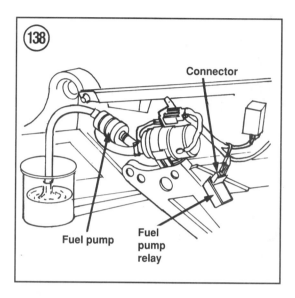

9. If the fuel pump relay fails either of these tests, there is either an open circuit (repair the circuit) or the fuel pump relay is faulty and must be replaced as described in the following:

   a. Disconnect the electrical connector from the fuel pump relay.
   b. Connect the electrical connector to the new fuel pump relay and install the relay into the rubber mounting bracket on the electrical panel.

10. Install by reversing these removal steps, making sure the electrical connectors are free of corrosion and are tight.

**Fuel Reserve Sensor
(1986-1989 Models)**

Testing

1. Remove the right-hand side cover.
2. Remove the seat as described in Chapter Thirteen.
3. Remove the fuel tank rear mounting bolt (**Figure 139**) and loosen the front mounting bolt.
4. Prop the rear of the fuel tank up to gain access to the fuel reserve sensor 2-pin red electrical connector containing 2 wires (1 gray/black and 1 green/black).
5. Disconnect this electrical connector.
6. Connect a jumper wire to the wiring harness side of the fuel reserve sensor electrical connector.
7. Turn the ignition switch ON.
8. The fuel reserve indicator light (**Figure 140**) on the instrument cluster should come on.
9. If the fuel reserve light comes on, the fuel reserve sensor in the fuel tank is faulty and must be replaced as described in this chapter.
10. Remove the jumper wire from the connector, then reconnect the electrical connector.
11. Lower the fuel tank and install the rear bolt. Tighten the bolt securely.
12. Install the seat and the right-hand side cover.

Removal/installation

1. Drain the fuel from the fuel tank and then remove the fuel tank as described under *Fuel Tank Removal/Installation* in Chapter Seven.
2. Lay a blanket or shop cloths on the workbench to protect the painted finish of the fuel tank.
3. Turn the fuel tank upside down on the blanket or shop cloths.

4. Remove the nuts (A, **Figure 141**) securing the fuel reserve sensor to the underside of the fuel tank.
5. Remove the fuel level sensor (B, **Figure 141**) and O-ring seal.
6. Install a new fuel level sensor (B, **Figure 141**) and new O-ring seal. Tighten the nuts securely.
7. Add some fuel into the tank and check for leaks. Fix any fuel leak prior to reinstalling the fuel tank.
8. Install by reversing these removal steps.

Fuel Level Sensor/Fuel Gauge Removal/Testing/Installation (1990-on Models)

1. Drain the fuel from the fuel tank and then remove the fuel tank as described under *Fuel Tank Removal/Installation* in Chapter Seven.
2. Lay a blanket or shop cloths on the workbench to protect painted finish of the fuel tank.
3. Turn the fuel tank upside down on the blanket or shop cloths.
4. Remove the nuts (A, **Figure 142**) securing the fuel level sensor (B, **Figure 142**) from the underside of the fuel tank.
5. Reconnect the fuel level sensor electrical connector to the wiring harness.
6. Turn the ignition switch ON.
7. Hold the fuel level sensor in the same position as it would be mounted in the fuel tank (**Figure 143**). Carefully move the float arm up and down from the full "F" to the empty "E" positions and observe the fuel gauge (B, **Figure 127**) on the instrument panel.
8. If the fuel needle does not move, disconnect the fuel level sensor electrical connector from the wiring harness. Then inspect the fuel level sensor as follows:
   a. Connect an ohmmeter test leads to the electrical terminals on the fuel gauge sensor as shown in **Figure 144**.
   b. Carefully move the float arm and check for the following resistance readings:
   c. Float at the top (full tank): 4-10 ohms.
   d. Float at the bottom (empty tank): 90-100 ohms.
9. If the fuel sensor fails either of these tests, the sensor must be replaced.
10. If the fuel sensor passes these tests, then there could be an open circuit between the fuel level sensor and the fuel gauge in the instrument panel. Repair or replace the circuit.

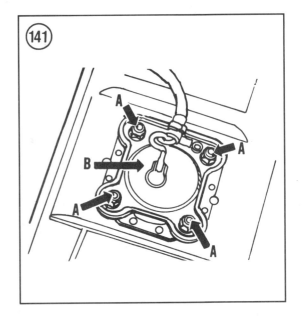

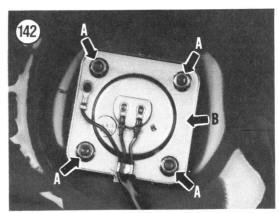

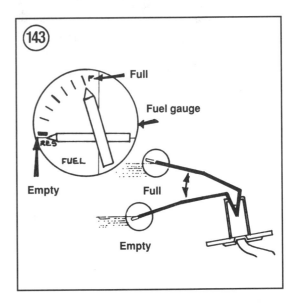

ELECTRICAL SYSTEM

11. If the electrical circuit is okay, then the fuel gauge (B, **Figure 127**) in the instrument cluster is faulty and must be replaced.

12. Install by reversing these removal steps. Make sure the electrical connectors are free of corrosion and are tight.

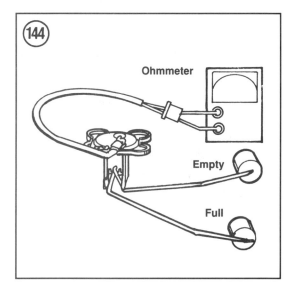

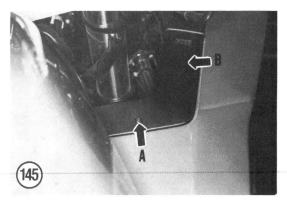

Horn Removal/Installation

1. Remove the front fairing as described under *Front Fairing Removal/Installation* in Chapter Thirteen.
2. Disconnect the electrical connections from the horn.
3. Remove the bolt securing the horn to the lower fork bridge.
4. Remove the horn.
5. Install by reversing these removal steps, noting the following.
6. Make sure the electrical connectors are free of corrosion and are tight.

Horn Testing

Remove the horn as described in this chapter. Connect a 12-volt battery to the horn. If the horn is good, it will sound. If not, replace it.

FUSES

The number of fuses varies among the various models. They are located in the fuse holder on the right-hand side of the front fairing

All models also have a main fuse located on the starter switch relay.

> *CAUTION*
> *When replacing a fuse, make sure the ignition switch is in the OFF position. This will lessen the chance of a short circuit.*

Fuse Replacement

If a fuse in the fuse holder blows, perform the following.

1A. On 1986-1989 models, perform the following:
  a. Remove the screw and remove the fuse panel cover.
  b. Hinge the cover forward to expose the fuses.

1B. On 1990-1993 models, perform the following:
  a. Remove the screw (A, **Figure 145**) securing the front fairing inner panel and remove the inner panel (B, **Figure 145**).
  b. Remove the fuse panel cover (**Figure 146**).

1C. On 1994-on models, perform the following:
  a. Remove the screw (A, **Figure 147**) and remove the fuse panel outer cover (B, **Figure 147**).

b. Pull up on the front edge of the fuse panel cover and hinge it back to expose the fuses.

2. Remove the blown fuse (**Figure 148**) and install a new one.

Main Fuse Replacement

If the main fusible link blows, perform the following.

1986-1989 models

1. Remove right-hand side cover.
2. Move the rubber boot (A, **Figure 149**) off the starter relay switch.
3. Release the tabs and remove the electrical connector and main fuse assembly (B, **Figure 149**) from the top of the starter relay switch.
4. Remove the main fuse and install a new one.
5. Reconnect the electrical connector and make sure it is secure.
6. Move the rubber boot back into position.
7. Install the right-hand side cover.

1990-on models

1. Remove the seat.
2. Disconnect the electrical connector (**Figure 150**) from the top of the starter relay switch.
3. Release the tabs and remove the electrical connector and main fuse assembly from the top of the starter relay switch.
4. Remove the main fuse and install a new one.
5. Reconnect the electrical connector and make sure it is secure.
6. Install the seat.

Whenever a fuse blows, find out the reason for the failure before replacing the fuse. Usually the trouble is a short circuit in the wiring. This may be caused by worn-through insulation or a disconnected wire shorted to ground.

CAUTION
Never substitute aluminum foil or wire for a fuse. Never use a higher amperage fuse than specified. An overload could cause a fire and complete loss of the motorcycle.

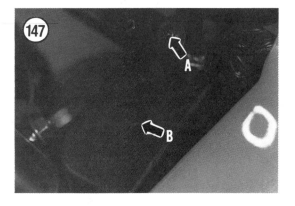

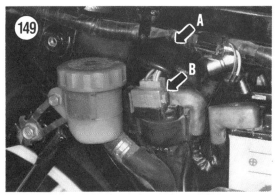

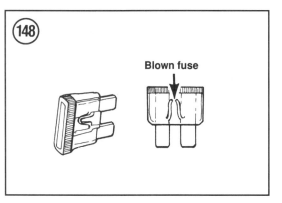

ELECTRICAL SYSTEM

Table 1 CHARGING SYSTEM SPECIFICATIONS

Alternator capacity	350W/5,000 rpm
Regulator/rectifier	Transistorized, non-adjustable
Regulated voltage	
1986-1989	13.7-15.3 V
1990-on	13.5-16 V
Charging start rpm (no load)	900-1,100 rpm
Stator coil resistance	
1986-1989	0.2-0.5 ohms
1990-on	0.1-1.0 ohms

Table 2 IGNITION SYSTEM SPECIFICATIONS

Camshaft pulse generator resistance (1986 models only)	400-500 ohms
Pulse generator resistance	
1986-1989	450-500 ohms
1990-on	200-400 ohms
Ignition coil resistance	
Primary resistance	
1986-1989	2.6-3.2 ohms
1990-on	2-4 ohms
Secondary resistance	
With spark plug cap	
1986-1989	15,000-21,000 ohms
1990-on	17,000-24,000 ohms
Without spark plug cap	
1986-1989	11,000-15,000 ohms
1990-on	13,000-17,000 ohms

Table 3 REPLACEMENT BULBS

1986-1987 U.S. and Canadian Models	
Item	Voltage/wattage
Headlight (high/low beam)	12V 60/55W
Taillight/brakelight	12V 8/27W
Directional signal	
Front	12V 23/8W
Rear	12V 23W
License plate light	12V 8W
Instrument and indicator lights	12V 3.4W

1990-on U.S. and Canadian Models	
Item	Voltage/wattage/candle power
Headlight (high/low beam)	12V 45/45W
Taillight/brakelight	12V 8/27W
1990-1993	12V 32/3cp
1994-on	12V 32/2cp
Directional signal	
Front	
1990-1993	12V 32/3cp
1994-on	12V 23/8W
Rear	
1990-1993	12V 32cp
1994-on	12V 23W

(continued)

Table 3 REPLACEMENT BULBS (continued)

1990-on U.S. and Canadian Models (continued)

Item	Voltage/wattage/candle power
License plate light	
1990-1993	12V 4cp
1994-on	12V 8W
Instrument and indicator lights	
1990-1993	12V 3.4W
1994-on	12V 1.7W

1986-1989 Other than U.S. and Canadian Models

Item	Voltage/wattage
Headlight (high/low beam)	12V 60/55W
Position light	12V 4W
Taillight/brakelight	12V 5/21W
Directional signal	12V 21W
Instrument and indicator lights	12V 3.4W

1990-on Other than U.S. and Canadian Models

Item*	Voltage/wattage/candle power
Headlight (high/low beam)	
1990-1991	
E, IT, SA, SW	12V 60/55W
G, ED, F, FI, SD, SP, U	12V 60W, 12V 60/55W
1992-on	
E, IT, SP	12V 60/55W
AR, ED, F, G, SW	12V 60W, 12V 60/55W
U	12V 45/45W
Position light	12V 5W
Taillight/brakelight	12V 5/21W
Directional signal	12V 21W
Instrument, clock lights	12V 1.7W
Indicator lights	12V 3.4W

* AR= Austria, E= United Kingdom, ED= Europe, F= France, FI= Finland, G= Germany, IT= Italy, ND= No. Europe, SP= Spain, SW= Switzerland, U Australia.

Table 4 TEMPERATURE GAUGE SENSOR READINGS

Temperature	Resistance (ohms)
60° C (140° F)	104.0
85° C (185° F)	43.9
110° C (230° F)	20.3
120° C (248° F)	16.1

CHAPTER NINE

LIQUID COOLING SYSTEM

The pressurized liquid cooling system consists of a radiator, water pump, thermostat, electric cooling fan and a coolant reserve tank. **Figure 1** shows the major components of the cooling system.

The system uses a radiator fill cap with a designed relief pressure of 93-123 kPa (14-18 psi). The radiator fill cap is designed to operate with a 180° F (82° C) thermostat.

The water pump requires no routine maintenance and is replaced as a complete unit if found defective. Replacement parts are not available for the unit.

It is important to keep the coolant level to the "UPPER" mark on the coolant reserve tank. Refer to **Figure 2** for 1986-1989 models or **Figure 3** for 1990-on models. Always add coolant to the reserve tank, *not* to the radiator.

CAUTION
*Drain and flush the cooling system at least every 2 years. Refer to **Coolant Change** in Chapter Three. Refill with a mixture of ethylene glycol antifreeze (formulated for aluminum engines) and purified water. Do not reuse the old coolant as it deteriorates with use. **Do not** operate the cooling system with only purified water (even in climates where antifreeze protection is not required). This is important because the engine is all aluminum; it will not rust but it will oxidize internally and have to be replaced. Refer to **Coolant Change** in Chapter Three.*

This chapter describes the repair and replacement of the cooling system components. **Table 1** at the end of this chapter lists all of the cooling system specifications. For routine maintenance of the system, refer to Chapter Three.

The cooling system must be cool prior to removing any component of the system.

WARNING
*Do **not** remove the radiator fill cap (**Figure 4**) when the engine is hot. The coolant is very hot and is under pressure. Severe scalding could result if the coolant comes in contact with your skin.*

HOSES AND HOSE CLAMPS

The small diameter coolant hoses are very stiff and are sometimes difficult to install onto the metal

CHAPTER NINE

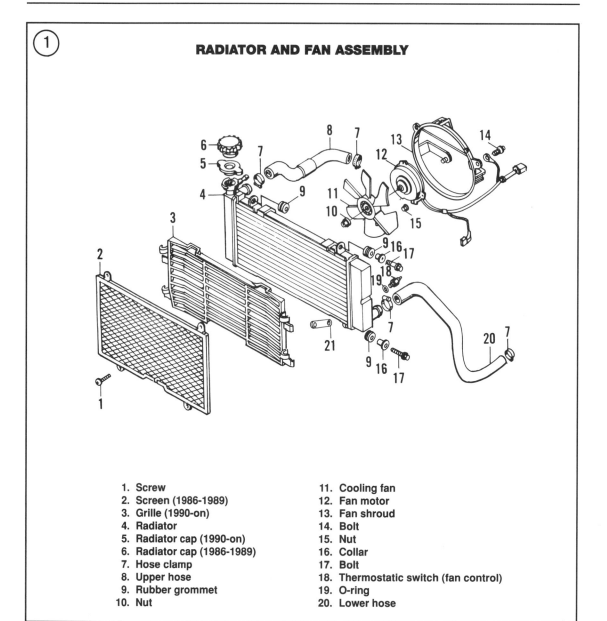

RADIATOR AND FAN ASSEMBLY

1. Screw
2. Screen (1986-1989)
3. Grille (1990-on)
4. Radiator
5. Radiator cap (1990-on)
6. Radiator cap (1986-1989)
7. Hose clamp
8. Upper hose
9. Rubber grommet
10. Nut
11. Cooling fan
12. Fan motor
13. Fan shroud
14. Bolt
15. Nut
16. Collar
17. Bolt
18. Thermostatic switch (fan control)
19. O-ring
20. Lower hose

fittings of the various cooling system parts. Prior to installing the hoses, apply a small amount of Armor All or rubber lube to the inside surface of these hoses and they will slide on much easier.

Different types of hose clamps are used on the various hoses, either the clamping screw type that is released with a screwdriver or the clamping band type where the ends must be pinched open with a pair of gas pliers. These clamps are used at specific locations due to space limitations around a specific part. Be sure to reinstall the correct type of clamp at the correct location.

COOLING SYSTEM CHECK

Two checks should be made before disassembly if a cooling system fault is suspected.
1. Run the engine until it reaches operating temperature. While the engine is running, a pressure surge should be felt when the radiator hose coming from the water pump is squeezed.
2. If a substantial coolant loss is noted, one of the head gaskets may be blown. In extreme cases, sufficient coolant will leak into a cylinder(s) when the bike is left standing for several hours so the engine cannot be turned over with the starter. White smoke (steam) might also be observed at the muffler(s) when the engine is running. Coolant may also find its way into the oil. Check the dipstick; if it looks like green chocolate malt (milky or foamy) there is coolant in the oil system. If so, correct the cooling system immediately.

CAUTION
After the cooling system is corrected, drain and thoroughly flush the engine oil system to eliminate all coolant residue. Refill with fresh engine oil; refer to Chapter Three.

PRESSURE CHECK

If the cooling system requires repeated refilling, there is probably a leak somewhere in the system. Perform *Cooling System Inspection* in Chapter Three.

RADIATOR

Removal/Installation

1. Remove both lower sections of the front fairing as described under *Front Fairing Removal/Installation* in Chapter Thirteen.
2. Drain the cooling system as described under *Coolant Change* in Chapter Three.
3. Remove the seat as described in Chapter Thirteen.
4. Disconnect the battery negative lead as described under *Battery* in Chapter Three.
5. Remove the fuel tank as described under *Fuel Tank Removal/Installation* in Chapter Seven.
6. Disconnect the overflow tube from the filler neck.
7. Disconnect the cooling fan and thermostatic switch 2-pin electrical connectors containing 2 wires.
8. Loosen the clamping screw on the upper hose clamp (**Figure 5**). Move the clamp back onto the hose and off of the neck of the radiator and remove the upper hose from the radiator.
9. Loosen the clamping screw on the lower hose clamp (A, **Figure 6**). Move the clamp back onto the hose and off of the neck of the radiator and remove the hose from the radiator.

10. Remove the bolts and collars securing the radiator at the top (**Figure 7**) and at the bottom (B, **Figure 6**).

11. Carefully pull the radiator slightly forward and down, then remove the radiator from the frame.

12. Install by reversing these removal steps while noting the following:
   a. Replace both radiator hoses if either is starting to deteriorate or is damaged.
   b. Make sure the cooling fan electrical connections are free of corrosion and are tight.
   c. Refill the cooling system with the recommended type and quantity of coolant as described in Chapter Three.

Inspection

1. If not already removed, remove the screws securing the grille (**Figure 8**) and remove the grille from the radiator.

2. If compressed air is available, use short spurts of air directed to the backside of the radiator and blow out dirt and bugs.

3. Flush off the exterior of the radiator with a garden hose on low pressure. Spray both the front and the back to remove all road dirt and bugs. Carefully use a whisk broom or stiff paint brush to remove any stubborn dirt.

> *CAUTION*
> *Do not press too hard or the cooling fins and tubes may be damaged, causing a leak.*

4. Carefully straighten out any bent cooling fins with a broad tipped screwdriver or putty knife.

5. Check for cracks or leakage (usually a moss-green colored residue) at the filler neck, the inlet and outlet hose fittings and the upper and lower tank seams (**Figure 9**).

6. If the condition of the radiator is doubtful, have it checked as described under *Pressure Check* in Chapter Three. The radiator can be pressure checked while removed or installed on the bike.

7. To prevent oxidation to the radiator, touch up any area where the black paint is worn off. Use a good quality spray paint and apply several *light* coats of paint. Do not apply heavy coats as this will cut down on the cooling efficiency of the radiator.

8. If necessary, unscrew the thermostatic switch from the radiator. Apply a silicone based sealant to the threads of the switch and install the switch in the radiator and tighten securely.

COOLING FAN

Removal/Installation

1. Remove the radiator as described in this chapter.

2. Remove the bolts securing the fan shroud and fan assembly and remove the assembly.

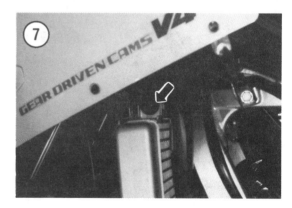

LIQUID COOLING SYSTEM

3. To remove the fan blade from the motor, remove the nut securing the fan blade. Remove the fan blade from the motor.

4. If necessary, remove the nuts securing the fan assembly to the fan shroud and remove the fan assembly.

5. Install by reversing these removal steps while noting the following:

   a. Apply Loctite Threadlocker to the threads on the fan motor shaft prior to installing the fan

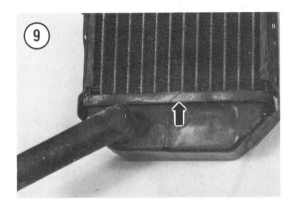

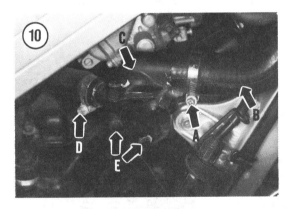

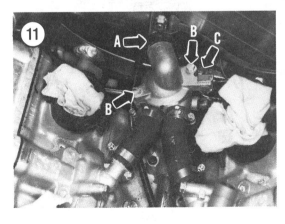

   blade nut. Install the nut and tighten the nut securely.

   b. Install the fan motor and shroud and tighten the nuts securely.

   c. Refill the cooling system with the recommended type and quantity of coolant as described in Chapter Three.

THERMOSTAT AND HOUSING

Thermostat
Removal/Installation

The thermostat is located on the right-hand side on 1986-1989 models and on the left-hand side on 1990-on models.

1. Remove both lower sections of the front fairing as described under *Front Fairing Removal/Installation* in Chapter Thirteen.

2. Drain the cooling system as described under *Coolant Change* in Chapter Three.

3. Remove the seat as described in Chapter Thirteen.

4. Disconnect the battery negative lead as described under *Battery* in Chapter Three.

5. Remove the fuel tank as described under *Fuel Tank Removal/Installation* in Chapter Seven.

6. On 1990-on models, remove the carburetor assembly as described under *Carburetor Removal/Installation* in Chapter Seven.

7A. On 1986-1989 models, perform the following:

   a. Loosen the clamping screw on the radiator upper hose clamp (A, **Figure 10**) and move the band back off of the thermostat cover neck.

   b. Remove the radiator upper hose (B, **Figure 10**) from the thermostat cover.

   c. Remove the bolts securing the thermostat housing cover (C, **Figure 10**) to the thermostat housing.

   d. Remove the thermostat housing cover and O-ring seal.

   e. Remove the thermostat from the housing.

7B. On 1990-on models, perform the following:

   a. Disconnect the electrical connector from the temperature sensor on the backside of the thermostat housing.

   b. Loosen the clamping screw on the radiator upper hose clamp (A, **Figure 11**) and move the band back off of the thermostat cover neck.

c. Remove the radiator upper hose from the thermostat cover.

d. Remove the bolts (B, **Figure 11**) securing the thermostat housing cover to thermostat housing.

e. Remove the bolt (C, **Figure 11**) securing the thermostat housing cover to the frame.

f. Remove the thermostat housing cover and O-ring seal.

g. Remove the thermostat from the housing.

8. Install by reversing these removal steps while noting the following:

   a. Install a new O-ring seal in the thermostat housing cover.

   b. On 1990-on models, position the thermostat with the hole facing toward the front of the bike.

   c. Refill the cooling system with the recommended type and quantity of coolant as described in Chapter Three.

Thermostat Testing

Test the thermostat to ensure proper operation. The thermostat should be replaced if it remains open at normal room temperature or stays closed after the specified temperature has been reached during the test procedure.

1. Place the thermostat on a small piece of wood in a pan of water (**Figure 12**).

2. Place a thermometer in the pan of water (use a cooking or candy thermometer that is rated higher than the test temperature).

3. Gradually heat the water and continue to gently stir the water until it reaches 80-84° C (176-183° F). At this temperature the thermostat valve should open.

NOTE
Valve operation is sometimes sluggish; it usually takes 3-5 minutes for the valve to operate properly.

4. If the valve fails to open, the thermostat should be replaced (it cannot be serviced). Be sure to replace it with one of the same temperature rating.

Thermostat Housing Removal/Installation

The thermostat housing is located on the right-hand side on 1986-1989 models and on the left-hand side on 1990-on models.

1. Remove both lower sections of the front fairing as described under *Front Fairing Removal/Installation* in Chapter Thirteen.

2. Drain the cooling system as described under *Coolant Change* in Chapter Three.

3. Remove the seat as described in Chapter Thirteen.

4. Disconnect the battery negative lead as described under *Battery* in Chapter Three.

5. Remove the fuel tank as described under *Fuel Tank Removal/Installation* in Chapter Seven.

6. On 1990-on models, remove the carburetor assembly as described under *Carburetor Removal/Installation* in Chapter Seven.

7A. On 1986-1989 models, perform the following:

   a. Loosen the clamping screw on the radiator upper hose clamp (A, **Figure 10**) and move the band back off of the thermostat cover neck.

   b. Remove the radiator upper hose (B, **Figure 10**) from the thermostat cover.

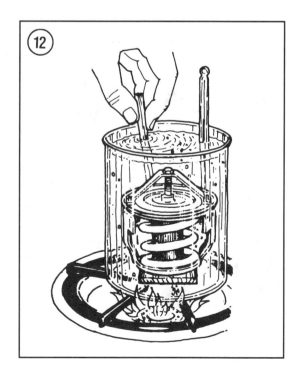

LIQUID COOLING SYSTEM

c. Disconnect the electrical connector from the temperature sensor on the backside of the thermostat housing.

d. Loosen the clamping screw on the rear cylinder head hose clamp (D, **Figure 10**) and move the band back off of the thermostat housing neck.

e. Remove the hose from the thermostat housing.

f. Remove the bolts (E, **Figure 10**) securing the thermostat housing to the front cylinder head.

g. Remove the thermostat housing and O-ring.

7B. On 1990-on models, perform the following:

a. Disconnect the electrical connector from the temperature sensor on the backside of the thermostat housing.

b. Loosen the clamping screw on the radiator upper hose clamp (A, **Figure 13**) and move the band back off of the thermostat cover neck.

c. Remove the radiator upper hose from the thermostat cover.

d. Remove the bolts securing the thermostat housing cover to the mounting bracket. Remove the bracket.

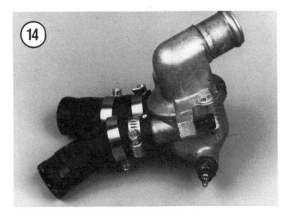

e. Loosen the clamping screws (B, **Figure 13**) on the 2 cylinder hoses and move the bands back off of the fittings on the cylinder heads.

f. Remove the hoses from the fittings on the cylinder heads.

g. Remove the thermostat housing and hoses (**Figure 14**) from the engine and frame.

8. Install by reversing these removal steps while noting the following:

a. On 1986-1989 models, install a new O-ring seal in the thermostat housing where it attaches to the cylinder head.

b. Refill the cooling system with the recommended type and quantity of coolant as described in Chapter Three.

WATER PUMP

Removal/Installation

Refer to the following illustrations for this procedure:

a. **Figure 15**: 1986-1989 models.
b. **Figure 16**: 1990-on models.

1. Remove both lower sections of the front fairing as described under *Front Fairing Removal/Installation* in Chapter Thirteen.

2. Drain the cooling system as described under *Coolant Change* in Chapter Three.

3. Loosen the clamping screw (A, **Figure 17**) on the water pump cover hose (B, **Figure 17**) and move the band back off of the water pump cover neck. Remove the hose from the water pump cover.

4. Loosen both clamping screws (**Figure 18**) on the water pump housing short hose and slide the hose forward on the metal pipe.

5. Remove the bolts securing the water pump cover and housing to the crankcase.

6. Remove the cover (**Figure 19**). Don't lose the locating dowels.

7. Withdraw the water pump from the crankcase.

Inspection

1. Inspect the water pump assembly for wear or damage. Rotate the impeller shaft (**Figure 20**) to make sure the bearings are not worn or damaged. If the bearings are damaged, the assembly must be replaced, as it cannot be serviced.

CHAPTER NINE

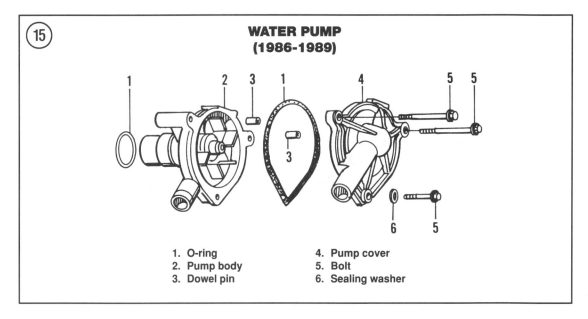

WATER PUMP (1986-1989)

1. O-ring
2. Pump body
3. Dowel pin
4. Pump cover
5. Bolt
6. Sealing washer

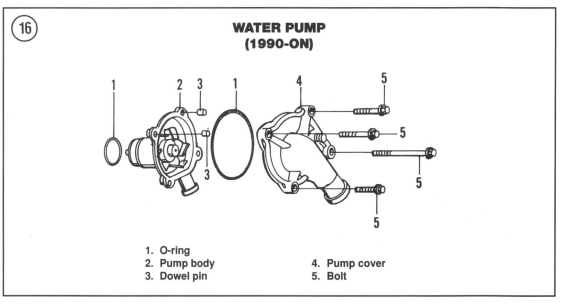

WATER PUMP (1990-ON)

1. O-ring
2. Pump body
3. Dowel pin
4. Pump cover
5. Bolt

LIQUID COOLING SYSTEM

2. Check the impeller blades (**Figure 21**). Straighten any that are bent.
3. Remove the O-ring seal (**Figure 22**) from the cover. This seal must be replaced each time the water pump is removed to prevent an oil leak. Install a new O-ring seal.
4. Remove the O-ring seal from the pump body. This seal must be replaced each time the water pump is removed to prevent an oil leak. Install a new O-ring seal.

Installation

1. Within the crankcase, rotate the oil pump shaft so the tab on the end of the shaft is vertical (A, **Figure 23**).
2. Apply a coat of clean engine oil to the new O-ring seal (B, **Figure 23**) on the water pump housing.
3. Position the groove on the water pump shaft (C, **Figure 23**) vertical so it will align with the tab on the oil pump shaft.
4. Install the water pump into the crankcase and slightly wiggle the water pump impeller to assure proper alignment of the tab and groove. Push the water pump assembly all the way on until it is properly seated against the crankcase. The assembly should completely bottom out against the crankcase without using any force. If it will not fit properly, withdraw the assembly and realign the tab of the oil pump shaft and the groove on the water pump.

CAUTION
Do not install the cover nor any bolts until the assembly is completely seated against the crankcase. Do not try to force the assembly into place with the mounting screws as both the oil pump and the water pump will be damaged.

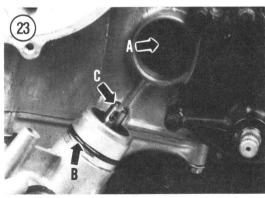

5. If removed, install the dowel pins on the water pump body.

6. Make sure the new O-ring seal is in place in the water pump cover.

7. Install the water pump cover (**Figure 19**) and bolts. Tighten the bolts securely.

8. Move the short section of water hose (on the metal pipe) onto the water pump housing and tighten the hose clamps (**Figure 18**) at this time.

9. On 1986-1989 models, be sure to install the washer onto the front lower bolt and install the bolts and tighten them securely.

10. Install the hose (B, **Figure 17**) onto the water pump cover and tighten the hose clamp screw (A, **Figure 17**).

11. Refill the cooling system with the recommended type and quantity of coolant. Refer to *Coolant Change* in Chapter Three.

12. Start the bike and check for leaks.

13. Install both lower sections of the front fairing as in Chapter Thirteen.

ENGINE COOLANT CROSSOVER PIPE (1986-1989 MODELS)

Replacement

Refer to **Figure 24** for this procedure.

1. Remove both lower sections of the front fairing as described under *Front Fairing Removal/Installation* in Chapter Thirteen.

2. Drain the cooling system as described under *Coolant Change* in Chapter Three.

3. Remove the seat as described in Chapter Thirteen.

4. Disconnect the battery negative lead as described under *Battery* in Chapter Three.

5. Remove the fuel tank as described under *Fuel Tank Removal/Installation* in Chapter Seven.

6. Remove the carburetor assembly as described under *Carburetor Removal/Installation* in Chapter Seven.

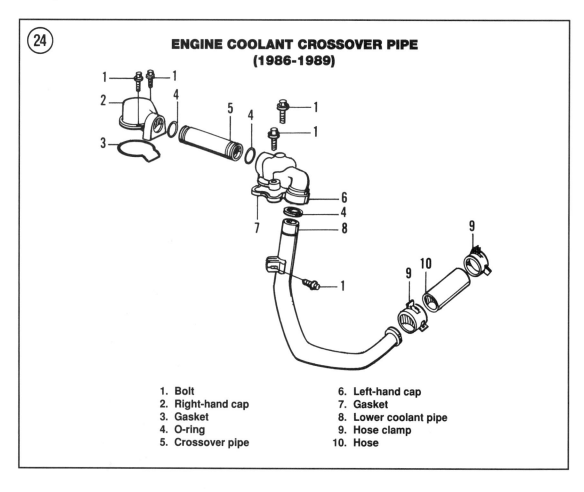

ENGINE COOLANT CROSSOVER PIPE (1986-1989)

1. Bolt
2. Right-hand cap
3. Gasket
4. O-ring
5. Crossover pipe
6. Left-hand cap
7. Gasket
8. Lower coolant pipe
9. Hose clamp
10. Hose

LIQUID COOLING SYSTEM

NOTE
The following steps are shown with the engine removed from the frame for clarity. The assembly can be removed with the engine in the frame.

7. Remove the bolts securing the right- and left-hand caps (A, **Figure 25**) to the top of the cylinder block.

8. Remove the caps and connecting pipe (B, **Figure 25**) assembly from the cylinder block. Remove the O-ring seals from the cylinder block and discard them.

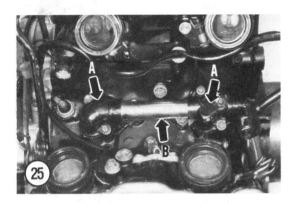

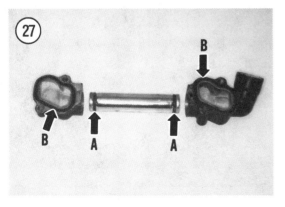

9. To remove the lower coolant pipe, perform the following:
   a. Loosen the clamping screw on the water pump housing hose where it connects to the coolant lower metal pipe attached to the engine. Leave this hose attached to the water pump housing.
   b. Remove the bolt securing the metal pipe to the cylinder head and remove the metal pipe assembly (**Figure 26**).
   c. Remove the upper seal where the metal pipe attaches to the left-hand cap. Discard the seal.

10. Install by reversing these removal steps while noting the following:
   a. Install a new upper seal on the metal pipe.
   b. Install a new O-ring seal (A, **Figure 27**) on the connecting pipe.
   c. Install new O-ring seals (B, **Figure 27**) under the right- and left-hand caps.
   d. Apply a liquid sealant to the cap threads prior to installation and tighten them securely.
   e. Refill the cooling system with the recommended type and quantity of coolant. Refer to *Coolant Change* in Chapter Three.
   f. Start the engine and check for leaks.

HOSES

Hoses deteriorate with age and should be replaced periodically or whenever they show signs of cracking or leakage. To be safe, replace the hoses every 2 years. The spray of hot coolant from a cracked hose can injure the rider and passenger. Loss of coolant can also cause the engine to overheat causing damage.

Whenever any component of the cooling system is removed, inspect the hose(s) and determine if replacement is necessary.

Replacement

NOTE
This procedure is shown on a 1986 model. Other models are similar.

1. Remove both lower sections of the front fairing as described under *Front Fairing Removal/Installation* in Chapter Thirteen.
2. Drain the cooling system as described under *Coolant Change* in Chapter Three.
3. Remove the seat as described in Chapter Thirteen.

4. Disconnect the battery negative lead as described under *Battery* in Chapter Three.

5. Remove the fuel tank as described under *Fuel Tank Removal/Installation* in Chapter Seven.

6. To remove the upper hose, perform the following:
   a. At the radiator, loosen the clamping screw on the upper hose clamp (A, **Figure 28**). Move the clamp back onto the hose and off of the neck of the radiator and remove the upper hose from the radiator.
   b. Loosen the clamping screw (B, **Figure 28**) at the thermostat and move the band back off of the thermostat cover neck.
   c. Remove the radiator upper hose (C, **Figure 28**) from the thermostat cover.
   d. Remove the hose from both fittings and remove the hose.

7. To remove the lower hose, perform the following:
   a. At the radiator, loosen the clamping screw on the lower hose clamp (A, **Figure 29**). Move the clamp back onto the hose and off of the neck of the radiator and remove the lower hose (B, **Figure 29**) from the radiator.
   b. Loosen the clamping screw (A, **Figure 30**) at the water pump cover and move the band back off of the cover neck.
   c. Remove the radiator lower hose from the wire bracket (B, **Figure 30**).
   d. Remove the radiator lower hose from the water pump cover.
   e. Remove the hose from both fittings and remove the hose (B, **Figure 29**).

8. To remove the short section of hose (**Figure 31**) between the water pump housing and the metal pipe, remove the water pump as described in this chapter. The section of hose is too short to remove without first removing the water pump housing.

9. To remove the short section of hose between the thermostat housing and the cylinder heads, remove the thermostat housing as described in this chapter. The section(s) of hose is (are) too short to remove without first removing the thermostat housing.

10. Install the new hoses along with the correct type of hose clamp. Tighten the clamps securely, but not so tight that the clamps cut into the new hose.

11. Refill the cooling system with the recommended type and quantity of coolant. Refer to *Coolant Change* in Chapter Three.

12. Start the engine and check for leaks.

13. Install all items removed.

LIQUID COOLING SYSTEM

Table 1 COOLING SYSTEM SPECIFICATIONS

Coolant capacity	
Total system	2.63 liters (2.75 U.S. qt.)
Radiator and engine	2.3 liters (2.4 U.S. qt.)
Reserve tank	0.33 liters (0.35 U.S. qt.)
Radiator cap relief pressure	95-125 kPa (14-18 psi)
Thermostat	
Begins to open	80-84° C (176-183° F)
Valve lift	Minimum of 8 mm @ 95° C (203° F)
Boiling point (50/50 mixture)	
Un pressurized:	107.7° C (226° F)
Pressurized (cap on)	125.6° C (258° F)
Freezing point (hydrometer test)	
Water-to-antifreeze ratio	
55:45	–32° C (–25° F)
50:50	–37° C (–34° F)
45:55	–44.5° C (–48° F)

CHAPTER TEN

FRONT SUSPENSION AND STEERING

This chapter describes procedures for the repair and maintenance of the front wheel, front forks and the steering components.

Front suspension torque specifications are covered in **Table 1**. **Tables 1-4** are at the end of this chapter.

NOTE
Where differences occur relating to the United Kingdom (U.K.) models, they are identified. If there is no (U.K.) designation relating to a procedure, photo or illustration, it is identical to the United States (U.S.) models.

FRONT WHEEL

Removal

1. On models so equipped, place the bike on the centerstand. On all other models, remove the lower section of the front fairing, then place wood blocks under the engine or frame to support it securely with the front wheel off the ground.
2. On 1986-1989 models, remove the speedometer cable set screw. Pull the speedometer cable (**Figure 1**) free from the speedometer gear box.

3A. On 1986-1989 models, remove the right-hand brake caliper assembly (A, **Figure 2**) from the front fork as described in Chapter Twelve. Tie the caliper assembly up with Bungee cord to take the strain off the hydraulic brake hose.
3B. On 1990-on models, remove the left-hand brake caliper assembly (A, **Figure 3**) from the front fork as described in Chapter Twelve. Tie the caliper assembly up with Bungee cord to take the strain off the hydraulic brake hose.

NOTE
Insert a piece of vinyl tubing or wood in the caliper in place of the brake disc.

FRONT SUSPENSION AND STEERING

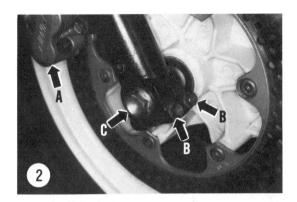

That way if the brake lever is inadvertently squeezed, the pistons will not be forced out of the cylinder. If this does happen, the caliper may have to be disassembled to reseat the pistons and the system will have to be bled. By using the wood, bleeding the brake is not necessary when installing the wheel.

4A. On 1986-1989 models, perform the following:
  a. Loosen the front axle pinch bolts (B, **Figure 2**) on the right-hand side.
  b. Loosen then remove the front axle bolt (C, **Figure 2**) on the right-hand side.
  c. Loosen the front axle pinch bolts (A, **Figure 4**) on the left-hand side.
  d. Insert a drift into the hole in the front axle and withdraw the front axle (B, **Figure 4**) from the left-hand side.

4B. On 1990-on models, perform the following:
  a. Loosen the front axle pinch bolt (A, **Figure 5**) on the right-hand side.
  b. Loosen then remove the front axle bolt (B, **Figure 5**) on the right-hand side.
  c. Loosen the front axle pinch bolt (B, **Figure 3**) on the left-hand side.
  d. Insert a drift into the hole in the front axle and withdraw the front axle (C, **Figure 3**) from the left-hand side.

5. Pull the wheel down and forward and remove it.

6A. On 1986-1989 models, perform the following:
  a. Remove the right-hand side collar.
  b. Remove the speedometer drive gear from the left-hand side.

6B. On 1990-on models, remove the spacer (**Figure 6**) from the right- and left-hand side of the hub.

CAUTION
*Do not set the wheel down on the disc surface as it may get scratched or warped. Set the tire sidewalls on 2 wood blocks as shown in **Figure 7**.*

Installation

1. Make sure the axle bearing surfaces of both fork sliders, both axle holders and the axle are free from burrs and nicks.
2A. On 1986-1989 models, perform the following:
   a. Install the right-hand side collar (**Figure 8**).
   b. Install the speedometer drive gear on the left-hand side.
   c. Position the wheel into place with the speedometer drive gear on the left-hand side.
   d. Position the speedometer housing tang *behind* the raised boss on the left-hand fork.
2B. On 1990-on models, install the spacer (**Figure 6**) into the right- and left-hand side of the hub.
3. Move the front wheel into place. Carefully insert the brake disc between the brake pads on the caliper still attached to the front fork.
4. Install the front axle from the left-hand side and push it in until it stops.
5. On the right-hand side, install the axle bolt. Insert a drift into the hole in the front axle to prevent it from turning.
6. Tighten the front axle bolt to the torque specification listed in **Table 1**.
7. Tighten the front axle pinch bolt(s) to the torque specification listed in **Table 1**.
8. Remove the vinyl tubing or pieces of wood from the brake calipers that were removed.
9A. On 1986-1989 models, install the right-hand brake caliper assembly as described in Chapter Twelve.
9B. On 1990-on models, install the left-hand brake caliper assembly as described in Chapter Twelve.
10. After the brake caliper and axle holders are installed and tightened to the correct torque specifications, check the caliper bracket-to-disc clearance as follows:
   a. Measure the distance between each surface of the right-hand brake disc and the brake caliper bracket with a flat feeler gauge (**Figure 9**).
   b. The clearance must be 0.7 mm (0.028 in.) or more on each side.
   c. If the clearance is insufficient, loosen the clamp bolt(s) on the side where the brake caliper was removed.
   d. Move right- or left-hand fork leg in or out until the correct clearance is obtained.
   e. Tighten the axle clamp bolt(s) and described in Step 7.
   f. Recheck the clearance again. Readjust if necessary.

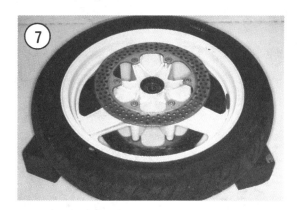

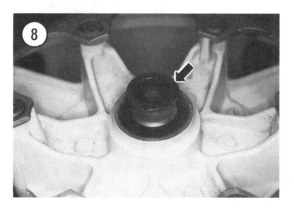

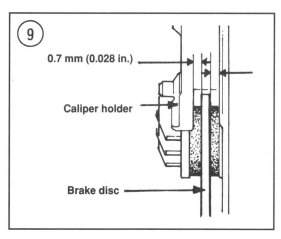

FRONT SUSPENSION AND STEERING

11. On 1986-1989 models, slowly rotate the wheel and install the speedometer cable into the speedometer housing. Install the cable set screw and tighten securely.

12. After the wheel is completely installed, rotate it several times and apply the brakes a couple of times to make sure the wheel rotates freely and that the brake pads are against the discs correctly.

13. If removed, install lower section of the front fairing.

Inspection

Measure the axial and radial runout of the wheel with a dial indicator as shown in **Figure 10**. The maximum axial and radial runout is 2.0 mm (0.08 in.). If the runout exceeds this dimension, check the wheel bearing condition.

If the wheel bearings are okay, the alloy wheel will have to be replaced as it cannot be serviced. Inspect the wheel for signs of cracks, fractures, dents or bends. If it is damaged in any way, it must be replaced.

WARNING
Do not try to repair any damage to the alloy wheel as it will result in an unsafe riding condition.

Check axle runout as described under *Front Hub Inspection* in this chapter.

FRONT HUB

Inspection

Inspect each wheel bearing prior to removing it from the wheel hub.

CAUTION
Do not remove the wheel bearings for inspection purposes as they will be damaged during the removal process. Remove wheel bearings only if they are to be replaced.

1. Perform Steps 1-3 of *Disassembly* in this chapter.
2. Turn each bearing by hand. Make sure the bearings turn smoothly. Replace the bearing(s) if they are noisy or have excessive play (**Figure 11**).
3. On non-sealed bearings, check the balls for evidence of wear, pitting or excessive heat (bluish tint). Replace the bearings if necessary; always replace as a complete set. When replacing the bearings, be sure to take your old bearings along to ensure a perfect matchup.

NOTE
Fully sealed bearings are available from many bearing specialty shops. Fully sealed bearings provide better protection from dirt and moisture that may get into the hub.

4. Check the axle for wear and straightness. Use V-blocks and a dial indicator as shown in **Figure 12**. If the runout is 0.2 mm (0.01 in.) or greater, the axle should be replaced.

Disassembly

Refer to the following illustrations for this procedure:

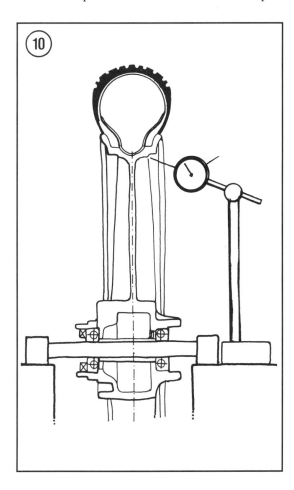

a. **Figure 13**: 1986-1989 models.
b. **Figure 14**: 1990-1993 models.
c. **Figure 15**: 1994-on models.

1. Remove the front wheel as described in this chapter.

2A. On 1986-1989 models, perform the following:
   a. If still installed, remove the speedometer gear housing and the right-hand side collar (**Figure 8**).
   b. Remove the dust seal (A, **Figure 16**) and the speedometer retainer (B, **Figure 16**) from the left-hand side.

2B. On 1990-on models, if still installed, remove the spacer (**Figure 6**) from the right- and left-hand side of the hub.

3. Before proceeding further, inspect the wheel bearings as described in this chapter. If they must be replaced, proceed as follows.

NOTE
The front disc on 1986-1989 models does not have a mark indicating which side of the wheel the disc belongs on. It is suggested that they be marked with either an "R" (right-hand side) or "L" (left-hand side) so they will be reinstalled on the same side of the wheel from which they were removed.

4. Remove the bolts securing the brake disc (**Figure 17**) on each side. Remove both discs and on 1986-1989 models, remove the damping shims located between the disc and the hub.

5. Remove the grease seal (**Figure 18**) from each side.

6. To remove the right- and left-hand bearings and distance collar, perform the following:
   a. Insert a soft aluminum or brass drift into one side of the hub.
   b. Push the distance collar over to one side and place the drift on the inner race of the lower bearing.
   c. Tap the bearing out of the hub with a hammer, working around the perimeter of the inner race.
   d. Repeat for the other bearing.

7. Clean the inside and the outside of the hub with solvent. Dry with compressed air.

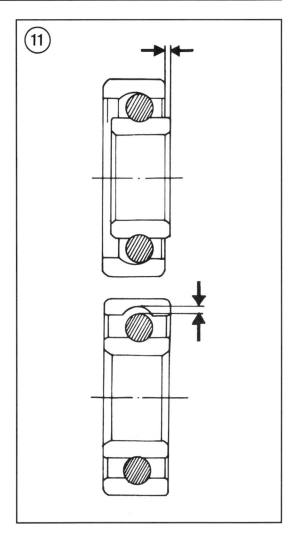

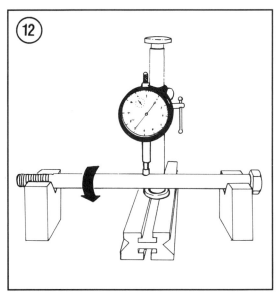

FRONT SUSPENSION AND STEERING

FRONT WHEEL (1986-1989)

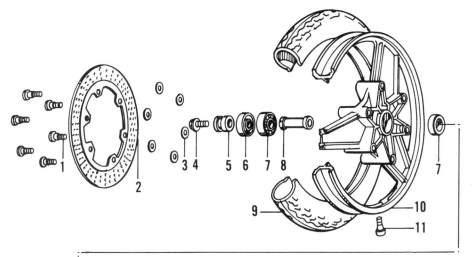

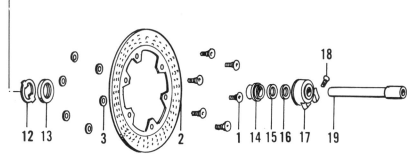

1. Bolt
2. Brake disc
3. Shim
4. Axle bolt
5. Side collar
6. Grease seal
7. Wheel bearing
8. Distance collar
9. Tire
10. Wheel
11. Valve stem
12. Speedometer retainer
13. Dust seal
14. Speedometer gear
15. Washer
16. Washer
17. Speedometer gear box
18. Screw
19. Front axle

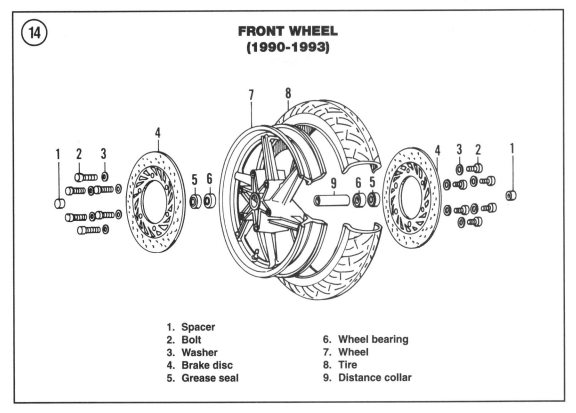

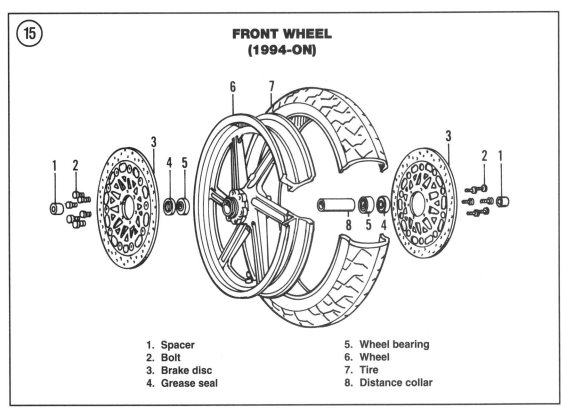

FRONT SUSPENSION AND STEERING

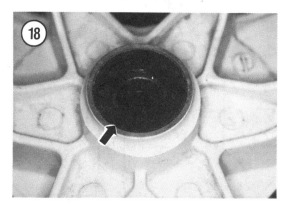

Assembly

1. On non-sealed bearings, pack the bearings with a good quality bearing grease. Work the grease in between the balls thoroughly; turn the bearing by hand a couple of times to make sure the grease is distributed evenly inside the bearing.

2. Blow any dirt or foreign matter out of the hub prior to installing the bearings.

CAUTION
*Install non-sealed bearings with the single sealed side facing outward. Tap the bearings squarely into place and tap on the outer race only. Use a socket (**Figure 19**) that matches the outer race diameter. Do not tap on the inner race or the bearing might be damaged. Be sure that the bearings are completely seated.*

3. First, install the right-hand bearing and press the distance collar into place.

4. Install the left-hand bearing.

5A. On the 1986-1989 front wheel, if the existing discs are being reinstalled, refer to the "R" or "L" marks made prior to removal and install the discs on the correct side of the wheel.

5B. On the 1990-1993 front wheel, note that the brake discs have either an "R" (right-hand side) or "L" (left-hand side) stamped on them. Be sure to install the disc with this mark facing outward and on the correct side of the wheel.

5C. On the 1994-on front wheel, note that the brake discs have an arrow indicating the proper direction of rotation. Be sure to install the disc with this mark facing outward and on the correct side of the wheel so the arrow is pointing in the correct direction.

5D. On the 1986-1989 front wheel, install the damping shims on the hub then install the disc and bolts.

5E. Tighten the Allen bolts to the torque specification listed in **Table 1**.

6. Install a new grease seal (**Figure 18**) on each side.

7A. On 1986-1989 models, perform the following:
 a. Pull the speedometer gear out of the speedometer gear box. Pack the cavity with multipurpose grease and reinstall the drive gear.
 b. Into the left-hand side, install the speedometer retainer (B, **Figure 16**) and the dust seal (A, **Figure 16**).

c. Align the slots of the speedometer drive gear with the raised tangs of the speedometer retainer and install the speedometer gear box.

d. Install the spacer (**Figure 8**) on the right-hand side.

7B. On 1990-on models, install the spacer (**Figure 6**) into the right- and left-hand side of the hub.

8. Install the front wheel as described in this chapter.

WHEELS

Wheel Balance

An unbalanced wheel is unsafe. Depending on the degree of unbalance and the speed of the motorcycle, the rider may experience anything from a mild vibration to a violent shimmy which may even result in loss of control.

On alloy wheels, weights are attached to the rim. A kit of weights may be purchased from most motorcycle supply stores. Some kits contain test weights and strips of adhesive-backed weights that can be cut to the desired weight and attached directly to the rim. Other weights are crimped directly onto the raised center rib of the wheel.

Before you attempt to balance the wheel, check to be sure that the wheel bearings are in good condition and properly lubricated and that the brakes do not drag. The wheel must rotate freely.

NOTE
When balancing the wheels, do so with the brake disc(s) (front and rear wheel) attached and on the rear wheel with the driven sprocket assembly attached. These components rotate with the wheels and they affect the balance.

1. Remove the wheel as described in this chapter or Chapter Eleven.

NOTE
The rear wheel on 1990 and later models requires a special holding fixture. Have this procedure performed by a Honda dealer's service department.

2. Mount the wheel on a fixture such as the one shown in **Figure 20** so it can rotate freely.

3. Give the wheel a spin and let it coast to a stop. Mark the tire at the lowest point.

4. Spin the wheel several more times. If the wheel keeps coming to rest at the same point, it is out of balance.

5. Attach a test weight to the upper (or light) side of the wheel.

6. Experiment with different weights until the wheel, when spun, comes to a rest at a different position each time.

7. Remove the test weight and install the correct size adhesive-backed or clamp-on weight (**Figure 21**).

Wheel Alignment

Refer to **Figure 22** for this procedure.

1. Measure the tires at their widest point.
2. Subtract the small dimension from the larger dimension.

FRONT SUSPENSION AND STEERING

3. Make an alignment tool out of wood, approximately 7 feet long, with an offset equal to one-half of the dimension obtained in Step 2. Refer to (D).

4. If the wheels are not aligned as in (A) and (C), the rear wheel must be shifted to correct the alignment.

5. Remove the cotter pin and loosen the rear axle nut.

6. To provide slack in the drive chain, refer to *Drive Chain Adjustment* in Chapter Three. Loosen the rear wheel and move the rear wheel until the wheels align.

7. Adjust the drive chain as described under *Drive Chain Adjustment* in Chapter Three.

TIRES

Tire Rating and Warnings

The Honda VFR700F and VFR750F models are factory equipped with tires rated for high speed running. When replacing the factory-equipped tires, be sure to purchase a tire of comparable rating. Refer to the *TIRE INFORMATION* label attached to the bike or listed in the Owner's Manual. Installing a lesser rated tire may result in instant tire failure at high speed riding that could result in loss of control.

After installing new tires on the bike, break them in correctly. Remember that a new tire has relatively poor adhesion to the road surface until it is broken in properly. Don't subject a new tire to any high speed riding for at least the first 60 miles (100 km).

Even after the tires are broken in properly, always warm them up prior to any high speed runs. This will lessen the possibility of loss of control of the bike. If you have purchased a tire brand other than those originally installed by the factory, maintain the correct tire inflation pressure recommended by *that tire manufacturer* and not those listed in **Table 2** located in Chapter Three. **Table 2** is for original equipment tires only.

Tubeless Tires

> *WARNING*
> *Do not install an inner tube inside a tubeless tire. The tube will cause an abnormal heat buildup in the tire.*

Tubeless tires have the word "TUBELESS" molded in the tire sidewall (**Figure 23**) and the rims have "SUITABLE FOR TUBELESS TIRES," "TUBELESS TIRE APPLICABLE," or equivalent cast on them.

When a tubeless tire is flat, it should be removed from the rim to inspect the inside of the tire and to apply a combination plug/patch from the inside. Don't rely on a plug or cord repair applied from outside the tire. They might be okay on a car, but they're too dangerous on a motorcycle.

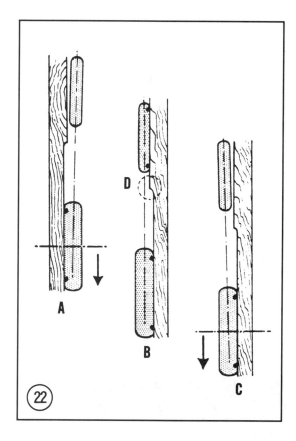

After repairing a tubeless tire, don't exceed 50 mph (80 kph) for the first 24 hours. Never race on a repaired tubeless tire. The patch could work loose from tire flexing and heat.

TUBELESS TIRE CHANGING

The wheels can easily be damaged during tire removal. Special care must be taken with tire irons when changing a tire to avoid scratches and gouges to the outer rim surface. Insert scraps of leather between the tire iron and the rim to protect the rim from damage. The stock cast wheels are designed for use with tubeless tires.

When removing a tubeless tire, take care not to damage the tire beads, inner liner of the tire or the wheel rim flange. Use tire levers or flat handled tire irons with rounded ends.

WARNING
Do not install tubeless tires on wheels designed for use only with tube-type tires. Personal injury and tire failure may result from rapid tire deflation while riding. Wheels for use with tubeless tires are so marked.

Removal

1. Mark the valve stem location on the tire (A, **Figure 24**), so the tire can be installed in the same position for easier balancing.
2. Remove the valve stem (B, **Figure 24**) core to deflate the tire.

NOTE
Removal of tubeless tires from their rims can be very difficult because of the exceptionally tight bead/rim seal. Breaking the bead seal may require the use of a special tool (Figure 25). If you are unable to break the seal loose, take the wheel to a motorcycle dealer and have them break it loose.

CAUTION
The inner rim and tire bead area are sealing surfaces on the tubeless tire. Do not scratch the inside of the rim or damage the tire bead.

3. Press the entire bead on both sides of the tire into the center of the rim.

4. Lubricate the beads with soapy water.

CAUTION
Use rim protectors or insert scraps of leather between the tire irons and the rim to protect the rim from damage.

5. Insert the tire iron under the bead next to the valve (**Figure 26**). Force the bead on the opposite side of the tire into the center of the rim and pry the bead over the rim with the tire iron.
6. Insert a second tire iron next to the first to hold the bead over the rim. Then work around the tire with the first tire iron, prying the bead over the rim (**Figure 27**).
7. Turn the tire over. Insert the tire iron between the second bead and the side of the rim that the first bead was pried over (**Figure 28**). Force the bead on the opposite side from the tire iron into the center of the rim. Pry the second bead off the rim, working around as with the first.
8. Inspect the valve stem seal. Because rubber deteriorates with age, it is advisable to replace the valve stem when replacing the tire.

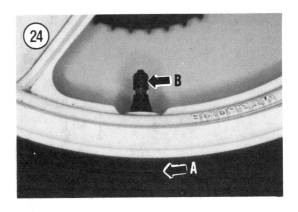

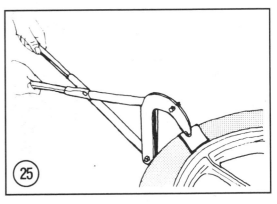

FRONT SUSPENSION AND STEERING

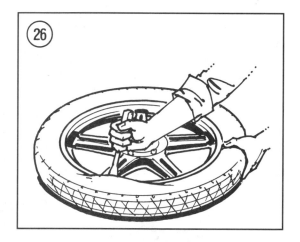

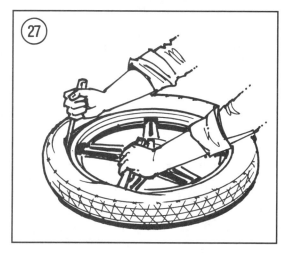

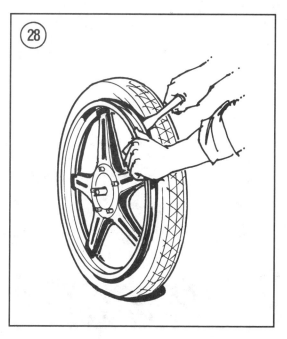

9. Remove the old valve stem and discard it. Inspect the valve stem hole in the rim. Remove any dirt or corrosion from the hole and wipe dry with a clean cloth.

Tire and Rim Inspection

1. Wipe off the inner surfaces of the wheel rim. Clean off any rubber residue or any oxidation.
2. If a can of pressurized tire sealant was used for a temporary fix of a flat, thoroughly clean off all sealant residue. Any remaining residue will present a problem when reinstalling the tire and achieving a good seal of the tire bead against the rim.
3. Inspect the rim inner flange. Smooth any scratches on the sealing surface with emery cloth. If a scratch is deeper than 0.5 mm (0.020 in.), the wheel should be replaced.

> *WARNING*
> *Since the VFR700F and VFR750F models are a high-performance bike, carefully consider whether a tire should be patched or replaced. If there is any doubt about the quality of the existing tire, **replace it with a new one**. Don't take a chance on a tire failure during a "canyon run."*

4. If a tire is going to be patched, thoroughly inspect the tire. If any one of the following is observed, do not repair the tire; *replace it with a new one*:
   a. A puncture or split whose total length or diameter exceeds 6 mm (0.24 in.).
   b. A scratch or split on the sidewall.
   c. Any type of ply separation.
   d. Tread separation or excessive abnormal wear pattern.
   e. Tread depth of less than 1.6 mm (0.06 in.) in the front tire or less than 2.0 mm (0.08 in.) in the rear tire on original equipment tires. Aftermarket tires' tread depth minimum may vary.
   f. Scratches on either sealing bead.
   g. The cord is cut in any place.
   h. Flat spots in the tread from skidding.
   i. Any abnormality in the inner liner.
5. Do not relay on a plug or cord patch applied from outside the tire. Use a combination plug/patch applied from inside the tire (**Figure 29**). Apply the plug/patch, following the instructions supplied with the patch kit.

6. Remove the valve stem from the rim.

7. If the valve stem is removed, inspect the valve hole in the wheel for dirt, rust or damage. Clean out the hole thoroughly prior to installing a new valve stem.

Installation

1. Carefully inspect the tire for any damage, especially inside.

2. A new tire may have balancing rubbers inside. These are not patches and should not be disturbed or removed.

3. Lubricate both beads of the tire with soapy water.

4. When installing the tire onto the rim make sure the correct tire, either front or rear is installed onto the correct wheel and also that the direction arrow (**Figure 30**) faces the direction of wheel rotation.

5. If remounting the old tire, align the mark made in Step 1, *Removal* with the valve stem. If a new tire is being installed, align the colored spot near the bead (indicating a lighter point on the tire) with the valve stem. Refer to **Figure 31**.

6. Place the backside of the tire into the center of the rim. The lower bead should go into the center of the rim and the upper bead outside. Work around the tire in both directions (**Figure 32**). Use a tire iron for the last few inches of bead (**Figure 33**).

7. Press the upper bead into the rim opposite the valve stem (**Figure 34**). Pry the bead into the rim on both sides of the initial point with a tire iron, working around the rim to the valve (**Figure 35**).

8. Check the bead on both sides of the tire for even fit around the rim.

9. Bounce the wheel several times, rotating it each time. This will force the tire beads against the rim flanges. After the tire beads are in contact with the rim evenly, inflate the tire to seat the beads.

10. Place an inflatable band around the circumference of the tire. Slowly inflate the band until the tire beads are pressed against the rim. Inflate the tire enough to seat it, deflate the band and remove it.

WARNING
In the next step never exceed 56 psi (40 kPa) inflation pressure as the tire could burst, causing severe injury. Never stand directly over a tire while inflating it.

11. After inflating the tire, check to see that the beads are fully seated and that the tire rim lines are the same distance from the rim all the way around the tire. If the beads won't seat, deflate the tire and re-lubricate the rim and beads with soapy water.

12. Re-inflate the tire to the required pressure. Install the valve stem cap.

13. Balance the wheel as described in this chapter.

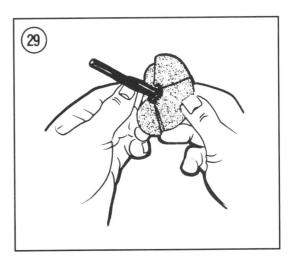

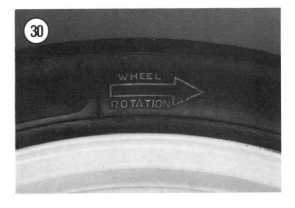

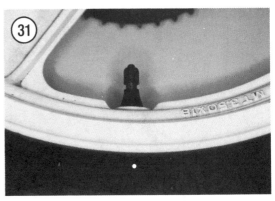

FRONT SUSPENSION AND STEERING

WARNING
*If you have repaired a tire, do not ride the bike any faster than 50 mph (80 km/h) for the first 24 hours. It takes at least 24 hours for a patch to cure. Also **never** ride the bike faster than 80 mph (130 km/h) with a repaired tire.*

TIRE REPAIRS

Patching a tubeless tire on the road is very difficult. If both beads are still against the rim, a can of pressurized tire sealant may inflate the tire and seal the hole, although this is only a temporary fix. The beads must be against the rim for this method to work. Another solution is to carry a spare inner tube that could be installed and inflated. This will enable you to get to a service station where the tire can be correctly repaired. Be sure that the inner tube is designed for use with tubeless tires.

Honda (and the tire industry) recommends that the tubeless tire be patched from the inside. Use a combination plug/patch applied from the inside the tire (**Figure 29**). Do not patch the tire with an external type plug. If you find an external patch on the tire, it is recommended that it be patch-reinforced from the inside. Due to the variations of material supplied with different tubeless tire repair kits, follow the instructions and recommendations supplied with the repair kit.

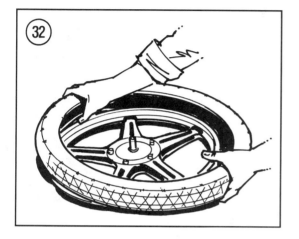

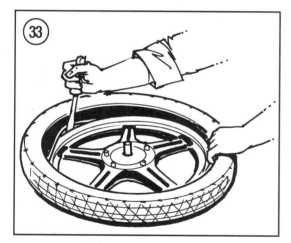

HANDLEBAR

Handlebar Assembly
Removal/Installation

NOTE
*If it is not necessary to remove the components from each handlebar for service, perform this procedure. If component removal is necessary, refer to the **Disassembly/Assembly** procedure in this chapter.*

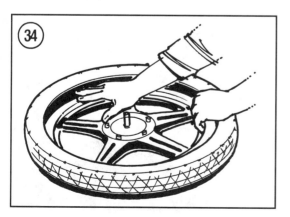

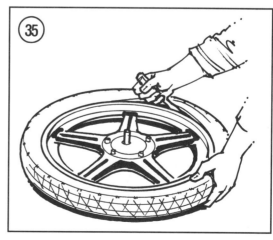

CAUTION
Cover the surrounding area with a heavy cloth or plastic tarp to protect it from accidental spilling of brake fluid from the brake and clutch master cylinders. Wash any spilled brake fluid off any painted or plated surface immediately, as it will destroy the finish. Use soapy water and rinse thoroughly.

1. Disconnect the battery negative lead as described under *Battery* in Chapter Three.

2A. On the right-hand handlebar, disconnect the brake light switch electrical connector (**Figure 36**).

2B. On the left-hand handlebar, disconnect the starter interlock switch electrical connector (**Figure 37**) on the clutch lever.

3. Remove the retaining ring from the top of the fork tube as follows:
    a. **Figure 38**: 1986-1989 models.
    b. A, **Figure 39**: 1990-1993 models.
    c. A, **Figure 40**: 1994-on models.

4. Loosen the handlebar pinch bolt as follows:
    a. **Figure 41**: 1986-1989 models.
    b. B, **Figure 39**: 1990-1993 models.
    c. B, **Figure 40**: 1994-on models.

5. Remove the handlebar assembly from the fork tube and upper fork bridge.

6. On the right-hand handlebar assembly, tie the handlebar assembly up to the front fairing to keep the front brake master cylinder horizontal in the upright position. This is to minimize loss of brake fluid and to keep air from entering into the brake system. It is not necessary to remove the hydraulic brake line.

7. Repeat for the other handlebar assembly.

8. On the left-hand handlebar assembly, tie the handlebar assembly up to the front fairing to keep the clutch master cylinder horizontal in the upright position. This is to minimize loss of hydraulic fluid and to keep air from entering into the clutch system. It is not necessary to remove the hydraulic brake line.

9. Install by reversing these removal steps while noting the following:
    a. Tighten the mounting bolts to the torque specification listed in **Table 1**.
    b. Adjust the throttle operation as described in Chapter Three.

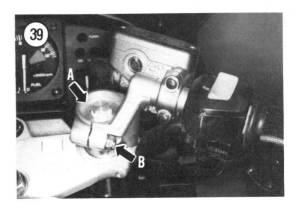

FRONT SUSPENSION AND STEERING

WARNING
*After installation is completed, make sure the brake lever does not come in contact with the throttle grip assembly when it is pulled on fully. If it does, the brake fluid may be low in the reservoir; refill as necessary. Refer to **Front Disc Brakes** in Chapter Eleven.*

Handlebar Disassembly/Assembly

NOTE
If it is necessary to remove the components from the handlebar for service, perform this procedure. If component removal is not necessary, refer to the preceding Handlebar Assembly Removal/Installation procedure as described in this chapter.

Right-hand handlebar

1. Disconnect the battery negative lead as described *Battery* in Chapter Three.

2. Disconnect the brake light switch electrical connector (**Figure 36**).

CAUTION
Cover the surrounding area with a heavy cloth or plastic tarp to protect it from accidental spilling of brake fluid. Wash any spilled brake fluid off any painted or plated surface immediately, as it will destroy the finish. Use soapy water and rinse thoroughly.

3. Remove the 2 bolts securing the brake master cylinder (A, **Figure 42**) and remove the assembly from the handlebar. Tie the brake master cylinder to the front fairing mounting bracket and keep the reservoir in the upright position. This is to minimize loss of brake fluid and to keep air from entering into the brake system. It is not necessary to remove the hydraulic brake line.

4. Remove the screws securing the right-hand handlebar switch assembly (B, **Figure 42**).

5. Remove the throttle assembly and carefully lay the throttle assembly and cables over the fender or back over the frame. Be careful that the cables do not get crimped or damaged.

6. Remove the retaining ring from the top of the fork tube as follows:
   a. **Figure 38**: 1986-1989 models.
   b. A, **Figure 39**: 1990-1993 models.
   c. A, **Figure 40**: 1994-on models.

7. Loosen the handlebar pinch bolt as follows:
   a. **Figure 41**: 1986-1989 models.
   b. B, **Figure 39**: 1990-1993 models.
   c. B, **Figure 40**: 1994-on models.

8. Remove the handlebar assembly from the fork tube and upper fork bridge.

9. Install by reversing these removal steps while noting the following:
   a. Apply a light coat of multipurpose grease to the throttle grip area on the handlebar prior to installing the throttle grip assembly.
   b. Align the locating pin the switch in the lower portion of the right-hand switch assembly with the hole in the handlebar and install the switch. Tighten the screws securely.
   c. Tighten all mounting bolts and clamping bolts to the torque specification listed in **Table 1**.
   d. Install the brake master cylinder onto the handlebar. Position the holder with the UP mark (A, **Figure 43**) facing up.
   e. Align the clamp with the index mark on the handlebar (B, **Figure 43**). Tighten the upper bolt first and then the lower bolt. Tighten the bolts securely.

   WARNING
   *After installation is completed, make sure the brake lever does not come in contact with the throttle grip assembly when it is pulled on fully. If it does, the brake fluid may be low in the reservoir; refill as necessary. Refer to **Front Disc Brakes** in Chapter Twelve.*

   f. Adjust the throttle operation as described in Chapter Three.

Left-hand handlebar

1. Disconnect the battery negative lead as described under *Battery* in Chapter Three.
2. Disconnect the starter interlock switch electrical connector (**Figure 37**) on the clutch lever.

   CAUTION
   Cover the surrounding area with a heavy cloth or plastic tarp to protect it from accidental spilling of clutch hydraulic fluid. Wash any spilled brake fluid off any painted or plated surface immediately, as it will destroy the finish. Use soapy water and rinse thoroughly.

3. Remove the 2 bolts securing the clutch master cylinder (A, **Figure 44**) and remove the assembly from the handlebar. Tie the clutch master cylinder to the front fairing mounting bracket and keep the reservoir in the upright position. This is to minimize

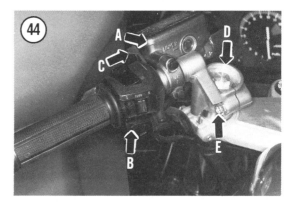

FRONT SUSPENSION AND STEERING

loss of hydraulic fluid and to keep air from entering into the clutch system. It is not necessary to remove the hydraulic clutch line.

4. Remove the screws securing the left-hand handlebar switch assembly (B, **Figure 44**).

5. Disconnect the choke cable from the choke lever assembly (C, **Figure 44**).

6. Remove the retaining ring from the top of the fork tube as follows:
   a. **Figure 45**: 1986-1989 models.
   b. D, **Figure 44**: 1990-1993 models.
   c. A, **Figure 46**: 1994-on models.

7. Loosen the handlebar pinch bolt as follows:
   a. **Figure 47**: 1986-1989 models.
   b. E, **Figure 44**: 1990-1993 models.
   c. B, **Figure 46**: 1994-on models.

8. Remove the handlebar assembly from the fork tube and upper fork bridge.

9. Install by reversing these removal steps while noting the following:
   a. Align the locating pin of the switch in the lower portion of the left-hand switch assembly with the hole in the handlebar and install the switch. Tighten the screws securely.
   b. Tighten all mounting bolts and clamping bolts to the torque specification listed in **Table 1**.
   c. Install the clutch master cylinder onto the handlebar. Position the holder with the UP mark (**Figure 48**) facing up.
   d. Align the clamp with the index mark on the handlebar (**Figure 49**). Tighten the upper bolt first and then the lower bolt. Tighten the bolts securely.

STEERING HEAD AND STEM

Disassembly

Refer to the following illustrations for this procedure:
   a. **Figure 50**: 1986-1989 models.
   b. **Figure 51**: 1990-on models.

1. Remove the front fairing as described under *Front Fairing Removal/Installation* in Chapter Thirteen.

2. Remove the bolts securing the brake hose and reflector mounting bracket (A, **Figure 52**) assembly to each fork leg.

3. Remove the bolts securing the front fender (B, **Figure 52**) and remove the front fender.

4. Remove the front wheel as described in this chapter.

5. Loosen the upper fork bridge clamp bolts (**Figure 53**).

6. Remove both handlebar assemblies (A, **Figure 54**) as described in this chapter.

7. Remove the steering stem nut cap (B, **Figure 54**).

8. Remove the front brake 2-way joint as described in Chapter Twelve.

9. Remove the horn assembly from the lower fork bridge.

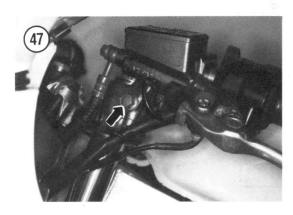

CHAPTER TEN

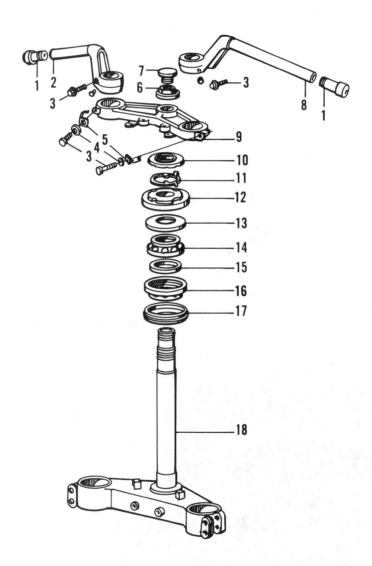

**STEERING STEM
(1986-1989)**

1. Weight/bolt
2. Handlebar—right-hand
3. Bolt
4. Washer
5. Wire clamp
6. Steering stem nut
7. Cap
8. Handlebar—left-hand
9. Upper fork bridge
10. Locknut
11. Lockwasher
12. Steering stem adjust nut
13. Dust seal
14. Upper bearing
15. Grease holder
16. Lower bearing
17. Lower race
18. Steering stem

FRONT SUSPENSION AND STEERING

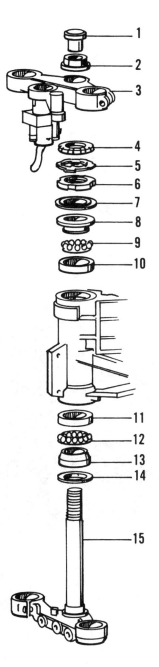

STEERING STEM (1990-ON)

1. Cap
2. Steering stem nut
3. Upper fork bridge
4. Locknut
5. Lockwasher
6. Steering stem adjust nut
7. Dust seal
8. Inner race
9. Upper bearing
10. Outer race
11. Outer race
12. Lower bearing
13. Inner race
14. Dust seal
15. Steering stem

10. Remove the steering stem nut (C, **Figure 54**).
11. On 1990-on models, disconnect the ignition switch electrical connector. The ignition switch will come off along with the upper fork bridge on these models.
12. Remove the upper fork bridge (D, **Figure 54**) from the fork tubes and steering stem.
13. Loosen the lower fork bridge clamp bolts (A, **Figure 55**) and remove both fork assemblies (B, **Figure 55**) from the lower fork bridge.
14. Bend down the locking tabs from the grooves in the lockwasher out from the grooves in the locknut.
15. Remove the locknut and the lockwasher. Discard the lockwasher.
16. Loosen the steering stem adjust nut. To loosen the nut, use a large drift and hammer or use the easily improvised tool shown in **Figure 56**. Honda offers a special tool for this purpose (Steering stem socket—part No. 07916-3710100).
17. Have an assistant hold onto the steering stem and remove the steering stem adjust nut and dust seal.
18. Lower the steering stem out of the steering head. Don't worry about catching any loose steel balls as the steering stem is equipped with assembled ball bearings.
19. Remove the upper bearing and grease holder from the top of the steering head.

Inspection

1. Clean the bearing races in the steering head and the bearings with solvent.
2. Check the welds around the steering head for cracks and fractures. If any are found, have them repaired by a competent frame shop or welding service.
3. Check the bearings for pitting, scratches or discoloration indicating wear or corrosion.
4. Check the races for pitting, galling and corrosion. If any of these conditions exist, replace the races as described in this chapter.
5. Check the steering stem for cracks and check its race for damage or wear. Replace if necessary.
6. Thread the steering stem adjust nut onto the steering stem. Make sure it screws on easily with no roughness. Unscrew the steering stem adjust nut. If necessary clean the threads on both parts with a wire brush or tap and die of the correct thread type and size.

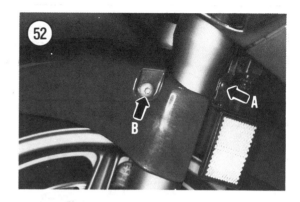

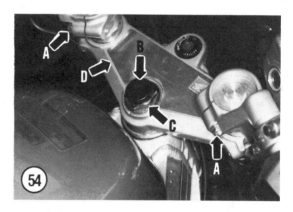

FRONT SUSPENSION AND STEERING

Assembly

Refer to the following illustrations for this procedure:
 a. **Figure 50**: 1986-1989 models.
 b. **Figure 51**: 1990-on models.

1. Make sure both steering head bearing outer races are properly seated in the steering head tube.
2. Pack the bearing cavities of both ball bearings with bearing grease. Coat the outer bearing races, within the steering head, with bearing grease also.
3. Apply a coat of grease to the threads of the steering stem and steering stem adjust nut.
4. Install the steering stem, with the lower bearing in place, into the steering head tube and hold it firmly in place.
5. Install a new grease holder and the upper roller bearing into the steering stem.
6. Install the steering stem adjust nut and tighten it to the torque specification listed in **Table 1**.
7. Turn the steering stem from lock-to-lock 5-6 times to seat the bearings.
8. Loosen the steering stem nut and repeat Step 6 and Step 7 twice more to make sure the bearings are properly seated.
9. Install a new lockwasher and insert 2 opposite tabs of the lockwasher into the notches in the steering stem adjust nut as shown in **Figure 57**. Always install a *new* lockwasher; never reinstall a used one as the tabs may break off, making the lockwasher ineffective.
10. Install the locknut and hand-tighten it. Further tighten the locknut just until the grooves align with 2 of the tabs of the lockwasher. Bend the 2 tabs up into the grooves in the locknut as shown in **Figure 57**.

NOTE
If the grooves in the locknut will not align easily with 2 of the tabs of the locknut, remove the locknut, turn it over and reinstall the locknut. Repeat Step 10.

11. Install the upper fork bridge and the steering stem nut. Tighten the steering stem nut only finger-tight at this time.

CAUTION
The temporary installation of the forks in Step 12 is necessary to properly align the upper fork bridge to the lower fork bridge. Do not eliminate this step as it will lead to improper steering alignment.

12. Temporarily install the fork tubes in the lower fork bridge and up through the upper fork bridge by about 1 inch. Tighten the lower fork bridge bolts securely.
13. Tighten the steering stem nut to the torque specification listed in **Table 1**.
14. Install the steering stem nut cap.
15. Remove, then properly install the front forks as described in this chapter.

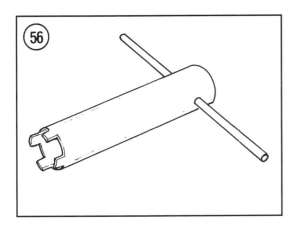

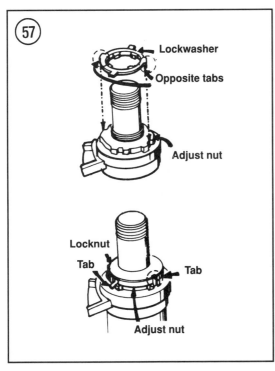

16. On 1990-on models, reconnect the ignition switch electrical connector.

17. Install the horn assembly from the lower fork bridge.

18. Install the front brake 2-way joint as described in Chapter Twelve.

19. Install both handlebar assemblies as described in this chapter.

20. Install the front fairing as described in Chapter Thirteen.

21. Install the front fender and tighten the bolts securely.

22. Install the front wheel as described in this chapter.

Steering Stem Adjustment

If play develops or there is binding in the steering system, it may only require adjustment. However, don't take a chance on it. Disassemble the steering stem assembly and look for possible damage as described in this chapter.

STEERING HEAD BEARING RACE

The headset and steering stem bearing races are pressed into place. Because they are easily bent, do not remove them unless they are worn and require replacement.

The top and bottom bearing races are not the same size. The bottom race has a larger inside diameter than the upper race. Be sure that you install them in the proper ends of the frame steering head tube.

Steering Head Bearing Outer Race Replacement

To remove the headset race, insert a hardwood stick or soft punch into the head tube (**Figure 58**) and carefully tap the race out from the inside. After it is started, tap around the race so that neither the race nor the steering head tube is damaged.

The inside diameter of the inner races are different. The lower bearing race has a *larger* inside diameter than the upper.

To install the steering head bearing race, tap it in slowly with a block of wood, a suitable size socket or piece of pipe (**Figure 59**). Make sure that the race is squarely seated in the steering head race bore before tapping it into place. Tap the race in until it is flush with the steering head surface.

Steering Stem Lower Bearing Assembly and Dust Seal Removal/Installation

CAUTION
*Do **not** move the steering stem lower bearing race unless it is going to be replaced with a new bearing race. Do **not** reinstall a bearing race that has been removed, as it is no longer true to alignment.*

1. Install the steering stem adjust nut onto the steering stem to protect the threads during this procedure.

2. To remove the steering stem lower bearing assembly, carefully pry it up from the base of the steering stem with a screwdriver; work around in a circle, prying a little at a time. Remove the bearing assembly and the dust seal.

3. Remove the steering stem adjust nut.

4. Slide a new dust seal over the steering stem.

5. Slide the lower bearing assembly over the steering stem.

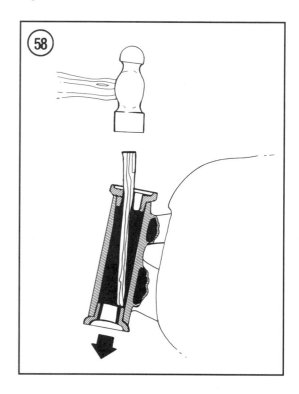

FRONT SUSPENSION AND STEERING

Tap the race down with a long piece of metal pipe that fits the inner race diameter or use a piece of hardwood; work around in a circle so the bearing and inner race will not be bent. Make sure it is seated squarely and is all the way down.

FRONT FORKS

The front suspension uses a spring controlled, hydraulically damped telescopic fork. On 1986-1989 models, there is air assist feature on both fork legs and an anti-dive feature is built into the left-hand fork leg. The anti-dive unit is covered separately from the fork procedure.

Before suspecting major trouble, drain the front fork oil and refill with the proper type and quantity. If you still have trouble, such as poor damping, a tendency to bottom or top out or leakage around the rubber seals, follow the service procedures in this section.

To simplify fork service and to prevent the mixing of parts, the legs should be removed, serviced and installed individually.

Removal

NOTE
Step 1 is not necessary but it does allow additional working space for ease of component removal. It also reduces the possibility of damage to the front fairing components during fork removal and installation.

1. If necessary, remove the front fairing as described under *Front Fairing Removal/Installation* in Chapter Thirteen.
2. Remove the bolts securing the brake hose and reflector mounting bracket (A, **Figure 52**) assembly to each fork leg.
3. Remove the bolts securing the front fender (B, **Figure 52**) and remove the front fender.
4. Remove the front wheel as described in this chapter.
5. Remove both handlebar assemblies (A, **Figure 60**) as described in this chapter.

WARNING
On 1986-1989 models, always bleed off all air pressure; failure to do so may cause personal injury when disassembling the fork assembly.

NOTE
On 1986-1989 models, release the air pressure gradually. If released too fast, fork oil will spurt out with the air. Protect your eyes and clothing accordingly.

6. On 1986-1989 models, remove the air valve cap (**Figure 61**) from each fork cap tube and bleed off

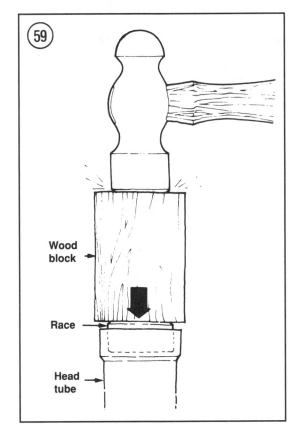

all air pressure by depressing the valve stem (**Figure 62**).

7. Loosen the upper (B, **Figure 60**) fork bridge bolts. If the fork legs are going to be disassembled, loosen the fork cap bolt at this time.
8. Loosen the lower (A, **Figure 55**) fork bridge bolts.
9. Lower the fork assembly (B, **Figure 55**) from the upper and lower fork bridges. It may be necessary to slightly rotate the fork tube while pulling it down and out.
10. Repeat Steps 7-9 for the other fork assembly.

Installation

1. Install the fork tubes up through the lower fork bridge and then the upper fork bridge.
2A. On 1986-1993 models, push the fork tube up until the groove (**Figure 63**) in the top of the fork tube is flush with the top surface of the upper fork bridge.
2B. On 1994 models, push the fork tube up until the top of the fork tube is 39 mm (1.53 in.) above the top surface (dimension "A") of the upper fork bridge (**Figure 64**).
3. Tighten the lower fork bridge bolt(s) to the torque specification listed in **Table 1**.
4. Tighten the upper fork bridge bolt to the torque specification listed in **Table 1**.
5. Install the front fender and tighten the bolts securely.
6. Install the handlebar assemblies as described in this chapter.
7. Install the front wheel as described in this chapter.
8. Install the front fairing as described in Chapter Thirteen.

> *WARNING*
> *Never use any type of compressed gas, as an explosion may be lethal. Never heat the fork assembly with a torch or place it near an open flame or extreme heat, as this will also result in an explosion.*

> *CAUTION*
> *Never exceed an air pressure of 30 kPa (43 psi), as damage may occur to internal components of the fork assembly.*

9. Make sure the front wheel is off the ground and inflate the forks to 0-4 kPa (0-6 psi). Do not use

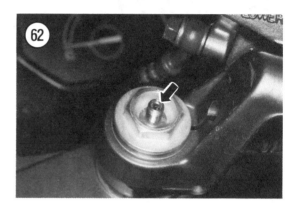

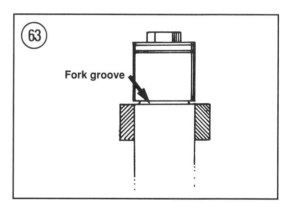

Fork groove

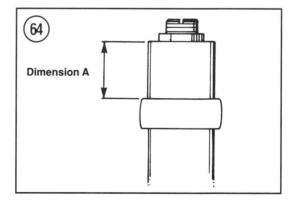

Dimension A

FRONT SUSPENSION AND STEERING

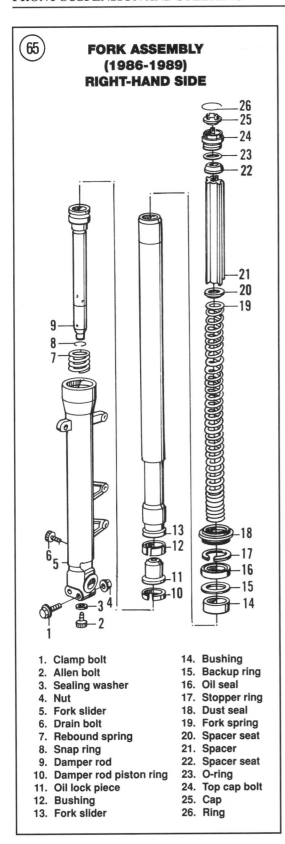

FORK ASSEMBLY (1986-1989) RIGHT-HAND SIDE

1. Clamp bolt
2. Allen bolt
3. Sealing washer
4. Nut
5. Fork slider
6. Drain bolt
7. Rebound spring
8. Snap ring
9. Damper rod
10. Damper rod piston ring
11. Oil lock piece
12. Bushing
13. Fork slider
14. Bushing
15. Backup ring
16. Oil seal
17. Stopper ring
18. Dust seal
19. Fork spring
20. Spacer seat
21. Spacer
22. Spacer seat
23. O-ring
24. Top cap bolt
25. Cap
26. Ring

compressed air, only use a small hand-operated air pump.

10. Apply the front brake and pump the forks several times. Recheck the air pressure and readjust if necessary.

FRONT FORKS
(1986-1989)

Disassembly

Refer to the following illustrations for this procedure:

a. **Figure 65**: right-hand fork leg.
b. **Figure 66**: left-hand fork leg.

> *WARNING*
> *Always bleed off all air pressure; failure to do so may cause personal injury when disassembling the fork assembly.*

> *NOTE*
> *Release the air pressure gradually. If released too fast, fork oil will spurt out with the air. Protect your eyes and clothing accordingly.*

1. If the air pressure was not released prior to removing the fork assembly, remove the air valve cap (**Figure 61**) from each fork cap tube and bleed off *all* air pressure by depressing the valve stem (**Figure 62**).

2. Clamp the slider in a vise with soft jaws.

> *NOTE*
> *This Allen head bolt has been secured with a locking compound and is often very difficult to remove because the damper rod will turn inside the slider. It sometimes can be removed with an air impact driver. If you are unable to remove it, take the fork tubes to a dealer and have the screws removed.*

3. *Loosen* the Allen head bolt at the bottom of the slider. Do not remove it at this time, as the fork oil will drain out.

4. If the fork cap bolt was not loosened during removal, hold the upper fork tube in a vise with soft jaws and loosen the fork cap bolt.

CHAPTER TEN

**FORK ASSEMBLY
(1986-1989)
LEFT-HAND SIDE**

1. Allen bolt
2. Sealing washer
3. Bolt
4. Washer
5. Spring
6. Check ball
7. Clamp bolt
8. Allen screw
9. Knob
10. O-ring
11. Orifice
12. Nut
13. Drain screw
14. Spring
15. O-ring
16. Piston
17. Case
18. O-ring
19. Boot
20. Needle bearing
21. Collar
22. Fork slider
23. Circlip
24. Oil lock piece
25. Spring
26. Spring seat
27. Rebound spring
28. Circlip
29. Damper rod
30. Piston seal
31. Piston seal
32. Fork spring
33. Bushing
34. Fork tube
35. Bushing
36. Backup ring
37. Oil seal
38. Stopper ring
39. Dust seal
40. Spacer seat
41. Spacer
42. Spacer seat
43. O-ring
44. Top cap bolt
45. Cap
46. Ring

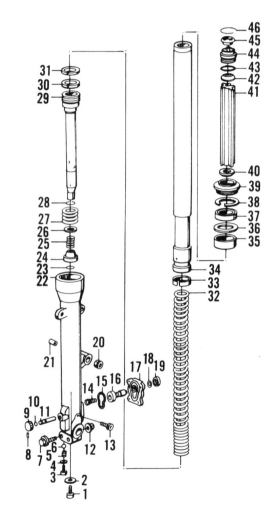

FRONT SUSPENSION AND STEERING

WARNING
Be careful when removing the fork cap bolt as the spring is under pressure. Protect your eyes accordingly.

5. Remove the fork cap bolt (**Figure 67**) from the fork.
6. Remove the spacer seat, spacer, spacer seat and the fork spring.
7. Remove the fork from the vise, pour the fork oil out and discard it. Pump the fork several times by hand to expel most of the remaining oil.
8. Remove the dust seal.
9. Using circlip pliers, remove the stopper ring (**Figure 68**).

NOTE
On this type of fork, force is needed to remove the fork tube from the slider.

10. Remove the Allen head bolt and gasket from the base of the slider.
11. Install the fork slider in a vise with soft jaws.
12. There is an interference fit between the bushing in the fork slider and the bushing on the fork tube. In order to remove the fork tube from the slider, pull hard on the fork tube using quick in and out strokes (**Figure 69**). Doing this will withdraw the bushing, backup ring and oil seal from the slider.

NOTE
It may be necessary to slightly heat the area on the slider around the oil seal prior to removal. Use a rag soaked in hot water; do not apply a flame directly to the fork slider.

13. Withdraw the fork tube from the slider.

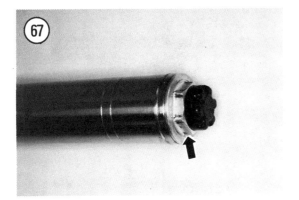

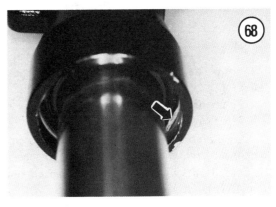

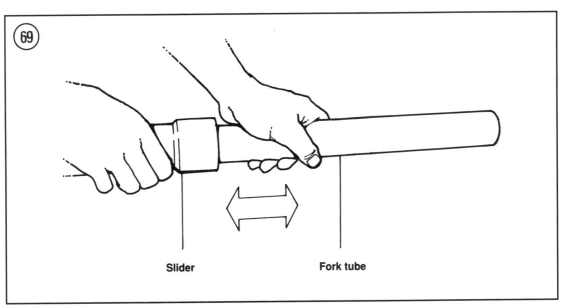

CHAPTER TEN

NOTE
Do not remove the fork tube bushing unless it is going to be replaced. Inspect it as described in this chapter.

14. Turn the fork tube upside down and slide off the oil seal, backup ring and slider bushing from the fork tube.
15A. On the left-hand fork leg, remove the lower circlip, oil lock valve, spring, spring seat and upper circlip from the damper rod.
15B. On the right-hand fork leg, remove the oil lock piece and circlip from the damper rod.
16. Remove the damper rod and rebound spring from the slider.
17. Inspect all parts as described in this chapter.
18. On the left-hand fork leg, if necessary, disassemble the anti-dive unit as described in this chapter.
19. Inspect all parts as described in this chapter.

Assembly

Refer to the following illustrations for this procedure:
  a. **Figure 65**: right-hand fork leg.
  b. **Figure 66**: left-hand fork leg.
1. On the left-hand fork leg, if disassembled, assemble the anti-dive unit as described in this chapter.
2. Coat all parts with fresh automatic transmission fluid (ATF) or fork oil prior to installation.
3. If removed, install a new fork tube bushing.
4. Install the rebound spring (A, **Figure 70**) onto the damper rod and insert this assembly (B, **Figure 70**) into the fork tube.
5A. On the left-hand fork leg, refer to **Figure 71** and install the upper circlip (A), spring seat (B), spring (C), oil lock valve (D) (shoulder end going on last) and the lower circlip (E). Make sure both circlips are correctly seated in the damper rod grooves (**Figure 72**).
5B. On the right-hand fork leg, install the circlip and the oil lock piece. Make sure the circlip is correctly seated in the damper rod groove.
6. Temporarily install the fork spring, spacer seat, spacer and spacer seat.
7. Install the fork cap bolt and push down on it to compress the spring. Start the bolt slowly, don't cross thread it. Tighten the cap bolt securely but not to the specified torque specifications at this time.

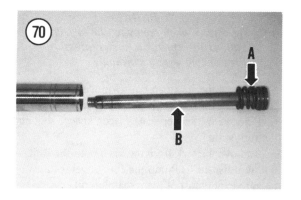

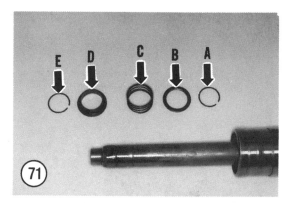

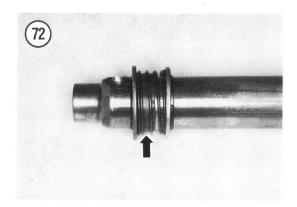

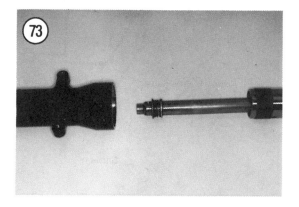

FRONT SUSPENSION AND STEERING

74

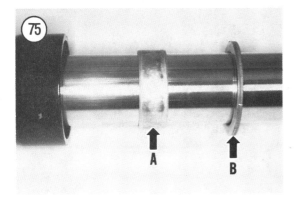

75

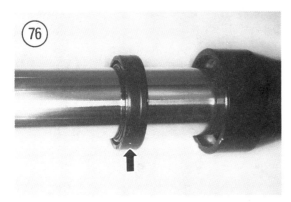

76

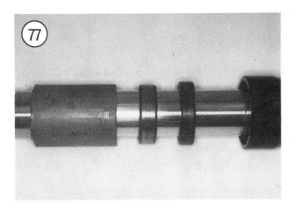

77

8. Install the upper fork assembly into the slider (**Figure 73**).

9. Make sure the gasket is on the Allen head bolt (**Figure 74**).

10. Apply red Loctite (No. 271) to the threads of the Allen head bolt prior to installation. Install it in the fork slider and tighten to the torque specification listed in **Table 1**.

11. To install the fork slider bushing and back-up ring, perform the following:
   a. Slide the slider bushing (A, **Figure 75**) and back-up ring (B, **Figure 75**) down the fork tube.
   b. If you have an old fork slider bushing, place it on top of the back-up ring.
   c. Drive the bushing into the fork slider with the Honda fork seal driver (part No. 07747-0010100) and attachment (part No. 07747-0010600) or an equivalent driver assembly.
   d. Drive the bushing into place until it seats completely in the recess in the slider.
   e. Remove the installation tool and the old fork slider bushing (if used).

NOTE
To avoid damaging the fork seal and dust seal when installing them over the top of the fork tube, place a plastic bag over the fork tube and coat it thoroughly with ATF or fork oil. You can then slide both seals over the plastic bag without damaging them.

12. To install the fork seal, perform the following:
   a. Coat the new seal with ATF or fork oil.
   b. Install the oil seal (**Figure 76**) over the fork tube with the manufacturer's name and size code facing up. Slide it down the fork tube.
   c. Drive the oil seal into the slider with the same tool used during Step 11 as shown in **Figure 77**.
   d. Drive the oil seal in until the groove in the slider can be seen above the top surface of the oil seal.
   e. Remove the installation tool and the old fork slider bushing (if used).

13. Position the stopper ring (**Figure 78**) with the sharp side facing up and install the stopper ring. Make sure the stopper ring is completely seated in the groove in the fork slider (**Figure 68**).

14. Install the dust seal (**Figure 79**). Push it on until it is completely seated.

15. Remove the fork cap bolt from the fork.

16. Remove the spacer seat, spacer, spacer seat and the fork spring.

17. Fill the fork tube with the correct quantity of automatic transmission fluid (ATF). Refer to **Table 3** for specified quantity and oil level.

18. Check the fork oil level in each fork assembly as follows:
   a. Hold the fork tube vertical and *completely* compress the fork tube into the slider.
   b. Use an accurate ruler or a measuring device and measure the distance from the top surface of the oil to the top surface of the fork tube. Adjust the oil level as necessary.

NOTE
*An oil level measuring device can be made as shown in **Figure 80**. Position the lower edge of the hose clamp the specified oil level distance up from the small diameter hole. Fill the fork with a few ml's more than the required amount of oil. Position the hose clamp on the top edge of the fork tube and draw out the excess oil. Oil is sucked out until the level reaches the small diameter hole. A*

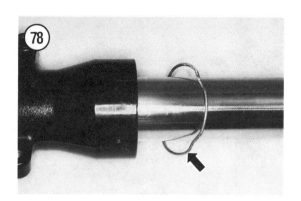

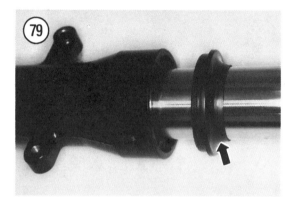

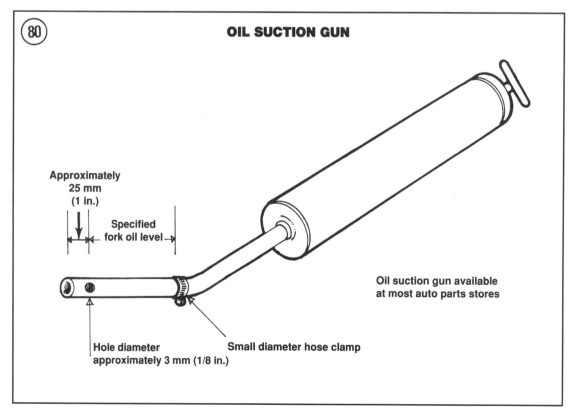

FRONT SUSPENSION AND STEERING

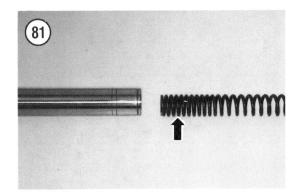

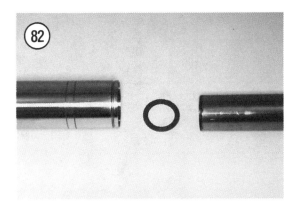

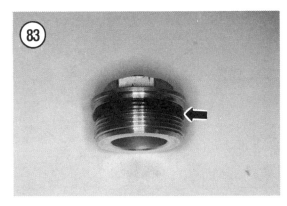

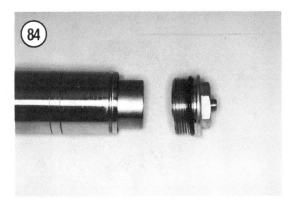

precise oil level can be achieved with this simple device.

19. Position the fork spring with the tapered end pointing *down* toward the slider (**Figure 81**) and install the spring.

20. Position each fork spring spacer seat with the cupped side facing toward the spacer. Install the fork spring lower spacer seat, the spacer and the upper spacer seat (**Figure 82**).

21. Inspect the O-ring seal (**Figure 83**) on the fork cap bolt; replace if necessary.

22. Install the fork cap bolt (**Figure 84**) and push down on it to compress the spring. Start the bolt slowly, don't cross thread it.

23. Place the slider in a vise with soft jaws and tighten the fork cap bolt (**Figure 67**) to the torque specifications listed in **Table 1**.

24. Install the fork assembly as described in this chapter.

Inspection

1. Thoroughly clean all parts in solvent and dry them. Check the fork tube for signs of wear or scratches.

2. Check the damper rod for straightness. **Figure 85** shows one method. The rod should be replaced if the runout is 0.2 mm (0.01 in.) or greater.

3. Make sure the damper rod oil passage hole (A, **Figure 86**) is clear. If clogged or congested, clean out with solvent and dry with compressed air.

4. Inspect the damper rod circlip groove(s) (B, **Figure 86**) to ensure it is free of burrs. Clean out if necessary.

5. On the left-hand fork leg damper rod, refer to **Figure 87** inspect the upper circlip (A), spring seat (B), spring (C), oil lock valve (D) and the lower circlip (E).

6. Carefully check the damper rod, piston ring(s) grooves (A, **Figure 88**) and piston ring(s) (B, **Figure 88**) for wear or damage. Install the piston ring(s) (**Figure 89**) and make sure they are properly seated.

7. On the left-hand fork leg slider, inspect the caliper bracket pivot needle bearing, collar and oil seals (**Figure 90**) for wear or damage. Replace if necessary.

8. Inspect the fork oil seal (**Figure 91**) for wear or deterioration. Replace if necessary.

9. Check the fork tube (**Figure 92**) for straightness. If bent or severely scratched, it should be replaced.

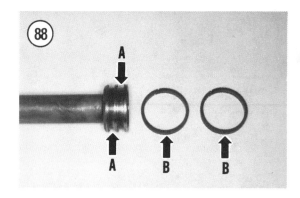

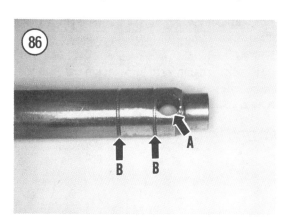

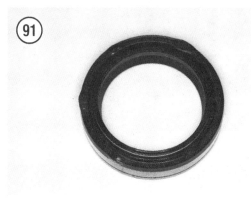

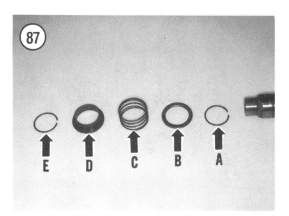

FRONT SUSPENSION AND STEERING

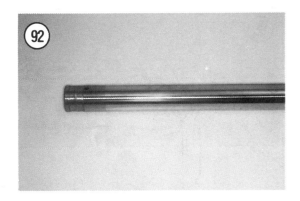

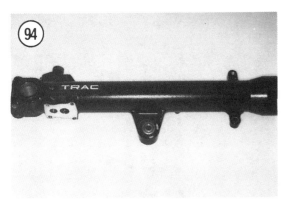

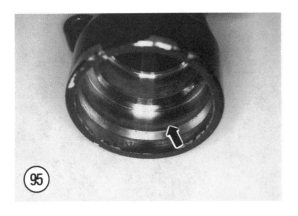

10. Inspect the cap bolt threads (**Figure 93**) in the fork tube. Clean out if necessary with the appropriate size metric tap.

11. Check the slider (**Figure 94**) for dents or exterior damage that may cause the fork tube to hang up during riding. Replace if necessary.

12. Check the fork seal area (**Figure 95**) in the slider for wear or damage. Replace if necessary.

13. Measure the un-compressed length of the fork spring (not rebound spring) as shown in **Figure 96**. If the spring has sagged to the service limit dimensions listed in **Table 4**, the spring must be replaced.

14. Inspect the slider and fork tube bushings (**Figure 97**). If either is scratched or scored it must be replaced. If the Teflon coating is worn off so that the copper base material is showing on approximately 3/4 of the total surface, the bushing must be replaced. Also check for distortion on the check points of the backup ring; replace as necessary. Refer to **Figure 98**.

15. Inspect the air valve (**Figure 99**) in the fork cap for damage. Replace if necessary.

16. Any parts that are worn or damaged should be replaced. Simply cleaning and reinstalling unserv-

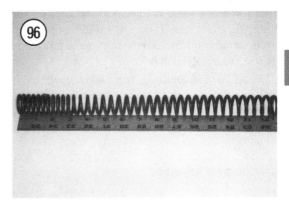

iceable components will not improve performance of the front suspension.

ANTI-DIVE FRONT SUSPENSION (1986-1989 MODELS)

The 1986-1989 models are equipped with the anti-dive control system integrated into the left-hand fork leg. The system reacts to the forward weight transfer of the bike and rider(s) during braking.

The left-hand caliper assembly is pivot-mounted on the fork slider. As the brake is applied, the caliper tries to move, or ride, with the disc thus pivoting the caliper assembly toward the anti-dive unit. This action forces a tab on the caliper assembly against the piston and main spring in the anti-dive unit.

As the anti-dive piston moves in, it uncovers the oil control orifice to restrict the fork leg's compression-damping passageway, thus diverting the fork oil through a small secondary valve (oil control orifice). The internal damping action increases, the fork resists compression and the anti-dive action is created. The harder the brake is applied, the further the valve moves and the greater the anti-dive action. The secondary valve is adjustable and controls the damping effect rate. There are 4 different settings, from soft to extra firm and the adjustment procedure is covered in this chapter.

If the forks encounter a bump when the brake is applied, the hydraulic pressure inside the fork leg progressively forces the main valve to open. By doing this, the fork can move to absorb the shock.

Damping Adjustment

The fork damping rate can be adjusted to 4 different settings from soft to extra firm. The oil control orifice has 4 different diameter holes that control the flow rate of the fork oil, to either increase or decrease the damping rate.

Turn the adjustment knob (**Figure 100**) on the front of the left-hand fork to the desired damping position. Refer to **Table 5** for the different settings and their damping effect.

Disassembly/Assembly

Refer to **Figure 101** for this procedure.

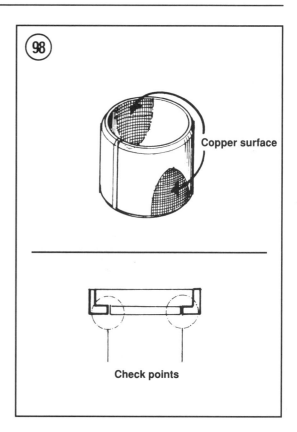

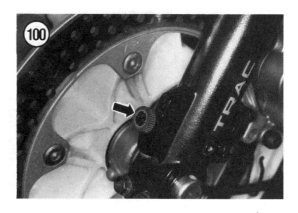

FRONT SUSPENSION AND STEERING

FORK ASSEMBLY (1986-1989) LEFT-HAND SIDE

1. Allen bolt
2. Sealing washer
3. Bolt
4. Washer
5. Spring
6. Check ball
7. Clamp bolt
8. Allen screw
9. Knob
10. O-ring
11. Orifice
12. Nut
13. Drain screw
14. Spring
15. O-ring
16. Piston
17. Case
18. O-ring
19. Boot
20. Needle bearing
21. Collar
22. Fork slider
23. Circlip
24. Oil lock piece
25. Spring
26. Spring seat
27. Rebound spring
28. Circlip
29. Damper rod
30. Piston seal
31. Piston seal
32. Fork spring
33. Bushing
34. Fork tube
35. Bushing
36. Backup ring
37. Oil seal
38. Stopper ring
39. Dust seal
40. Spacer seat
41. Spacer
42. Spacer seat
43. O-ring
44. Top cap bolt
45. Cap
46. Ring

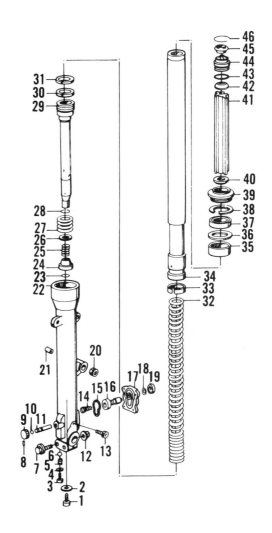

1. Remove the left-hand fork assembly from the bike and drain the fork oil as described in this chapter.
2. Remove the Allen bolts (**Figure 102**) securing the anti-dive case to the fork slider and remove the anti-dive case.
3. Remove the spring (**Figure 103**) from the slider.
4. Remove the stopper ring (**Figure 104**) from the piston and remove the bushing (**Figure 105**) from the anti-dive case.
5. Remove the O-ring seal (**Figure 106**) from the case.
6. Remove the boot (**Figure 107**) from the piston and anti-dive case.
7. From the case, remove the piston (**Figure 108**) and the return spring.
8. Remove the set screw (A, **Figure 109**) from the adjustment knob (B, **Figure 109**) and remove the adjustment knob.
9. Withdraw the oil control orifice from the fork slider.
10. From the bottom of the slider, remove the Allen bolt and O-ring seal, then the check ball spring and the check ball.
11. Inspect all components as described in this chapter.
12. Assemble by reversing these removal steps while noting the following:
    a. Apply blue Loctite (No. 242) to all screw and Allen bolt threads prior to installation.
    b. Apply automatic transmission fluid (ATF) to all O-ring seals prior to installation.
    c. Apply a light coat of silicone grease to the pivot bolt collar prior to installation.
    d. Install the piston collar with the large end on the side that will be next to the wheel when the fork assembly is reinstalled.

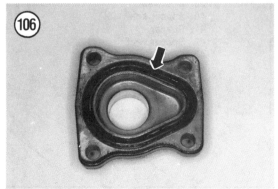

FRONT SUSPENSION AND STEERING

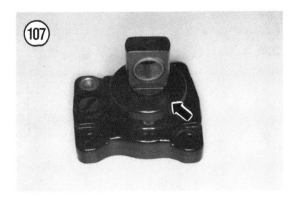

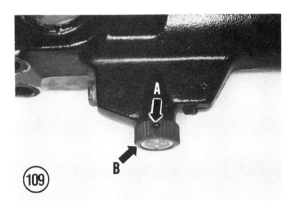

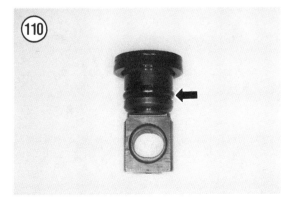

e. Tighten all screws and Allen bolts securely.
f. After the assembly is complete, push on the piston and make sure it moves freely. Turn the adjustment knob to all 4 settings. Make sure it moves freely.

Inspection

1. Clean all parts in solvent and thoroughly dry with compressed air.
2. Inspect the piston return spring (**Figure 103**) and the check ball spring for wear or damage.
3. Inspect the O-ring seal (**Figure 110**) on the piston and the oil control orifice for wear or deterioration. Replace if necessary.
4. Inspect the O-ring seal on the case (**Figure 106**) for wear or deterioration. Replace if necessary.
5. Inspect the pivot bolt collar boots and holders for wear or deterioration. Replace if necessary.
6. Make sure the oil flow holes (**Figure 111**) in the oil control orifice in the slider are clean and unobstructed. Blow out with compressed air; do not use a piece of wire as it may gouge the interior surface and disrupt the flow path.

FRONT FORKS (1990-ON MODELS)

Disassembly

Refer to **Figure 112** for this procedure.
1. Remove the drain bolt (**Figure 113**) and washer at the bottom of both fork tubes and drain the fork oil into a clean container. When the oil starts to drip out, compress the fork a few times to force out as much oil as possible. Reinstall the drain bolts and washers.

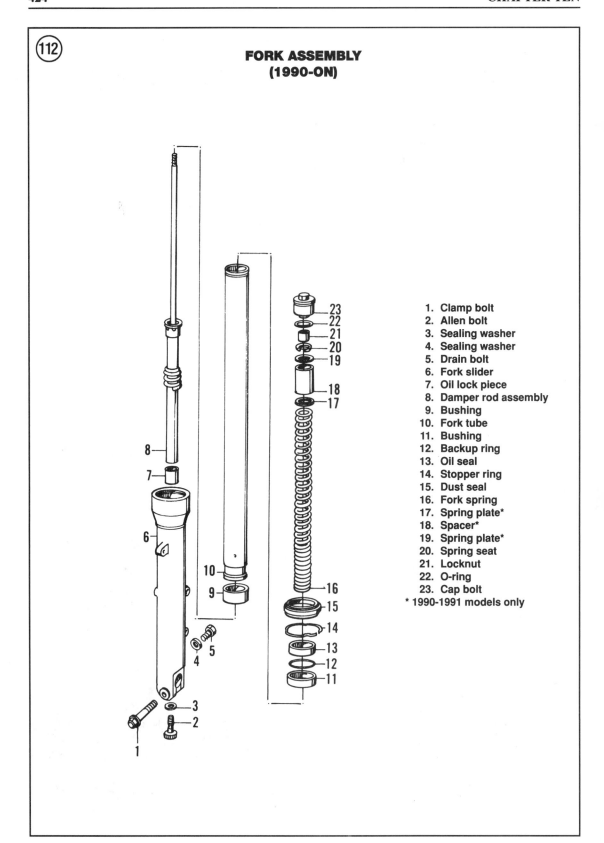

FRONT SUSPENSION AND STEERING

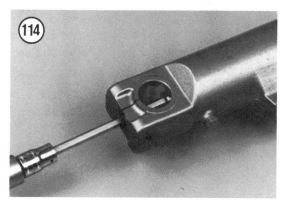

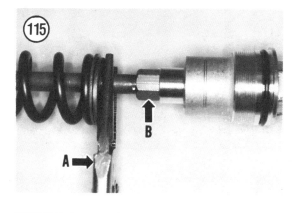

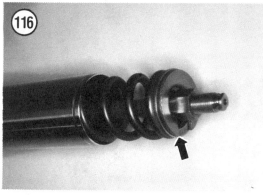

2. Remove the fork tube as described in this chapter.
3. Clamp the slider in a vise with soft jaws.

NOTE
This Allen head bolt has been secured with a locking compound and is often very difficult to remove because the damper rod will turn inside the slider. It sometimes can be removed with an air impact driver. If you are unable to remove it, take the fork tubes to a dealer and have the screws removed.

4. Remove the Allen head bolt (**Figure 114**) at the bottom of the slider.
5. If the fork cap bolt was not loosened during removal, hold the upper fork tube in a vise with soft jaws and loosen the fork cap bolt.

WARNING
Be careful when removing the fork cap bolt as the spring is under pressure. Protect your eyes accordingly.

6. Unscrew the fork cap bolt from the fork tube. Let the bolt and the damper rod extend out through the top of the fork tube.
7A. On 1990-1991 models, push the spring seat, spring plate and spring away from the fork cap and secure the pushrod with a pair of locking pliers as shown in A, **Figure 115**.
7B. On 1992-on models, push the spring seat and spring away from the fork cap and secure the pushrod with a pair of locking pliers as shown in A, **Figure 115**.
8. Hold the fork cap with a wrench and loosen the locknut (B, **Figure 115**) with another wrench.
9. Unscrew the fork cap bolt from the pushrod and remove it.
10. Extend the fork tubes and remove the locking pliers from the pushrod; allow the spring to rebound slowly as you remove the pliers.
11. Remove the spring seat (**Figure 116**) from the pushrod.
12A. On 1990-1991 models, remove the spring seat, spring plate and spring seat from the pushrod.
12B. On 1992-on models, remove the spring seat (**Figure 117**) from the pushrod.
13. Remove the fork spring (**Figure 118**).
14. Turn the fork assembly over the drain pan and pour out any remaining fork oil.

15. Twist the dust seal (**Figure 119**) and slide it out of the slider and off the fork tube.

16. Slip the tip of a small screwdriver behind the stopper ring (**Figure 120**) and carefully pry the ring out of the slider.

17. Using an Allen wrench, remove the Allen bolt (previously loosened) and washer from the base of the slider (**Figure 114**).

NOTE
On this type of fork, force is needed to remove the fork tube from the slider.

18. Hold the slider in one hand and the fork tube in the other hand (**Figure 121**). Pull the fork tube out until resistance is felt. This is where the slider and fork tube bushings are contacting each other.

CAUTION
When performing Step 18, do not bottom out the fork tube or you may damage the oil lock piece installed on the bottom of the damper rod.

19. Hold the slider and pull hard on the fork tube, using quick in-and-out strokes (**Figure 121**). Doing so will withdraw the oil seal, back-up ring and slider bushing from the slider (**Figure 122**).

20. Remove the slider and pour any remaining oil in the oil pan.

NOTE
Do not remove the fork tube bushing unless it is going to be replaced. Inspect it as described in this chapter.

21. Remove the oil lock piece (**Figure 123**) from the end of the damper rod.

22. Turn the fork tube over and slide out the damper rod and spring (**Figure 124**). The spring is fixed to the damper rod. Do not attempt to remove it.

23. Slide the dust seal, stopper ring, oil seal, back-up ring and slider bushing off of the fork tube.

24. Inspect the components as described in this chapter.

Inspection

1. Thoroughly clean all parts (**Figure 125**) in solvent and dry them.

2. Check the fork tube for severe wear or scratches. Check the chrome for flaking or other damage.

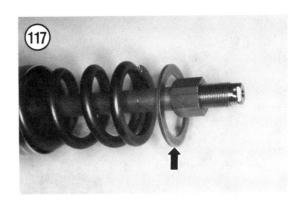

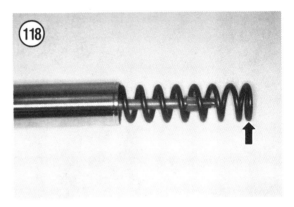

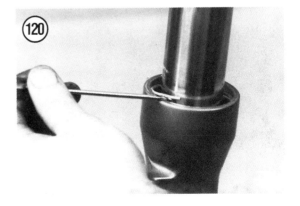

FRONT SUSPENSION AND STEERING

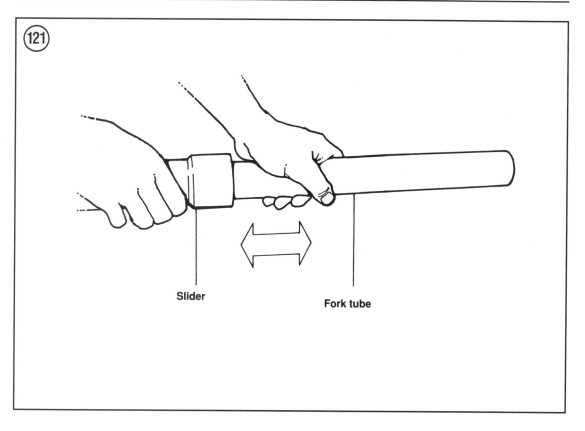

Slider   Fork tube

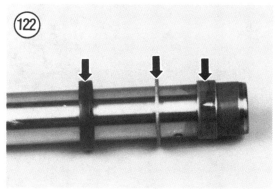

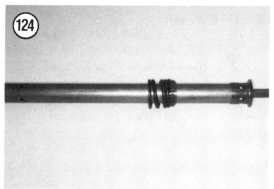

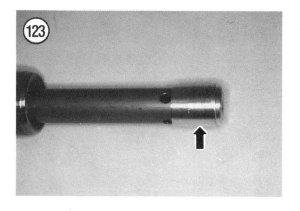

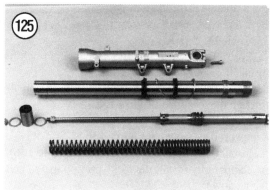

3. Check the fork tube for straightness. Place the fork tube on V-blocks and check runout with a dial indicator. If the runout meets or exceeds the service limit in **Table 4**, have it straightened by a Honda dealer. If the fork tube is bent to the point that it has creased or the chrome has flaked, the fork tube must be replaced.

4. Check the slider (**Figure 126**) for dents or exterior damage. Check the stopper ring groove (**Figure 127**) for cracks or damage. Check the oil seal area for dents or other damage. Replace the slider if necessary.

5. Check the damper rod and pushrod assembly (**Figure 128**) for straightness. Check the threads in both rods for damage; see (**Figure 129**) and (**Figure 130**).

6. Measure the free length of the fork spring (not rebound spring) as shown in **Figure 131**. If the spring has sagged to the service limit dimension in **Table 4**, replace the spring.

7. Inspect the fork tube (**Figure 132**) and slider (**Figure 133**) bushings. If the Teflon coating is worn off so that the copper base material is showing on approximately 3/4 of the total surface, the bushing must be replaced. Also check for distortion on the check points of the washer; replace as necessary. Refer to **Figure 134**.

8. To replace the fork tube bushing (**Figure 132**), open the bushing slot with a screwdriver and slide the bushing off the fork tube. Wipe the new bushing with fork oil, then open its slot slightly and slide it onto the fork tube.

9. Replace the fork cap bolt O-ring if worn or damaged.

Assembly

When fork oil is called for in the following steps, use a suitable cartridge fork oil.

1. If removed, install the fork tube bushing (**Figure 132**) onto the fork tube.

2. Coat all parts with new ATF or fork oil before installation.

3. Insert the damper rod (with spring attached) through the fork tube (**Figure 135**).

4. Install the oil lock piece onto the end of the damper rod as shown in **Figure 136**.

5. Install the fork tube into the slider (**Figure 136**).

6. Temporarily install the fork spring (tapered end facing down).

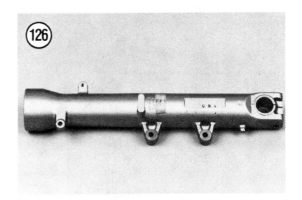

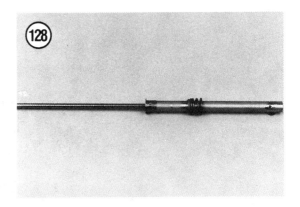

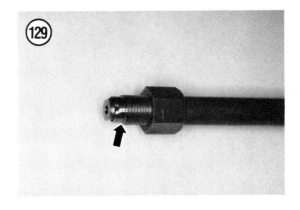

FRONT SUSPENSION AND STEERING

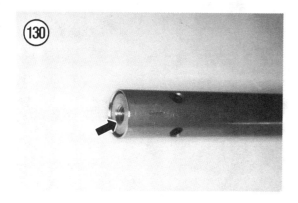

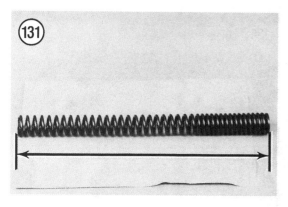

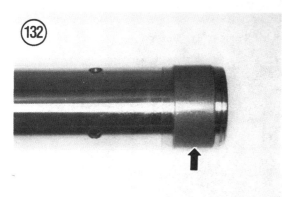

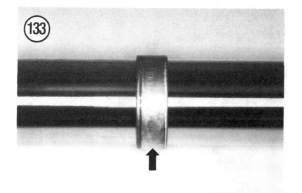

7A. On 1990-1991 models, perform the following:
   a. Install the spring plate, spacer, spring plate and spring seat onto the pushrod.
   b. Push all of these components down and secure the pushrod with a pair of locking pliers as shown in A, **Figure 115**.
7B. On 1992-on models, perform the following:
   a. Install the spring seat onto the pushrod.
   b. Push all of these components down and secure the pushrod with a pair of locking pliers as shown in A, **Figure 115**.
8. Screw the fork cap bolt onto the pushrod.
9. Hold the fork cap with a wrench and tighten the locknut (B, **Figure 115**) with another wrench.
10. Remove the locking pliers from the pushrod.
11. Install the fork cap bolt and push down on it to compress the spring. Start the bolt slowly, don't cross thread it. Tighten the cap bolt securely but not to the specified torque at this time.
12. Mount the slider in a vise with soft jaws.
13. Install a new washer onto the Allen bolt.
14. Apply blue Loctite (No 242) to the threads of the Allen bolt prior to installation. Install it in the fork slider (**Figure 137**) and tighten to the torque specification in **Table 1**.
15. Unscrew the fork cap bolt.

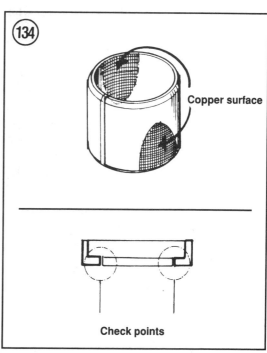

16A. On 1990-1991 models, push the spring seat, spring plate and spring away from the fork cap and secure the pushrod with a pair of locking pliers as shown in A, **Figure 115**.

16B. On 1992-on models, push the spring seat and spring away from the fork cap and secure the pushrod with a pair of locking pliers as shown in A, **Figure 115**.

17. Hold the fork cap with a wrench and loosen the locknut (B, (**Figure 115**) with another wrench.

18. Unscrew the fork cap bolt from the pushrod and remove it.

19. Extend the fork tubes and remove the locking pliers from the pushrod; allow the spring to rebound slowly as you remove the pliers.

20. Remove the spring seat (**Figure 116**) from the pushrod.

21A. On 1990-1991 models, remove the spring seat, spring plate and spring seat from the pushrod.

21B. On 1992-on models, remove the spring seat (**Figure 117**) from the pushrod.

22. Remove the fork spring (**Figure 118**).

23. To install the fork slider bushing and back-up ring, perform the following:
    a. Slide the slider bushing (A, **Figure 138**) and back-up ring (B, **Figure 138**) down the fork tube. Install the back-up ring so that its chamfered side faces down.
    b. If you have an old fork slider bushing, place it on top of the back-up ring.
    c. Drive the bushing into the fork slider with the Honda fork seal driver (part No. 07947-KA50100) and attachment (part No. 07947-KF00100) or an equivalent driver assembly (**Figure 139**).
    d. Drive the bushing into place until it seats completely in the recess in the slider.
    e. Remove the installation tool and the old fork slider bushing (if used).

NOTE
To avoid damaging the fork seal and dust seal when installing them over the top of the fork tube, place a plastic bag (A, Figure 140) over the fork tube and coat it thoroughly with fork oil. You can then slide both seals over the plastic bag without damaging them.

24. To install the fork seal (C, **Figure 138**), perform the following:

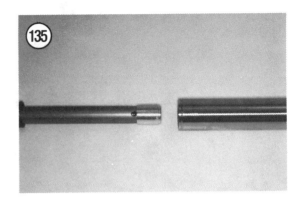

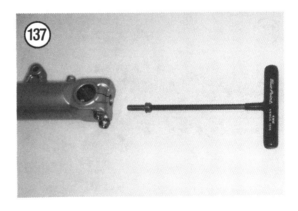

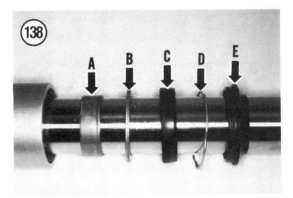

FRONT SUSPENSION AND STEERING

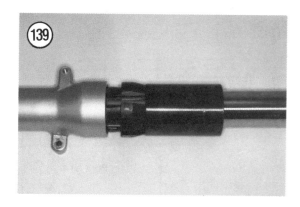

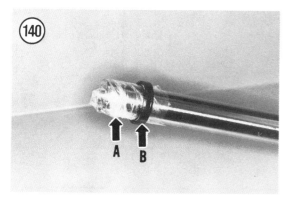

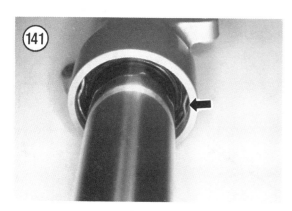

a. Coat the new seal with ATF or fork oil.
b. Install the oil seal (B, **Figure 140**) over the fork tube with the manufacturer's name and size code facing up. Slide it down the fork tube.
c. Drive the oil seal into the slider with the same tool (**Figure 139**) used during Step 23.
d. Drive the oil seal in until the groove in the slider can be seen above the top surface of the oil seal.

25. Slide the stopper ring (D, **Figure 138**) over the fork tube and install it into the groove in the slider. Make sure the stopper ring is completely seated in the slider groove (**Figure 141**).

26. Slide the dust seal (E, **Figure 138** and **Figure 142**) down the fork tube and seat it into the slider. See **Figure 143**.

27. Add fork oil, bleed and adjust the oil level as follows:
  a. Push the fork tube down to bottom it out. Then push the pushrod all the way down.
  b. Position the fork vertically and pour fork oil into the fork slowly. Continue until the oil level is about 50 mm (2 in.) from the top (with fork tube bottomed out).
  c. Hold the slider with one hand and slowly extend the fork tube with your other hand. Place your hand over the fork tube and compress it slowly. Remove your hand when the tube is at the bottom of its stroke. Repeat this step 8-10 times. Check the oil level and top it off to maintain the oil level specified in sub-step b.
  d. With the fork tube bottomed out, thread a pushrod puller onto the end of the pushrod as shown in **Figure 144**, if available.

NOTE
While the fork can be bled without the pushrod puller, the puller does help you

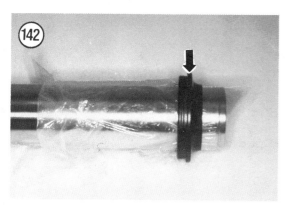

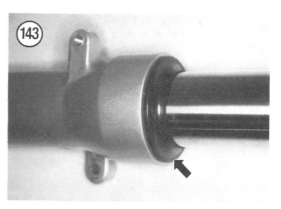

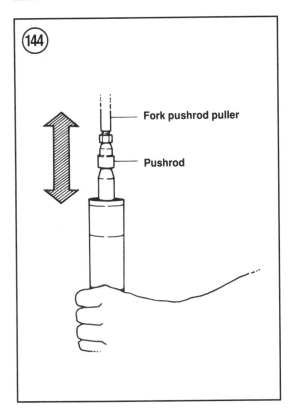

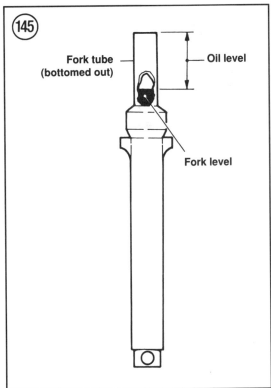

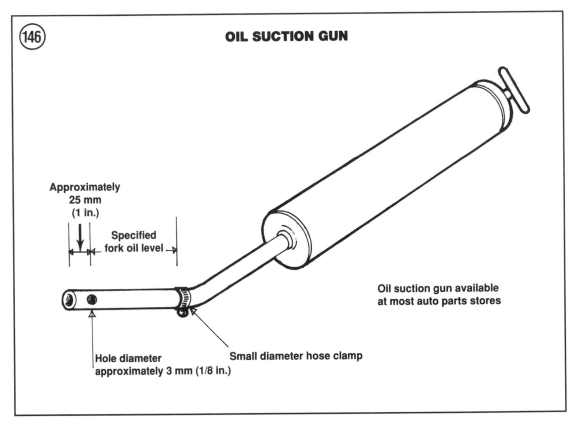

FRONT SUSPENSION AND STEERING

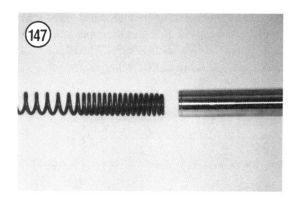

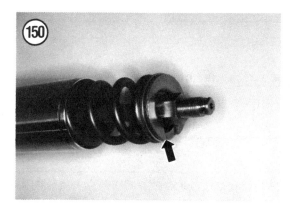

get a good feel of the bleeding procedure.

e. Slowly pump the pushrod up and down (**Figure 144**). Continue until the pushrod moves smoothly with noticeable tension through the compression and rebound travel strokes. Stop with the pushrod at the bottom of its stroke. Remove the pushrod puller, if used.

f. Set the fork tube aside for approximately 5 minutes to allow any suspended air bubbles in the oil to surface.

g. With the fork tube compressed in a vertical position, measure the oil level (**Figure 145**), from the top of the fork tube with an oil level gauge (**Figure 146**). Using the oil level gauge, adjust the oil level, maintaining it within the oil level range specified in **Table 3**.

h. Repeat for the opposite fork tube.

28. Pull the pushrod all the way up. Then install the fork spring so that the end with the closer wound springs faces toward the bottom (**Figure 147**).

29. Pull the pushrod once again so that the locknut (**Figure 148**) is positioned above the fork spring.

30. Screw the locknut (**Figure 148**) all the way down.

31A. On 1990-1991 models, perform the following:

a. Install the spring plate, spacer, spring plate and spring seat (**Figure 149**) onto the pushrod.

b. Push all of these components down and and secure the pushrod with a pair of locking pliers as shown in A, **Figure 115**.

31B. On 1992-on models, perform the following:

a. Install the spring seat onto the pushrod (**Figure 150**).

b. Push all of these components down and secure the pushrod with a pair of locking pliers as shown in **Figure 151**.

32. Screw the fork cap bolt onto the pushrod.
33. Hold the fork cap with a wrench and tighten the locknut with another wrench. Tighten the locknut to the torque specification listed in **Table 1**.
34. Remove the locking pliers from the pushrod.
35. Apply fork oil to the fork cap bolt O-ring.
36. Slowly thread the cap bolt and push down on it to compress the spring. Start the bolt slowly, don't cross thread it. Tighten the cap bolt securely but not to the specified torque at this time.
37. Install the fork tube through the steering stem until the fork cap is higher than the upper fork bridge and tighten the pinch bolt securely. Then tighten the fork cap to the torque specification in **Table 1**.
38. Loosen the fork tube pinch bolts and remove the fork tube.
39. Repeat for the other fork assembly.
40. Install the fork tubes as described in this chapter.

Table 1 FRONT SUSPENSION TIGHTENING TORQUES

Item	N•m	ft.-lb.
Front axle		
Bolt	55-65	40-47
Pinch bolt	18-25	13-18
Brake disc bolts and nuts		
1986-1989	37-43	27-31
1990-1993	43	31
1994-on	20	14
Master cylinder clamp bolts	5-8	3.5-6.0
Handlebar pinch bolts	35-45	25-33
Steering stem		
Adjust nut	23-27	17-20
Nut	90-120	65-87
Fork bridge clamp bolts		
1986-1989		
Upper bolt	9-13	6.5-9
Lower bolt	30-35	22-25
1990-on		
Upper bolt	23	17
Lower bolt	50	36
Front fork		
Fork cap bolt		
1986-1989	30-40	21.5-29
1990-on	23	17
Damper rod Allen bolt	15-25	11-18
Damper rod lock nut (1990-on)	20	14

Table 2 TIRE INFLATION PRESSURE (COLD)*

	Tire pressure			
	Front		Rear	
Load	psi	kPa	psi	kPa
Solo riding	36	250	42	290
Dual riding	36	250	42	290

*Tire inflation pressure for factory equipped tires. Aftermarket tires may require different inflation pressure.

FRONT SUSPENSION AND STEERING

Table 3 FORK OIL CAPACITY AND DIMENSIONS

Front fork oil capacity (each fork leg)	
1986-1989	
Right-hand fork	358 ml (12.1 oz.)
Left-hand fork	370 ml (12.5 oz.)
1990-1991	
U.S.	383 ml (13.4 oz.)
U.K. and Canada	394 ml (13.8 oz.)
1992-1993	386 ml (13.5 oz.)
1994-on	412 ml (14.5 oz.)
Front fork oil level dimension	
1986-1989	153 mm (6.02 in.)
1990-1991	
U.S. and U.K.	175 mm (6.89 in.)
Canada	187 mm (7.36 in.)
1992-1993	
U.S., Canada and U.K.	178 mm (7.01 in.)
1994-on	177 mm (6.97 in.)
Fork oil type	
1986-1989	ATF (automatic transmission fluid)
1990-on	Pro Honda Suspension fluid SS-7

Table 4 FRONT SUSPENSION SPECIFICATIONS

Item	Wear limit
Front axle runout	0.2 mm (0.01 in.)
Front wheel rim runout	
Radial	2.0 mm (0.08 in.)
Axial	2.0 mm (0.08 in.)
Front fork tube runout	0.20 mm (0.01 in.)
Front fork spring free length	
1986-1989	365.0 mm (14.37 in.)
1990-1991	405 mm (15.96 in.)
1992-1993	418.5 mm (16.48 in.)
1994-on	330 mm (13.0 in.)

Table 5 ANTI-DIVE ADJUSTMENT CHART (1986-1989)*

Position	Damping effect
1	Light anti-dive
2	Medium
3	Hard
4	Maximum anti-dive

* Do not position the adjuster between the numbered detent adjustment points.

CHAPTER ELEVEN

REAR SUSPENSION

This chapter includes procedures for the repair and replacement of the rear wheel and the rear suspension components. Power from the engine is transmitted to the rear wheel by a drive chain and the drive and driven sprockets.

Tire changing, tire repair and wheel balancing are covered in Chapter Ten.

Refer to **Table 1** for rear suspension torque specifications. **Table 1** and **Table 2** are located at the end of this chapter.

NOTE
Where differences occur relating to the United Kingdom (U.K.) models, they are identified. If there is no (U.K.) designation relating to a procedure, photo or illustration, it is identical to the United States (U.S.) models.

REAR WHEEL

Removal/Installation
(1986-1989 Models)

1. Place the bike on the centerstand (optional) or block up the engine so that the rear wheel clears the ground.

2. Remove the rear caliper as described under *Rear Caliper Removal/Installation* in Chapter Twelve.

NOTE
Insert a piece of wood or vinyl tubing in the caliper between the brake pads in place of the disc. That way, if the brake pedal is inadvertently depressed, the pistons will not be forced out of the cylinders. If this does happen, the caliper might have to be disassembled to reseat the pistons and the system will have to be bled. By using the wood or

REAR SUSPENSION

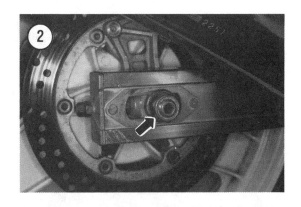

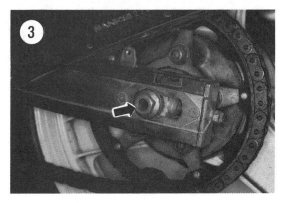

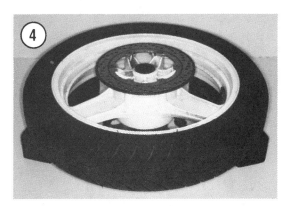

vinyl tubing, bleeding the brake is not necessary when installing the wheel.

3. Loosen the drive chain adjuster locknut and the adjuster nut (**Figure 1**) on each side of the swing arm.

4. Remove the rear axle self-locking nut (**Figure 2**) and locator.

5. Push the rear wheel forward until the drive chain is loose.

6. Partially withdraw the rear axle (**Figure 3**) from the left-hand side until the axle is free of the rear brake caliper bracket.

7. Slide the caliper and bracket off of the rear disc. Tie the caliper bracket up to the frame with a piece of wire or a Bungee cord.

8. Completely withdraw the rear axle from the wheel and swing arm.

9. Pull the rear wheel toward the rear and remove the rear wheel assembly. Don't lose the drive chain adjusters on the end of the swing arm.

10. Remove the spacer from each side of the hub.

NOTE
*Never set the wheel and brake disc assembly directly onto the brake disc, as it may be damaged. Place the outer edge of the tire on wood blocks (**Figure 4**).*

11. Install by reversing these removal steps while noting the following:
   a. If removed, install the drive chain adjuster (**Figure 5**) into the end of the swing arm on each side.
   b. Be sure to install the right-hand spacer (**Figure 6**) and left-hand spacer (**Figure 7**) into the hub.

c. Make sure the locator is properly indexed into the slot in the swing arm prior to tightening the rear axle nut.
d. Untie the rear caliper bracket from the frame and position it correctly next to the rear wheel (**Figure 8**).
e. Tighten the rear axle nut to the torque specifications listed in **Table 1**.
f. After the wheel is installed, completely rotate it and apply the brake several times to make sure it rotates freely and that the brakes work properly.
g. If used, remove the block(s) from under the engine.

Removal/Installation (1990-on Models)

Refer to **Figure 9** for this procedure.
1. With the rear wheel still on the ground, loosen the nuts (**Figure 10**) securing the rear wheel.
2. Place the bike on the centerstand (optional) or block up the engine so that the rear wheel clears the ground.

NOTE
Figure 11 shows only one of the bolts, be sure to loosen both bolts on the muffler clamp.

3. On 1994 models, loosen the 2 bolts (**Figure 11**) clamping the front of the muffler to the rear set of exhaust pipes.
4. Remove the muffler mounting bolt, washer and nut (**Figure 12**).
5. Pivot the muffler out away from the rear wheel.
6. Remove the nuts (**Figure 10**) securing the rear wheel.
7. Carefully pull the rear wheel straight off the threaded studs on the rear axle and remove the rear wheel.

NOTE
Never set the wheel and brake disc assembly directly onto the brake disc, as it may be damaged. Place the outer edge of the tire on wood blocks (Figure 4).

8. While the rear wheel is removed, inspect the rear brake pad thickness as described in Chapter Three.
9. Install by reversing these removal steps while noting the following:

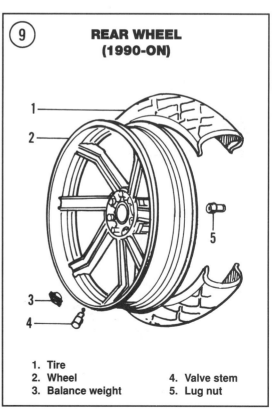

REAR WHEEL (1990-ON)

1. Tire
2. Wheel
3. Balance weight
4. Valve stem
5. Lug nut

REAR SUSPENSION

a. Tighten the rear wheel nuts to the torque specifications listed in **Table 1**.
b. After the wheel is installed, completely rotate it to make sure it rotates freely and that the brake work properly.
c. If used, remove the block(s) from under the engine.
d. On 1994 models, move the muffler back into position and maintain a distance (Dimension A) of 25-35 mm (1-1 3/8 in.) between the muffler and the rear tire (**Figure 13**).

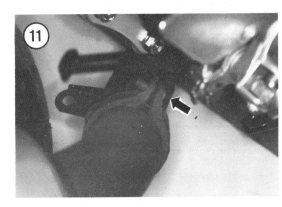

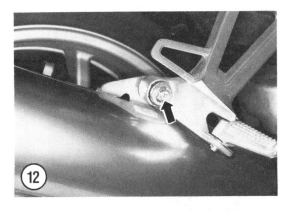

e. Tighten the muffler bolts securely.

Inspection
(1986-1989 Models)

Measure the axial and radial runout of the wheel with a dial indicator as shown in **Figure 14**. The maximum axial and radial runout is 2.0 mm (0.08 in.). If the runout exceeds this dimension, check the wheel bearing condition.

If the wheel bearings are okay, the wheel will have to be replaced, as it cannot be serviced. Inspect the wheel for signs of cracks, fractures, dents or bends. If it is damaged in any way, it must be replaced.

WARNING
Do not try to repair any damage to an alloy wheel as it will result in an unsafe riding condition.

Check axial runout as described under *Rear Hub Inspection* in this chapter.

REAR HUB
(1986-1989 MODELS)

Inspection

Inspect each wheel bearing prior to removing it from the wheel hub.

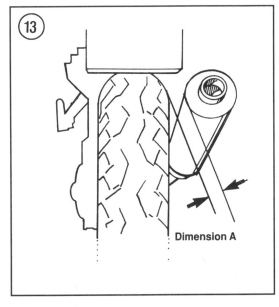

CAUTION
Do not remove the wheel bearings for inspection purposes as they will be damaged during the removal process. Remove wheel bearings only if they are to be replaced.

1. Perform Steps 1-6 of *Disassembly* in this chapter.
2. Turn each bearing by hand. Make sure the bearings turn smoothly.
3. On non-sealed bearings, check the balls for evidence of wear, pitting or excessive heat (bluish tint). Replace the bearings if necessary; always replace as a complete set. When replacing the bearings, be sure to take your old bearings along to ensure a perfect matchup.

NOTE
Fully sealed bearings are available from many bearing specialty shops. Fully sealed bearings provide better protection from dirt and moisture that may get into the hub.

4. Check the axle for wear and straightness. Use V-blocks and a dial indicator as shown in **Figure 15**. If the runout is 0.2 mm (0.01 in.) or greater, the axle should be replaced.
5. Inspect the rubber damper bosses (**Figure 16**) for cracks, fractures or other damage. If damage is severe, replace the rear wheel.

Disassembly

Refer to **Figure 17** for this procedure.
1. Remove the rear wheel as described in this chapter.
2. Remove the right-hand spacer and left-hand spacer (**Figure 7**) from the hub.

NOTE
If the driven flange assembly is difficult to remove, tap on the backside of the sprocket (from the opposite side of the wheel through the wheel spokes) with the wooden handle of a hammer. Tap evenly around the perimeter of the sprocket until the assembly is free.

3. Pull the driven flange assembly (**Figure 18**) straight up and remove it from the hub.
4. Remove the O-ring (A, **Figure 19**) from the left-hand side bearing.

5. Remove the final drive flange rubber dampers (**Figure 20**) from the left-hand side of the hub. It is not necessary to remove them, but they will probably fall out during bearing removal.
6. Remove the grease seal (**Figure 21**) from the right-hand side.

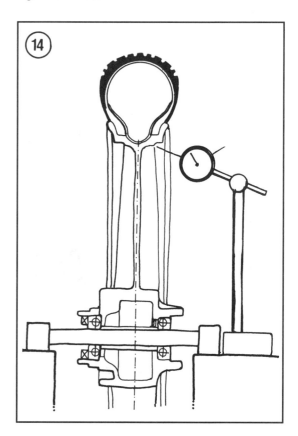

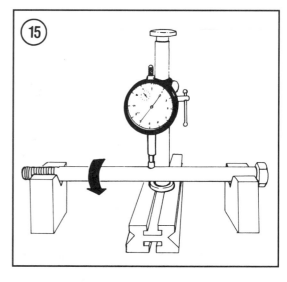

REAR SUSPENSION

7. Before proceeding further, inspect the wheel bearings as described in this chapter. If they must be replaced, proceed as follows.

8. Remove the bolts securing the brake disc (**Figure 22**) and remove the brake disc.

9. To remove the right- and left-hand bearings and distance collar, perform the following:

    a. Insert a soft aluminum or brass drift into one side of the hub.

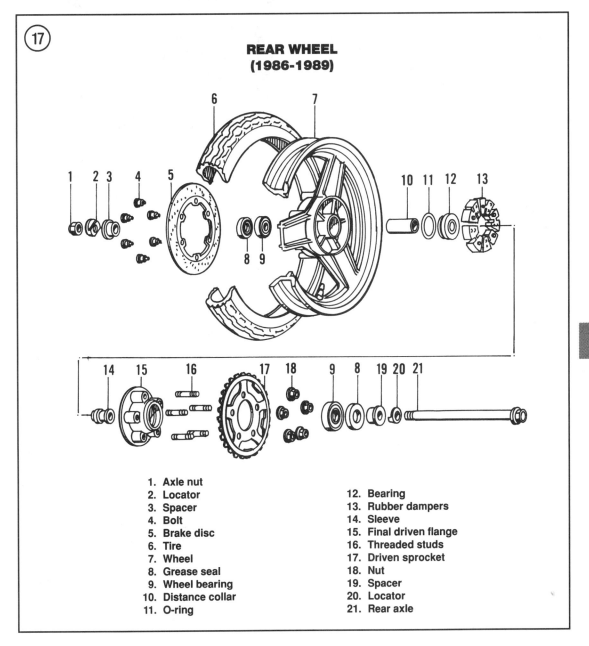

REAR WHEEL (1986-1989)

1. Axle nut
2. Locator
3. Spacer
4. Bolt
5. Brake disc
6. Tire
7. Wheel
8. Grease seal
9. Wheel bearing
10. Distance collar
11. O-ring
12. Bearing
13. Rubber dampers
14. Sleeve
15. Final driven flange
16. Threaded studs
17. Driven sprocket
18. Nut
19. Spacer
20. Locator
21. Rear axle

b. Push the distance collar over to one side and place the drift on the inner race of the lower bearing.

c. Tap the bearing out of the hub with a hammer, working around the perimeter of the inner race.

d. Repeat for the other bearing.

10. Clean the inside and the outside of the hub with solvent. Dry with compressed air.

Assembly

1. On non-sealed bearings, pack the bearings with a good quality bearing grease. Work the grease in between the balls thoroughly; turn the bearing by hand a couple of times to make sure the grease is distributed evenly inside the bearing.

2. Blow any dirt or foreign matter out of the hub prior to installing the bearings.

CAUTION
*Install non-sealed bearings with the single sealed side (B, **Figure 19**) facing outward.*

3. Pack the hub with multipurpose grease.

CAUTION
*Install the standard bearings (they are sealed on one side only) with the sealed side facing out. Tap the bearings squarely into place and tap on the outer race only. Use a socket (**Figure 23**) that matches the outer race diameter. Do not tap on the inner race or the bearing might be damaged. Be sure that the bearings are completely seated.*

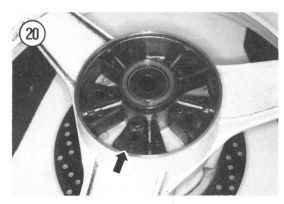

4. First, install the right-hand bearing into the hub.
5. Press the distance collar into the hub from the left-hand side.
6. Install the left-hand bearing into the hub.
7. Install the new grease seal (**Figure 21**) into the right-hand side.
8. If removed, install all final drive flange rubber dampers (**Figure 20**) into the left-hand side of the hub.
9. Apply a light coat of grease to the new O-ring and install the new O-ring (A, **Figure 19**) into the left-hand bearing.
10. Install the brake disc and tighten the bolts to the torque specification listed in **Table 1**.

REAR SUSPENSION

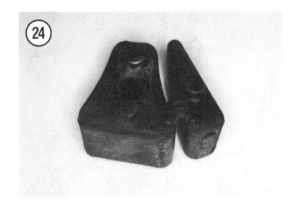

11. Install the driven flange assembly (**Figure 18**) into the hub. Push it in then tap the flange in with a soft-faced mallet and make sure it is completely seated in the hub.

12. Install the spacer on each side of the rear hub.

13. Install the rear wheel as described in this chapter.

DRIVEN FLANGE ASSEMBLY (1986-1989 MODELS)

Removal/Installation

Refer to **Figure 17** for this procedure.

1. Remove the rear wheel as described in this chapter.

2. If the driven sprocket requires replacement, loosen the nuts securing the sprocket to the driven flange assembly.

> *NOTE*
> *If the driven flange assembly is difficult to remove, tap on the backside of the sprocket (from the opposite side of the wheel through the wheel spokes) with the wooden handle of a hammer. Tap evenly around the perimeter of the sprocket until the assembly is free.*

3. Pull the driven flange assembly (**Figure 18**) straight up and remove it from the hub.

4. Inspect all parts as described in this chapter.

5. Install by reversing these removal steps while noting the following:

   a. Make sure *all* rubber dampers (**Figure 20**) are in place in the rear hub prior to installing the driven sprocket.

   b. If the driven sprocket was removed, tighten the mounting nuts to the torque specification listed in **Table 1**.

Inspection

1. Visually inspect the rubber dampers (**Figure 24**) for signs of damage, hardness or deterioration. Replace as a complete set even though only one or two require replacement.

2. Inspect the driven flange assembly housing (A, **Figure 25**) for cracks or damage, replace if necessary.

3. Inspect the teeth of the driven sprocket (B, **Figure 25**). If the teeth are worn, remove the nuts and replace the sprocket.

4. If the driven sprocket requires replacement, also replace the drive chain and the drive sprocket.

Bearing Replacement

1. Prior to removing the bearing in the final driven flange, inspect it as described under *Rear Hub Inspection* in this chapter.

2. If still in place, remove the rear axle sleeve (**Figure 26**) from the driven flange assembly.

3. To remove the bearing, perform the following:
   a. Remove the grease seal (A, **Figure 27**).
   b. Remove the circlip.
   c. Turn the driven flange with the sprocket side facing down.
   d. Insert a soft aluminum or brass drift into the side of the driven flange that is facing up.
   e. Tap the bearing (B, **Figure 27**) out of the driven flange with a hammer, working around the perimeter of the inner race.

4. Clean the inside and the outside of the driven flange with solvent. Dry with compressed air.

5. Pack the driven flange with multipurpose grease.

CAUTION
Install the standard bearing (it is sealed on one side only) with the sealed side facing out. Tap the bearing squarely into place and tap on the outer race only. Use a socket that matches the outer race diameter. Do not tap on the inner race or the bearing might be damaged. Be sure that the bearing is completely seated.

6. Install the bearing (B, **Figure 27**) into the final driven flange.

7. Install the circlip and make sure it is properly seated in its groove.

8. Install the grease seal (A, **Figure 27**).

9. Install the rear axle sleeve (**Figure 26**).

DRIVE SPROCKET AND DRIVE CHAIN

Removal/Installation

CAUTION
The original factory equipped drive chain is manufactured as a continuous closed loop with no master link. Do not cut the chain with a chain cutter as this will result in future chain failure and possible loss of control of the bike under riding conditions.

1. Remove the drive sprocket from the transmission shaft as described under *Engine Drive Sprocket and Cover* in Chapter Six.

2. Remove the rear wheel as described in this chapter.

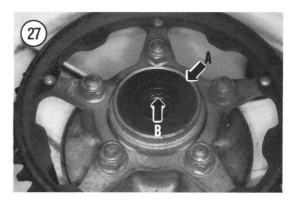

REAR SUSPENSION

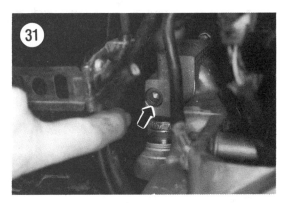

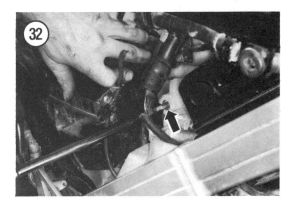

3. Remove the swing arm as described in this chapter.
4. Remove the drive chain.
5. Install by reversing these removal steps while noting the following:
   a. Positioned the drive chain over the left-hand side of the swing arm and install the swing arm as described in this chapter.
   b. Adjust the drive chain as described under *Drive Chain Adjustment* in Chapter Three.

SHOCK ABSORBER (1986-1989 MODELS)

Spring Preload Adjustment

The spring preload adjust knob can be moved to any position between the LOW or HIGH positions. The LOW setting is the softest and the HIGH is the hardest providing the maximum spring preload.

1. Remove the frame left-hand side cover as described in Chapter Thirteen.
2. Rotate the knob (**Figure 28**) to any of the settings from completely *counterclockwise* LOW or completely *clockwise* HIGH or any setting in between.
3. Always position the knob into one of the detents, NEVER in between detents.

Removal

1. Place wood block(s) under the engine to support the bike securely with the rear wheel off of the ground.
2. Remove the rear wheel as described in this chapter.
3. Remove the seat and both side covers as described in Chapter Thirteen.
4. Remove the bolt (**Figure 29**) securing the spring preload adjuster assembly to the frame.
5. Remove the battery as described under *Battery Removal/Installation* in Chapter Three.
6. Remove the bolt (**Figure 30**) securing the battery box to the frame.
7. Push the front section of the battery box toward the rear to gain access to the shock absorber's upper mounting bolt (**Figure 31**).
8. Remove the upper mounting flange bolt (**Figure 32**) and nut (**Figure 33**) securing the shock to the frame.

9. Remove the bolt (A, **Figure 34**) and nut securing the shock arm to the shock link and pivot the shock link (B, **Figure 34**) down to expose the shock absorber lower mounting bolt and nut.

10. Remove the lower mounting flange bolt (C, **Figure 34**) and nut securing the shock absorber to the shock arm.

NOTE
Prior to removing the shock absorber from the frame, note the routing of the spring preload cable through the frame. Make a drawing or take a Polaroid picture so you won't forget. It must be reinstalled in the same path so that it will operate correctly.

11. Raise the swing arm and place a wood block under it in the raised position.

12. Carefully remove the shock absorber and spring preload adjuster assembly out through the frame and through the bottom of the shock linkage.

13. Inspect the shock absorber unit as described in this chapter.

Installation

1. Apply a light coat of molybdenum disulfide paste grease to the upper mounting bracket on the frame.

2. Position the shock absorber assembly in the frame with the spring preload adjuster assembly facing toward the left-hand side of the bike.

3. Install the upper mounting flange bolt (**Figure 31**) and install the nut (**Figure 33**). Tighten the nut to the torque specification listed in **Table 1**.

4. Apply a coat of molybdenum disulfide paste grease to the pivot points of the shock link.

5. Install the shock absorber lower mounting flange bolt (C, **Figure 34**). Install the nut and tighten to the torque specification listed in **Table 1**.

6. Move the shock link (B, **Figure 34**) up and align it with the shock arm, then install the bolt (A, **Figure 34**) and nut securing the 2 parts. Tighten the bolt and nut to the torque specification listed in **Table 1**.

7. Reinstall the rear wheel as described in this chapter.

8. Remove the wood block(s) from under the engine. Push down on the rear of the bike and make sure the rear suspension is operating properly.

9. Install the bolt securing the battery box to the frame. Tighten the bolt securely.

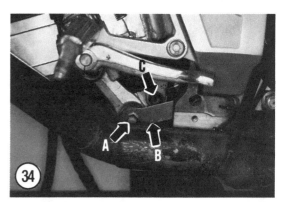

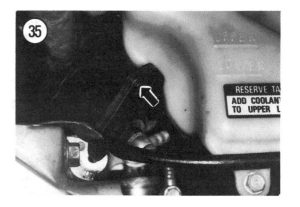

REAR SUSPENSION

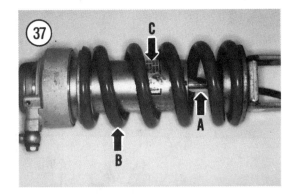

10. Install the battery as described in Chapter Three.

11. Move the spring preload adjuster assembly into place and align the locating pin (**Figure 35**) on the mounting bracket with the hole in the frame. Install the bolt (**Figure 29**) and tighten securely.

12. Install the seat and both side covers as described in Chapter Thirteen.

Preliminary Inspection

1. Inspect the upper mount bushing and collar (A, **Figure 36**) for wear or damage. Replace the bushing and collar if necessary.

2. Inspect the lower mounting yoke (B, **Figure 36**) for wear or damage; replace if necessary.

3. Check the damper unit and rod (A, **Figure 37**) for dents, oil leakage or other damage. Make sure the damper rod is straight. If either is damaged, replace the damper unit.

4. Check the spring adjuster cable (**Figure 38**) for wear, damage or kinks. Replace the spring adjuster if necessary.

5. Rotate the adjuster knob (**Figure 39**) and check for free operation. Make sure it rotates freely and that the spring adjuster operates properly.

6. Inspect the rubber stopper (**Figure 40**) for wear, damage or deterioration; replace if necessary.

7. Check the spring (B, **Figure 37**) for damage or sagging. If necessary, disassemble the shock absorber and measure the spring. Replace the spring if it has sagged to the service limit listed in **Table 2** or less.

Disassembly/Inspection/Assembly

Refer to **Figure 41** for this procedure.

WARNING
*The shock absorber damper unit is a sealed unit and cannot be rebuilt. It contains highly compressed nitrogen gas. Do not tamper with or attempt to open the cylinder. Do not place it near an open flame or other extreme heat. Do not weld on the frame near it. Do not dispose of the shock absorber yourself. Take it to a Honda dealer where it can be deactivated and disposed of properly. Refer to WARNING label (C, **Figure 37**) on damper unit.*

SHOCK ABSORBER (1986-1989)

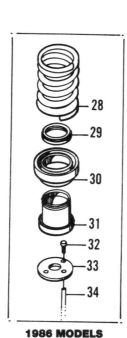

1986 MODELS

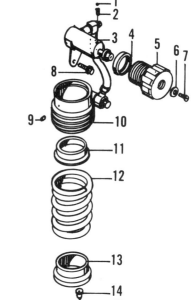

1. Steel ball
2. Spring
3. Spring pre-load adjuster
4. Dust seal
5. Adjust knob
6. Washer
7. Screw
8. Bolt
9. Allen screw
10. Spring pre-load adjuster
11. Upper spring seat
12. Spring
13. Lower spring seat
14. Drain hose fitting
15. Spring seat stopper
16. Drain hose
17. Bolt
18. Dust seal cap
19. Dust seal
20. Stopper ring
21. Collar
22. Bushing
23. Damper unit
24. Nut
25. Rubber stopper
26. Lower yoke
27. Bolt
28. Spring*
29. Dust seal*
30. Spring seat*
31. Spring guide*
32. Drain hose fitting*
33. Spring seat stopper*
34. Drain hose*
  * 1986 models only

REAR SUSPENSION

1. Remove the dust seal cap, dust seal and bushing (A, **Figure 36**) from the upper mount.
2. Install the shock absorber in a compression tool as shown in **Figure 42**. This is a special tool and is available from a Honda dealer. It is the Shock Absorber Compressor (part No. 07959-3290001) and Attachment (part No. 07959-MB10000).
3. Compress the spring approximately 20 mm (3/4 in.).
4. Place a wrench on the damper rod locknut and loosen, then remove the lower yoke. The locknut may be difficult to break loose, as a thread locking agent was applied during assembly.
5. Loosen the compressor tool to release the spring tension and remove the tool from the shock absorber.
6A. On 1986 models, remove the spring seat stopper, spring guide, spring seat, dust seal and spring.
6B. On 1987-1989 models, remove the spring seat stopper, lower spring seat, spring and the upper spring seat.
7. Measure the spring free length (**Figure 43**). The spring must be replaced if it has sagged to the service limit listed in **Table 2** or less.

NOTE
The damper unit cannot be rebuilt; it must be replaced as a unit.

8. Check the damper unit for leakage and make sure the damper rod is straight.
9. Inspect the rubber stopper (**Figure 40**) for wear, damage or deterioration; replace if necessary.
10. Assemble by reversing these disassembly steps while noting the following:
   a. Apply red loctite (No. 271) to the threads of the locknut prior to installation. Temporarily screw the locknut all the way on until it stops.
   b. Install the lower yoke and screw it on until it stops. Hold onto the lower yoke and tighten the locknut against the lower yoke. Tighten the locknut to the specification listed in **Table 1**.
   c. Position the spring adjuster so the cable fitting is parallel with the upper mount bolt hole.
   d. Loosen the spring compressor tool gradually and align the spring seat stopper locating pin with the lower joint shoulder. Also make sure the drain tube is facing toward the front.
   e. Apply molybdenum disulfide grease to the upper mount bushing.

SHOCK ABSORBER (1990-ON MODELS)

Adjustment

Spring preload

1. Use the 8 × 12 mm open end wrench in the owner's tool kit and rotate the adjuster (**Figure 44**) in either direction to achieve the desired spring preload.
2. Turn the adjuster to any of the settings from completely *clockwise* HIGH or completely *counterclockwise* LOW or any setting in between.
3. Always position the knob into one of the detents, NEVER in between detents.

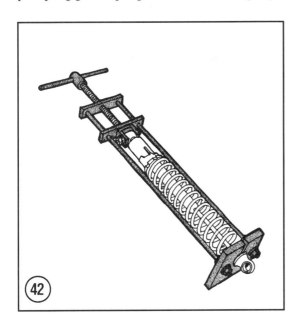

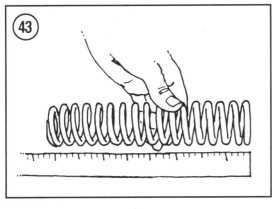

1990-on damping rebound

1. Use a flat-blade screwdriver and rotate the damping rebound adjuster (**Figure 45**) completely *clockwise*. This is the hardest setting. Rotate the adjuster completely *counterclockwise*. This is the softest setting.
2. The standard setting is when the adjuster is turned *counterclockwise* one full turn from the hardest setting. At this point the punch mark (A) will align with the reference mark (B) shown in **Figure 46**.

Removal

1. Remove the rear wheel as described in this chapter.
2. Remove the starter relay from its mount on the frame and move it out of the way.
3. Remove the battery as described under *Battery Removal/Installation* in Chapter Three.
4. Remove the screws securing the battery case and remove it from the frame.
5. Remove the bolt (A, **Figure 47**) and nut securing the shock link and shock arm together. Pivot the shock link (B, **Figure 47**) down.
6. Remove the bolt (C, **Figure 47**) and nut securing the lower mount of the shock absorber to the shock arm.
7. Remove the bolt and nut (A, **Figure 48**) securing the upper mount to the frame.
8. Carefully remove the shock absorber assembly up and out through the top of the frame.

Installation

1. Apply a light coat of molybdenum disulfide paste grease to the upper mounting bracket on the frame.
2. Position the shock absorber assembly in the frame with the spring preload adjuster assembly (B, **Figure 48**) facing toward the left-hand side of the bike.
3. Install the upper mounting flange bolt from the left-hand side and install the nut (A, **Figure 48**). Tighten the nut to the torque specification listed in **Table 1**.
4. Apply a coat of molybdenum disulfide paste grease to the pivot points of the shock link.
5. Install the shock absorber lower mounting flange bolt (C, **Figure 47**) from the left-hand side. Install the nut and tighten to the torque specification listed in **Table 1**.
6. Pivot the shock link (B, **Figure 47**) up and align the holes in the shock link, shock arm and shock absorber. Install the bolt (A, **Figure 47**) from the

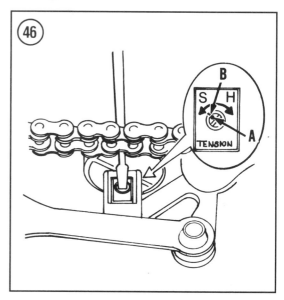

REAR SUSPENSION

left-hand side and install nut. Tighten to the torque specification listed in **Table 1**.
7. Install the battery case and screws. Tighten the screws securely.
8. Install the battery as described in Chapter Three.
9. Install the starter relay into its mount on the frame.
10. Reinstall the rear wheel as described in this chapter.
11. Remove the wood block(s) from under the engine. Push down on the rear of the bike and make sure the rear suspension is operating properly.

Preliminary Inspection

1. Inspect the upper rubber mount for wear or damage. If damaged, replace the shock absorber.
2. Inspect the lower mounting yoke for wear or damage. If the yoke is damaged on 1990-1991 models, it can be replaced. On all other years, if it is damaged, replace the shock absorber.
3. Check the damper unit and rod for dents, oil leakage or other damage. Make sure the damper rod is straight. If either is damaged, replace the damper unit.
4. Check the spring preload adjuster assembly for wear. If the spring preload adjuster is damaged on 1990-1993 models, it can be replaced. On 1994-on models, if it is damaged, replace the shock absorber.
5. Inspect the rubber stopper for wear, damage or deterioration; replace if necessary.
6. Check the spring for damage or sagging. If necessary, disassemble the shock absorber (1990-1993 models only) and measure the spring. Replace the spring if it has sagged to the service limit listed in **Table 2** or less.

Disassembly/Inspection/Assembly

Refer to the following illustrations for this procedure:
  a. **Figure 49**: 1990 and 1991 models.
  b. **Figure 50**: 1992 and 1993 models.

NOTE
The shock absorber used on 1994-on models cannot be disassembled. If any portion of the shock is faulty, the entire assembly must be replaced.

WARNING
The shock absorber damper unit is a sealed unit and cannot be rebuilt. It contains highly compressed nitrogen gas. Do not tamper with or attempt to open the cylinder. Do not place it near an open flame or other extreme heat. Do not weld on the frame near it. Do not dispose of the shock absorber yourself. Take it to a Honda dealer where it can be deactivated and disposed of properly.

1. Install the shock absorber in a compression tool as shown in **Figure 42**. This is a special tool and is available from a Honda dealer. It is the Shock Absorber Compressor (part No. 07GME-0010000) and Attachment (part No. 07GME-0010100).
2. Compress the spring approximately 20 mm (3/4 in.).
3A. On 1990 and 1991 models, place a wrench on the damper rod locknut and loosen, then remove the lower yoke. The locknut may be difficult to break loose, as a thread locking agent was applied during assembly.

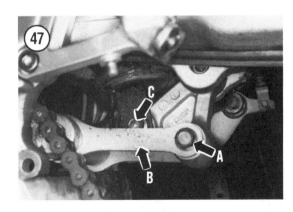

3B. On 1992 and 1993 models, remove the stopper plates located below the lower spring seat.

4. Loosen the compressor tool to release the spring tension and remove the tool from the shock absorber.

5A. On 1990 and 1991 models, perform the following:
   a. Remove the spring seat stopper, lower spring seat, spring and upper spring seat.
   b. If necessary, remove the set screw and slide the spring preload adjuster assembly off the bottom of the damper unit.

5B. On 1992 and 1993 models, perform the following:
   a. Remove the lower spring seat, spring and the upper spring seat.
   b. If necessary, remove the set screw and the stopper ring, then slide the spring preload adjuster assembly off the top of the damper unit.

6. Measure the spring free length (**Figure 43**). The spring must be replaced if it has sagged to the service limit listed in **Table 2** or less.

NOTE
The damper unit cannot be rebuilt; it must be replaced as a unit.

7. Check the damper unit for leakage and make sure the damper rod is straight.

8. Inspect the rubber stopper for wear, damage or deterioration. On 1990 and 1991 models, replace if necessary.

9A. On 1990 and 1991 models, assemble by reversing these disassembly steps while noting the following:
   a. If removed, install the spring preload adjuster. Align the adjuster to the damper unit, install the set screw and tighten securely.
   b. Apply red loctite (No. 271) to the threads of the locknut prior to installation. Temporarily screw the locknut all the way on until it stops.
   c. Install the lower yoke and screw it on until it stops. Hold onto the lower yoke and tighten the locknut against the lower yoke. Tighten the locknut to the specification listed in **Table 1**.
   d. Loosen the spring compressor tool gradually and align the spring seat stopper locating pin with the lower joint shoulder. Also make sure the drain tube is facing toward the front.
   e. Apply molybdenum disulfide grease to the upper mount bushing.

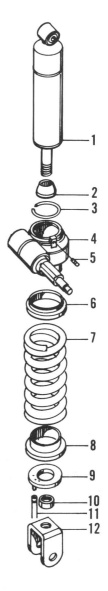

SHOCK ABSORBER (1990-1991)

1. Damper unit
2. Rubber stopper
3. Stopper ring
4. Spring pre-load adjuster
5. Set screw
6. Upper spring seat
7. Spring
8. Lower spring seat
9. Spring seat stopper
10. Locknut
11. Drain tube
12. Lower yoke

REAR SUSPENSION

9B. On 1992 and 1993 models, assemble by reversing these disassembly steps while noting the following:

a. If removed, install the spring preload adjuster. Align the adjuster to the damper unit (**Figure 51**), install the set screw and tighten securely.

b. Install the stopper ring and make sure it seats correctly in the damper unit groove.

c. Install the spring with the tapered end facing up toward the adjuster assembly.

d. Make sure the stopper plates are seated correctly in the lower spring seat.

e. Loosen the spring compressor tool gradually.

f. Apply molybdenum disulfide grease to the upper mount.

SHOCK ABSORBER LINKAGE (1986-1989 MODELS)

Removal

Refer to **Figure 52** for this procedure.

1. Remove the rear wheel as described in this chapter.
2. Remove the shock arm shaft pinch bolt (**Figure 53**).
3. Push the shock arm shaft (**Figure 54**) out through the mounting bracket on the left-hand side of the swing arm and through the shock arm and remove the shaft.
4. Remove the bolt (**Figure 55**) and nut (A, **Figure 56**) securing the shock arm to the frame mounting bracket. Don't lose the hose clamp (B, **Figure 56**) under the nut.
5. Lower the shock arm and remove the bolt and nut securing the shock absorber lower mount to the shock arm.
6. Remove the shock arm and shock link assembly from the frame.
7. Inspect the components as described in this chapter.

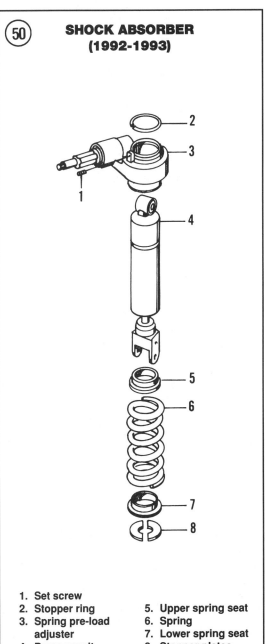

50 SHOCK ABSORBER (1992-1993)

1. Set screw
2. Stopper ring
3. Spring pre-load adjuster
4. Damper unit
5. Upper spring seat
6. Spring
7. Lower spring seat
8. Stopper plates

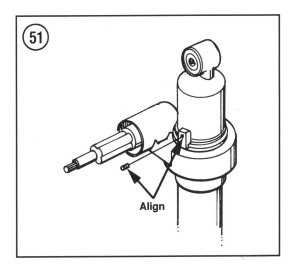

51 Align

Inspection

1. Remove the dust seals at all pivot points and push out the bushings.
2. Clean all parts in solvent and thoroughly dry with compressed air.
3. Inspect the shock arm (**Figure 57**) and shock link for cracks or damage; replace as necessary.
4. Inspect the bushings for scratches, abrasion or abnormal wear; replace as necessary.
5. Inspect the collars (A, **Figure 58**) for scratches, abrasion or abnormal wear; replace as necessary.
6. Inspect the dust seals in the shock link (**Figure 59**) and shock arm (**Figure 60**). Replace all of them as a set if any are worn or starting to deteriorate. If the dust seals are in poor condition they will allow dirt to enter into the pivot areas and cause the bushings to wear.
7. Inspect the needle bearings (**Figure 61**) for abnormal wear. The needle bearings are not sold separately. If worn or damaged, replace the part that the damaged bearing is installed in.
8. Inspect the shock arm shaft (B, **Figure 58**) for scratches, abrasion or abnormal wear. Remove any rust with emery cloth and thoroughly clean off all

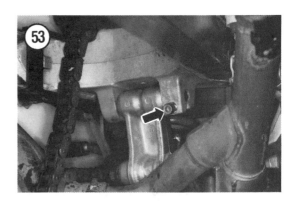

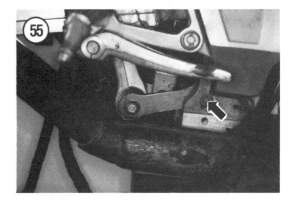

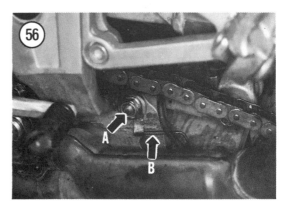

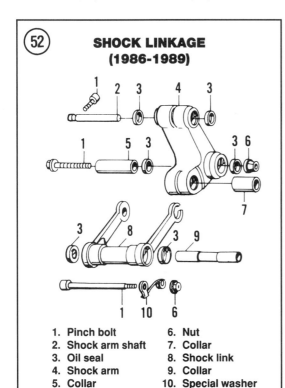

SHOCK LINKAGE (1986-1989)

1. Pinch bolt
2. Shock arm shaft
3. Oil seal
4. Shock arm
5. Collar
6. Nut
7. Collar
8. Shock link
9. Collar
10. Special washer

REAR SUSPENSION

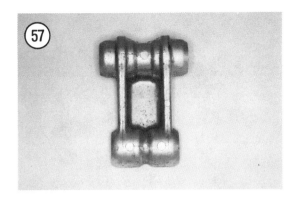

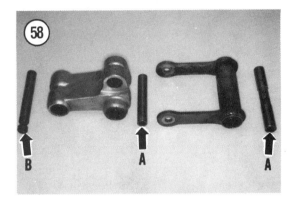

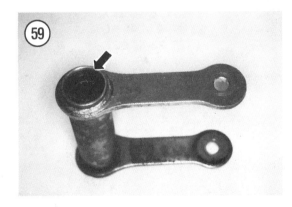

residue in solvent. If rust is deep or excessive wear is evident; replace the shaft.

9. Coat all surfaces of the pivot receptacles, the needle bearings, the collars and the inside of the dust seals with molybdenum disulfide paste grease. Insert the collars into the shock link and the shock arms and install the dust seals.

NOTE
Make sure the dust seal lips seat correctly. If not, they will allow dirt and moisture into the bearing areas and cause wear.

Installation

CAUTION
Do not tighten the bolt and nut securing the shock link to the shock arm at this time. The bolt and nut must be tightened after these parts are installed on the bike and all components attached to them. If the bolt and nut are tightened at this time, the two parts will not be in the proper alignment to each other and this will create abnormal stress on the rubber mount in the shock arm pivot area. This would lead to premature fatigue and failure of the rubber mount.

1. Assemble the shock arm and shock link as shown in **Figure 62**. Install the bolt and nut—do *not* tighten at this time.

2. Install the shock arm and shock link assembly into place and install the shock absorber's lower mounting bolt and nut. Tighten the bolt and nut to the torque specification listed in **Table 1**.

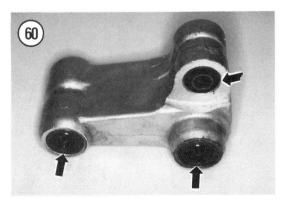

3. Move the shock link into position on the frame mounting bracket. Install the bolt (**Figure 55**) from the right-hand side.
4. Place the hose clamp (B, **Figure 56**) on the bolt and install the nut (A, **Figure 56**). Tighten the bolt and nut finger-tight at this time.
5. Move the shock arm up into position in the swing arm and install the shock arm shaft (**Figure 54**) from the left-hand side.
6. Install the shock arm shaft pinch bolt (**Figure 53**). Tighten the pinch bolt and nut to the torque specification listed in **Table 1**.
7. Tighten the shock link to frame bolt and nut to the torque specification listed in **Table 1**.
8. Install the rear wheel as described in this chapter.
9. With the rear wheel on the ground, tighten the shock link to shock arm bolt (**Figure 63**) and nut to the torque specification listed in **Table 1**.
10. Push down on the seat several times to make sure all components are installed correctly and that the suspension is operating correctly.

SHOCK ABSORBER LINKAGE (1990-1993 MODELS)

Removal

Refer to **Figure 64** for this procedure.
1. Remove the rear wheel as described in this chapter.
2. Remove the bolts securing the exhaust chamber guard and remove the guard.
3. Remove the bolt (A, **Figure 65**) and nut (A, **Figure 66**) securing the shock arm to the shock link.
4. Remove the bolt (B, **Figure 65**) and nut (B, **Figure 66**) securing the shock absorber lower mount to the shock arm.
5. Remove the bolt (C, **Figure 65**) and nut (C, **Figure 66**) securing the shock arm to the swing arm and remove the shock arm.
6. Remove the bolt and nut (D, **Figure 66**) securing the shock link (D, **Figure 65**) to the frame and remove the shock link.
7. Inspect the components as described in this chapter.

Inspection

1. Remove the dust seals at all pivot points and push out the collars.

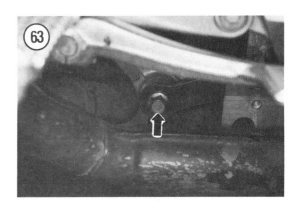

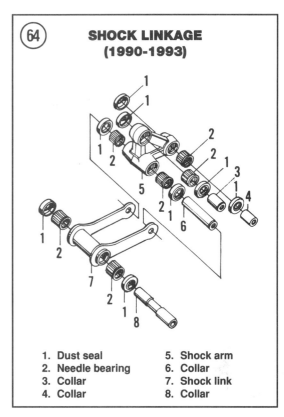

SHOCK LINKAGE (1990-1993)

1. Dust seal
2. Needle bearing
3. Collar
4. Collar
5. Shock arm
6. Collar
7. Shock link
8. Collar

REAR SUSPENSION

2. Clean all parts in solvent and thoroughly dry with compressed air.

3. Inspect the shock arm and shock link for cracks or damage; replace as necessary.

4. Inspect the collars for scratches, abrasion or abnormal wear; replace as necessary.

5. Inspect the needle bearings for abnormal wear. If worn or damaged, replace the damaged bearing(s).

6. Inspect the dust seals. Replace all of them as a set if any are worn or starting to deteriorate. If the dust seals are in poor condition, they will allow dirt to enter into the pivot areas and cause the needle bearings and collars to wear.

7. Coat all surfaces of the pivot receptacles, the needle bearings, the collars and the inside of the dust seals with molybdenum disulfide paste grease. Insert the collars into the shock link and the shock arms and install the dust seals.

NOTE
Make sure the dust seal lips seat correctly. If not, they will allow dirt and moisture into the bearing areas and cause wear.

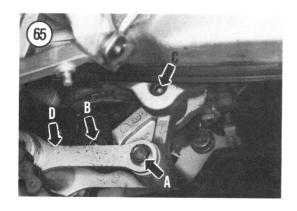

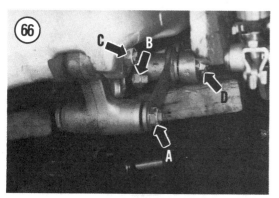

Installation

1. Install the shock link onto the frame mounting area and install the bolt and nut (D, **Figure 66**). Tighten the bolt and nut finger-tight at this time.

2. Install the shock arm onto the swing arm mounting area and install the bolt and nut (C, **Figure 66**). Tighten the bolt and nut finger-tight at this time.

3. Move the shock arm into position with the shock absorber lower mount and install the bolt and nut (B, **Figure 66**). Tighten the bolt and nut finger-tight at this time.

4. Tighten all bolts and nuts to the torque specification listed in **Table 1**.

5. Move the shock link onto the shock arm mounting area and install the bolt and nut (A, **Figure 66**). Tighten the bolt and nut to the torque specification listed in **Table 1**.

6. Install the exhaust chamber guard and tighten the bolts securely.

7. Install the rear wheel as described in this chapter.

SHOCK ABSORBER LINKAGE (1994-ON MODELS)

Removal

Refer to **Figure 67** for this procedure.

1. Remove the rear wheel as described in this chapter.

2. Remove the centerstand as described under *Centerstand Removal/Installation* in Chapter Thirteen.

3. Remove the bolt (A, **Figure 68**) and nut securing the shock arm plates to the shock link.

4. Remove the bolt (B, **Figure 68**) and nut securing the shock absorber lower mount to the shock arm plates.

5. Remove the bolt (C, **Figure 68**) and nut securing the shock arm plates to the swing arm and remove the shock arm plates (D, **Figure 68**).

6. Remove the bolt and nut securing the shock link to the frame and remove the shock link (E, **Figure 68**).

7. Inspect the components as described in this chapter.

Inspection

1. Remove the dust seals from the pivot points on the shock link.

458

2. Remove the collar from each pivot point on the shock link.

3. Clean all parts in solvent and thoroughly dry with compressed air.

4. Inspect the shock arm plates and the shock link for cracks or damage; replace as necessary.

5. Inspect the collars for scratches, abrasion or abnormal wear; replace as necessary.

6. Inspect the needle bearings for abnormal wear. If worn or damaged, replace the damaged bearing(s).

7. Inspect the dust seals. Replace all of them as a set if any are worn or starting to deteriorate. If the dust seals are in poor condition, they will allow dirt to enter into the pivot areas and cause the needle bearings and collars to wear.

8. Coat all surfaces of the pivot receptacles, the needle bearings, the collars and the inside of the dust seals with molybdenum disulfide paste grease. Insert the collars into the shock link and install the dust seals.

NOTE
Make sure the dust seal lips seat correctly. If not, they will allow dirt and moisture into the bearing areas and cause wear.

Installation

1. Install the shock link (E, **Figure 68**) onto the frame mounting area and install the bolt and nut. Tighten the bolt and nut finger-tight at this time.

2. Install the shock arm plates (D, **Figure 68**) onto the swing arm mounting area and install the bolt and nut (C, **Figure 68**). Tighten the bolt and nut finger-tight at this time.

3. Move the shock arm plates into position with the shock absorber lower mount and install the bolt and nut (B, **Figure 68**). Tighten the bolt and nut finger-tight at this time.

4. Move the shock link onto the shock arm plates mounting area and install the bolt and nut (A, **Figure 68**).

5. Tighten all bolts and nuts to the torque specification listed in **Table 1**.

6. Install the centerstand as described in this chapter.

7. Install the rear wheel as described in this chapter.

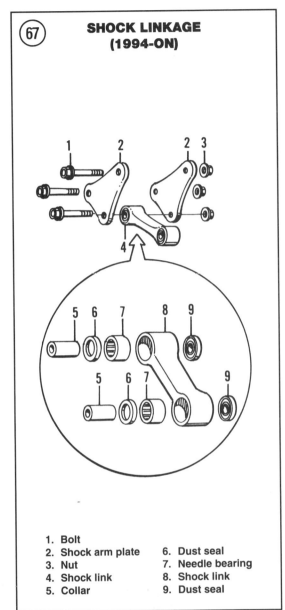

SHOCK LINKAGE (1994-ON)

1. Bolt
2. Shock arm plate
3. Nut
4. Shock link
5. Collar
6. Dust seal
7. Needle bearing
8. Shock link
9. Dust seal

REAR SUSPENSION

SWING ARM
(1986-1989 MODELS)

In time, the left-hand needle bearing and right-hand ball bearings will wear and will have to be replaced. The condition of the bearings can greatly affect handling performance and if worn parts are not replaced they can produce erratic and dangerous handling. Common symptoms are wheel hop, pulling to one side during acceleration and pulling to the other side during braking.

Refer to **Figure 69** for these procedures.

Removal

1. Place the bike on the centerstand (optional) or block up the engine so that the rear wheel clears the ground.

2. Remove the muffler(s) as described under *Exhaust System Removal/Installation* in Chapter Seven.

3. Remove the bolts and washers securing the drive chain guard to the swing arm and remove the chain guard.

4. Remove the rear brake caliper as described under *Rear Brake Caliper Removal/Installation* in Chapter Twelve.

5. Remove the rear wheel as described in this chapter.

6. Remove the rear brake caliper bracket as described under *Caliper Bracket Removal/Installation* in Chapter Twelve.

7. Remove the shock absorber linkage as described in this chapter.

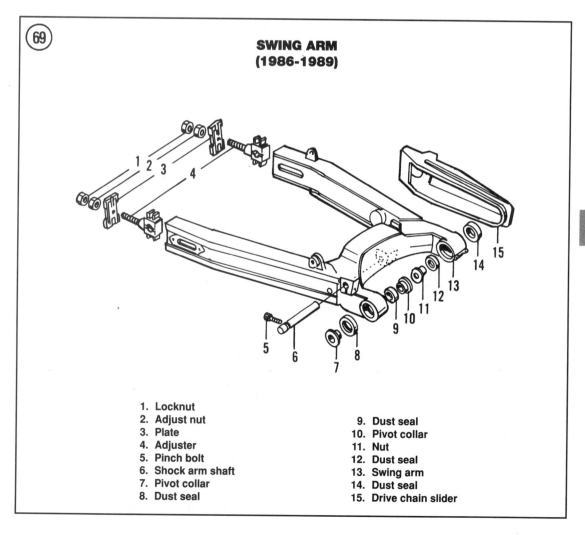

SWING ARM (1986-1989)

1. Locknut
2. Adjust nut
3. Plate
4. Adjuster
5. Pinch bolt
6. Shock arm shaft
7. Pivot collar
8. Dust seal
9. Dust seal
10. Pivot collar
11. Nut
12. Dust seal
13. Swing arm
14. Dust seal
15. Drive chain slider

8. Grasp the rear end of the swing arm and try to move it from side to side in a horizontal arc. There should be no noticeable side play. If play is evident and the pivot adjusting bolt is tightened correctly, the bearings should be replaced.

9. Remove the bolt and clamp securing the brake hydraulic hose to the torque link.

10. Remove the trim plug from the swing arm pivot bolt on the right-hand (**Figure 70**) and left-hand (**Figure 71**) sides.

11. Loosen both the right-hand pivot bolt (**Figure 72**) and left-hand pivot bolt (**Figure 73**), then remove both pivot bolts.

12. Remove the swing arm from the frame. Don't lose the pivot collars on the right-hand side of the swing arm.

13. Inspect the swing arm as described in this chapter.

Installation

1. If removed, install the brake torque link (**Figure 74**) onto the swing arm. Install the collar and bolt. Tighten the bolt to the torque specification listed in **Table 1**. Install the lockpin.

2. If removed, install the pivot collars (**Figure 75**) on the right-hand side of the swing arm.

3. Position the drive chain over the left-hand side of the swing arm.

4. Position the swing arm into the mounting area of the frame. Align the holes in the swing arm with the holes in the frame.

5. Apply a light coat of grease to the inner tip of both the right- and left-hand pivot bolts. Install the right-hand pivot bolt (**Figure 72**) and left-hand pivot bolt (**Figure 73**).

6. Make sure the swing arm is properly located in the frame and then tighten the right-hand pivot bolt to the torque specifications listed in **Table 1**.

7. Tighten the left-hand pivot bolt to the torque specification listed in **Table 1**.

8. Move the swing arm up and down several times to make sure all components are properly seated.

9. Install the trim plug into the swing arm pivot bolt on the right-hand (**Figure 70**) and left-hand (**Figure 71**) sides.

10. Install the brake hydraulic hose onto the torque link and install the bolt and clamp. Tighten the bolt securely.

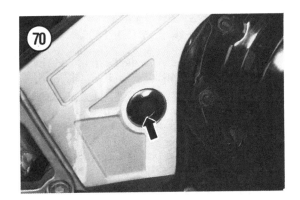

REAR SUSPENSION

11. Install the shock absorber linkage as described in this chapter.
12. Install the rear brake caliper bracket as described in Chapter Twelve.
13. Install the rear wheel as described in this chapter.
14. Install the rear brake caliper as described in Chapter Twelve.
15. Install the drive chain guard to the swing arm and install the bolts, collars and nuts.
16. Install the muffler(s) as described in Chapter Seven.

Inspection

1. Inspect the swing arm weld joints (**Figure 76**) for cracks, fractures or fatigue. Replace if necessary.
2. Inspect the drive chain slider (**Figure 77**) for wear or damage. Replace if necessary.
3. Inspect the shock arm pivot shaft mounting bosses (**Figure 78**) for wear, cracks or damage. If damaged, replace the swing arm.
4. Inspect the pivot bolts for wear, cracks or damage. If the threads are damaged, clean out the threads with the correct size and pitch thread die or replace if necessary.
5. Inspect the drive chain adjusters (**Figure 79**) for wear, cracks or damage. Replace if necessary.
6. Inspect the rear brake torque link (**Figure 74**) for wear, cracks or damage. Replace if necessary.

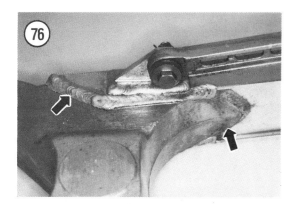

Bearing Replacement

The swing arm is equipped with a roller bearing on the left-hand side and 2 ball bearings on the right-hand side.

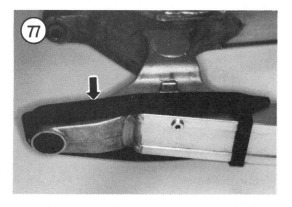

Several Honda special tools are required for bearing removal and installation. They are listed in this procedure.

1. Remove the swing arm as described in this chapter.
2. Remove the bolts, washers and collar securing the drive chain slider (**Figure 77**) and remove the slider.
3. On the right-hand side, perform the following:
   a. Remove the pivot collars (**Figure 80**) and the dust seals from each side of the pivot point.
   b. Remove the snap ring.
   c. Secure the swing arm in a vise with soft jaws.
   d. From the inside surface of the swing arm, drive out both ball bearing assemblies with a suitable size socket, an extension and a hammer.
4. On the left-hand side, perform the following:
   a. Remove the dust seal (A, **Figure 81**) from each side of the pivot point.
   b. Secure the swing arm in a vise with soft jaws.
   c. From the outside surface of the swing arm, drive out the needle bearing assembly (B, **Figure 81**) with a suitable size socket, an extension and a hammer.
5. Thoroughly clean out the inside surfaces of the pivot portions of the swing arm with solvent and dry with compressed air.
6. Apply a light coat of waterproof grease to all parts prior to installation.

NOTE
Drive the bearings into each side of the swing arm from the outside surface.

CAUTION
Never reinstall a bearing that has been removed. During removal it becomes slightly damaged and is no longer true to alignment. If installed, it will create an unsafe riding condition.

CAUTION
In order to prevent damage, the swing arm must be supported with the wood block under the pivot area when installing the bearings.

7. On the right-hand side, perform the following:
   a. Place a wood block under the inside surface of the swing arm pivot area.

NOTE
*The ball bearings can also be installed with Honda special tools (driver, part No. 07749-0010000), (32 × 35 mm attachment, part No. 07746-0010100) and (pilot, part No. 07746-0040300) as shown in **Figure 82**.*

b. Drive the ball bearings, one at a time, into place slowly and squarely with a suitable size socket, an extension and a hammer. Make sure the bearings are properly seated.

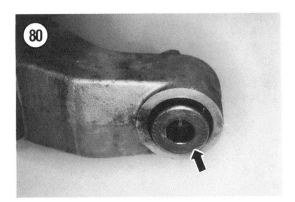

REAR SUSPENSION

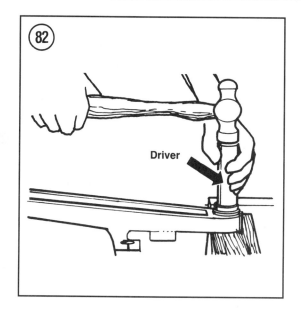

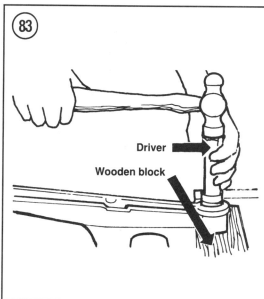

c. Install the snap ring. Make sure the snap is properly seated in the groove in the swing arm.
d. Install both dust seals into the outside surface of the pivot point.
e. Install the pivot collars (**Figure 80**).
8. On the left-hand side, perform the following:
a. Place a wood block under the inside surface of the swing arm pivot area.

NOTE
*The needle bearing can also be installed with Honda special tools (driver, part No. 07749-0010000), (32 × 35 mm attachment, part No. 07746-0010100) and (22 mm pilot, part No. 07746-0041000) as shown in **Figure 83**.*

b. Drive the needle bearings into place slowly and squarely with a suitable size socket, an extension and a hammer. Make sure they are properly seated.
c. Install the dust seals (**Figure 84**) into the outside surface of the pivot point.
9. Install the drive chain slider. Be sure to install the collars with the bolts. Tighten the bolts securely.
10. Install the swing arm as described in this chapter.

SWING ARM (1990-ON MODELS)

In time, the left-hand needle bearing and right-hand ball bearings will wear and will have to be replaced. The condition of the bearings can greatly affect handling performance and if worn parts are not replaced they can produce erratic and dangerous handling. Common symptoms are wheel hop, pulling to one side during acceleration and pulling to the other side during braking.

Refer to **Figure 85** for these procedures.

Removal

1. Place the bike on the centerstand (optional) or block up the engine so that the rear wheel clears the ground.
2. Remove the muffler as described under *Exhaust System Removal/Installation* in Chapter Seven.
3. Remove the bolts and washers securing the drive chain guard to the swing arm and remove the chain guard.

4. Remove the rear brake caliper as described under *Rear Brake Caliper Removal/Installation* in Chapter Twelve.

5. Remove the rear wheel as described in this chapter.

6A. On 1990-1993 models, perform the following:
   a. Remove the shock arm-to-swing arm bolt and nut (A, **Figure 86**).
   b. Remove the shock absorber-to-shock arm bolt and nut (B, **Figure 86**).
   c. Separate the shock arm from the swing arm.

6B. On 1994-on models, perform the following:
   a. Remove the shock arm plates-to-swing arm bolt and nut (A, **Figure 87**).
   b. Remove the shock absorber-to-shock arm plates bolt and nut (B, **Figure 87**).
   c. Separate the shock arm plates (C, **Figure 87**) from the swing arm and shock absorber.

7. Grasp the rear end of the swing arm and try to move it from side to side in a horizontal arc. There

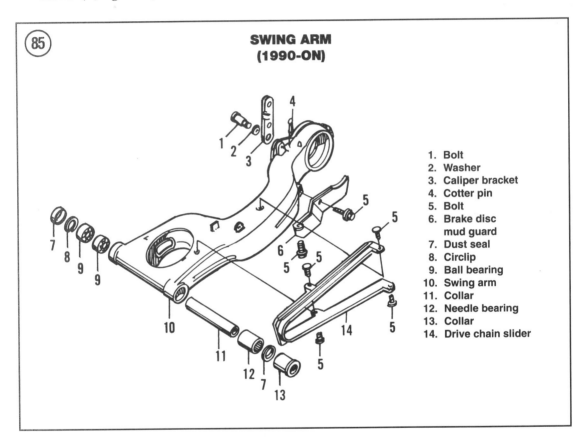

SWING ARM (1990-ON)

1. Bolt
2. Washer
3. Caliper bracket
4. Cotter pin
5. Bolt
6. Brake disc mud guard
7. Dust seal
8. Circlip
9. Ball bearing
10. Swing arm
11. Collar
12. Needle bearing
13. Collar
14. Drive chain slider

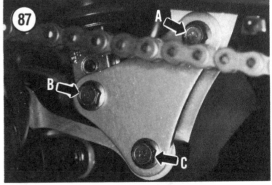

REAR SUSPENSION

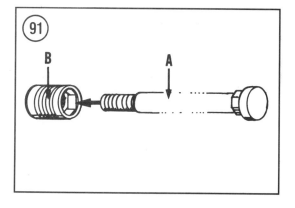

should be no noticeable side play. If play is evident and the pivot adjusting bolt is tightened correctly, the bearings should be replaced.

8. Remove the brake hydraulic hose from the clamps on the swing arm.
9. Remove the pivot bolt nut (**Figure 88**) from the left-hand side.
10. Remove the adjust bolt locknut (A, **Figure 89**) from the swing arm adjust bolt on the right-hand side.
11. Remove the adjust bolt (B, **Figure 89**) from the right-hand side.
12. Remove the pivot bolt from the right-hand side.
13. Remove the swing arm from the frame.
14. Inspect the swing arm as described in this chapter.

Installation

1. If removed, install the pivot collar on the left-hand side of the swing arm.
2. Position the drive chain (**Figure 90**) over the left-hand side of the swing arm.
3. Position the swing arm into the mounting area of the frame. Align the holes in the swing arm with the holes in the frame.
4. Apply a light coat of grease to the pivot bolt.
5. Make sure the swing arm is properly located in the frame and then install the adjust bolt in the right-hand side. Tighten the adjust bolt fully by hand.
6. From the right-hand side, insert the swing arm pivot bolt (A, **Figure 91**) through the adjust bolt so that the hex portions mate (B, **Figure 91**).
7. Using the pivot bolt (B, **Figure 89**), tighten the adjusting bolt to the torque specification listed in **Table 1**.
8. Install the adjust bolt locknut (A, **Figure 89**) onto the adjust bolt and tighten by hand.

NOTE
*The locknut can be tightened with an Allen wrench (A, **Figure 92**) and Honda special tool (swing arm pivot locknut wrench, part No. 07908-4690002) (B, **Figure 92**).*

9. Hold the swing arm pivot (and adjust bolt) stationary and tighten the locknut to the torque specification listed in **Table 1**.
10. Install the pivot bolt nut (**Figure 88**).

11. Have an assistant hold onto the pivot bolt to keep it from rotating, then tighten the pivot bolt nut to the torque specification listed in **Table 1**.

12. Move the swing arm up and down several times to make sure all components are properly seated.

13. Install the brake hydraulic hose onto the clamps on the swing arm.

14A. On 1990-1993 models, perform the following:
  a. Move the shock arm up into position on the shock absorber and install the bolt and nut (B, **Figure 86**). Tighten the bolt nut to the torque specification listed in **Table 1**.
  b. Move the shock arm up into position on the swing arm.
  c. Install the shock arm-to-swing arm bolt and nut (A, **Figure 86**). Tighten the bolt nut to the torque specification listed in **Table 1**.

14B. On 1994-on models, perform the following:
  a. Move the shock plates up into position on the shock absorber and install the bolt and nut (B, **Figure 87**). Tighten the bolt nut to the torque specification listed in **Table 1**.
  b. Align the shock arm plates with the swing arm.
  c. Install the shock arm plates-to-swing arm bolt and nut (A, **Figure 87**). Tighten the bolt nut to the torque specification listed in **Table 1**.

15. Install the rear wheel as described in this chapter.

16. Install the rear brake caliper as described under *Rear Brake Caliper Removal/Installation* in Chapter Twelve.

17. Install the drive chain guard onto the swing arm and tighten the bolts securely.

18. Install the muffler as described under *Exhaust System Removal/Installation* in Chapter Seven.

Inspection

1. Inspect the swing arm for wear, cracks or damage. Replace if necessary.

2. Inspect the drive chain slider for wear or damage. Replace if necessary.

3. Inspect the shock arm (or shock arm plates) pivot shaft mounting bosses for wear, cracks or damage. If damaged, replace the swing arm.

4. Inspect the pivot bolt, adjust bolt and adjust bolt locknut for wear, cracks or damage. If the threads are damaged, clean out the threads with the correct size and pitch thread die or replace if necessary.

Bearing Replacement

The swing arm is equipped with a roller bearing on the left-hand side and 2 ball bearings on the right-hand side.

Several Honda special tools are required for bearing removal and installation. They are listed in this procedure.

1. Remove the swing arm as described in this chapter.

2. Remove the bolts and washers securing the drive chain slider and remove the slider.

3. On the right-hand side, perform the following:
  a. Remove the dust seals from the pivot point.
  b. Remove the snap ring.
  c. Secure the swing arm in a vise with soft jaws.
  d. From the outside surface of the swing arm, install Honda special tool (bearing remover set, part No. 07936-371001) into the right-hand side of the swing arm.
  e. Expand the bearing tool behind both ball bearings.
  f. Use the slide hammer portion of the tool and withdraw both bearings from the pivot area.

4. On the left-hand side, perform the following:
  a. Remove the collar and the dust seal from the pivot point.
  b. From the outside surface of the swing arm, install Honda special tool (needle bearing remover, part No. 07HMC-MR70100) into the left-hand side of the swing arm.

CAUTION
In order to prevent damage, the swing must be supported with the wood block

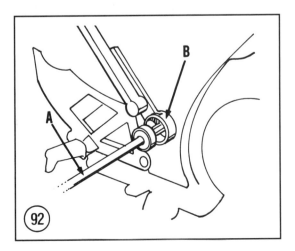

REAR SUSPENSION

under the pivot area when removing the bearing.

c. Place a wood block under the outside surface of the swing arm pivot area.
d. From the right-hand side of the swing arm, insert Honda special tool (driver shaft, part No. 07946-MJ00100) and place it on the bearing remover.
e. Drive the bearing out of the left-hand side.

5. Thoroughly clean out the inside surfaces of the pivot portions of the swing arm with solvent and dry with compressed air.

6. Apply a light coat of waterproof grease to all parts prior to installation.

NOTE
Drive the bearings into each side of the swing arm from the outside surface.

CAUTION
Never reinstall a bearing that has been removed. During removal it becomes slightly damaged and is no longer true to alignment. If installed, it will create an unsafe riding condition.

CAUTION
In order to prevent damage the swing arm must be supported with the wood block under the pivot area when installing the bearings.

7. On the right-hand side, perform the following:
a. Place a wood block under the inside surface of the swing arm pivot area.

NOTE
The ball bearings can also be installed with Honda special tools (driver, part No. 07749-0010000; 37 × 40 mm attachment, part No. 07746-0010200; and 28 mm pilot, part No. 07746-0040500) as shown in **Figure 82***.*

b. Drive the ball bearings, one at a time, into place slowly and squarely with a suitable size socket an extension and hammer. Make sure they are properly seated.
c. Install the snap ring. Make sure the snap is properly seated in the groove in the swing arm.
d. Install the dust seal into the outside surface of the pivot point.

8. On the left-hand side, perform the following:

a. Place a wood block under the inside surface of the swing arm pivot area.

NOTE
The needle bearing can also be installed with Honda special tools (driver, part No. 07749-0010000; 37 × 40 mm attachment, part No. 07746-0010200; and 28 mm pilot, part No. 07746-0041100).

b. Drive the needle bearings into place slowly and squarely with a suitable size socket, an extension and a hammer. Drive the bearing in until it is 4 mm (0.15 in.) below the outer surface of the pivot point.
c. Install the dust seals and collar into the outside surface of the pivot point.

9. Install the drive chain slider and bolts. Tighten the bolts securely.

10. Install the swing arm as described in this chapter.

REAR AXLE BEARING HOLDER AND DRIVEN SPROCKET (1990-ON MODELS)

Refer to **Figure 93** for these procedures.

Removal

1. Place the bike on the centerstand (optional) or block up the engine so that the rear wheel clears the ground.
2. Remove the muffler as described under *Exhaust System Removal/Installation* in Chapter Seven.
3. Remove the rear axle nut trim cap (**Figure 94**).
4. Un-stake the rear axle nut from the rear axle groove.
5. Have an assistant apply the rear brake, then loosen the rear axle nut. Do not remove the nut at this time.
6. Remove the bolts and washers securing the drive chain guard to the swing arm and remove the chain guard.
7. Remove the rear brake caliper as described under *Rear Brake Caliper Removal/Installation* in Chapter Twelve.
8. Remove the rear wheel as described in this chapter.

9. Remove the rear axle nut, lockwasher and collar from the left-hand side of the rear axle.

10. Slide the driven sprocket off the rear axle.

11. From the right-hand side, withdraw the rear axle/brake disc assembly from the bearing holder.

12. Remove the large snap ring from the right-hand side of the bearing assembly.

13. Remove the bolt securing the rear caliper bracket, rotate the bracket down and slide it off the bearing assembly.

14. Loosen the bearing assembly pinch bolt. It is not necessary to remove the bolt.

15. Withdraw the bearing assembly from the left-hand side of the swing arm and remove it.

16. Inspect the bearing assembly as described in this chapter.

Inspection

1. Clean all parts in solvent and thoroughly dry with compressed air.

2. Inspect the driven sprocket splines on the rear axle. Check for excessive wear, burrs or pitting. If damage is minor, clean up with a fine-cut file. If damage is severe, replace the rear axle.

3. Inspect the rear axle nut threads for stripped threads or damage. If necessary, clean up with the proper size metric die, then clean with solvent.

4. Make sure the rear brake disc mounting bolts and nuts are tight. If necessary, tighten to the torque specification listed in **Table 1**.

5. Inspect the driven sprocket inner splines. Check for excessive wear, burrs or pitting. If damage is minor, clean up with a fine-cut file. If damage is severe, replace the driven sprocket assembly.

6. Inspect the teeth of the driven sprocket. If the teeth are worn, remove the nuts and washers and remove driven sprocket from the assembly. Install the sprocket and tighten the nuts to the torque specification listed in **Table 1**.

7. If the driven sprocket requires replacement, also replace the drive chain and the drive sprocket.

8. Check the outer surface of the bearing housing and the inner surface of the swing arm where the

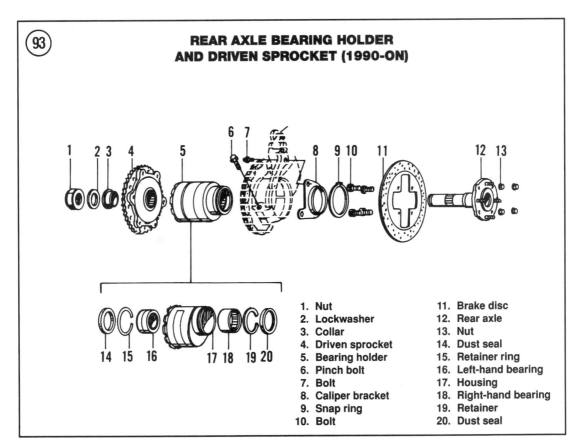

REAR AXLE BEARING HOLDER AND DRIVEN SPROCKET (1990-ON)

1. Nut
2. Lockwasher
3. Collar
4. Driven sprocket
5. Bearing holder
6. Pinch bolt
7. Bolt
8. Caliper bracket
9. Snap ring
10. Bolt
11. Brake disc
12. Rear axle
13. Nut
14. Dust seal
15. Retainer ring
16. Left-hand bearing
17. Housing
18. Right-hand bearing
19. Retainer
20. Dust seal

REAR SUSPENSION

bearing housing rides. Both of these surfaces must be smooth and free of any burrs so the bearing housing can rotate freely during drive chain adjustment.

> *CAUTION*
> *The needle bearings in the housing are very large in diameter and must be pressed out and pressed in to prevent damage to the bearing housing. Do not try to replace the bearing without the use of a hydraulic press and the special tools. Have the bearings replaced by a Honda dealer or qualified machine shop.*

9. Inspect the needle bearings for abnormal wear. If worn or damaged, have the damaged bearings replaced.
10. Inspect the dust seals. Replace both of them as a set if either is worn or starting to deteriorate. If the dust seals are in poor condition, they will allow dirt to enter and cause the needle bearings to wear.

> *NOTE*
> *Make sure the dust seal lips seat correctly. If not, they will allow dirt and moisture into the bearing areas and cause wear.*

11. Apply multipurpose grease to the needle bearings and to the lips of the dust seals.

Installation

1. Apply a light coat of multipurpose grease to the exterior of the bearing housing and to the inner surface of the swing arm where the bearing rides.

2. Install the bearing assembly from the left-hand side of the swing arm.
3. Temporarily tighten the bearing assembly pinch bolt. It will be tightened to the correct torque specification after the drive chain is adjusted.
4. Onto the right-hand side, slide the rear caliper bracket with the flanged side going on last. Rotate the bracket into the position and install the retaining bolt. Tighten the bolt to the torque specification listed in **Table 1**.
5. Install the large snap ring next to the bracket on the right-hand side of the bearing assembly. Make sure the snap ring is correctly seated in the bearing housing groove.
6. Install the rear axle/brake disc assembly into the bearing holder from the right-hand side. Push it in until it bottoms out.
7. Hold onto the end of the rear axle and install the driven sprocket onto the left-hand end of the rear axle.
8. Remove the rear axle nut, lockwasher and collar from the left-hand side of the rear axle. Push it on until it bottoms out.
9. Position the lockwasher with the dished side facing out and install the lockwasher onto the rear axle.
10. Install the rear axle nut and tighten only finger-tight at this time.
11. Install the rear brake caliper as described in Chapter Twelve.
12. Install the rear wheel as described in this chapter.
13. Have an assistant apply the rear brake, then tighten the rear axle nut to the torque specification listed in **Table 1**.
14. Stake the rear axle nut into the rear axle groove.
15. Install the rear axle nut trim cap.
16. Install the drive chain guard, bolts and washers. Tighten the bolts securely.
17. Install the muffler as described in Chapter Seven.

DRIVEN SPROCKET (1990-ON MODELS)

Disassembly/Assembly

Refer to **Figure 95** for these procedures.
1. Remove the rear axle bearing assembly as described in this chapter.

2. Remove the collar from the left-hand side.

3. Remove the hub from the driven sprocket/driven flange assembly.

4. Remove the rubber dampers from the driven sprocket/driven flange assembly.

5. Inspect the rubber dampers for signs of damage, hardness or deterioration. Replace as a complete set even though only one or two require replacement.

CAUTION
The bearing is very large and must be pressed out and pressed in to prevent damage to the driven sprocket/driven flange assembly. Do not try to replace the bearing without the use of a hydraulic press and the special tools. Have the bearings replaced by a Honda dealer or qualified machine shop.

6. Inspect the bearing for abnormal wear. If worn or damaged, have the damaged bearing replaced.

7. Inspect the dust seal and replace if it is worn or starting to deteriorate. If the dust seal is in poor condition, it will allow dirt to enter and cause the needle bearing to wear.

NOTE
Make sure the dust seal lips seat correctly. If not, it will allow dirt and moisture into the bearing area and cause wear.

8. Inspect the O-ring seal for wear or deterioration. Replace if necessary.

9. Assemble by reversing these disassembly steps while noting the following:

   a. Apply multipurpose grease to the lips of the dust seal and to the O-ring seal.

   b. Make sure all rubber dampers are installed in the driven sprocket/driven flange assembly.

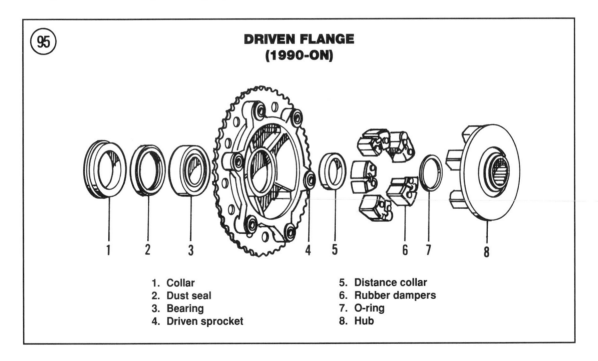

DRIVEN FLANGE (1990-ON)

1. Collar
2. Dust seal
3. Bearing
4. Driven sprocket
5. Distance collar
6. Rubber dampers
7. O-ring
8. Hub

REAR SUSPENSION

Table 1 REAR SUSPENSION TIGHTENING TORQUES

Item	N•m	ft.-lb.
Rear axle nut		
1986-1989	90-105	65-77
1990-on	195	141
Rear wheel nuts	35	25
Rear caliper bracket bolt		
1990-on	27	20
Brake disc bolts and nuts	35	25
1986-1989	37-43	27-31
1990-on	35	25
Driven sprocket nuts		
1986-1989	80-100	58-72
1990-on	33	24
Brake torque rod bolt	30-40	22-29
Shock absorber mounting bolts		
Upper and lower	40-50	29-36
Shock absorber damper rod-to-lower		
yoke locknut (1989-1991)	60-75	47-54
Shock linkage		
Shock arm pinch bolt (1986-1989)	20-30	14-22
Shock link-to-frame	40-50	29-36
Shock absorber-to-shock arm	40-50	29-36
Shock arm-to-shock link	40-50	29-36
Swing arm pivot bolts (1986-1989)		
Right-hand	55-65	40-47
Left-hand	85-105	62-77
Swing arm (1990-on)		
Adjust bolt	15	16
Adjust bolt locknut	80	58
Pivot bolt nut	95	69

Table 2 REAR SUSPENSION SPECIFICATIONS

Item	Standard	Service limit
Rear shock absorber spring		
Free length		
1986	–	147.0 mm (5.79 in.)
1987-1989	–	159.8 mm (6.29 in.)
1990-1991	–	191.4 mm (7.54 in.)
1992-1993	–	181.1 mm (7.13 in.)
1994-on	–	–

CHAPTER TWELVE

BRAKES

The brake system consists of dual discs on the front wheel and a single disc brake on the rear. This chapter describes repair and replacement procedures for all brake components.

Table 1 contains the brake system torque specifications and **Table 2** contains brake system specifications. **Table 1** and **Table 2** are located at the end of this chapter.

DISC BRAKES

The disc brakes are actuated by hydraulic fluid and are controlled by a hand lever for the front brakes or foot pedal for the rear brake that is connected to the master cylinder. As the brake pads wear, the brake fluid level drops in the reservoir and automatically adjusts for wear.

When working on hydraulic brake systems, it is necessary that the work area and all tools be absolutely clean. Any tiny particles of foreign matter and grit in the caliper assembly or the master cylinder can damage the components.

NOTE
*If you recycle your old engine oil **never** add used brake fluid to the old engine oil. Most oil retailers that accept old oil for recycling may not accept the oil if other fluids (fork oil, brake fluid or any other type of petroleum based fluids) have been combined with it.*

Consider the following when servicing the front and rear brake systems.

1. Disc brake components rarely require disassembly, so do not disassemble them unless necessary.
2. Use only DOT 4 brake fluid from a sealed container.

WARNING
Do not intermix silicone based (DOT 5) brake fluid as it can cause brake component damage leading to brake system failure.

3. Do not allow disc brake fluid to contact any plastic or painted or plated surfaces or surface damage will occur.

BRAKES

4. Always keep the master cylinder's reservoir cover closed to prevent dust or moisture from entering.

5. Use only DOT 4 brake fluid to wash parts. Never clean any internal brake components with solvent or any other petroleum based cleaners. Solvents will cause the seals to swell and distort and require replacement.

6. Whenever *any* component has been removed from the brake system the system is considered "opened" and must be bled to remove the air bubbles. Also if the brake feels "spongy," this usually means there is air in the system and it must be bled. For safe brake operation, refer to *Bleeding the System* as described in this chapter.

WARNING
*When working on the brake system, do **not** inhale brake dust. It may contain asbestos, which can cause lung injury and cancer. Wear a face mask that meets OSHA requirements for trapping asbestos particles, and wash your hands and forearms thoroughly after completing the work.*

FRONT BRAKE PAD REPLACEMENT

There is no recommended mileage interval for changing the friction pads in the disc brake. Pad wear depends greatly on riding habits and conditions. The pads should be checked for wear every 6,400 km (4,000 miles) and replaced when the wear indicator reaches the edge of the brake disc. To maintain an even brake pressure on the disc, always replace both pads in each caliper at the same time.

CAUTION
Watch the pads more closely when the wear line approaches the disc. On some pads the wear line is very close to the metal backing plate. If pad wear happens to be uneven for some reason, the backing plate may come in contact with the disc and cause damage.

Refer to the following illustrations for this procedure:
  a. **Figure 1**: 1986-1989 models.
  b. **Figure 2**: 1990-on models.

NOTE
When the brake pads are removed, if the front brake lever is inadvertently applied, the caliper pistons will be forced out of the cylinders in the caliper assemblies. If this does happen, the caliper assembly may have to be disassembled to reseat the pistons.

NOTE
This procedure is shown on a 1986-1989 model caliper and applies to all front caliper models. Where differences occur they are noted.

1. To prevent the accidental application of the front brake lever, place a spacer between the front brake lever and the hand grip. Hold the spacer in place with tape or a large rubber band.

2. Remove the pad pin plug(s) (A, **Figure 3**) and loosen the pad pins.

3. Remove the brake caliper bracket bolts (B, **Figure 3**).

4. Slide the brake caliper and bracket assembly off of the brake disc.

NOTE
On 1986-1989 models left-hand fork leg, don't lose the needle bearing and pivot collar in the fork slider nor the collar in the anti-dive piston.

5A. On 1986-1989 models, remove the 2 pad pins (**Figure 4**).

5B. On 1990-on models, remove the pad pin.

6. Remove the brake pads (**Figure 5**) and on 1986 models, remove the brake pad shim located behind the inboard brake pad.

7. Remove the anti-rattle spring (**Figure 6**).

8. Clean the pad recess and the ends of the pistons with a shop cloth. Do not use solvent, a wire brush or any hard tool which would damage the cylinders or pistons.

9. Carefully remove any rust or corrosion from the disc.

10. Lightly coat the end of the pistons and the backs of the new pads *(not the friction material)* with disc brake lubricant.

NOTE
When purchasing new pads, check with your dealer to make sure the friction compound of the new pad is compatible

with the disc material. Remove any roughness from the backs of the new pads with a fine-cut file; blow them clean with compressed air.

11. When new pads are installed in the caliper, the master cylinder brake fluid will rise as the caliper pistons are repositioned. Perform the following:
   a. Clean the top of the master cylinder of all dirt and foreign matter. Remove the screws securing the cover (**Figure 7**) and remove the cover, diaphragm plate and the diaphragm (**Figure 8**) from the front master cylinder.
   b. Slowly push both pistons into the caliper.
   c. Constantly check the reservoir to make sure brake fluid does not overflow. Siphon off brake fluid, if necessary, before it overflows.
   d. The pistons should move freely. If they don't, and there is evidence of them sticking in the cylinder, the caliper should be removed and serviced as described in this chapter.

12. Push the caliper pistons in all the way to allow room for the new pads.

13. Install the anti-rattle spring as shown in **Figure 6**.

14. Insert the brake pads into the caliper housing so that the friction material faces each other (**Figure 5**).

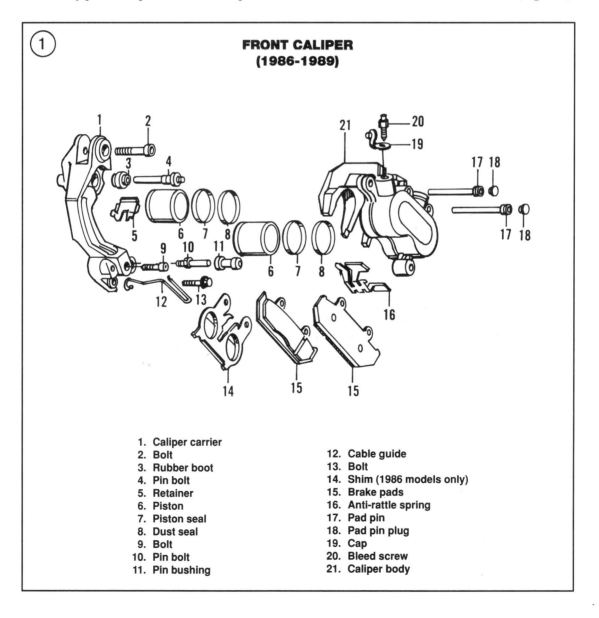

FRONT CALIPER (1986-1989)

1. Caliper carrier
2. Bolt
3. Rubber boot
4. Pin bolt
5. Retainer
6. Piston
7. Piston seal
8. Dust seal
9. Bolt
10. Pin bolt
11. Pin bushing
12. Cable guide
13. Bolt
14. Shim (1986 models only)
15. Brake pads
16. Anti-rattle spring
17. Pad pin
18. Pad pin plug
19. Cap
20. Bleed screw
21. Caliper body

BRAKES

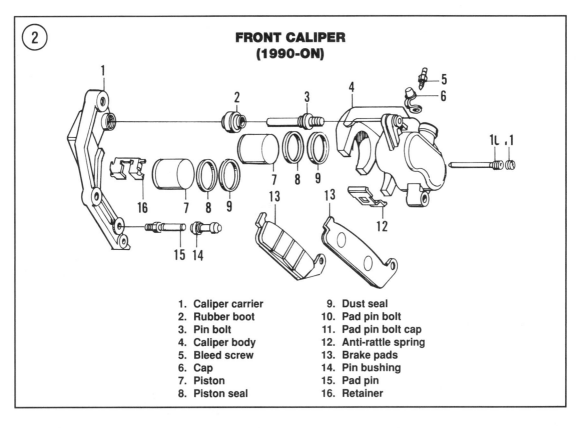

FRONT CALIPER (1990-ON)

1. Caliper carrier
2. Rubber boot
3. Pin bolt
4. Caliper body
5. Bleed screw
6. Cap
7. Piston
8. Piston seal
9. Dust seal
10. Pad pin bolt
11. Pad pin bolt cap
12. Anti-rattle spring
13. Brake pads
14. Pin bushing
15. Pad pin
16. Retainer

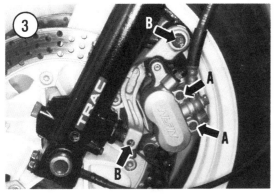

15. On 1986 models, install the brake pad shim behind the inboard brake pad.

16A. On 1986-1989 models, install one brake pad pin, then the other (**Figure 4**). Screw the pad pins in all the way.

16B. On 1990-on models, install the pad pin in all the way.

17. Apply silicone grease to the inside surface of the caliper pin boots.

18. On 1986-1989 models' left-hand fork leg, perform the following:
   a. Apply multipurpose grease to the needle bearing and pivot collar and install the collar in the fork slider where the caliper assembly attaches.
   b. If removed, install the collar into the backside of the anti-dive piston.

19. Align the brake pads with the brake disc and install the brake caliper onto the disc. Be careful not to damage the leading edge of the pads during installation.

20. Tighten the caliper bracket bolts (B, **Figure 3**) to the torque specification in **Table 1**.

21. Tighten the pad pin(s) to the torque specification in **Table 1**.

22. Install the pad pin plug(s) (A, **Figure 3**) and tighten securely.

23. Carefully roll the bike back and forth and apply the brake lever as many times as it takes to refill the cylinder in the caliper and correctly locate the pads.

WARNING
Use brake fluid clearly marked DOT 4 from a sealed container. Other types may vaporize and cause brake failure. Always use the same brand name. Do not intermix silicone based (DOT 5) brake fluid as it can cause brake component damage leading to brake system failure.

24. Refill the master cylinder reservoir, if necessary, to maintain the correct fluid level. Install the diaphragm, diaphragm plate and top cover. Tighten the screws securely.

25. After the caliper assemblies are installed and the brake pads correctly seated the following inspection must be made on the *left-hand caliper only* to check the caliper bracket-to-disc clearance:
   a. Measure the distance between each surface of the right-hand brake disc and the brake caliper bracket with a flat feeler gauge (**Figure 9**).
   b. The clearance must be 0.70 mm (0.028 in.) or more on each side.
   c. If the clearance is insufficient, loosen the left-hand axle clamp bolts and move the left-hand fork leg in or out until the correct clearance is obtained.
   d. Tighten the axle clamp bolts to the torque specification listed in **Table 1**.

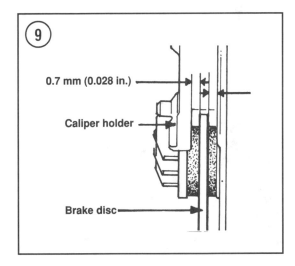

BRAKES

e. Recheck the clearance again. Readjust if necessary.

> **WARNING**
> *Do not ride the motorcycle until you are sure the brakes are working correctly.*

26. Bed the pads in gradually for the first 80 km (50 miles) by using only light pressure as much as possible. Immediate hard application will glaze the new friction pads and greatly reduce the effectiveness of the brake.

FRONT BRAKE CALIPER

Removal/Installation

Refer to the following illustrations for this procedure:

a. **Figure 1**: 1986-1989 models.
b. **Figure 2**: 1990-on models.

> **CAUTION**
> *Do not spill any brake fluid on the front fork or front wheel. Wash off any spilled brake fluid immediately, as it will destroy the finish. Use soapy water and rinse completely.*

1. If the caliper assembly is going to be disassembled for service, perform the following:

> **NOTE**
> *By performing Step 1b, compressed air may not be necessary for piston removal during caliper disassembly.*

   a. Remove the brake pads as described in this chapter.

> **CAUTION**
> *Do not allow the pistons to travel out far enough to come in contact with the brake disc. If this happens the pistons may scratch the disc during caliper removal.*

   b. Slowly apply the brake lever to push the pistons part way out of the caliper assembly for ease of removal during caliper service.

2. Clean the top of the master cylinder of all dirt and foreign matter.
3. Loosen the screws securing the master cylinder cover (**Figure 7**). Slightly loosen the cover, diaphragm plate and the diaphragm (**Figure 8**). This will allow air to enter the reservoir and allow the brake fluid to drain out more quickly in the next step.
4. Remove the union bolt and sealing washers (**Figure 10**) attaching the brake hose (A, **Figure 11**) to the front caliper and let the brake fluid drain out into the container. Dispose of this brake fluid—never reuse brake fluid.
5. Remove the bolts (B, **Figure 11**) securing the brake caliper assembly to the front fork as described in this chapter.
6. Place the loose end of the brake hose in a reclosable plastic bag to prevent brake fluid from dribbling out.
7. Installation is the reverse of these steps while noting the following:

   a. Tighten the caliper mounting bolts to the torque specification in **Table 1**.
   b. Install the brake hose using new washers (**Figure 12**).
   c. Tighten the brake union bolt to the torque specification in **Table 1**.
   d. Bleed the brakes as described under *Bleeding the System* in this chapter.

WARNING
Do not ride the motorcycle until you are sure that the brakes are operating properly.

Disassembly

Refer to the following illustrations for this procedure:
 a. **Figure 1**: 1986-1989 models.
 b. **Figure 2**: 1990-on models.
1. Remove the brake caliper as described in this chapter.
2. Pull the caliper bracket out of the housing.

NOTE
If the pistons were partially forced out of the caliper body during removal, Steps 5-7 may not be necessary. If the piston or caliper bore is corroded or very dirty, additional compressed air may be necessary to completely remove the pistons from the body.

3. Place a shop cloth or piece of soft wood over the end of the piston.
4. Perform this step over and close down to a workbench top. Hold the caliper body with the pistons facing away from you.

WARNING
*In the next step, the piston may shoot out of the caliper body like a bullet. Keep your fingers out of the way. Wear shop gloves and apply air pressure gradually. Do **not** use high pressure air or place the air hose nozzle directly against the hydraulic line fitting inlet in the caliper body. Hold the air nozzle away from the inlet allowing some of the air to escape.*

5. Apply the air pressure in short spurts to the hydraulic fluid passageway or brake hose inlet (**Figure 13**) and force the piston out (**Figure 14**). Use a service station air hose if you don't have an air compressor.

CAUTION
In the following step, do not use a sharp tool to remove the dust and piston seals from the caliper cylinders. Do not damage the cylinder surface.

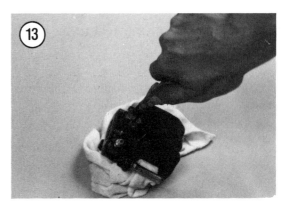

BRAKES

6. Use a piece of plastic or wood and carefully push the piston dust and piston seals (**Figure 15**) in toward the caliper cylinder and out of its grooves. Remove the seals from the caliper and discard both seals.

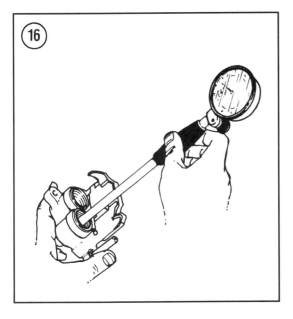

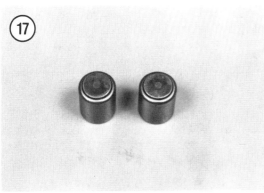

NOTE
Never reuse the old dust seals or piston seals. Very minor damage or age deterioration can make the seals useless.

7. Inspect the caliper as described in this chapter.

Inspection

1. Clean all caliper parts (except brake pads) in new DOT 4 brake fluid. Place the parts on a clean, lint-free cloth while performing the following inspection procedures.
2. Check the caliper bore (**Figure 15**) for cracks, deep scoring or excessive wear. Measure the cylinder bore (**Figure 16**) with a bore gauge. Replace the caliper housing if the bore exceeds the service limit in **Table 2**.
3. Check the caliper pistons (**Figure 17**) for deep scoring, excessive wear or rust. Then measure the piston outside diameter with a micrometer (**Figure 18**). Replace the pistons if the outside diameter exceeds the specifications given in **Table 2**.
4. The piston seal (A, **Figure 19**) helps to maintain correct brake pad to disc clearance. If the seal is worn or damaged, the brake pads will drag and cause excessive pad wear and brake fluid temperatures. Replace the piston seals (A, **Figure 19**) and dust seals (B, **Figure 19**) if the following conditions exist:
   a. Brake fluid leaks around the inner brake pad.
   b. Stuck piston seal(s).
   c. There is a large difference in inner and outer brake pad thickness (**Figure 20**).
5. Check the caliper bracket (A, **Figure 21**) for cracks or other damage; replace the support if necessary. Replace the dust boot (B, **Figure 21**) in the caliper bracket if torn or damaged.

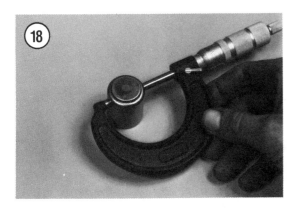

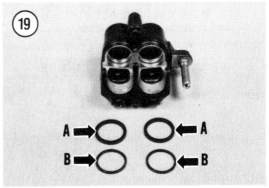

6. Check the pad pin(s) for cracks, deep scoring or excessive wear. Replace the pins if necessary.
7. Check the anti-rattle spring (**Figure 22**) for cracks or other damage; replace if necessary.
8. Remove the bleed screw. Make sure it is clean and open. Apply compressed air to the opening and make sure it is clear. Clean out if necessary with fresh brake fluid.

Assembly

1. Coat the seals, pistons and each piston bore with clean DOT 4 brake fluid.
2. See **Figure 19**. Install the piston seals (A) and dust seals (B) as follows:
   a. Install the piston seals (**Figure 23**) in the rear piston bore grooves.
   b. Install the dust seals (B, **Figure 19**) in the front piston bore grooves.
3. Install the pistons so that the closed end with the metal surface faces to the outside as shown in **Figure 24**.
4. Coat the caliper bracket pin (C, **Figure 21**) with a high-temperature silicone grease specified for brake use.
5. Install the caliper bracket onto the caliper housing.
6. Install the brake pads and the caliper housing as described under *Front Brake Pad Replacement* in this chapter.
7. Install the brake hose (A, **Figure 11**) onto the caliper. Be sure to place a new sealing washer on each side of the hose fitting (**Figure 12**) and install the union bolt (**Figure 10**). Tighten the union bolt to the torque specification in **Table 1**.
8. Bleed the brake system as described under *Bleeding the System* in this chapter.

> **WARNING**
> *Do not ride the motorcycle until the front brake is operating correctly.*

FRONT MASTER CYLINDER

Removal/Installation

> **CAUTION**
> *Cover the surrounding area with a heavy cloth or plastic tarp to protect them from accidental brake fluid spills. Wash brake fluid off any painted or*

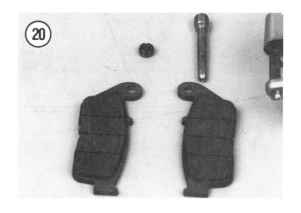

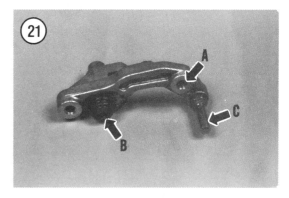

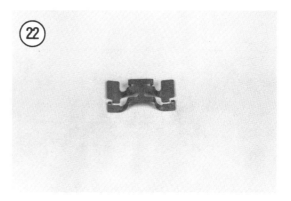

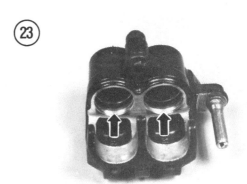

BRAKES

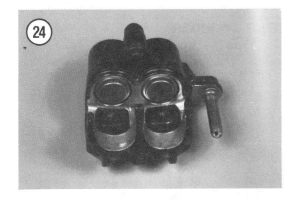

plated surfaces immediately, as it will destroy the finish. Use soapy water and rinse completely.

1. Disconnect the electrical wires from the brake light switch.

2. Pull back the rubber boot (**Figure 25**) and remove the union bolt (A, **Figure 26**) securing the brake hose to the master cylinder. Remove the brake hose. Tie the brake hose up and cover the end with a reclosable plastic bag to prevent the entry of foreign matter.

3. Remove the clamping bolts and clamp (B, **Figure 26**) securing the master cylinder to the handlebar and remove the master cylinder.

4. Install by reversing these removal steps while noting the following:

  a. Install the clamp with the UP arrow facing up (**Figure 27**). Align the raised boss on the clamp with the punch mark on the handlebar (**Figure 28**). Tighten the upper bolt first, then the lower to the torque specification listed in **Table 2**.

  b. Install the brake hose onto the master cylinder. Be sure to place a sealing washer on each side of the fitting and install the union bolt. Tighten the union bolt to the torque specifications listed in **Table 1**.

  c. Bleed the brake as described in this chapter.

Disassembly

Refer to **Figure 29** for this procedure.

1. Remove the master cylinder as described in this chapter.

2. Remove the screw securing the brake switch (A, **Figure 30**) and remove the switch.

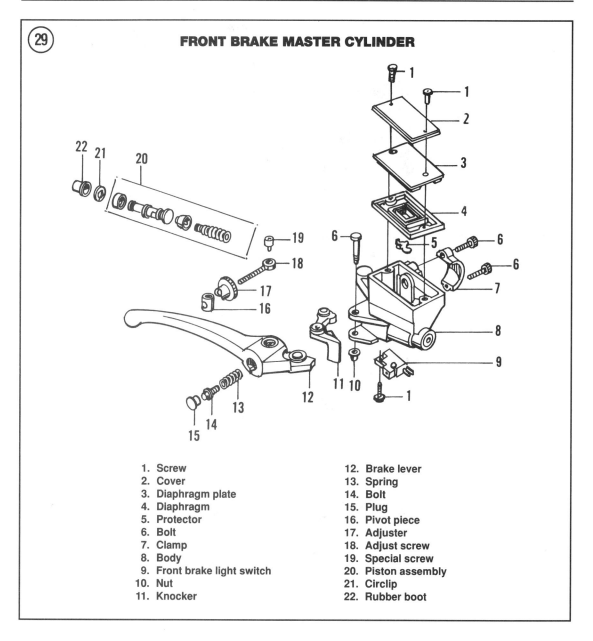

FRONT BRAKE MASTER CYLINDER

1. Screw
2. Cover
3. Diaphragm plate
4. Diaphragm
5. Protector
6. Bolt
7. Clamp
8. Body
9. Front brake light switch
10. Nut
11. Knocker
12. Brake lever
13. Spring
14. Bolt
15. Plug
16. Pivot piece
17. Adjuster
18. Adjust screw
19. Special screw
20. Piston assembly
21. Circlip
22. Rubber boot

BRAKES

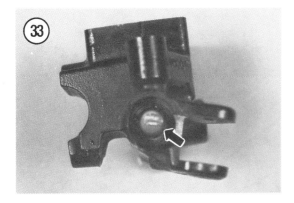

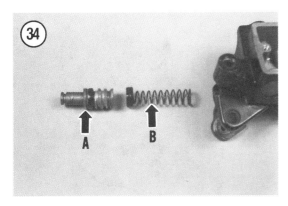

3. Remove the bolt and nut (B, **Figure 30**) securing the brake lever and remove the lever.

4. Remove the screws securing the cover (**Figure 31**) and remove the cover, diaphragm plate (**Figure 32**) and diaphragm; pour out the brake fluid and discard it. *Never reuse brake fluid.*

5. Remove the rubber boot from the area where the hand lever actuates the internal piston.

6. Using circlip pliers, remove the internal circlip (**Figure 33**) from the body.

7. Remove the secondary cup and the piston assembly (A, **Figure 34**).

8. Remove the primary cup and spring (B, **Figure 34**).

9. Remove the protector (**Figure 35**) from the bottom of the reservoir.

Inspection

1. Clean all parts in denatured alcohol or fresh brake fluid. Inspect the cylinder bore and piston contact surfaces for signs of wear and damage. If either part is less than perfect, replace it.

2. Check the end of the piston (A, **Figure 36**) for wear caused by the hand lever. Replace if worn.

3. Replace the piston if the secondary cup (B, **Figure 36**) requires replacement.

4. Inspect the primary cup and spring (C, **Figure 36**) for wear or deterioration. Replace if necessary.

5. Make sure the passages (**Figure 37**) on the bottom of the brake fluid reservoir are clear. Clean out if necessary.

6. Check the reservoir cap, diaphragm plate and diaphragm (**Figure 38**) for damage and deterioration and replace as necessary.

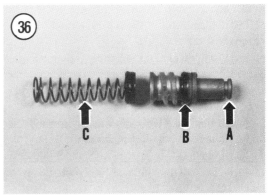

7. Inspect the threads in the bore for the brake hose union bolt. If the threads are slightly damaged; clean them up with a tap.
8. Check the hand lever pivot lugs (**Figure 39**) on the master cylinder body for elongation or cracks. Replace the body if necessary.
9. Measure the cylinder bore (**Figure 40**). Replace the master cylinder if the bore exceeds the specifications given in **Table 2**.
10. Measure the outside diameter of the piston as shown in **Figure 41** with a micrometer. Replace the piston assembly if it is less than the specifications given in **Table 2**.
11. Inspect the pivot hole (**Figure 42**) in the hand lever. If worn or elongated it must be replaced.

Assembly

1. Soak the new cups in fresh brake fluid for at least 15 minutes to make them pliable. Coat the inside of the cylinder with fresh brake fluid prior to the assembly of parts.

> *CAUTION*
> *When installing the piston assembly, do not allow the cups to turn inside out as they will be damaged and allow brake fluid leakage within the cylinder bore.*

2. Install the spring, primary cup and piston assembly into the reservoir cylinder together. Install the spring (B, **Figure 34**) with the tapered end facing toward the primary cup.

> *NOTE*
> *Be sure to install the primary cup with the open end in first, toward the spring.*

3. Install the circlip (**Figure 33**) and slide in the rubber boot.
4. Install the protector (**Figure 35**) onto the bottom of the reservoir.
5. Install the diaphragm, diaphragm plate (**Figure 32**) and cover (**Figure 31**). Do not tighten the cover screws at this time as fluid will have to be added later.
6. Install the brake lever onto the master cylinder body. Tighten the bolt and nut securely.
7. Install the brake light switch. Tighten the screw securely but not too tight as the switch may be damaged.

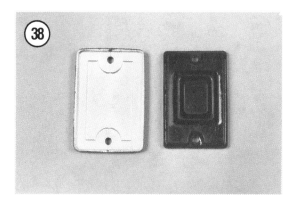

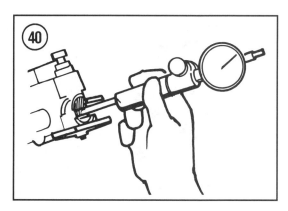

BRAKES

8. Install the master cylinder as described in this chapter.

REAR DISC BRAKE

The rear disc brake is actuated by hydraulic fluid and is controlled by the foot-operated pedal that is linked to the master cylinder. As the brake pads wear, the brake fluid level drops in the reservoir and automatically adjusts for wear.

REAR BRAKE PAD REPLACEMENT

There is no recommended mileage interval for changing the friction pads in the disc brake. Pad wear depends greatly on riding habits and conditions. The pads should be checked for wear every 6,400 km (4,000 miles) and replaced when the wear indicator reaches the edge of the brake disc. To maintain an even brake pressure on the disc, always replace both pads in the caliper at the same time.

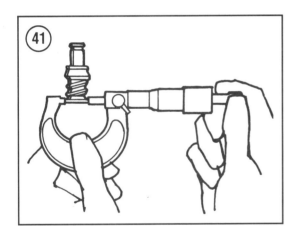

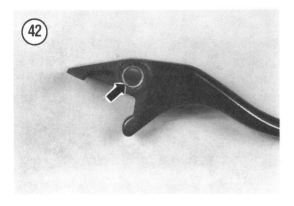

CAUTION
Watch the pads more closely when the wear line approaches the disc. On some pads the wear line is very close to the metal backing plate. If pad wear happens to be uneven for some reason, the backing plate may come in contact with the disc and cause damage.

1986-1989 models

Refer to **Figure 43** for this procedure.
1. Loosen the bolt (**Figure 44**) securing the pin retainer.
2. Remove the caliper upper (**Figure 45**) and lower (**Figure 46**) mounting bolts.
3. Pivot the caliper assembly up and off the disc.
4. Pull the caliper assembly off of the caliper bracket.
5. Remove the bolt (A, **Figure 47**) securing the pin retainer to the caliper assembly and remove the pin retainer (B, **Figure 47**).
6. Remove both pad pins and both brake pads.
7. Clean the pad recess and the end of the pistons (**Figure 48**) with a soft brush. Do not use solvent, wire brush or any hard tool which would damage the cylinders or pistons.
8. Carefully remove any rust or corrosion from the disc.
9. Lightly coat the end of the pistons and the backs of the new pads *(not the friction material)* with disc brake lubricant.

NOTE
When purchasing new pads, check with your dealer to make sure the friction compound of the new pad is compatible with the disc material. Remove any roughness from the backs of the new pads with a fine-cut file; blow them clean with compressed air.

10. When new pads are installed in the caliper, the master cylinder brake fluid level will rise as the caliper pistons are repositioned. Perform the following:
   a. Remove the frame right-hand side cover.
   b. Clean the top of the master cylinder reservoir of all dirt and foreign matter.
   c. Unscrew the cover (**Figure 49**) and remove the cover, diaphragm plate and diaphragm from the reservoir.

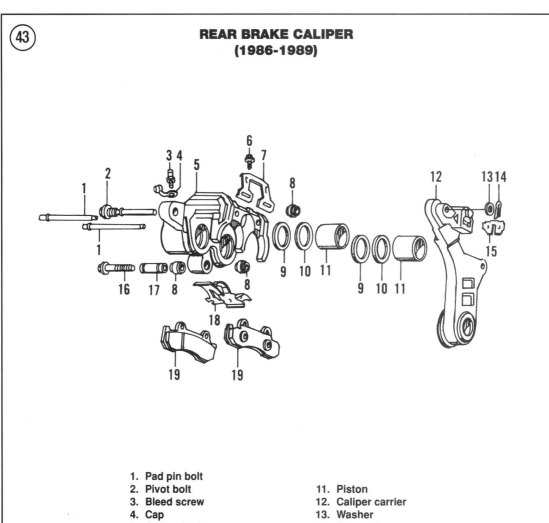

REAR BRAKE CALIPER (1986-1989)

1. Pad pin bolt
2. Pivot bolt
3. Bleed screw
4. Cap
5. Caliper body
6. Bolt
7. Pad pin retainer
8. Rubber boot
9. Piston seal
10. Dust seal
11. Piston
12. Caliper carrier
13. Washer
14. Cotter pin
15. Retainer
16. Bolt
17. Pivot collar
18. Anti-rattle spring
19. Brake pads

BRAKES

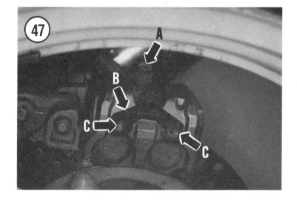

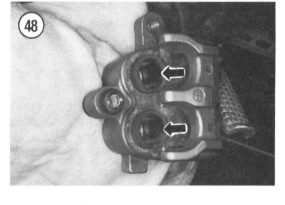

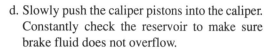

d. Slowly push the caliper pistons into the caliper. Constantly check the reservoir to make sure brake fluid does not overflow.

e. Siphon off fluid, if necessary, prior to it overflowing.

f. The pistons should move freely. If they don't, and there is evidence of them sticking in the cylinders, the caliper should be removed and serviced as described under *Rear Caliper Rebuilding* in this chapter.

11. Push the caliper pistons in all the way to allow room for the new pads.

12. Make sure the anti-rattle spring (**Figure 50**) is in place.

13. Install the outboard and inboard pads (**Figure 51**).

NOTE
Position the pad pins with the pin retainer groove going in first.

14. Push both pads down against the anti-rattle spring and install the front pad pin (**Figure 52**) then the rear pad pin (**Figure 53**).

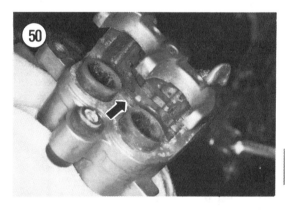

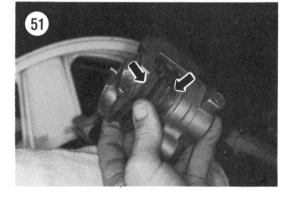

15. Install the pad pin retainer (B, **Figure 47**) onto the ends of the pins. Push the pin retainer down and make sure it seats completely on the groove in each pin (C, **Figure 47**).
16. Install the pad pin retaining bolt (A, **Figure 47**). Do not tighten at this time.
17. Make sure the retaining clip (A, **Figure 54**) is installed on the caliper bracket.
18. Inspect the pivot bolt boot (B, **Figure 54**) in the caliper bracket for wear or damage, replace if necessary.
19. Lubricate the caliper pivot bolt and pivot boot (B, **Figure 54**) on the caliper bracket with silicone grease.
20. Insert the caliper pivot bolt into the pivot bolt boot on the caliper bracket. Push the caliper on all the way until it stops.
21. Carefully pivot the caliper assembly down onto the disc. Be careful not to damage the leading edge of the pads during installation.
22. Install the caliper upper (**Figure 45**) and lower (**Figure 46**) mounting bolts. Tighten the bolts to torque specifications listed in **Table 1**.
23. Securely tighten the bolt (**Figure 44**) securing the pin retainer.
24. Carefully roll the bike back and forth and press the brake pedal as many times as it takes to refill the cylinder in the caliper and correctly locate the pads.

WARNING
Use brake fluid clearly marked DOT 4 from a sealed container. Other types may vaporize and cause brake failure. Always use the same brand name; do not intermix as many brands are not compatible. Do not intermix silicone based (DOT 5) brake fluid as it can cause brake component damage leading to brake system failure.

25. Refill the master cylinder reservoir, if necessary, to maintain the correct fluid level. Install the diaphragm, diaphragm plate and top cover (**Figure 49**). Tighten the cover securely.

WARNING
Do not ride the motorcycle until you are sure the rear brake is operating correctly with full hydraulic advantage. If necessary, bleed the brake as described in this chapter.

26. Install the frame right-hand side cover.
27. Bed the pads in gradually for the first 80 km (50 miles) by using only light pressure as much as possible. Immediate hard application will glaze the new friction pads and greatly reduce the effectiveness of the brake.

1990-on models

Refer to **Figure 55** for this procedure.
1. Remove the rear wheel as described under *Rear Wheel Removal/Installation (1990-on Models)* in Chapter Eleven.

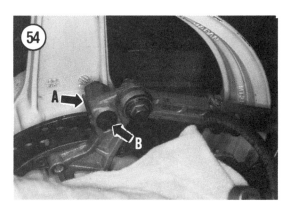

BRAKES

2. Remove the caliper mounting bolts (A, **Figure 56**) securing the caliper assembly and the caliper bracket to the swing arm.

3. Disengage the brake hose from the retainer (B, **Figure 56**) on the swing arm.

4. Pull the caliper assembly up and off the disc.
5. Remove the pad pin cap (**Figure 57**).
6. Remove the pad pin bolt (**Figure 58**).
7. Remove the pad pin, both brake pads and the pad shims (on models so equipped).

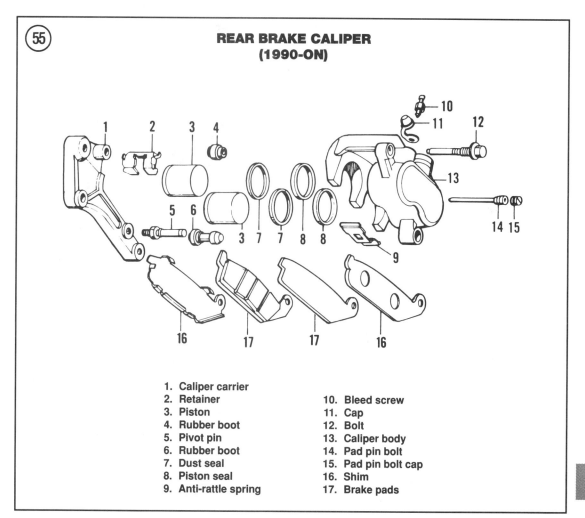

REAR BRAKE CALIPER (1990-ON)

1. Caliper carrier
2. Retainer
3. Piston
4. Rubber boot
5. Pivot pin
6. Rubber boot
7. Dust seal
8. Piston seal
9. Anti-rattle spring
10. Bleed screw
11. Cap
12. Bolt
13. Caliper body
14. Pad pin bolt
15. Pad pin bolt cap
16. Shim
17. Brake pads

8. Clean the pad recess and the end of the pistons (A, **Figure 59**) with a soft brush. Do not use solvent, wire brush or any hard tool which would damage the cylinders or pistons.

9. Carefully remove any rust or corrosion from the disc.

10. Lightly coat the end of the pistons and the backs of the new pads *(not the friction material)* with disc brake lubricant.

NOTE
When purchasing new pads, check with your dealer to make sure the friction compound of the new pad is compatible with the disc material. Remove any roughness from the backs of the new pads with a fine-cut file; blow them clean with compressed air.

11. When new pads are installed in the caliper, the master cylinder brake fluid level will rise as the caliper pistons are repositioned. Perform the following:
   a. Clean the top of the master cylinder reservoir of all dirt and foreign matter.
   b. Remove the screws securing the cover (**Figure 60**) and remove the cover, diaphragm plate and diaphragm from the reservoir.
   c. Slowly push the caliper pistons into the caliper. Constantly check the reservoir to make sure brake fluid does not overflow.
   d. Siphon off fluid, if necessary, prior to it overflowing.
   e. The pistons should move freely. If they don't, and there is evidence of them sticking in the cylinders, the caliper should be removed and serviced as described under *Rear Caliper Rebuilding* in this chapter.

12. Push the caliper pistons in all the way to allow room for the new pads.

13. If removed, install the anti-rattle spring as shown in B, **Figure 59**.

14. On models so equipped, install the shims onto the brake pads.

15. Install the outboard pad (A, **Figure 61**) and inboard pad (B, **Figure 61**).

16. Hook the front end of the brake pad into the caliper housing and push the rear end of both pads down, then install the pad pin (**Figure 62**) into the caliper housing and through the hole in each pad.

17. Push the pin all the way in, then tighten (**Figure 58**) to the torque specification listed in **Table 1**.

18. Install the pad pin cap (**Figure 63**) and tighten securely.

19. Install the caliper assembly onto the disc. Be careful not to damage the leading edge of the pads during installation.

20. Install the caliper assembly and the caliper bracket mounting bolts (A, **Figure 56**). Tighten the bolt to torque specifications listed in **Table 1**.

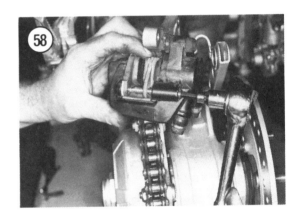

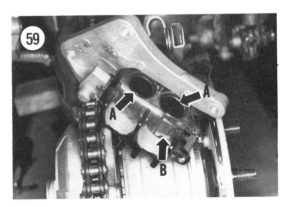

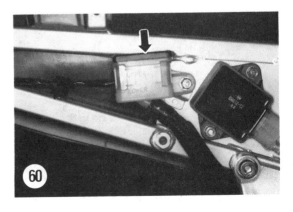

BRAKES

21. Install the brake hose into the retainer (B, **Figure 56**).
22. Install the rear wheel as described in Chapter Eleven.
23. Carefully roll the bike back and forth and press the brake pedal as many times as it takes to refill the cylinder in the caliper and correctly locate the pads.

WARNING
Use brake fluid clearly marked DOT 4 from a sealed container. Other types may vaporize and cause brake failure.

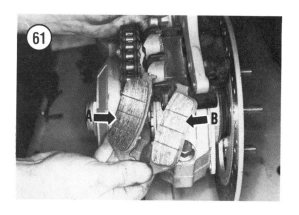

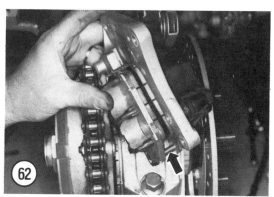

Always use the same brand name; do not intermix as many brands are not compatible. Do not intermix silicone based (DOT 5) brake fluid as it can cause brake component damage leading to brake system failure.

24. Refill the master cylinder reservoir, if necessary, to maintain the correct fluid level. Install the diaphragm, diaphragm plate and top cover. Tighten the screws securely.

WARNING
Do not ride the motorcycle until you are sure the rear brake is operating correctly with full hydraulic advantage. If necessary, bleed the brake as described in this chapter.

25. Bed the pads in gradually for the first 80 km (50 miles) by using only light pressure as much as possible. Immediate hard application will glaze the new friction pads and greatly reduce the effectiveness of the brake.

REAR CALIPER

Refer to the following illustrations for this procedure:
 a. **Figure 43**: 1986-1989 models.
 b. **Figure 55**: 1990-on models.

Removal

CAUTION
Do not spill any brake fluid on the painted portion of the rear wheel. Wash any spilled brake fluid immediately, as it will destroy the finish. Use soapy water and rinse completely.

1A. On 1986-1989 models, remove the right-hand muffler as described under *Exhaust System Removal/Installation* in Chapter Seven.
1B. On 1990-on models, remove the rear wheel as described under *Rear Wheel Removal/Installation (1990-on Models)* in Chapter Eleven.
2. Place a container under the brake hose at the caliper. Remove the union bolt and sealing washers securing the brake hose to the caliper assembly. Refer to **Figure 64** for 1986-1989 models or A, **Figure 65** for 1990-on models.

3. Remove the brake hose and let the brake fluid drain out into the container. Dispose of this brake fluid—never reuse brake fluid.

4. To prevent the entry of moisture and dirt, cap the end of the brake hose. Place the loose end in a plastic reclosable bag and tie the loose end up to the frame.

5A. On 1986-1989 models, perform the following:
   a. Remove the caliper upper (**Figure 45**) and lower (**Figure 46**) mounting bolts.
   b. Pivot the caliper assembly up and off the disc.
   c. Pull the caliper assembly off of the caliper bracket.

5B. On 1990-on models, perform the following:
   a. Remove the caliper mounting bolts (B, **Figure 65**) securing the caliper assembly and the caliper bracket to the swing arm.
   b. Pull the caliper assembly (C, **Figure 65**) up and off the disc.

Installation

1A. On 1986-1989 models, perform the following:
   a. Lubricate the caliper pivot bolt and pivot boot on the caliper bracket with silicone grease.
   b. Insert the caliper pivot bolt into the pivot bolt boot on the caliper bracket. Push the caliper on all the way until it stops.
   c. Carefully pivot the caliper assembly down onto the disc. Be careful not to damage the leading edge of the pads during installation.
   d. Install the caliper upper (**Figure 45**) and lower (**Figure 46**) mounting bolts. Tighten the bolt to torque specifications listed in **Table 1**.

1B. On 1990-on models, perform the following:
   a. Carefully install the caliper assembly onto the disc. Be careful not to damage the leading edge of the pads during installation.
   b. Install the caliper assembly and the caliper bracket mounting bolts (A, **Figure 56**). Tighten the bolt to torque specifications listed in **Table 1**.
   c. Install the brake hose into the retainer (B, **Figure 56**).
   d. Install the rear wheel as described in Chapter Eleven.

2. Install the brake hose, with a sealing washer on each side of the fitting, onto the caliper. Install the union bolt and tighten to the torque specifications listed in **Table 1**.

3. Bleed the brake as described in this chapter.

WARNING
Do not ride the motorcycle until you are sure that the brake is operating properly.

Rebuilding

Refer to the following illustrations for this procedure:
   a. **Figure 43**: 1986-1989 models.
   b. **Figure 55**: 1990-on models.

BRAKES

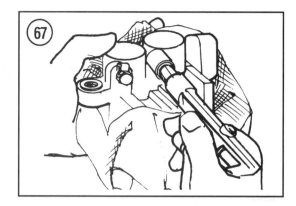

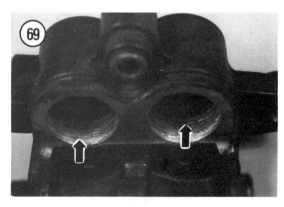

1. Remove the caliper assembly as described in this chapter.
2. Remove the brake pads as described in this chapter.
3. Unscrew and remove the bleed screw and cap (**Figure 66**).
4. Place a shop cloth or piece of soft wood over the ends of the pistons.
5. Perform this step over and close down to a workbench top. Hold the caliper body with the piston facing away from you.

WARNING
*In the next step, the pistons may shoot out of the caliper body like bullets. Keep your fingers out of the way. Wear shop gloves and apply air pressure gradually. Do **not** use high pressure air or place the air hose nozzle directly against the hydraulic hose fitting inlet in the caliper body. Hold the air nozzle away from the inlet allowing some of the air to escape during the procedure.*

6. Apply the air pressure (**Figure 67**) in short spurts to the union bolt hole (**Figure 68**) and force the pistons out of the caliper. Use a service station air hose if you don't have an air compressor.

CAUTION
In the following step, do not use a sharp tool to remove the dust and piston seals from the caliper cylinders. Do not damage the cylinder surfaces.

7. Use a piece of plastic or wood and carefully push the dust seals and the piston seals in toward the caliper cylinder and out of their grooves. Remove the dust and piston seals from the cylinders and discard both seals.
8. Inspect the seal grooves in caliper body (**Figure 69**) for damage. If damaged or corroded, replace the caliper assembly.

NOTE
The caliper body cannot be replaced separately. If it is damaged in any way, the entire caliper assembly must be replaced.

9. Inspect the caliper body (A, **Figure 70**) for damage, replace the caliper body if necessary.
10. Inspect the hydraulic fluid passageways in the base of each cylinder bore. Make sure they are clean

and open. Apply compressed air to the openings and make sure they are clear. Clean out if necessary with fresh brake fluid.

11. Inspect the cylinder walls and the pistons (**Figure 71**) for scratches, scoring or other damage. If either is rusty or corroded, replace either the pistons or the caliper assembly.

12. Measure the outside diameter of the pistons with a caliper (**Figure 72**). Replace the piston(s) if the dimension is less than the specifications given in **Table 2**.

13. Measure each cylinder bore (**Figure 73**). Replace the caliper assembly if the bore exceeds the specifications given in **Table 2**.

14. Inspect the caliper mounting bolt holes (B, **Figure 70**). If worn or damaged, replace the caliper assembly.

15. On 1986-1989 models, inspect the rubber boots (**Figure 74**) for damage or deterioration. Replace if necessary.

16. Make sure the hole in the bleed screw (A, **Figure 75**) and brake hose union bolt (B, **Figure 75**) are clean and open. Apply compressed air to the openings and make sure they are clear. Clean out if necessary with fresh brake fluid.

17. If serviceable, clean the caliper body with rubbing alcohol and rinse with clean brake fluid.

NOTE
Never reuse a dust seal or piston seal that has been removed. Very minor damage or age deterioration can make the seals useless.

18. Coat the new dust and piston seals with fresh DOT 4 brake fluid.

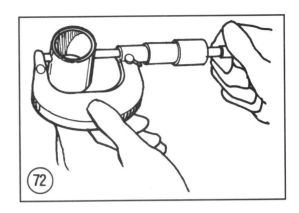

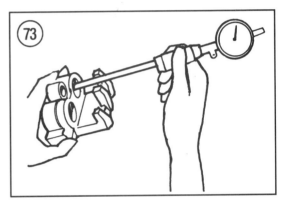

BRAKES

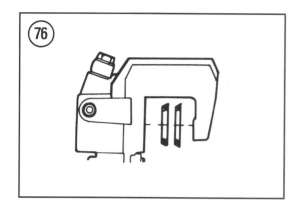

NOTE
*On 1986-1989 models, install the piston and dust seals with the smaller diameter side (**Figure 76**) going in first.*

19. Carefully install the new piston seals (**Figure 77**) and new dust seals (**Figure 78**) in the grooves in the caliper cylinders. Make sure the seals are properly seated in their respective grooves.

20. Coat the pistons and the caliper cylinders with fresh DOT 4 brake fluid.

21. Position the pistons with the *open end facing out* toward the brake pads and install the pistons into the caliper cylinders (**Figure 79**). Push the pistons in until they bottom out.

22. Install the bleed screw and cap (**Figure 66**).

23. Install the anti-rattle spring (**Figure 80**) into the caliper.

24. Install the brake pads as described in this chapter.

25. Install the brake caliper as described in this chapter.

Caliper Bracket Removal/Installation (1986-1989 Models)

Refer to **Figure 81** for this procedure.

1. Remove the rear caliper assembly as described in this chapter.
2. Remove the cotter pin and washer (A, **Figure 82**) from the end of the bolt, then remove the bolt (B, **Figure 82**) and washer from the brake torque arm.
3. Lift the torque arm (C, **Figure 82**) up and off the caliper bracket.
4. Remove the rear wheel as described in Chapter Eleven and remove the caliper bracket.

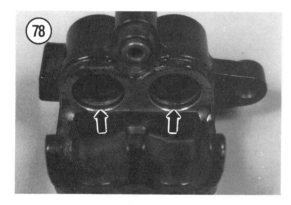

5. Inspect the caliper bracket (**Figure 83**) for damage or cracks. Replace if necessary.

6. Make sure the retainer (**Figure 84**) is in place and in good condition. Replace if necessary.

7. Install by reversing these removal steps while noting the following:

a. Position the caliper bracket as shown in A, **Figure 85** during rear wheel installation.

b. Make sure the retainer (B, **Figure 85**) is in place on the bracket.

c. Be sure to install a washer on each side of the hole in the brake torque arm, then install the bolt. Tighten the bolt securely.

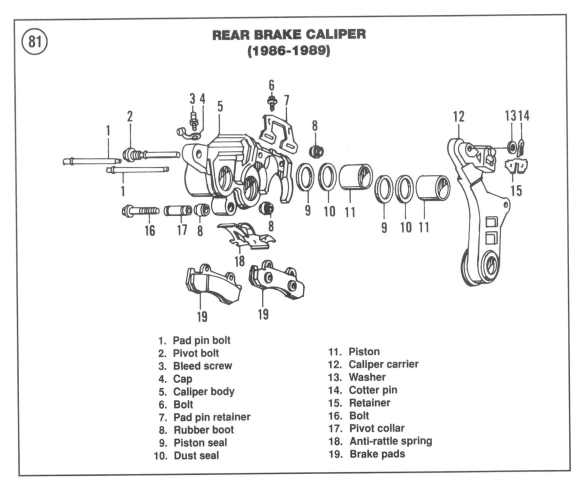

REAR BRAKE CALIPER (1986-1989)

1. Pad pin bolt
2. Pivot bolt
3. Bleed screw
4. Cap
5. Caliper body
6. Bolt
7. Pad pin retainer
8. Rubber boot
9. Piston seal
10. Dust seal
11. Piston
12. Caliper carrier
13. Washer
14. Cotter pin
15. Retainer
16. Bolt
17. Pivot collar
18. Anti-rattle spring
19. Brake pads

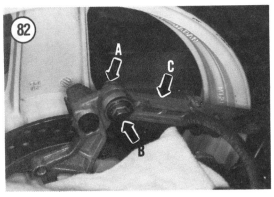

BRAKES

Caliper Bracket Removal/Installation (1990-On Models)

Refer to **Figure 86** for this procedure.

1. Remove the rear caliper assembly as described in this chapter.
2. Remove the bolt (A, **Figure 87**) securing the caliper to the caliper bracket.
3. Pull the caliper straight off the caliper bracket (B, **Figure 87**).
4. Inspect the caliper bracket for damage or cracks. Replace if necessary.
5. Install by reversing these removal steps while noting the following:
   a. Lubricate the caliper pivot bolt and pivot boot on the caliper bracket with silicone grease.

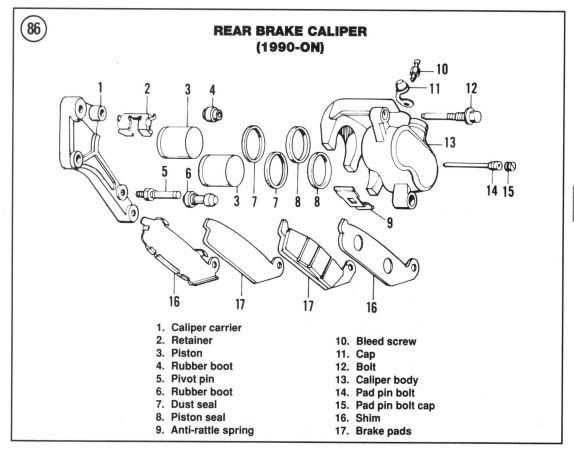

REAR BRAKE CALIPER (1990-ON)

1. Caliper carrier
2. Retainer
3. Piston
4. Rubber boot
5. Pivot pin
6. Rubber boot
7. Dust seal
8. Piston seal
9. Anti-rattle spring
10. Bleed screw
11. Cap
12. Bolt
13. Caliper body
14. Pad pin bolt
15. Pad pin bolt cap
16. Shim
17. Brake pads

b. Tighten the caliper-to-caliper bracket bolt to the torque specification listed in **Table 1**.

REAR MASTER CYLINDER

Removal/Installation

Refer to **Figure 88** for this procedure.

NOTE
This procedure is shown on a 1991 model. All other models are similar.

1A. On 1986-1989 models, remove the seat and the frame right-hand side cover as described in Chapter Thirteen.

1B. On 1990-on models, remove the seat and the tailpiece/side cover as described in Chapter Thirteen.

CAUTION
Cover the surrounding area of the frame and the wheel with a heavy cloth or plastic tarp to protect them from accidental brake fluid spills. Wash brake fluid off any painted or plated surfaces immediately, as it will destroy the finish. Use soapy water and rinse completely.

2. Place a container under the brake hose at the master cylinder.
3. Remove the bolt (A, **Figure 89**) securing the reservoir hose to the master cylinder. Disconnect the hose (B, **Figure 89**) from the master cylinder.
4. Loosen the union bolt and sealing washers (**Figure 90**) securing the brake hose to the top of the master cylinder.
5. Remove the cotter pin and washer from the pivot pin (C, **Figure 89**) on the rod eye.

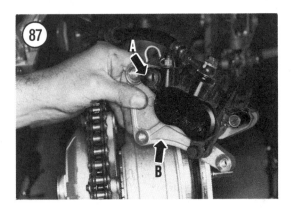

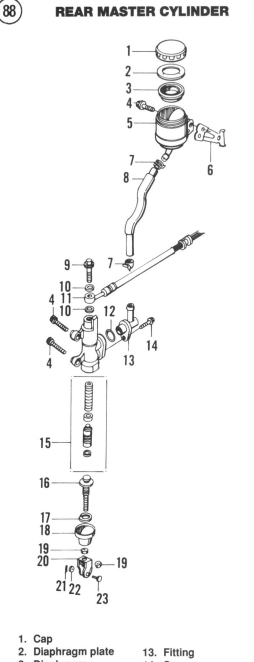

REAR MASTER CYLINDER

1. Cap
2. Diaphragm plate
3. Diaphragm
4. Bolt
5. Reservoir
6. Bracket
7. Hose clamp
8. Reservoir hose
9. Union bolt
10. Sealing washer
11. Caliper hose
12. O-ring
13. Fitting
14. Screw
15. Piston assembly
16. Pushrod
17. Circlip
18. Rubber boot
19. Nut
20. Rod eye
21. Cotter pin
22. Washer
23. Pivot pin

BRAKES

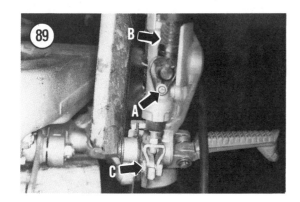

6. Remove the pivot pin and remove the brake pedal actuating arm from the rod eye (**Figure 91**).
7. Remove the union bolt and sealing washers (A, **Figure 92**) loosened in Step 4.

NOTE
Drain the brake fluid from the hose and discard it—never reuse brake fluid. Contaminated brake fluid may cause brake failure.

8. Cover the end of the brake hose to prevent the entry of foreign matter. Place the loose end in a reclosable plastic bag and tie the loose end of the hose up to the frame.
9. Remove the Allen bolts (B, **Figure 92**) securing the master cylinder to the rider's right-hand footpeg bracket.
10. Remove the master cylinder and drain out any residual brake fluid.
11. To remove the master cylinder reservoir, perform the following:
    a. Remove the flange bolt securing the master cylinder reservoir to the frame. Refer to **Figure 93** for 1986-1989 models or **Figure 94** for 1990-on models.

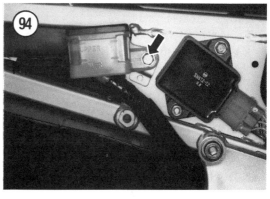

b. Remove the reservoir and the hose assembly from the frame.
c. Wipe off any spilled brake fluid from the frame after removing the reservoir and hose assembly.

12. Install by reversing these removal steps while noting the following:
   a. Install a new cotter pin on the joint pin and bend the ends over completely.
   b. Install a new O-ring seal into the fitting and install the brake fluid reservoir hose and fitting onto the master cylinder.
   c. Be sure to install a sealing washer on each side of the brake hose fitting and install the union bolt into the top of the master cylinder. Tighten the union bolt to the torque specification listed in **Table 2**.
   d. Fill the reservoir and bleed the brake as described in this chapter.

Disassembly

Refer to **Figure 88** for this procedure.

1. Remove the master cylinder as described in this chapter.
2. If still attached, remove the bolt securing the reservoir hose to the master cylinder. Disconnect the hose and remove the hose and reservoir assembly (**Figure 95**) from the master cylinder.
3. Slide the rubber boot (**Figure 96**) off the base of the master cylinder. It is not necessary to remove the boot.

> *CAUTION*
> *When the circlip is removed, the pushrod will be pushed out by the internal spring pressure. Protect yourself accordingly.*

4. Using circlip pliers, remove the internal circlip (**Figure 97**) from the body.
5. Remove the pushrod (**Figure 98**) from the body.
6. Remove the piston, primary cup and spring assembly (**Figure 99**).

> *NOTE*
> *It may be necessary to apply a small amount of air pressure to the brake fluid outlet to remove the piston and primary cup. If necessary, apply the air in short spurts and catch the piston as it comes out.*

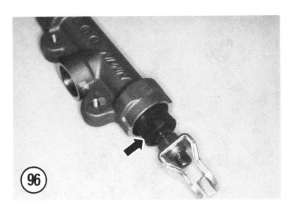

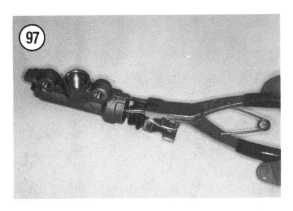

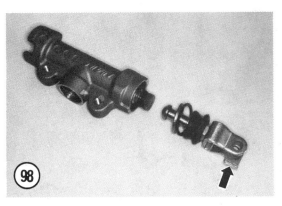

BRAKES

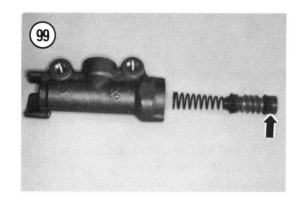

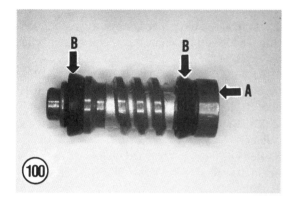

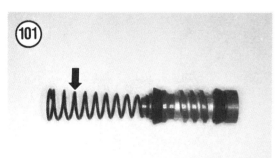

Inspection

1. Clean all parts in denatured alcohol or fresh brake fluid.

2. Apply compressed air to all openings in the master cylinder body to thoroughly dry it out.

3. Inspect the cylinder bore and piston contact surfaces for signs of wear and damage. If either part is less than perfect, replace it.

4. Check the end of the piston (A, **Figure 100**) for wear caused by the pushrod. Replace if worn.

5. Check the cups (B, **Figure 100**) for damage, softness or for swollen conditions. Replace the piston assembly if necessary.

6. Check the spring (**Figure 101**) for cracks or other damage; replace if necessary.

7. Inspect the pushrod assembly (**Figure 102**) for wear or damage. Make sure the dust boot is in good condition. Check that the circlip is not bent or damaged. Replace worn or damaged parts as necessary.

8. Inspect the cylinder bore for signs of wear and damage. If less than perfect, replace the master cylinder assembly. The body cannot be replaced separately. If the bore is satisfactory, perform Step 9.

9. Measure the cylinder bore (**Figure 103**). Replace the master cylinder if the bore exceeds the specifications given in **Table 1**.

10. Measure the outside diameter of the piston with a micrometer (**Figure 104**). Replace the piston assembly if it is less than the specifications given in **Table 1**.

11. Make sure the passages (**Figure 105**) in the bottom of the brake fluid reservoir are clear. Check

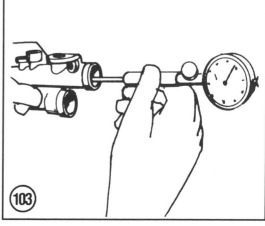

the reservoir cap and diaphragm for damage and deterioration and replace as necessary.

12. Inspect the brake hose threads in the body. If damaged the master cylinder must be replaced.

Assembly

1. Soak the new cups (B, **Figure 100**) in fresh brake fluid for at least 15 minutes to make them pliable. Coat the inside of the cylinder with fresh brake fluid prior to the assembly of parts.

CAUTION
When installing the piston assembly, do not allow the cup to turn inside out as it will be damaged and allow brake fluid leakage within the cylinder bore.

2. Place the master cylinder in a vise with soft jaws. Do not tighten the jaws too tight or the master cylinder may be distorted or damaged.

NOTE
Be sure to install the primary cup with the open end in first, toward the spring.

3. Install the spring, primary cup and piston assembly into the cylinder together. Install the spring with the tapered end facing toward the primary cup (**Figure 99**).
4. Install the pushrod (**Figure 98**) and press it into the body.
5. Install the circlip (**Figure 97**) and slide in the rubber boot. Make sure the rubber boot is properly seated in the body to form a good seal.
6. Install the master cylinder as described in this chapter.

BRAKE HOSE REPLACEMENT

There is no factory-recommended replacement interval but it is a good idea to replace all brake hoses every four years or when they show signs of cracking or damage.

CAUTION
Cover the surrounding area with a heavy cloth or plastic tarp to protect it from accidental spilling of brake fluid. Wash brake fluid off of any painted or plated surface immediately, as it will destroy the finish. Use soapy water and rinse completely.

Front Hoses and 2-Way Joint Removal/Installation

Refer to the following illustrations for this procedure:
  a. **Figure 106**: 1986-1989 models.
  b. **Figure 107**: 1990-on models.

1. Remove the front fairing as described under *Front Fairing Removal/Installation* in Chapter Thirteen.
2. On models so equipped, move the rubber boot (**Figure 108**) off the union bolt on the master cylinder union bolt.
3. Remove the union bolt (A, **Figure 109**) securing the upper hose to the master cylinder and remove the hose (B, **Figure 109**).
4. Place a container under the brake hose at the caliper.
5. Remove the union bolt and sealing washer (**Figure 110**) securing the brake hose to the caliper assembly.

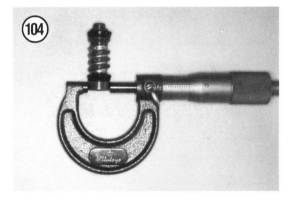

BRAKES

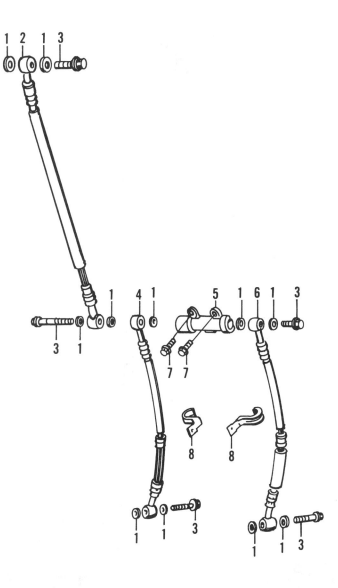

FRONT BRAKE LINES (1986-1989)

1. Sealing washer
2. Upper hose
3. Union bolt
4. Lower right-hand hose
5. Three-way joint
6. Lower left-hand hose
7. Bolt
8. Hose guide

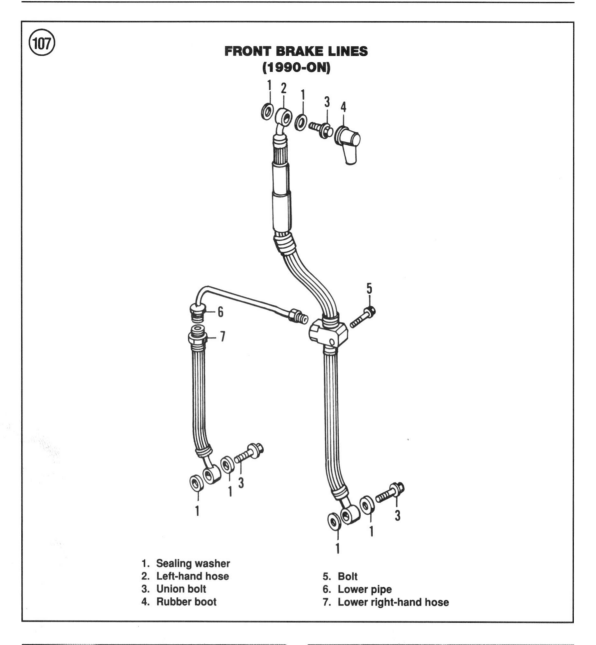

FRONT BRAKE LINES (1990-ON)

1. Sealing washer
2. Left-hand hose
3. Union bolt
4. Rubber boot
5. Bolt
6. Lower pipe
7. Lower right-hand hose

BRAKES

6. Remove brake hose from the clip or bracket on the fork leg.

7. Remove the brake hose and let the brake fluid drain out into the container.

8. To prevent the entry of moisture and dirt, cap the end of the brake hose. Place the loose end in a reclosable plastic bag and tie the loose end up to the forks.

WARNING
Dispose of this brake fluid—never reuse brake fluid. Contaminated brake fluid can cause brake failure.

9. Repeat Steps 4-8 for the other caliper.

10A. On 1986-1989 models, perform the following:
   a. Remove the union bolt securing the left-hand brake hose to the 2-way joint.
   b. Remove the union bolt securing the right-hand lower hose and upper hose to the fitting on the 2-way joint and remove them.
   c. If necessary, remove the bolts securing the 2-way joint to the lower fork bridge and remove the 2-way joint.

10B. On 1990 and later models, perform the following:
   a. Hold onto the lower right-hand brake hose fitting with an open end wrench. Loosen the fitting on the lower pipe.
   b. Unscrew the lower pipe from the lower right-hand hose. Remove the lower right-hand hose from the mounting bracket on the fork slider and remove it.
   c. Unscrew the lower pipe from the fitting on the left-hand hose and remove the lower pipe.
   d. Remove the bolt securing the left-hand hose center connection to the left-hand fork slider.
   e. Carefully remove the left-hand hose from the steering head assembly and frame and remove the hose.

11. Install new hoses, sealing washers and union bolts in the reverse order of removal. Be sure to install *new* sealing washers in the correct positions.

12. Tighten all union bolts to torque specifications listed in **Table 1**.

13. Refill the master cylinder with fresh brake fluid clearly marked DOT 4. Bleed the brake as described in this chapter.

WARNING
Do not ride the motorcycle until you are sure that the brakes are operating properly.

14. Install the front fairing as described in Chapter Thirteen.

Rear Brake Hose Removal/Installation

Refer to **Figure 88** for this procedure.

1. On 1990-on models, remove the rear wheel (A, **Figure 111**) as described under *Rear Wheel Removal/Installation* in Chapter Eleven.

2. Place a container under the brake hose at the caliper.

3A. On 1986-1989 models, perform the following:
   a. Remove the union bolt (A, **Figure 112**) and sealing washers securing the brake hose to the caliper assembly.
   b. Remove bolt and clip (B, **Figure 112**) securing the brake hose to the caliper torque link.

3B. On 1990-on models, perform the following:

a. Remove the union bolt (B, **Figure 111**) and sealing washers securing the brake hose to the caliper assembly.

b. Remove brake hose from the clip on the caliper bracket (C, **Figure 111**) and drive chain guard (D, **Figure 111**).

WARNING
Dispose of this brake fluid—never reuse brake fluid. Contaminated brake fluid can cause brake failure.

4. Remove the brake hose from the caliper and let the brake fluid drain out into the container.

5. To prevent the entry of moisture and dirt, cap the union bolt hole in the caliper.

6A. On 1986-1989 models, perform the following:
   a. Remove the union bolt and sealing washers (**Figure 113**) securing the brake hose to the top of the master cylinder.
   b. Remove the hose.

6B. On 1990-on models, perform the following:
   a. Remove the union bolt and sealing washers (**Figure 114**) securing the brake hose to the top of the master cylinder.
   b. Remove the hose.

7. Install a new hose, sealing washers and the union bolts in the reverse order of removal. Be sure to install new sealing washers in the correct positions; refer to **Figure 88**.

8. Tighten all union bolts to torque specifications listed in **Table 2**.

9A. On 1986-1989 models, to replace the master cylinder-to-reservoir hose, perform the following:
   a. Remove the frame right-hand side cover.
   b. Loosen the hose clamps (A, **Figure 115**) at the reservoir and at the master cylinder.
   c. Remove the hose (B, **Figure 115**) from both fittings.
   d. Install a new hose and tighten the hose clamps securely.

9B. On 1990-on models, to replace the master cylinder-to-reservoir hose, perform the following:
   a. Remove the frame tailpiece/side cover assembly as described in Chapter Thirteen.
   b. Loosen the hose clamp (A, **Figure 116**) at the reservoir and at the master cylinder (**Figure 117**).
   c. Remove the hose (B, **Figure 116**) from both fittings.

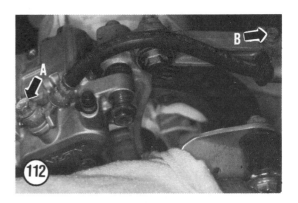

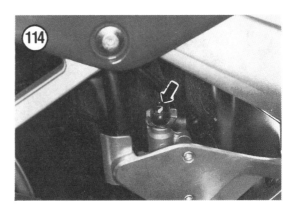

BRAKES

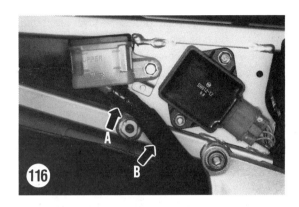

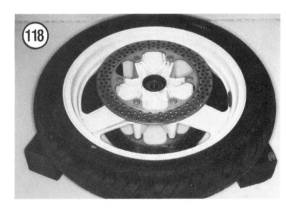

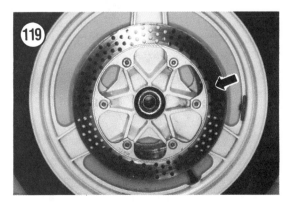

d. Install a new hose and tighten the hose clamps securely.

10. Refill the master cylinder with fresh brake fluid clearly marked DOT 4 only. Bleed the brake as described in this chapter.

WARNING
Do not ride the motorcycle until you are sure that the brakes are operating properly.

11. Install all items removed.

BRAKE DISC—FRONT AND REAR

Removal/Installation

1. Remove the front or rear wheel as described in Chapter Ten or Chapter Eleven.

NOTE
Place a piece of wood or vinyl tube in the caliper(s) in place of the disc(s). This way, if the brake lever is inadvertently squeezed, or the brake pedal depressed, the pistons will not be forced out of the cylinders. If this does happen, the caliper may have to be disassembled to reseat the pistons and the system will have to be bled. By using the wood or vinyl tube, bleeding the system is not necessary when installing the wheel.

CAUTION
*Do not set the wheel down on the disc surface, as it may get scratched or warped. Set the tire sidewall on 2 blocks of wood (**Figure 118**).*

NOTE
The front discs on 1986-1989 models do not have a mark indicating which side of the wheel the discs belong. It is suggested that they be marked with either an "R" (right-hand side) or "L" (left-hand side) so they will be reinstalled on the same side of the wheel from which they were removed.

2. On the front wheel, remove the bolts securing the brake disc (**Figure 119**) on each side. Remove both discs and on 1986-1989 models, remove the damping shims located between the disc and the hub.

3A. On 1986-1989 models, on the rear wheel, remove the Allen bolts securing the disc (**Figure 120**) to the wheel. Remove the brake disc.

3B. On 1990-on models, on the rear disc, perform the following:

    a. Remove the rear axle as described under *Rear Axle Removal/Installation* in Chapter Eleven.

    b. Remove the Allen bolts and nuts securing the disc to the rear axle. Remove the brake disc.

4. On the front wheel, install by reversing these removal steps while noting the following:

    a. On the 1986-1989 front wheel, if the existing discs are being reinstalled, refer to the "R" or "L" marks made prior to removal and install the disc on the correct side of the wheel.

    b. On the 1990-1993 front wheel, note that the brake discs have either an "R" (right-hand side) or "L" (left-hand side) stamped on them. Be sure to install the disc with this mark facing outward and on the correct side of the wheel.

    c. On the 1994-on front wheel, note that the brake discs have an arrow indicating the proper direction of rotation. Be sure to install the disc with this mark facing outward and on the correct side of the wheel so the arrow is pointing in the correct direction.

    d. On the 1986-1989 front wheel, install the damping shims on the hub then install the disc and bolts.

    e. Tighten the Allen bolts to the torque specification listed in **Table 1**.

    f. Repeat for the other brake disc.

5. On the rear wheel, install by reversing these removal steps while noting the following:

    a. On 1986-1989 models, install the brake disc and the disc mounting Allen bolts. Tighten the bolts to the torque specification listed in **Table 2**.

    b. On 1990-on models, install the brake disc and the disc mounting Allen bolts and nuts. Tighten the bolts and nuts to the torque specification listed in **Table 2**. Install the rear axle as described in Chapter Eleven.

Inspection

It is not necessary to remove the disc from the wheel to inspect it. Small marks on the disc are not important, but deep radial scratches, deep enough to snag a fingernail, reduce braking effectiveness and increase brake pad wear. If these grooves are found, the disc should be replaced.

1. Measure the thickness of the disc at several locations around the disc with a micrometer (**Figure 121**) or vernier caliper. The disc must be replaced if the thickness in any area is less than that specified in **Table 2**.

2. Make sure the disc bolts (and nuts) are tight prior to running this check.

3. Check the disc runout with a dial indicator as shown in **Figure 122**.

4. Slowly rotate the wheel, or rear disc (1990-on models) and watch the dial indicator. On all models, if the runout exceeds that listed in **Table 2** or greater the disc(s) must be replaced.

5. Clean the disc of any rust or corrosion and wipe clean with lacquer thinner. Never use an oil based solvent that may leave an oil residue on the disc.

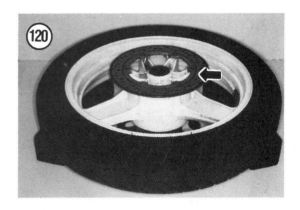

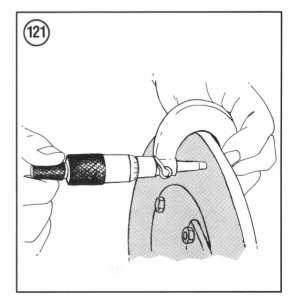

BRAKES

BLEEDING THE SYSTEM

This procedure is not necessary unless the brakes feel spongy, there has been a leak in the system, a component has been replaced or the brake fluid has been replaced.

1. Remove the dust cap from the bleed valve on the caliper assembly as follows:

   a. **Figure 123**: the front caliper.
   b. **Figure 124**: 1986-1989 rear caliper.
   c. **Figure 125**: 1990-on rear caliper.

2. Connect a piece of clear tubing to the bleed valve on the caliper assembly.

CAUTION
Cover the surrounding area with a heavy cloth or plastic tarp to protect it from the accidental spilling of brake fluid. Wash any brake fluid off of any plastic, painted or plated surface immediately; as it will destroy the finish. Use soapy water and rinse completely.

3. Clean the top cover or cap of the master cylinder of all dirt and foreign matter.

4A. On the front brake, remove the screws securing the cover (**Figure 126**). Remove the cover, diaphragm plate and the diaphragm (**Figure 127**).

4B. On the 1986-1989 and 1994 rear brake, unscrew the cap **Figure 128**. Remove the cap, diaphragm plate and the diaphragm.

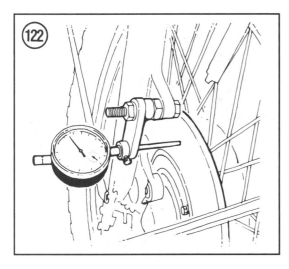

4C. On the 1990-1993 rear brake, remove the screws securing the cover (**Figure 129**). Remove the cover, diaphragm plate and the diaphragm.

5. Fill the reservoir almost to the top lip; insert the diaphragm, diaphragm plate and the cover or cap loosely. Leave the cover or cap in place during this procedure to prevent the entry of dirt.

6. Place the other end of the tube into a clean container (**Figure 130**).

WARNING
Use brake fluid from a sealed container marked DOT 4 only (specified for disc brakes). Other types may vaporize and cause brake failure. Do not intermix different brands or types as they may not be compatible. Do not intermix a silicone based (DOT 5) brake fluid as it can cause brake component damage leading to brake system failure.

NOTE
During this procedure, it is very important to check the fluid level in the brake master cylinder reservoir often. If the reservoir runs dry, you'll introduce more air into the system which will require starting over.

7. Fill the container with enough fresh brake fluid to keep the end submerged.

8. If the master cylinder was drained, it must be bled first as follows:
   a. Remove the union bolt and hose from the master cylinder. Refer to **Figure 131** for the front brake or **Figure 132** for the rear.
   b. Slowly apply the brake lever or pedal several times while holding your thumb over the opening in the master cylinder.
   c. With the lever or pedal applied, slightly release your thumb pressure. Some of the brake fluid and air bubbles will escape.
   d. Apply thumb pressure and pump lever once more.
   e. Repeat this procedure until you can feel resistance at the lever.

9. Quickly reinstall the hose, sealing washers and the union bolt. Refill the master cylinder.

10. Tighten the union bolt and pump the lever or pedal again and perform the following:
    a. Loosen the union bolt 1/4 turn. Some brake fluid and air bubbles will escape.
    b. Tighten the union bolt and repeat this procedure until no air bubbles escape.

11. Tighten the union bolts to the torque specification listed in **Table 1**.

12. Slowly apply the brake lever, or pedal, several times as follows:
    a. Pull the lever in or apply the pedal and hold it in the applied position.
    b. Open the bleed valve about one-half turn. Allow the lever or pedal to travel to its limit.

BRAKES

c. When this limit is reached, tighten the bleed valve.

13. As the fluid enters the system, the level will drop in the reservoir. Maintain the level to just about the top of the reservoir to prevent air from being drawn into the system.

14. Continue to pump the lever or pedal and fill the reservoir until the fluid emerging from the hose is completely free of bubbles.

NOTE
Do not allow the reservoir to empty during the bleeding operation or more air will enter the system. If this occurs, the entire procedure must be repeated.

NOTE
If you are having trouble getting all of the bubbles out of the system, refer to the Reverse Flow Bleeding at the end of this section.

15. With the lever held in, or the pedal applied, tighten the bleed valve, remove the bleed tube and install the bleed valve dust cap.

16. If necessary, add fluid to correct the level in the reservoir.

17. Install the diaphragm, diaphragm plate and cover (**Figure 127**) or cap (**Figure 128**). Tighten the cap or cover screws securely.

18. Test the feel of the brake lever or pedal. It should be firm and should offer the same resistance each time it's operated. If it feels spongy, it is likely that there is still air in the system and it must be bled again. When all air has been bled from the system and the fluid level is correct in the reservoir, double-check for leaks and tighten all fittings and connections.

WARNING
Before riding the bike, make certain that the brakes are operating correctly. Roll the bike back and forth and apply the lever and the pedal several times. The wheels must come to a complete stop each time.

19. Test ride the bike slowly at first to make sure that the brakes are operating properly.

Reverse Flow Bleeding

This bleeding procedure can be used if you are having a difficult time freeing the system of all bubbles.

Using this procedure, the brake fluid will be forced into the system in a reverse direction. The fluid will enter the caliper, flow through the brake hose and into the master cylinder reservoir. If the system is already filled with brake fluid, the existing fluid will be flushed out of the top of the master cylinder by the new brake fluid being forced into the caliper. Siphon the fluid from the reservoir, then hold a shop cloth under the master cylinder reservoir to catch any additional fluid that will be forced out.

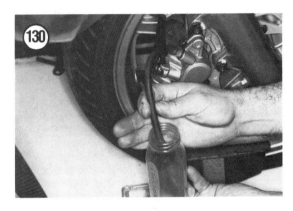

A special reverse flow tool called the EZE Bleeder is available, or a homemade tool can be fabricated for this procedure.

To make this homemade tool, perform the following:

NOTE
The brake fluid container must be plastic—not metal because it will be squeezed to force out the brake fluid. Use vinyl tubing of the correct inner diameter to ensure a tight fit on the caliper bleed valve.

a. Purchase a 12 oz. *plastic* bottle of DOT 4 brake fluid.
b. Remove the cap, drill an appropriate size hole and adapt a vinyl hose fitting onto the cap.
c. Attach a section of vinyl hose to the hose fitting on the cap and secure it with a hose clamp. This joint must be a tight fit as the plastic brake fluid bottle will be squeezed to force the brake fluid out past this fitting and through the hose.
d. Remove the moisture seal from the plastic bottle of brake fluid and screw the cap and hose assembly onto the bottle.

1. Remove the dust cap from the bleed valve on the caliper assembly as follows:
   a. **Figure 123**: the front caliper.
   b. **Figure 124**: 1986-1989 rear caliper.
   c. **Figure 125**: 1990-on rear caliper.
2. Clean the top cover of the master cylinder of all dirt and foreign matter.
3A. On the front brake, remove the screws securing the cover (**Figure 126**). Remove the cover, diaphragm plate and the diaphragm.
3B. On the 1986-1989 and 1994 rear brake, unscrew the cap (**Figure 128**). Remove the cap, diaphragm plate and the diaphragm.
3C. On the 1990-1993 rear brake, remove the screws securing the cover (**Figure 129**). Remove the cover, diaphragm plate and the diaphragm.
4. Attach the vinyl hose to the bleed valve on the caliper. Make sure the hose is tight on the bleed valve.
5. Open the bleed valve and squeeze the plastic bottle forcing this brake fluid into the system.

NOTE
If necessary, siphon brake fluid from the reservoir to avoid overflow of fluid.

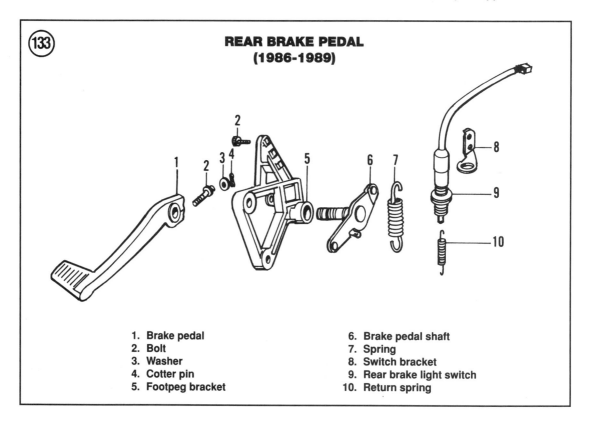

REAR BRAKE PEDAL (1986-1989)

1. Brake pedal
2. Bolt
3. Washer
4. Cotter pin
5. Footpeg bracket
6. Brake pedal shaft
7. Spring
8. Switch bracket
9. Rear brake light switch
10. Return spring

BRAKES

6. Observe the brake fluid entering the master cylinder reservoir. Continue to apply pressure from the tool, or bottle, until the fluid entering the reservoir is free of all air bubbles.

7. Close the bleed valve and disconnect the bleeder or hose from the bleed valve.

8. Install the dust cap onto the bleed valve on the caliper.

9. Install the diaphragm, diaphragm plate and the cover or cap. Tighten the cap, or cover screws securely.

10. At this time the system should be free of bubbles. Apply the brake lever and check for proper brake operation. If the system still feels spongy, perform the typical bleeding procedure in the beginning of this section.

REAR BRAKE PEDAL

Removal/Installation
(1986-1989 Models)

Refer to **Figure 133** for this procedure.

1. Remove the frame right-hand side cover.

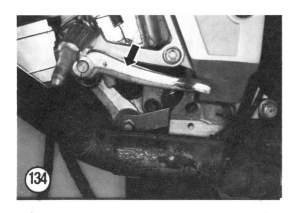

2. Disconnect the rear brake light switch electrical connector.

3. Remove the clamping bolt and remove the rear brake pedal (**Figure 134**).

4. Loosen, but do not remove, the Allen bolts (A, **Figure 135**) securing the master cylinder to the rider's right-hand footpeg bracket.

5. Remove the Allen bolts securing the rider's right-hand footpeg bracket (B, **Figure 135**) to the frame.

NOTE
It is not necessary to remove the hydraulic hose from the master cylinder.

6. Remove the Allen bolts loosened in Step 4 and remove the master cylinder from the footpeg bracket. Move the master cylinder out of the way.

7. Partially pull the footpeg assembly away from the frame.

8. Unhook the return spring from the brake light switch.

WARNING
In the next step, protect your hands and eyes as the return spring is under tension.

9. Using a small pair of vise-grip pliers, unhook the brake pedal return spring from the hook on the brake pedal shaft arm.

10. Remove the brake pedal shaft from the footpeg bracket.

11. Install by reversing these removal steps while noting the following:
   a. Apply a light coat of multi-purpose grease to all pivot areas of the brake pedal prior to installation.
   b. Install the rider's right-hand footpeg bracket and tighten the bolts to the torque specification listed in **Table 2**.
   c. Align the punch marks on the brake pedal pivot arm to the brake pedal shaft and tighten the bolt to the torque specification listed in **Table 2**.

Removal/Installation
(1990-on Models)

Refer to the following illustrations for this procedure:
   a. **Figure 136**: 1990-1993 models.
   b. **Figure 137**: 1994 models.

1. Remove the rear wheel as described under *Rear Wheel Removal/Installation* in Chapter Eleven.

2. Remove the cotter pin (A, **Figure 138**) and withdraw the pivot pin (**Figure 139**) from the brake pedal.

3. Remove the Allen bolts (A, **Figure 140**) securing the rider's right-hand footpeg bracket to the frame.

4. Partially pull the footpeg assembly (B, **Figure 140**) away from the frame.

5. Remove the bolts securing the heat shield and remove the heat shield (B, **Figure 138**).

6. Unhook the return spring (C, **Figure 138**) from the brake light switch.

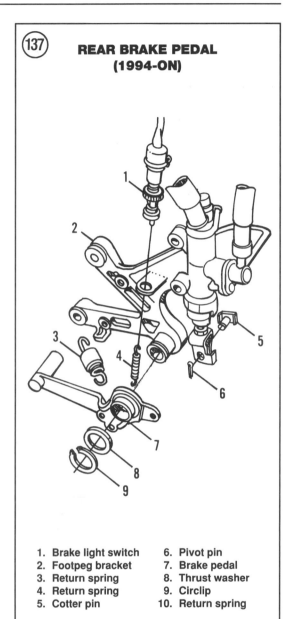

REAR BRAKE PEDAL (1994-ON)

1. Brake light switch
2. Footpeg bracket
3. Return spring
4. Return spring
5. Cotter pin
6. Pivot pin
7. Brake pedal
8. Thrust washer
9. Circlip
10. Return spring

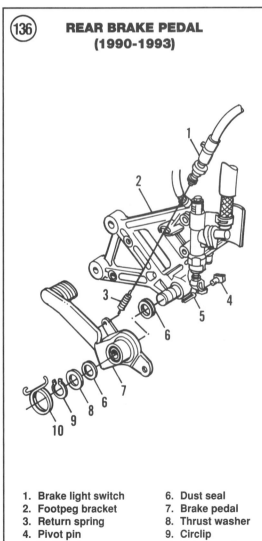

REAR BRAKE PEDAL (1990-1993)

1. Brake light switch
2. Footpeg bracket
3. Return spring
4. Pivot pin
5. Cotter pin
6. Dust seal
7. Brake pedal
8. Thrust washer
9. Circlip
10. Return spring

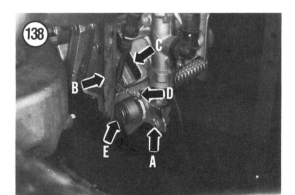

BRAKES

WARNING
In the next step, protect your hands and eyes as the return spring is under tension.

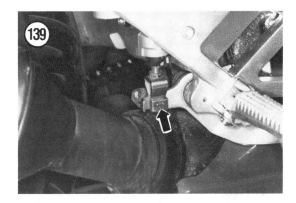

7A. On 1990-1993 models, using a screwdriver, pry the brake pedal return spring off the post (D, **Figure 138**) on the footpeg bracket.

7B. On 1994 models, using a small pair of vise-grip pliers, unhook the brake pedal return spring from the hook on the brake pedal or from the mounting tab on the footpeg bracket.

8. Remove the circlip and thrust washer (E, **Figure 138**) from the end of the shaft.

9. Remove the brake pedal from the pivot post on the footpeg bracket.

10. On 1990-1993 models, inspect the dust seals on each side of the brake pedal pivot point. Replace if necessary.

11. Install by reversing these removal steps while noting the following:

   a. On 1990-1993 models *only*, apply a light coat of multi-purpose grease to the pivot areas of the brake pedal prior to installation.

   b. On 1994 models, if the brake pedal return spring was disconnected from the mounting tab on the footpeg bracket, attach the spring by bringing the spring end up from the bottom to attach it. Do *not* come down from the top as the spring coils and protective sleeve will bind on the footpeg bracket and not work properly.

   c. Install the rider's right-hand footpeg bracket and tighten the bolts to the torque specification listed in **Table 2**.

Table 1 BRAKE SYSTEM TIGHTENING TORQUES

Item	N•m	ft.-lb.
Front master cylinder		
Clamping bolts	5-8	3-6
Union bolt	20-25	14-18
Front caliper		
Mounting bolts	24-30	17-22
Pad pins	15-20	11-14
Anti-dive piston bolt		
1986-1989	10-14	7.2-10
Rear caliper		
Mounting bolts	20-30	14-18
Pad pin (1990-on)	18	13
Caliper-to-bracket bolt		
1990-on	23	17
Miscellaneous (all models)		
Union bolt	20-25	14-18
Bleed valve	6-9	4-7
(continued)		

Table 1 BRAKE SYSTEM TIGHTENING TORQUES (continued)

Item	N•m	ft.-lb.
Brake disc bolts		
Front and rear		
1986-1989	37-43	27-31
Front		
1990-1993	43	31
1994	20	14
Rear (1990-on)	35	25
Rear brake pedal bolt		
1986-1989	10-14	7.2-10
Right-hand footpeg bracket		
Allen bolts	24-30	17-22

Table 2 BRAKE SYSTEM SPECIFICATIONS

Item	Specifications	Wear limit
Front master cylinder		
1986-1989		
Cylinder bore ID	15.870-15.913 mm (0.6248-0.6265 in.)	15.93 mm (0.627 in.)
Piston OD	15.827-15.854 mm (0.6231-0.6242 in.)	15.82 mm (0.623 in.)
1990-on		
Cylinder bore ID	12.700-12.743 mm (0.5000-0.5017 in.)	12.76 mm (0.502 in.)
Piston OD	12.657-12.684 mm (0.4983-0.4994 in.)	12.65 mm (0.498 in.)
Rear master cylinder		
Cylinder bore ID	12.700-12.743 mm (0.5000-0.5017 in.)	12.76 mm (0.502 in.)
Piston OD	12.657-12.684 mm (0.4983-0.4994 in.)	12.65 mm (0.498 in.)
Front caliper		
1986-1989		
Cylinder bore ID	30.230-30.280 mm (1.1902-1.1921 in.)	30.290 mm (1.1925 in.)
Piston OD	30.165-30.198 mm (1.1876-1.1889 in.)	30.16 mm (1.187 in.)
1990-on		
Cylinder bore ID	25.400-25.450 mm (1.0000-1.0020 in.)	25.460 mm (1.0024 in.)
Piston OD	25.335-25.368 mm (0.9974-0.9987 in.)	25.33 mm (0.997 in.)
Rear caliper		
Cylinder bore ID	27.000-27.050 mm (1.0630-1.0650 in.)	27.060 mm (1.0654 in.)
Piston OD	26.918-26.968 mm (1.0598-1.0617 in.)	26.910 mm (1.0594 in.)
Brake disc thickness		
Front		
1986-1989	4.0 mm (0.16 in.)	3.5 mm (0.14 in.)
1990-1993	5.0 mm (0.20 in.)	4.0 mm (0.16 in.)
1994-on	4.5 mm (0.18 in.)	3.5 mm (0.14 in.)
Rear		
1986-1989	5.0 mm (0.20 in.)	4.0 mm (0.16 in.)
1990-on	6.0 mm (0.24 in.)	5.0 mm (0.20 in.)
Disc runout	–	0.3 mm (0.012 in.)

CHAPTER THIRTEEN

FAIRING COMPONENTS

This chapter includes removal and installation procedures for all fairing and body panels.

SEAT

Removal/Installation

Refer to **Figure 1** for this procedure.

1. On models equipped with the optional seat cover, remove the bolt (A, **Figure 2**) and remove the rear seat cover (B, **Figure 2**).

2A. On 1986-1989 models, insert the ignition key into the seat lock and turn it clockwise to release the seat.

2B. On 1990-1993 models, insert the ignition key into the seat lock (A, **Figure 3**) and pull down on the release hook (B, **Figure 3**).

2C. On 1994-on models, insert the ignition key into the seat lock (A, **Figure 4**) and pull down on the lock lever (B, **Figure 4**).

3. Pull the seat (**Figure 5**) toward the rear and remove it.

4. Install by reversing these removal steps while noting the following:

a. Make sure the locking tab on the front of the seat is correctly hooked into the metal bracket on the fuel tank (**Figure 6**) or frame.
b. Make sure the rear retaining hook on each side is secure in the locking mechanism. Refer to **Figure 7** and **Figure 8**.

WARNING
*After the seat in installed, pull up on it firmly in the front and back (**Figure 9**) to make sure it is securely locked in place. If the seat is not correctly locked in place, it may slide to one side or the other when riding the bike. This could lead to the loss of control of the bike and a possible accident.*

SIDE COVERS
(1986-1989 MODELS)

Removal/Installation

Refer to **Figure 10** for this procedure.

NOTE
The 1986-1989 models are the only models equipped with separate side covers. On 1990 and later models, the

CHAPTER THIRTEEN

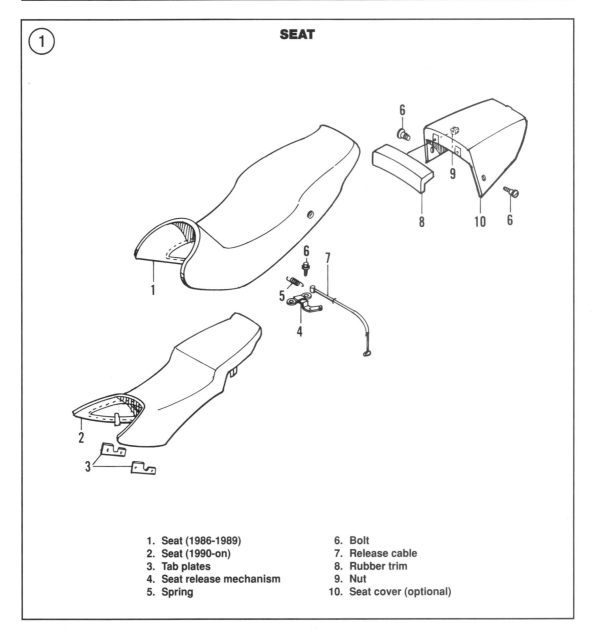

SEAT

1. Seat (1986-1989)
2. Seat (1990-on)
3. Tab plates
4. Seat release mechanism
5. Spring
6. Bolt
7. Release cable
8. Rubber trim
9. Nut
10. Seat cover (optional)

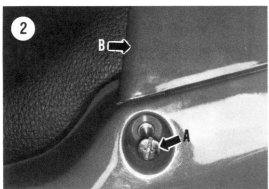

FAIRING COMPONENTS

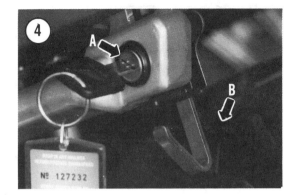

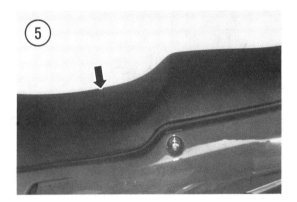

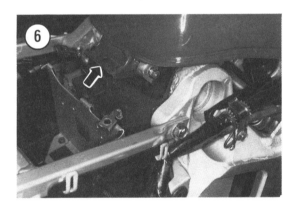

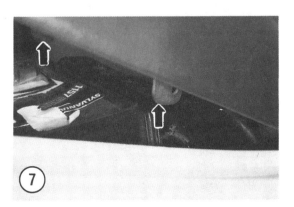

side covers are integrated into the tailpiece.

1. Remove the seat as described in this chapter.
2. Remove the bolt (A, **Figure 11**) securing the side cover. Don't lose the plastic retainer under the bolt.
3. Pull the front end of the side cover (**Figure 12**) out to release the post from the rubber grommet on the frame.
4. Carefully pull the side cover forward and release the rear locating tab and rubber stopper (**Figure 13**) from the locating slot (**Figure 14**) in the tailpiece.
5. Remove the side cover (B, **Figure 11**).
6. Install by reversing these removal steps.

TAILPIECE

Removal/Installation
1986-1989 Models

Refer to **Figure 15** for this procedure.

1. Remove the side covers and the seat as described in this chapter.
2. Remove the front bolt (**Figure 16**) on each side securing front portion of the tailpiece to the frame.

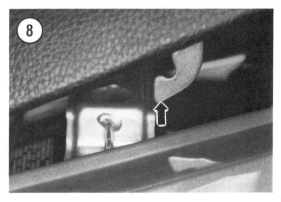

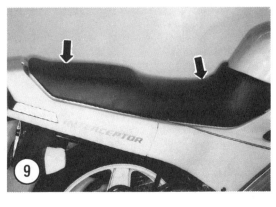

CHAPTER THIRTEEN

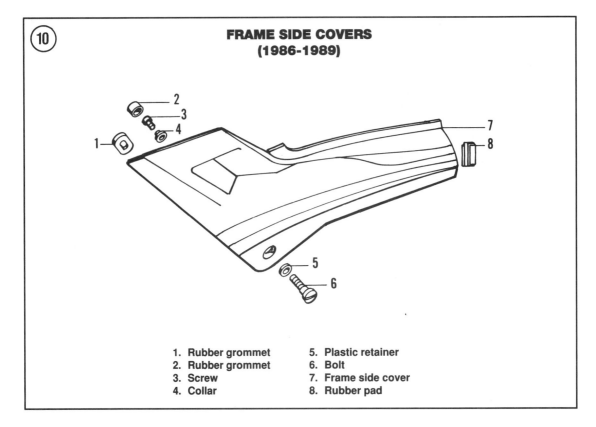

FRAME SIDE COVERS (1986-1989)

1. Rubber grommet
2. Rubber grommet
3. Screw
4. Collar
5. Plastic retainer
6. Bolt
7. Frame side cover
8. Rubber pad

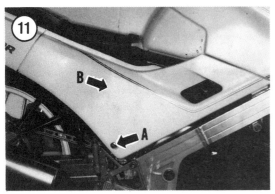

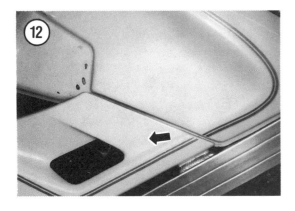

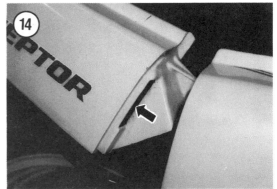

FAIRING COMPONENTS

3. Remove the bolts and washers (A, **Figure 17**) at the rear.

4. Disconnect the taillight electrical connector.

5. Remove the tailpiece (B, **Figure 17**) from the frame.

6. Don't lose the rubber grommet and collar at the rear bolt mounting areas.

7. If necessary, remove the bolts securing the tailpiece and rear directional signal mounting bracket and remove the bracket assembly.

8. Install by reversing these removal steps while noting the following:

    a. Make sure the metal collar is in place in both rubber grommets at the rear mounting areas.

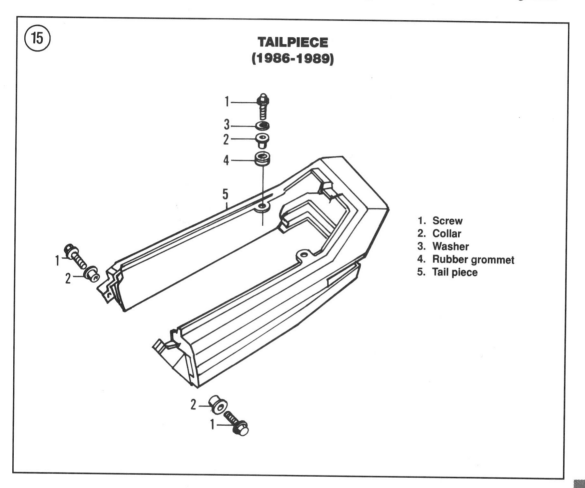

TAILPIECE (1986-1989)

1. Screw
2. Collar
3. Washer
4. Rubber grommet
5. Tail piece

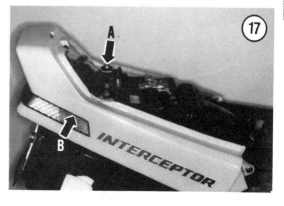

b. Tighten the bolts securely but do not overtighten, as the plastic mounting area may fracture.

**Removal/Installation
1990-1993 Models**

Refer to **Figure 18** for this procedure.
1. Remove seat as described in this chapter.
2. Remove the front bolt (**Figure 19**) on each side securing front portion of the tailpiece to the frame.
3. Remove the center bolt (**Figure 20**) on each side securing middle portion of the tailpiece to the frame.
4. Disconnect the taillight electrical connectors (A, **Figure 21**).
5. On models so equipped, remove the bolts and washers securing the individual hand grips. Remove both hand grips.
6. Remove the bolts and washers (B, **Figure 21**) at the rear.
7. Pull the front end of the tailpiece out to release the post from the rubber grommet on the frame.
8. Remove the tailpiece (C, **Figure 21**) from the frame.
9. Don't lose the collars at each bolt mounting area.

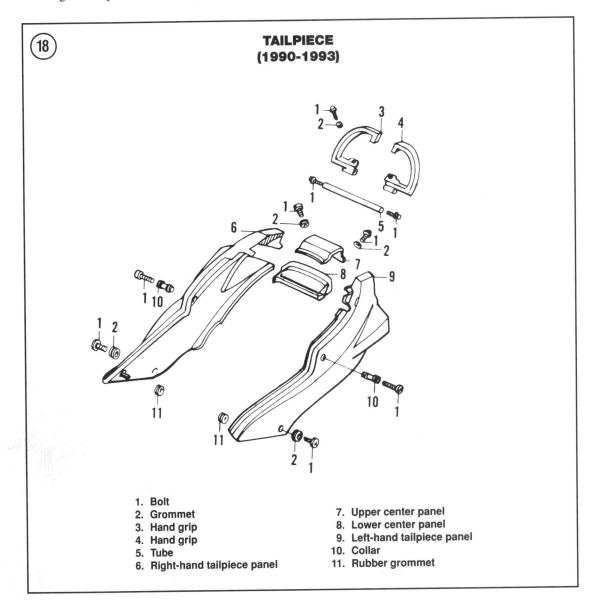

TAILPIECE (1990-1993)

1. Bolt
2. Grommet
3. Hand grip
4. Hand grip
5. Tube
6. Right-hand tailpiece panel
7. Upper center panel
8. Lower center panel
9. Left-hand tailpiece panel
10. Collar
11. Rubber grommet

FAIRING COMPONENTS

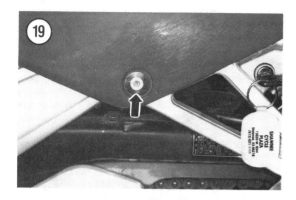

10. Install by reversing these removal steps while noting the following:
    a. Inspect the mounting post (**Figure 22**) for wear or damage.
    b. Make sure the metal collar is in place at the mounting areas.
    c. Tighten the bolts securely but do not overtighten as the plastic mounting area may fracture.

Removal/Installation
1994-on Models

Refer to **Figure 23** for this procedure.
1. Remove seat as described in this chapter.
2. On models so equipped, remove the bolts and washers securing the individual hand grips. Remove both hand grips.
3. Remove the front bolt (**Figure 24**) on each side securing front portion of the tailpiece to the frame.
4. Pull the front end of the side cover out to release the post (A, **Figure 25**) from the rubber grommet (B, **Figure 25**) on the frame.
5. Carefully pull the left-hand front section away from the frame and disconnect the taillight electrical connector (**Figure 26**).
6. Remove the bolts and washers (**Figure 27**) at the rear.
7. Carefully pull the tailpiece straight up and off the frame.
8. Don't lose the collars at each bolt mounting area.
9. Install by reversing these removal steps while noting the following:
    a. Inspect the mounting post (**Figure 28**) for wear or damage.
    b. Make sure the electrical connector (**Figure 29**) is free of corrosion and is tight.
    c. Tighten the bolts securely but do not overtighten as the plastic mounting area may fracture.

FRONT FAIRING

Front Fairing Components
Removal/Installation
(1986-1989 Models)

Lower side fairing sections

Refer to **Figure 30** for this procedure.
1. At the front lower section (**Figure 31**), remove the spring clips holding both lower sections together.

CHAPTER THIRTEEN

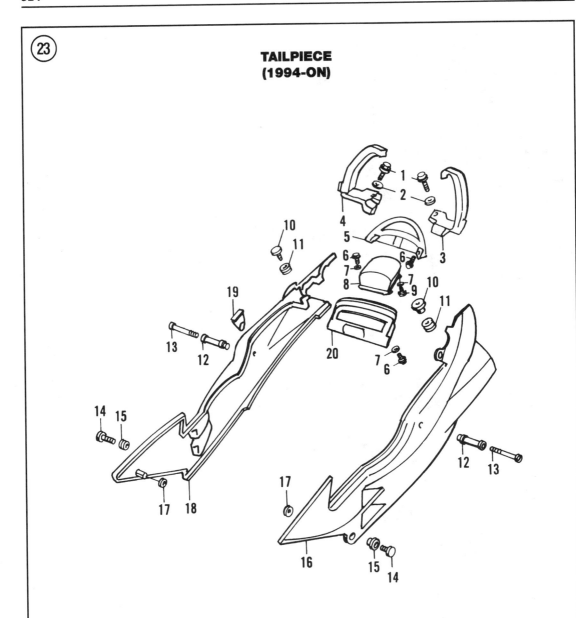

㉓ TAILPIECE (1994-ON)

1. Bolt
2. Washer
3. Hand grip
4. Hand grip
5. Center panel trim
6. Bolt
7. Washer
8. Upper center panel
9. Screw
10. Collar
11. Rubber bushing
12. Collar
13. Screw
14. Screw
15. Collar
16. Left-hand tailpiece panel
17. Rubber grommet
18. Right-hand tailpiece panel
19. Tab
20. Lower center panel

FAIRING COMPONENTS

1. At the front lower section (**Figure 31**), remove the spring clips holding both lower sections together.
2. Remove the screws (A, **Figure 32**) securing the lower side section to the frame and upper fairing.
3. Turn the fasteners (B, **Figure 32**) 90° counterclockwise to release them.
4. Carefully remove the lower section from the frame.
5. Repeat Steps 2-3 for the other side, if necessary.
6. Install by reversing these removal steps and tighten the screws securely and lock the fasteners.

Upper fairing section

Refer to **Figure 30** for this procedure.

1. Remove the lower fairing side sections (A, **Figure 33**) as described in this chapter.
2. Disconnect the electrical connector from the backside of the headlight and from both front direction signals.

NOTE
It is not necessary to remove the windshield but it does decrease the overall

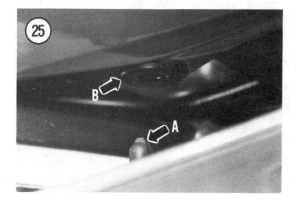

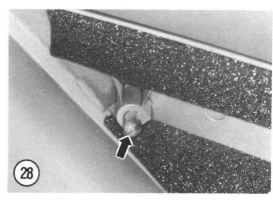

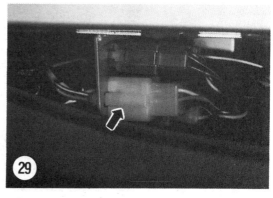

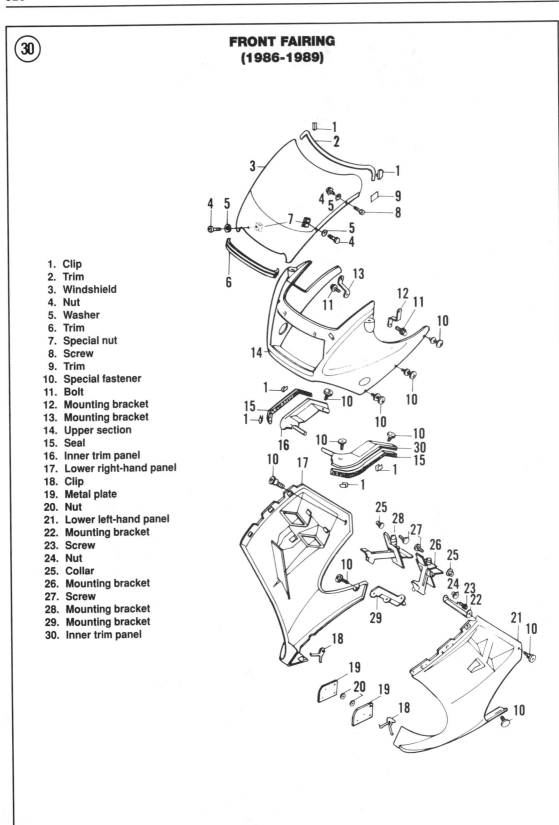

FAIRING COMPONENTS

mass of the upper fairing section and helps to eliminate damage to this fragile part during upper section removal and installation.

3. Remove the screws securing the windshield and remove the windshield.

4. Remove the nuts securing the directional signal assemblies to the upper section and to the fairing mounting bracket. Remove both directional signal assemblies (B, **Figure 33**).

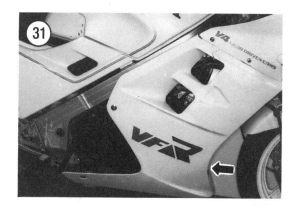

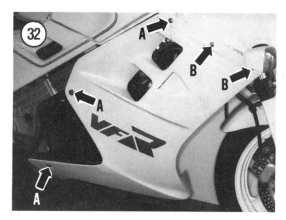

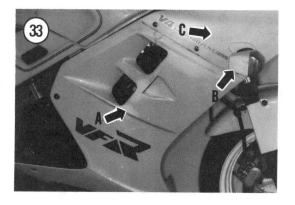

5. Remove the nut and lockwasher securing the rear view mirror to the upper section and to the fairing mounting bracket. Remove both mirror assemblies.

NOTE
The headlight assembly is mounted to the backside of the upper fairing section and will come off with the fairing as an assembly.

6. Carefully pull the fairing upper section (C, **Figure 33**) forward and off the fairing mounting bracket.

7. Install by reversing these removal steps and tighten all the fasteners securely.

Front Fairing Components Removal/Installation (1990-1993 Models)

Lower side fairing sections

Refer to **Figure 34** for this procedure.

CAUTION
***Completely** remove the lower screws in Step 1 from both body panels. If the screw is left in place, the mounting tab on the lower side fairing will be damaged when the panel is removed.*

1. At the front inner cowl completely unscrew the lower screw (A, **Figure 35**) from the front inner cowl (B, **Figure 35**) and the lower side section (C, **Figure 35**).

NOTE
***Figure 36** shows only 2 of the 3 fasteners on each side. Be sure to release all 3 fasteners.*

2. Turn the fasteners 90° counterclockwise to loosen them from the frame mounting tabs. Loosen the lower 3 fasteners (**Figure 36**) and the upper single fastener. Refer to **Figure 37** and **Figure 38**.

CAUTION
Be careful when disengaging the upper locating tabs from the locating grooves. These tabs and grooves are fragile and will easily break off if force is used during removal and installation.

528

CHAPTER THIRTEEN

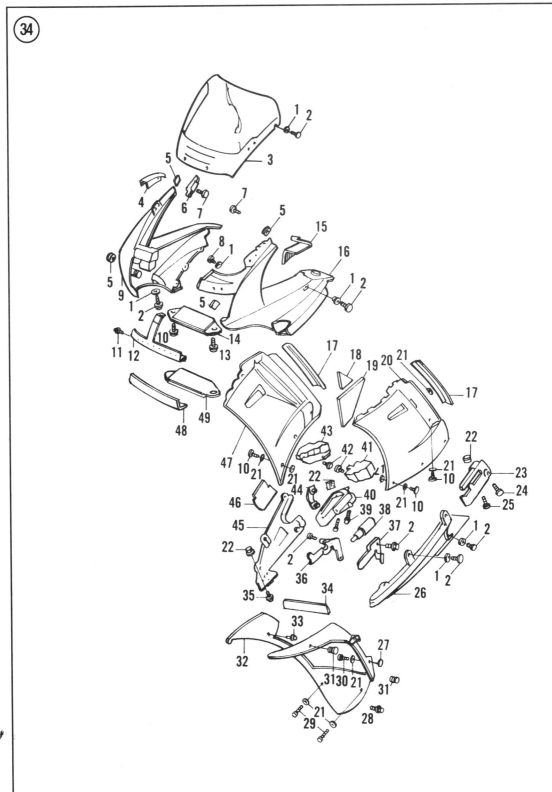

FAIRING COMPONENTS

FRONT FAIRING (1990-1993)

1. Collar
2. Screw
3. Windshield
4. Inner cover
5. Rubber grommet
6. Inner cover
7. Bolt
8. Screw
9. Upper right-hand section
10. Screw
11. Screw
12. Headlight trim panel
13. Screw
14. Upper center panel
15. Inner cover
16. Upper left-hand section
17. Trim
18. Insulator pad
19. Insulator pad
20. Upper right-hand section
21. Washer
22. Rubber stopper
23. Lower left-hand cover
24. Bolt
25. Bolt
26. Lower left-hand cowl
27. Plug
28. Fastener
29. Screw
30. Screw
31. Trim clip
32. Front inner cowl
33. Screw
34. Insulator
35. Bolt
36. Mounting bracket
37. Mounting bracket
38. Bracket
39. Bolt
40. Lower right-hand cover
41. Air duct
42. Screw
43. Air duct
44. Bracket
45. Lower right-hand cowl
46. Insulator pad
47. Upper left-hand section
48. Front center panel
49. Lower center panel

3. Carefully pull the lower portion of the lower side section out and then down to release the upper locating tabs from the locating grooves in the upper fairing section.
4. Remove the lower side section from the frame.
5. Repeat Steps 2-3 for the other side, if necessary.
6. Install by reversing these removal steps and lock the fasteners.

Front inner cowl section

Refer to **Figure 34** for this procedure.

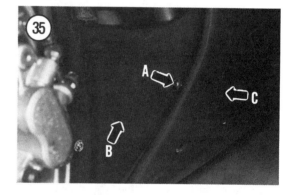

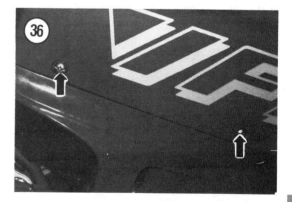

1. Remove the lower side fairing sections as described in this chapter.
2. Remove the Allen bolts securing the front inner cowl to the mounting brackets.

NOTE
The plastic fasteners tend to become brittle with age and may fracture during removal. If several break during removal, replace all of them as a set, as they are relatively inexpensive.

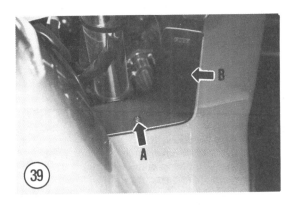

3. Use a flat blade screwdriver and turn the inner center pin to release the plastic fasteners. Remove all plastic fasteners
4. Remove the front inner cowl panel (B, **Figure 35**).
5. Install by reversing these removal steps and tighten the Allen bolts securely and lock the plastic fasteners.

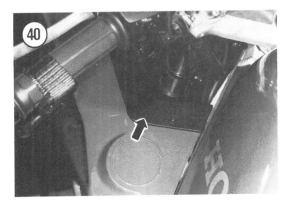

Upper fairing section

Refer to **Figure 34** for this procedure.
1. Remove the lower side fairing sections as described in this chapter.
2. Remove the screw (A, **Figure 39**) and remove the inner cover (B, **Figure 39**). Remove the inner cover (**Figure 40**) on the other side.
3. Roll the rubber section of the rear view mirror back (**Figure 41**) to expose the mounting nuts.
4. Remove the rear view mirror mounting nuts (**Figure 42**) and remove mirror, metal plate and rubber gasket from the fairing. Remove both mirrors.
5. Remove the screws (A, **Figure 43**) securing the inner cover and remove the cover (B, **Figure 43**). Remove both inner covers.

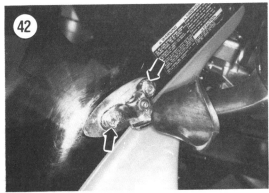

FAIRING COMPONENTS

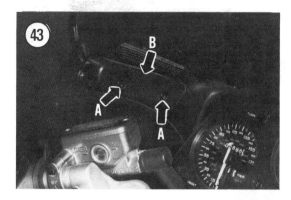

6. Remove the front screws (A, **Figure 44**) and the rear screws and washers securing the windshield and remove the windshield (B, **Figure 44**).

7. Disconnect the electrical connector from the backside of each headlight (**Figure 45**) and from both front directional signals.

8. Remove the headlight lower trim panel screw (**Figure 46**) on each side.

NOTE
The headlight assembly is mounted to the backside of the upper fairing section and will come off as an assembly.

9. Carefully pull the fairing upper section forward and off the fairing mounting bracket.

10. Install by reversing these removal steps while noting the following:
   a. Tighten all bolts and fasteners securely.
   b. Make sure all electrical connectors are free of corrosion and are tight.

Lower cowl and cover section

Refer to **Figure 34** for this procedure.

1. Remove both lower side fairing sections as described in this chapter.

2. On one side of the lower cowl, unscrew the front clip (**Figure 47**).

3. Remove the middle bolt (**Figure 48**), upper rear bolt (**Figure 49**) and lower rear bolt (**Figure 50**) securing the lower cowl to the frame.

4. Place a box under the cowl or have an assistant hold onto the lower cowl, then remove the clip and bolts on the other side.

5. Lower the cowl and remove it from the frame.

6. If necessary, remove the bolts (A, **Figure 51**) and remove the lower cover (B, **Figure 51**). Repeat for the other side if necessary.

7. Install by reversing these removal steps. Tighten the bolts and fasteners securely.

Front inner cowl

Refer to **Figure 34** for this procedure.

1. Remove both lower side fairing sections as described in this chapter.
2. Remove the upper fairing section as described in this chapter.
3. Remove the lower bolt (**Figure 52**) and upper bolt (A, **Figure 53**) and remove the front inner cowl (B, **Figure 53**) from the frame.
4. Install by reversing these removal steps. Tighten the bolts and fasteners securely.

Front Fairing Components Removal/Installation (1994-on Models)

Lower side fairing sections

Refer to **Figure 54** for this procedure.

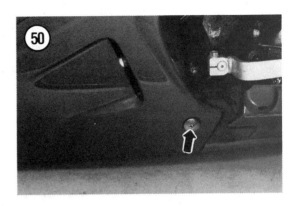

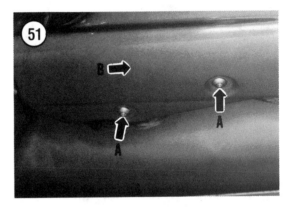

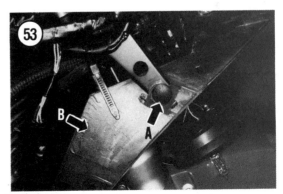

FAIRING COMPONENTS

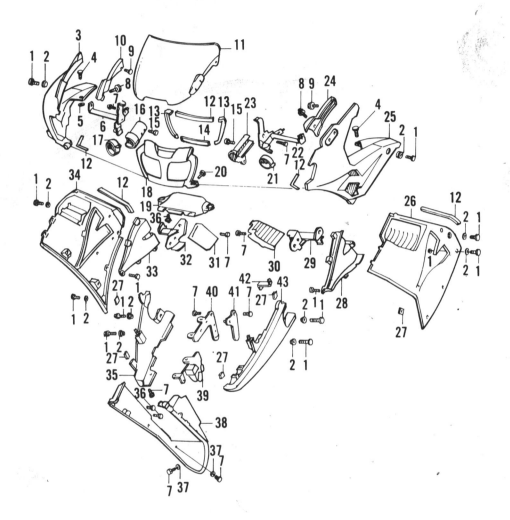

FRONT FAIRING (1994-ON)

1. Trim clip
2. Retainer
3. Upper left-hand section
4. Screw
5. Nut
6. Mounting bracket
7. Screw
8. Screw
9. Screw
10. Inner right-hand cover
11. Windshield
12. Trim
13. Trim
14. Trim
15. Screw
16. Air duct
17. Clamp
18. Headlight trim panel
19. Lower cover
20. Screw
21. Clamp
22. Mounting bracket
23. Air duct
24. Inner left-hand cover
25. Upper right-hand section
26. Lower left-hand side section
27. Clip
28. Air duct—left-hand side
29. Mounting bracket
30. Inner left-hand cover
31. Inner right-hand cover
32. Mounting bracket
33. Air duct—right-hand side
34. Lower right-hand side section
35. Lower right-hand cowl
36. Trim clip
37. Washer
38. Front inner cowl
39. Mounting bracket
40. Mounting bracket
41. Mounting bracket
42. Mounting bracket
43. Lower left-hand cowl

1. Turn the fasteners 90° counterclockwise to loosen them from the other fairing panel. Loosen the lower 3 fasteners (**Figure 55**), and remove the rear Allen bolt (**Figure 56**).

CAUTION
Be careful when disengaging the upper locating tabs from the locating grooves. These tabs and grooves are fragile and will easily break off if force is used during removal and installation.

2. Carefully pull the front lower portion of the lower side section out and away from the lower cowl.

3. Pull out and up on the lower portion and release the upper locating tabs (**Figure 57**) from the locating grooves (**Figure 58**) in the upper fairing section.

4. Carefully push down on the lower side fairing and release the lower side fairing tab (A, **Figure 59**) from the locking tab (B, **Figure 59**) on the upper fairing.

5. Slowly lower the lower side section and remove the lower side section from the frame.

6. Repeat Steps 2-5 for the other side, if necessary.

7. Install by reversing these removal steps while noting the following:
   a. Be sure to install a washer (**Figure 60**) under the lower fasteners.
   b. Tighten the Allen bolt securely and lock all fasteners.

Front inner cowl section

Refer to **Figure 54** for this procedure.

1. Remove the lower side fairing sections as described in this chapter.

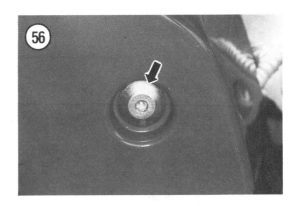

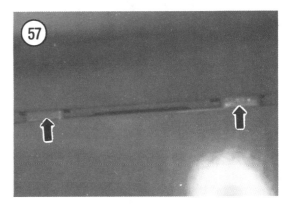

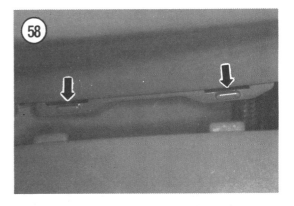

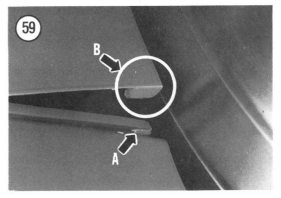

FAIRING COMPONENTS

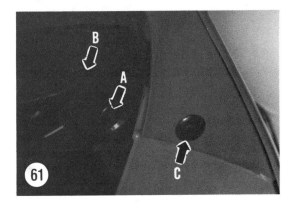

2. Remove the screws (A, **Figure 61**) and remove the lower cover (B, **Figure 61**) from under the headlight.

NOTE
The plastic fasteners tend to become brittle with age and may fracture during removal. If several break during removal, replace all of them as a set, as they are relatively inexpensive.

3. Push the center pin into the upper (C, **Figure 61**) and lower fasteners (**Figure 62**) to loosen them. Remove the fasteners from the panel.
4. Carefully release the locating tabs from the lower cowl.
5. Install by reversing these removal steps while noting the following:
   a. Push the center pin (**Figure 63**) back into the back of the fastener so it is sticking out of the front of the fastener (**Figure 64**). It is now ready for re-use.
   b. Place the panel into position.
   c. Install the fastener and push it all the way in through the panels until it bottoms out.
   d. Hold the fastener in place and push the center pin back into the fastener. This will lock the panels in place.
   e. Tighten the Allen bolts securely.

Upper fairing section

Refer to **Figure 54** for this procedure.
1. Remove the lower side fairing sections as described in this chapter.
2. Remove the screws securing the inner cover. Refer to (A, **Figure 65**) and **Figure 66**. Remove the inner cover (B, **Figure 65**) on both sides.

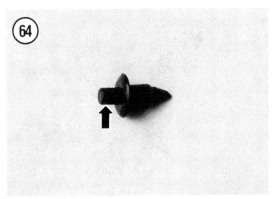

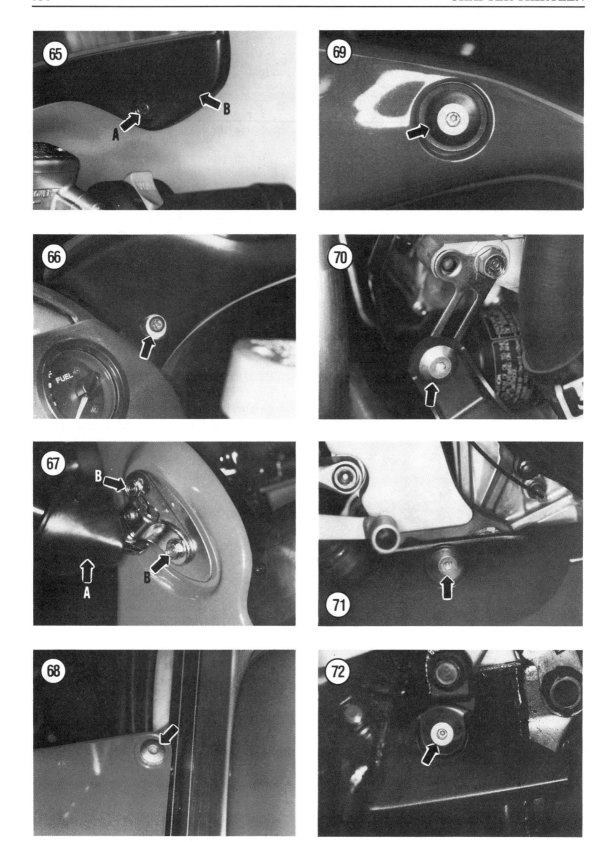

FAIRING COMPONENTS

3. Roll the rubber section of the rear view mirror back (A, **Figure 67**) to expose the mounting bolts.

4. Remove the rear view mirror mounting bolts (B, **Figure 67**) and remove mirror, mirror plate and rubber seat from the fairing. Remove both mirrors and keep the metal seat plate and rubber seat together with its respective mirror. These parts must be reinstalled on the correct side of the fairing.

5. Carefully pull the upper corners of the upper fairing panels away from the top of the windshield and remove the windshield. Don't lose the rubber cushions on the ends of the fairing mounting bracket after the windshield is removed. They must be in place prior to installing the windshield.

6. Disconnect the electrical connector from the backside of each headlight, both position lights and from both front directional signal assemblies.

7. Remove the screw (**Figure 68**) securing the upper panel to the mounting bracket on the frame.

8. Remove the rear Allen bolt (**Figure 69**) at the rear of the upper section.

NOTE
The headlight assembly is mounted to the backside of the upper fairing section and will come off as an assembly.

9. Carefully pull the fairing upper section forward and off the fairing mounting bracket.

10. Install by reversing these removal steps while noting the following:
   a. Install the rubber cushions on the ends of the fairing mounting bracket prior to installing the windshield.
   b. Position the upper section into place on the mounting bracket and align the holes in the headlight assembly with the mounting bosses on the mounting bracket. Push the upper section in until it bottoms out correctly.
   c. Install the rear view mirror rubber seat with the "R" (right-hand side) mark facing in and the "L" (left-hand side) mark facing out.
   d. Install the rear view mirror plate with the "arrow marks" facing in on the right-hand side and the marks facing out on the left-hand side.
   e. Tighten all bolts and fasteners securely.
   f. Make sure all electrical connectors are free of corrosion and are tight.

Lower cowl

Refer to **Figure 54** for this procedure.

1. Remove both lower side fairing sections as described in this chapter.

2. On one side of the lower cowl, unscrew the front bolt (**Figure 70**).

3. Remove the rear bolt securing the lower cowl to the frame. Refer to **Figure 71** for the right-hand side or **Figure 72** for the left-hand side.

4. Place box under the cowl or have an assistant hold onto the lower cowl, then remove the clip and bolts on the other side.

5. Lower the cowl and remove it from the frame.

6. Install by reversing these removal steps while noting the following:
   a. Align the tabs at the front of the lower cowl with the tabs on the front inner cowl.
   b. Tighten the bolts and fasteners securely.

INDEX

A

Air filter housing.................... 274-276
Alternator 185-188, 321-322
Anti-dive front suspension
    1986-1989 models................. 420-423
Axle bearing holder and driven sprocket,
    1990-on models, rear.............. 467-469

B

Ball bearing replacement 25-29
Battery............................. 68-74
Battery negative terminal 314-315
Bleeding the clutch system 240-241
Brake
    caliper
        front 477-480
        rear 491-498
    disc—front and rear................ 507-508
    hose replacement.................. 502-507
    pad replacement
        front 473-477
        rear 485-491
    pedal, rear 513-515
    problems 61-62
Brakes
    bleeding the system................ 509-513
    disc............................. 472-473
    disc, rear 485
Break-in procedure 215

C

Camshaft pulse generator
    1986 models only 328-329
Camshafts
    1986-1989 models................. 131-142
    1990-on models................... 142-151
Carburetor
    adjustment 114-117, 285-287

assembly 276-278
operation 276
overhaul......................... 278-284
service 276
troubleshooting 59-61
Charging system............... 49-51, 315-319
Choke cable replacement 288-289
Cleaning solvent 22-23
Clutch 44, 221-232
    bleeding......................... 240-241
    diode 338-339
    hydraulic system 232
    master cylinder 232-237
    slave cylinder 237-240
Cooling fan......................... 376-377
Cooling system
    check 375
    engine coolant crossover pipe
        1986-1989 models.............. 382-383
    fan 376-377
    hoses 383-384
    hoses and hose clamps 373-375
    pressure check...................... 375
    radiator 375-376
    thermostat and housing 377-379
    water pump 379-382
Crankcase breather system, U.S. only 297
Crankshaft........................ 206-211
Crankshaft pulse generator............ 326-328
Cylinder
    block and crankcase 188-195
    head cover 129-131
    heads 151-161

D

Disc brakes 472-473
    rear................................. 485
Drive sprocket and drive chain......... 444-445
Driven flange assembly
    1986-1989 models................. 443-444
Driven sprocket, 1990-on models....... 469-470

INDEX

E

Electrical system
- alternator 321-322
- battery negative terminal 314-315
- camshaft pulse generator
  - 1986 models only 328-329
- charging system 315-319
- clutch diode 338-339
- components 359-369
- connectors 313-314
- crankshaft pulse generator 326-328
- fuses 369-370
- ignition coil 325-326
- ignition control module
  - 1990-on models 324-325
- ignition spark unit,
  - 1986-1989 models 324
- lighting system 339-347
- problems 48-49
- starter motor 329-337
- starter relay switch 338
- starting system 329
- switches 347-358
- transistorized ignition system 322-324
- troubleshooting 45-46
- voltage regulator/rectifier 319-321

Emergency troubleshooting 38

Engine 124-129
- alternator 185-188
- break-in procedure 215
- camshafts, 1986-1989 models 131-142
- camshafts, 1990-on models 142-151
- coolant crossover pipe
  - 1986-1989 models 382-383
- crankshaft 206-211
- cylinder block and crankcase 188-195
- cylinder head cover 129-131
- cylinder heads 151-161
- drive sprocket and cover 242-245
- lubrication 43-44
- noises 42-43
- oil cooler 184-185
- oil pan, oil strainer and oil pump 175-184
- performance 40-42
- piston and connecting rods 195-206
- principles 122
- rocker arms assemblies
  - 1986-1989 models 161-163
- servicing in frame 124
- starter clutch assembly, starter
  - reduction gear and primary drive gear 211-215
- starting troubleshooting 39-40
- valves and valve components 163-175

Equipment, test 18-19

Evaporative emission control system
- California models only 298-300

Excessive vibration 61
Exhaust system 303-310
External shift mechanism 245-250

F

Fairing, front 523-537
Fasteners 7-11
Forks
- front 409-411
  - 1986-1989 411-420
  - 1990-on models 423-434
Front suspension and steering 61
Fuel
- filler cap 295-296
- filter 296
- pump 296
- shutoff valve 294-295
- tank 289-294
Fuses 369-370

G

Gasket remover 12-13
Gasoline/alcohol blend test 296-297
Gearshift linkage 44

H

Handlebar 399-403
Hoses 383-384
Hoses and hose clamps 373-375
Hub
- front 389-394
- rear, 1986-1989 models 439-443

I

Ignition
- coil 325-326
- control module, 1990-on models 324-325
- spark unit, 1986-1989 models 324
- system troubleshooting 51-55
- timing 112-114

Internal shift mechanism 267-271

L

Lighting system 339-347
Lubricants 11-12
Lubrication, periodic 74-82

M

Maintenance intervals 66
Maintenance, periodic 82-100
Master cylinder
- clutch 232-237
- front 480-485
- rear 498-502

Mechanic's tips 23-25

O

Oil cooler 184-185
Oil pan, oil strainer and oil pump 175-184
Oil seals 29
Operating requirements 35-36

P

Parts replacement 6
Piston and connecting rods 195-206
Pressure check 375

R

Radiator 375-376
Riding safety 29
Rocker arms assemblies,
  1986-1989 models 161-163

Routine checks 63-66
RTV gasket sealant 12

S

Seat 517
Secondary air supply system
  1986-on U.S., 1988-on Switzerland
  1992-on Austria models 300-302
Serial numbers 5-6
Shift mechanism
- external 245-250
- internal 267-271

Shock absorber
- 1986-1989 models 445-449
- 1990-on models 449-453

Shock absorber linkage
- 1986-1989 models 453-456
- 1990-1993 models 456-457
- 1994-on models 457-458

Side covers, 1986-1989 models 517-519
Slave cylinder, clutch 237-240
Specifications, torque 6
Starter
- clutch assembly, starter reduction gear
  and primary drive gear 211-215
- motor 329-337
- relay switch 338
- system troubleshooting 55-59

Starting system 329
Starting the engine 36-38
Steering head and stem 403-408
Steering head bearing race 408-409
Supplies, expendable 13
Suspension, front
- anti-dive, 1986-1989 models 420-423
- forks 409-411
  - 1986-1989 411-420
  - 1990-on models 423-434
- handlebar 399-403
- steering head and stem 403-408
- steering head bearing race 408-409

Suspension, rear
- drive sprocket and drive chain 444-445
- driven flange assembly
  - 1986-1989 models 443-444
- driven sprocket, 1990-on models 469-470
- shock absorber
  - 1986-1989 models 445-449
  - 1990-on models 449-453

INDEX

shock absorber linkage
    1986-1989 models 453-456
    1990-1993 models 456-457
    1994-on models 457-458
Swing arm
    1990-on models 463-467
    1986-1989 models 459-463
    1990-on models 463-467
Switches 347-358

T

Tailpiece 519-523
Test procedures, basic 47-48
Thermostat and housing 377-379
Threadlock 12
Throttle cable replacement 287-288
Tire repairs 399
    changing, tubeless 396-399
Tires and wheels 66-68, 395-396
Tools,
    basic hand 13-18
    precision measuring 19-22
    special 23
    test equipment 18-19, 46
Torque specifications 6
Transistorized ignition system 322-324
Transmission 44-45, 251-267
    internal shift operation 251
Troubleshooting
    basic test procedures 47-48
    brake problems 61-62
    carburetor 59-61

    charging system 49-51
    clutch 44
    electrical 45-46
    electrical problems 48-49
    emergency 38
    engine lubrication 43-44
    engine noises 42-43
    engine performance 40-42
    engine starting 39-40
    excessive vibration 61
    front suspension and steering 61
    gearshift linkage 44
    ignition system 51-55
    instruments 36
    starter system 55-59
    starting the engine 36-38
    test equipment 46
    transmission 44-45
Tune-up 100-112

V

Valves and valve components 163-175
Voltage regulator/rectifier 319-321

W

Water pump 379-382
Wheels 394-395
    front 386-389
    rear 436-439
Wheels and tires 66-68

VFR700F (1986) AND VFR750F (1986-1989) (U.S.)

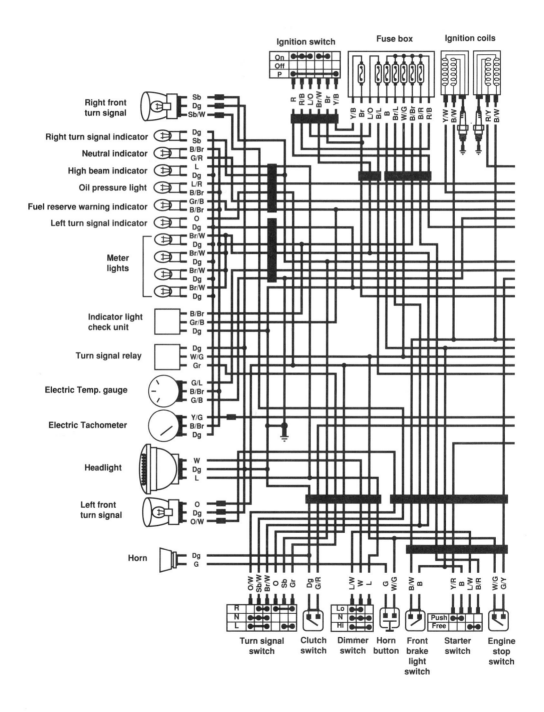

WIRING DIAGRAMS

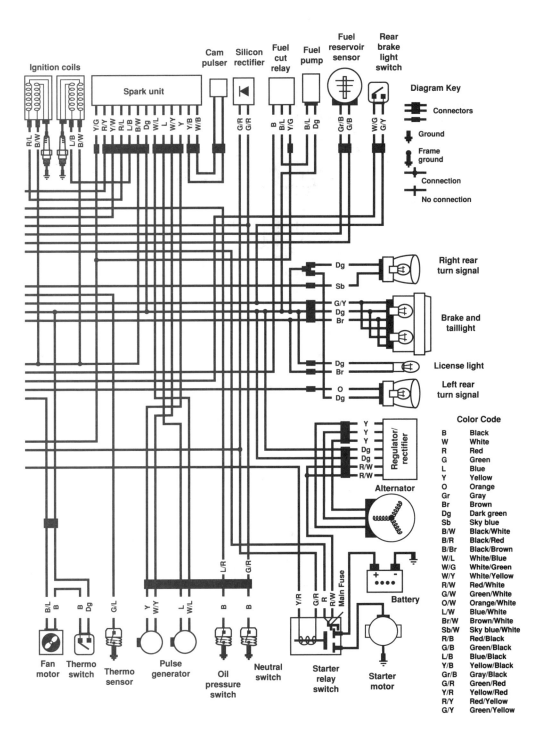

1990-1993 VFR750F (U.S.)

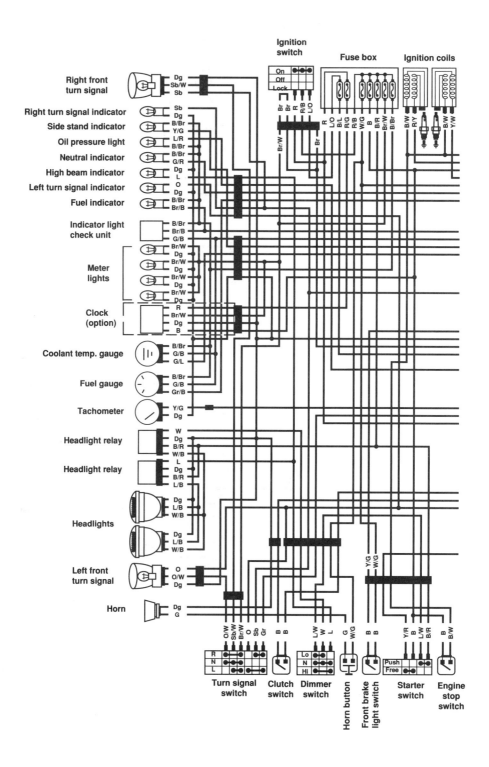

WIRING DIAGRAMS

545

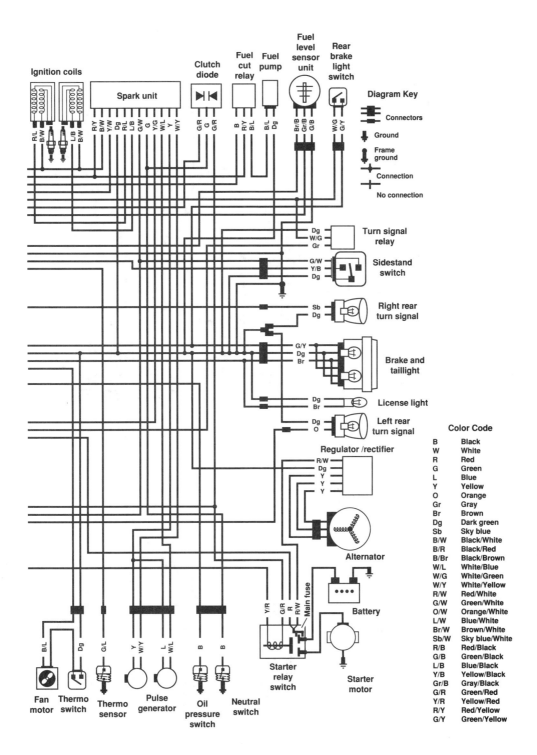

WIRING DIAGRAMS

1994-ON (U.S.)

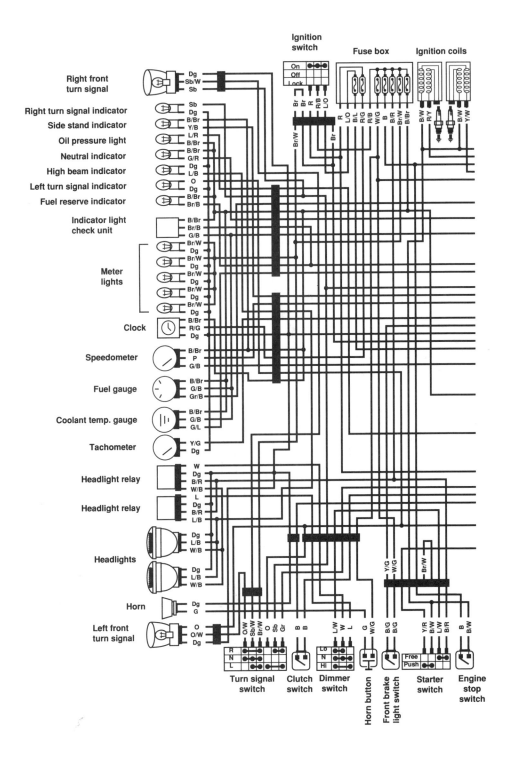

WIRING DIAGRAMS

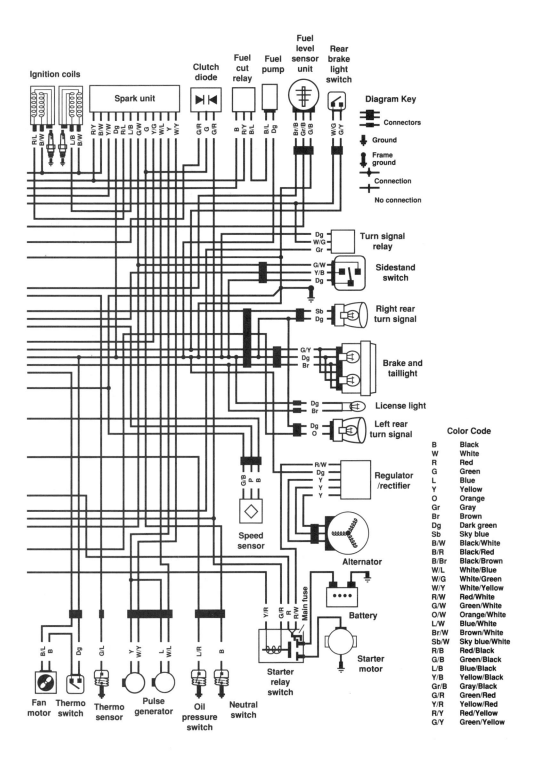

WIRING DIAGRAMS

1986 VFR700F2 (U.S.)

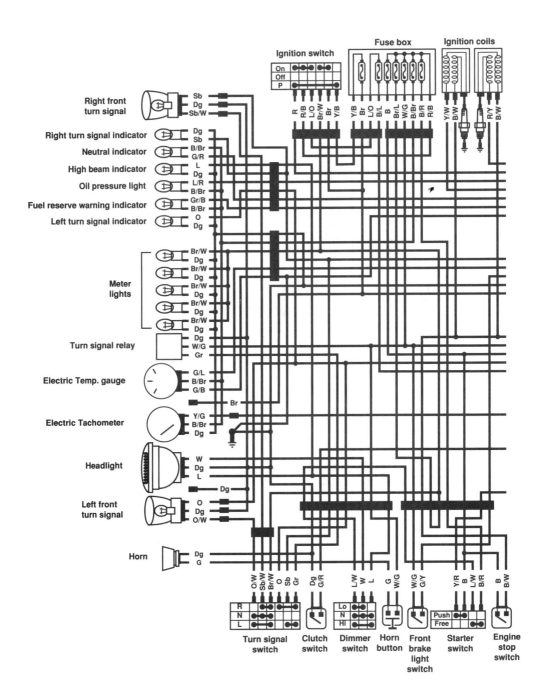

WIRING DIAGRAMS

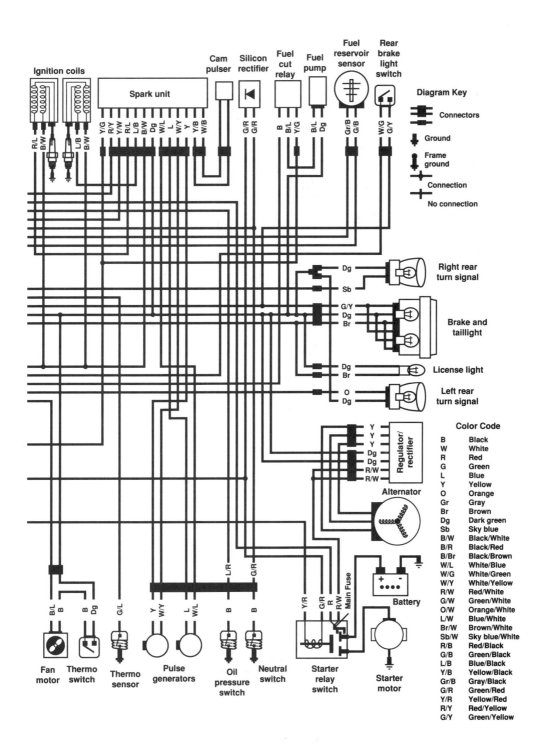

WIRING DIAGRAMS

1987-ON VFR700F2 (U.S.)

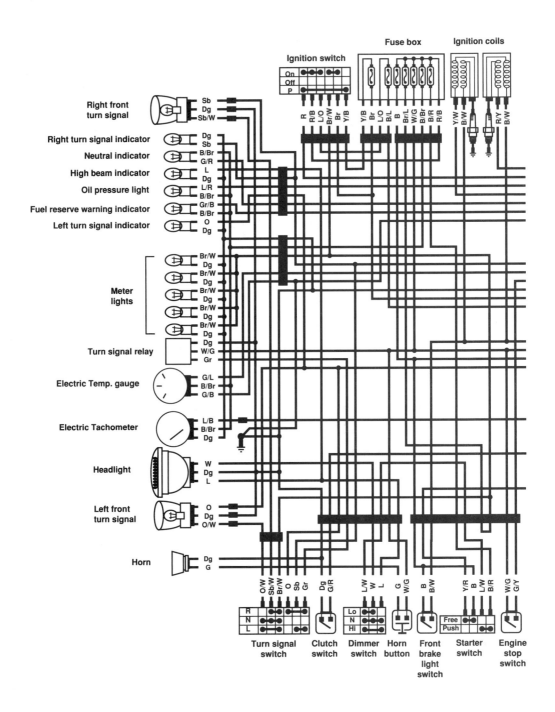

WIRING DIAGRAMS

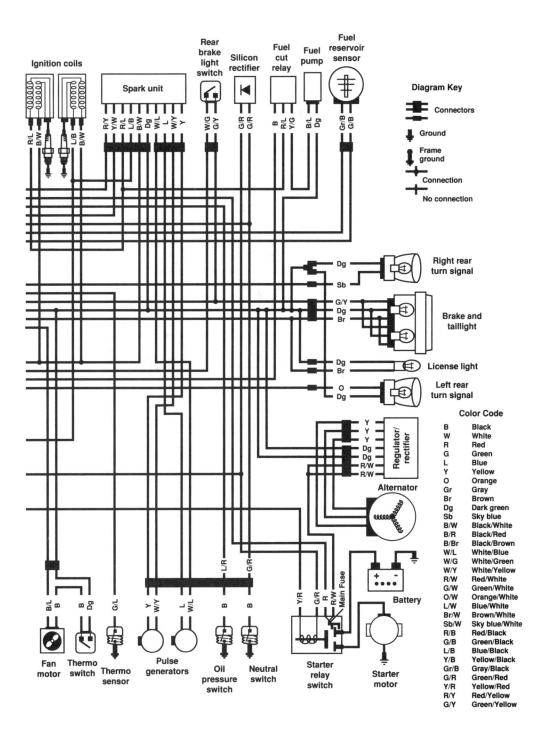

552 WIRING DIAGRAMS

1986 (NON-U.S.)

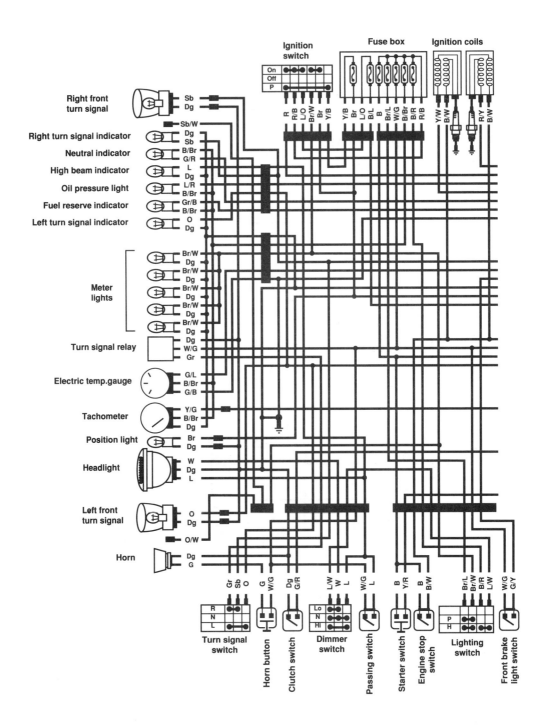

WIRING DIAGRAMS

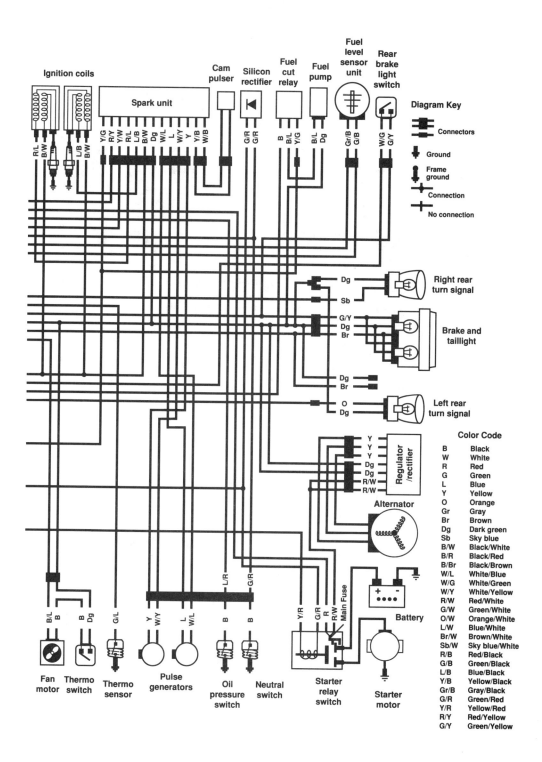

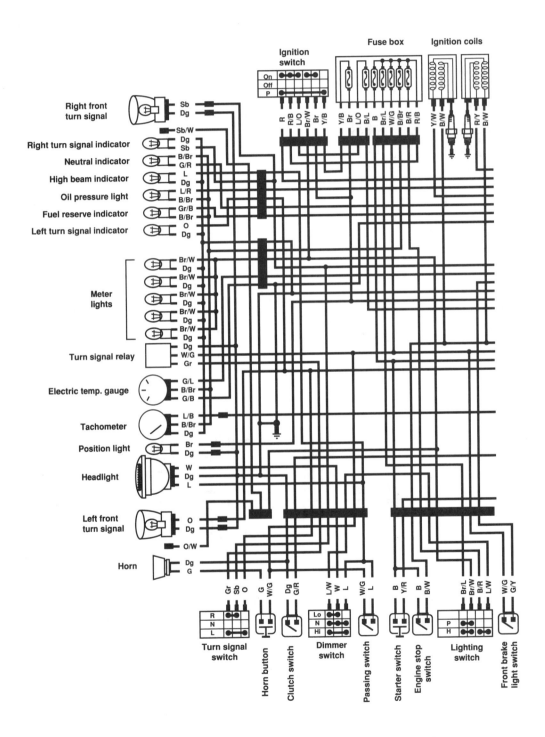

WIRING DIAGRAMS

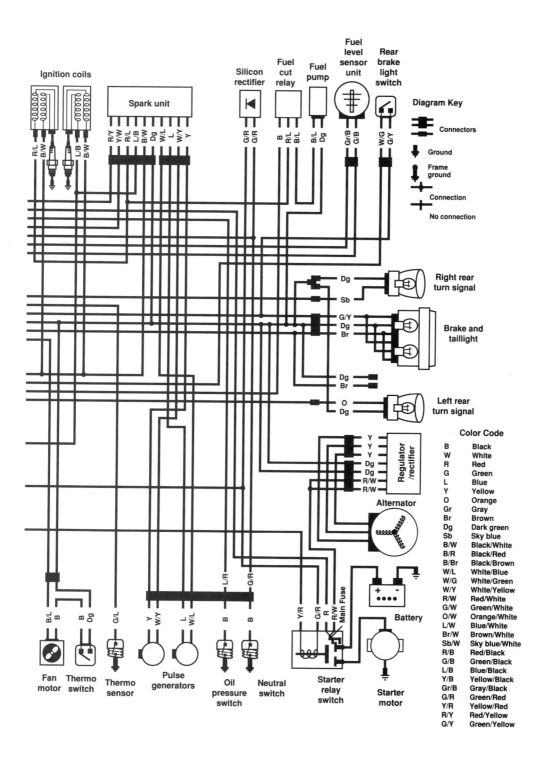

1988 (NON-U.S.)

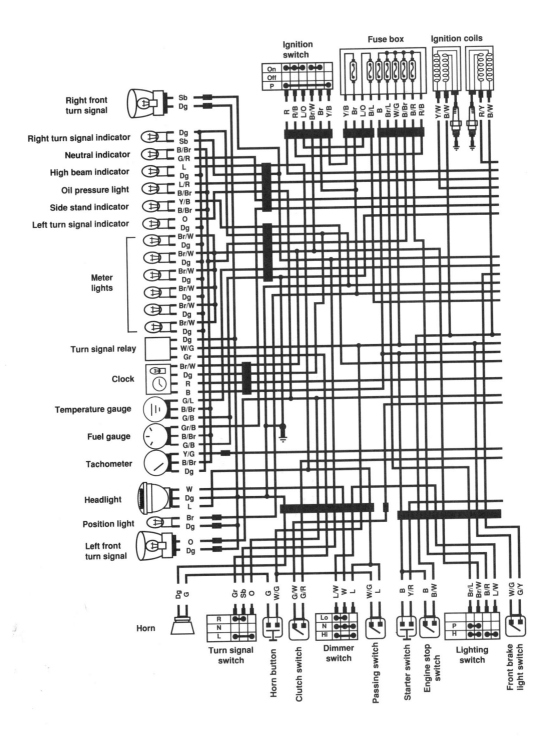

WIRING DIAGRAMS

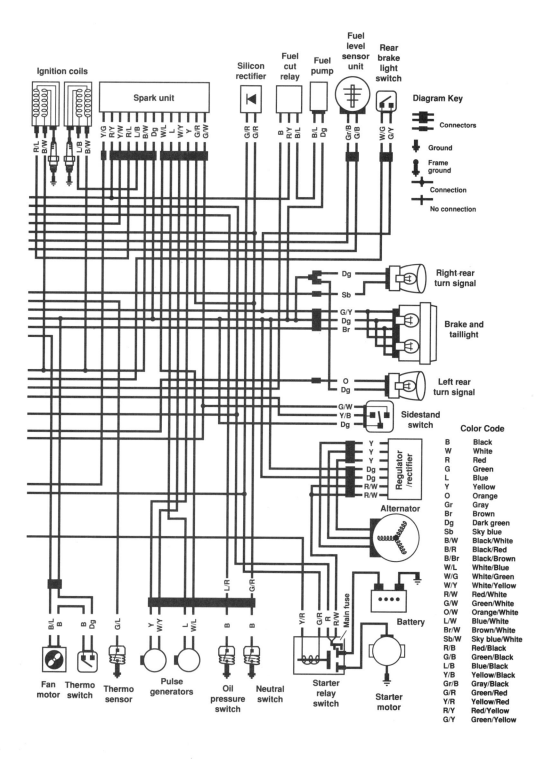

NOTES

MAINTENANCE LOG

Date	Miles	Type of Service

Check out *clymer.com* for our full line of powersport repair manuals.

BMW
- M308 500 & 600 CC twins, 55-69
- M309 F650, 1994-2000
- M502-3 BMW R-Series, 70-96
- M500-3 BMW K-Series, 85-97
- M503 R-850 & R-1100, 93-98

HARLEY-DAVIDSON
- M419 Sportsters, 59-85
- M428 Sportster Evolution, 86-90
- M429-3 Sportster Evolution, 91-02
- M418 Panheads, 48-65
- M420 Shovelheads, 66-84
- M421 FX/FL Softail Big-Twin Evolution, 84-94
- M422 FLT/FXR Big-Twin Evolution, 84-94
- M424 Dyna Glide, 91-95
- M425 Dyna Glide Twin Cam, 99-01
- M430 FLH/FLT 1999-2002

HONDA
- M316 Odyssey FL250, 77-84
- M311 ATC, TRX & Fourtrax 70-125, 70-87
- M433 Fourtrax 90 ATV, 93-00
- M326 ATC185 & 200, 80-86
- M347 ATC200X & Fourtrax 200SX, 86-88
- M455 ATC250 & Fourtrax 200/250, 84-87
- M342 ATC250R, 81-84
- M348 TRX250R/Fourtrax 250R & ATC250R, 85-89
- M456-2 TRX250X 1987-1992; TRX300EX 1993-2003
- M446 TRX250 Recon 1997-02
- M346-3 TRX300/Fourtrax 300 & TRX300FW/Fourtrax 4x4, 88-00
- M459-2 Fourtrax Foreman 1995-2001
- M454 TRX400EX 1999-02

- M310-13 50-110cc OHC Singles, 65-99
- M315 100-350cc OHC, 69-82
- M317 Elsinore, 125-250cc, 73-80
- M442 CR60-125R Pro-Link, 81-88
- M431-2 CR80R, 89-95, CR125R, 89-91
- M435 CR80, 96-02
- M457-2 CR125R & CR250R, 92-97
- M443 CR250R-500R Pro-Link, 81-87
- M432 CR250R & CR500R, 88-96
- M437 CR250R, 97-01
- M312-12 XL/XR75-100, 75-02
- M318 XL/XR/TLR 125-200, 79-87
- M328-4 XL/XR250, 78-00; XL/XR350R 83-85; XR200R, 84-85; XR250L, 91-96
- M320 XR400R, 96-00
- M339-6 XL/XR 500-650, 79-02

- M321 125-200cc, 65-78
- M322 250-350cc, 64-74
- M323 250-360cc Twins, 74-77
- M324-5 Twinstar, Rebel 250 & Nighthawk 250, 1978-2003
- M334 400-450cc, 78-87
- M333 450 & 500cc, 65-76
- M335 CX & GL500/650 Twins, 78-83
- M344 VT500, 83-88
- M313 VT700 & 750, 83-87
- M460-2 VT1100C2 A.C.E. Shadow, 95-99
- M440 Shadow 1100cc V-Twin, 85-96

- M332 350-550cc 71-78
- M345 CB550 & 650, 83-85
- M336 CB650, 79-82
- M341 CB750 SOHC, 69-78
- M337 CB750 DOHC, 79-82
- M436 CB750 Nighthawk, 91-93 & 95-99
- M325 CB900, 1000 & 1100, 80-83
- M439 Hurricane 600, 87-90
- M441-2 CBR600, 91-98
- M434 CBR900RR Fireblade, 93-98
- M329 500cc V-Fours, 84-86
- M438 Honda VFR800, 98-00
- M349 700-1000 Interceptor, 83-85
- M458-2 VFR700F-750F, 86-97
- M327 700-1100cc V-Fours, 82-88
- M340 GL1000 & 1100, 75-83
- M504 GL1200, 84-87
- M508 ST1100/PAN European, 90-02

- M505 GL1500 Gold Wing, 88-92
- M506 GL1500 Gold Wing, 93-95
- M462 GL1500C Valkyrie, 97-00

KAWASAKI
- M465 KLF220 Bayou, 88-95
- M466-2 KLF300 Bayou, 86-98
- M467 KLF400 Bayou, 93-99
- M470 KEF300 Lakota, 95-99
- M385 KSF250 Mojave, 87-95

- M350-9 Rotary Valve 80-350cc, 66-01
- M444-2 KX60, 1983-2002; KX80 1983-1990
- M351 KDX200, 83-88
- M447 KX125 & KX250, 82-91 KX500, 83-93
- M472 KX125, 92-98
- M473 KX250, 92-98

- M355 KZ400, KZ/Z440, EN450 & EN500, 74-95
- M360-3 EX500, GPZ500S, Ninja R, 1987-2002
- M356-3 700-750 Vulcan, 1985-2002
- M354 VN800 Vulcan 95-98
- M357 VN1500 Vulcan 87-98
- M471 VN1500 Vulcan Classic, 96-98

- M449 KZ500/550 & ZX550, 79-85
- M450 KZ, Z & ZX750, 80-85
- M358 KZ650, 77-83
- M359-3 900-1000cc Fours, 73-81
- M451 1000 &1100cc Fours, 81-85
- M452-3 ZX500 & 600 Ninja, 85-97
- M453-3 Ninja ZX900-1100 84-01
- M468 ZX6 Ninja, 90-97
- M469 ZX7 Ninja, 91-98
- M453-3 900-1100 Ninja, 84-01

POLARIS
- M496 Polaris ATV, 85-95
- M362 Polaris Magnum ATV, 96-98
- M363 Scrambler 500, 4X4 97-00
- M365 Sportsman/Xplorer, 96-00

SUZUKI
- M381 ALT/LT 125 & 185, 83-87
- M475 LT230 & LT250, 85-90
- M380 LT250R Quad Racer, 85-88
- M343 LTF500F Quadrunner, 98-00
- M483 Suzuki King Quad/ Quad Runner 250, 87-95

- M371 RM50-400 Twin Shock, 75-81
- M369 125-400cc 64-81
- M379 RM125-500 Single Shock, 81-88
- M476 DR250-350, 90-94
- M384 LS650 Savage Single, 86-88
- M386 RM80-250, 89-95
- M400 RM125, 1996-2000

- M372 GS400-450 Twins, 77-87
- M481-3 VS700-800 Intruder, 85-02
- M482 VS1400 Intruder, 87-98
- M484-3 GS500E Twins, 89-02

- M368 380-750cc, 72-77

- M373 GS550, 77-86
- M364 GS650, 81-83
- M370 GS750 Fours, 77-82
- M376 GS850-1100 Shaft Drive, 79-84
- M378 GS1100 Chain Drive, 80-81
- M383-3 Katana 600, 88-96 GSX-R750-1100, 86-87
- M331 GSX-R600, 97-00
- M478-2 GSX-R750, 88-92 GSX750F Katana, 89-96
- M485 GSX-R750, 96-99
- M338 GSF600 Bandit, 95-00
- M353 GSF1200 Bandit, 1996-2003
- M361 SV650, 1999-2002

YAMAHA
- M394 YTM/YFM200 & 225, 83-86
- M487-3 YFM350 Warrior, 87-02
- M486-3 YFZ350 Banshee, 87-02
- M488-4 Blaster ATV, 88-02
- M489-2 Timberwolf ATV, 89-00
- M490-2 YFM350 Moto-4 & Big Bear, 87-98
- M493 YFM400FW Kodiak, 93-98

- M492-2 PW50 & PW80, BW80 Big Wheel 80, 81-02
- M410 80-175 Piston Port, 68-76
- M415 250-400cc Piston Port, 68-76
- M412 DT & MX 100-400, 77-83
- M414 IT125-490, 76-86
- M393 YZ50-80 Monoshock, 78-90
- M413 YZ100-490 Monoshock, 76-84
- M390 YZ125-250, 85-87 YZ490, 85-90
- M391 YZ125-250, 88-93 WR250Z, 91-93
- M497-2 YZ125, 94-01
- M498 YZ250, 94-98 and WR250Z, 94-97
- M491 YZ400F, YZ426F & WR400F, 98-00
- M417 XT125-250, 80-84
- M480-3 XT/TT 350, 85-00
- M405 XT500 & TT500, 76-81
- M416 XT/TT 600, 83-89

- M403 650cc, 70-82
- M395-9 XV535-1100 Virago, 81-99
- M495 XVS650 V-Star, 98-00

- M404 XS750 & 850, 77-81
- M387 XJ550, XJ600 & FJ600, 81-92
- M494 XJ600 Seca II, 92-98
- M388 YX600 Radian & FZ600, 86-90
- M396 FZR600, 89-93
- M392 FZ700-750 & Fazer, 85-87
- M411 XS1100 Fours, 78-81
- M397 FJ1100 & 1200, 84-93

VINTAGE MOTORCYCLES
- M330 Vintage British Street Bikes, BSA, 500 & 650cc Unit Twins; Norton, 750 & 850cc Commandos; Triumph, 500-750cc Twins
- M300 Vintage Dirt Bikes, V. 1 Bultaco, 125-370cc Singles; Montesa, 123-360cc Singles; Ossa, 125-250cc Singles
- M301 Vintage Dirt Bikes, V. 2 CZ, 125-400cc Singles; Husqvarna, 125-450cc Singles; Maico, 250-501cc Singles; Hodaka, 90-125cc Singles
- M305 Vintage Japanese Street Bikes Honda, 250 & 305cc Twins; Kawasaki, 250-750cc Triples; Kawasaki, 900 & 1000cc Fours